"Jack Higgins is funny and serious. His cartoons are worth more than a thousand words. Higgins is the first thing I look for in Chicago's papers every morning. With Jack Higgins, everyone, and I mean everyone, is fair game. He can be warm and wonderful or he can be a brick to the head. He is Chicago."

—James "Skinny" Sheahan, Chicago political veteran

"Sometimes without a word, always with brilliant artistry, never ambivalent or ambiguous, humor is his sword, and Higgins's point of view cuts to the truth."

—Bob Sirott, anchor NBC5/News Chicago

"Chicago, city of big shoulders! They tell me that politics in this city has been elevated to an art form, and I believe them, for I have seen the faces of politicians in Jack Higgins's cartoons. If you want to see the soul of Chicago as it truly is, in its husky, brawling, crooked, proud heart, then this book has what you want. Jack Higgins portrays the essence of Chicago as only he can see it. I must admit, though, that I am still searching for the Nobel Prize Room at the University of Chicago."

—Roger Myerson, University of Chicago economist and 2007 Nobel Laureate

"Jack Higgins sees Chicago through a razored set of lenses—in shadows, around corners, and through keyholes and hearts, uncovering the antics and intentions of some of our city's most colorful characters. He sketches their legacies and their dreams, their proudest moments, secret ambitions, and darkest deeds. Nobody willingly poses for his portraits that read like a Rorschach test."

—Edward M. Burke, Chicago alderman

"Jack Higgins isn't just a brilliant editorial cartoonist . . . he's a brilliant reporter of the news, saying in one drawing what most of us can't say in a thousand words of copy."
—**Carol Marin, columnist,** ***Chicago Sun-Times,*** **and political editor, NBC5 Chicago**

"Like so many of his fans, I view Higgins's cartoons with wonder and awe. How does he consistently transform real-life triumphs and tragedy into elegant sketches of truth and humor? Higgins is the master of his craft."
—**Warner Saunders, NBC Universal, WMAQ**

"Jack Higgins is the one cartoonist who truly understands the Chicago way. On my office wall—on a hallowed spot next to last year's White Sox schedule and the takeout menu from CND Gyros and Lounge—there is a Jack Higgins cartoon based on one of my columns. It's the nicest journalism award a Chicago reporter can receive: a Jack Higgins cartoon. Thanks, Jack."
—**John Kass, columnist,** ***Chicago Tribune***

"Jack Higgins fills in what the editorial writers leave out. His commentary resonates more with the working people of Chicago than anyone else's."
—**Dennis Gannon, president of the Chicago Federation of Labor**

"Jack Higgins embodies the pursuit of consistent excellence. His soul flows from his pen."
— **John H. White,** ***Sun-Times*** **Pulitzer Prize–winning photographer**

MY KIND OF TOON, CHICAGO IS

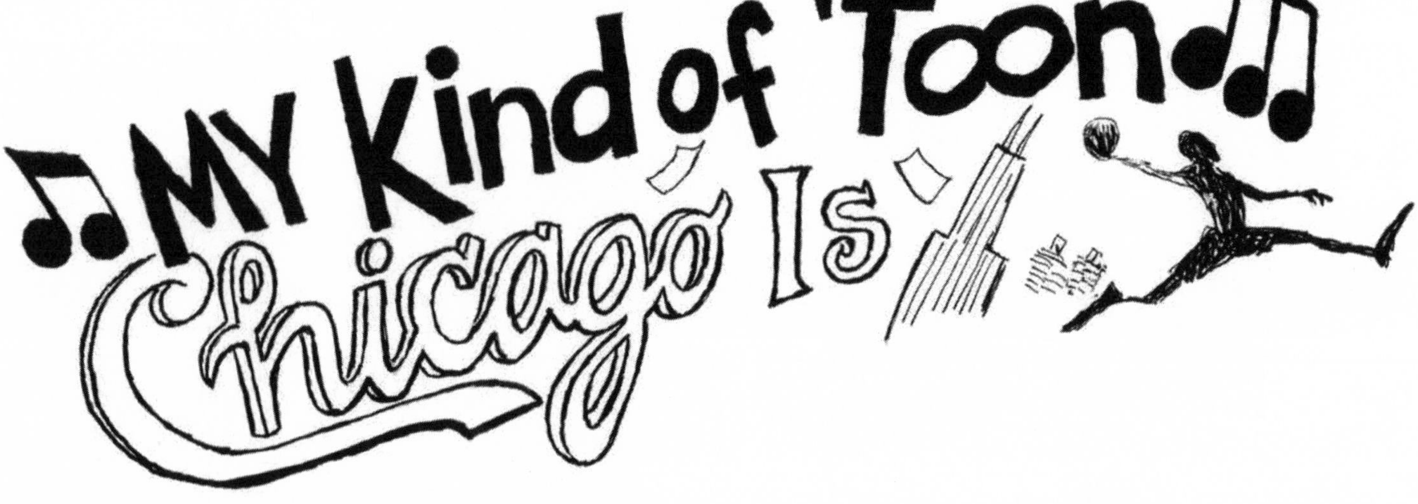
MY Kind of 'Toon
Chicago Is

POLITICAL CARTOONS

BY JACK HIGGINS

Foreword by Roger Ebert

Northwestern University Press
Evanston, Illinois

Northwestern University Press
www.nupress.northwestern.edu

Printed in the United States of America

10   9   8   7   6   5   4   3   2   1

ISBN 978-0-8101-2645-9

Library of Congress Cataloging-in-Publication Data

Higgins, Jack, 1954–
    My kind of 'toon, Chicago is : political cartoons /
  by Jack Higgins; foreword by Robert Ebert.
      p. cm.
    ISBN 978-0-8101-2645-9 (pbk. : alk. paper)
    1. Chicago (Ill.)—Politics and government—
  Caricatures and cartoons. 2. American wit and
  humor, Pictorial. I. Title.
  F548.3.H54 2009
  320.0207—dc22
                                        2009019633

∞ The paper used in this publication meets the
minimum requirements of the American National
Standard for Information Sciences—Permanence of
Paper for Printed Library Materials, ANSI Z39.48-1992.

To Tom McNamee, Steve Huntley, and the
late Ray Coffey—

The three best editors a guy could ever ask for.
Without whose encouragement, friendship,
correction, enthusiasm, and wisdom there
would be no body of work to include in this book.

You are, each one of you, the excellence of our
profession.

To my wife, Missy, for all the love, and to our children, Tommy, Brigid, Rose, Jackie, and Brendan, for all the laughter.

Truly there is a God.

CONTENTS

Preface ix

Foreword by Roger Ebert xi

In One Era & Out the Other 1

Only in Chicago . . . 11

All Politics Is Loco 25

Sports 101

Racism, Crime, & Gangs 129

Pretenders to the Throne 143

Economy & Culture 169

Environment & Health 191

Celebrities 203

Foreign Affairs 213

9-11 & After 251

Portraits & Passages 269

PREFACE

I was born and raised on Chicago's South Side. There you cannot escape being involved in politics, from cradle to grave and beyond. In my case, it seems that my attraction to local politics wasn't by any action of my own, but by political pull my mother had. The very same hands that yanked me into this world also delivered Mayor Richard M. Daley.

An election always seemed to be in the offing. I was only seven years old when I got my first job. My assignment was to put on a White Sox cap, sit near the entrance of the polling place, and slip palm cards to people as they passed by on their way to vote. I thought it was fun. I didn't question the legality of my actions. At the end of the day, the precinct captain would buy us ice cream and pop. It was like a game. Did we win? Of course! The Democrats always won! Eventually I moved into the world of journalism—

When I was eleven, I got a paper route.

A passion for local politics and art placed me in political cartooning. It served for me as an immediate means to express my exasperation. And because it was local, the reaction was always swift and strong. In Chicago, they don't stab you in the back, they fillet you in the belly. Now my salad days of ice cream are over. My precinct captain won't even talk to me.

The leap from local to national issues was a small one. Nepotism, greed, and racism still prevail on the national scene as well, and some of the faces are the same. It's just a wider screen.

In these days of canned pop-top logic and shopworn cliché, the impact of an original, slashing cartoon can be devastating. Although the shelf life of a newspaper is short, the political cartoon has a second life on refrigerator doors, office bulletin boards, through syndication, and on the Internet. In the muddle caused by the information glut, the cartoon is striking in its simplicity and poignancy. All these qualities make the political cartoon more memorable and describable than the column, the editorial, or the film at ten.

Most of all, our medium is timeless. Just as Thomas Nast educated illiterate immigrants, we today appeal to those sensory overloaded masses yearning to be free by Friday.

How successful I am is in the eye of the beholder. I don't kid myself by saying that a single political cartoon can change people's ways of thinking. But cartoonists are an influence that helps them shape their thoughts (or, for the uninformed, their prejudices). In a world of gray areas, in judgment and in brain matter, we glow—we turn on a light bulb. That makes the work more memorable. With humor as honey to go with the medicine, we keep a hold on the readers. Some cartoonists are more serious than funny. Others are so funny that they're not taken seriously. The best have something to say with the versatility of an artist's quill: using the plume to tickle and the point to prick. And in a rare moment of inspiration, some even manage to dip a sledgehammer into the ink well. I've yet to find a politician who can wash out India ink.

—Jack Higgins
Chicago Sun-Times

FOREWORD

by Roger Ebert

The mind of a great editorial cartoonist must resemble a busy crossroads: opinion and artistry intersect with wit. There are also lanes for satire and irony and, when they are called for, joy and sorrow. Jack Higgins is a great editorial cartoonist.

To regard the drawings in a book like this can be deceptive. Each cartoon rests on its page—finished, complete, on exhibit. That is true enough, but it conceals the most important ability of the editorial cartoonist, and that is to discover the *Eureka!* insight on deadline. The cartoon is almost always inspired by a day's events. The cartoonist absorbs the news, sits at his drafting board, sips a cup of coffee, arranges his drawing materials, looks out the window, muses, doodles, and waits.

He has a deadline. It is not flexible. The finished drawing must be delivered to the editors and then join the rush of material into the next day's paper. It is hard enough to create at all. It must be agonizing to create on deadline, day after day. Higgins was born and raised in Chicago, home of the Second City comedy troupe, and in his work he embodies Second City's definition of improvisation: "Something wonderful right away."

It takes a quick mind and a sure drawing hand, and (perhaps more important) the gift for lateral thinking, the ability to find the humor in the connection of two things you'd never think of connecting. One day President George Bush had a shoe thrown at him in Iraq. The next day Governor Rod Blagojevich was the target of national scorn. Higgins drew Blago as the target of a barrage of flying shoes. Perfect. There is a murder wave in the Englewood neighborhood, and Mayor Richard M. Daley makes an official visit there. Higgins writes the caption "Mayor Daley visits the people of Englewood" and shows him surrounded by body outlines on the sidewalk. Perfect. In Grant Park in 1968, protesters chant "The whole world is watching" and the city's image takes a hit that will hurt for four decades—until the park is filled with the Obama victory celebration. Higgins drew the hundreds of thousands against the skyline, with the words of 1968 as his caption.

The first President Bush gained some notoriety as a patrician who had not been in a supermarket for so long that he was unfamiliar with the workings of a grocery checkout scanner. Jack Higgins found a hilarious Chicago angle: Bush is visiting Chicago's most famous hamburger place, Billy Goat's, on the lower level of Michigan Avenue and only a two-minute walk from the back door of the old *Sun-Times* building. The president regards a dripping hamburger and asks, "What wine do you recommend?"

There's another thing about that drawing. The president is instantly recognizable—and so, as any Billy Goat regular can testify, is Sam Sianis, the owner. Higgins has a rare gift for inventing recognizable caricatures. Not all of his colleagues are so blessed. An editorial cartoon deflates if you don't immediately recognize the people in it.

Editorial cartoonists, like film critics and indeed editors, are an endangered species in these days of the Internet tsunami against the printed press. I am proud that my paper continues to be the home of one of the greatest. Jack is a Pulitzer Prize winner in a proud tradition at the *Sun-Times,* where both Jacob Burck and Bill Mauldin won the prize before him, while John Fischetti won it at our sister newspaper, the *Chicago Daily News.* This book shows why he so richly deserves it.

IN ONE ERA &
OUT THE OTHER

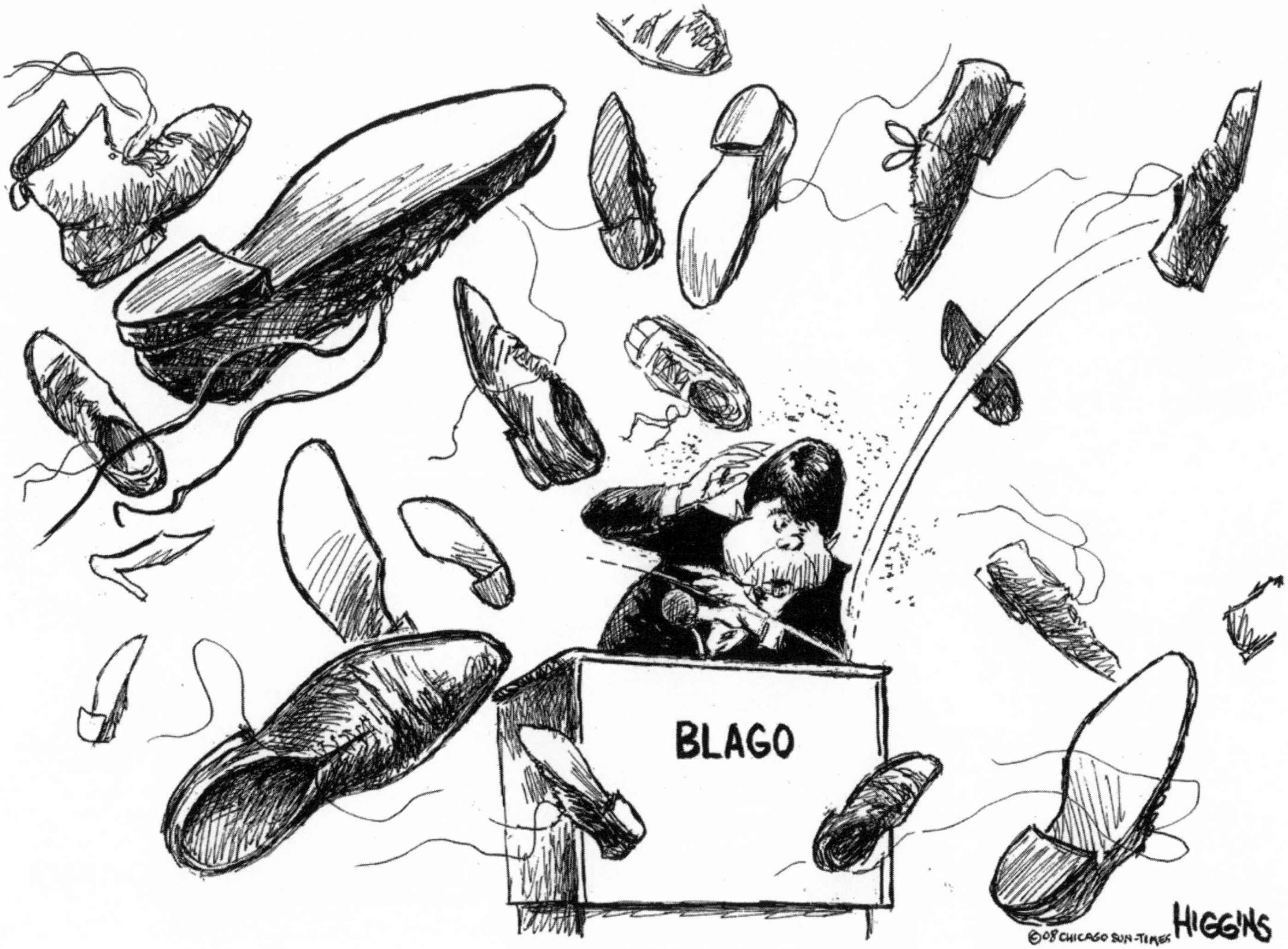
BLAGO
©08 CHICAGO SUN-TIMES
HIGGINS

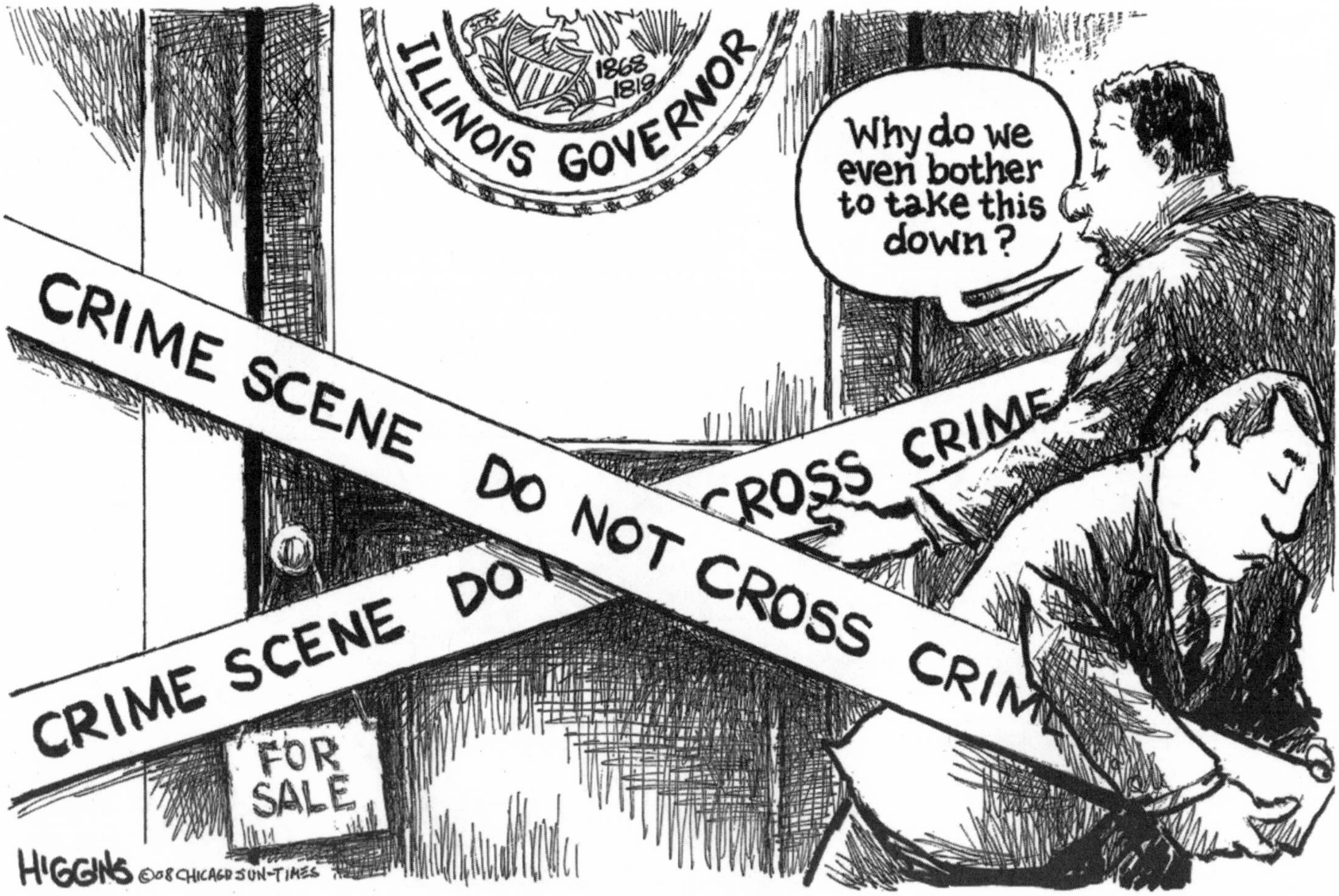
ILLINOIS GOVERNOR
1868
1819
Why do we even bother to take this down?
CRIME SCENE DO NOT CROSS CRIM
CRIME SCENE DO NOT CROSS CRIME
FOR SALE
HIGGINS ©08 CHICAGO SUN-TIMES

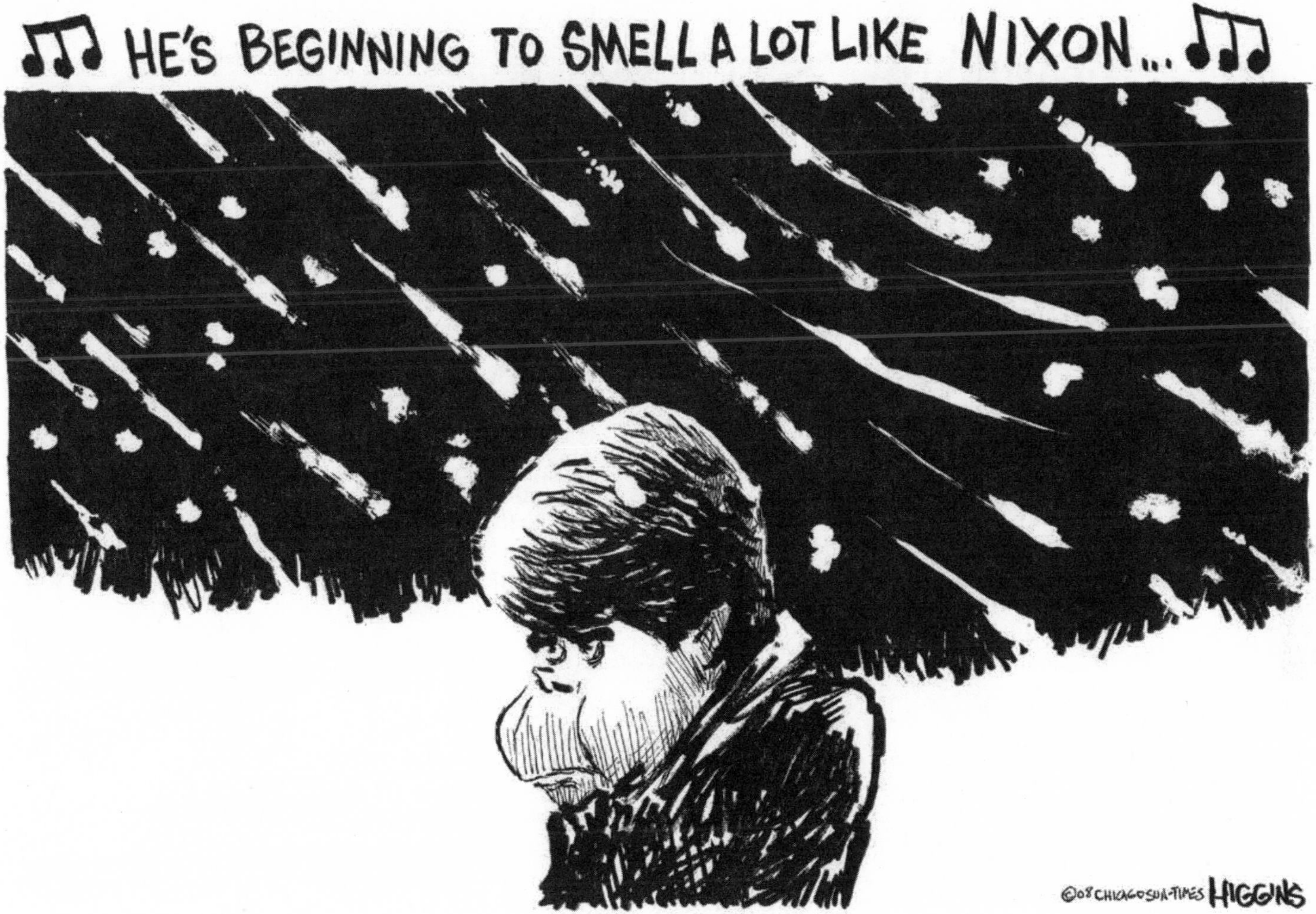
HE'S BEGINNING TO SMELL A LOT LIKE NIXON...
©08 CHICAGO SUN-TIMES HIGGINS

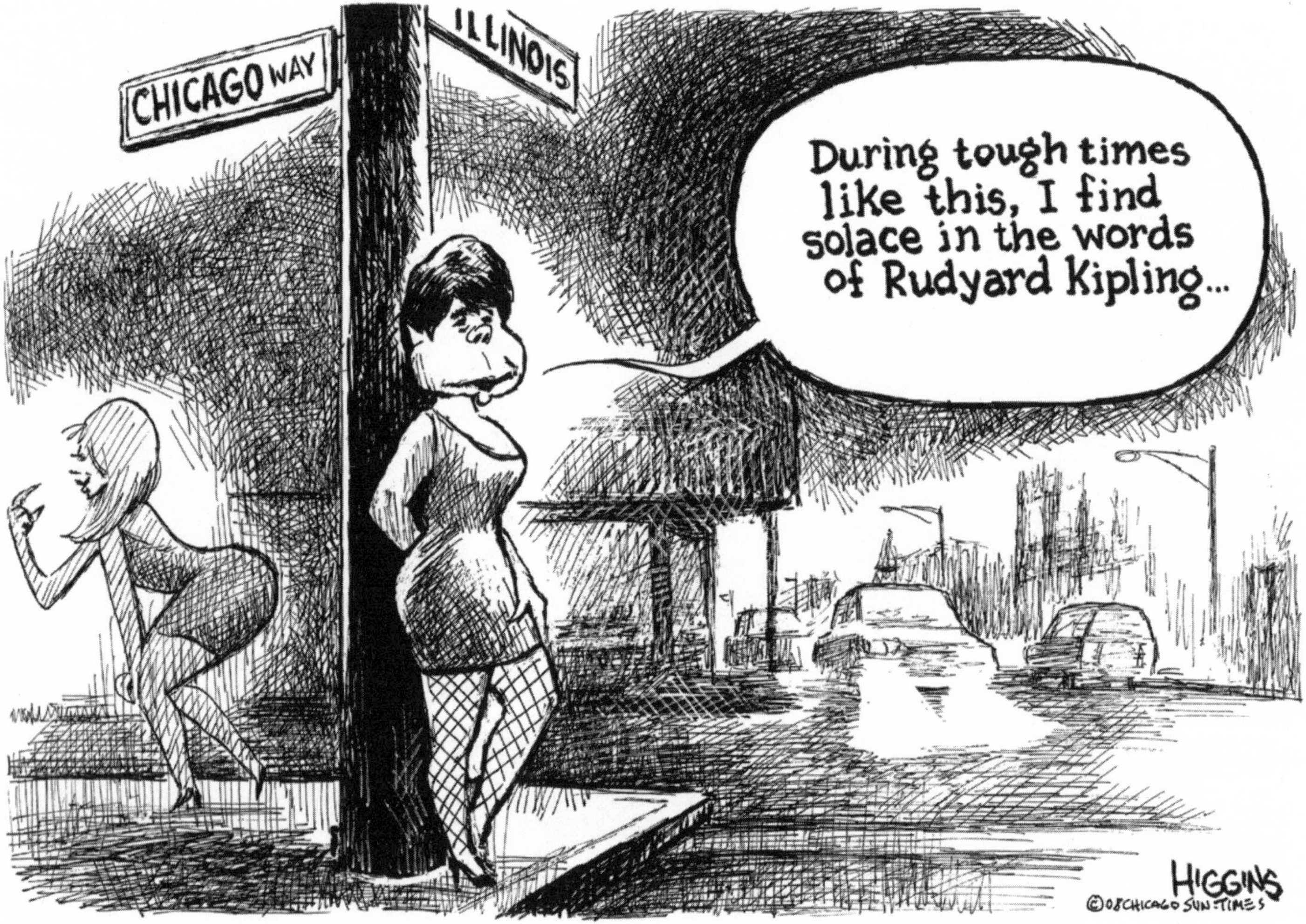
CHICAGO WAY
ILLINOIS
During tough times like this, I find solace in the words of Rudyard Kipling...
HIGGINS
©08 CHICAGO SUN-TIMES

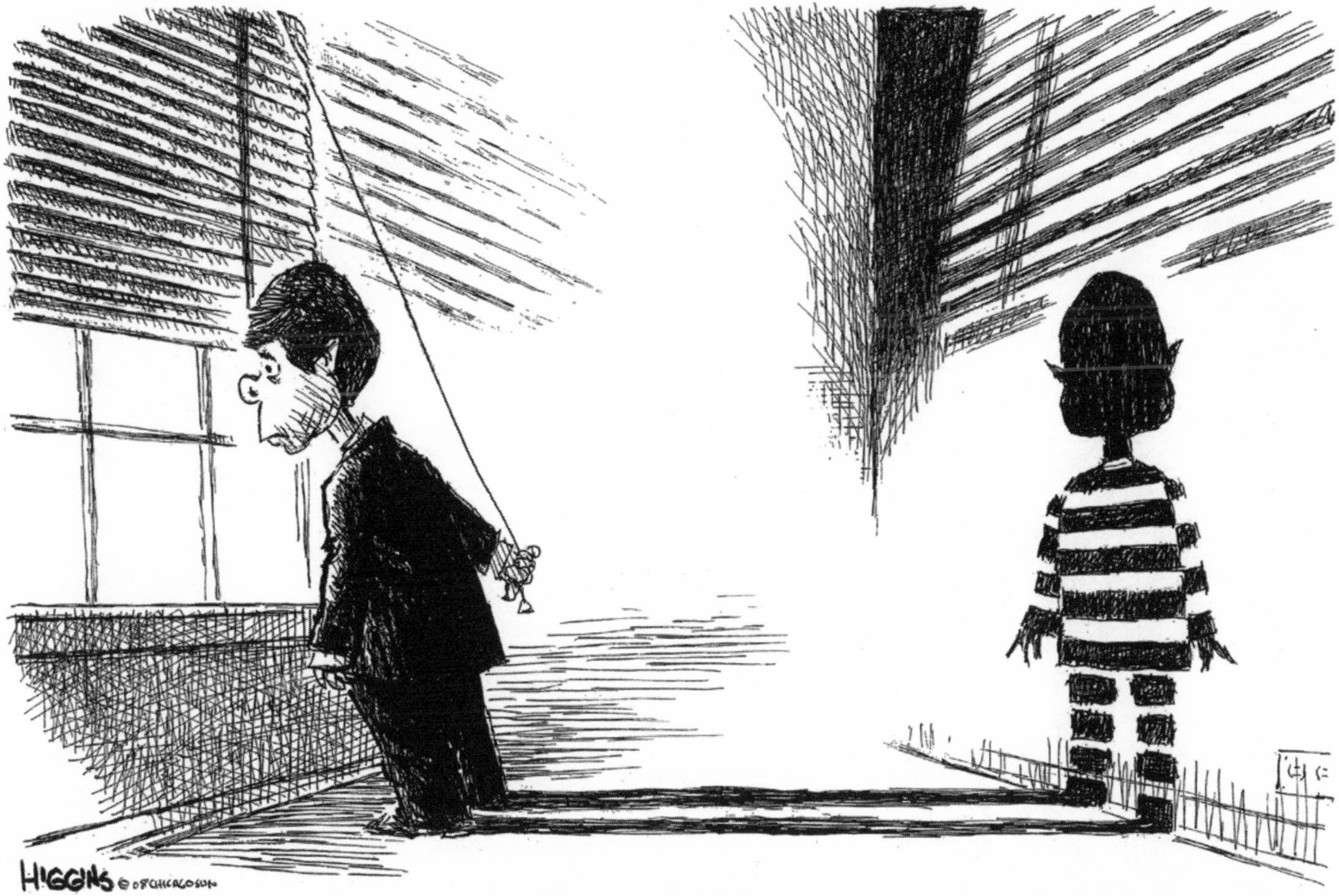
HIGGINS ©08CHICAGOSUN

FORESHADOW

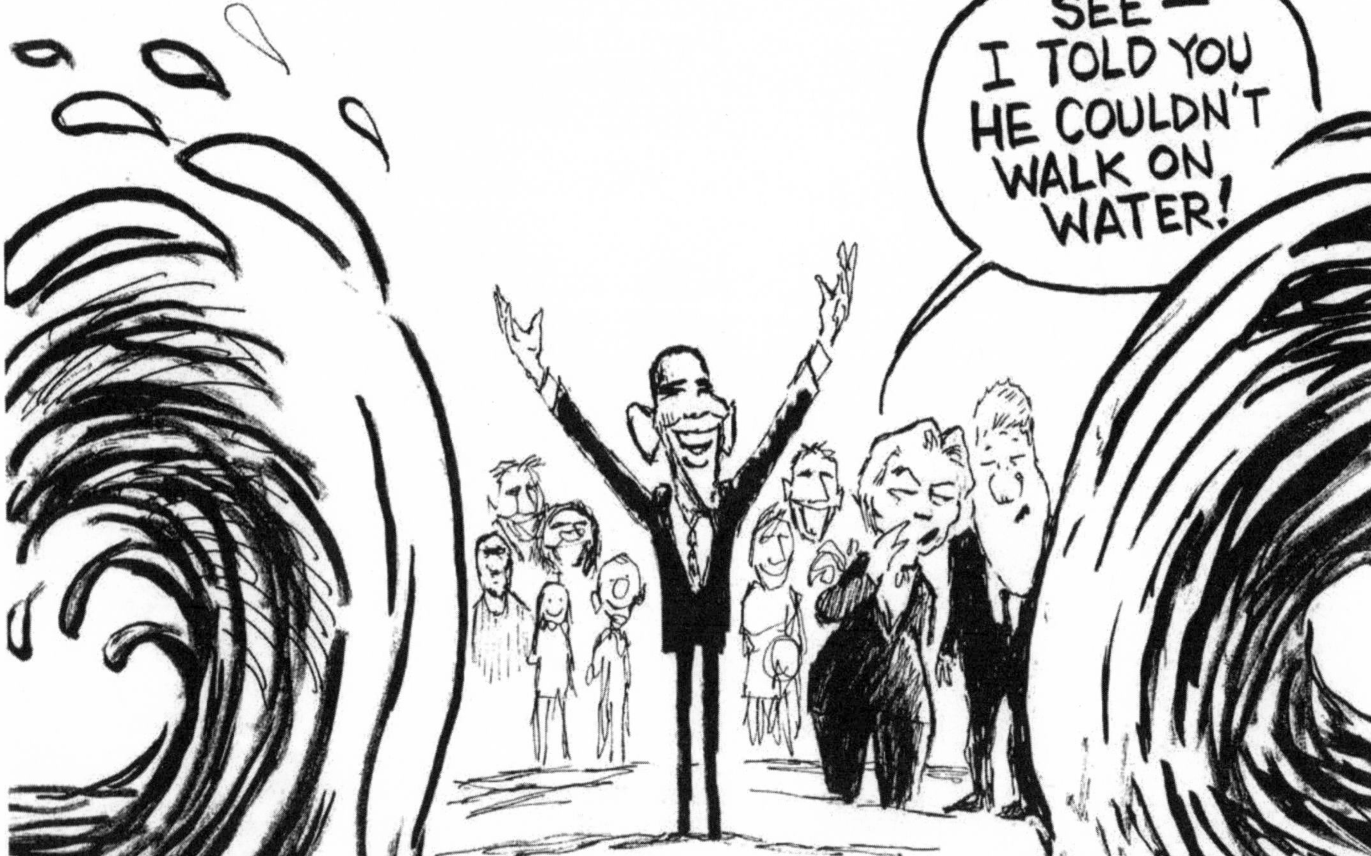
SEE — I TOLD YOU HE COULDN'T WALK ON WATER!
HIGGINS
©08 CHICAGO SUN-TIMES

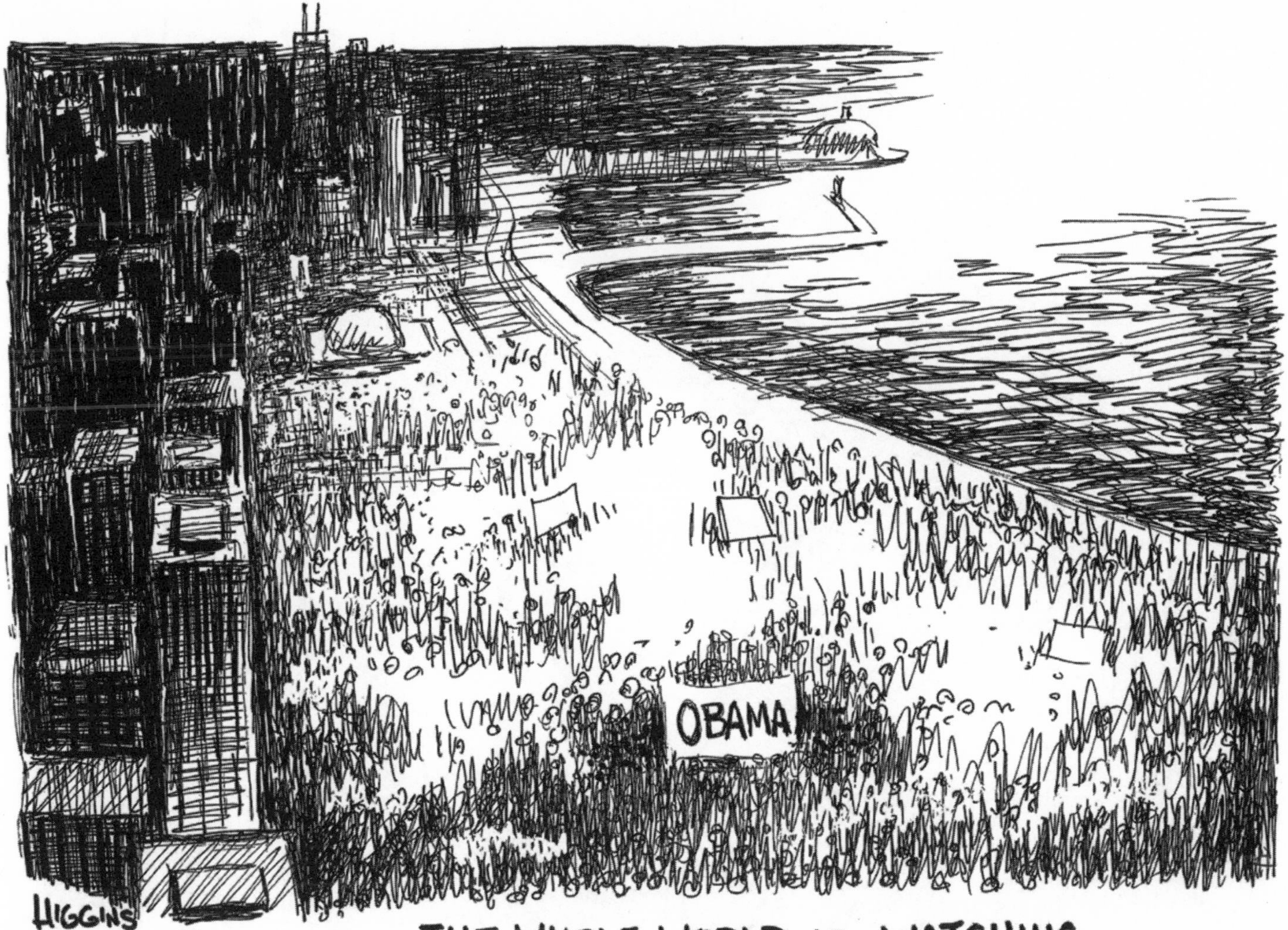
OBAMA
HIGGINS
©08 CHICAGO SUN-TIMES

... THE WHOLE WORLD IS WATCHING.

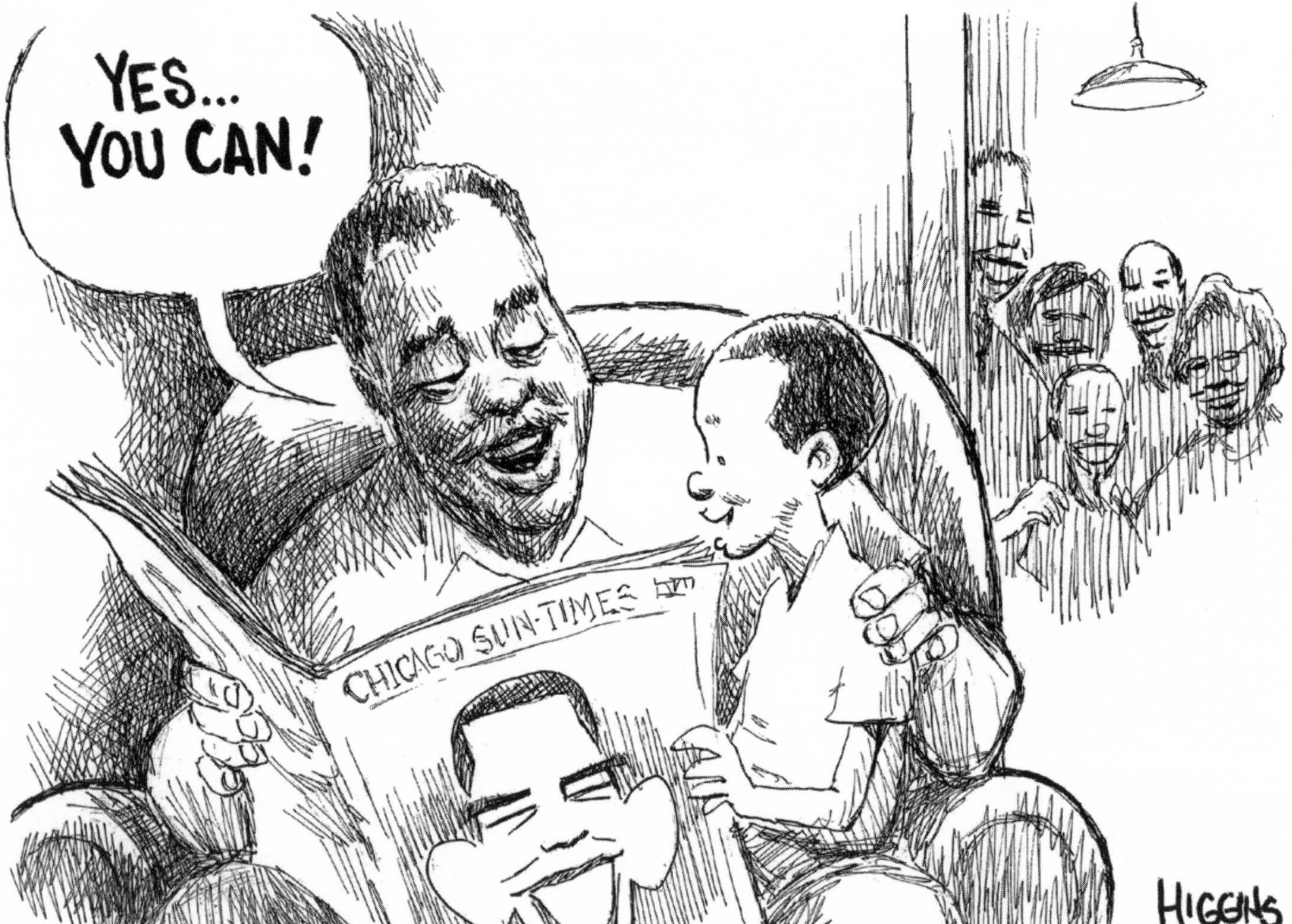
YES... YOU CAN!
CHICAGO SUN-TIMES
HIGGINS
©08 CHICAGO SUN-TIMES

ONLY IN
CHICAGO . . .

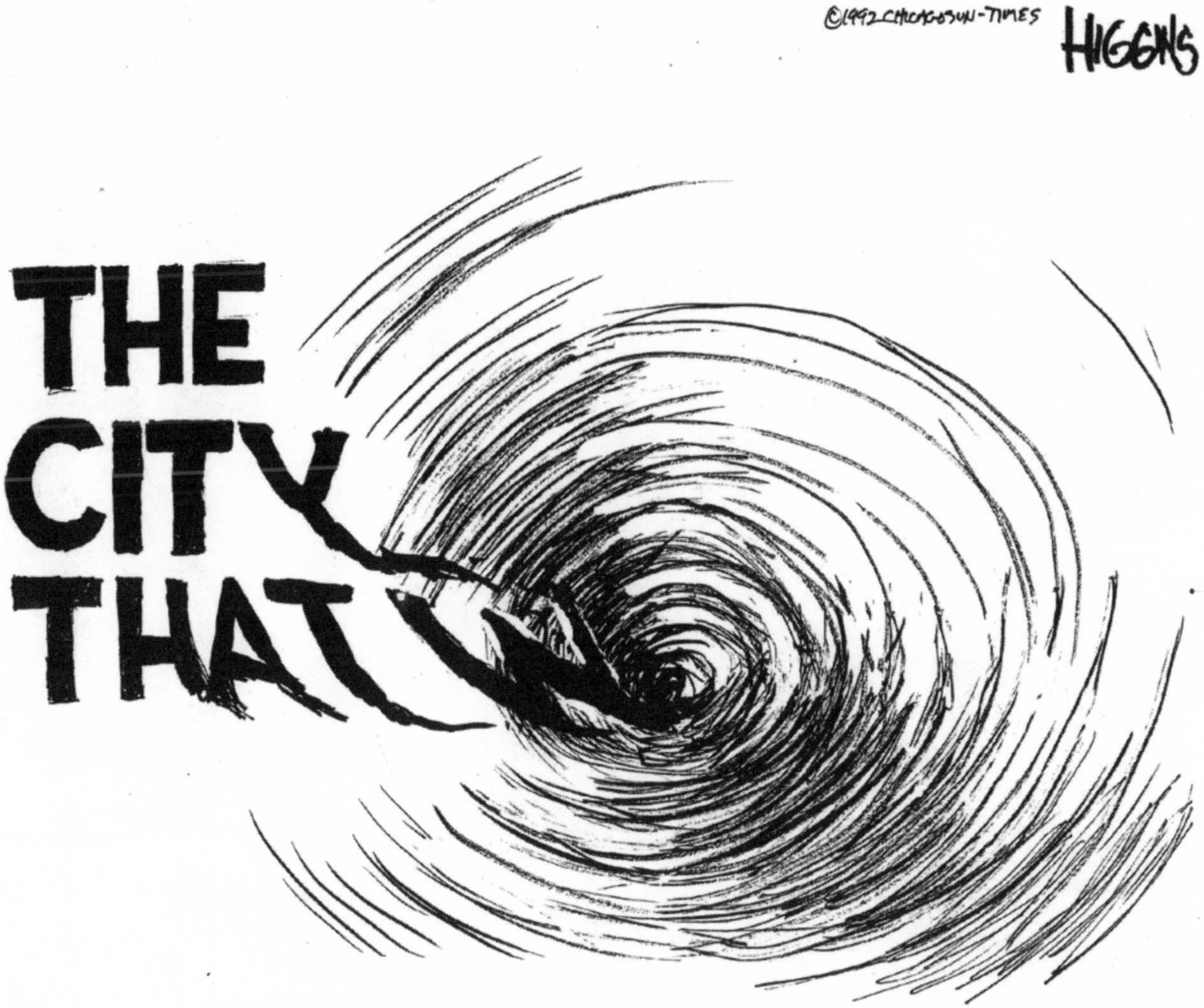
©1992 CHICAGO SUN-TIMES
HIGGINS
THE CITY THAT

. . . does a river sink (100 years after we reverse its flow).

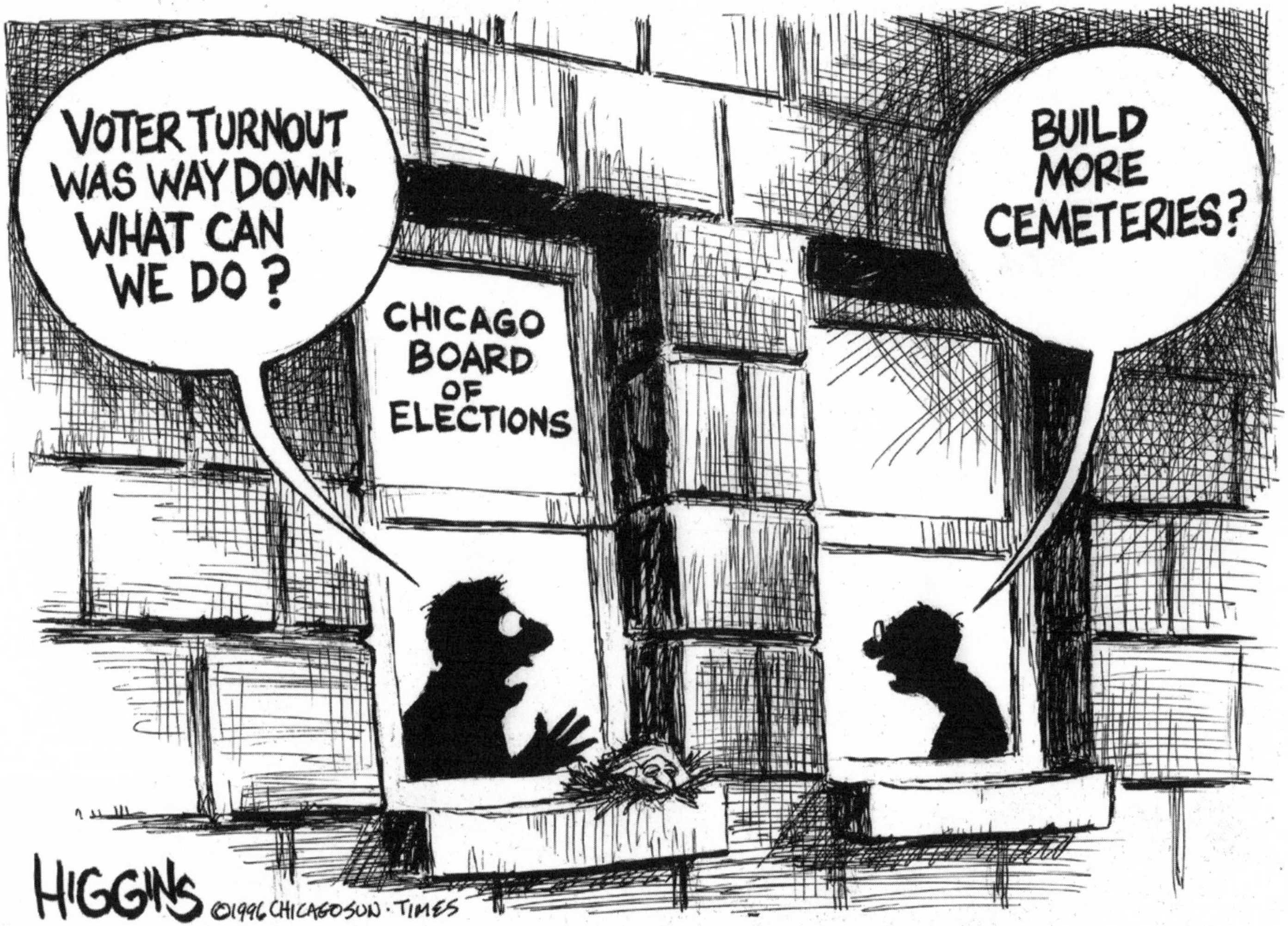
VOTER TURNOUT WAS WAY DOWN. WHAT CAN WE DO?
BUILD MORE CEMETERIES?
CHICAGO BOARD OF ELECTIONS
HIGGINS ©1996 CHICAGO SUN-TIMES

. . . could the coroner's office be part of the Board of Elections.

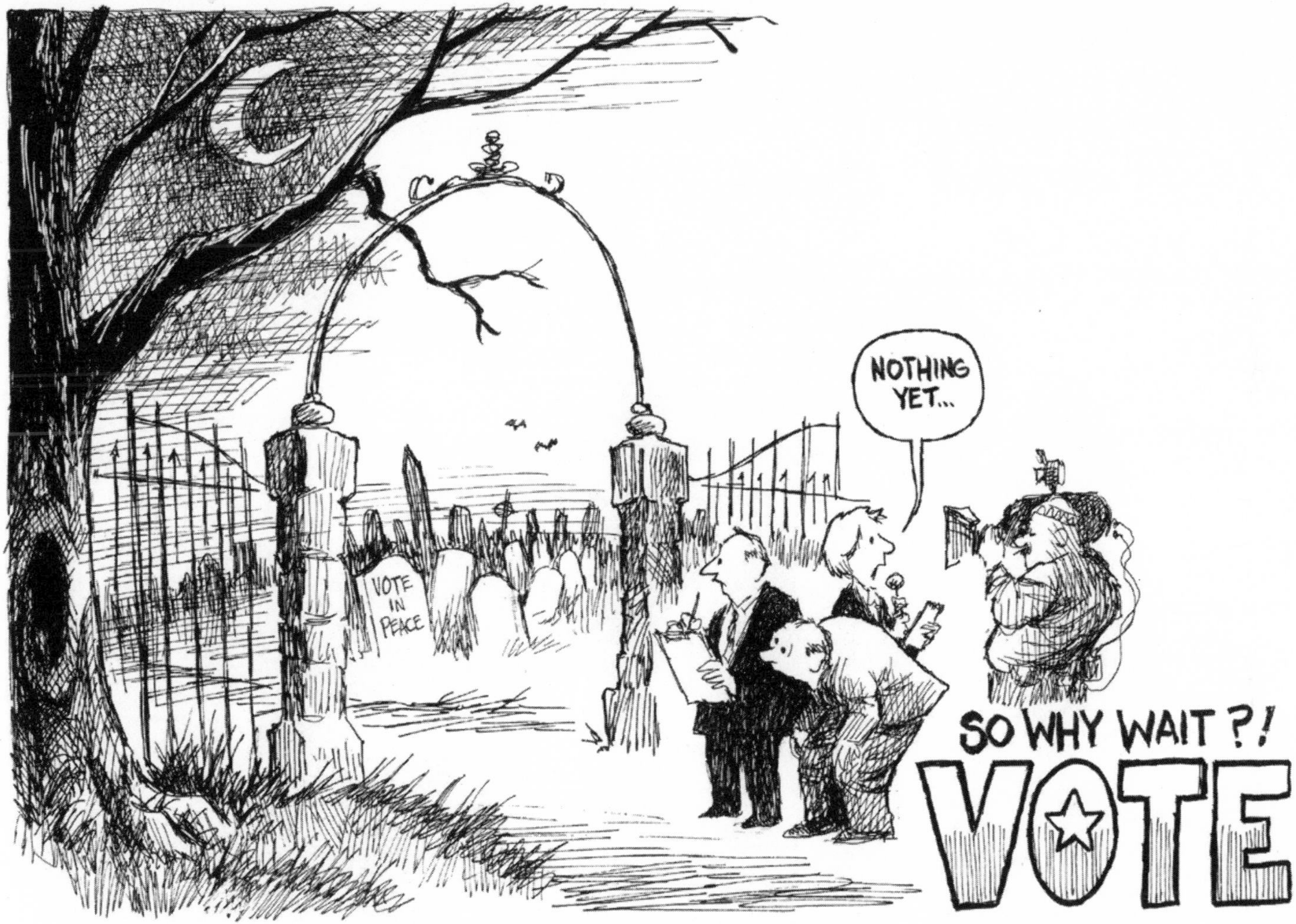
VOTE IN PEACE
NOTHING YET...
SO WHY WAIT ?!
VOTE

. . . are exit polls totally unreliable.

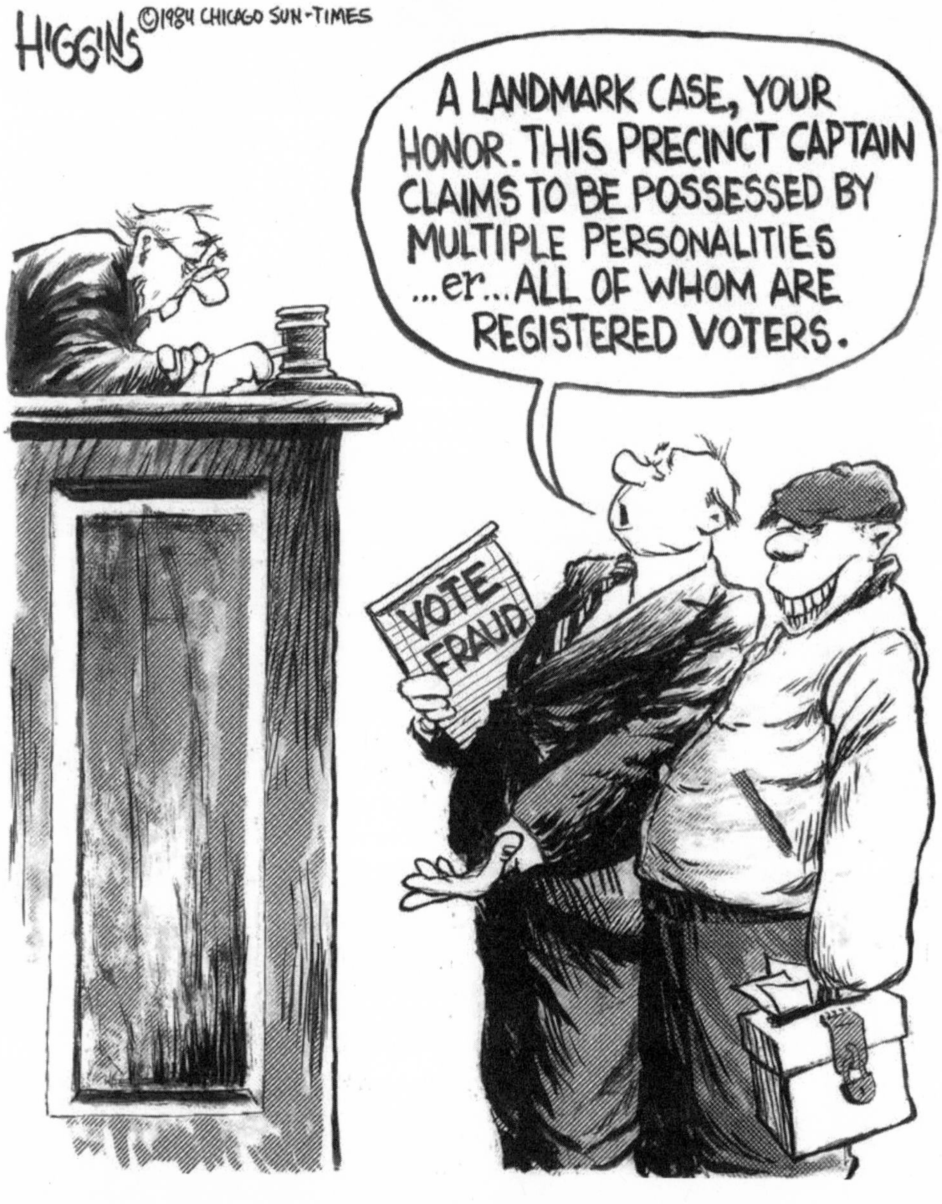
HIGGINS ©1984 CHICAGO SUN-TIMES
A LANDMARK CASE, YOUR HONOR. THIS PRECINCT CAPTAIN CLAIMS TO BE POSSESSED BY MULTIPLE PERSONALITIES ...er...ALL OF WHOM ARE REGISTERED VOTERS.
VOTE FRAUD

. . . can you have a
plurality of one.

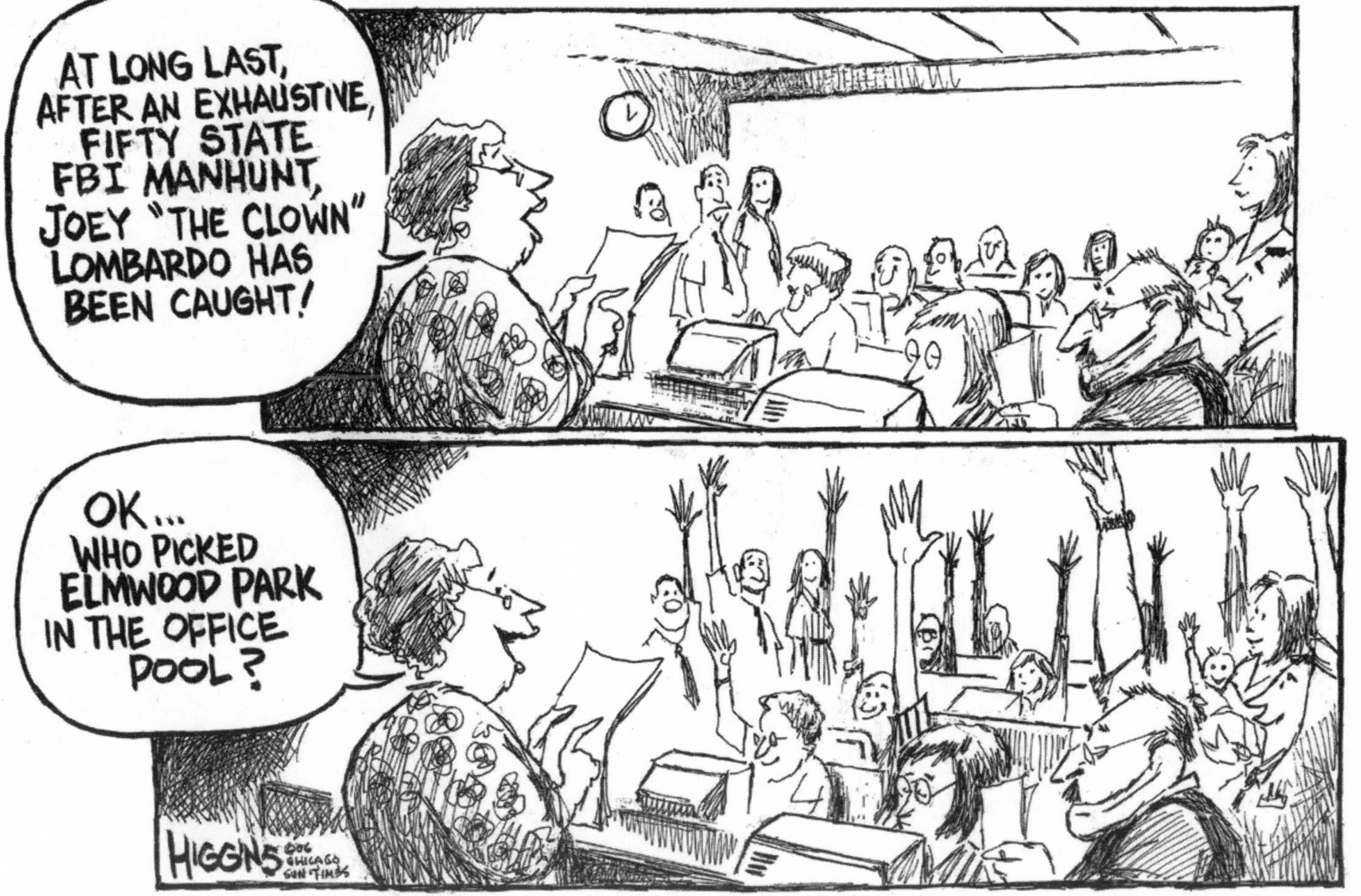
AT LONG LAST, AFTER AN EXHAUSTIVE, FIFTY STATE FBI MANHUNT, JOEY "THE CLOWN" LOMBARDO HAS BEEN CAUGHT!
OK... WHO PICKED ELMWOOD PARK IN THE OFFICE POOL?
HIGGINS ©06 CHICAGO SUN-TIMES

. . . does the mob sleep with the suburbanites and not with the fishes.

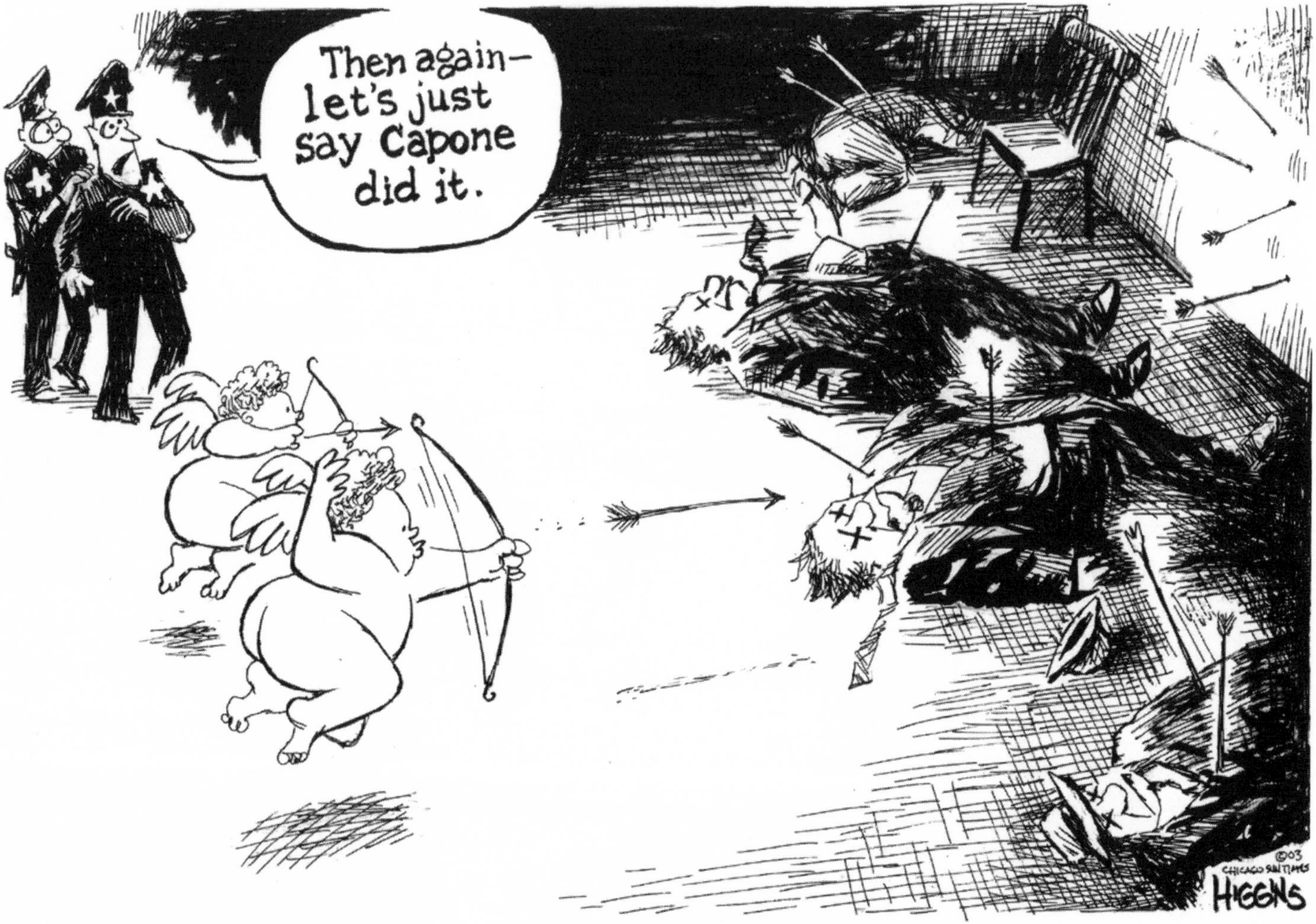
Then again— let's just say Capone did it.
HIGGINS

. . . do we romanticize mass murder every February 14th.

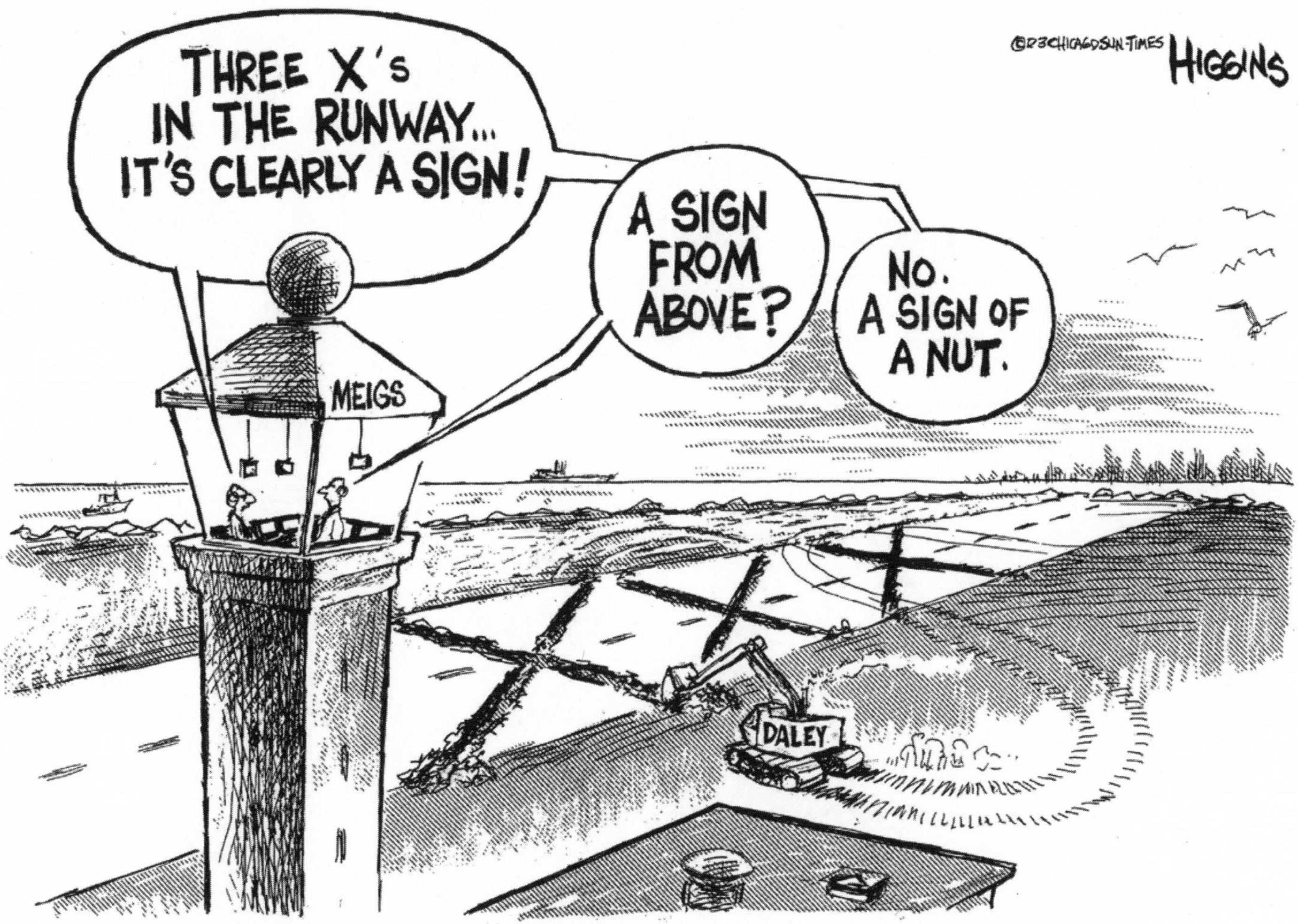
©03 CHICAGO SUN-TIMES HIGGINS
THREE X's IN THE RUNWAY... IT'S CLEARLY A SIGN!
A SIGN FROM ABOVE?
NO. A SIGN OF A NUT.
MEIGS
DALEY

. . . can one man truly make a difference.

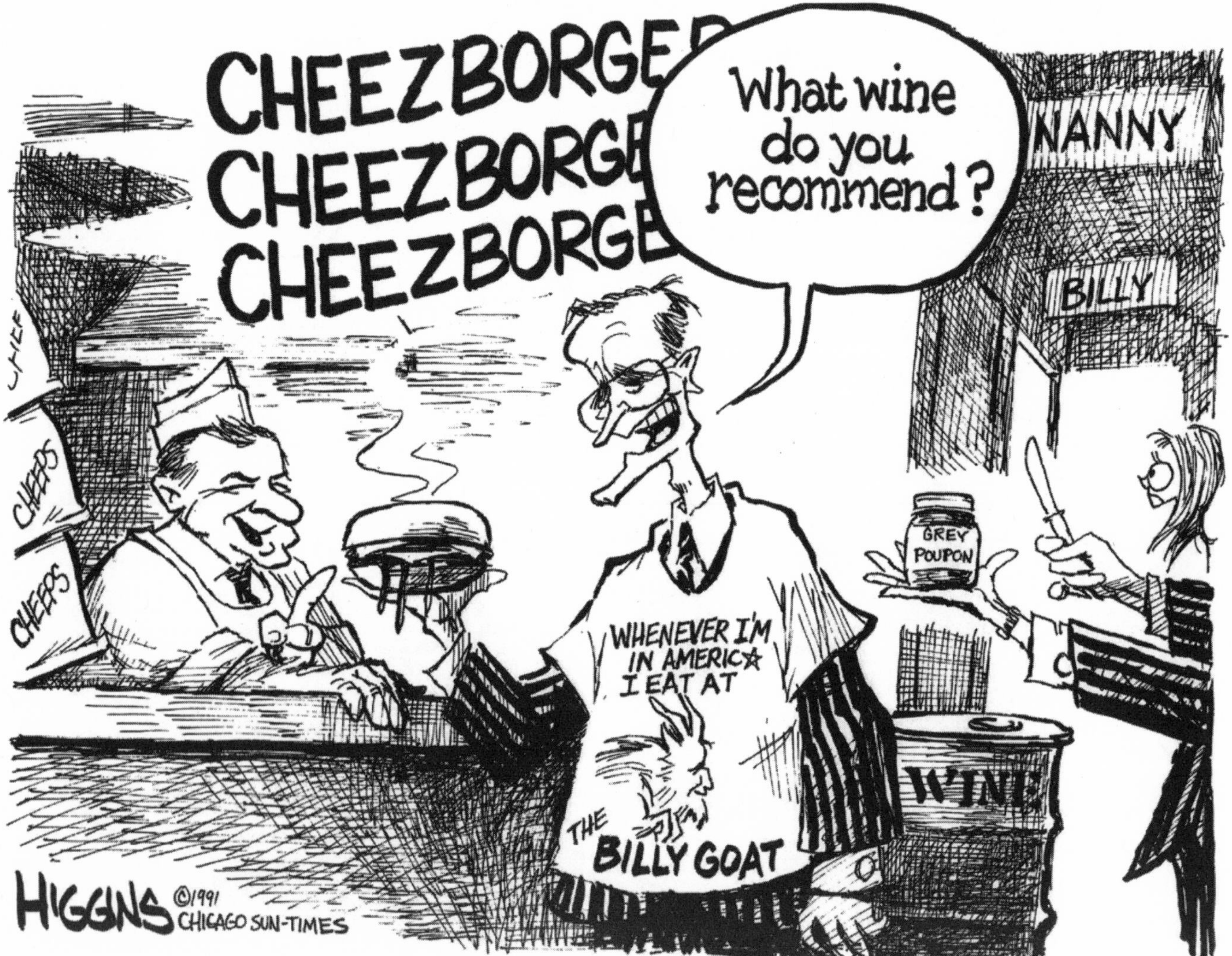
CHEEZBORGER
CHEEZBORGER
CHEEZBORGER
What wine do you recommend?
NANNY
BILLY
CHEERS
CHEERS
GREY POUPON
WHENEVER I'M IN AMERICA I EAT AT THE BILLY GOAT
WINE
HIGGINS ©1991 CHICAGO SUN-TIMES

. . . do we serve "cheezborger, no Coke, Pepsi."

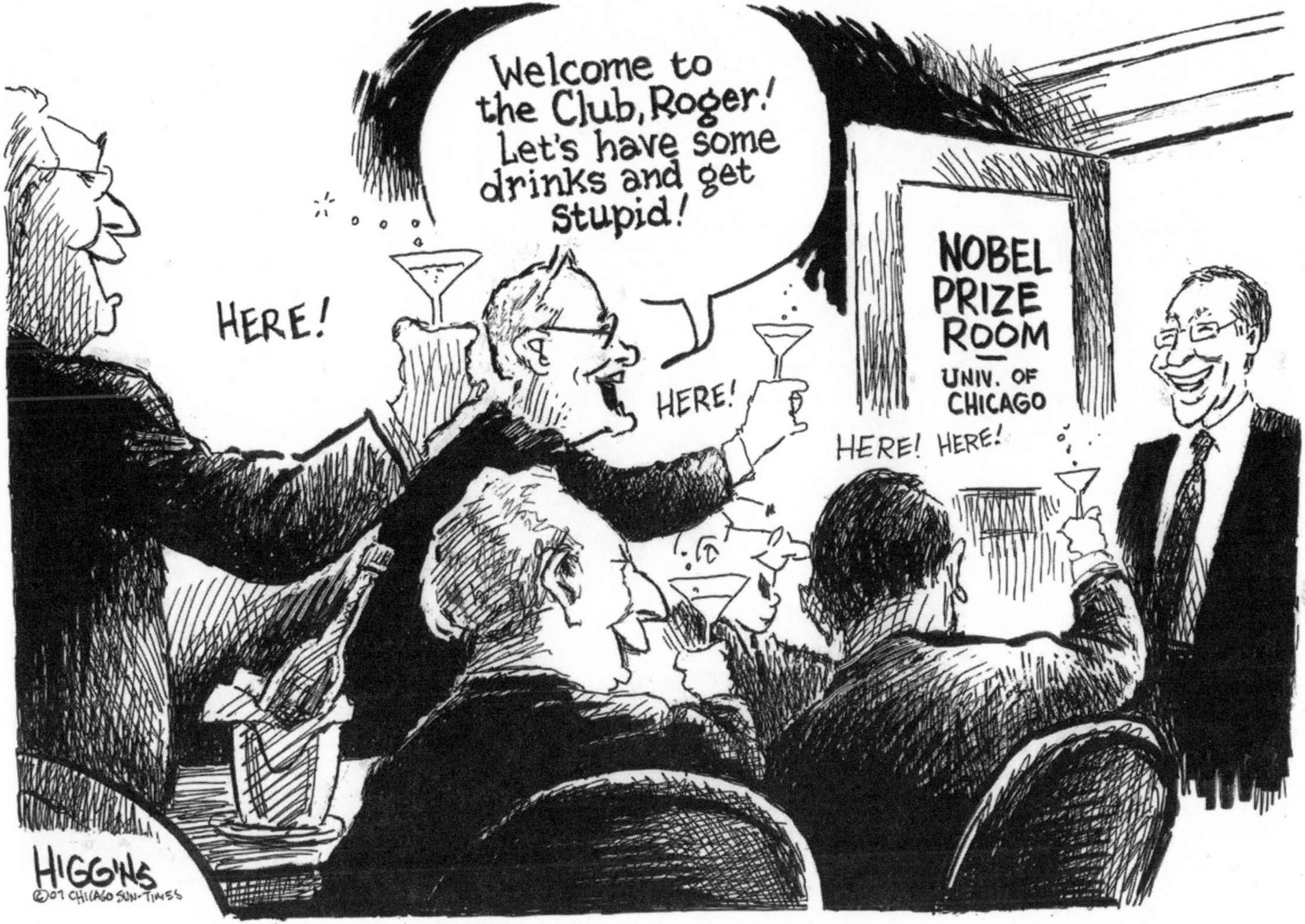
Welcome to the Club, Roger! Let's have some drinks and get stupid!
HERE!
HERE!
HERE! HERE!
NOBEL PRIZE ROOM
UNIV. OF CHICAGO
HIGGINS
©07 CHICAGO SUN-TIMES

. . . do two parties have a lock on winning.

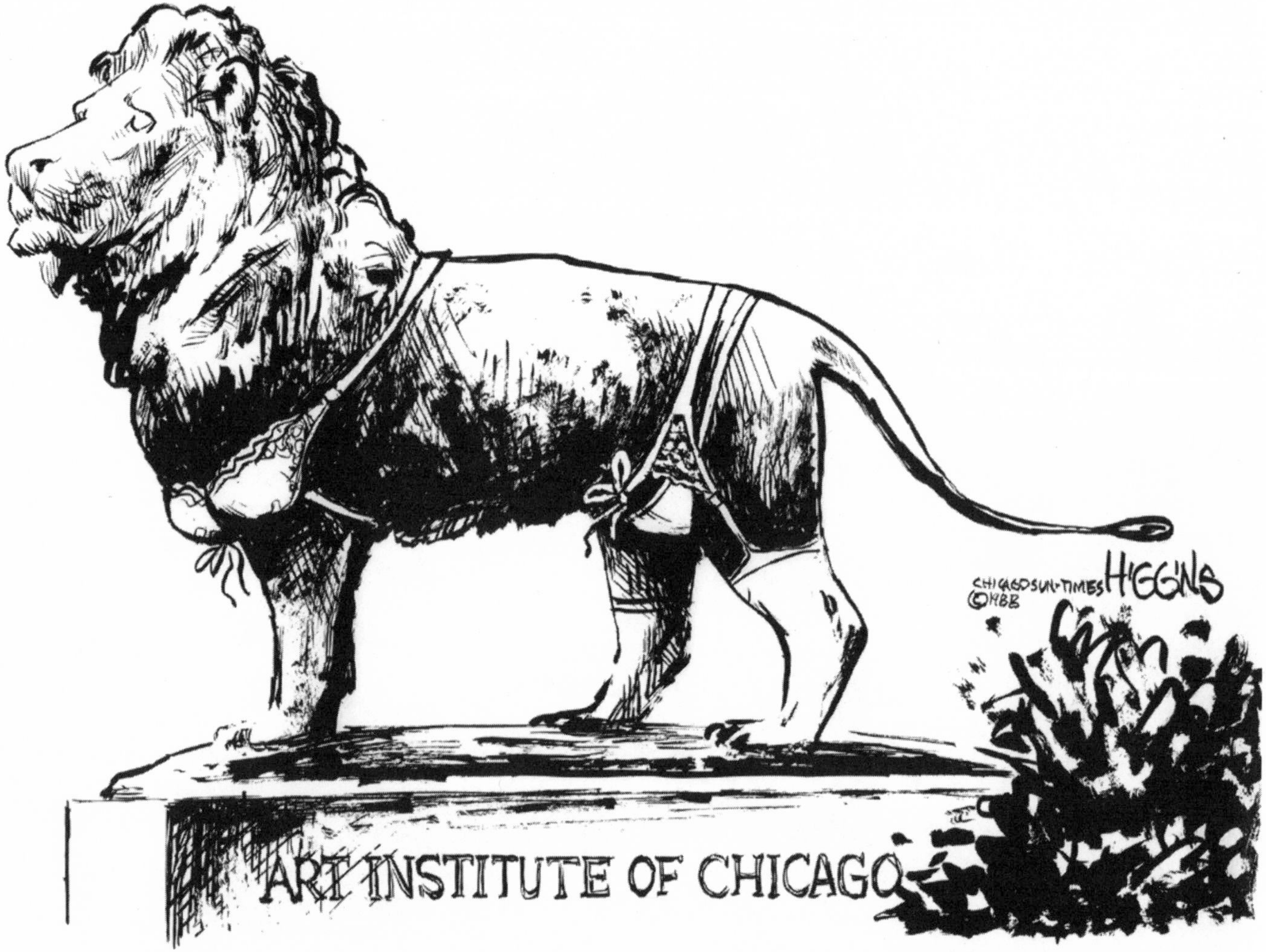
CHICAGO SUN-TIMES HIGGINS
©1988
ART INSTITUTE OF CHICAGO

. . . are our statues clothed for special occasions . . .

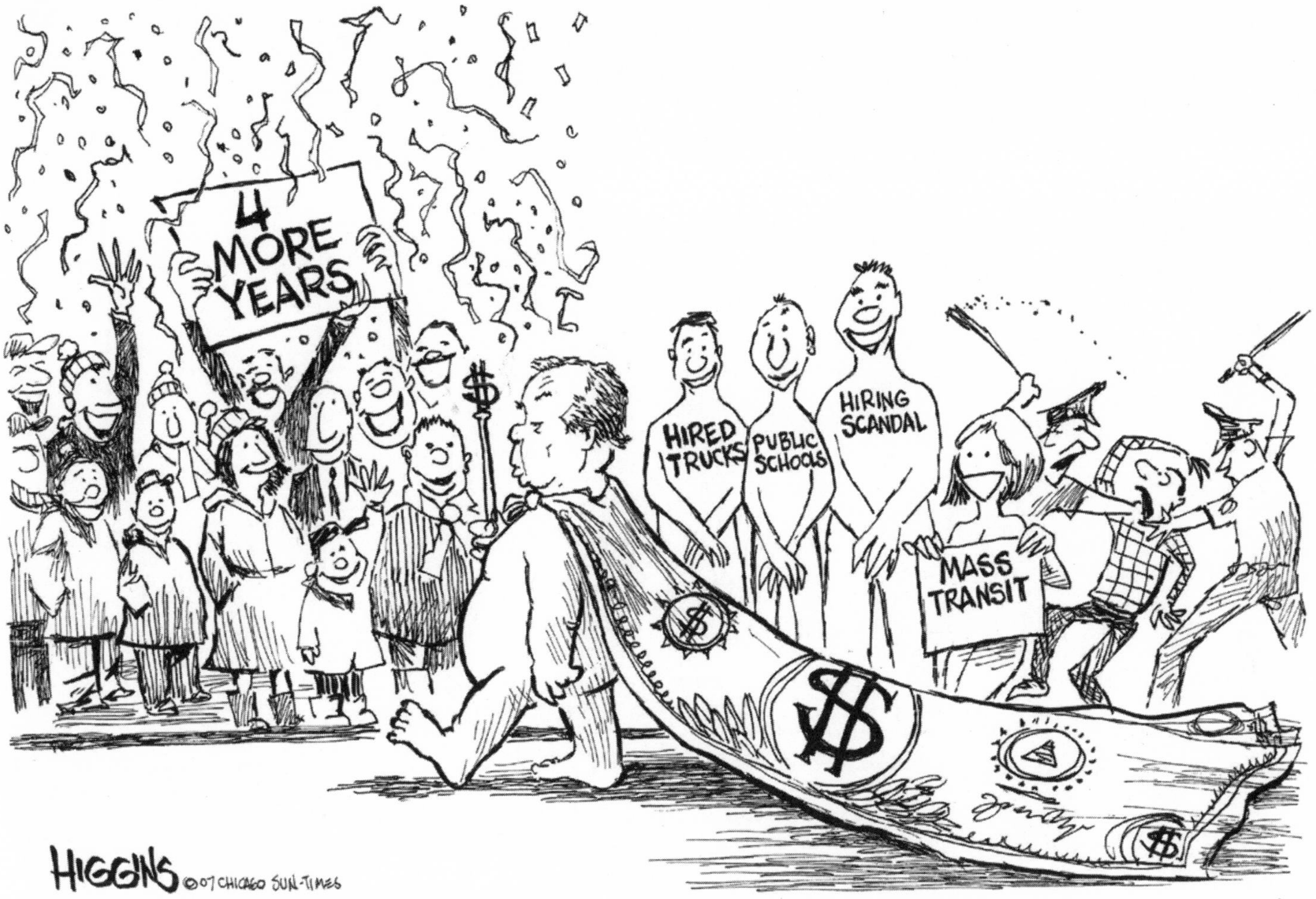
4
MORE
YEARS
$
HIRED
TRUCKS
PUBLIC
SCHOOLS
HIRING
SCANDAL
MASS
TRANSIT
$
$
$
HIGGINS ©07 CHICAGO SUN-TIMES

. . . and our emperors naked.

ALL POLITICS
IS LOCO

The U.S. Attorney's Office was conducting probes of state, county, and city governments in Illinois involving corruption, dishonest bidding practices, crooked contracts, rigged job interviews, phony minority front companies, tax fraud racketeering, and bribery.

The City of Chicago's water commissioner built a political army comprised of hundreds of city employees working city precincts to get out the vote for pro-Daley political candidates. They were rewarded with better paying city jobs, landed through rigged job interviews.

While Mayor Daley repeatedly declared that his administration was in compliance with a federal ban on political hiring and firing (the Shakman decrees), the city was in fact violating it.

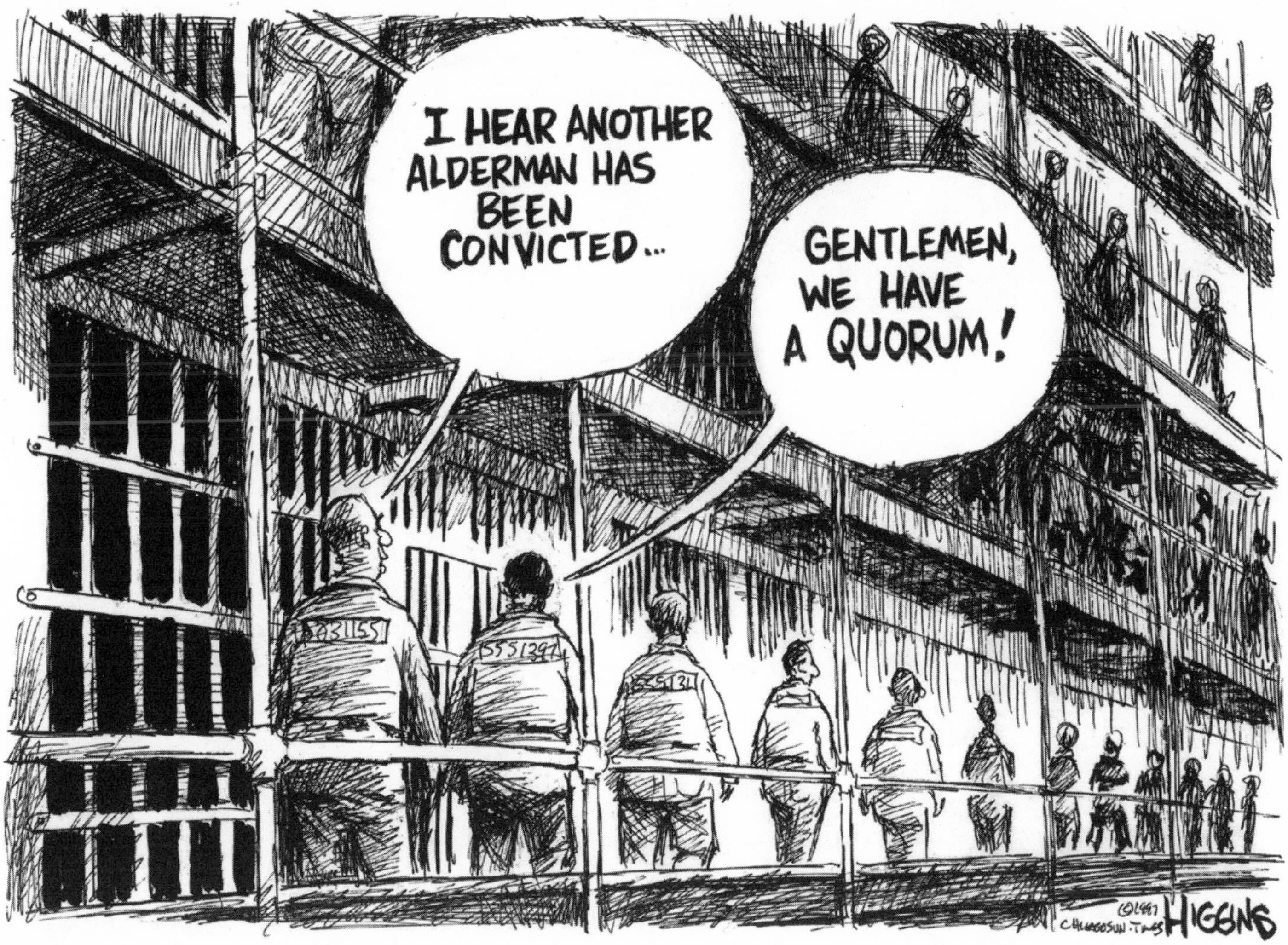
I HEAR ANOTHER ALDERMAN HAS BEEN CONVICTED...
GENTLEMEN, WE HAVE A QUORUM!
©1997 CHICAGO SUN-TIMES HIGGINS

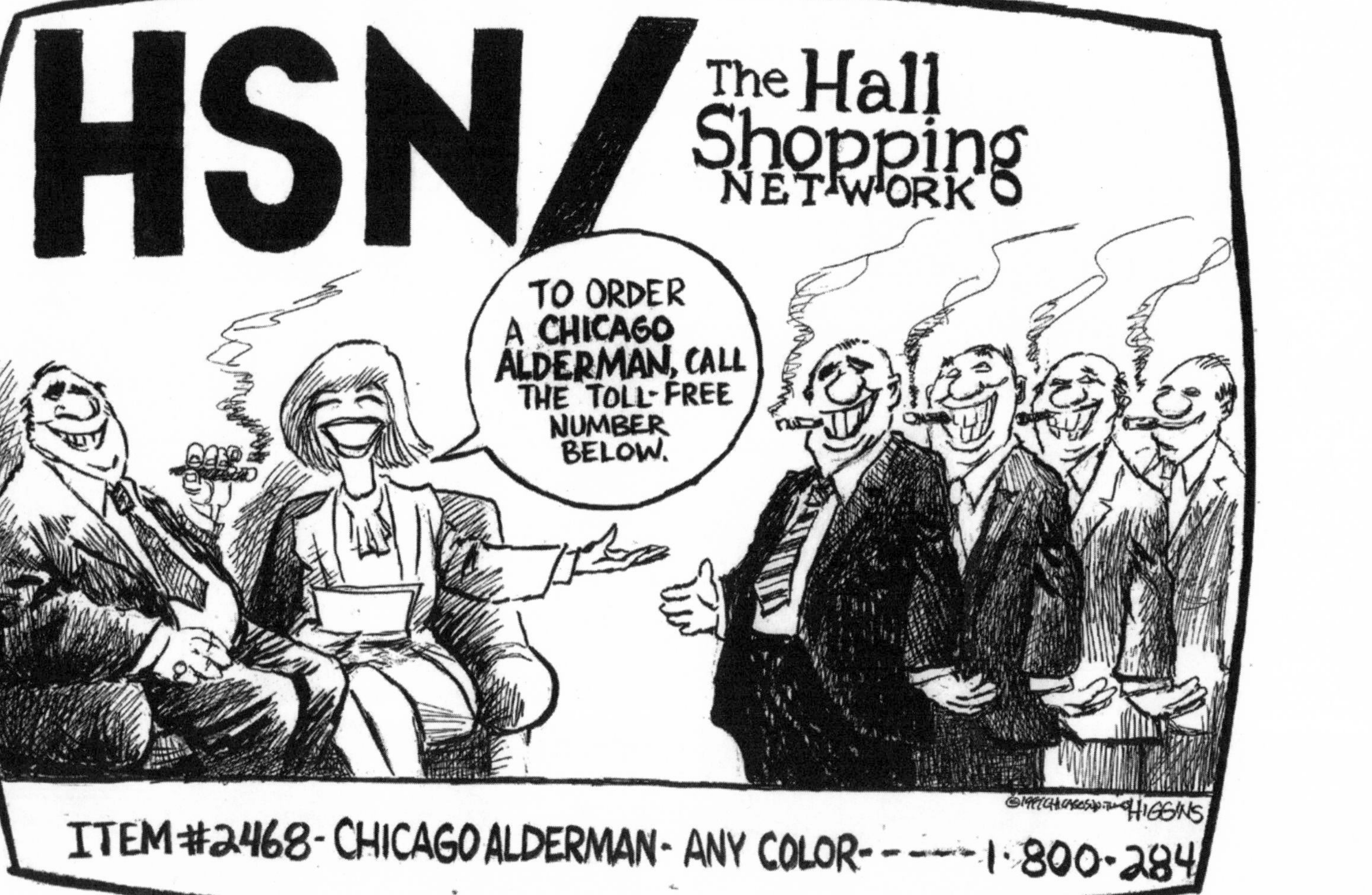
HSN/ The Hall Shopping NETWORK
TO ORDER A CHICAGO ALDERMAN, CALL THE TOLL-FREE NUMBER BELOW.
ITEM #2468- CHICAGO ALDERMAN- ANY COLOR----1-800-284
HIGGINS

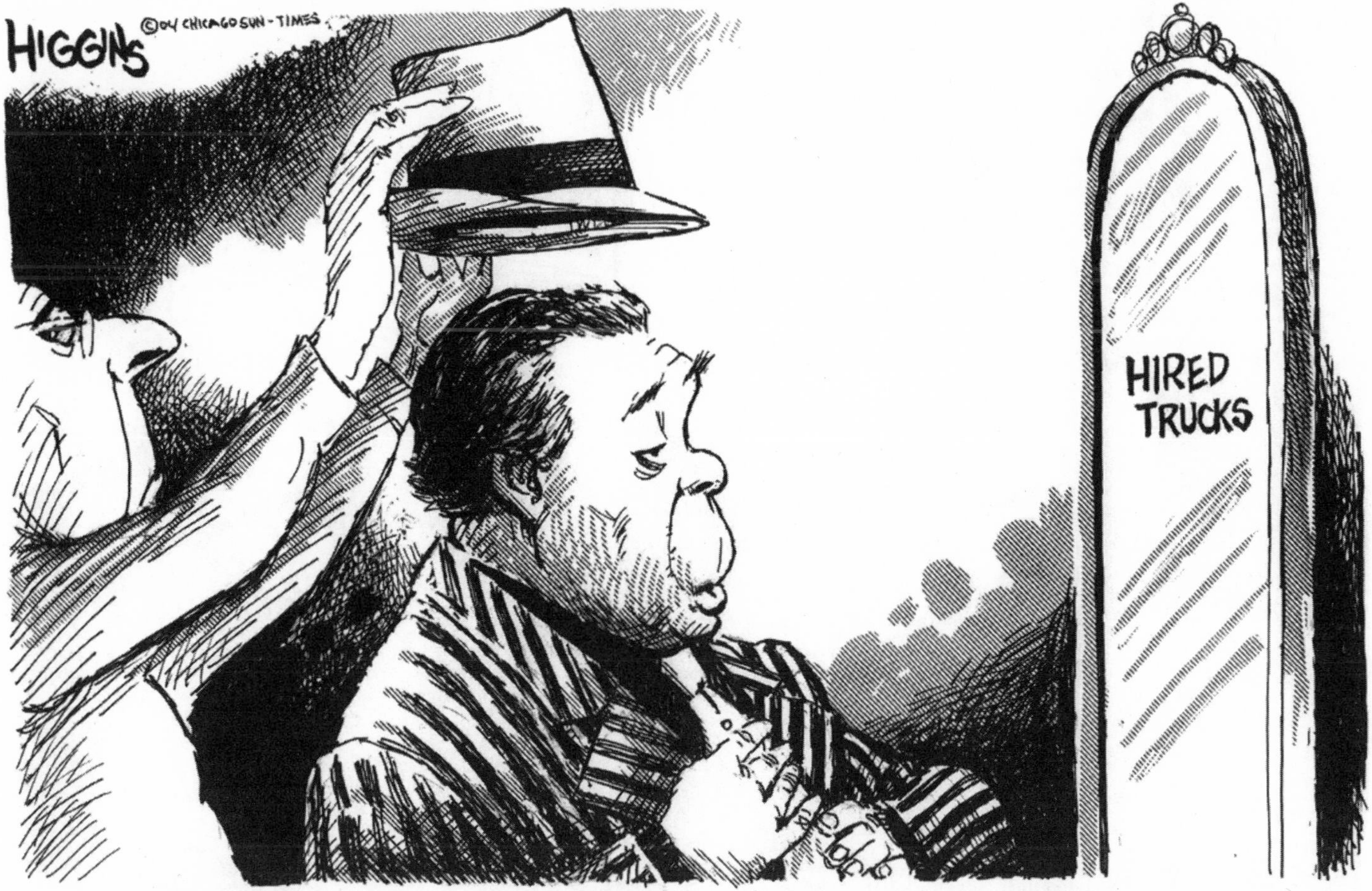
HIGGINS
©04 CHICAGO SUN-TIMES
HIRED TRUCKS

" DOES MY TIE LOOK CROOKED, OR IS IT JUST ME...? "

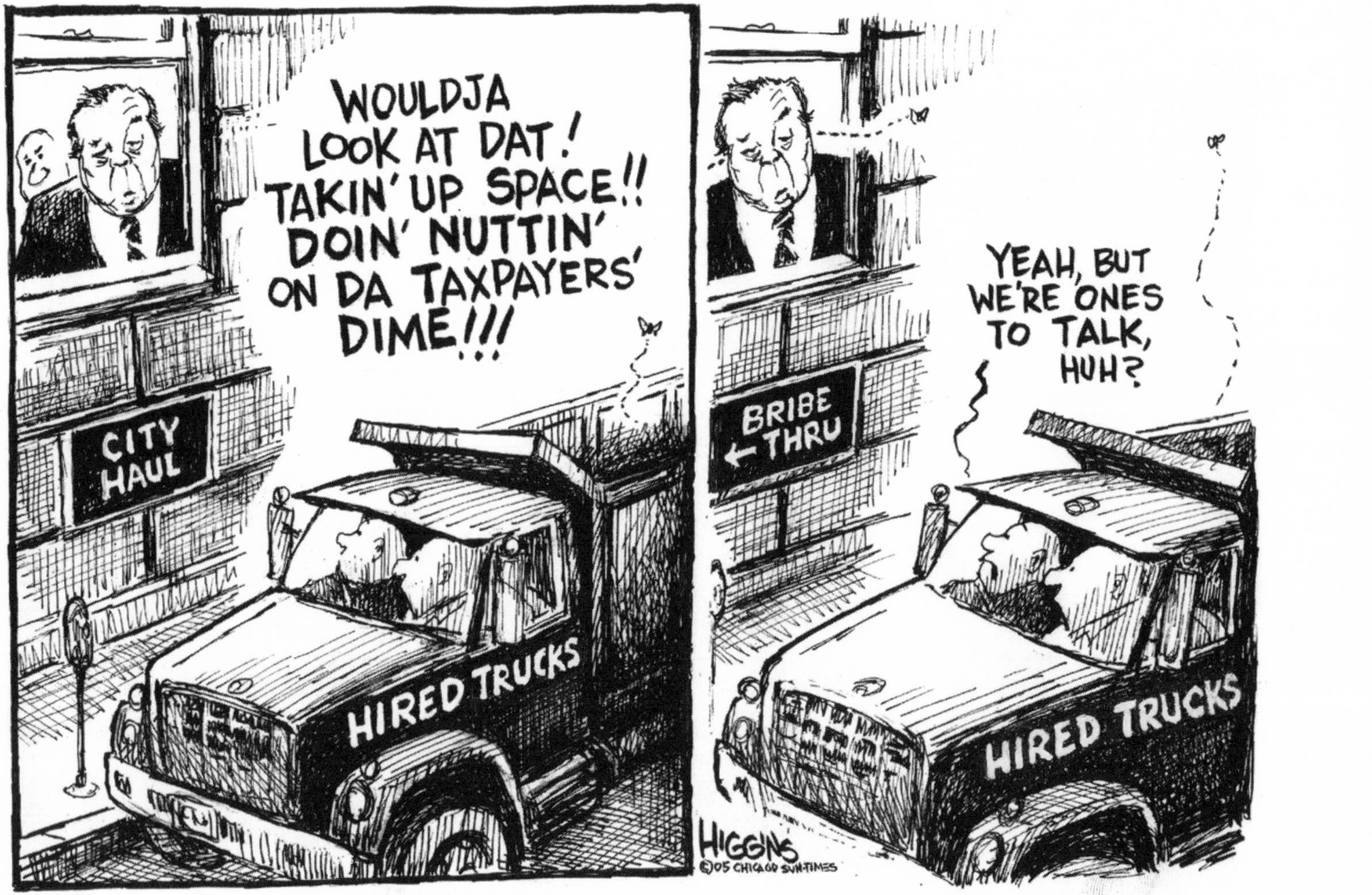
WOULDJA LOOK AT DAT! TAKIN' UP SPACE!! DOIN' NUTTIN' ON DA TAXPAYERS' DIME!!!
CITY HAUL
HIRED TRUCKS
BRIBE ← THRU
YEAH, BUT WE'RE ONES TO TALK, HUH?
HIRED TRUCKS
HIGGINS
©05 CHICAGO SUN-TIMES

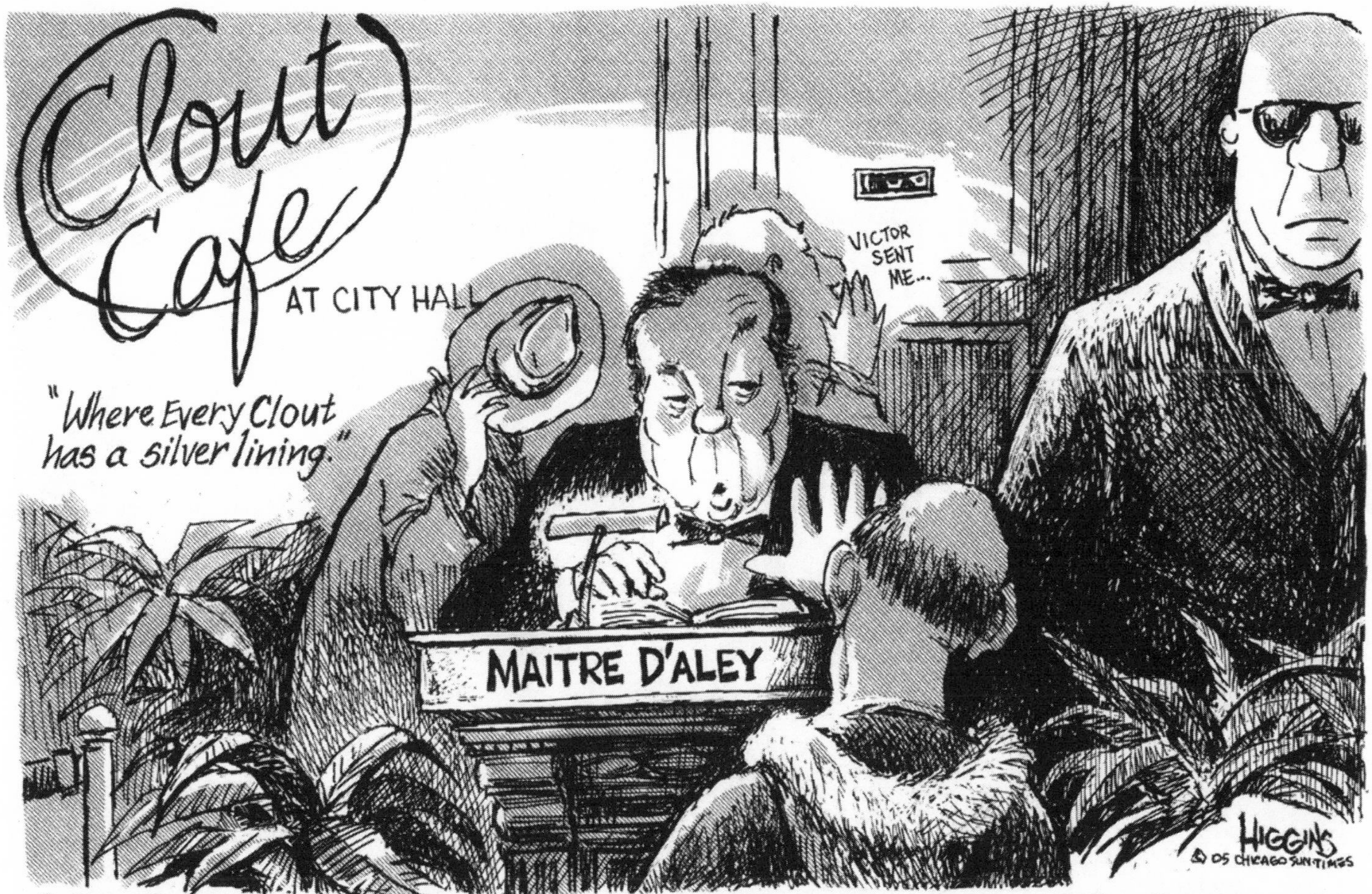
Clout Cafe
AT CITY HALL
"Where Every Clout has a silver lining."
VICTOR SENT ME...
MAITRE D'ALEY
HIGGINS
© 05 CHICAGO SUN-TIMES

"SO SORRY... I CAN'T SEEM TO FIND YOUR NAME... WHO SENT YA?"

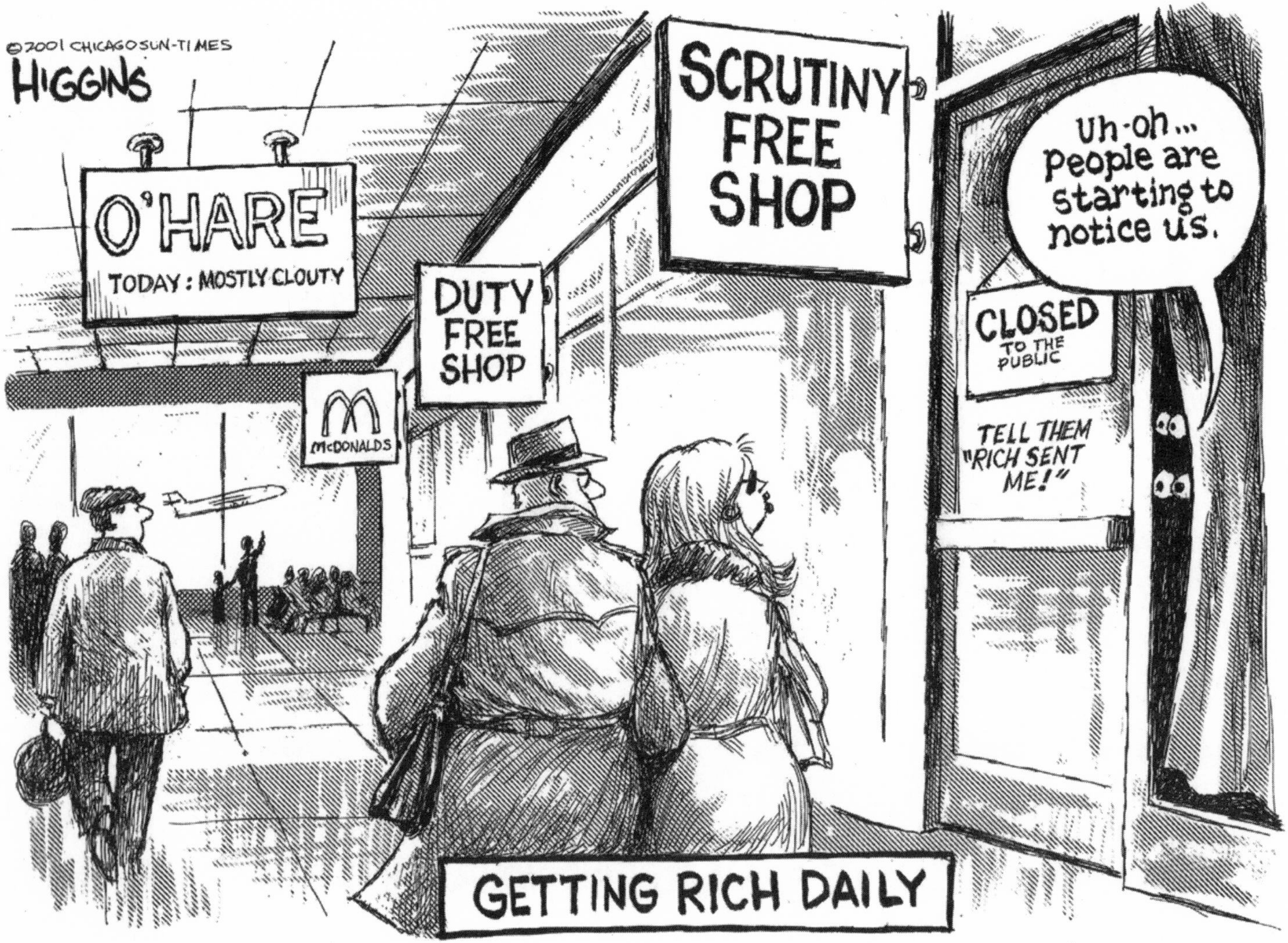
©2001 CHICAGO SUN-TIMES
HIGGINS
O'HARE
TODAY : MOSTLY CLOUTY
McDONALDS
DUTY FREE SHOP
SCRUTINY FREE SHOP
CLOSED TO THE PUBLIC
TELL THEM "RICH SENT ME!"
Uh-oh... People are starting to notice us.
GETTING RICH DAILY

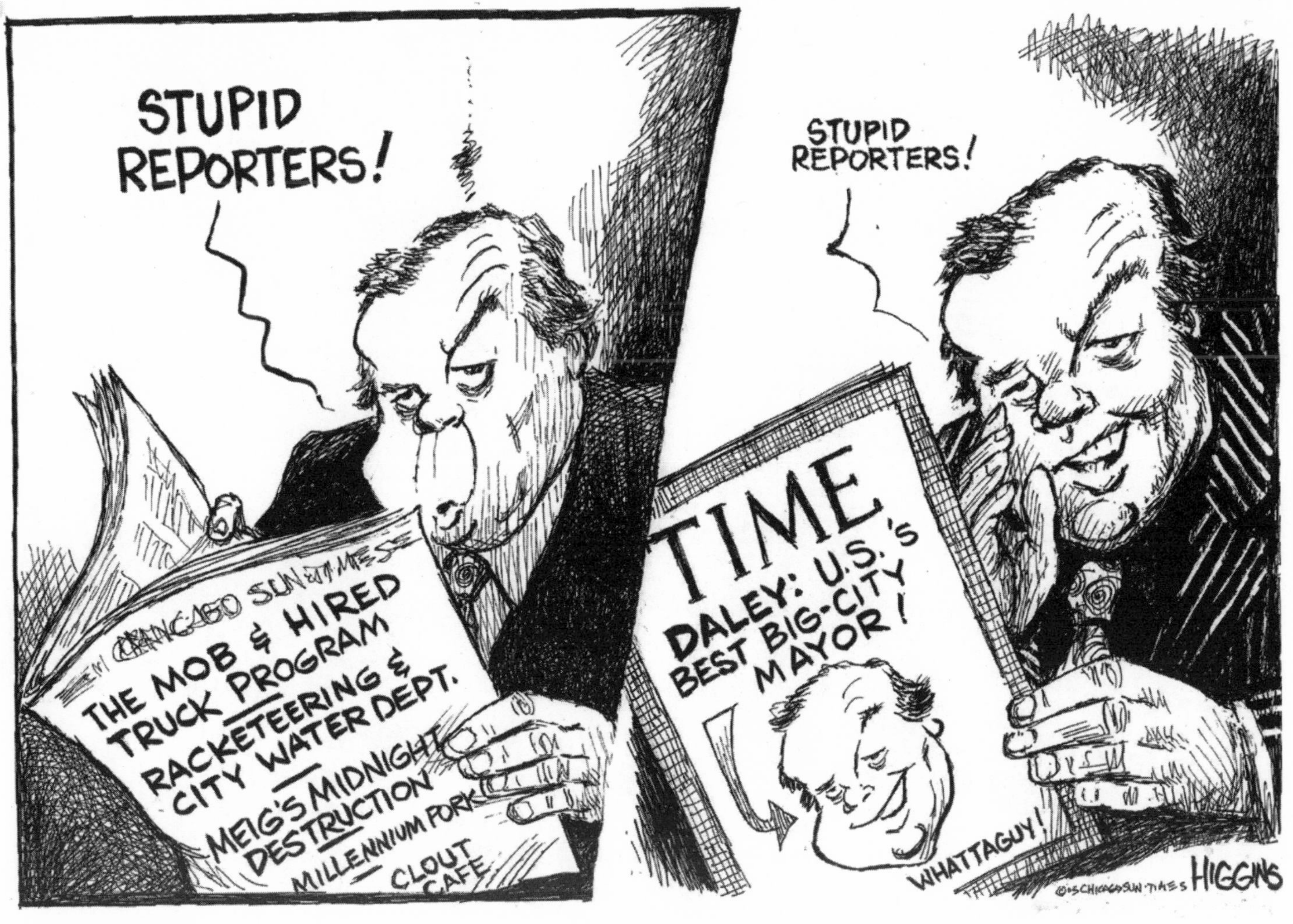
STUPID REPORTERS!
THE MOB & HIRED TRUCK PROGRAM
RACKETEERING & CITY WATER DEPT.
MEIG'S MIDNIGHT DESTRUCTION
MILLENNIUM PORK
CLOUT CAFE
STUPID REPORTERS!
TIME
DALEY: U.S.'s BEST BIG-CITY MAYOR!
WHATTAGUY!
HIGGINS

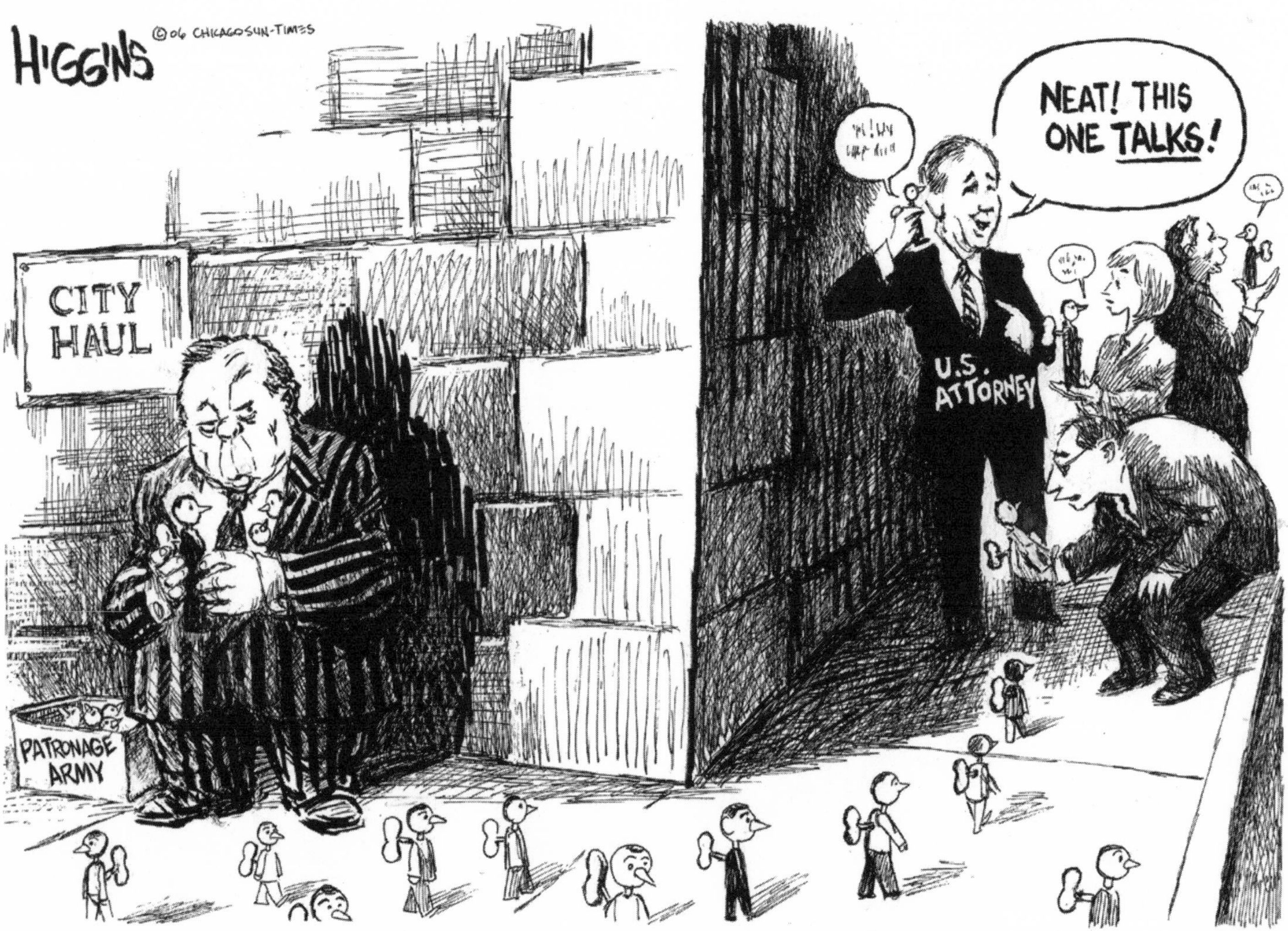
HIGGINS
©06 CHICAGO SUN-TIMES
CITY HAUL
PATRONAGE ARMY
U.S. ATTORNEY
NEAT! THIS ONE TALKS!

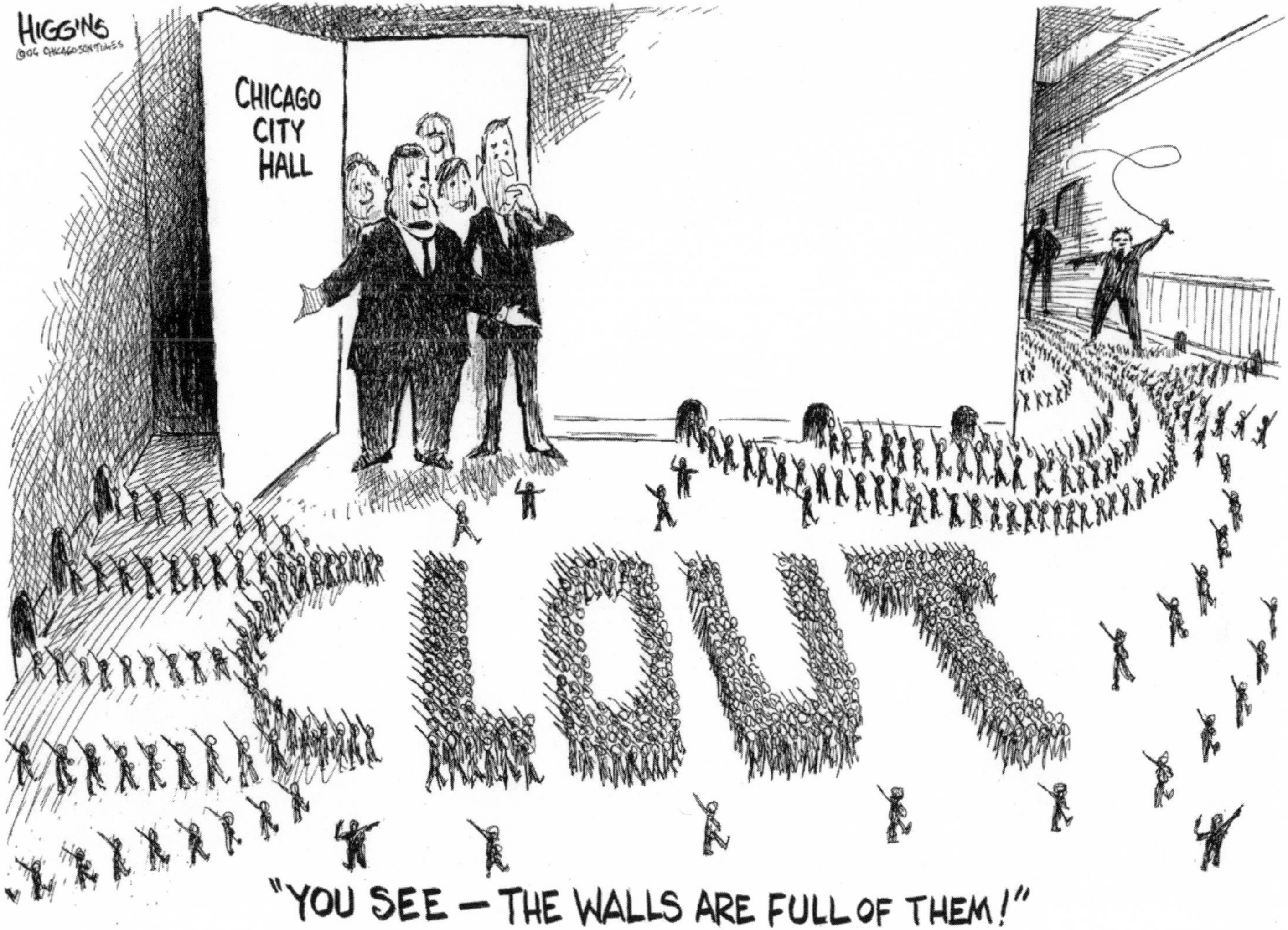
HIGGINS
©06 CHICAGO SUN-TIMES
CHICAGO CITY HALL
CLOUT
"YOU SEE — THE WALLS ARE FULL OF THEM!"

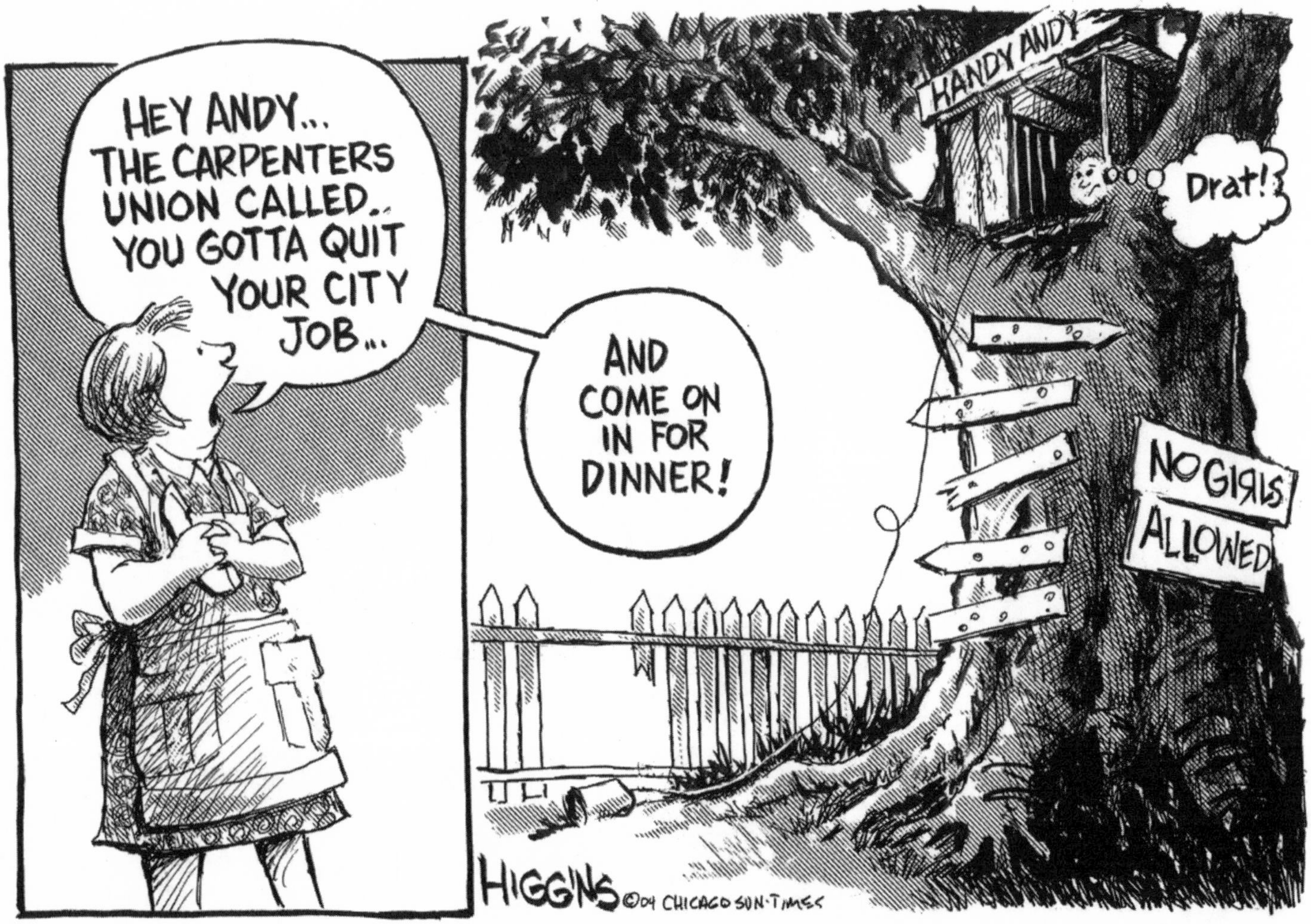
HEY ANDY... THE CARPENTERS UNION CALLED.. YOU GOTTA QUIT YOUR CITY JOB...
AND COME ON IN FOR DINNER!
HANDY ANDY
Drat!
NO GIRLS ALLOWED
HIGGINS ©04 CHICAGO SUN-TIMES

An 18-year-old gets a job as a city inspector.

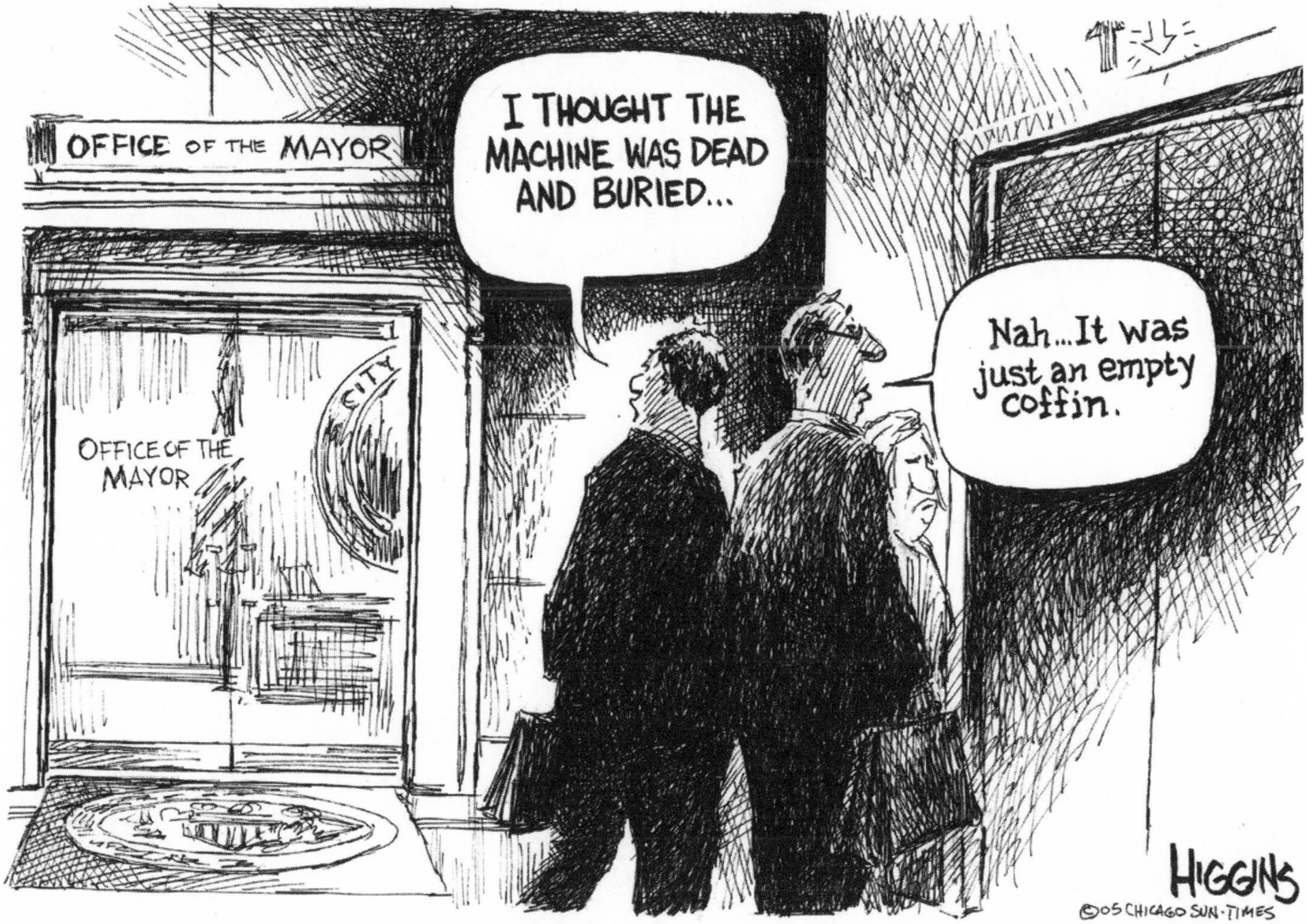
OFFICE OF THE MAYOR
OFFICE OF THE MAYOR
CITY
I THOUGHT THE MACHINE WAS DEAD AND BURIED...
Nah...It was just an empty coffin.
HIGGINS
©05 CHICAGO SUN-TIMES

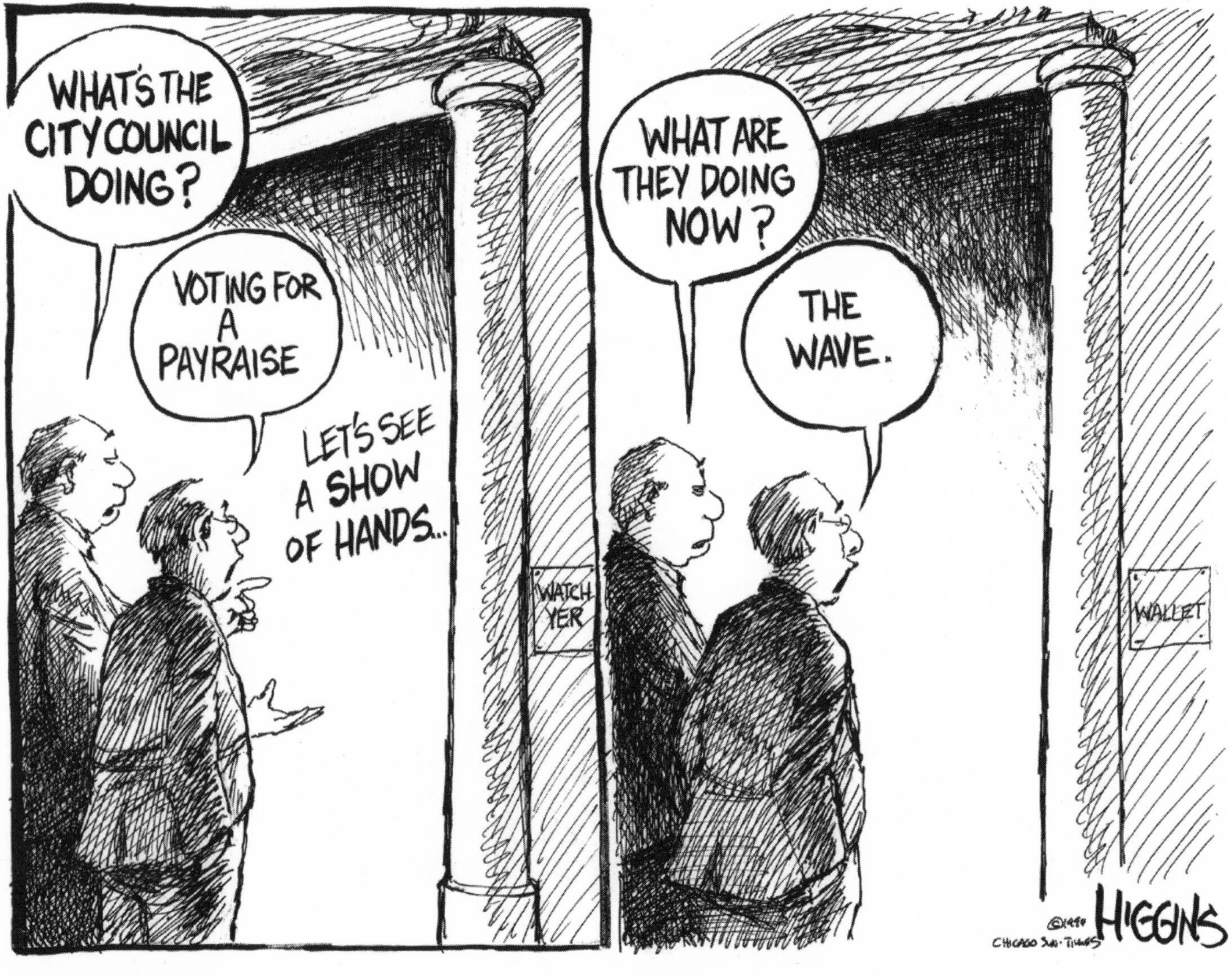
WHAT'S THE CITY COUNCIL DOING?
VOTING FOR A PAYRAISE
LET'S SEE A SHOW OF HANDS...
WATCH YER
WHAT ARE THEY DOING NOW?
THE WAVE.
WALLET
©1990 CHICAGO SUN-TIMES
HIGGINS

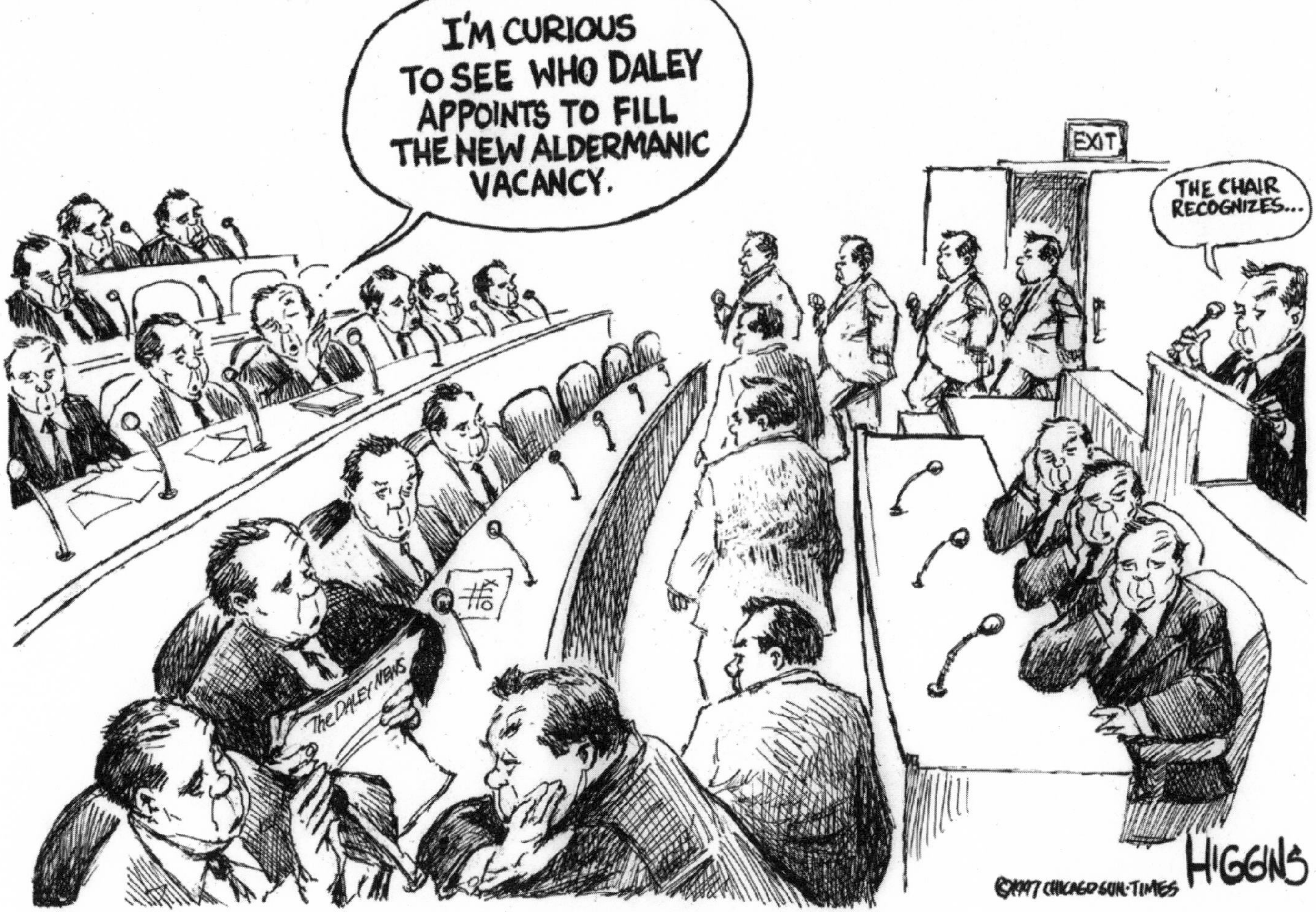
I'M CURIOUS TO SEE WHO DALEY APPOINTS TO FILL THE NEW ALDERMANIC VACANCY.
EXIT
THE CHAIR RECOGNIZES...
The DALEY NEWS
©1997 CHICAGO SUN-TIMES
HIGGINS

Daley puts his thumbprint on the City Council.

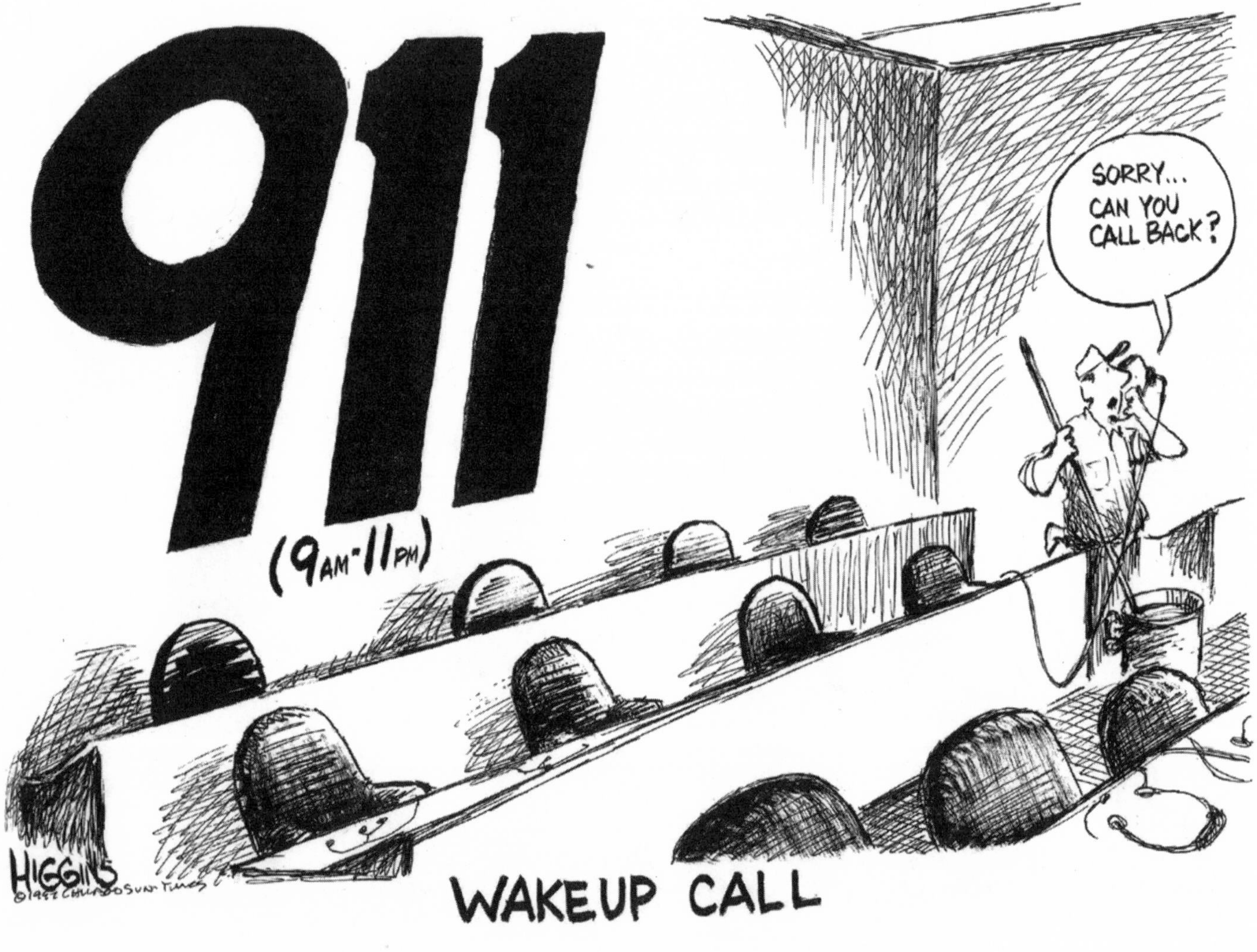

911
(9AM-11PM)
SORRY... CAN YOU CALL BACK?
HIGGINS
WAKEUP CALL

City's 9/11 Center is understaffed and underfunded.

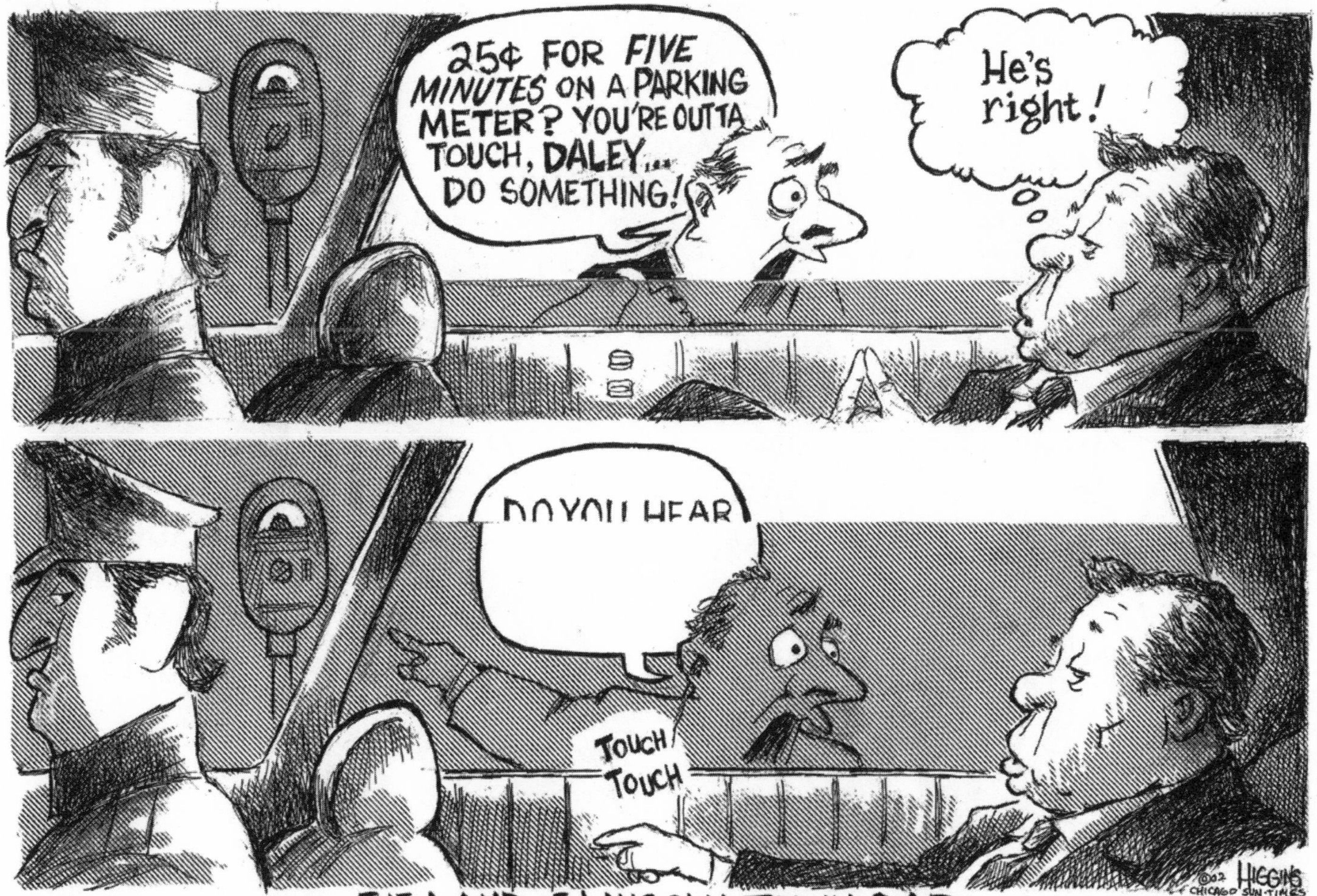
25¢ FOR FIVE MINUTES ON A PARKING METER? YOU'RE OUTTA TOUCH, DALEY... DO SOMETHING!
He's right!
DO YOU HEAR
TOUCH! TOUCH
©02 HIGGINS CHICAGO SUN-TIMES

THE LAND OF LINCOLN TOWN CAR

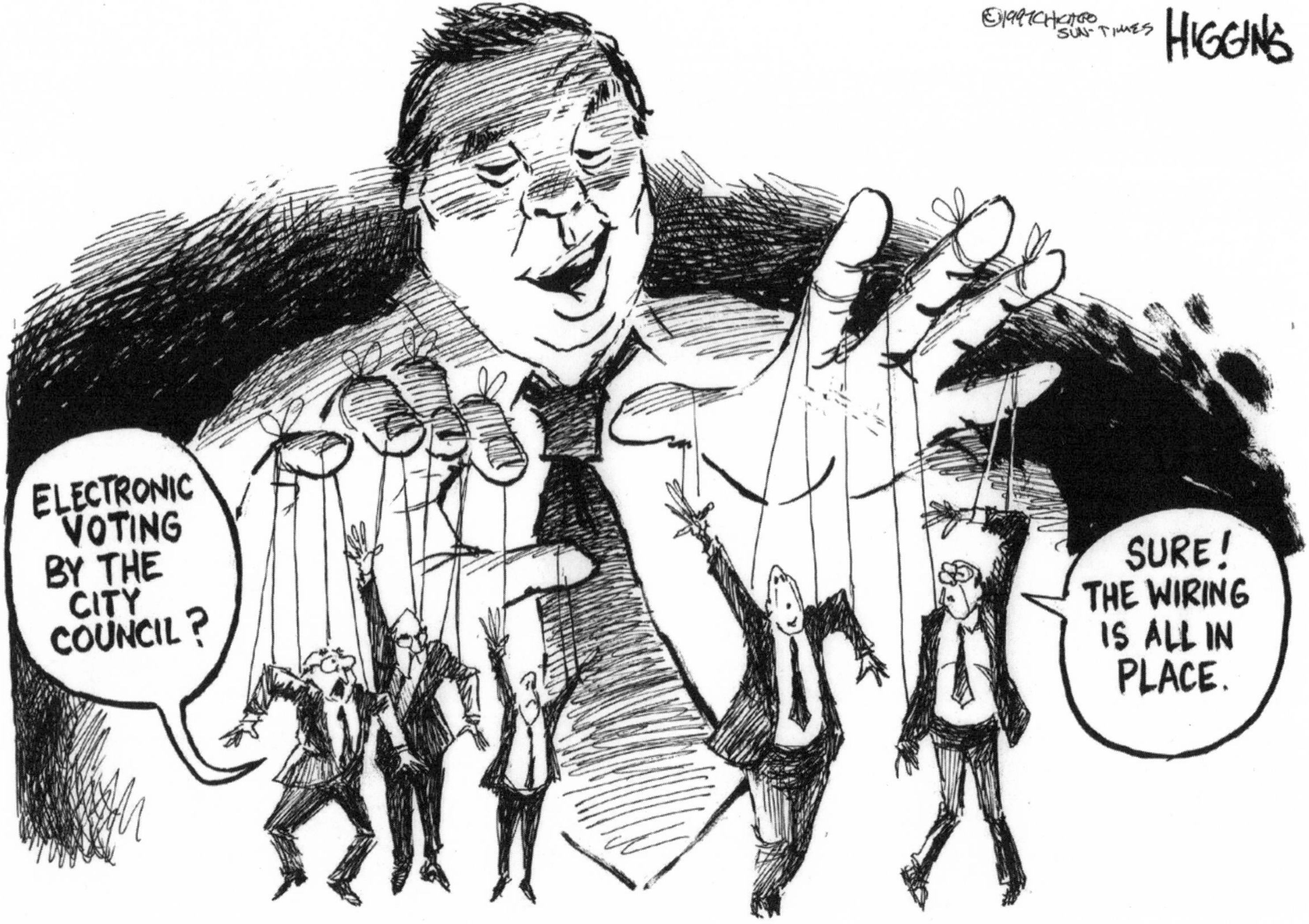
©1997 CHICAGO SUN-TIMES
HIGGINS
ELECTRONIC VOTING BY THE CITY COUNCIL?
SURE! THE WIRING IS ALL IN PLACE.

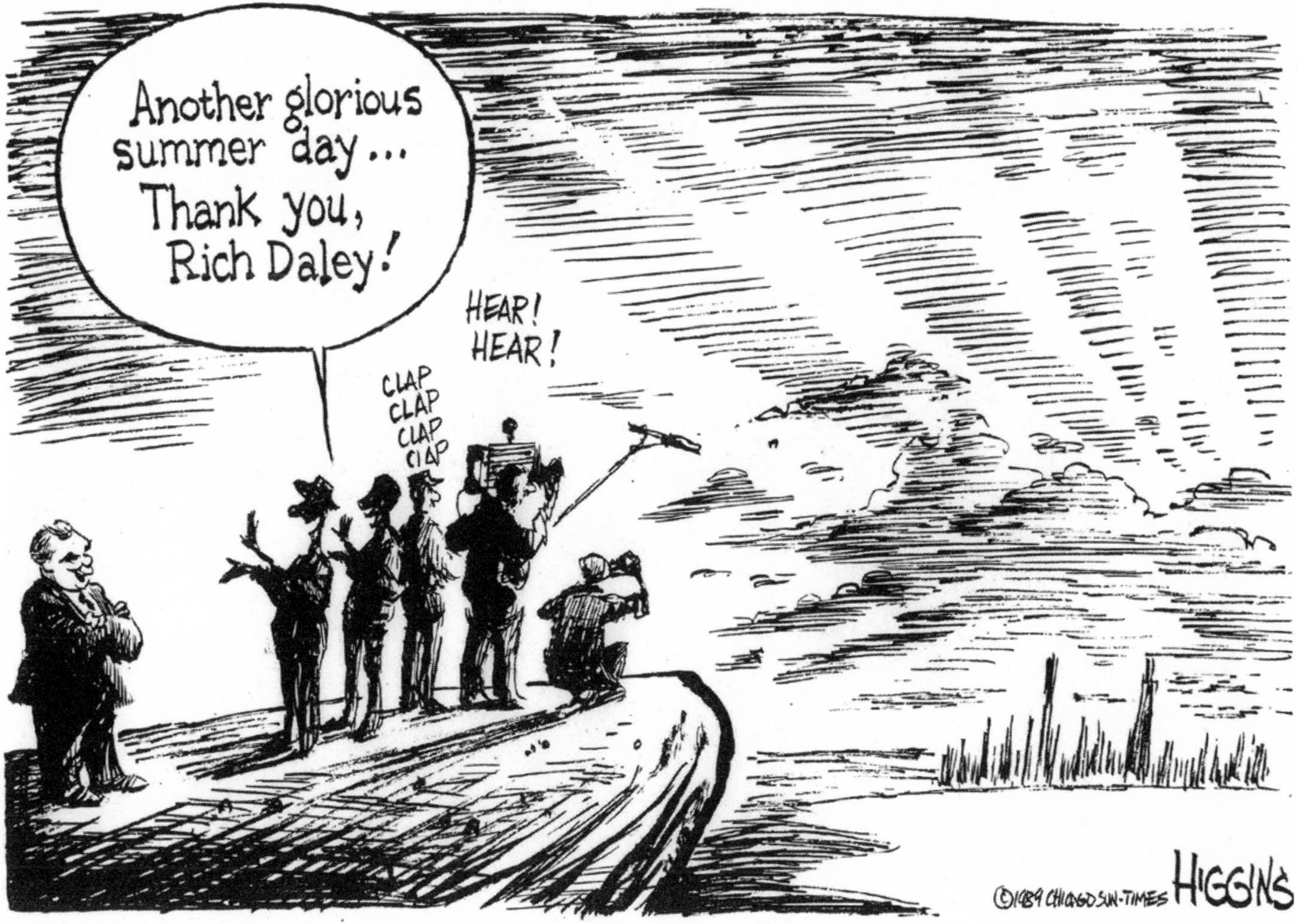
Another glorious summer day... Thank you, Rich Daley!
HEAR! HEAR!
CLAP CLAP CLAP CLAP
©1989 CHICAGO SUN-TIMES
HIGGINS

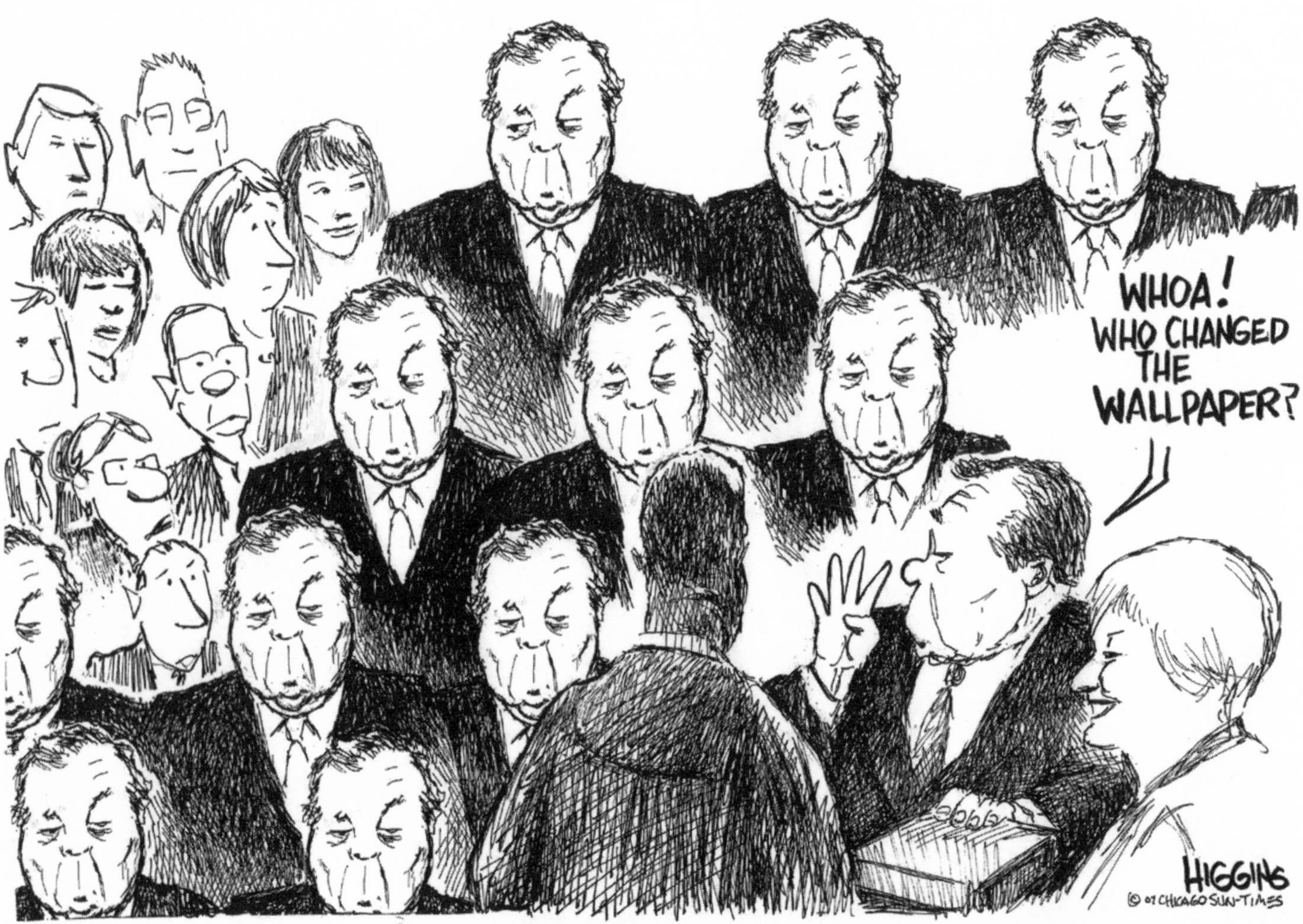
WHOA! WHO CHANGED THE WALLPAPER?
HIGGINS
© 07 CHICAGO SUN-TIMES

The changing face of the City Council.

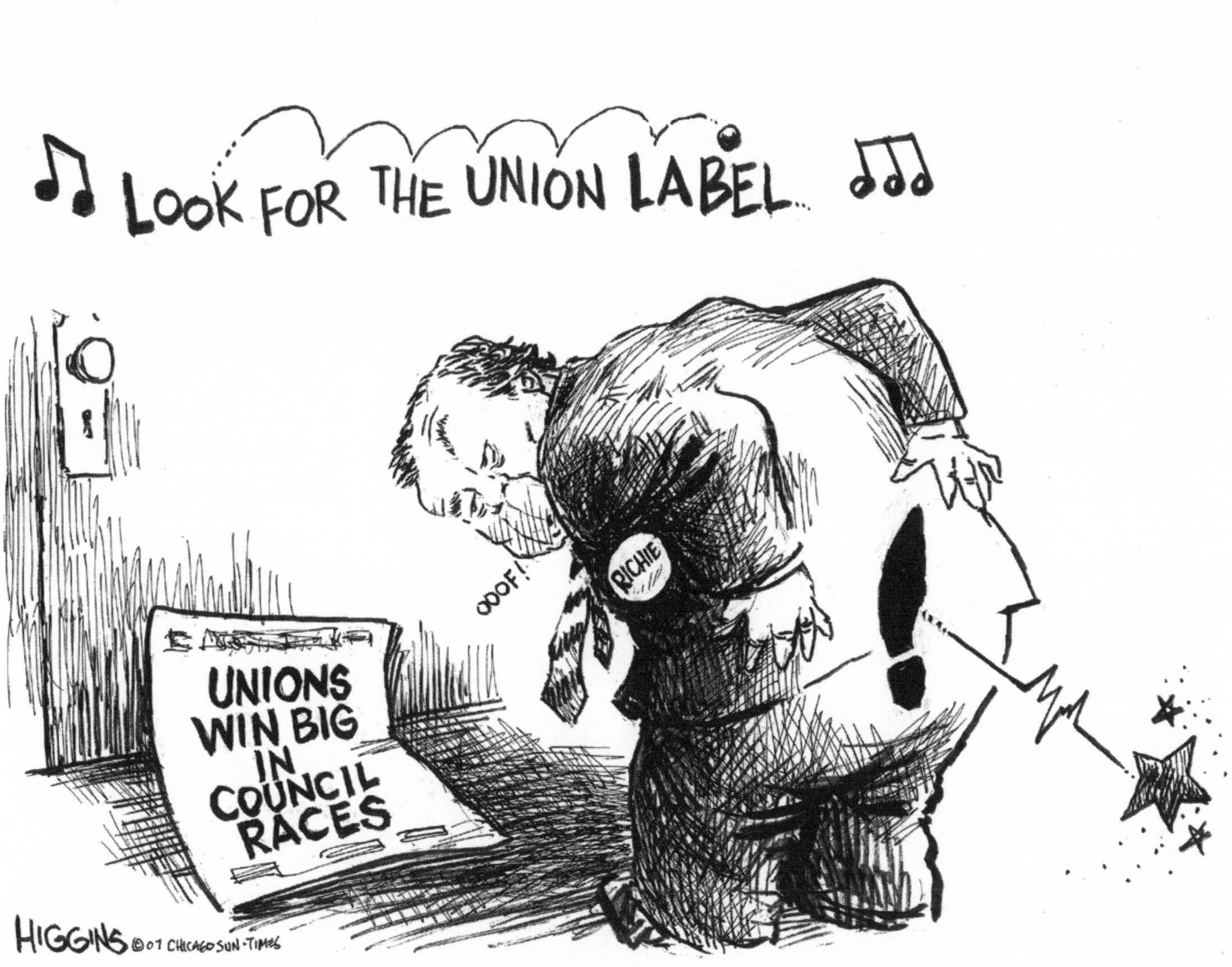
LOOK FOR THE UNION LABEL...
OOOF!
RICHIE
UNIONS WIN BIG IN COUNCIL RACES
HIGGINS ©07 CHICAGO SUN-TIMES

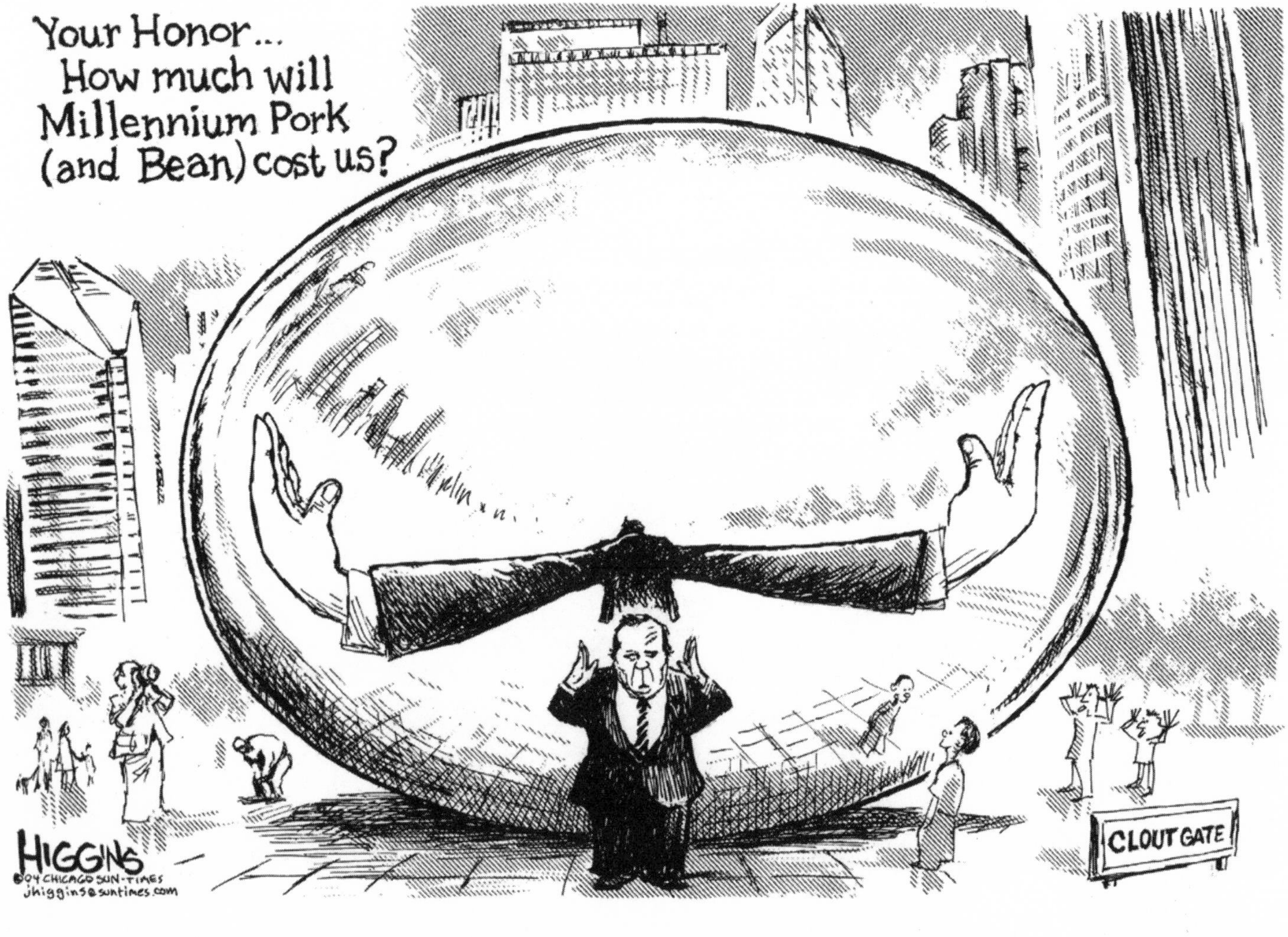

Your Honor...
How much will
Millennium Pork
(and Bean) cost us?
CLOUT GATE
HIGGINS
©04 CHICAGO SUN-TIMES
jhiggins@suntimes.com

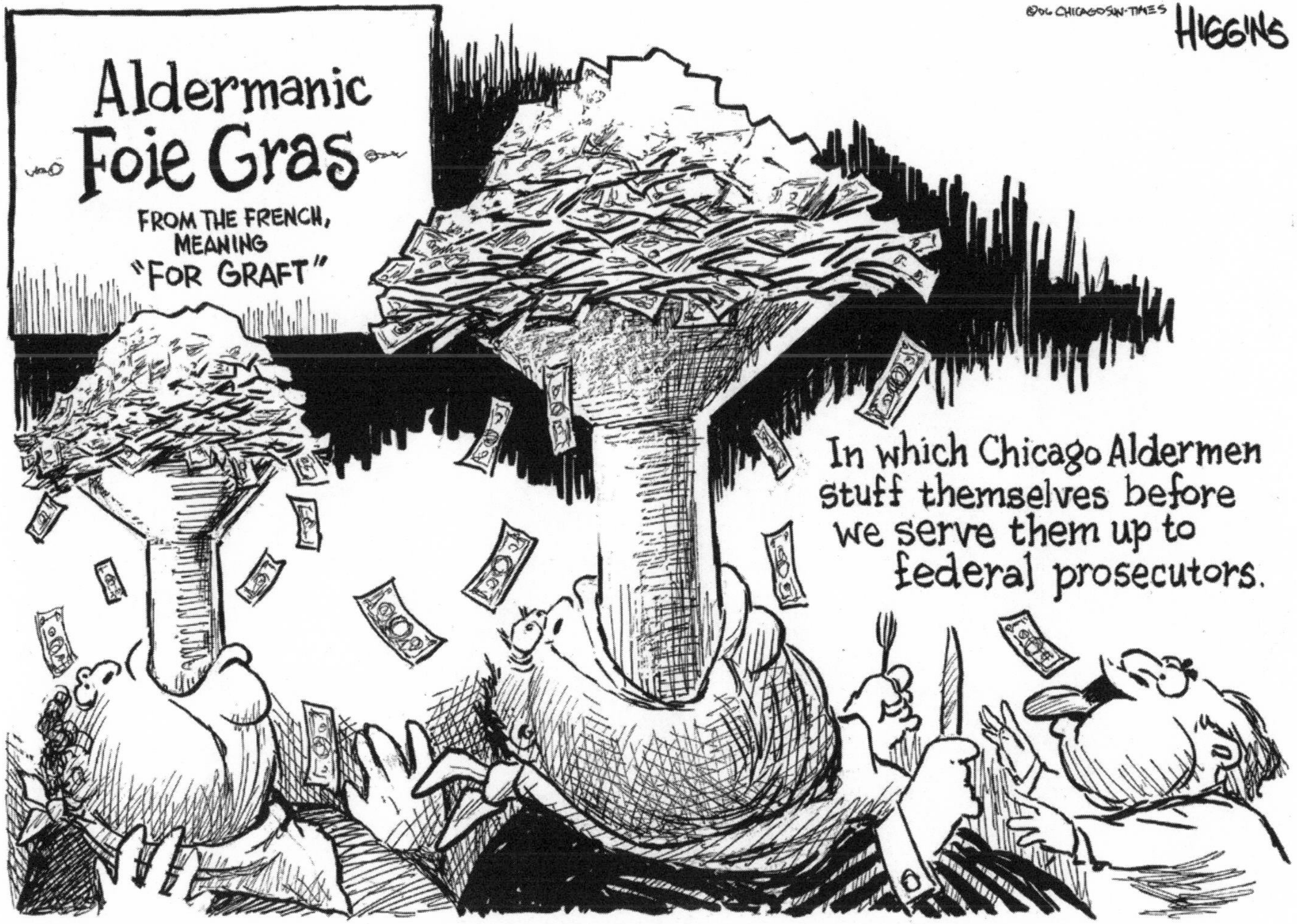
©06 CHICAGO SUN-TIMES
HIGGINS
Aldermanic
Foie Gras
FROM THE FRENCH, MEANING "FOR GRAFT"
In which Chicago Aldermen stuff themselves before we serve them up to federal prosecutors.

Foie gras is banned in Chicago, but not everyone complies.

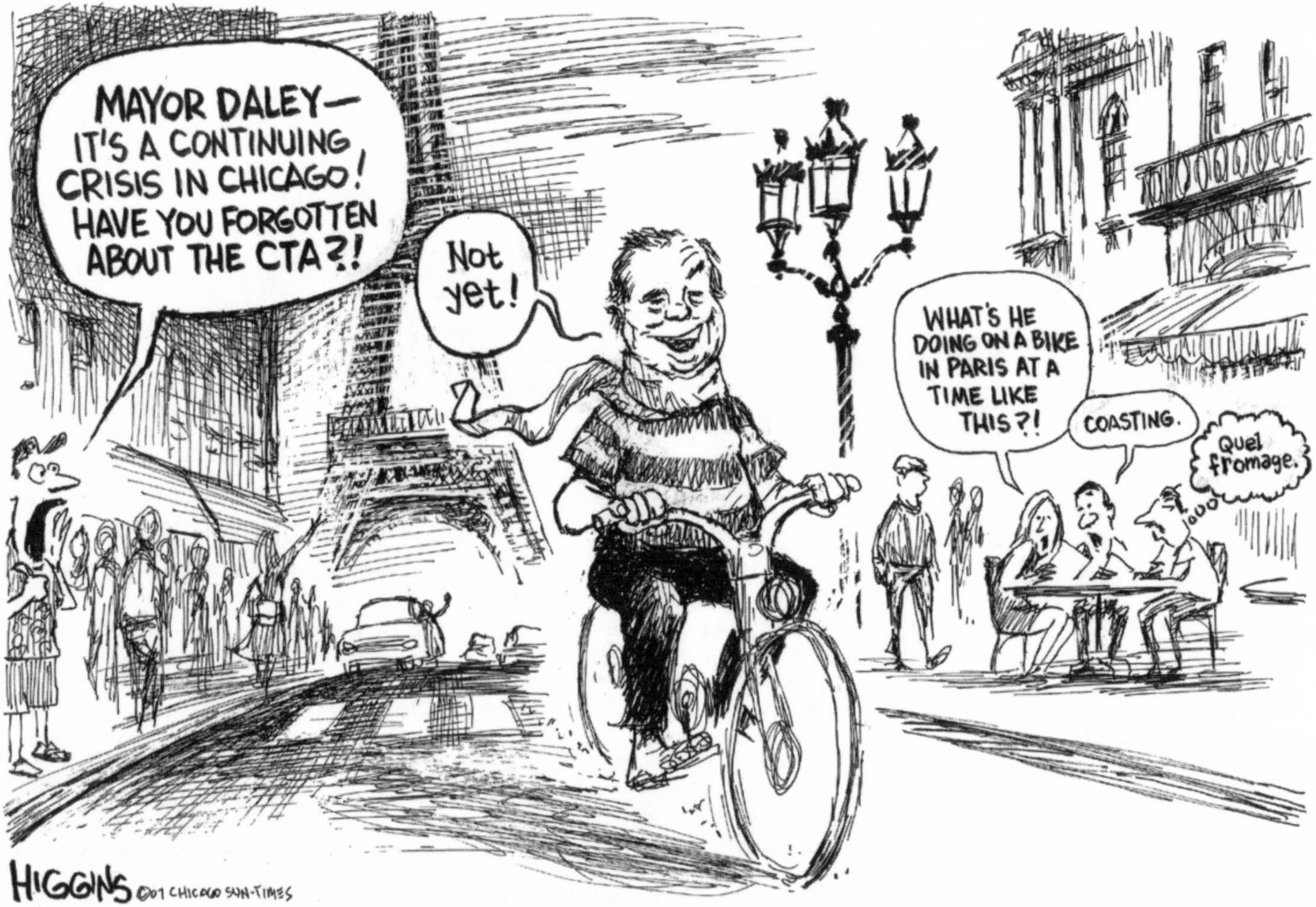
MAYOR DALEY— IT'S A CONTINUING CRISIS IN CHICAGO! HAVE YOU FORGOTTEN ABOUT THE CTA?!
Not yet!
WHAT'S HE DOING ON A BIKE IN PARIS AT A TIME LIKE THIS?!
COASTING.
Quel fromage.
HIGGINS ©07 CHICAGO SUN-TIMES

In the midst of a transit crisis in Chicago,
the mayor takes to bike riding in Paris.

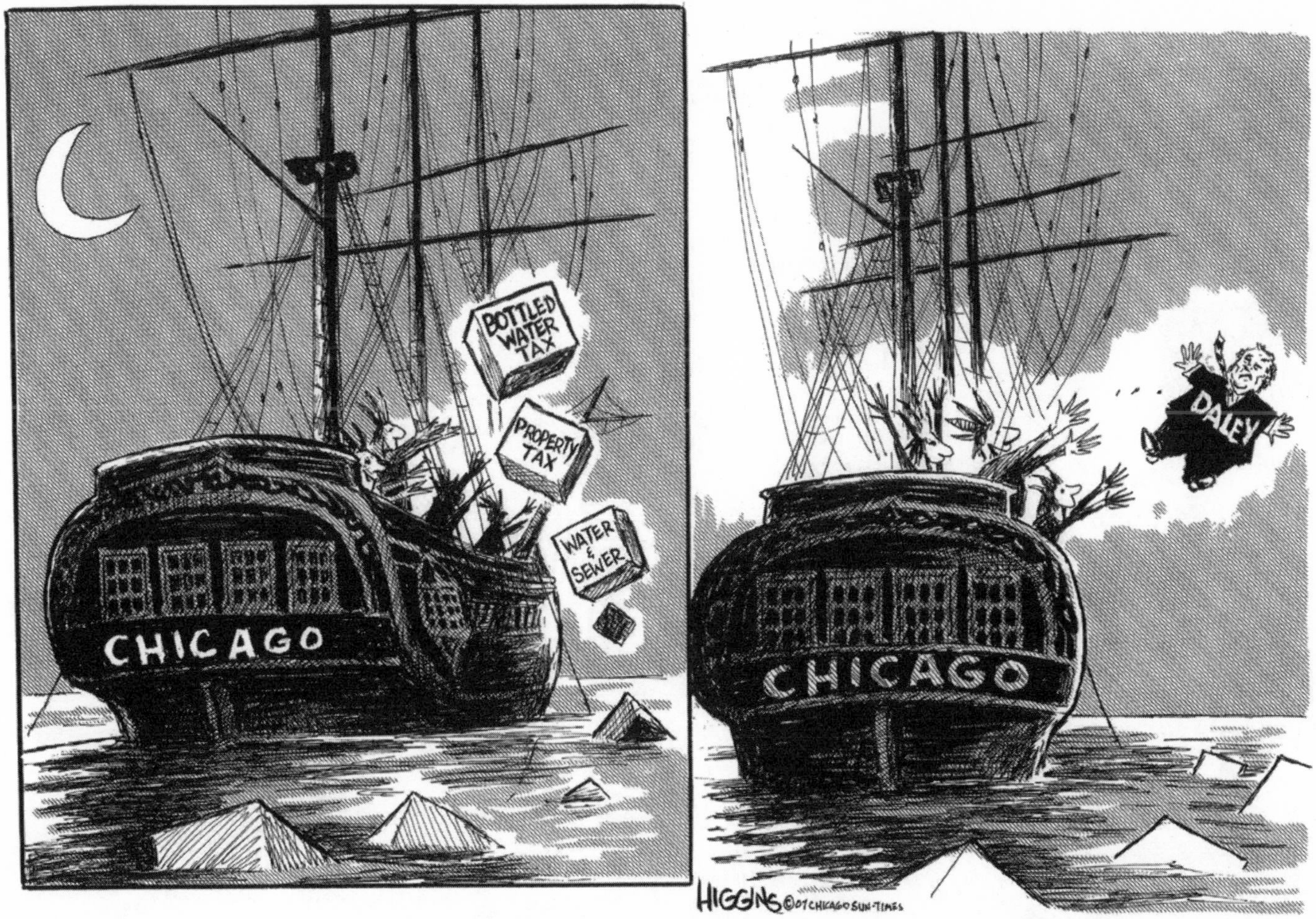
BOTTLED WATER TAX
PROPERTY TAX
WATER & SEWER
CHICAGO
CHICAGO
DALEY
HIGGINS ©07 CHICAGO SUN-TIMES

Daley announces his intention to raise sales, property, and utility taxes and an unprecedented uproar ensues citywide. After this cartoon ran, aldermen gathered on a bridge and tossed tea bags into the Chicago River. The mayor backed off on some of the taxes.

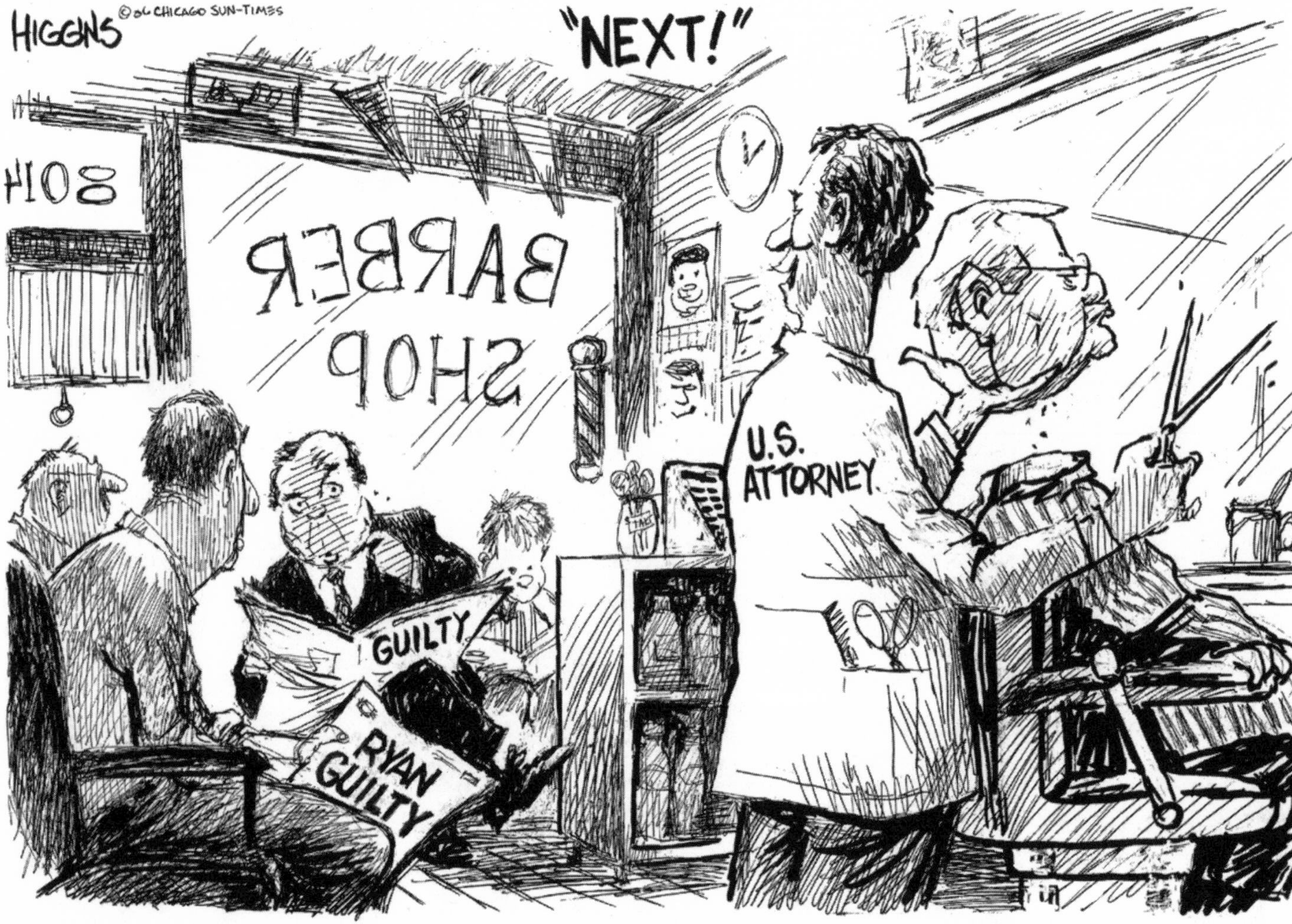
HIGGINS © 06 CHICAGO SUN-TIMES
"NEXT!"
BARBER SHOP
U.S. ATTORNEY
GUILTY
RYAN GUILTY

The trial of former Illinois governor George Ryan displayed how he financed his political aspirations by providing truck drivers with illegally obtained driver's licenses while he was secretary of state. Truckers who purchased those licenses, many of whom could not read or speak English, have been tied to vehicular accidents resulting in the deaths of nine people, six of whom were the children of Scott and Janet Willis.

Providing a sideshow to the trial were juror problems and rumors that George Ryan, who as governor commuted the sentences of all inmates on Illinois's death row, once again had been nominated for a Nobel Prize.

Ryan was found guilty of corruption and lost his state pension. His journey to prison in Wisconsin took Ryan past the site where the Willis children died.

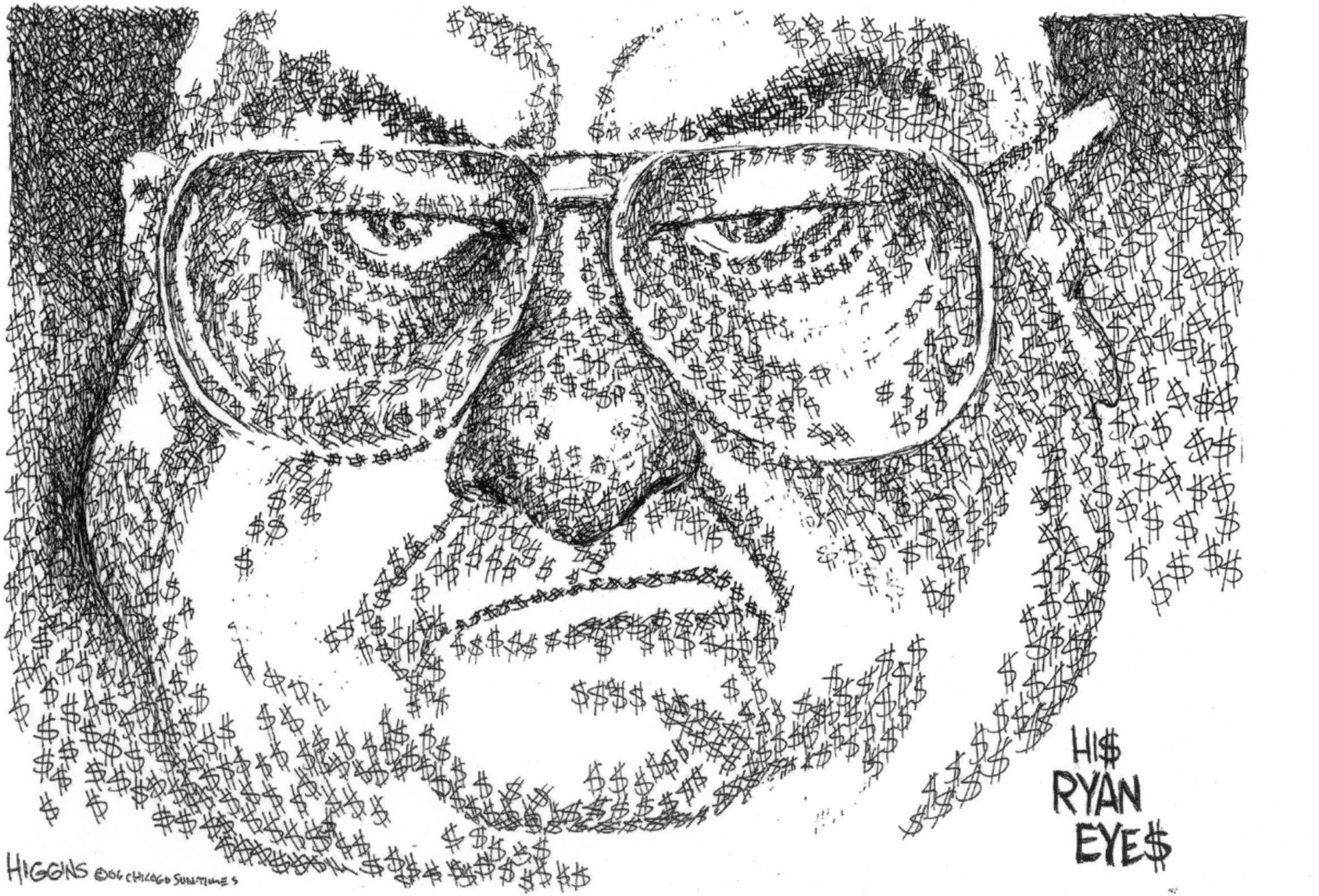
HI$
RYAN
EYE$
HIGGINS ©06 CHICAGO SUN-TIMES

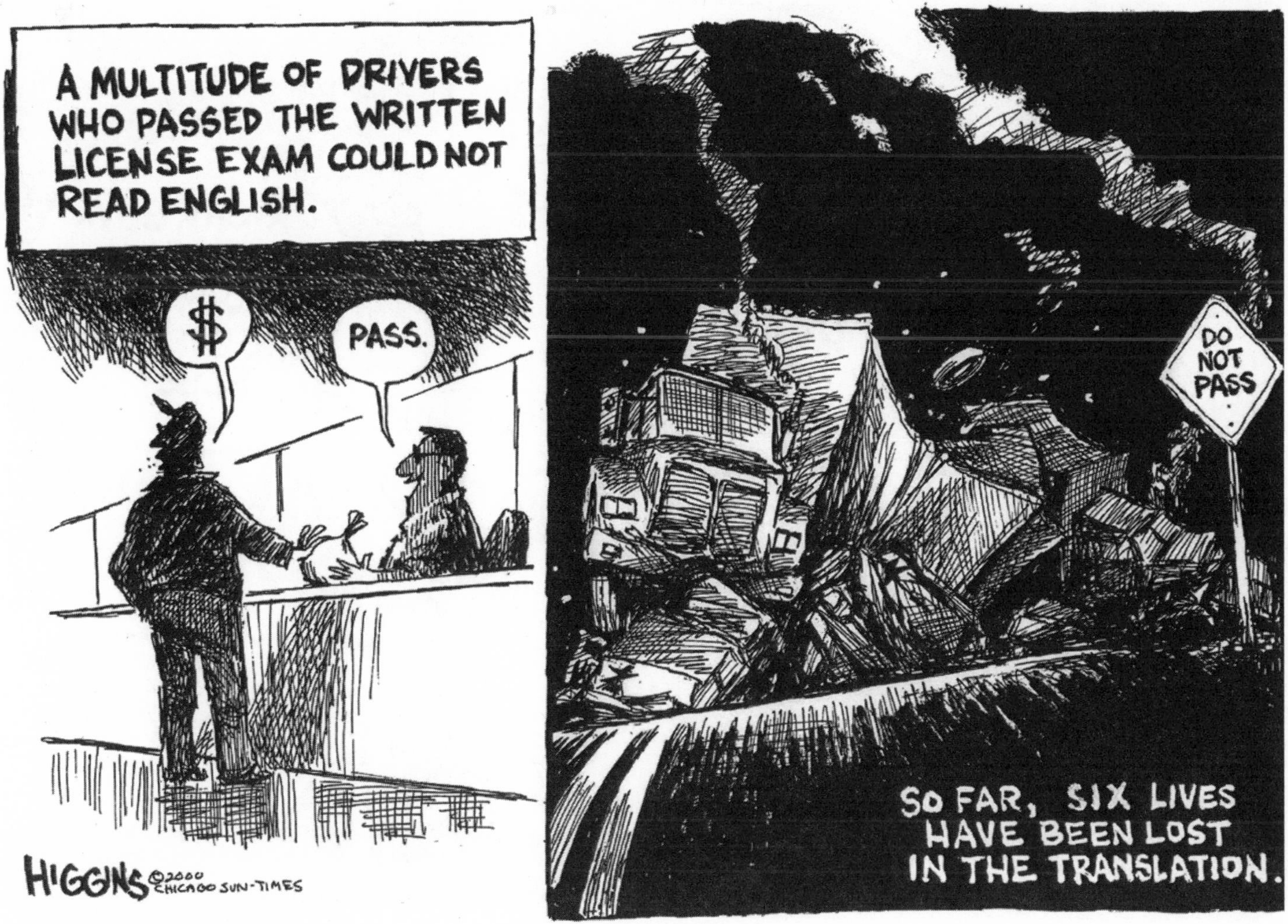
A MULTITUDE OF DRIVERS WHO PASSED THE WRITTEN LICENSE EXAM COULD NOT READ ENGLISH.
$
PASS.
HIGGINS ©2000 CHICAGO SUN-TIMES
DO NOT PASS
SO FAR, SIX LIVES HAVE BEEN LOST IN THE TRANSLATION.

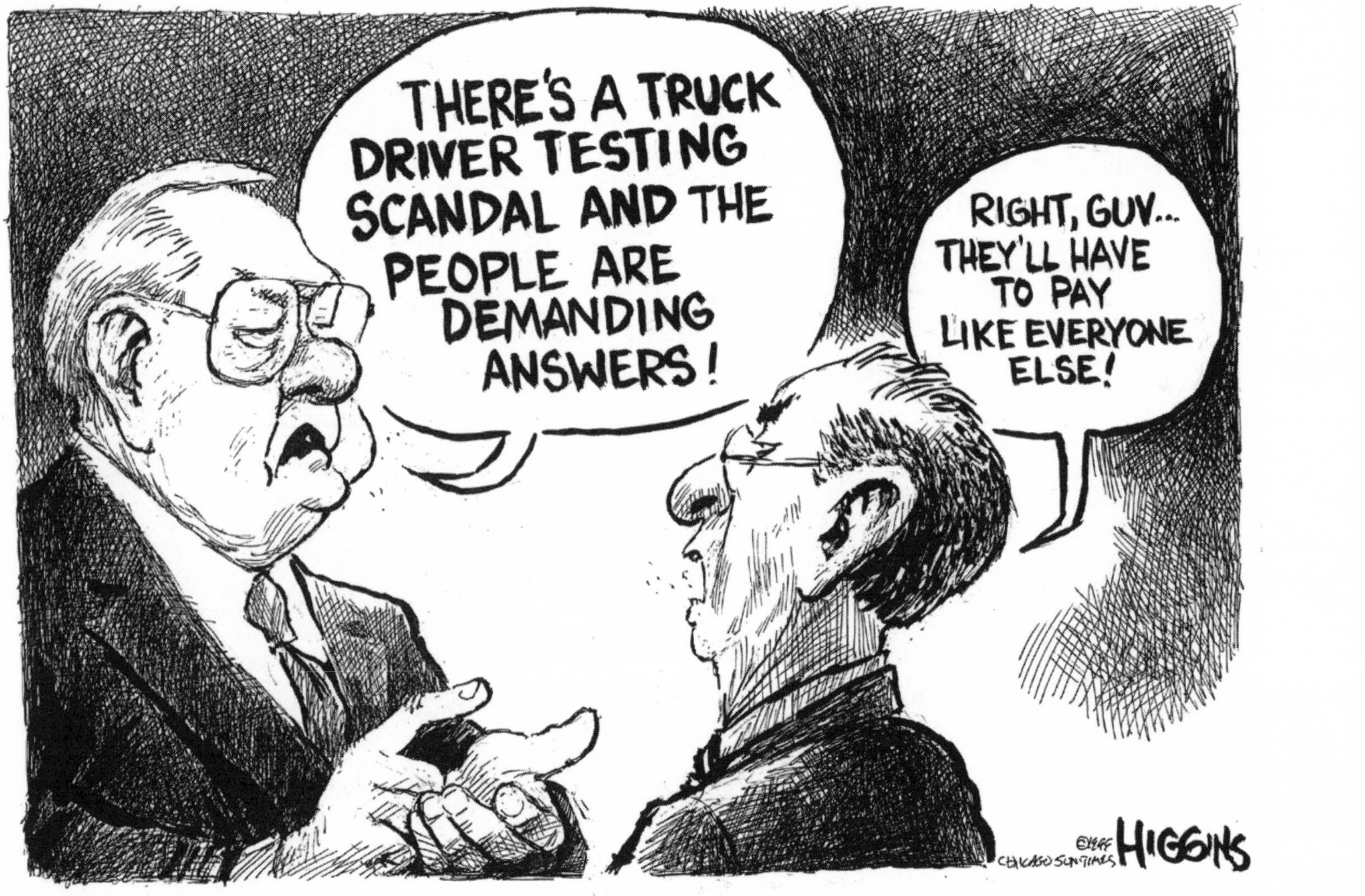
THERE'S A TRUCK DRIVER TESTING SCANDAL AND THE PEOPLE ARE DEMANDING ANSWERS!
RIGHT, GUV... THEY'LL HAVE TO PAY LIKE EVERYONE ELSE!
HIGGINS

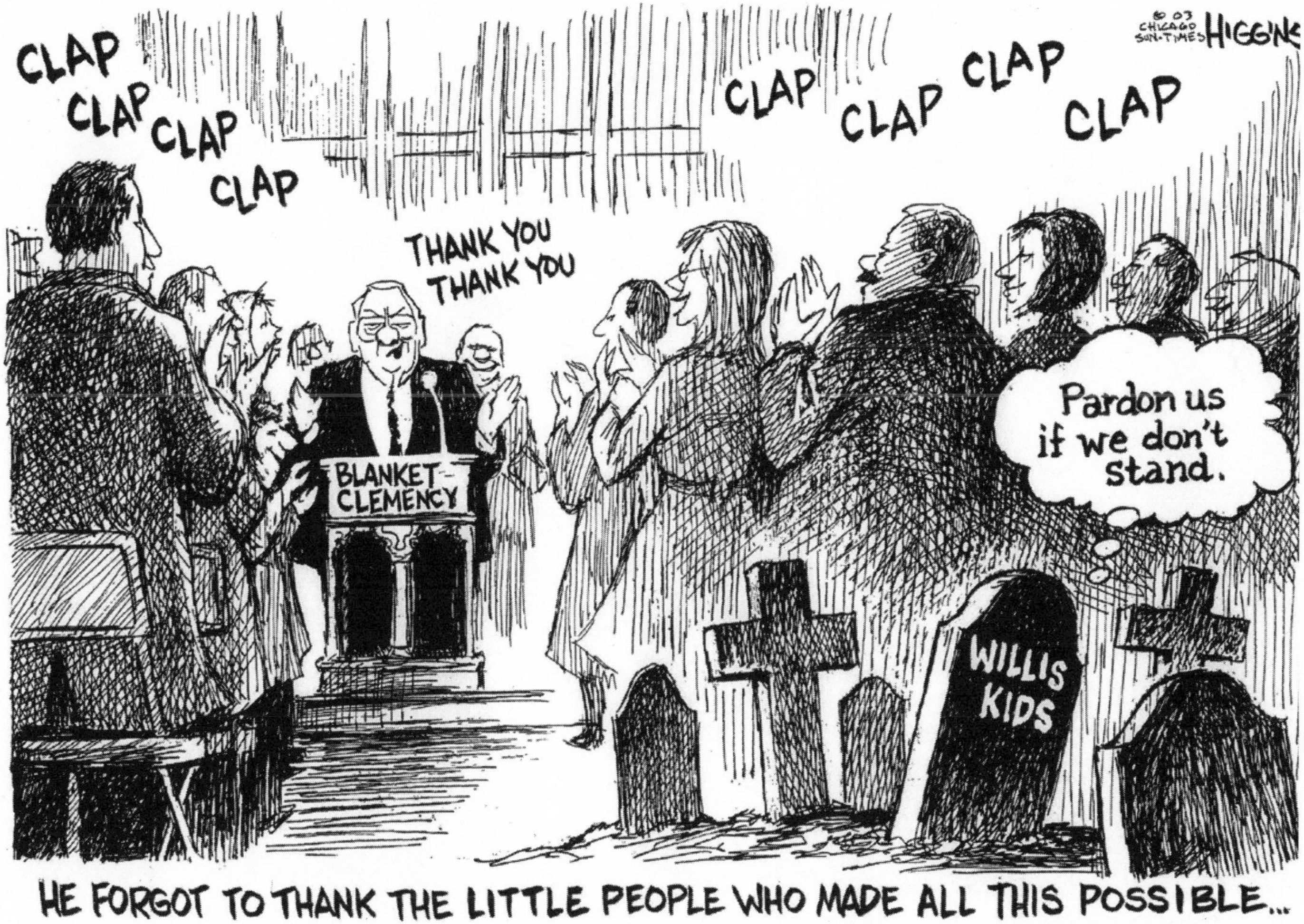
© 03 CHICAGO SUN-TIMES HIGGINS
CLAP
CLAP
CLAP
CLAP
CLAP
CLAP
CLAP
CLAP
THANK YOU THANK YOU
BLANKET CLEMENCY
Pardon us if we don't stand.
WILLIS KIDS
HE FORGOT TO THANK THE LITTLE PEOPLE WHO MADE ALL THIS POSSIBLE...

Blanket amnesty for death row inmates provides a popular diversion from the truck licenses for bribes scandal. Governor Ryan even gets nominated for the Nobel Peace Prize.

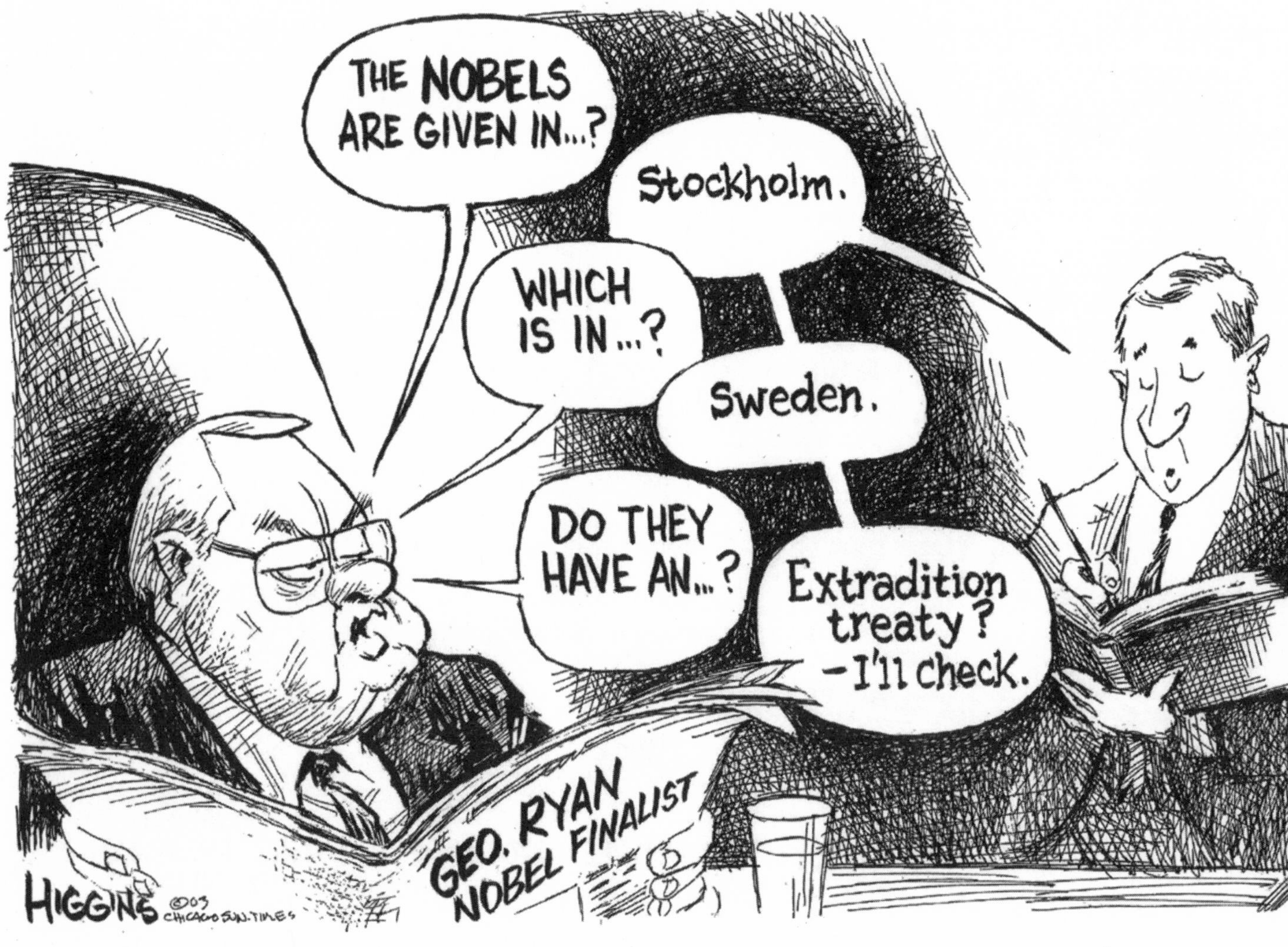
THE NOBELS ARE GIVEN IN...?
Stockholm.
WHICH IS IN...?
Sweden.
DO THEY HAVE AN...?
Extradition treaty? -I'll check.
GEO. RYAN NOBEL FINALIST
HIGGINS ©03 CHICAGO SUN-TIMES

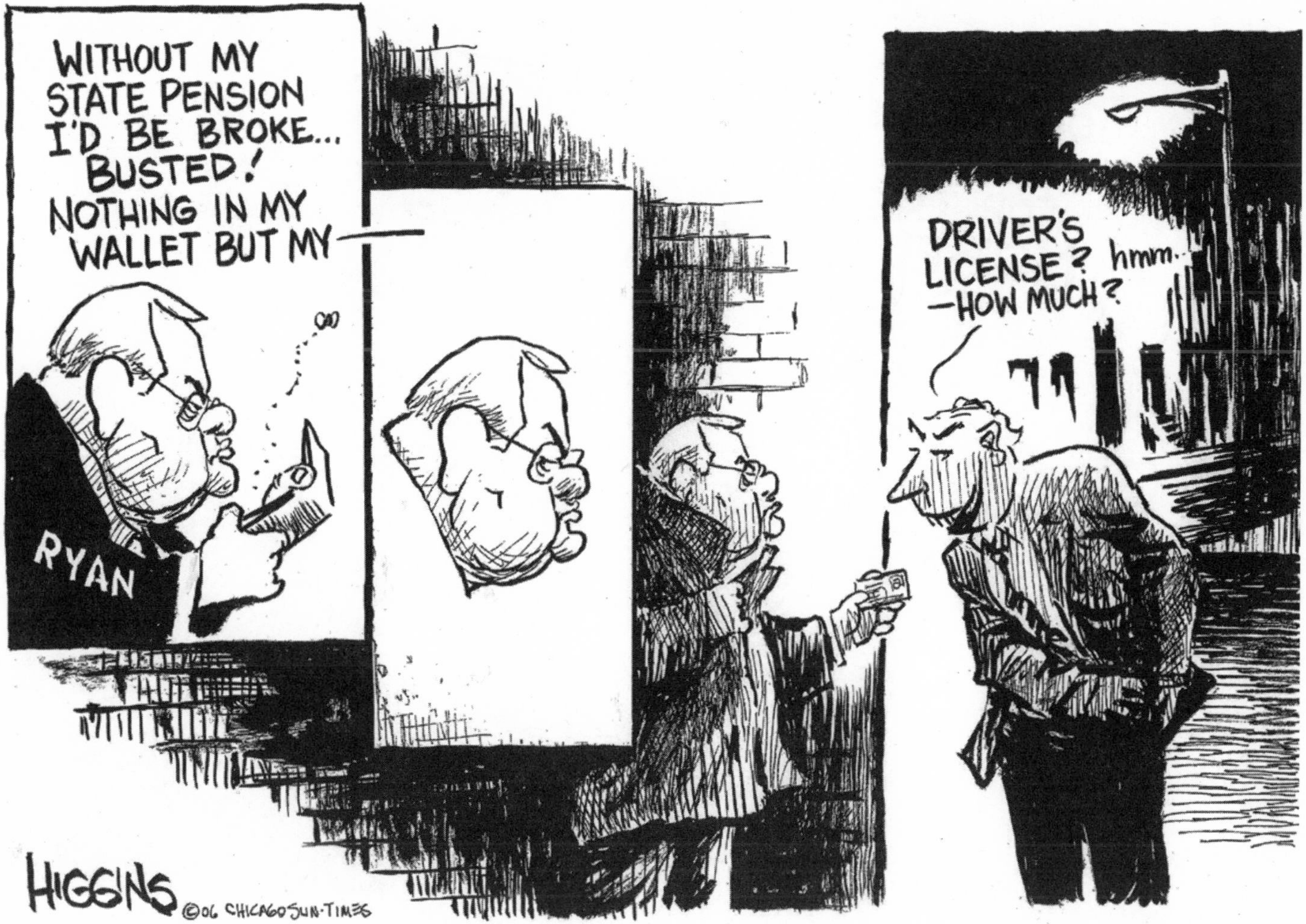
WITHOUT MY STATE PENSION I'D BE BROKE... BUSTED! NOTHING IN MY WALLET BUT MY—
RYAN
DRIVER'S LICENSE? hmm.. —HOW MUCH?
HIGGINS ©06 CHICAGO SUN-TIMES

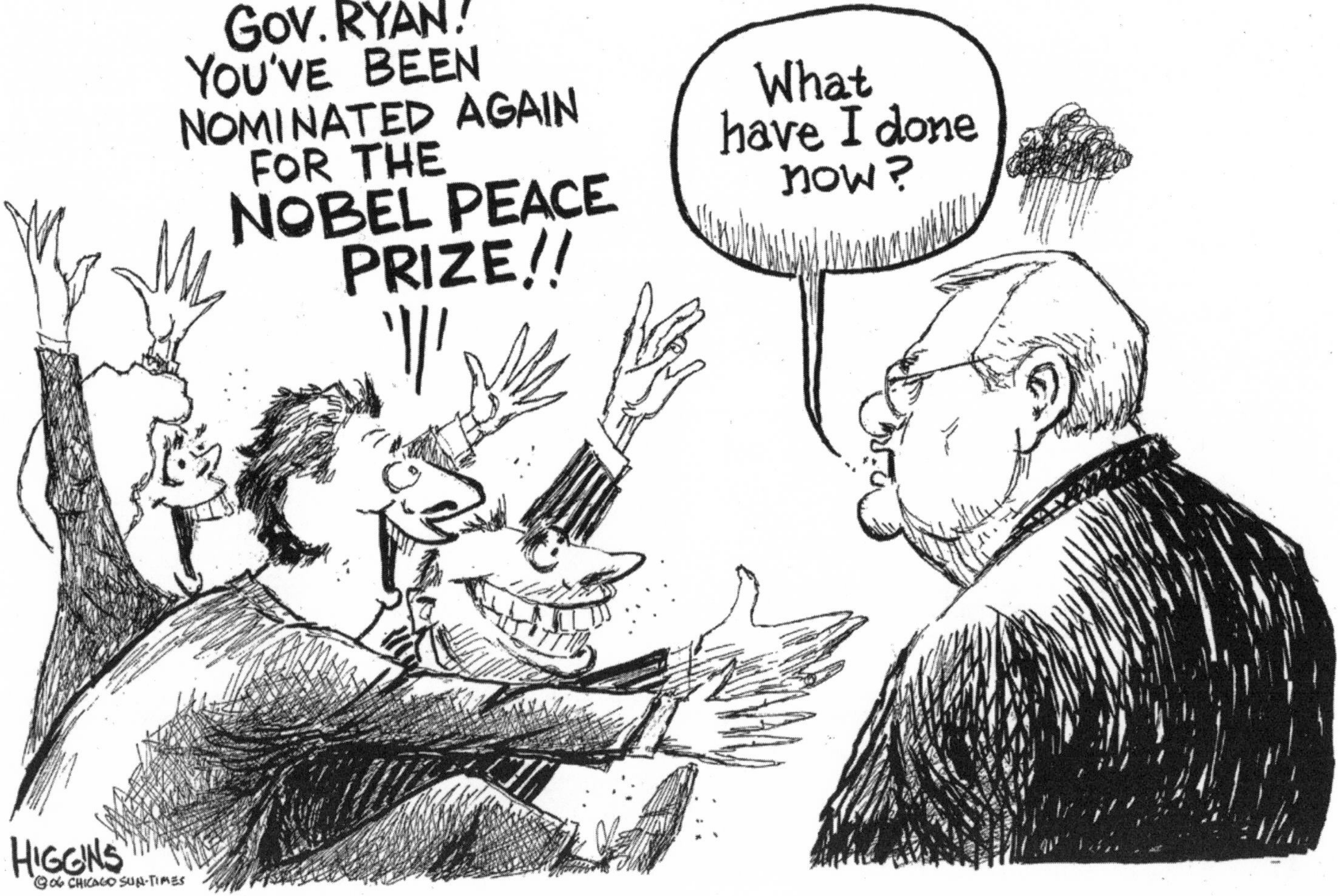
GOV. RYAN! YOU'VE BEEN NOMINATED AGAIN FOR THE NOBEL PEACE PRIZE!!
What have I done now?
HIGGINS
©06 CHICAGO SUN-TIMES

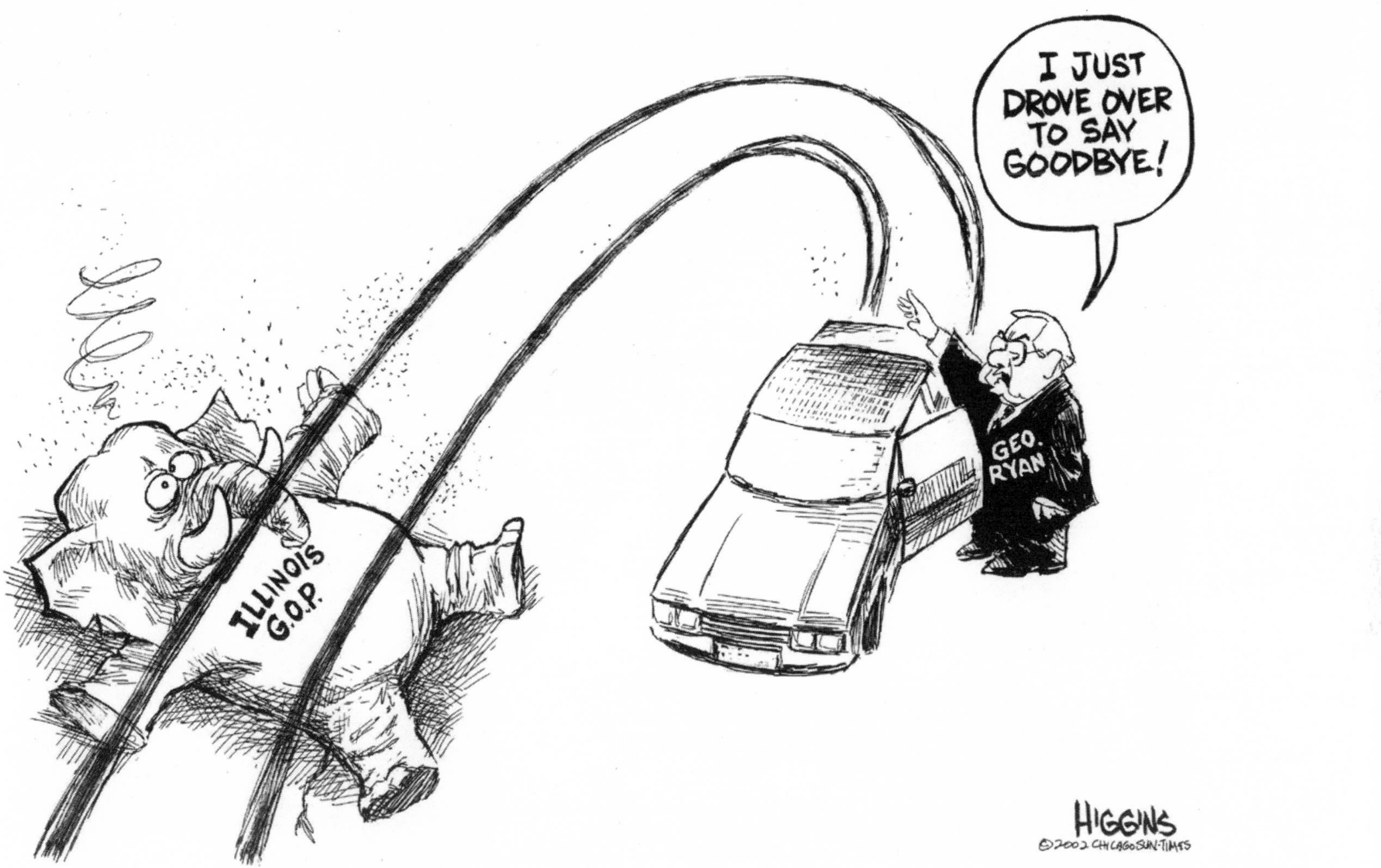
I JUST DROVE OVER TO SAY GOODBYE!
ILLINOIS G.O.P.
GEO. RYAN
HIGGINS
©2002 CHICAGO SUN-TIMES

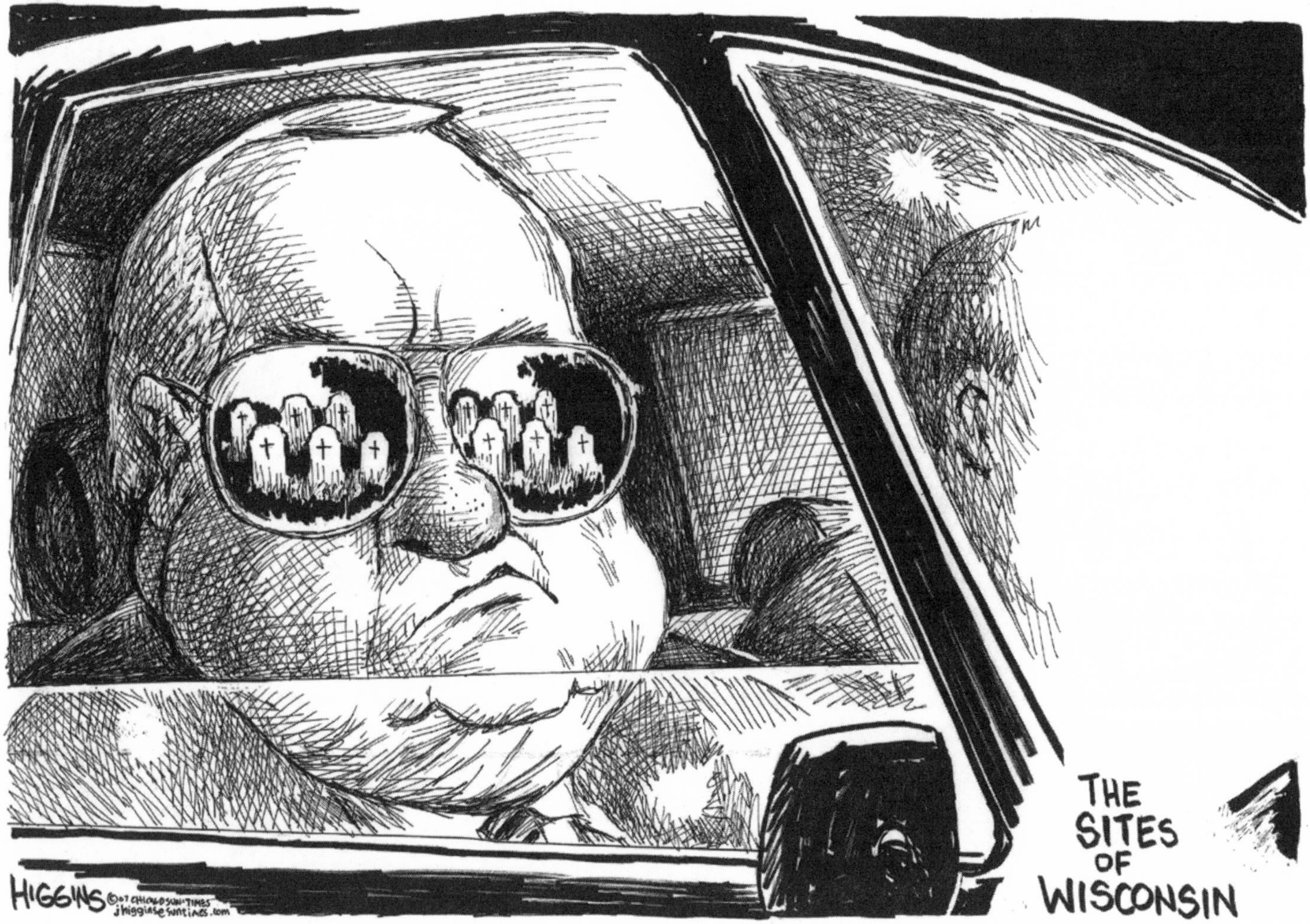
THE SITES OF WISCONSIN
HIGGINS ©07 CHICAGO SUN-TIMES
jhiggins@suntimes.com

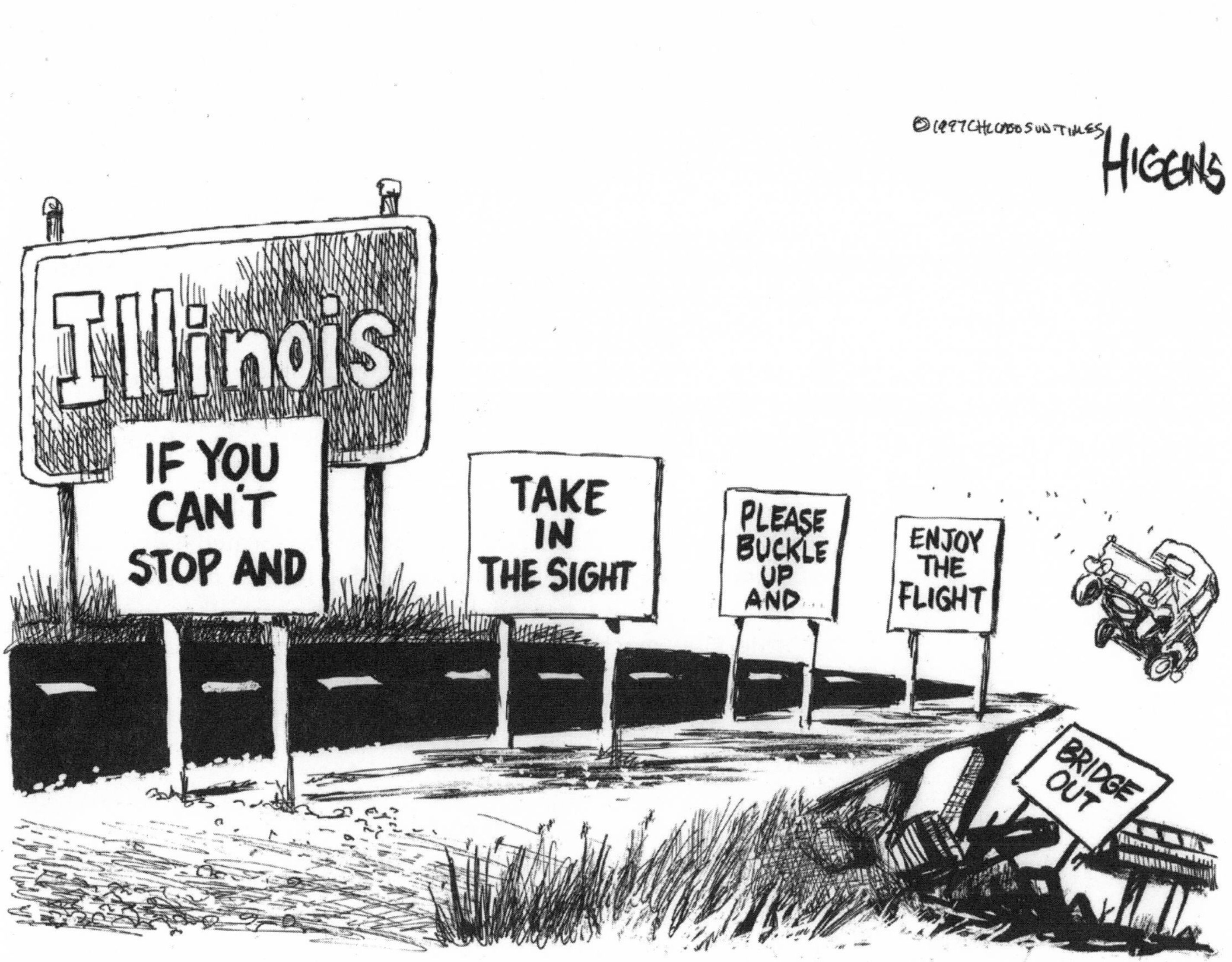
©1997 CHICAGO SUN-TIMES
HIGGINS
Illinois
IF YOU CAN'T STOP AND
TAKE IN THE SIGHT
PLEASE BUCKLE UP AND...
ENJOY THE FLIGHT
BRIDGE OUT

A 24-count indictment against one of Governor Rod Blagojevich's top fundraisers, Tony Rezko, lays out what U.S. Attorney Patrick Fitzgerald has termed a "pay-to-play scheme on steroids."

Rezko and his associates allegedly demanded kickbacks in the form of consulting fees from companies looking to do business with the Teachers Retirement System. Another transaction allegedly attempted to arrange political contributions to an unnamed public official, named by sources as Blagojevich.

Eventually, pay-to-play ended when business partner Stuart Levine turned on Rezko. Rezko left the country, and he was located doing business in the Middle East before finally turning himself in to authorities.

People here have always treated public corruption with a perverse sense of pride. How much our public officials get away with all boils down to how much we will tolerate.

Shame on them and shame on us.

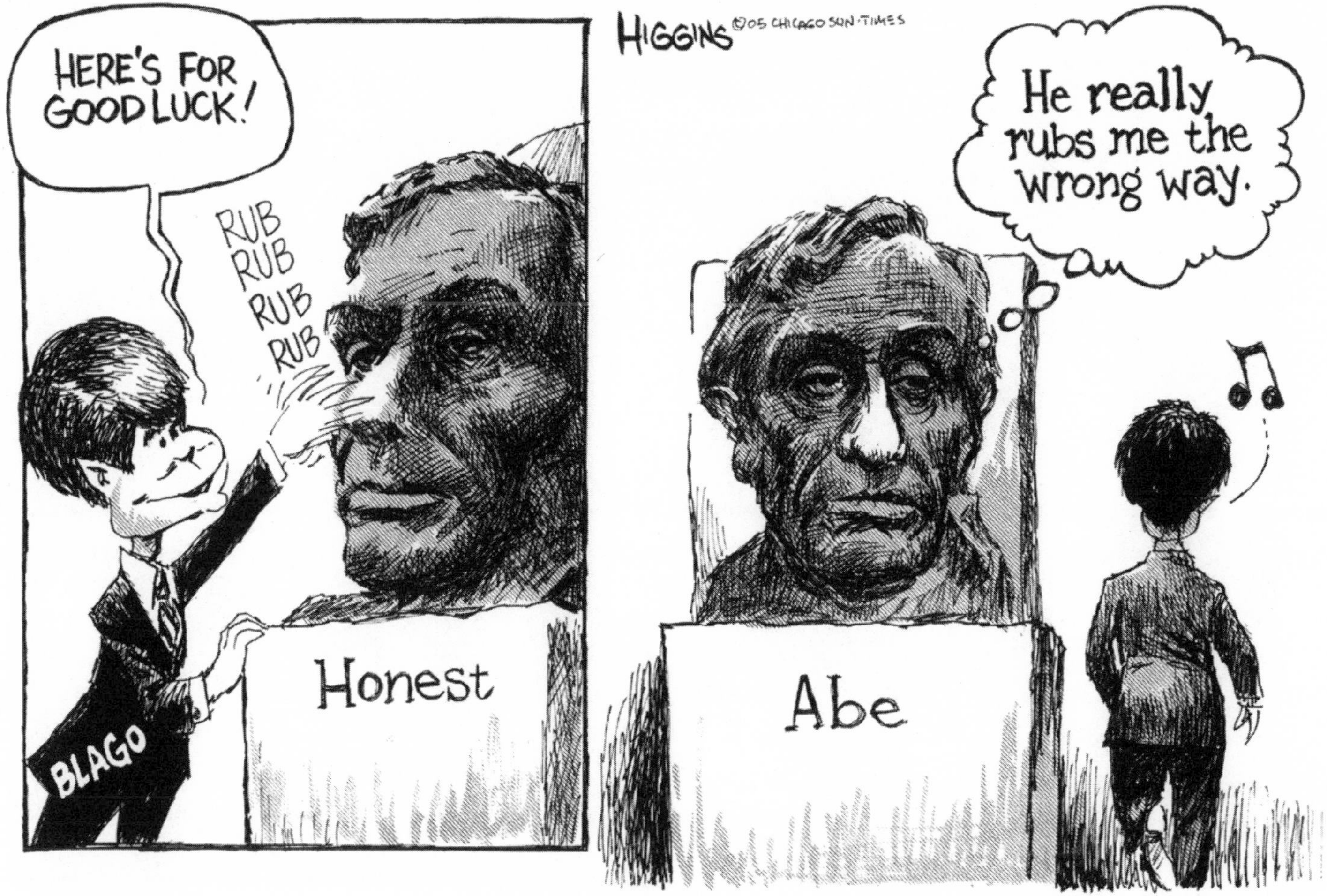
HIGGINS ©05 CHICAGO SUN-TIMES
HERE'S FOR GOOD LUCK!
RUB RUB RUB RUB
BLAGO
Honest
Abe
He really rubs me the wrong way.

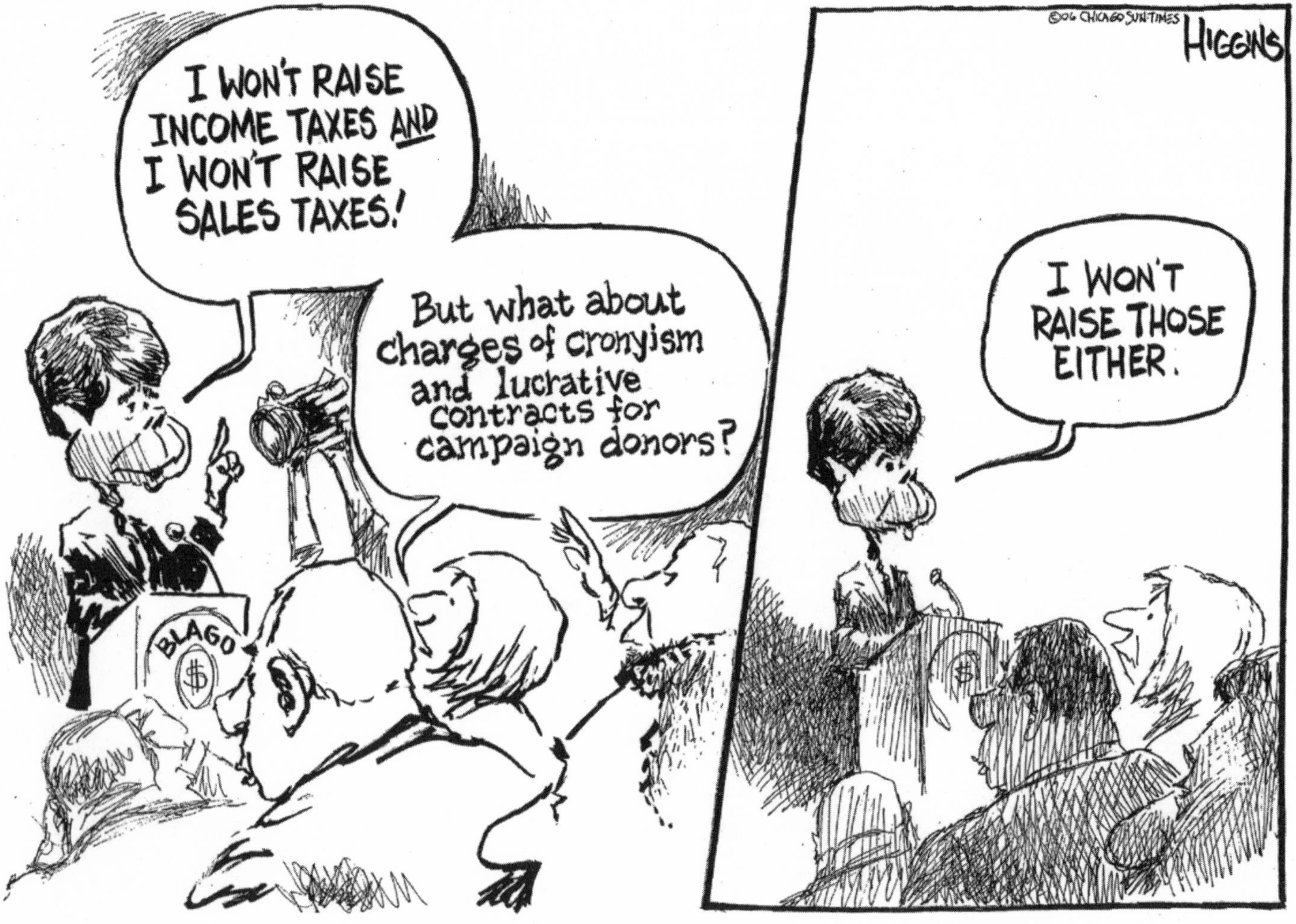
©06 CHICAGO SUN-TIMES
HIGGINS
I WON'T RAISE INCOME TAXES AND I WON'T RAISE SALES TAXES!
BLAGO
But what about charges of cronyism and lucrative contracts for campaign donors?
I WON'T RAISE THOSE EITHER.

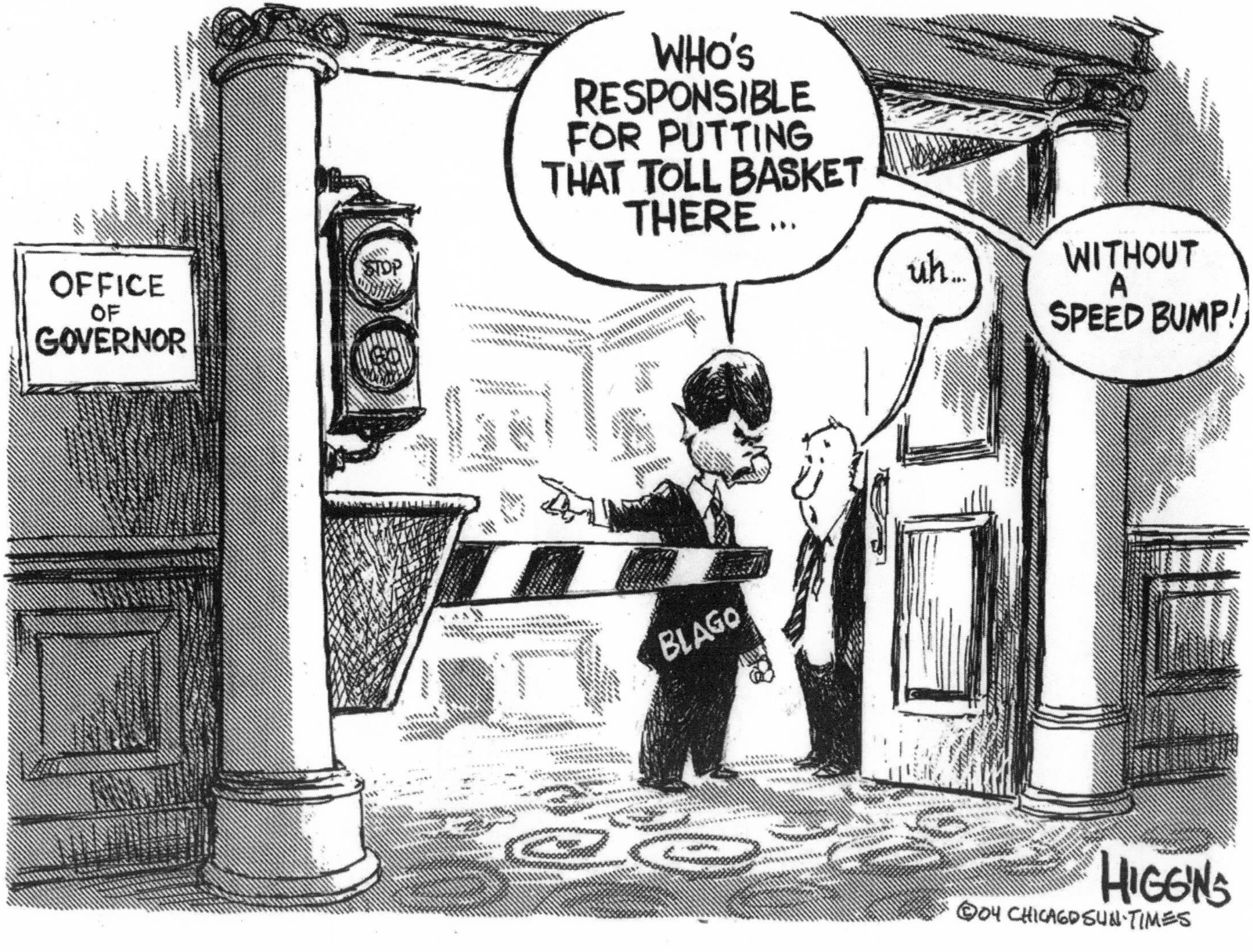
OFFICE OF GOVERNOR
STOP
GO
WHO'S RESPONSIBLE FOR PUTTING THAT TOLL BASKET THERE...
uh...
WITHOUT A SPEED BUMP!
BLAGO
HIGGINS
©04 CHICAGO SUN-TIMES

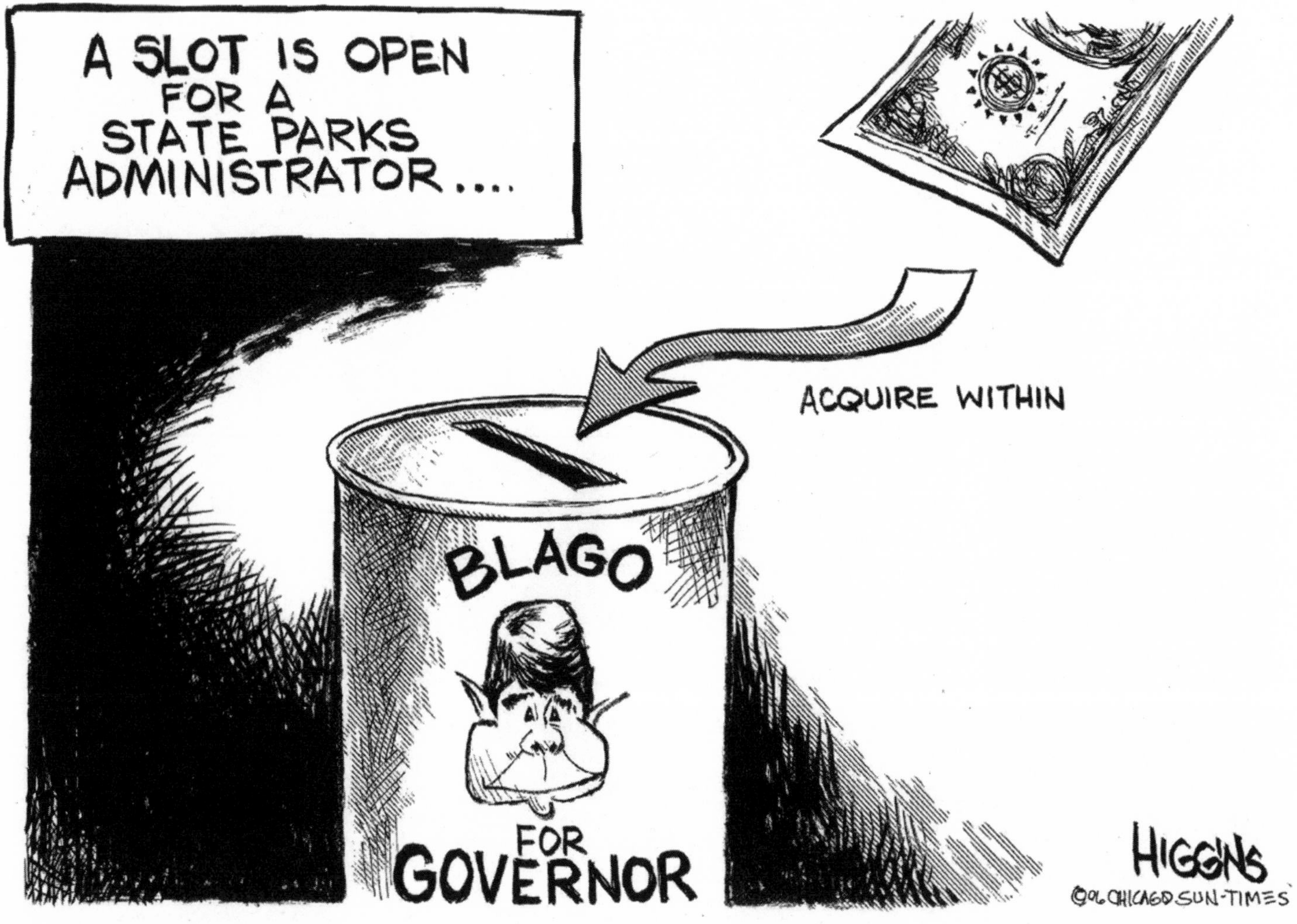
A SLOT IS OPEN
FOR A
STATE PARKS
ADMINISTRATOR....
ACQUIRE WITHIN
BLAGO
FOR
GOVERNOR
HIGGINS
©06 CHICAGO SUN-TIMES

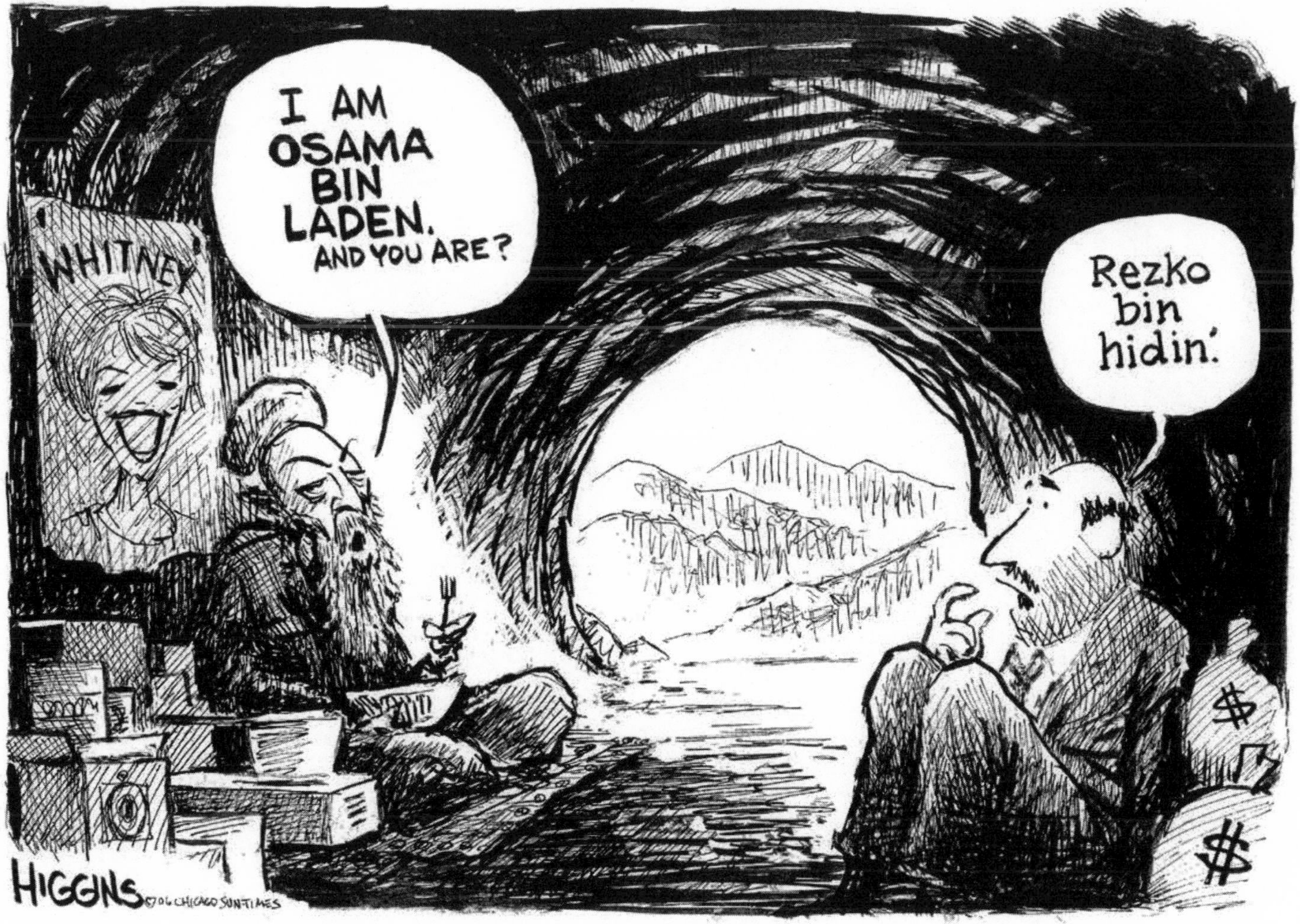
WHITNEY
I AM OSAMA BIN LADEN. AND YOU ARE?
Rezko bin hidin'
$
$
HIGGINS ©'06 CHICAGO SUN-TIMES

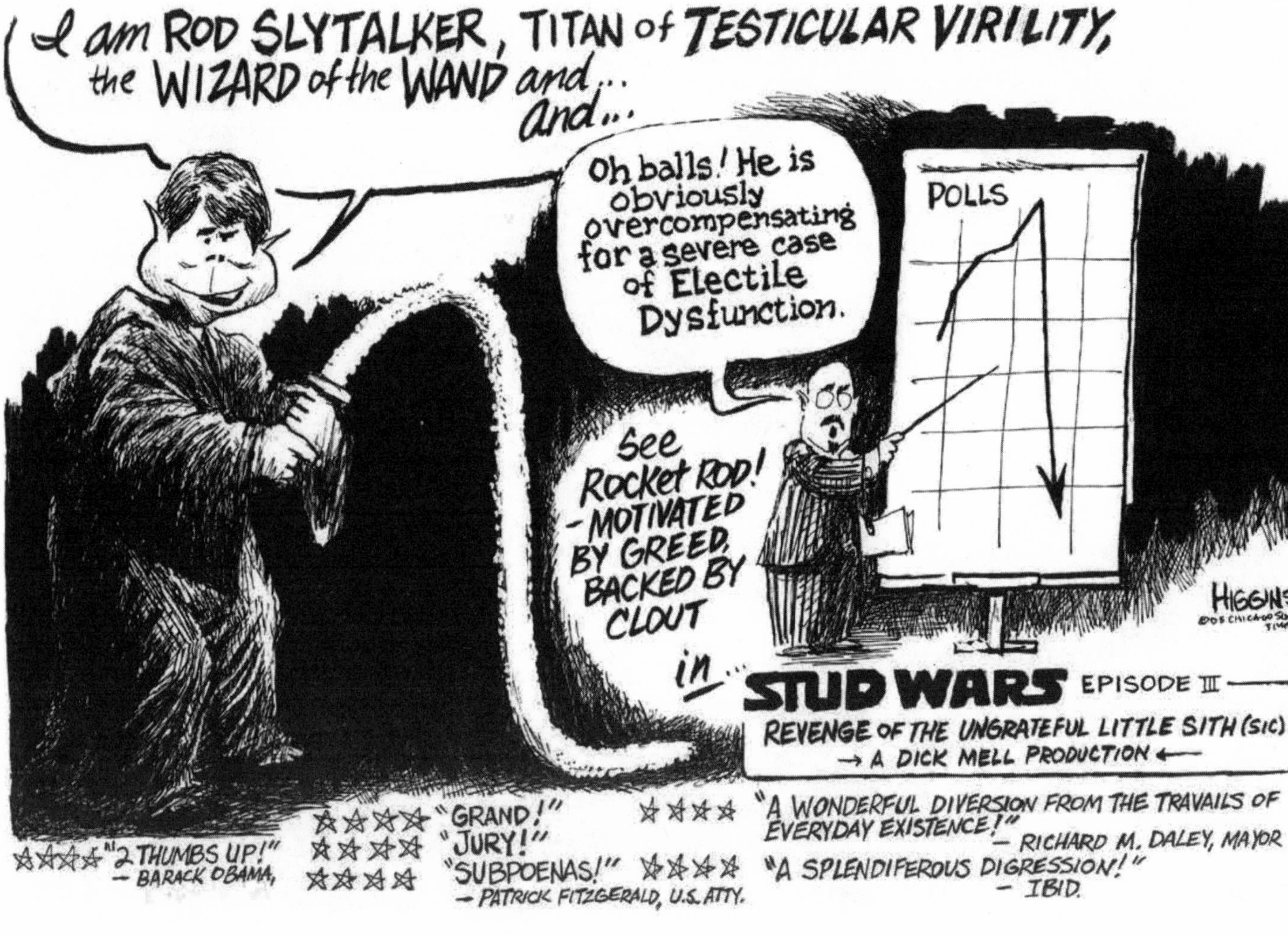
I am ROD SLYTALKER, TITAN of TESTICULAR VIRILITY, the WIZARD of the WAND and... and...
Oh balls! He is obviously overcompensating for a severe case of Electile Dysfunction.
POLLS
See Rocket ROD! -MOTIVATED BY GREED, BACKED BY CLOUT
in... STUD WARS EPISODE III
REVENGE OF THE UNGRATEFUL LITTLE SITH (SIC)
→ A DICK MELL PRODUCTION ←
HIGGINS
"2 THUMBS UP!" – BARACK OBAMA,
"GRAND!" "JURY!" "SUBPOENAS!" – PATRICK FITZGERALD, U.S. ATTY.
"A WONDERFUL DIVERSION FROM THE TRAVAILS OF EVERYDAY EXISTENCE!" – RICHARD M. DALEY, MAYOR
"A SPLENDIFEROUS DIGRESSION!" – IBID.

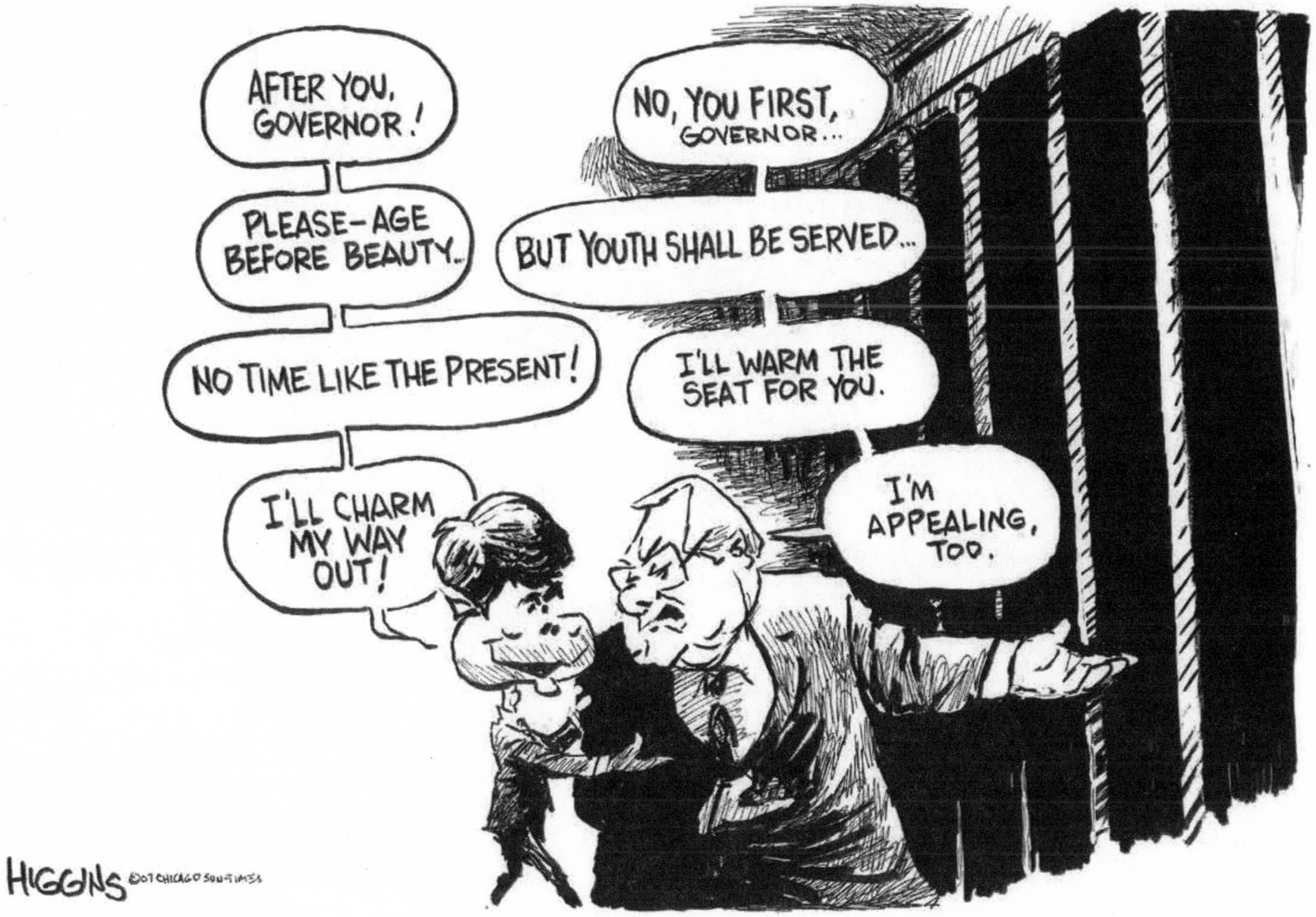
AFTER YOU, GOVERNOR!
NO, YOU FIRST, GOVERNOR...
PLEASE–AGE BEFORE BEAUTY..
BUT YOUTH SHALL BE SERVED...
NO TIME LIKE THE PRESENT!
I'LL WARM THE SEAT FOR YOU.
I'LL CHARM MY WAY OUT!
I'M APPEALING, TOO.
HIGGINS ©07 CHICAGO SUN-TIMES

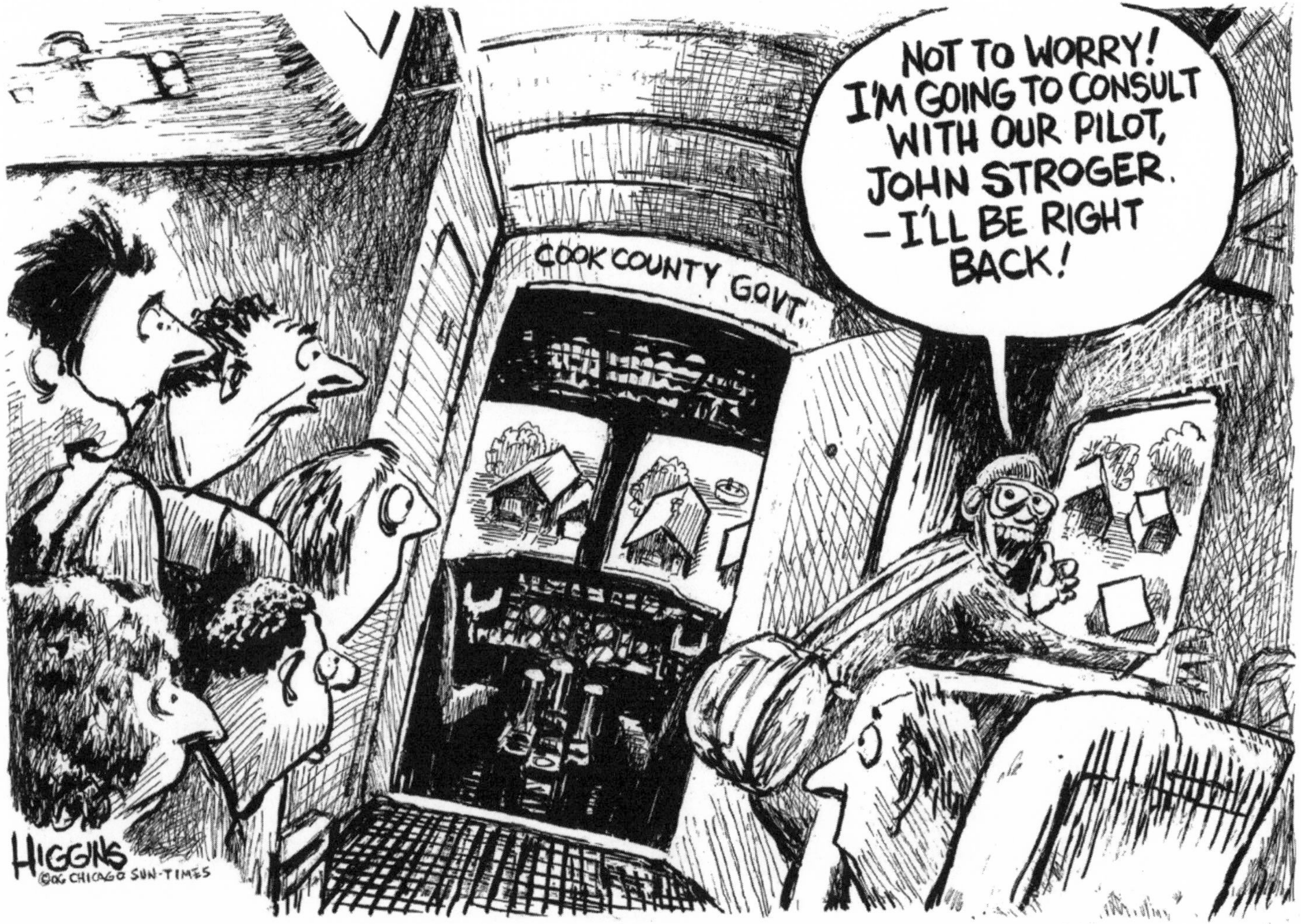
NOT TO WORRY! I'M GOING TO CONSULT WITH OUR PILOT, JOHN STROGER. – I'LL BE RIGHT BACK!
COOK COUNTY GOV'T.
HIGGINS
©06 CHICAGO SUN-TIMES

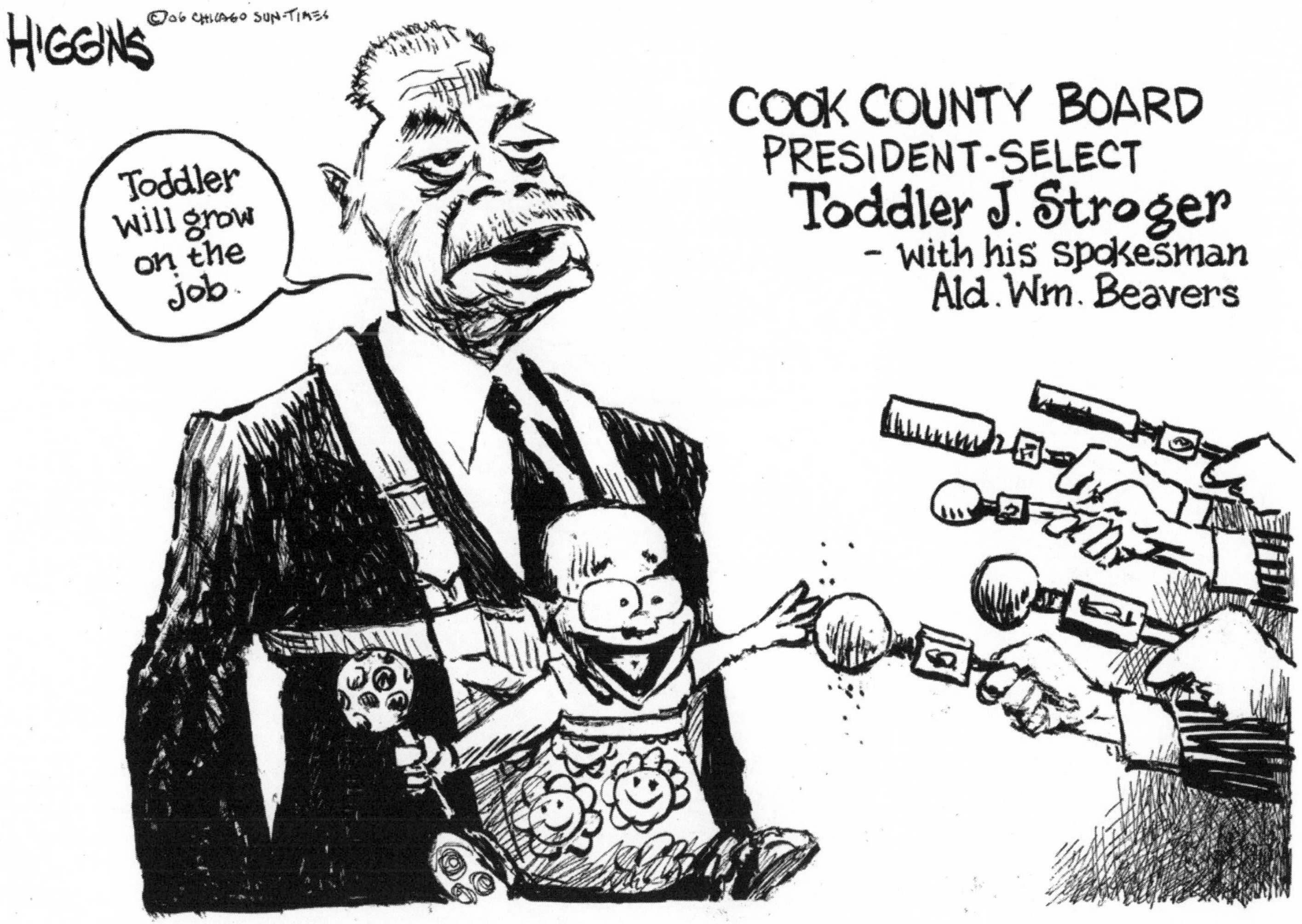
HIGGINS ©06 CHICAGO SUN-TIMES
COOK COUNTY BOARD PRESIDENT-SELECT Toddler J. Stroger - with his spokesman Ald. Wm. Beavers
Toddler will grow on the job.

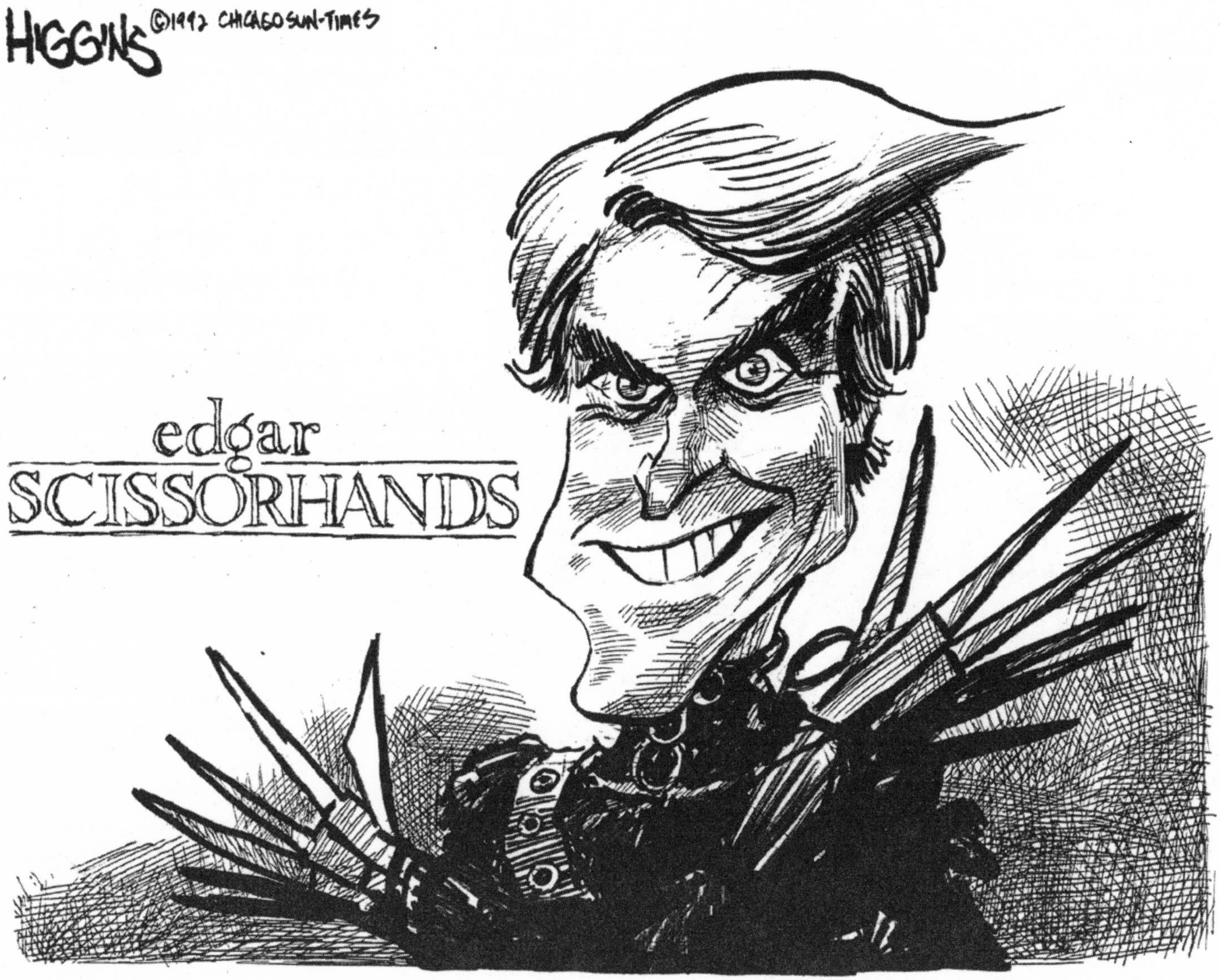
HIGGINS ©1992 CHICAGO SUN-TIMES
edgar
SCISSORHANDS

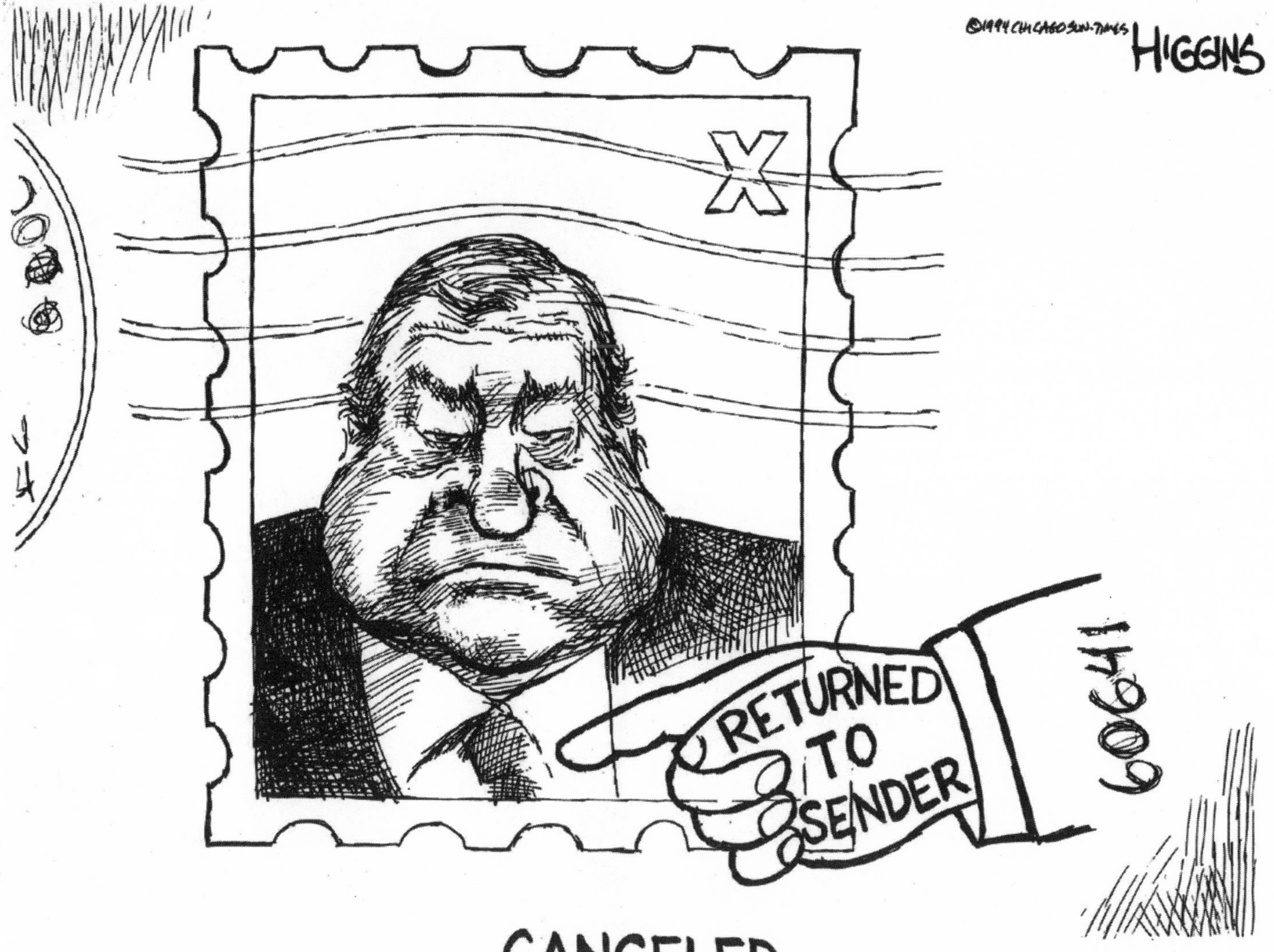
©1994 CHICAGO SUN-TIMES
HIGGINS
X
RETURNED TO SENDER
60641

CANCELED

The mishandling of snow removal services during the Great Snowstorm of '79 leads to Mayor Michael Bilandic's Democratic primary upset at the hands of former Consumer Affairs Commissioner Jane Byrne.

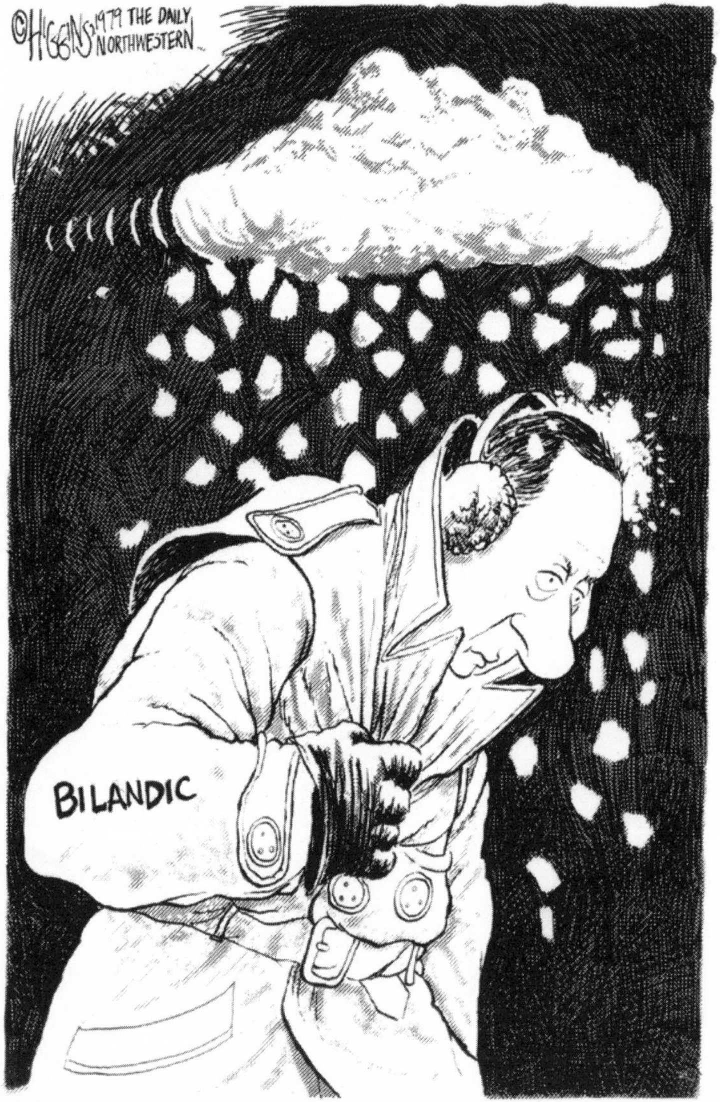

©HIGGINS 1979 THE DAILY NORTHWESTERN
BILANDIC

UNDER THE WEATHER

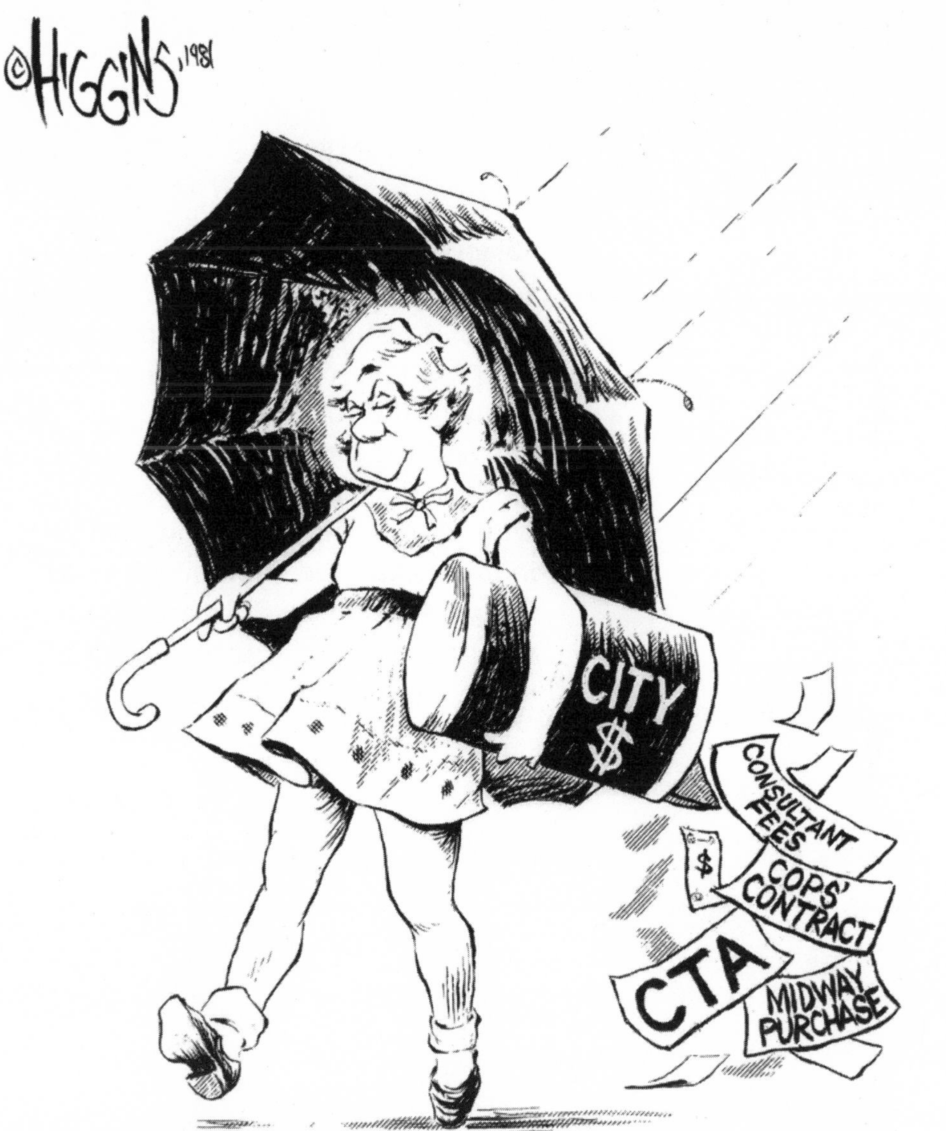
©HIGGINS, 1981
CITY $
CONSULTANT FEES
$
COPS' CONTRACT
CTA
MIDWAY PURCHASE
WHEN SHE REIGNS — IT POURS.

Blacks felt excluded from Jane Byrne's administration. In an effort to regain the African American vote, she moved into the Cabrini-Green Public Housing Project. By giving the appearance of effecting change, she hoped to resurrect her image as a reformer. Her 1983 Democratic primary strategy of Byrne for "All Chicago" also included an unholy alliance between the former reformer and a notorious street gang.

Harold Washington's Democratic primary victory in a three-way race with Mayor Jane Byrne and States Attorney Richard M. Daley also ushers in the unexpected, though temporary, rebirth of the Chicago Republican Party. Its candidate, Bernard Epton, runs a racially charged campaign with the slogan of "Epton: Before It's Too Late." Meanwhile, Mayor Byrne launches a "White-in" vote.

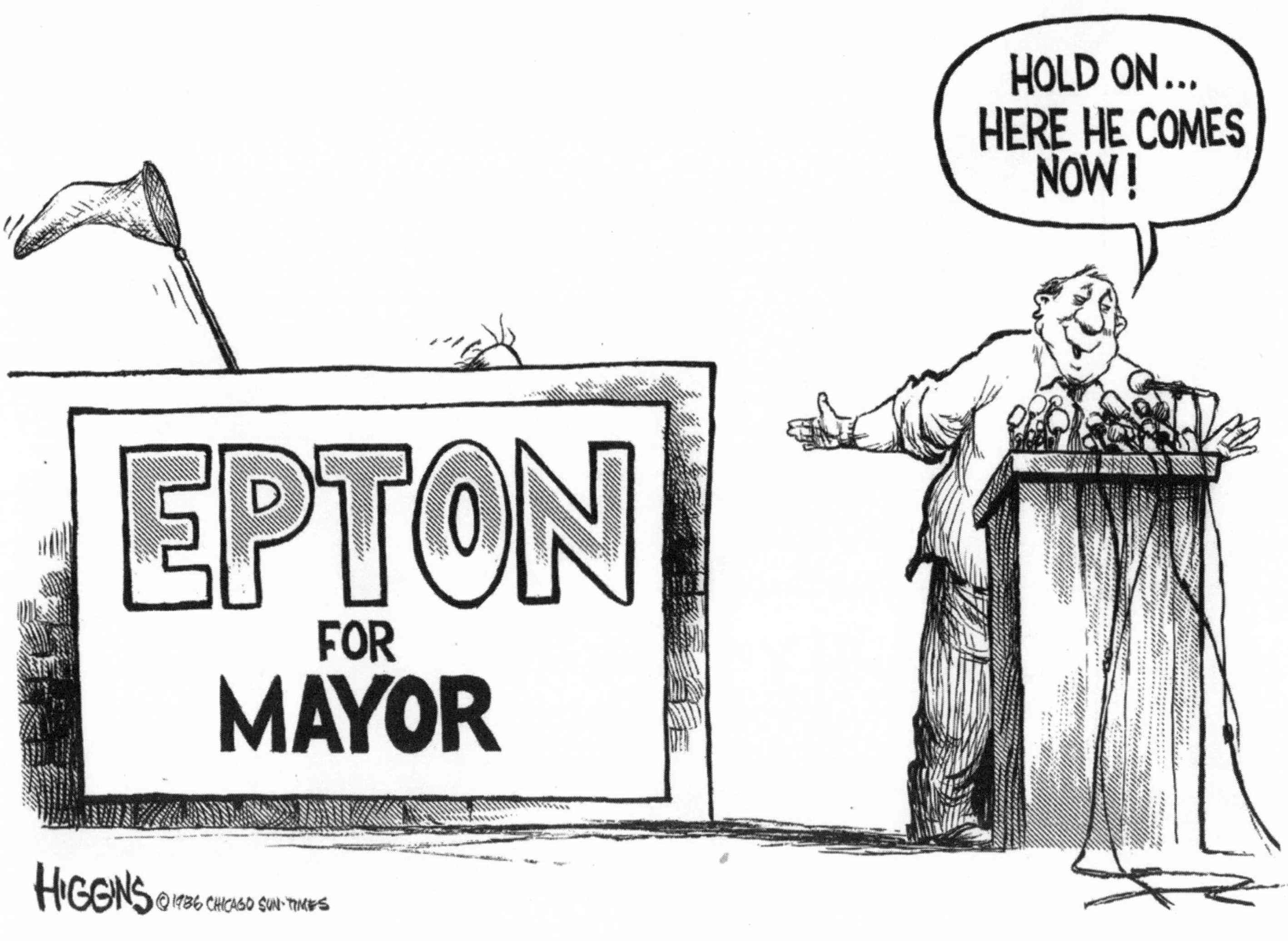

HOLD ON...
HERE HE COMES
NOW!
EPTON
FOR
MAYOR
HIGGINS © 1986 CHICAGO SUN-TIMES

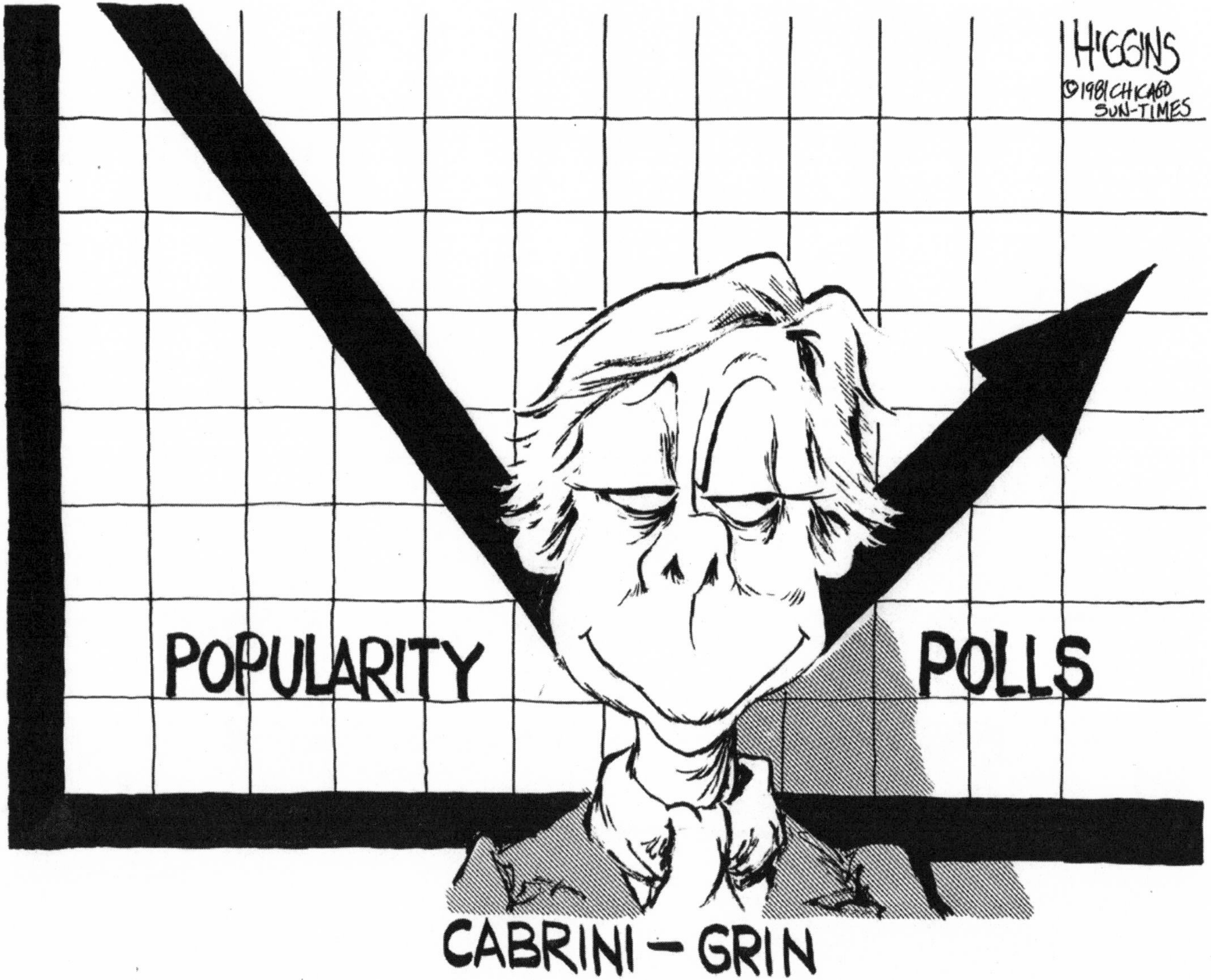
HIGGINS
©1981 CHICAGO SUN-TIMES
POPULARITY
POLLS
CABRINI - GRIN

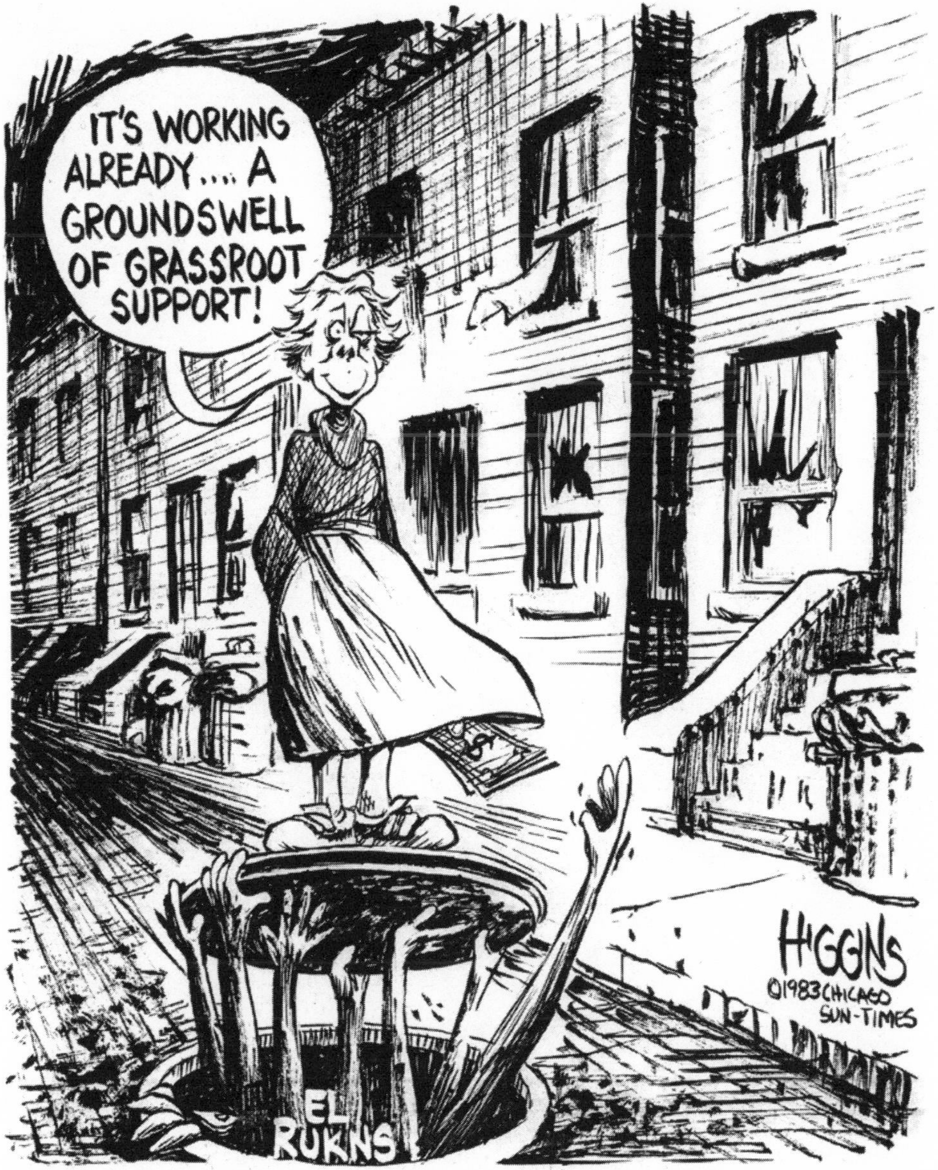
IT'S WORKING ALREADY.... A GROUNDSWELL OF GRASSROOT SUPPORT!
EL RUKNS
HIGGINS
©1983 CHICAGO SUN-TIMES

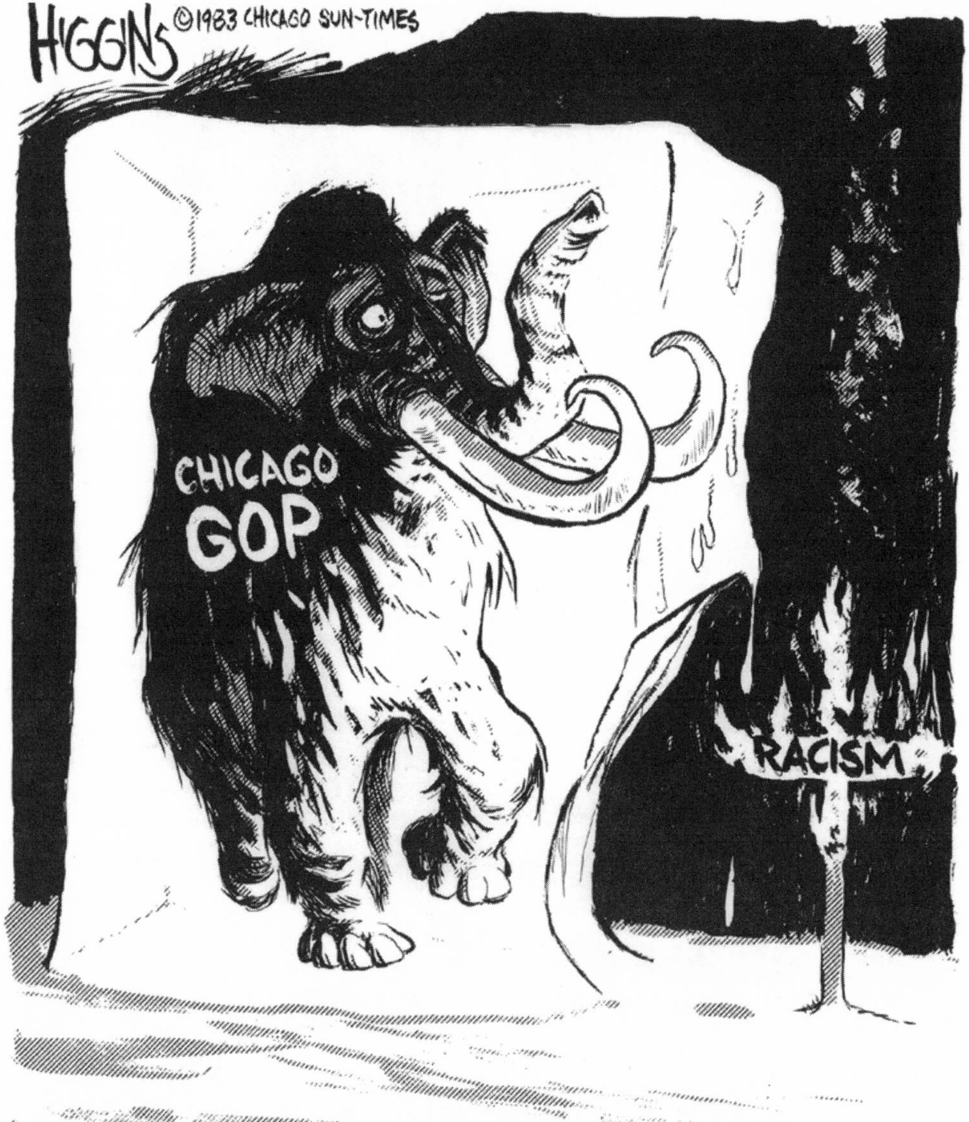
HIGGINS ©1983 CHICAGO SUN-TIMES
CHICAGO GOP
RACISM

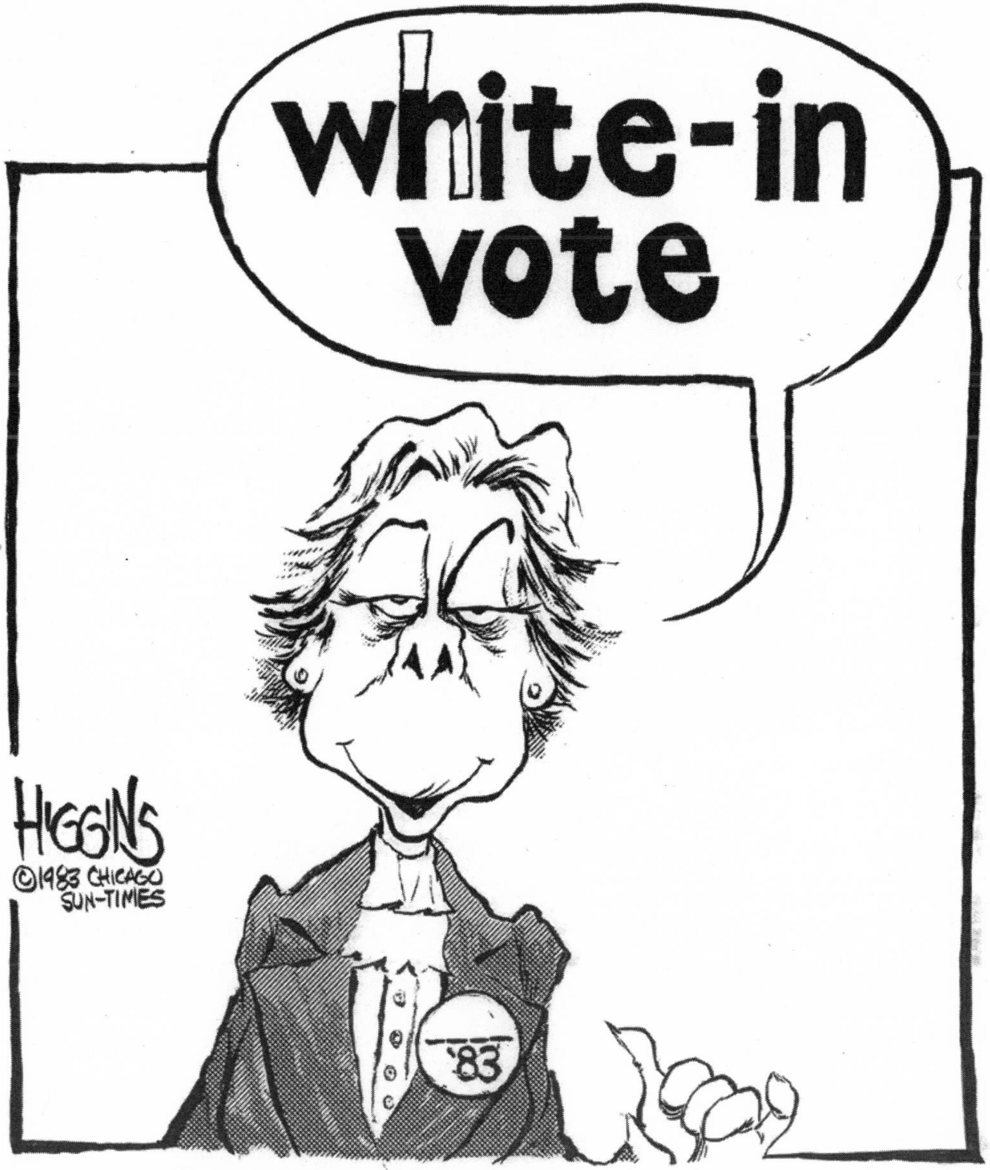
white-in vote
HIGGINS
©1983 CHICAGO SUN-TIMES
'83

Washington wins but tips his hand at his inauguration about his plans to reorganize the City Council. Aldermen Edward Vrdolyak and Edward Burke outmaneuver Washington by naming their own slate of committee chairmen, setting off a lengthy court battle and beginning a saga that came to be known as Council Wars. Votes of 29–21 would ring in Chicagoans' ears for the next three years. The battles would earn the city the nickname "Beirut by the Lake."

Vrdolyak considers running against Washington, and Jane Byrne flirts with running as a Republican. Mother Nature comes to her aid again, this time in the form of rainstorms bringing swells of water across Lake Shore Drive, exposing the city's weak breakwater walls.

Washington's image as a reformer takes a hit, but it does not harm him. Vrdolyak and Cook County Assessor Tom Hynes vie for his job but cancel each other out and Washington is reelected.

During the Washington administration the sun still rose over the city, the garbage was still picked up, the buses and trains still ran, and the city that worked still worked, only now for more people.

Before the year was over, Washington would die in his office of a heart attack. The contest for his successor began in a heartbeat.

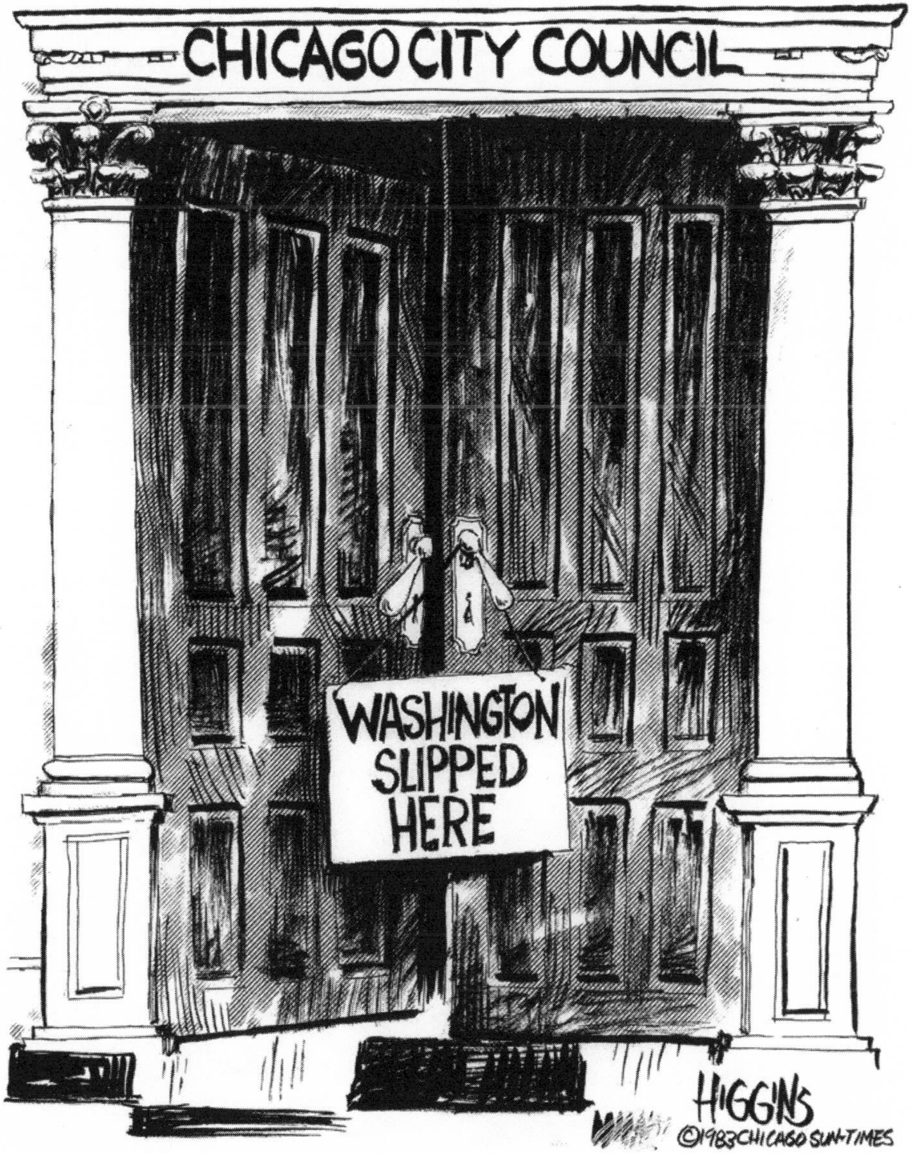
CHICAGO CITY COUNCIL
WASHINGTON SLIPPED HERE
HIGGINS
©1983 CHICAGO SUN-TIMES

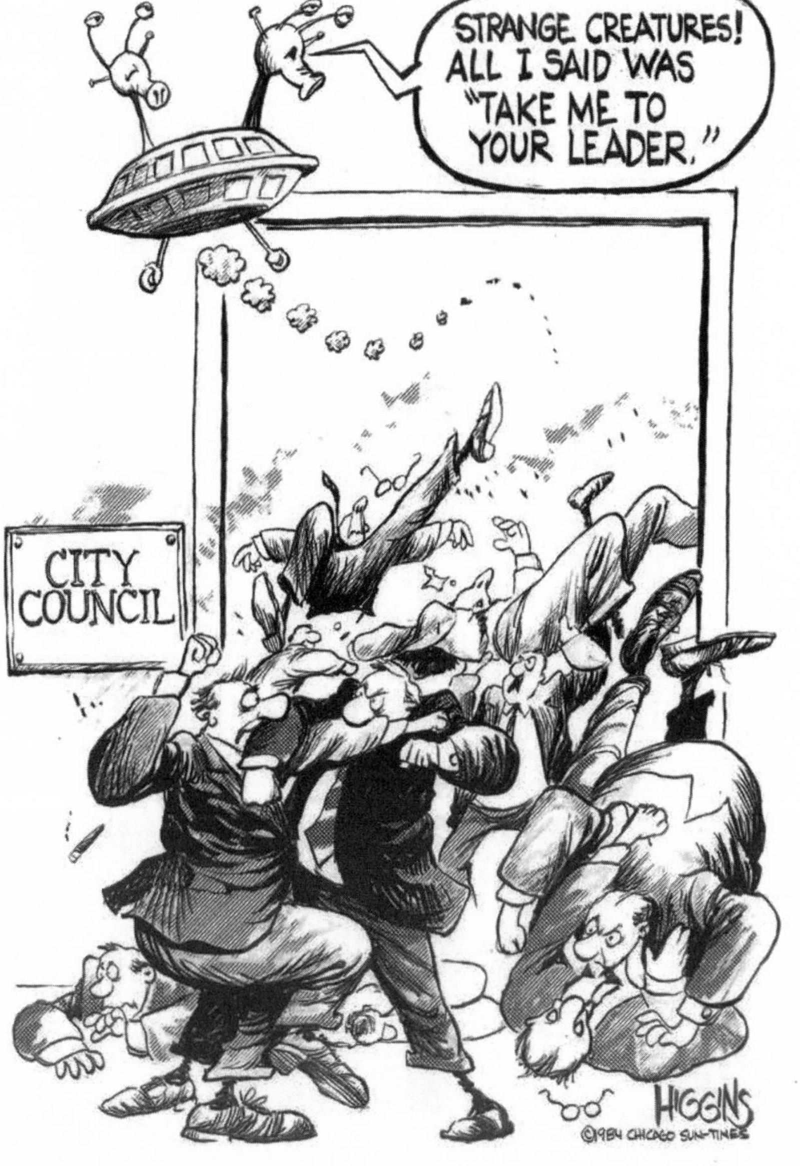

STRANGE CREATURES! ALL I SAID WAS "TAKE ME TO YOUR LEADER."
CITY COUNCIL
HIGGINS
©1984 CHICAGO SUN-TIMES

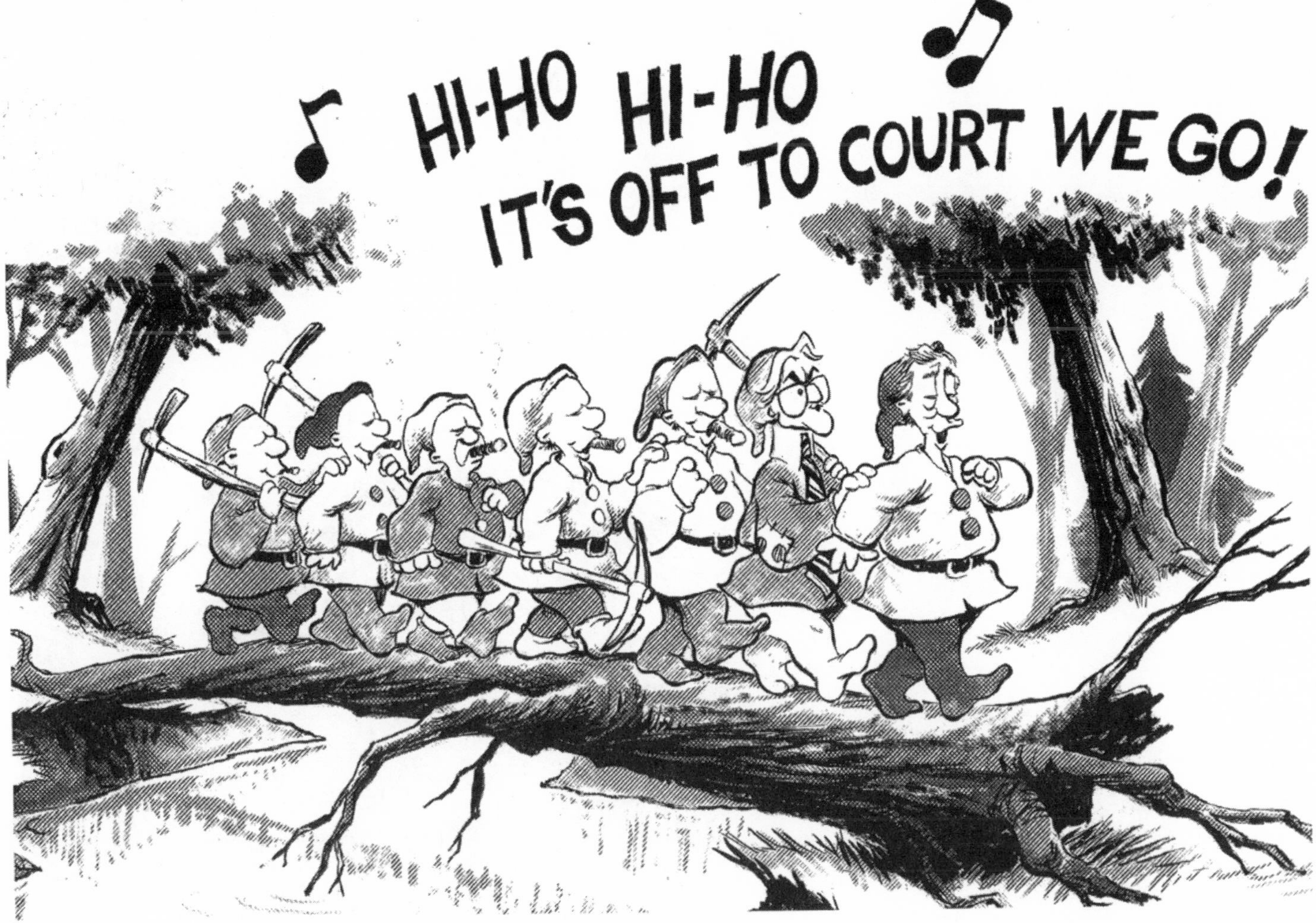
HI-HO HI-HO
IT'S OFF TO COURT WE GO!

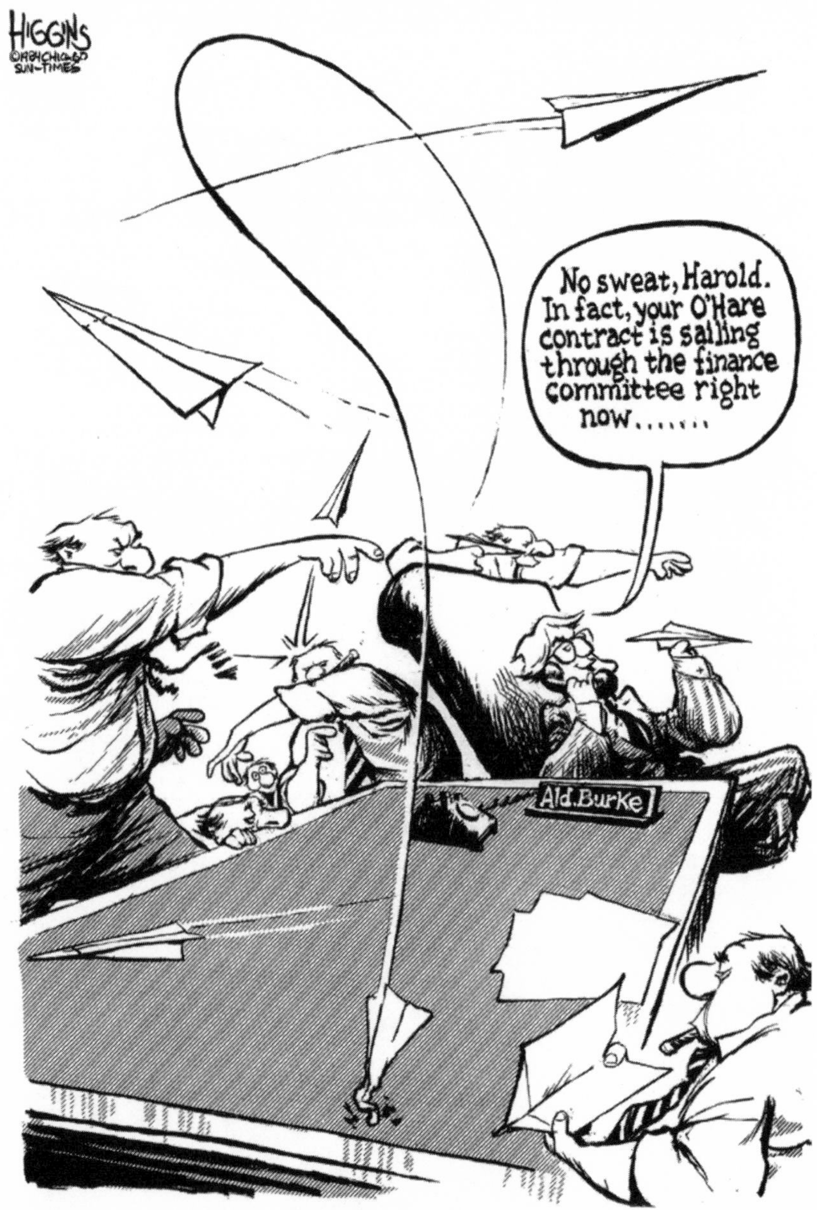
HIGGINS
©1984 CHICAGO SUN-TIMES
No sweat, Harold. In fact, your O'Hare contract is sailing through the finance committee right now.......
Ald. Burke

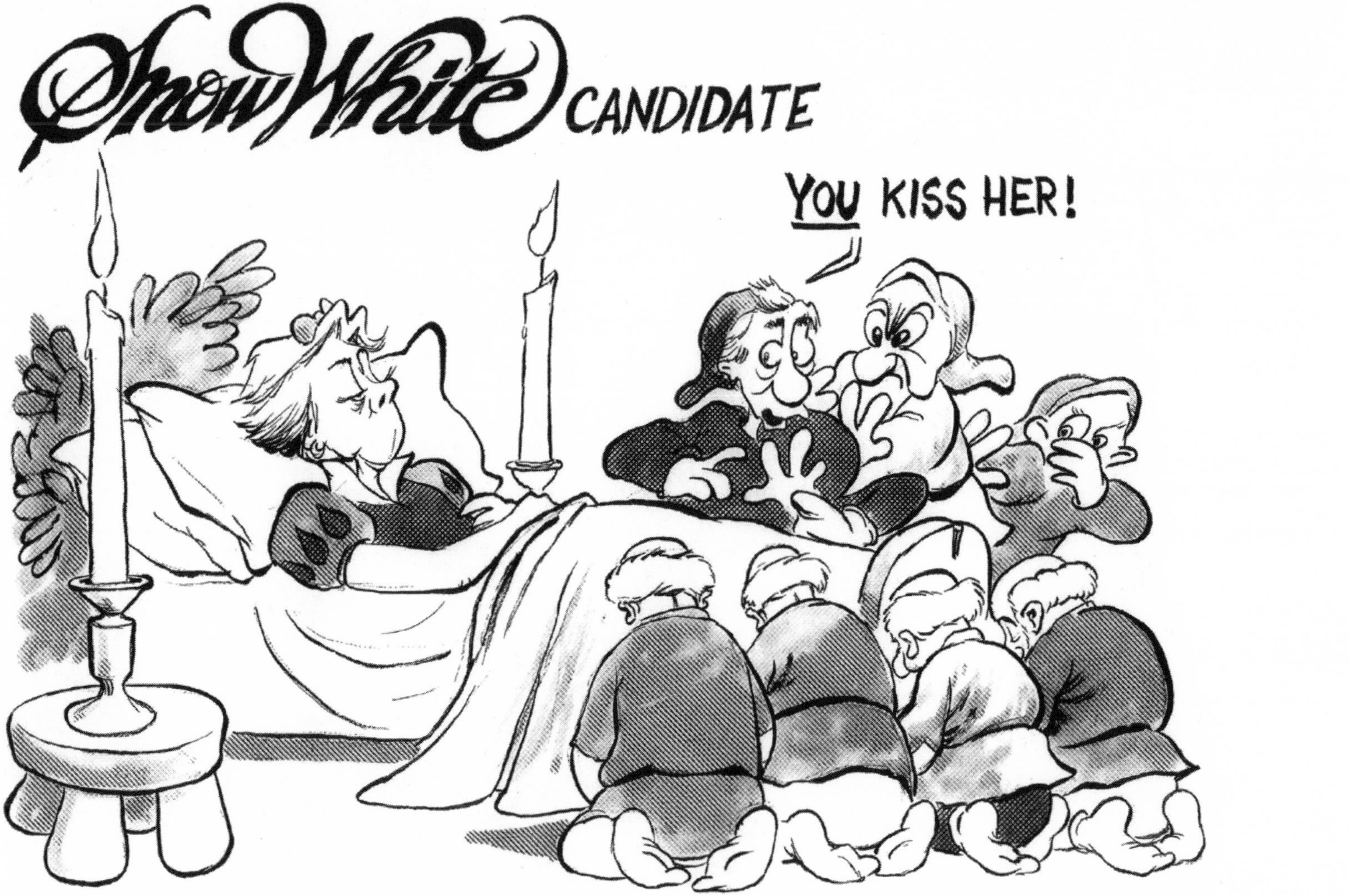
Snow White CANDIDATE
YOU KISS HER!

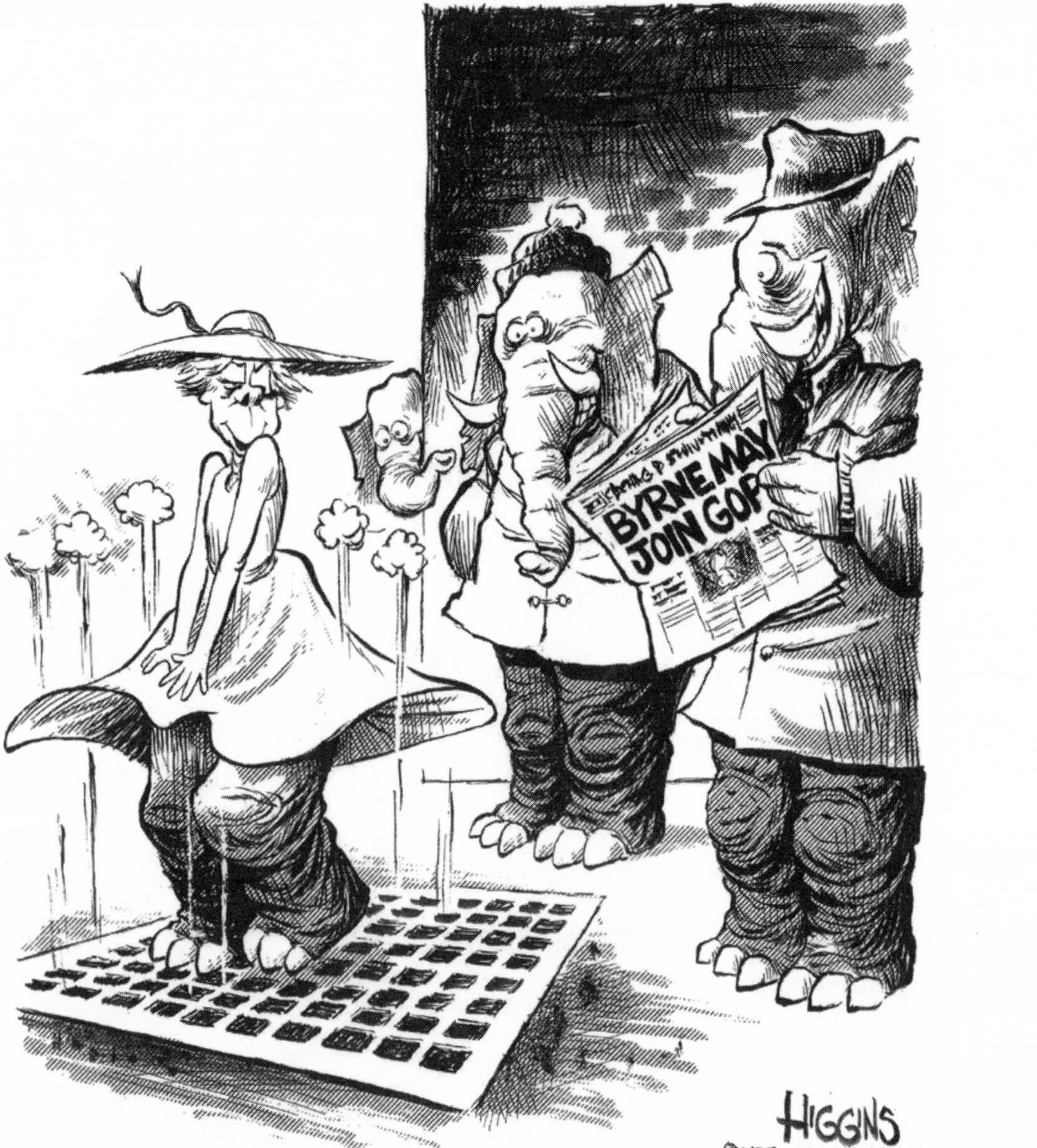
BYRNE MAY JOIN GOP
HIGGINS
©1985 CHICAGO SUN-TIMES

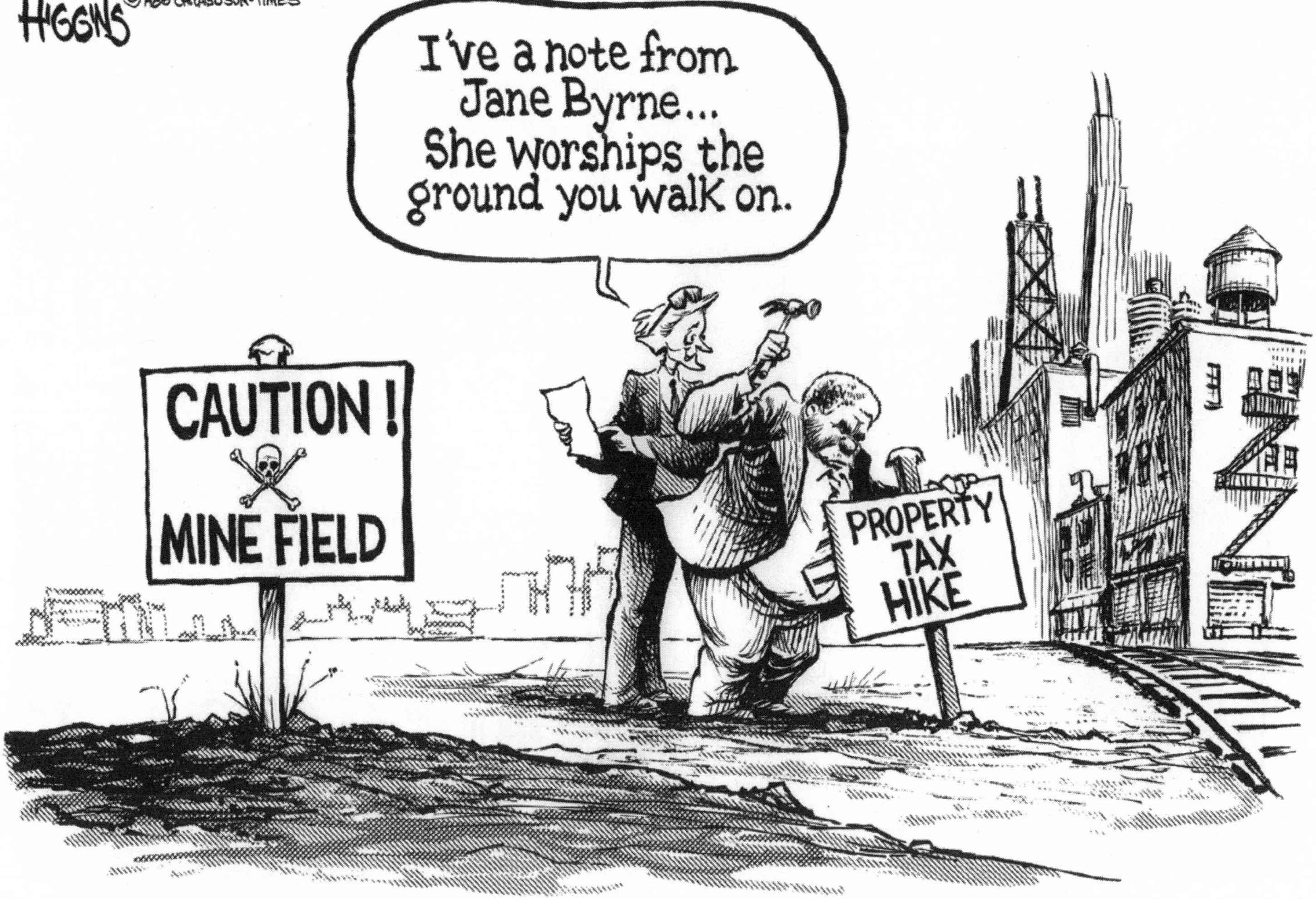
HIGGINS © 1986 CHICAGO SUN-TIMES
I've a note from Jane Byrne... She worships the ground you walk on.
CAUTION! MINE FIELD
PROPERTY TAX HIKE

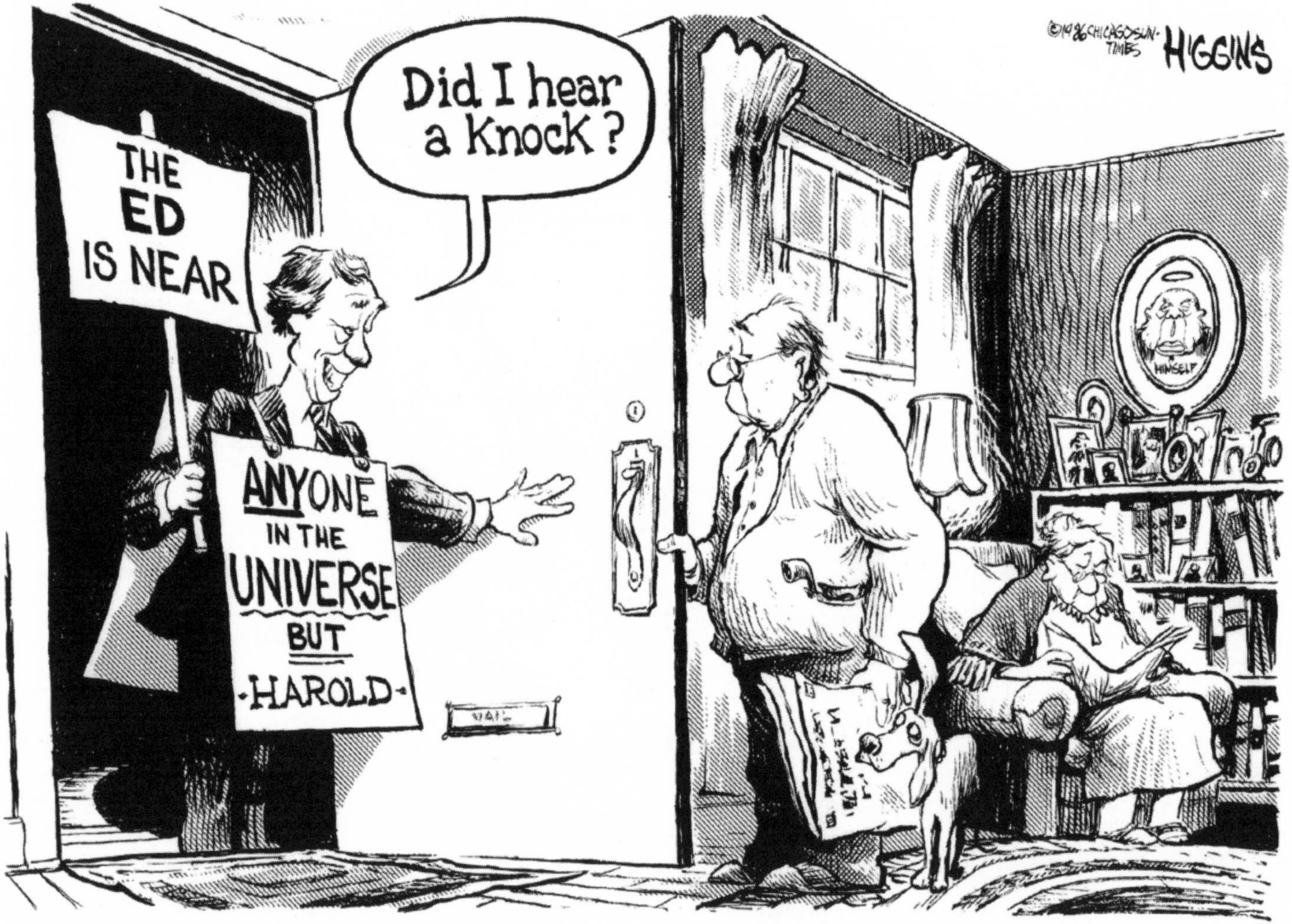
©1986 CHICAGO SUN-TIMES
HIGGINS
Did I hear a Knock?
THE ED IS NEAR
ANYONE IN THE UNIVERSE BUT HAROLD
HIMSELF

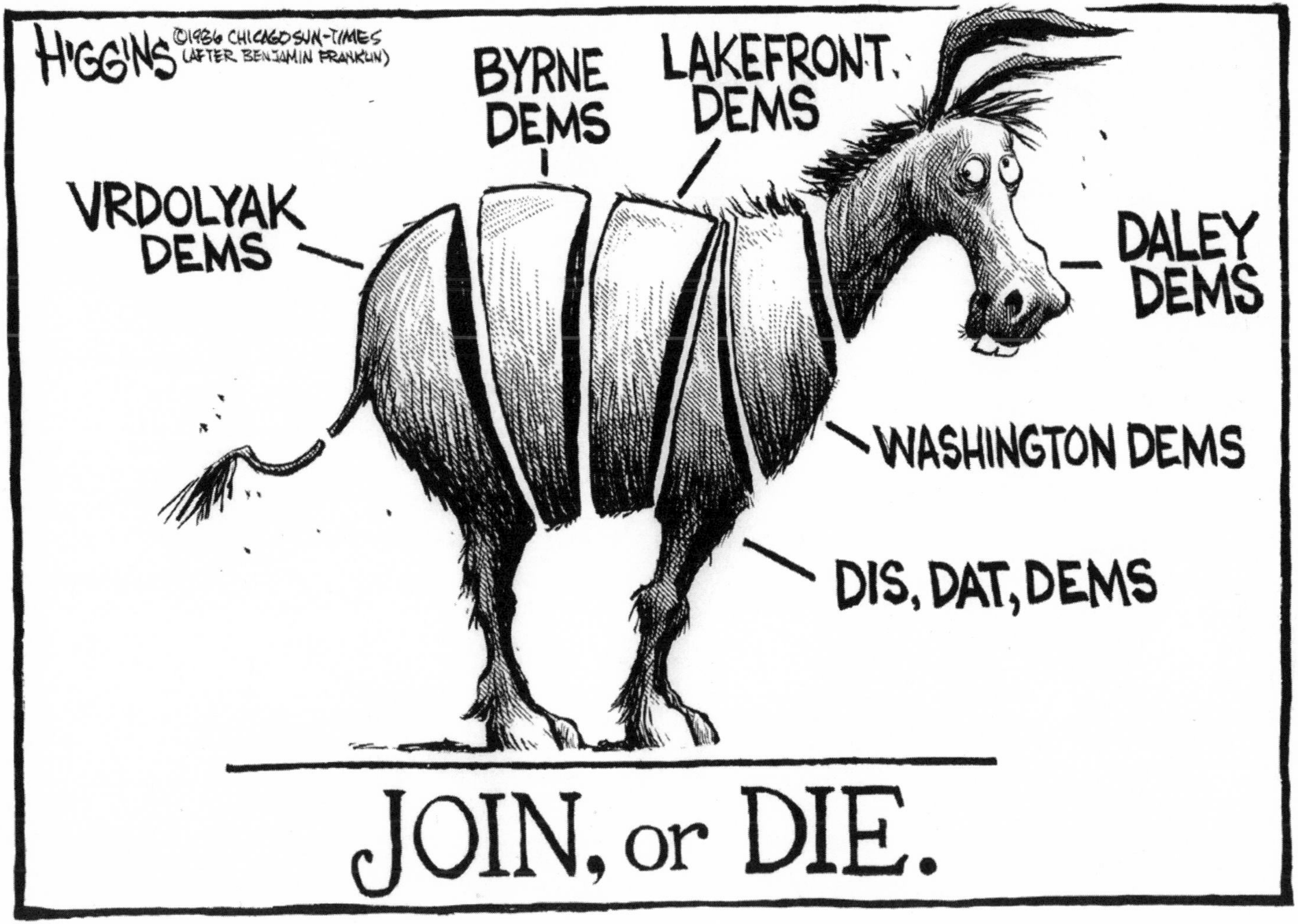
HIGGINS ©1986 CHICAGO SUN-TIMES (AFTER BENJAMIN FRANKLIN)
BYRNE DEMS
LAKEFRONT DEMS
VRDOLYAK DEMS
DALEY DEMS
WASHINGTON DEMS
DIS, DAT, DEMS
JOIN, or DIE.

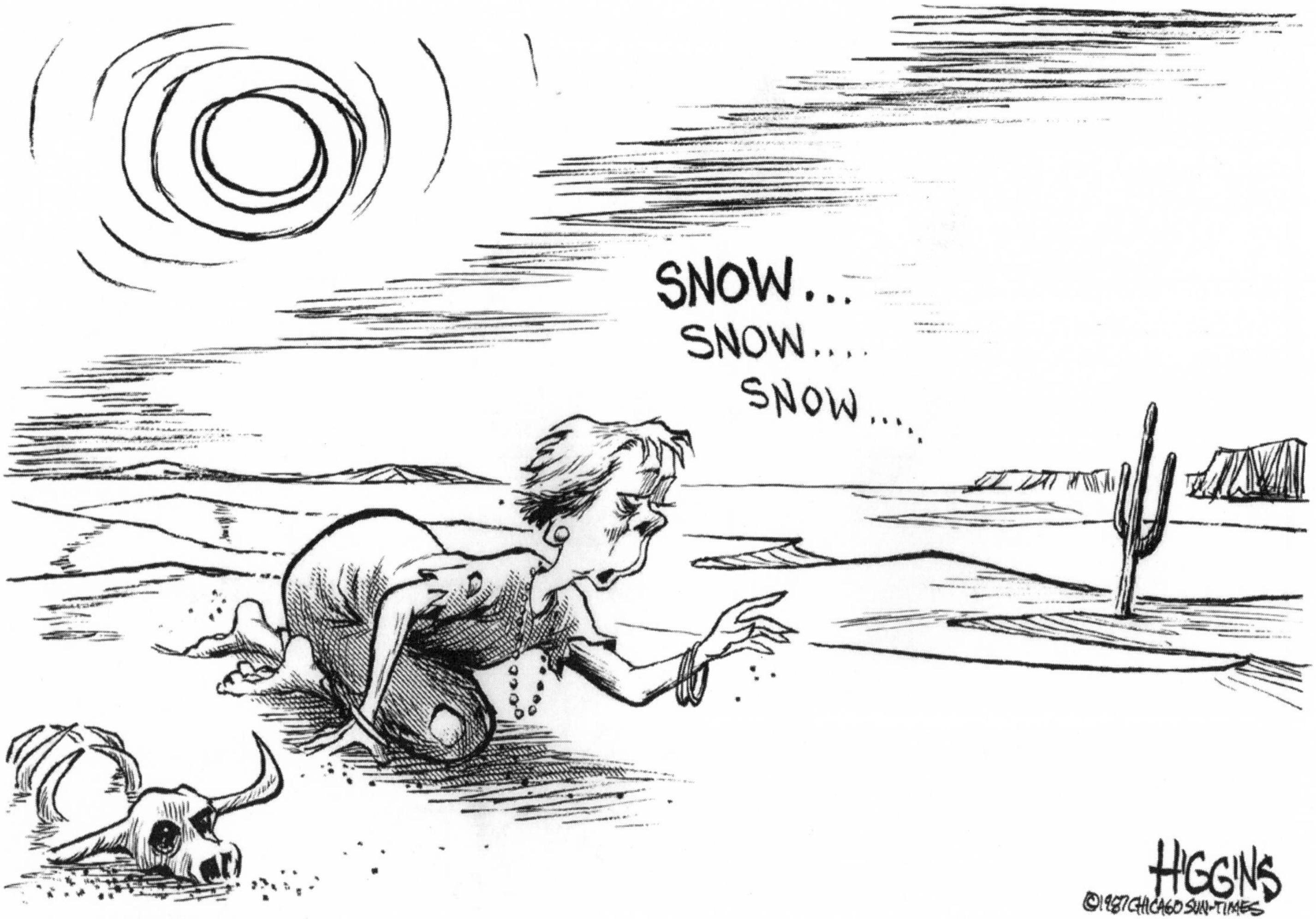
SNOW...
SNOW....
SNOW....
HIGGINS
©1987 CHICAGO SUN-TIMES

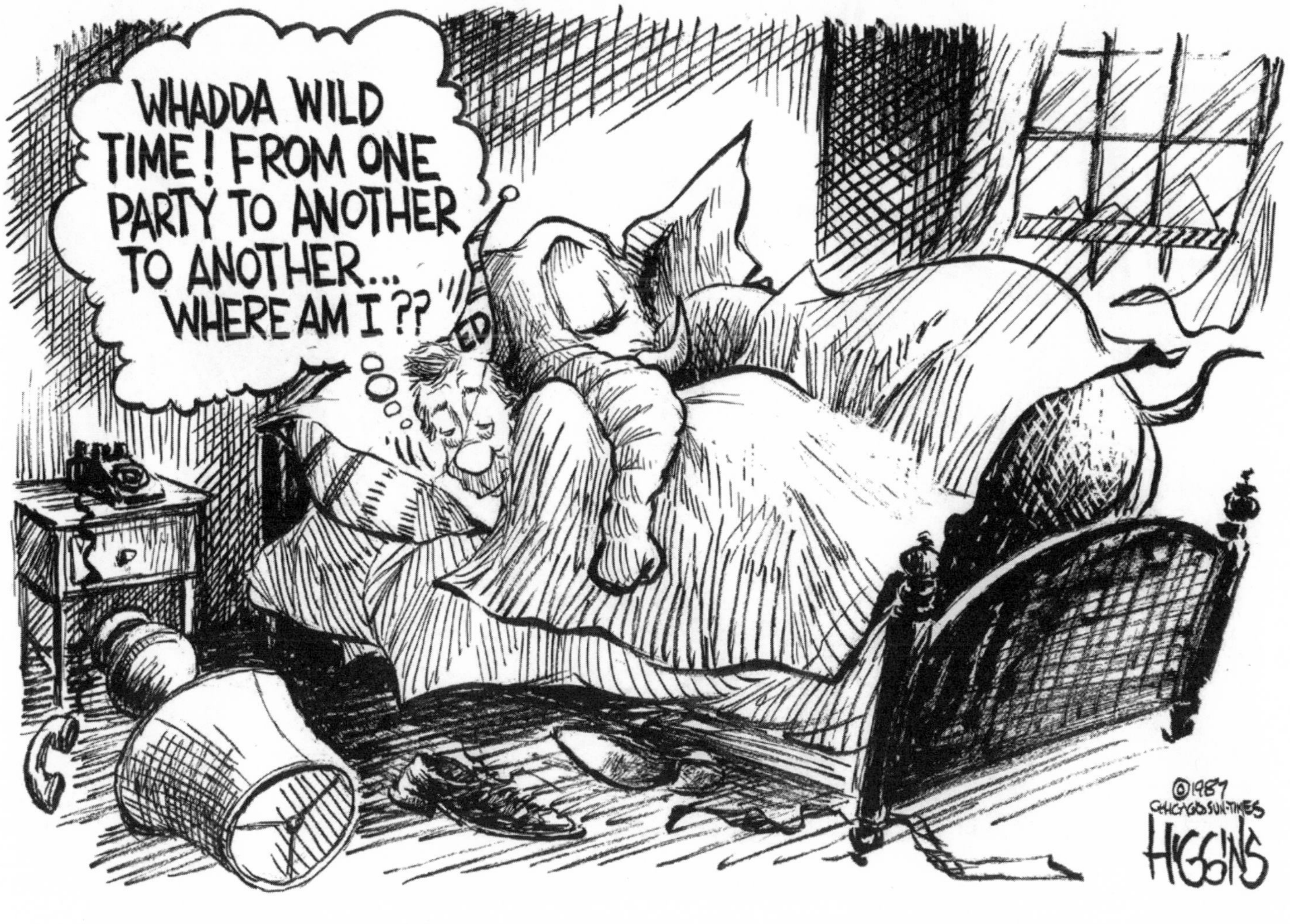
WHADDA WILD TIME! FROM ONE PARTY TO ANOTHER TO ANOTHER... WHERE AM I??
ED
©1987 CHICAGO SUN-TIMES
HIGGINS

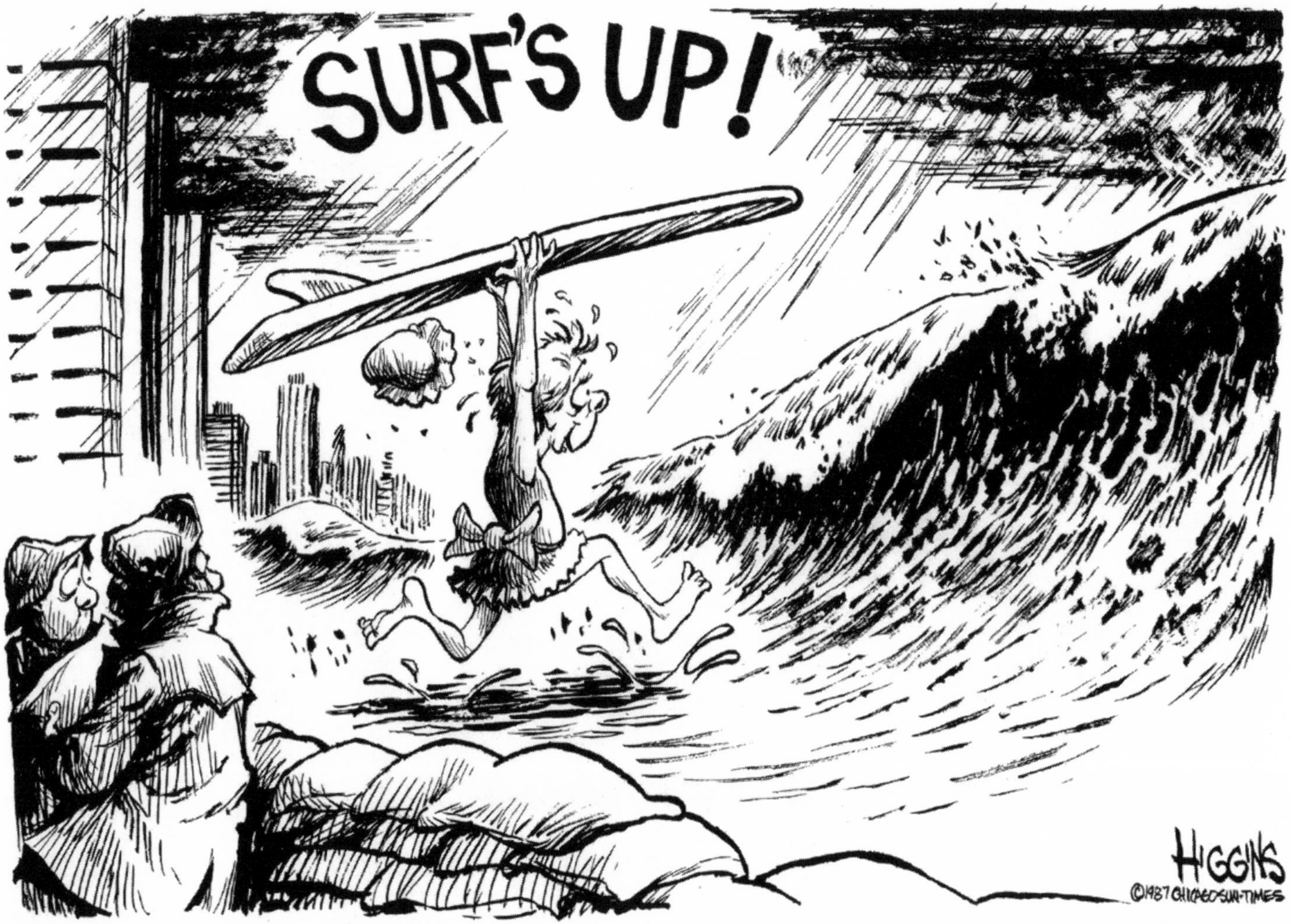
SURF'S UP!
HIGGINS
©1987 CHICAGO SUN-TIMES

Jane "Our Lady of the Lake" Byrne and
the 1987 flooding of Lake Shore Drive.

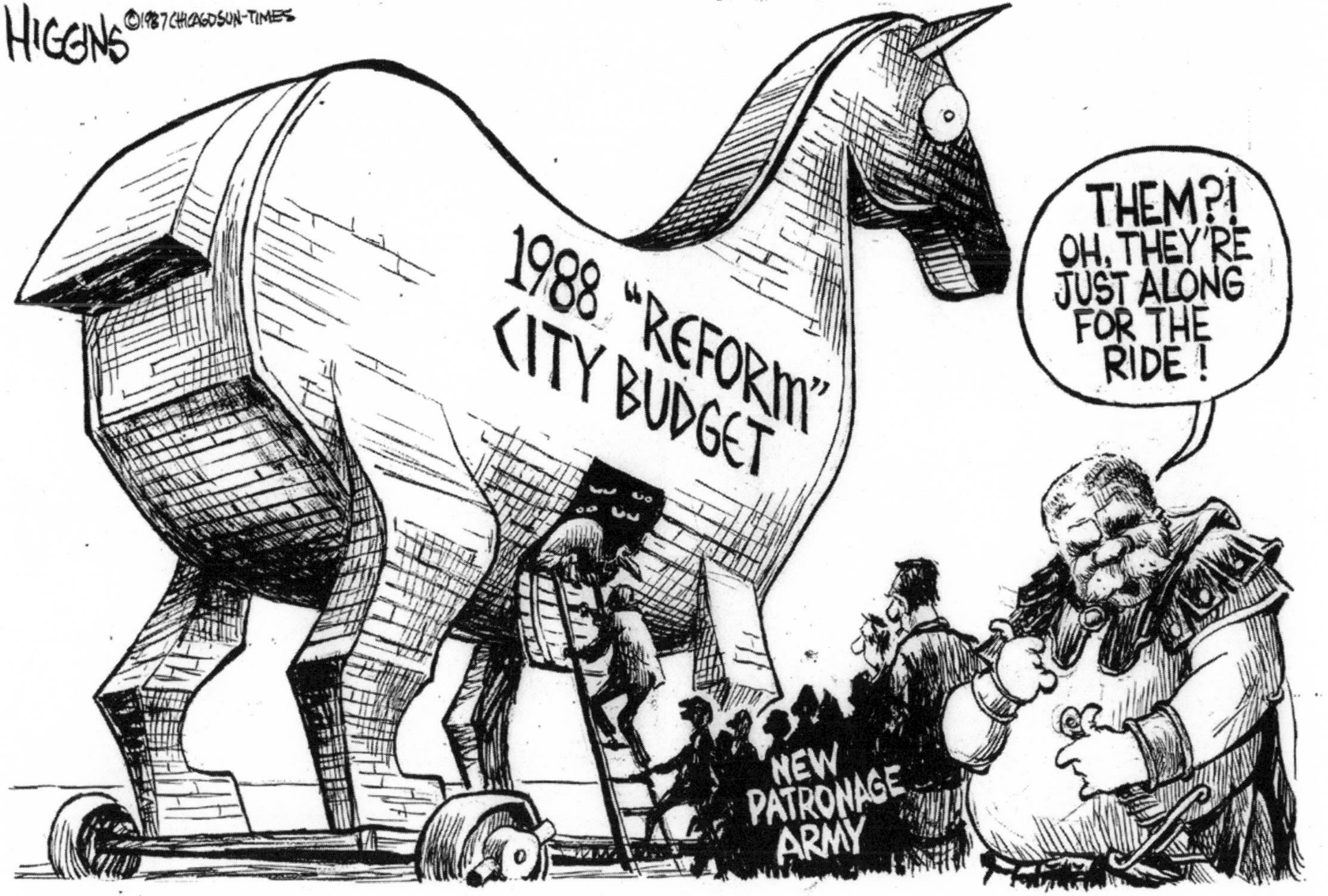
HIGGINS ©1987 CHICAGO SUN-TIMES
1988 "REFORM" CITY BUDGET
THEM?! OH, THEY'RE JUST ALONG FOR THE RIDE!
NEW PATRONAGE ARMY

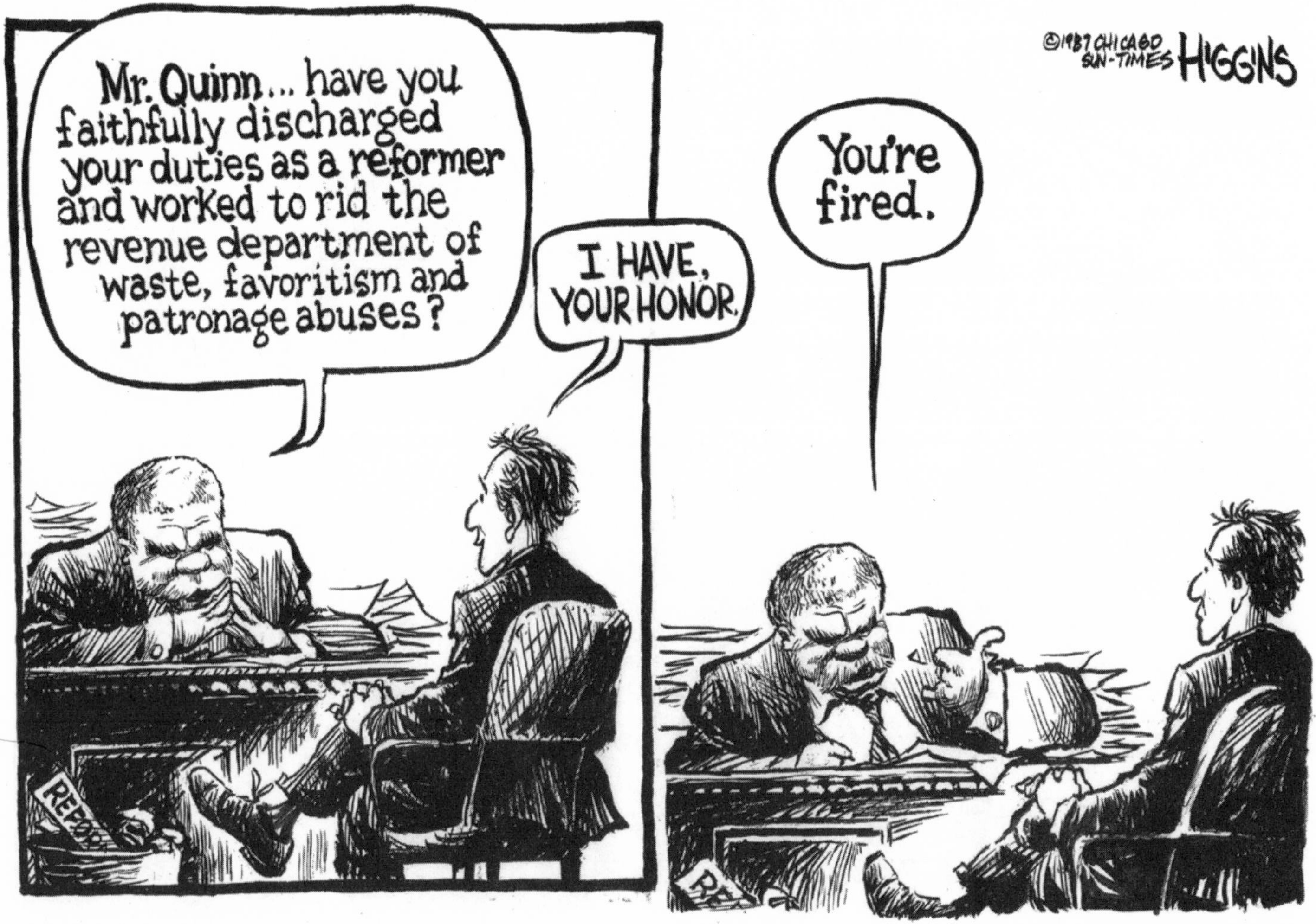
©1987 CHICAGO SUN-TIMES
HIGGINS
Mr. Quinn ... have you faithfully discharged your duties as a reformer and worked to rid the revenue department of waste, favoritism and patronage abuses?
I HAVE, YOUR HONOR.
You're fired.

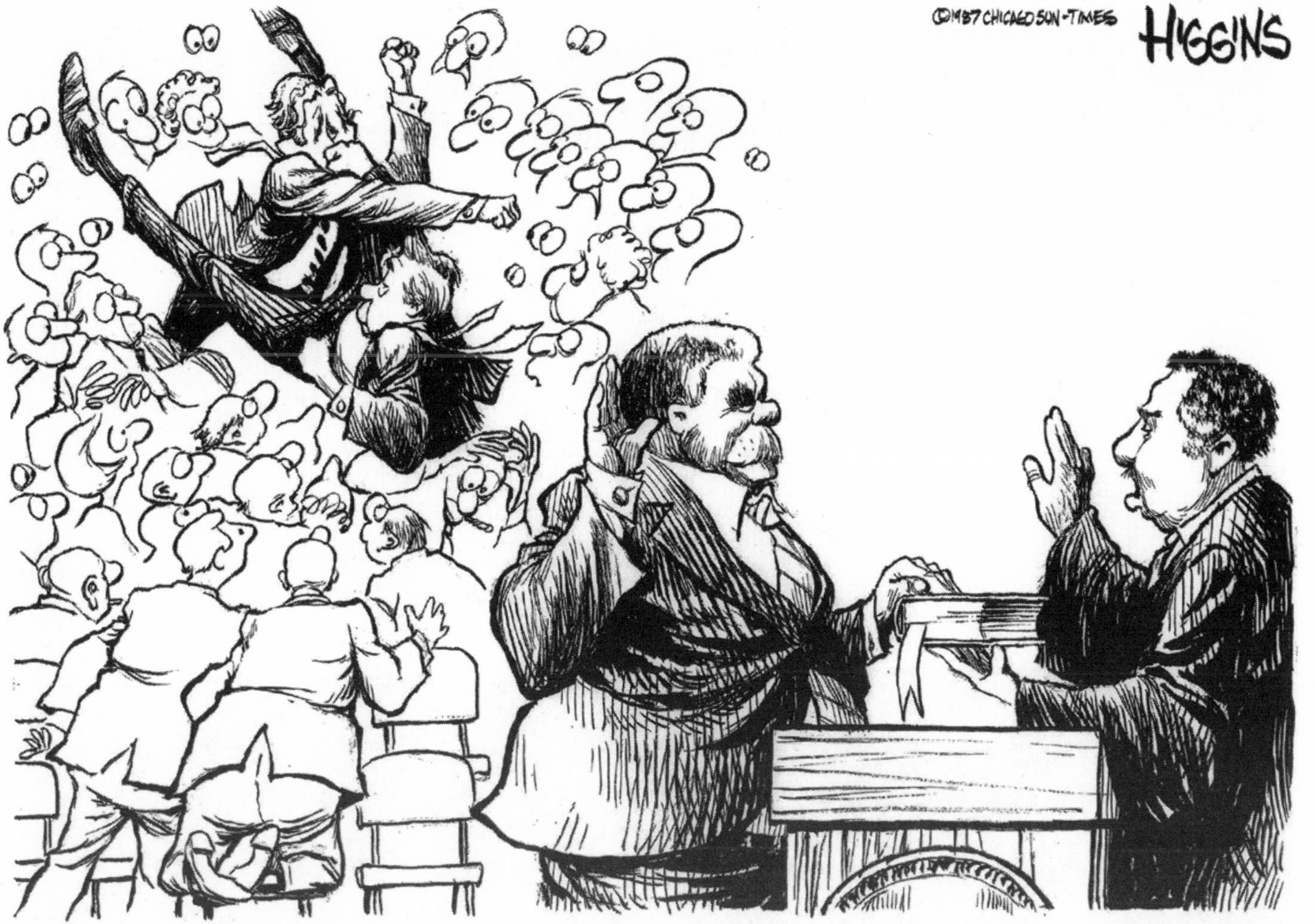

©1987 CHICAGO SUN-TIMES
HIGGINS

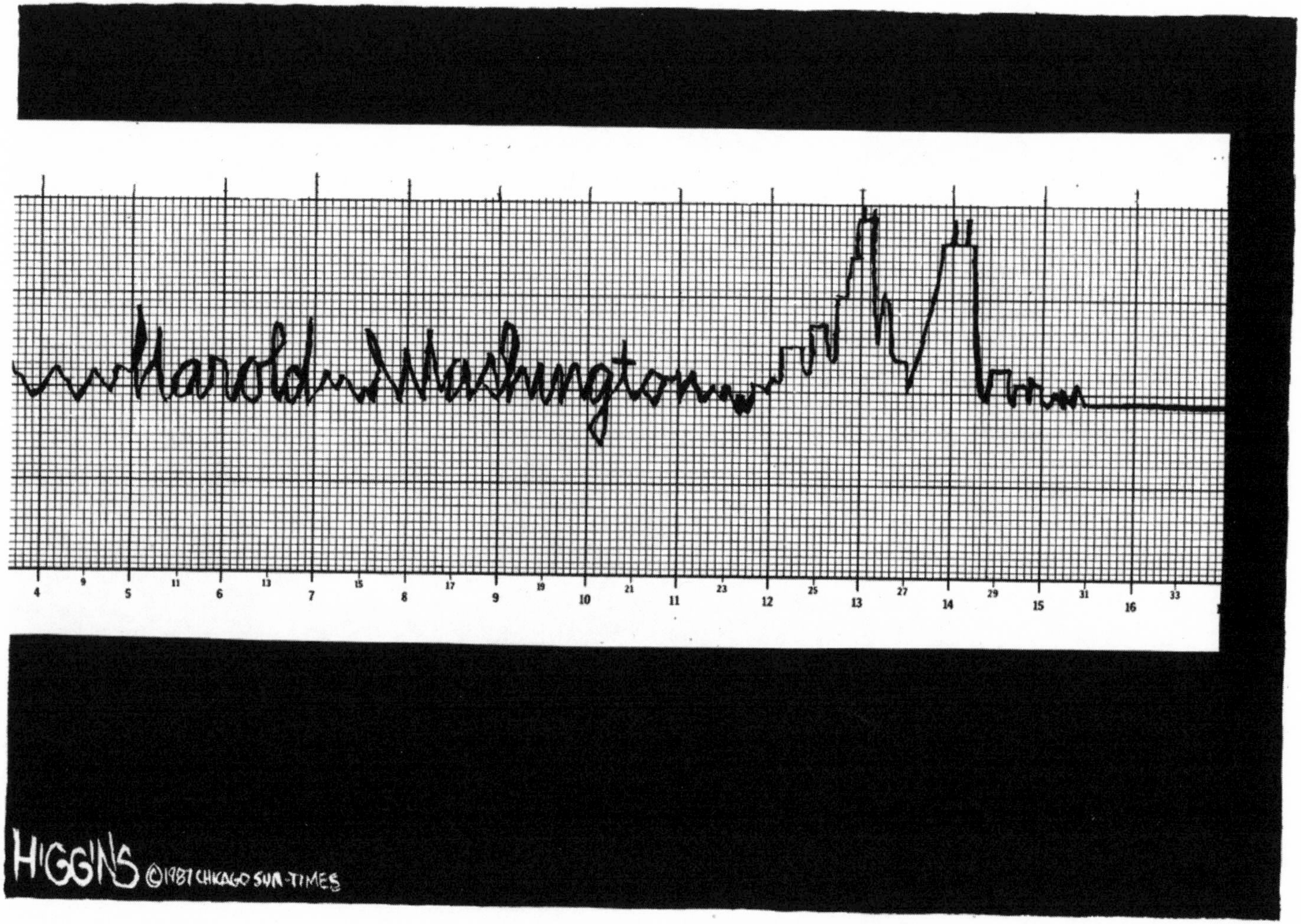
Harold Washington
HIGGINS ©1987 CHICAGO SUN-TIMES

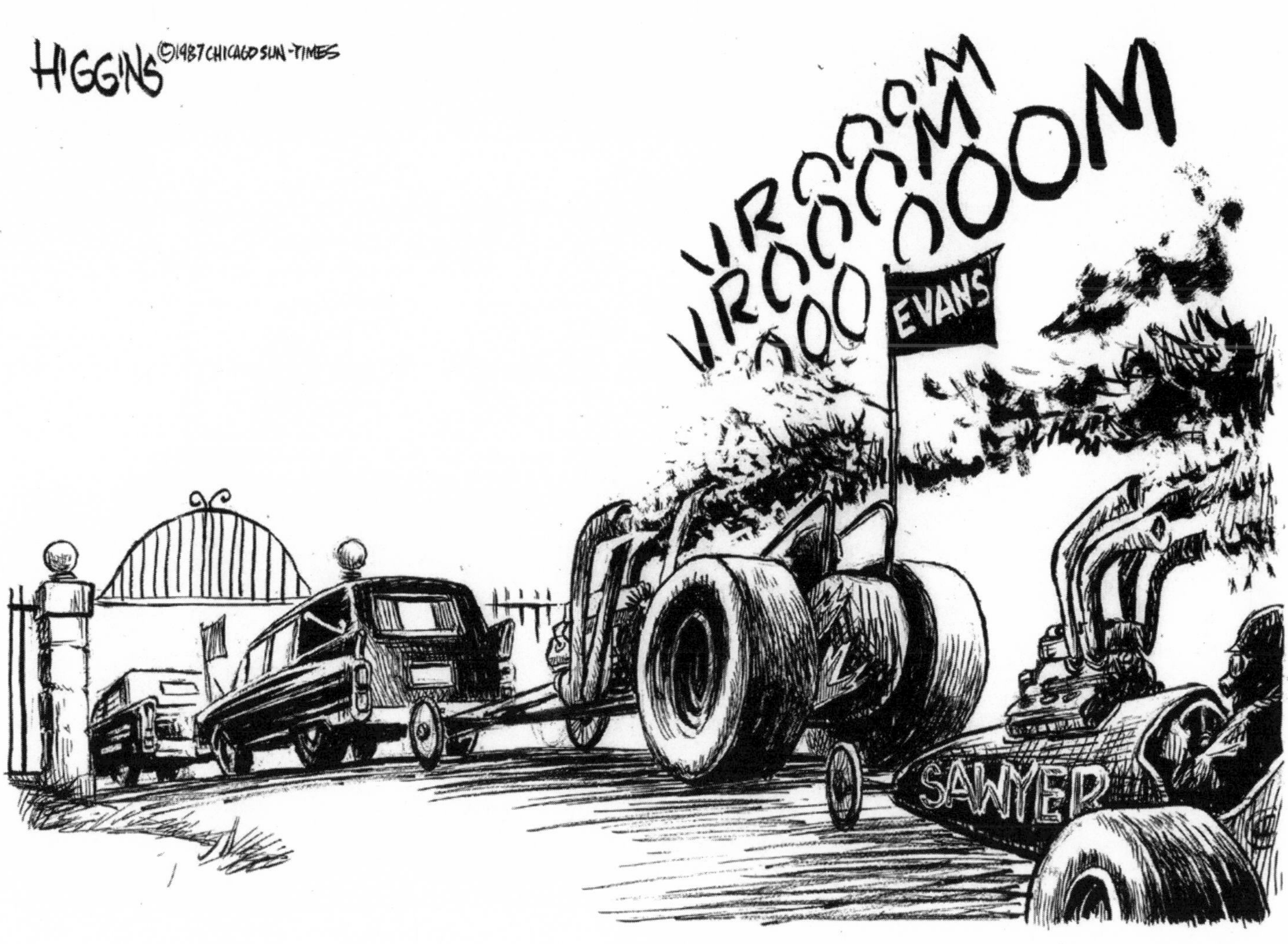
HIGGINS ©1987 CHICAGO SUN-TIMES
VROOOOM
VROOOOOOOOM
EVANS
SAWYER

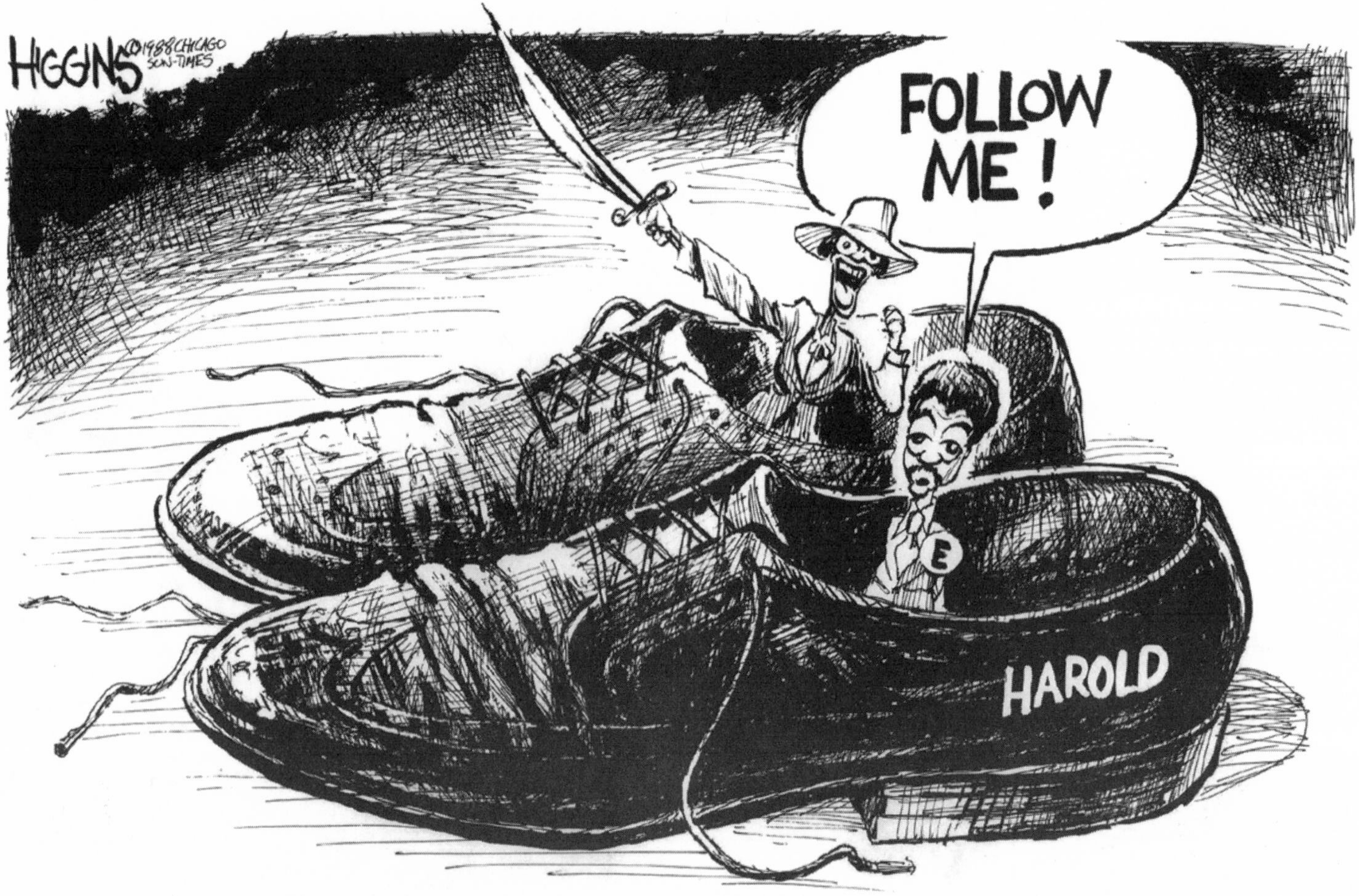
HIGGINS ©1988 CHICAGO SUN-TIMES
FOLLOW ME!
E
HAROLD

SPORTS

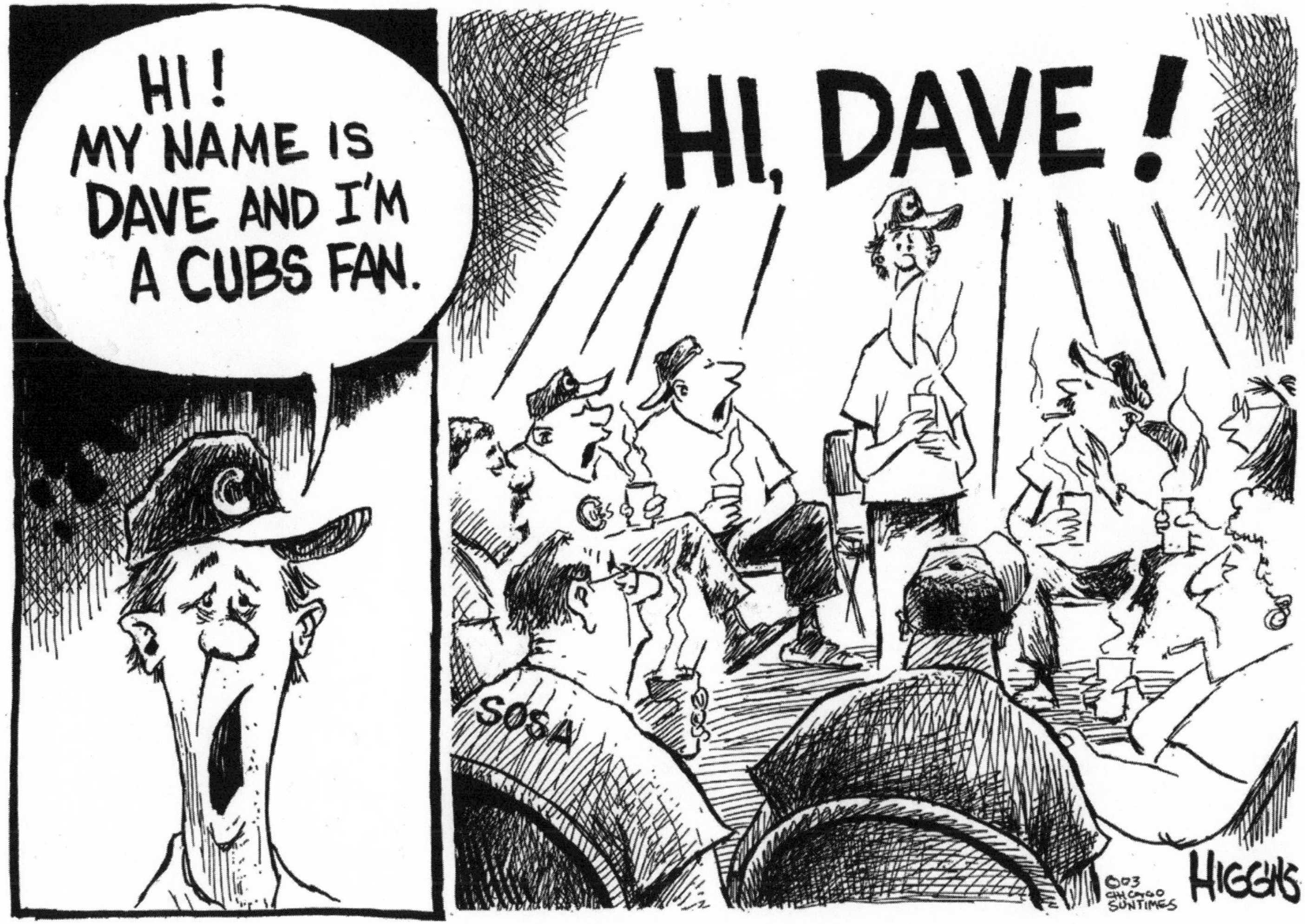
HI !
MY NAME IS
DAVE AND I'M
A CUBS FAN.
HI, DAVE !
SOSA
©03
CHICAGO
SUNTIMES
HIGGINS

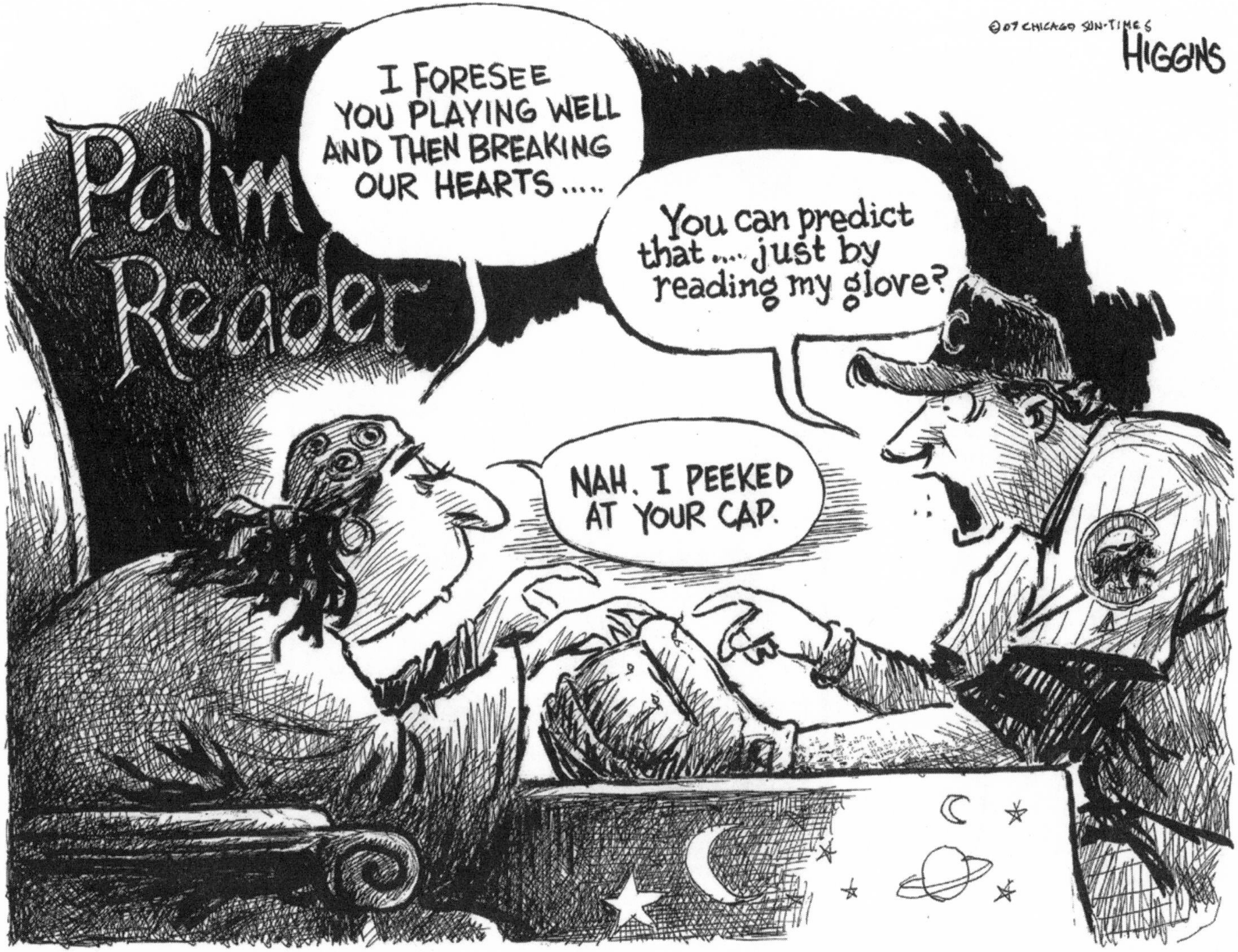
©07 CHICAGO SUN-TIMES
HIGGINS
Palm Reader
I FORESEE YOU PLAYING WELL AND THEN BREAKING OUR HEARTS.....
You can predict that..... just by reading my glove?
NAH. I PEEKED AT YOUR CAP.

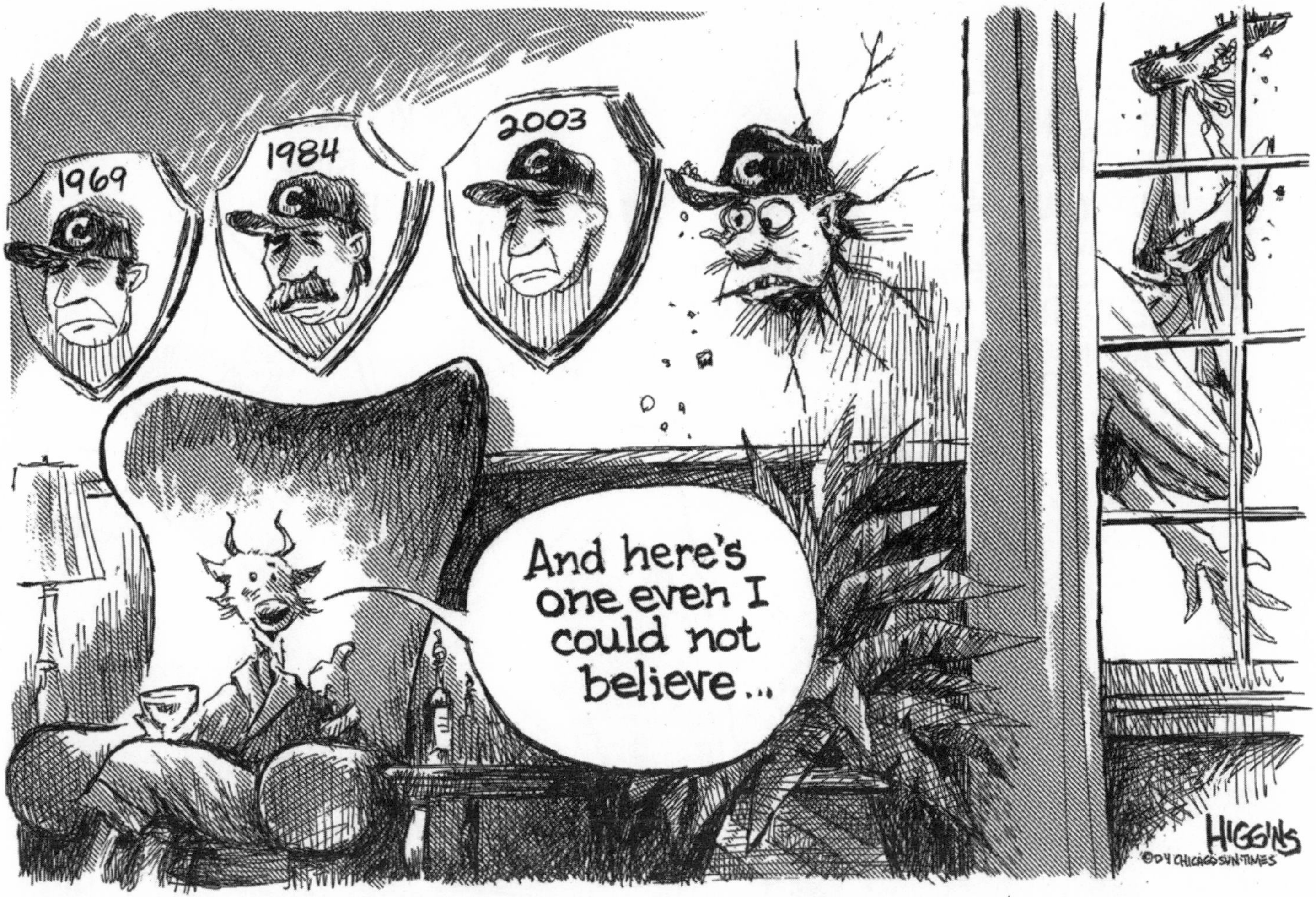
1969
1984
2003
And here's one even I could not believe...
HIGGINS
©04 CHICAGO SUN-TIMES

Steve Bartman becomes a household curse.

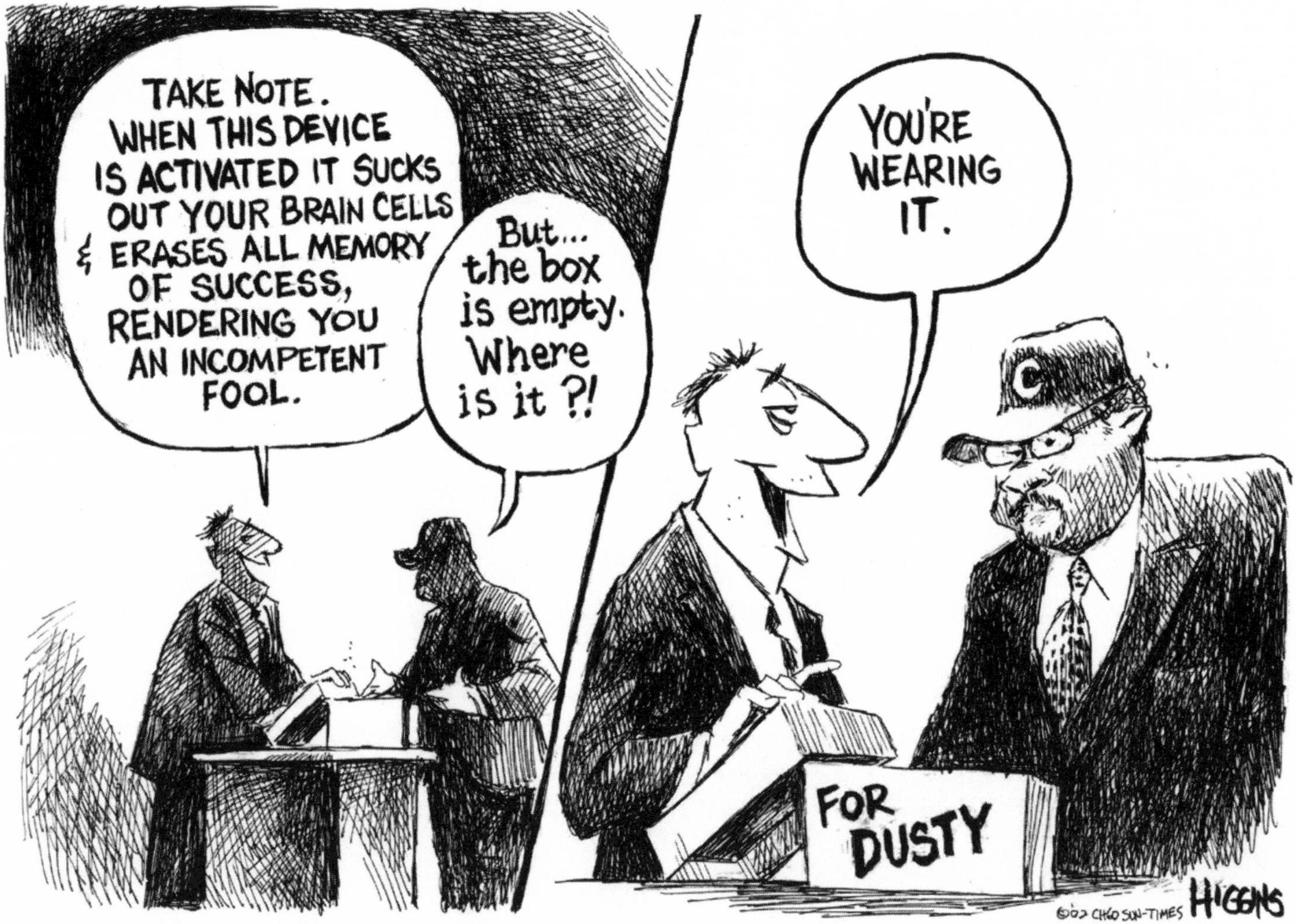
TAKE NOTE. WHEN THIS DEVICE IS ACTIVATED IT SUCKS OUT YOUR BRAIN CELLS & ERASES ALL MEMORY OF SUCCESS, RENDERING YOU AN INCOMPETENT FOOL.
But... the box is empty. Where is it ?!
YOU'RE WEARING IT.
FOR DUSTY
©02 CHGO SUN-TIMES HIGGINS

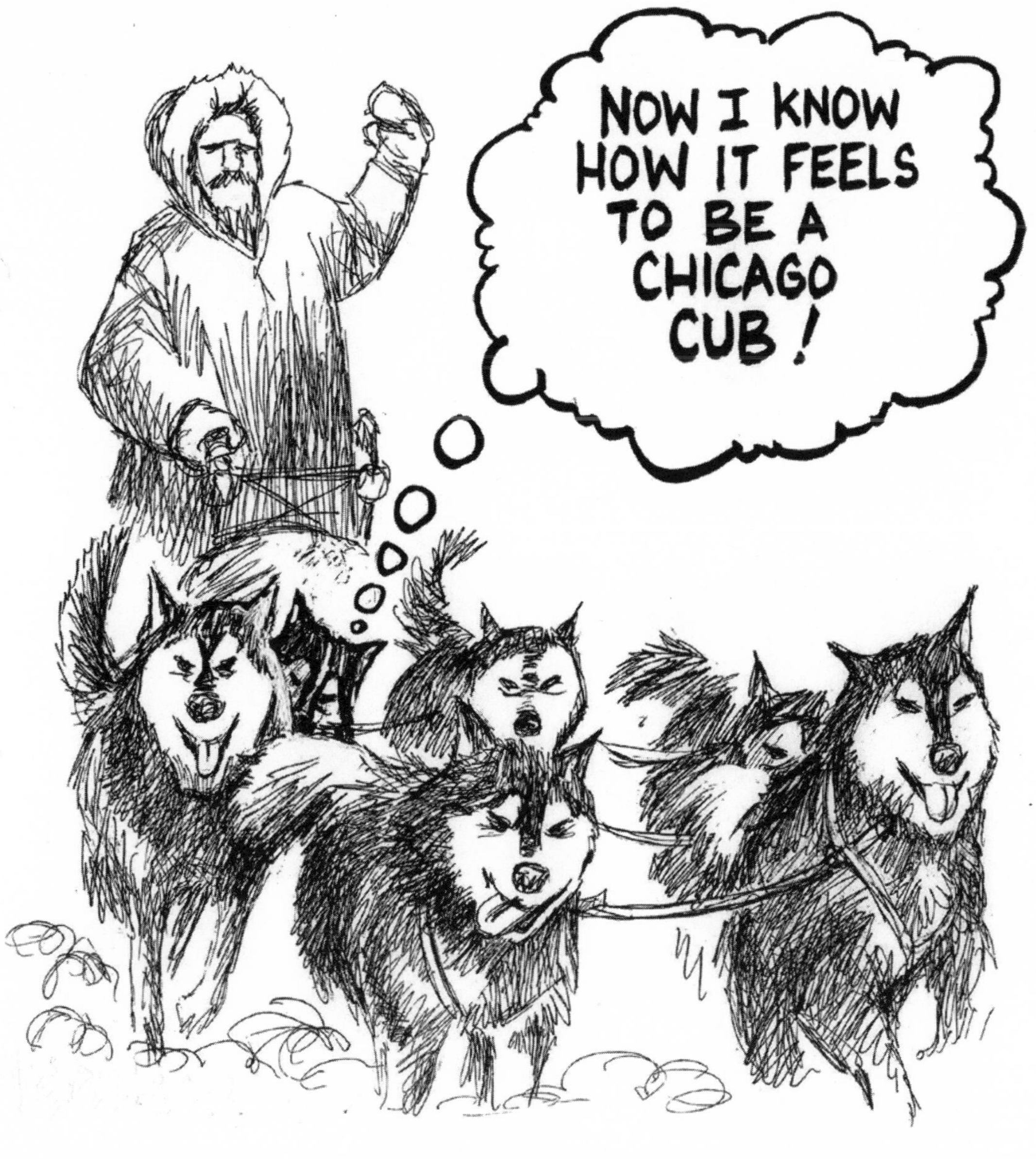
NOW I KNOW HOW IT FEELS TO BE A CHICAGO CUB!

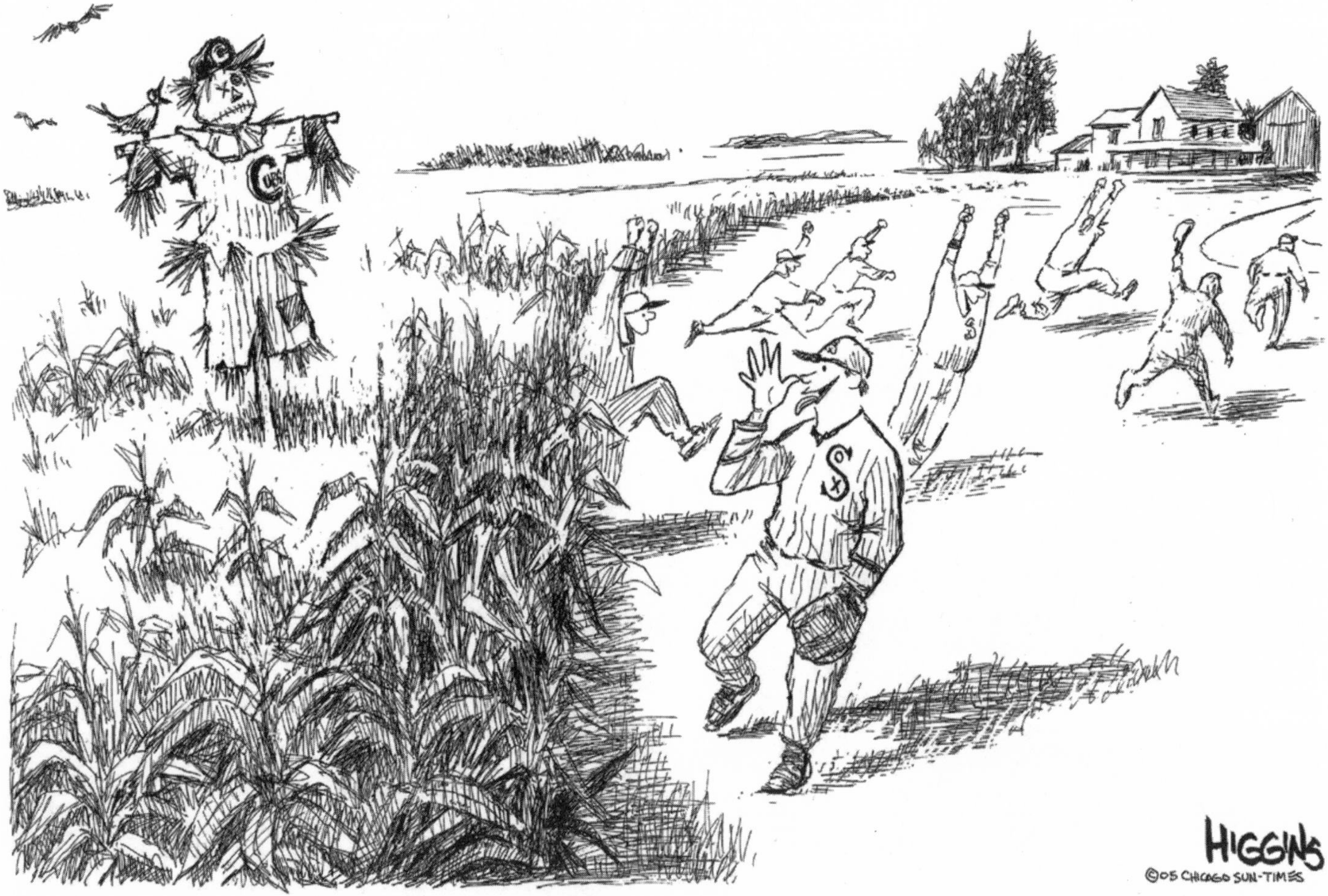
HIGGINS
©05 CHICAGO SUN-TIMES

Sox win the World Series.

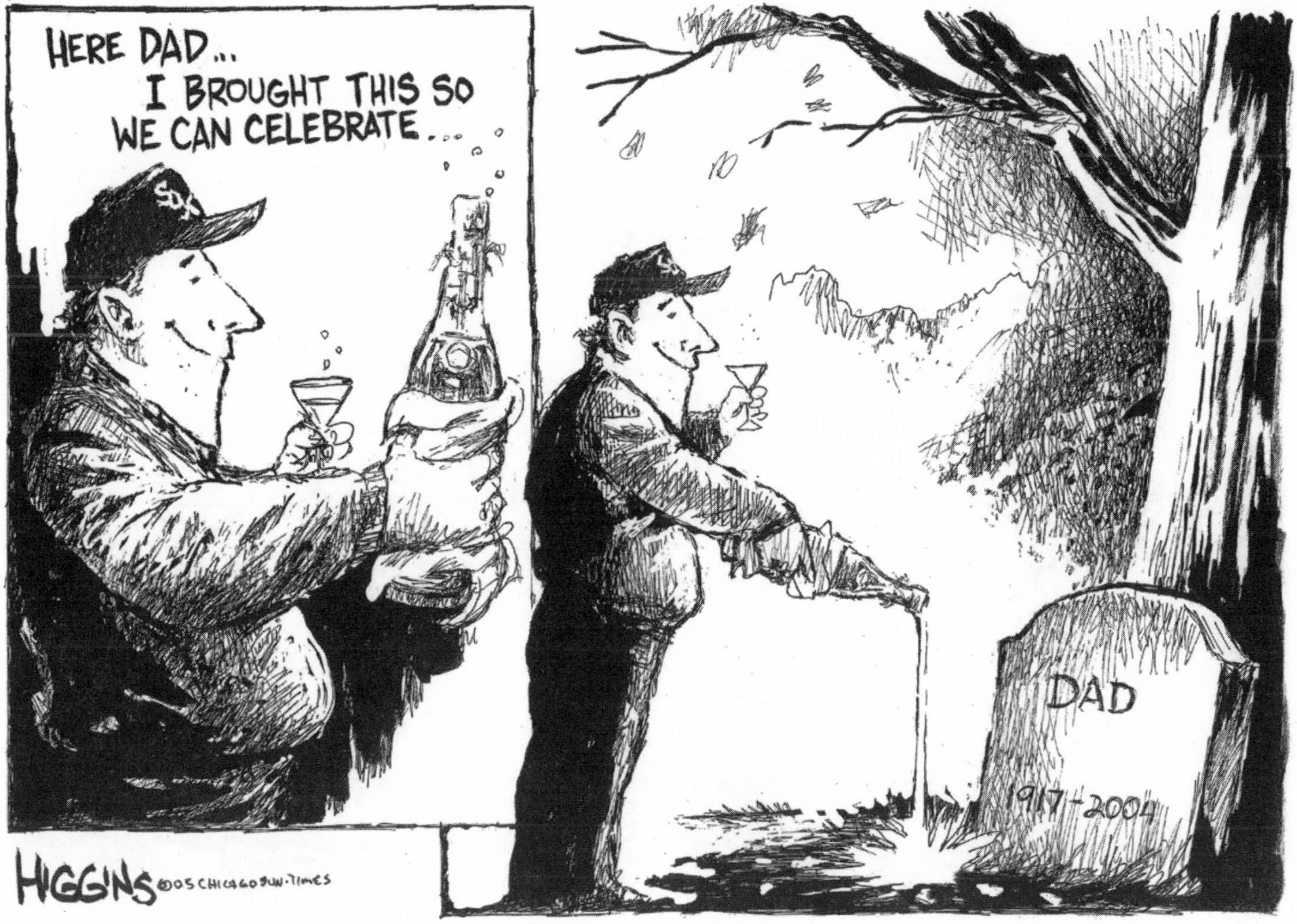
HERE DAD...
I BROUGHT THIS SO
WE CAN CELEBRATE...
SOX
DAD
1917-2004
HIGGINS ©05 CHICAGO SUN-TIMES

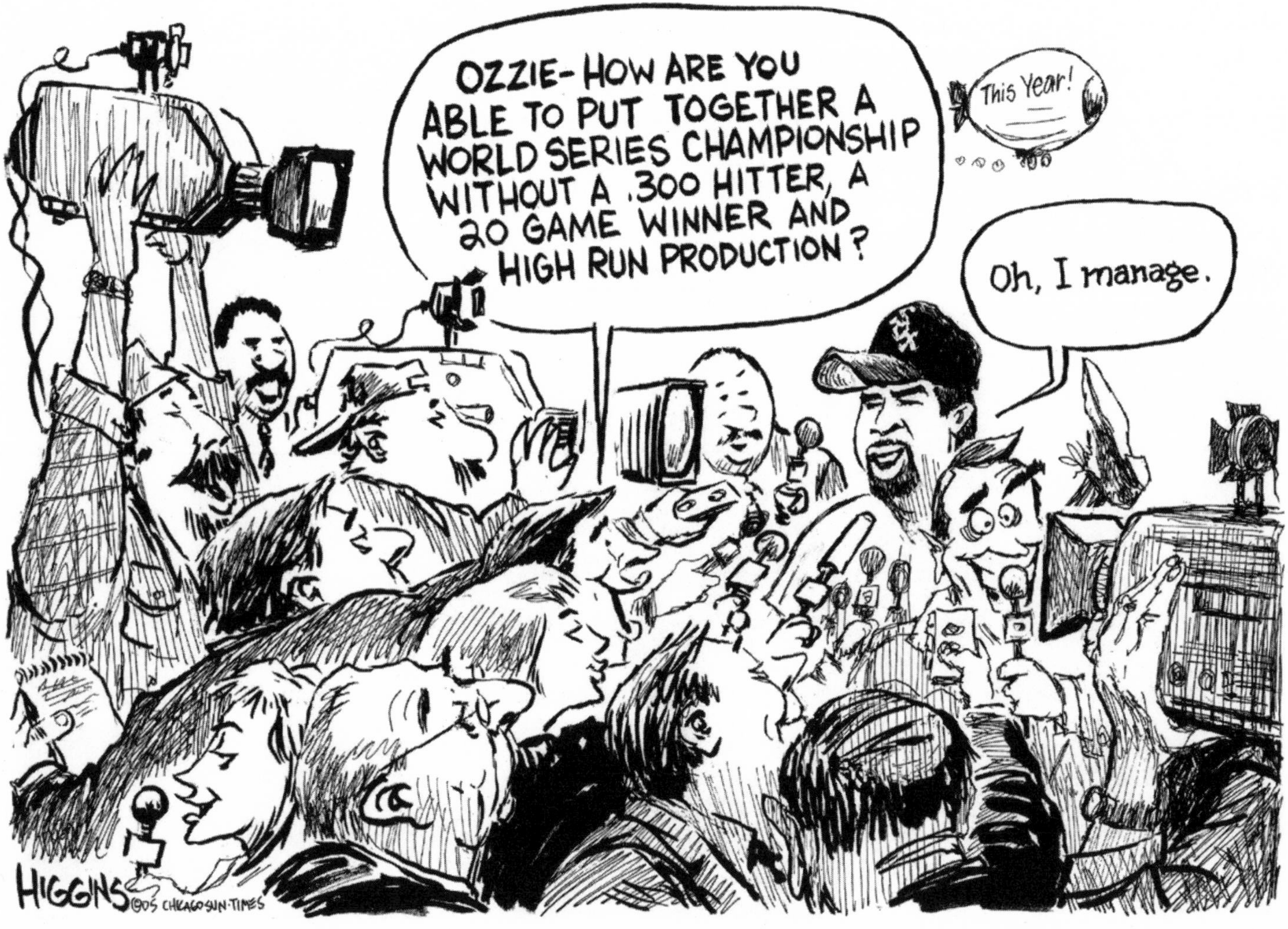
OZZIE- HOW ARE YOU ABLE TO PUT TOGETHER A WORLD SERIES CHAMPIONSHIP WITHOUT A .300 HITTER, A 20 GAME WINNER AND HIGH RUN PRODUCTION?
This Year!
Oh, I manage.
HIGGINS ©05 CHICAGO SUN-TIMES

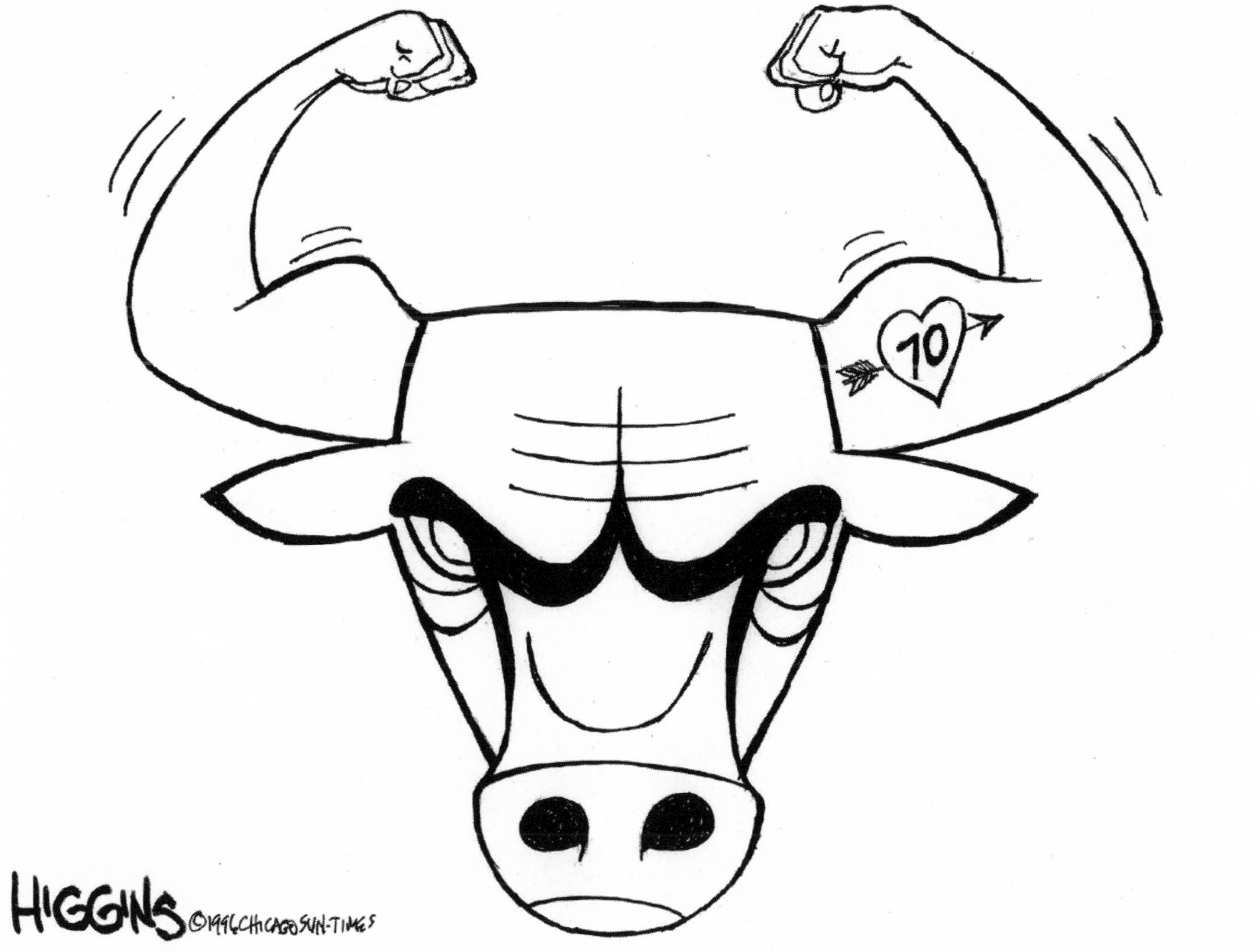
70
HIGGINS
©1996 CHICAGO SUN-TIMES

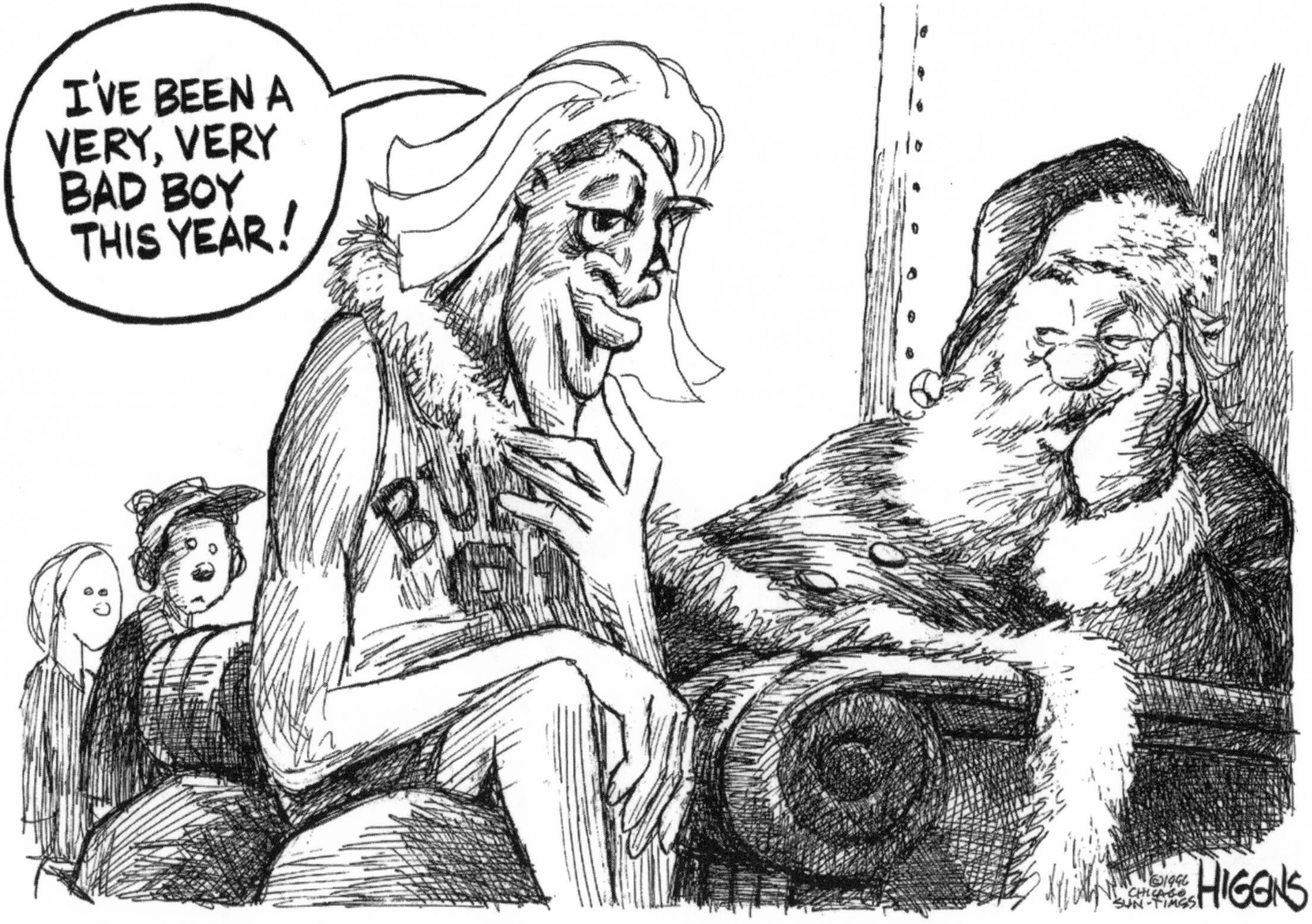
I'VE BEEN A VERY, VERY BAD BOY THIS YEAR!
©1996 CHICAGO SUN-TIMES
HIGGINS

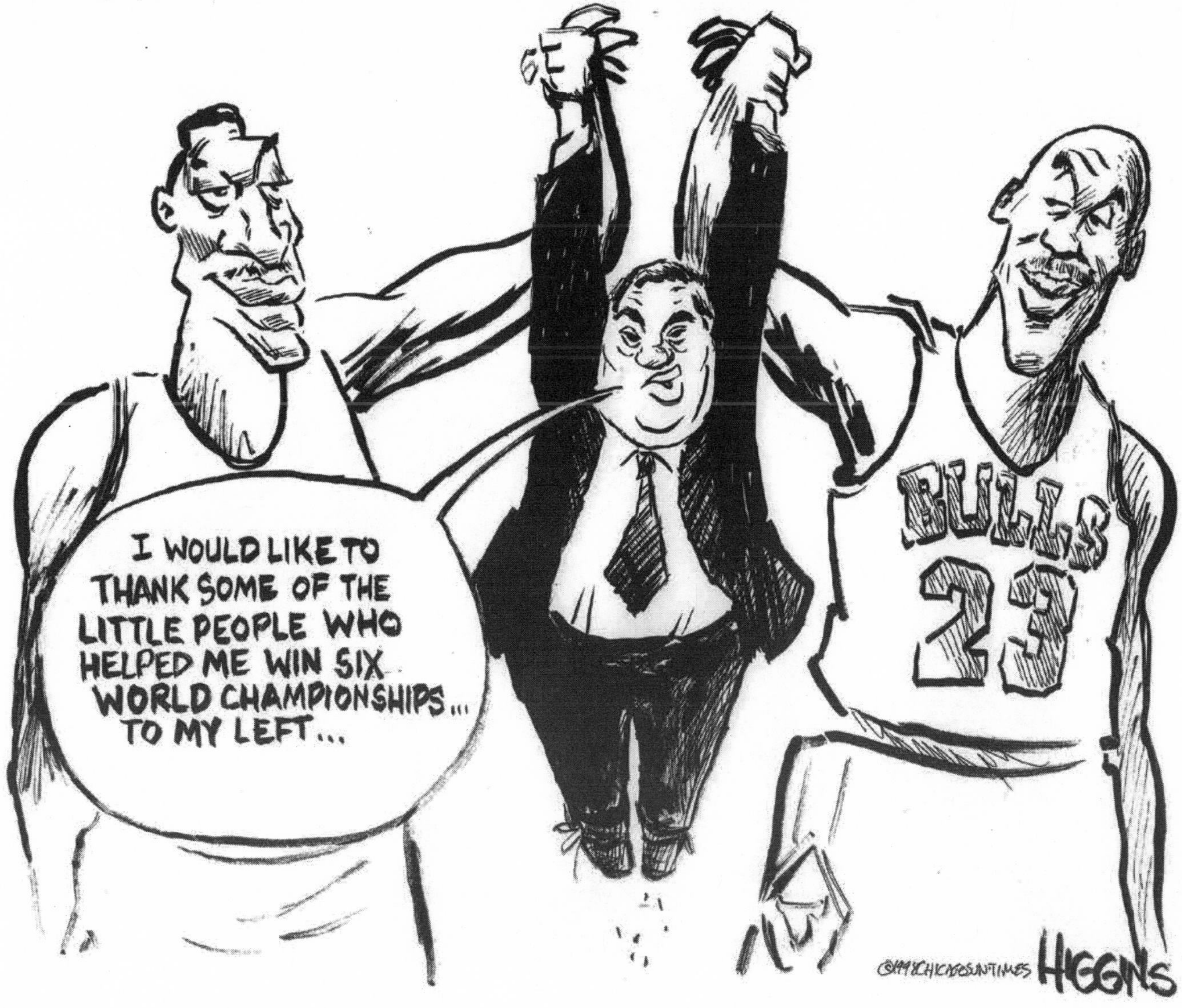
I WOULD LIKE TO THANK SOME OF THE LITTLE PEOPLE WHO HELPED ME WIN SIX WORLD CHAMPIONSHIPS... TO MY LEFT...
BULLS
23
©1998 CHICAGO SUN-TIMES
HIGGINS

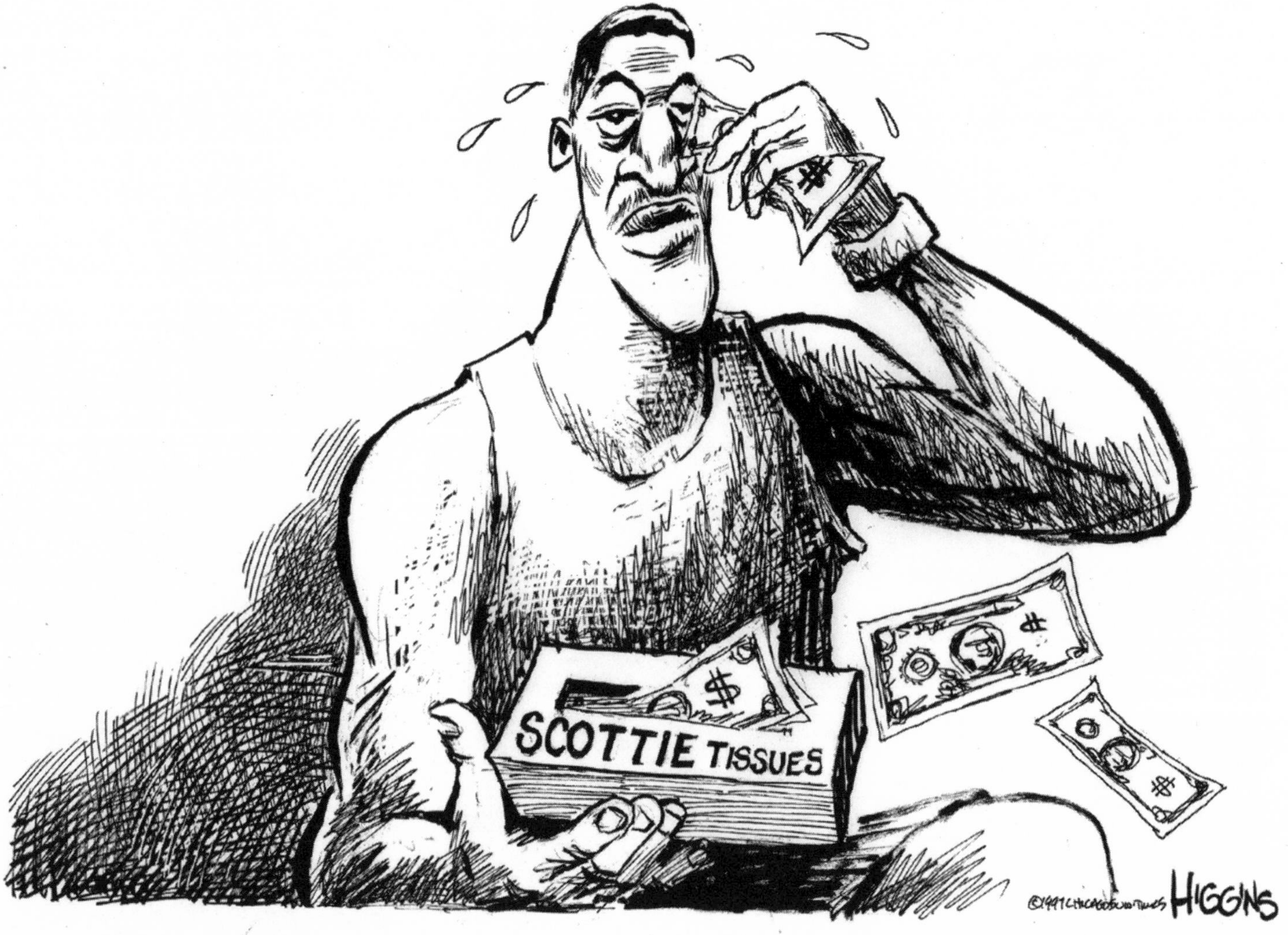
SCOTTIE TISSUES
HIGGINS

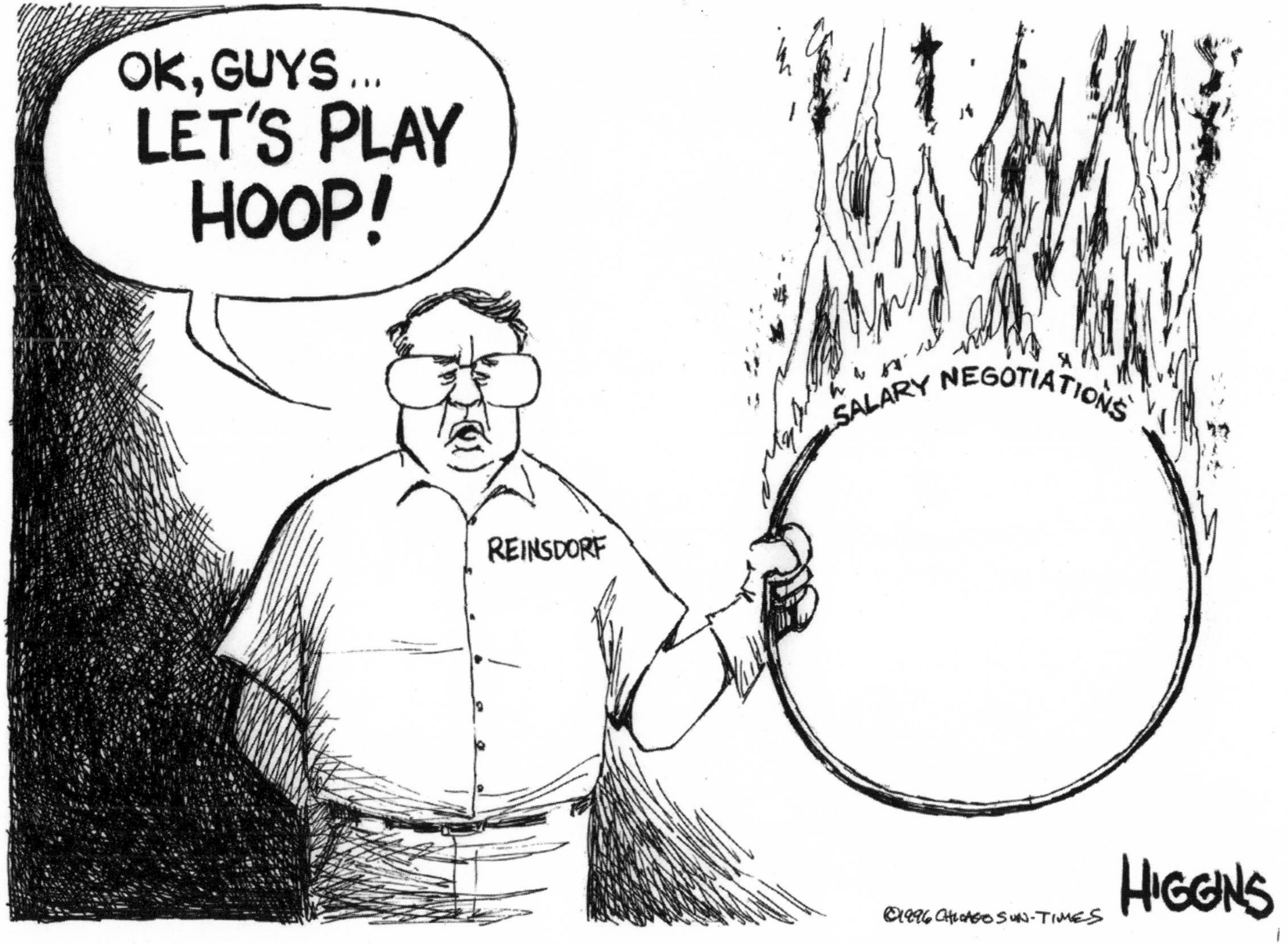
OK, GUYS...
LET'S PLAY
HOOP!
REINSDORF
SALARY NEGOTIATIONS
©1996 CHICAGO SUN-TIMES
HIGGINS

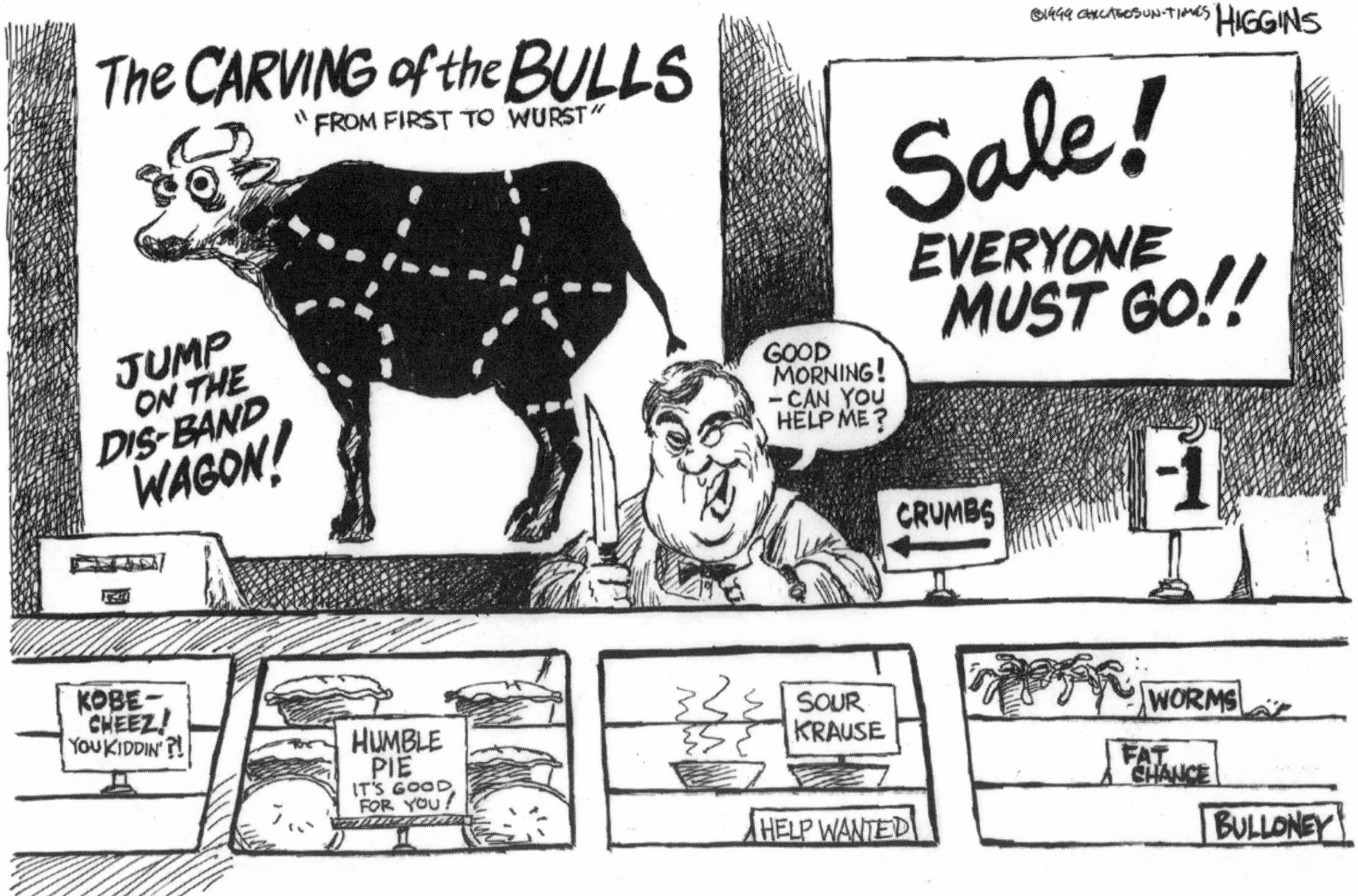
©1999 CHICAGO SUN-TIMES HIGGINS
The CARVING of the BULLS
"FROM FIRST TO WURST"
JUMP ON THE DIS-BAND WAGON!
GOOD MORNING! - CAN YOU HELP ME?
Sale! EVERYONE MUST GO!!
CRUMBS
-1
KOBE-CHEEZ! YOU KIDDIN'?!
HUMBLE PIE IT'S GOOD FOR YOU!
SOUR KRAUSE
HELP WANTED
WORMS
FAT CHANCE
BULLONEY

DEPLETE THE THREE-PEAT REPEAT

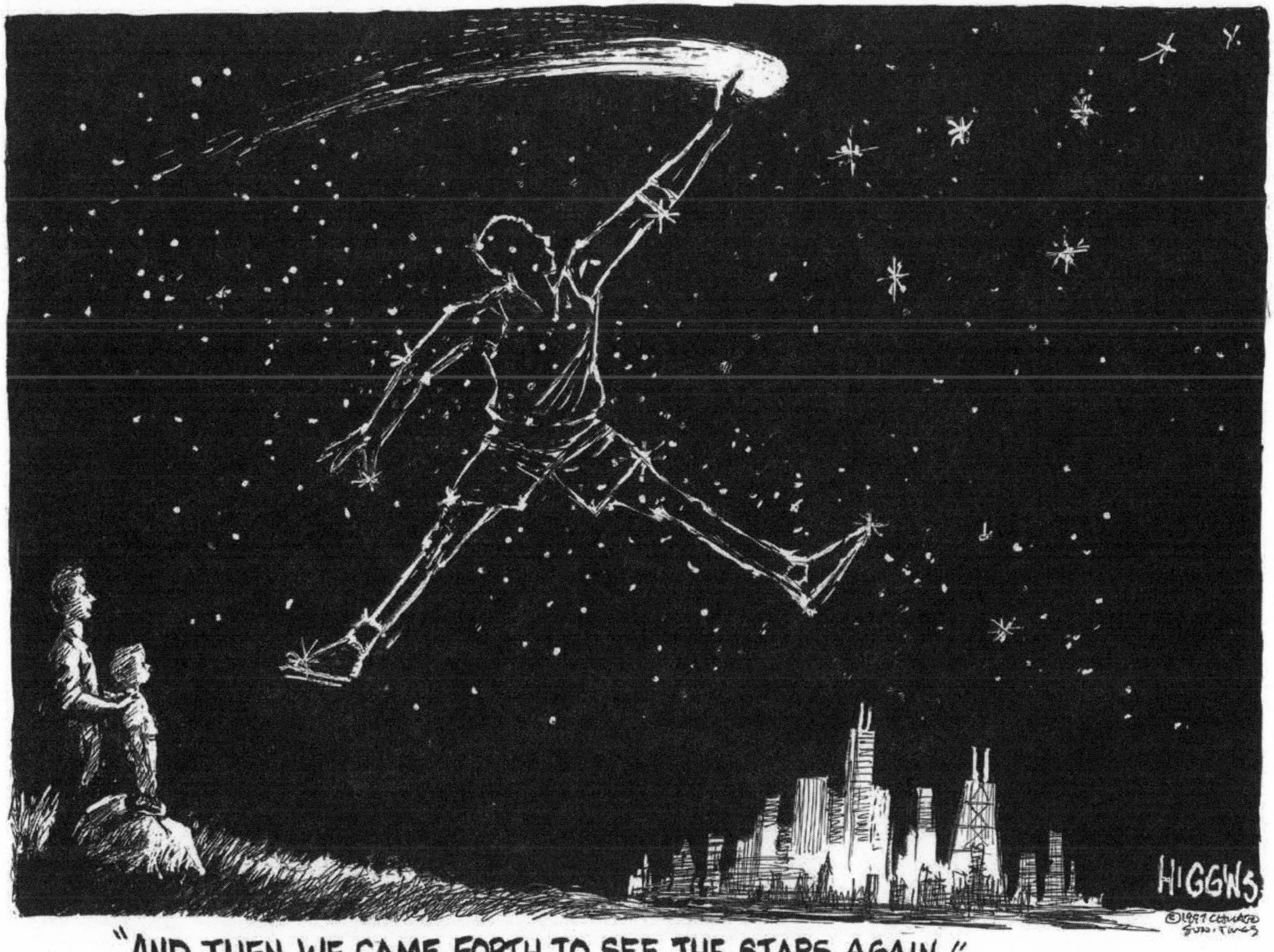
HIGGINS
©1997 CHICAGO SUN-TIMES

"AND THEN WE CAME FORTH TO SEE THE STARS AGAIN."
– DANTE'S DIVINE COMEDY

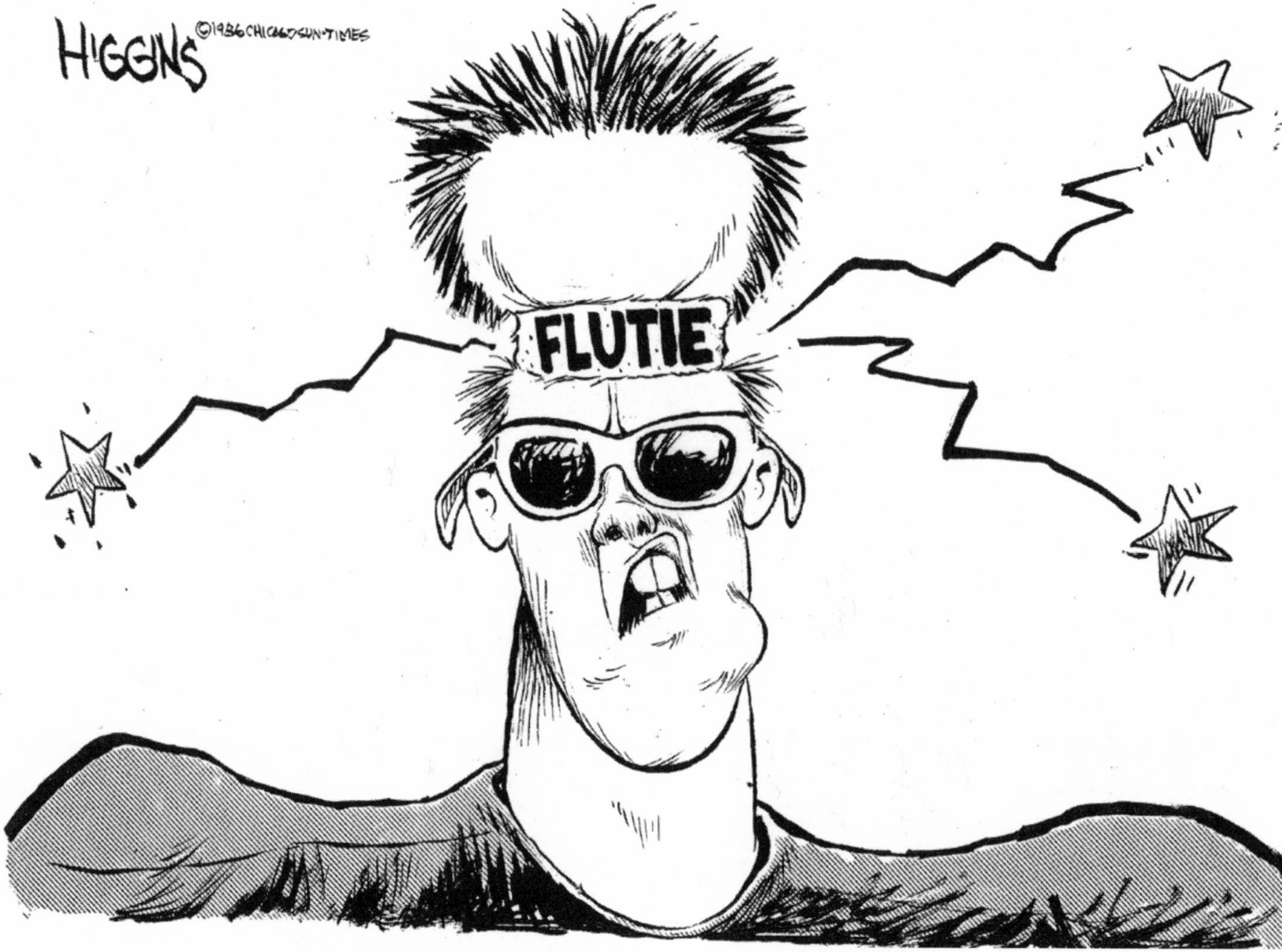
HIGGINS ©1986 CHICAGO SUN-TIMES
FLUTIE

HEY PATRIOT! EVER PLAY IN ONE OF THESE?
72
11
NEW ORLEANS
HIGGINS ©1986 CHICAGO SUN-TIMES

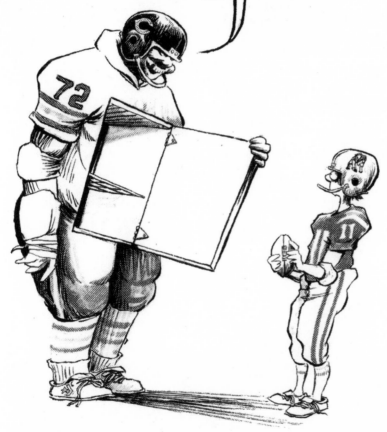

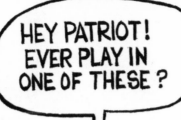

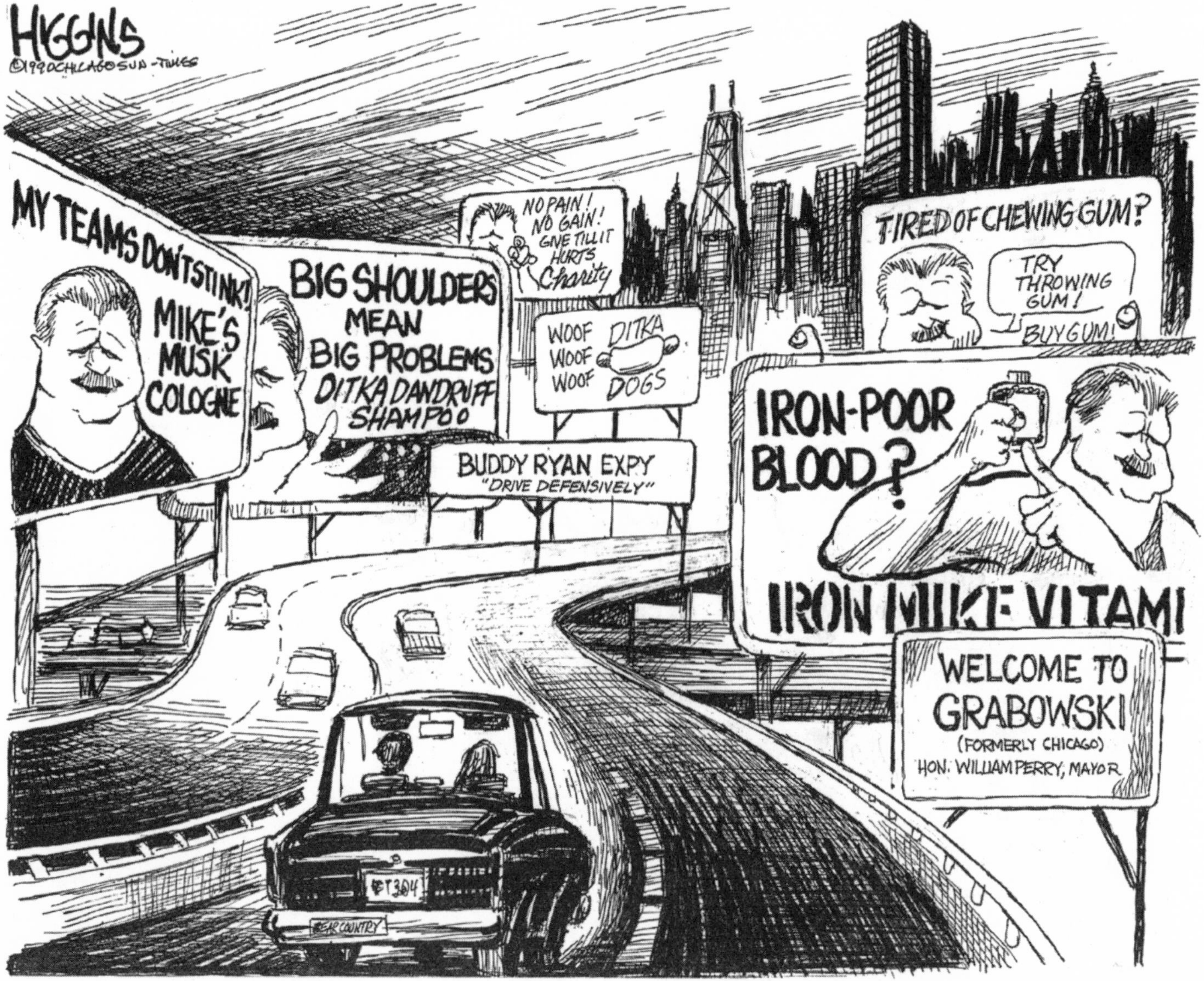

HIGGINS
©1990 CHICAGO SUN-TIMES
MY TEAMS DON'T STINK!
MIKE'S MUSK COLOGNE
BIG SHOULDERS MEAN BIG PROBLEMS
DITKA DANDRUFF SHAMPOO
NO PAIN! NO GAIN! GIVE TILL IT HURTS
Charity
WOOF WOOF WOOF
DITKA DOGS
BUDDY RYAN EXPY
"DRIVE DEFENSIVELY"
TIRED OF CHEWING GUM?
TRY THROWING GUM!
BUY GUM!
IRON-POOR BLOOD?
IRON MIKE VITAMI
WELCOME TO GRABOWSKI
(FORMERLY CHICAGO)
HON. WILLIAM PERRY, MAYOR
BEAR COUNTRY

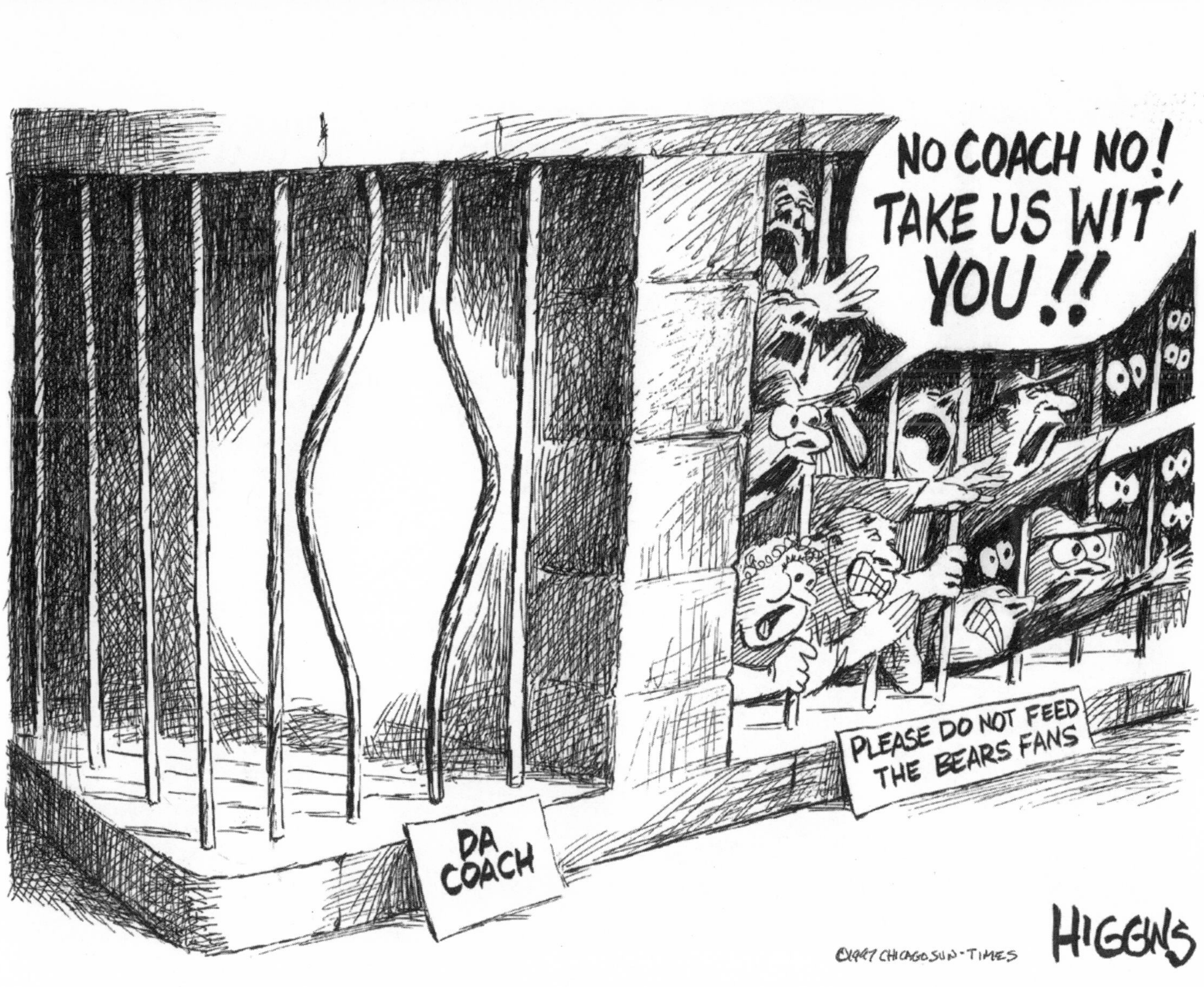
NO COACH NO! TAKE US WIT' YOU!!
DA COACH
PLEASE DO NOT FEED THE BEARS FANS
©1997 CHICAGO SUN-TIMES
HIGGINS

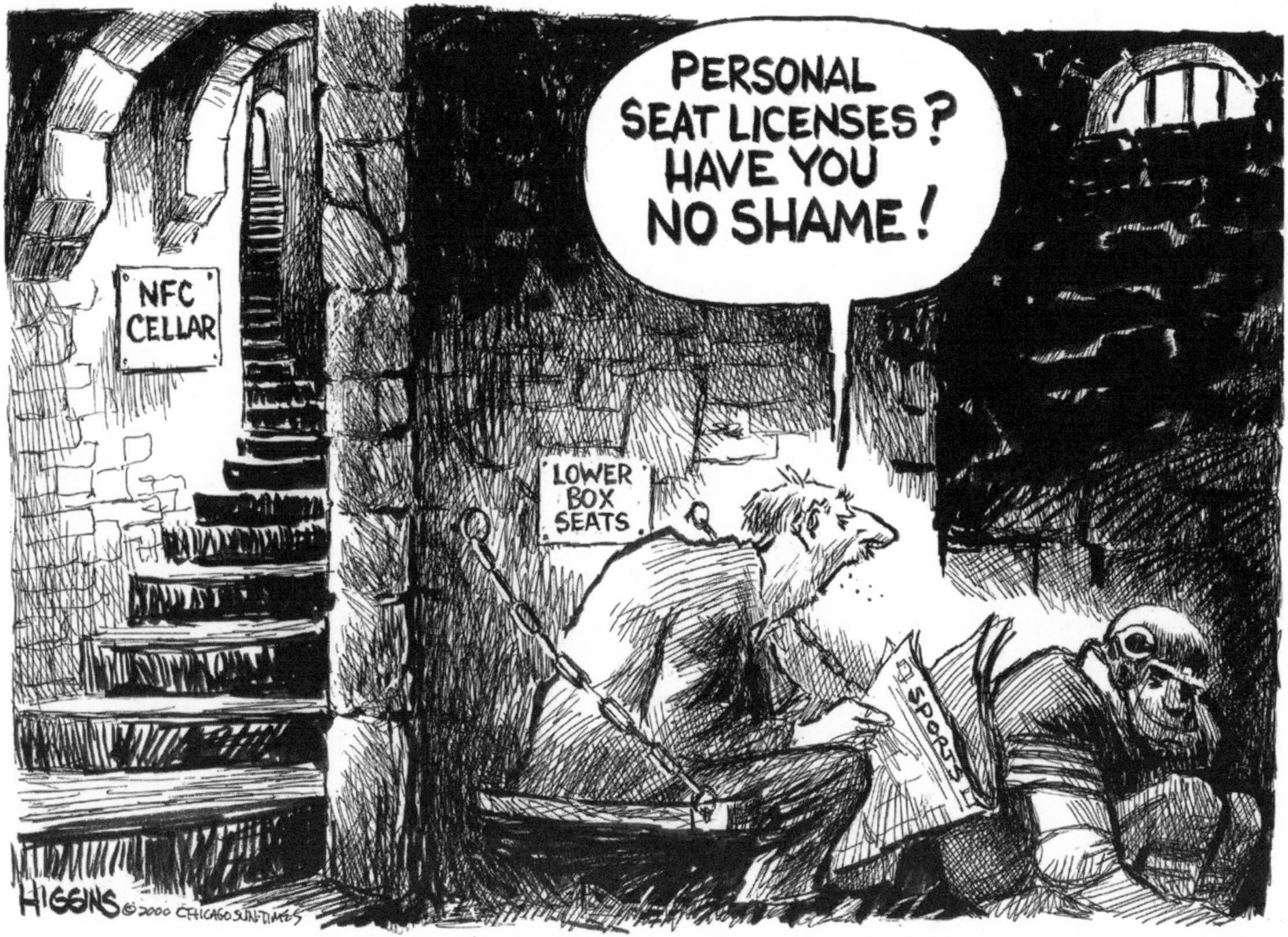
PERSONAL SEAT LICENSES? HAVE YOU NO SHAME!
NFC CELLAR
LOWER BOX SEATS
SPORTS
HIGGINS © 2000 CHICAGO SUN-TIMES

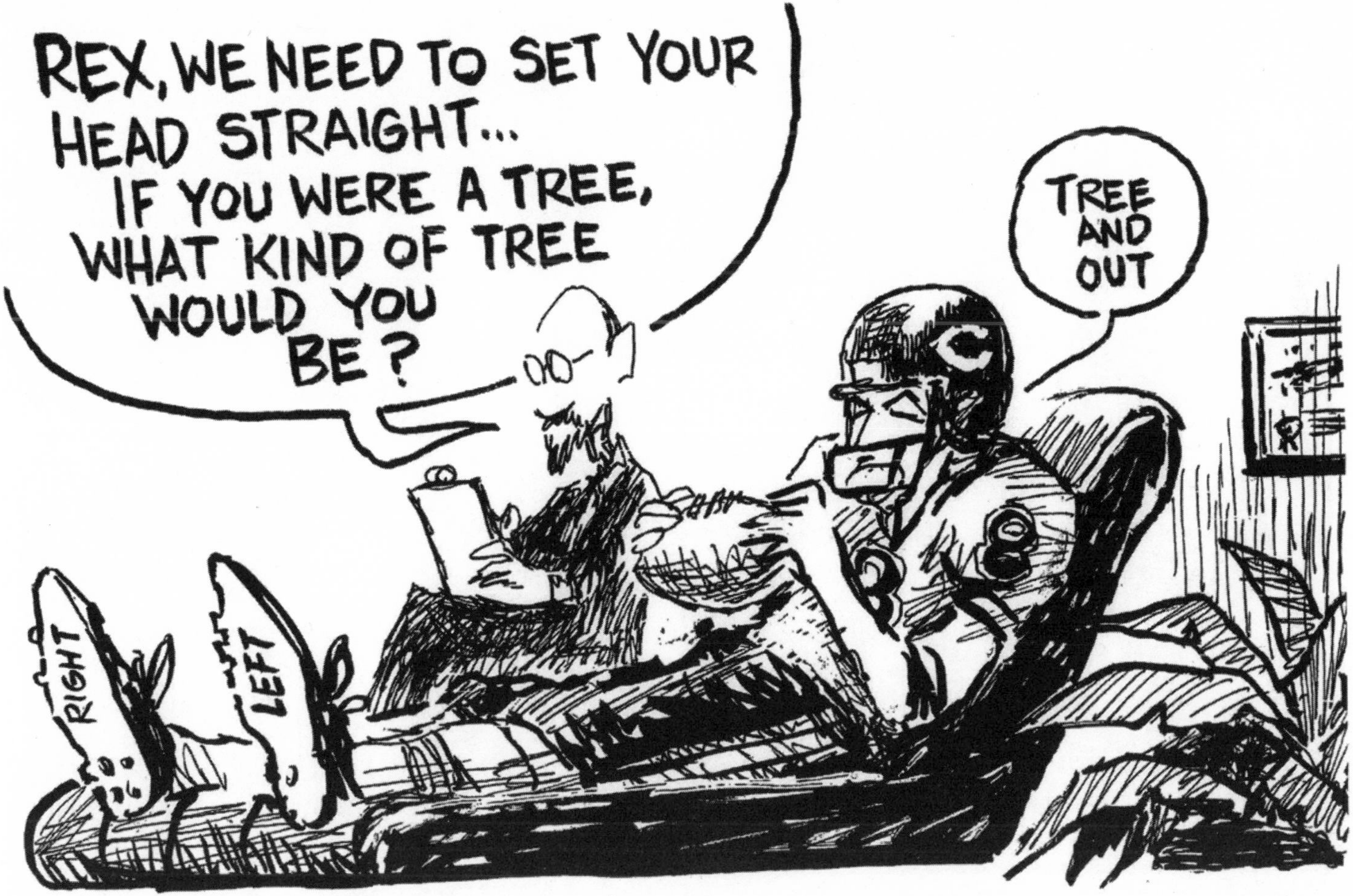
REX, WE NEED TO SET YOUR HEAD STRAIGHT... IF YOU WERE A TREE, WHAT KIND OF TREE WOULD YOU BE?
TREE AND OUT
RIGHT
LEFT

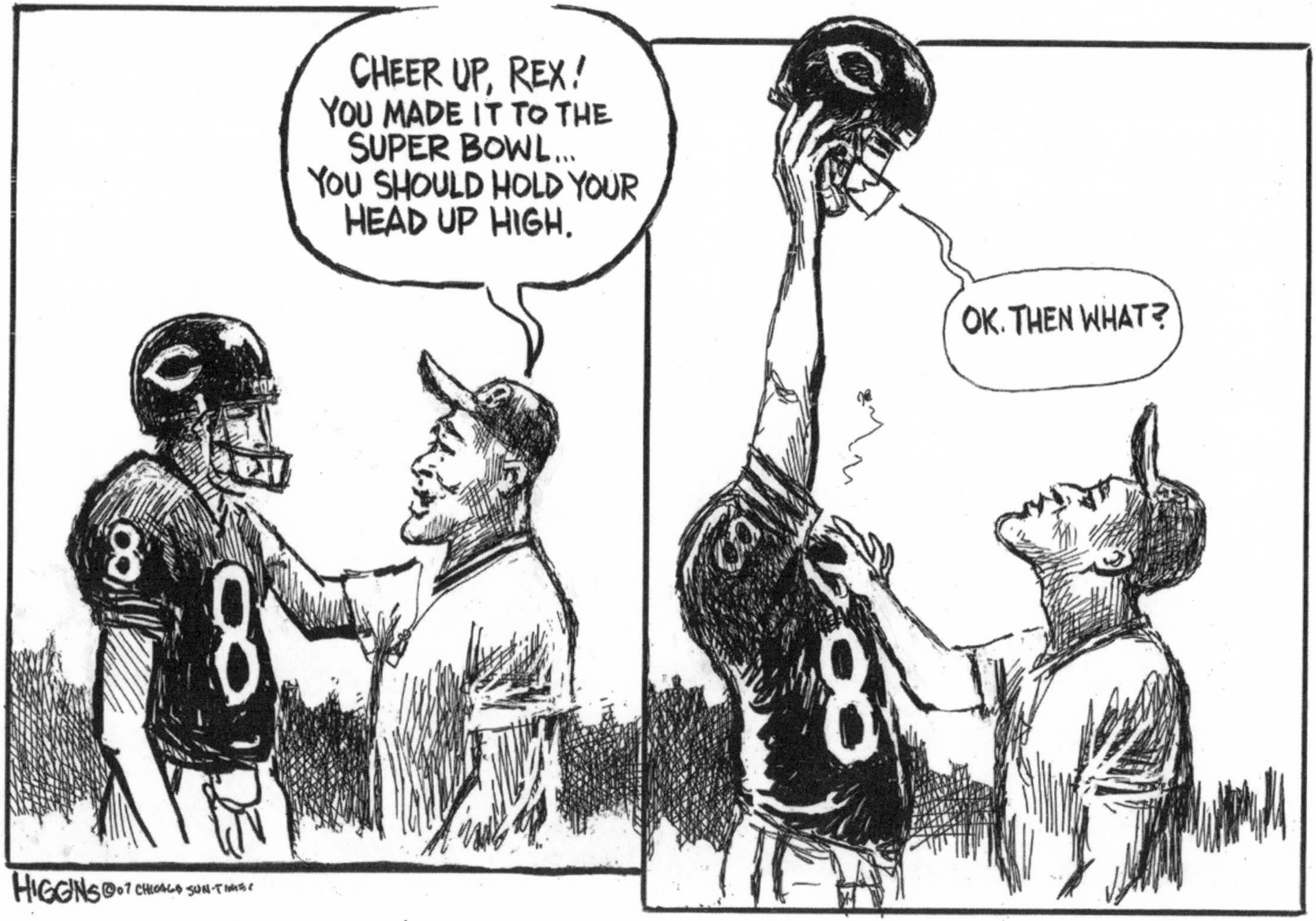
CHEER UP, REX! YOU MADE IT TO THE SUPER BOWL... YOU SHOULD HOLD YOUR HEAD UP HIGH.
OK. THEN WHAT?
HIGGINS ©07 CHICAGO SUN-TIMES

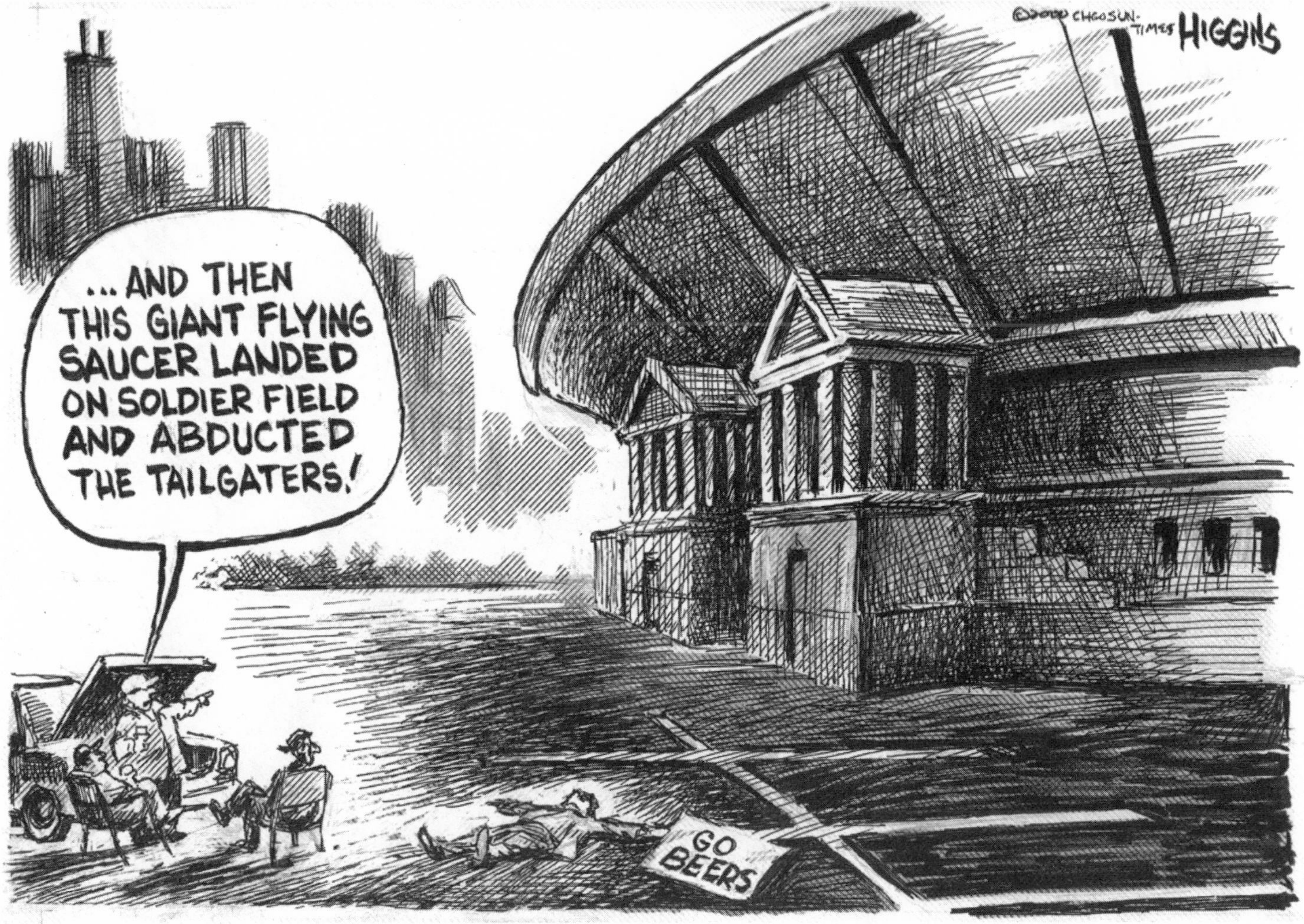
... AND THEN THIS GIANT FLYING SAUCER LANDED ON SOLDIER FIELD AND ABDUCTED THE TAILGATERS!
HIGGINS
GO BEERS

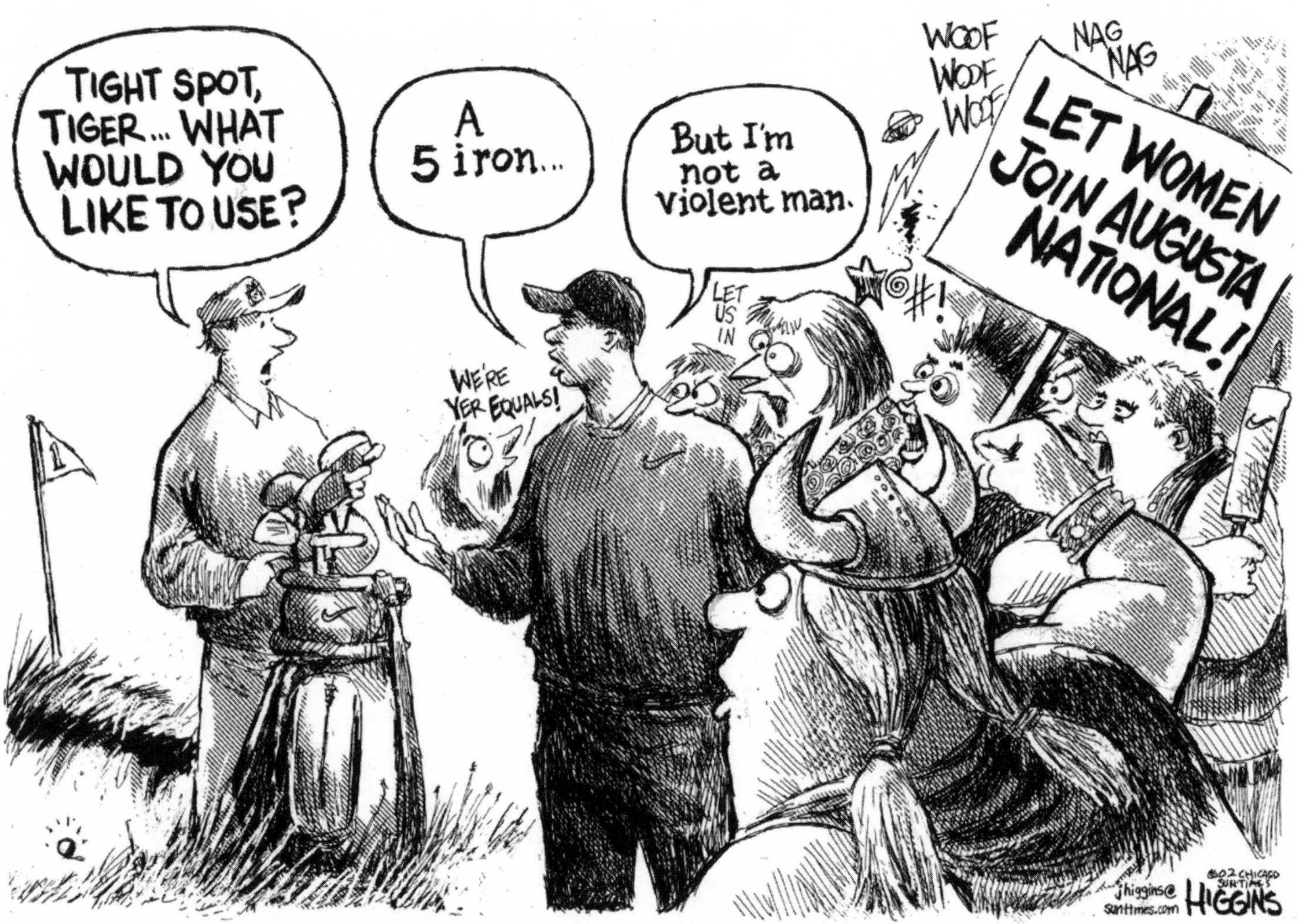
TIGHT SPOT, TIGER... WHAT WOULD YOU LIKE TO USE?
A 5 iron...
But I'm not a violent man.
WOOF WOOF WOOF
NAG NAG
LET WOMEN JOIN AUGUSTA NATIONAL!
LET US IN
WE'RE YER EQUALS!
#!
©02 CHICAGO SUN-TIMES
jhiggins@suntimes.com
HIGGINS

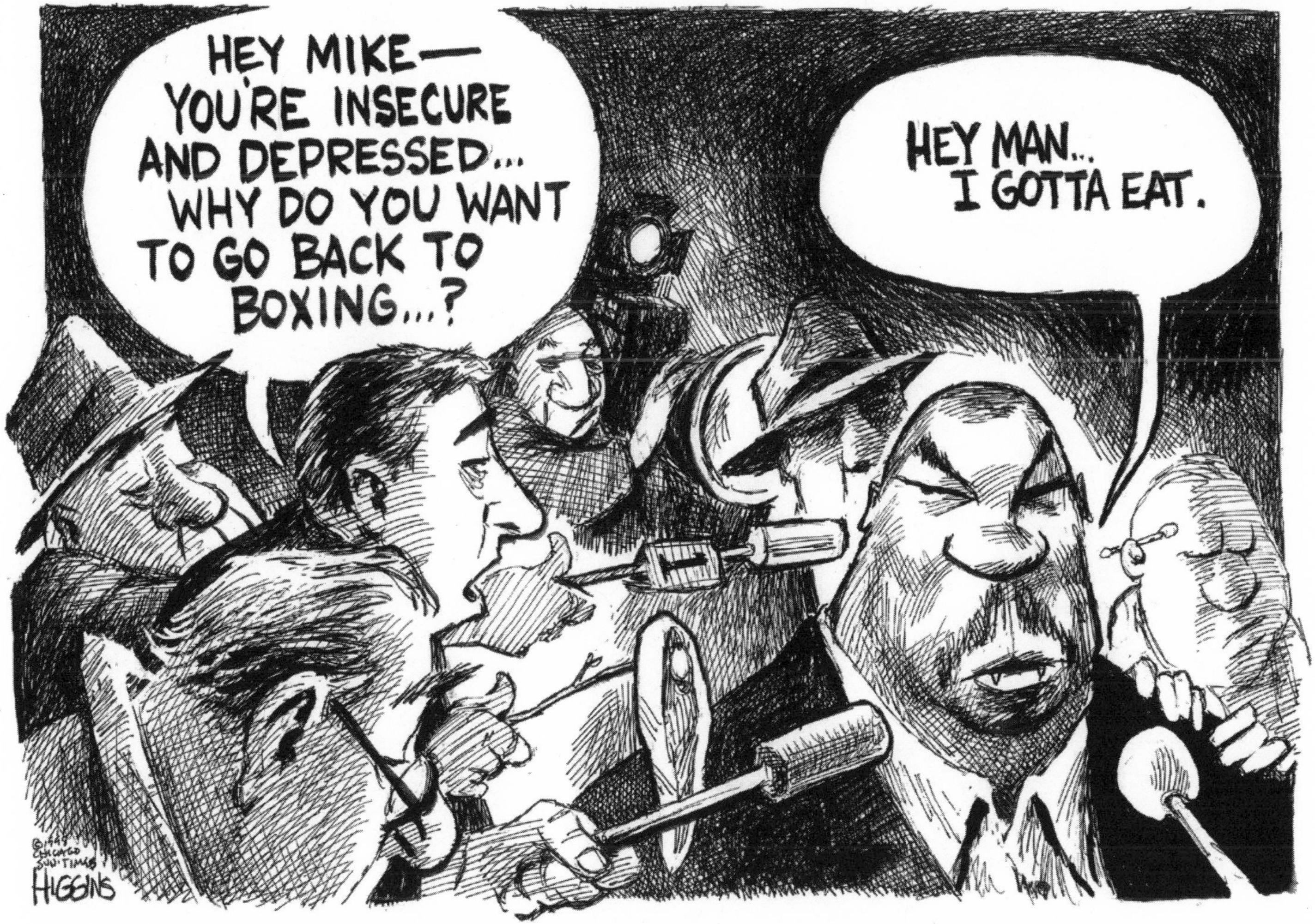
HEY MIKE— YOU'RE INSECURE AND DEPRESSED... WHY DO YOU WANT TO GO BACK TO BOXING...?
HEY MAN... I GOTTA EAT.
HIGGINS

Mike Tyson bites off a piece of Evander Holyfield's ear.

RACISM, CRIME, & GANGS

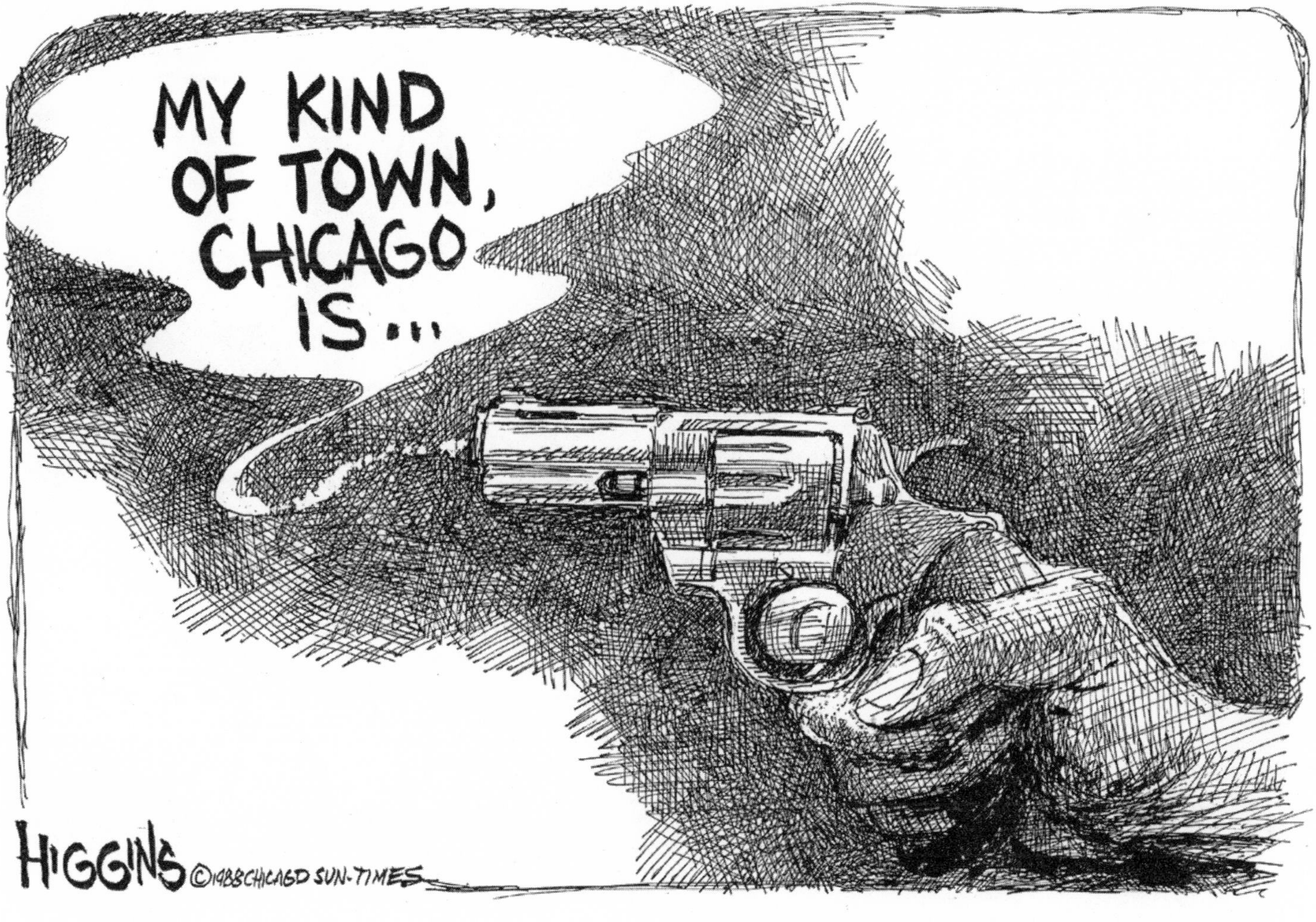
MY KIND OF TOWN, CHICAGO IS...
HIGGINS ©1988 CHICAGO SUN-TIMES

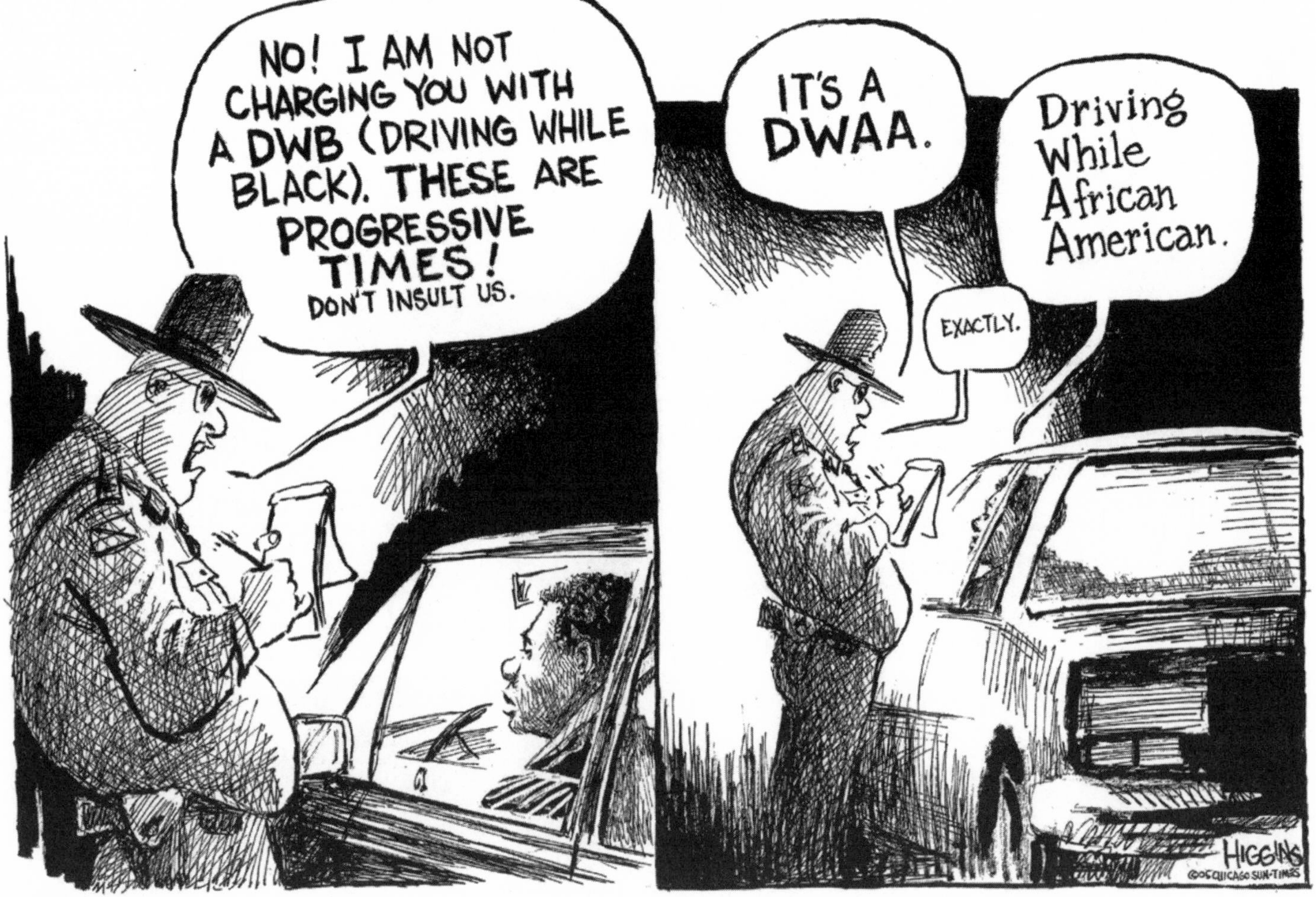
NO! I AM NOT CHARGING YOU WITH A DWB (DRIVING WHILE BLACK). THESE ARE PROGRESSIVE TIMES! DON'T INSULT US.
IT'S A DWAA.
Driving While African American.
EXACTLY.
HIGGINS
©05 CHICAGO SUN-TIMES

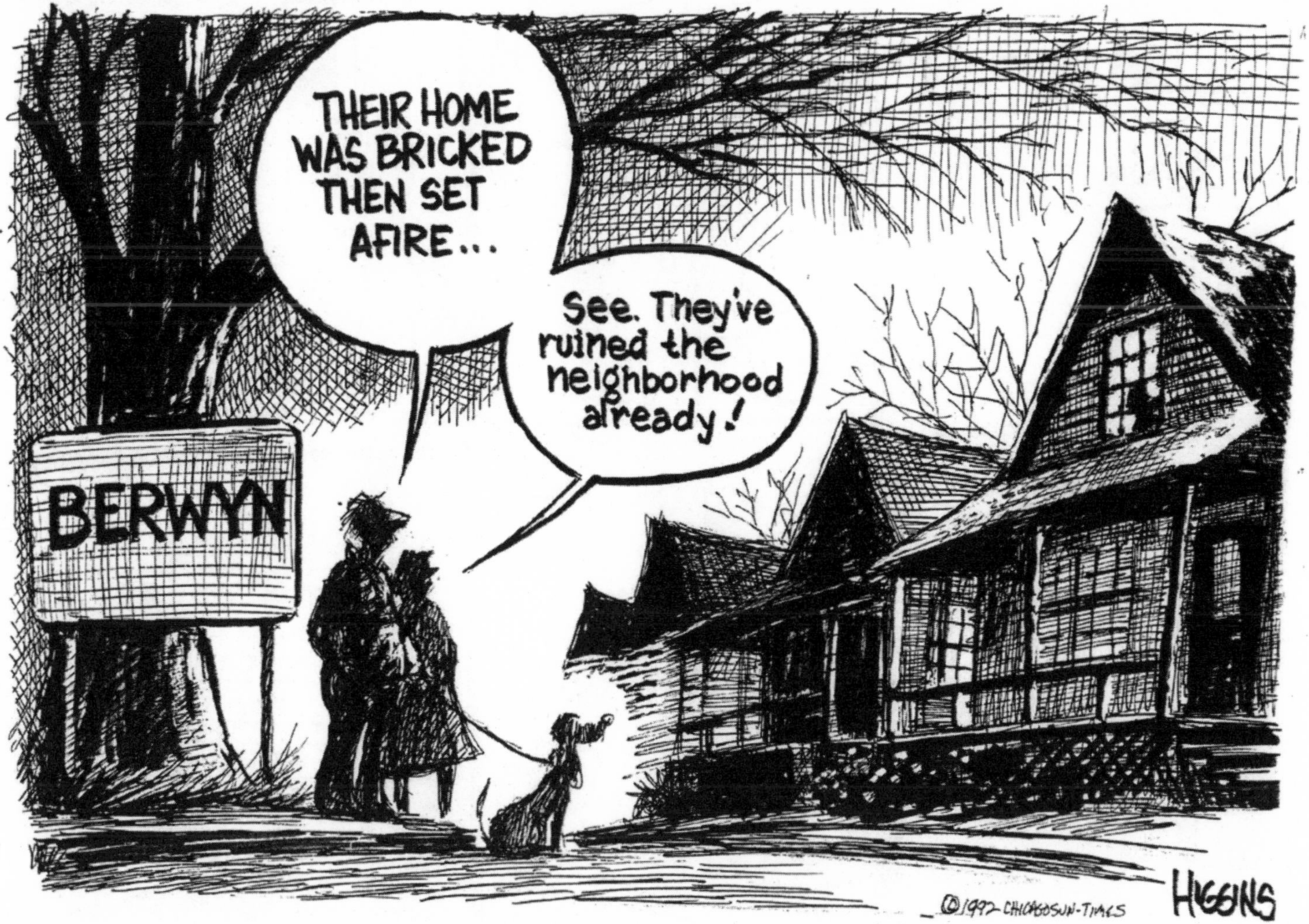
THEIR HOME WAS BRICKED THEN SET AFIRE...
See. They've ruined the neighborhood already!
BERWYN
©1992 CHICAGO SUN-TIMES
HIGGINS

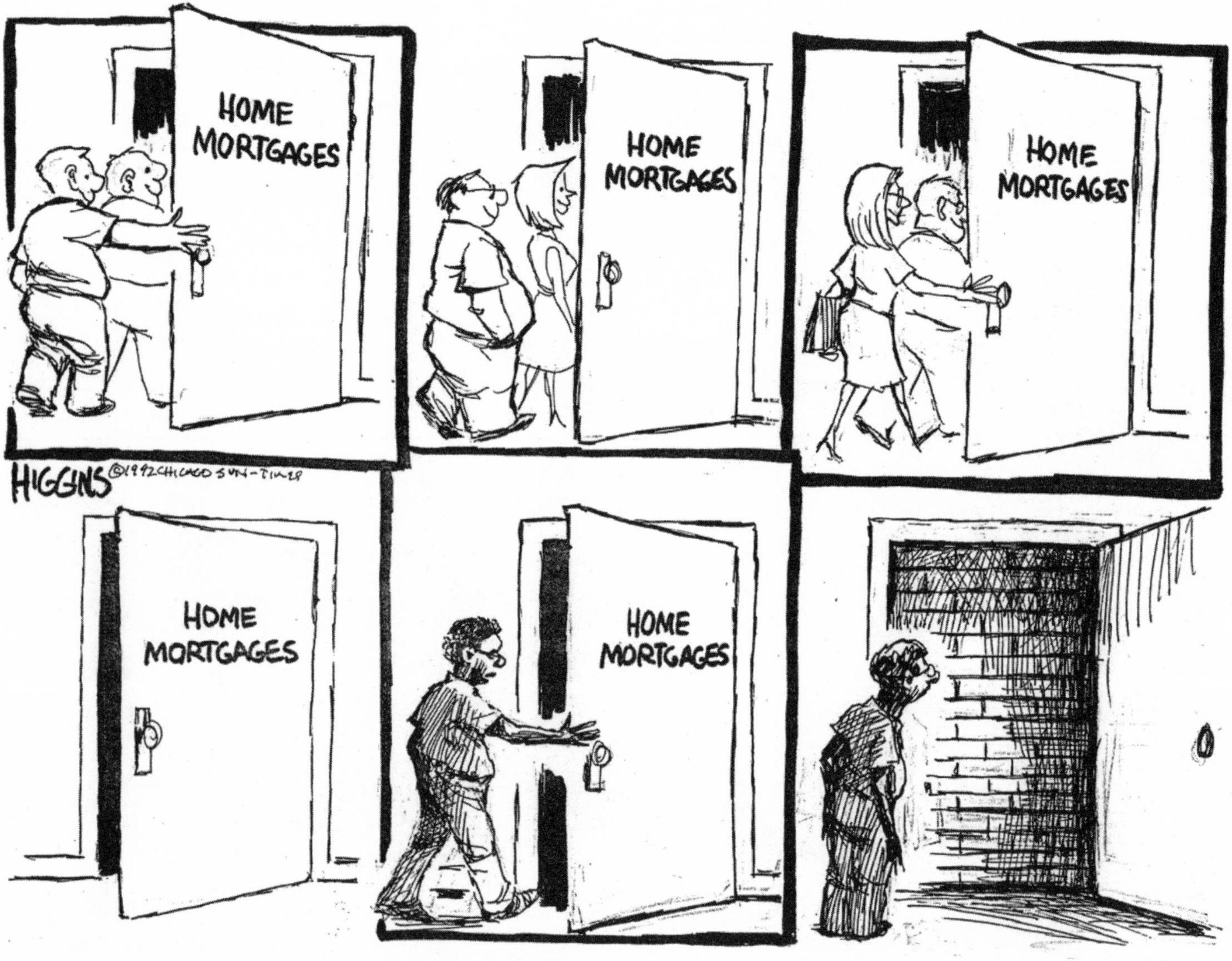
HOME MORTGAGES
HOME MORTGAGES
HOME MORTGAGES
HIGGINS ©1992 CHICAGO SUN-TIMES
HOME MORTGAGES
HOME MORTGAGES

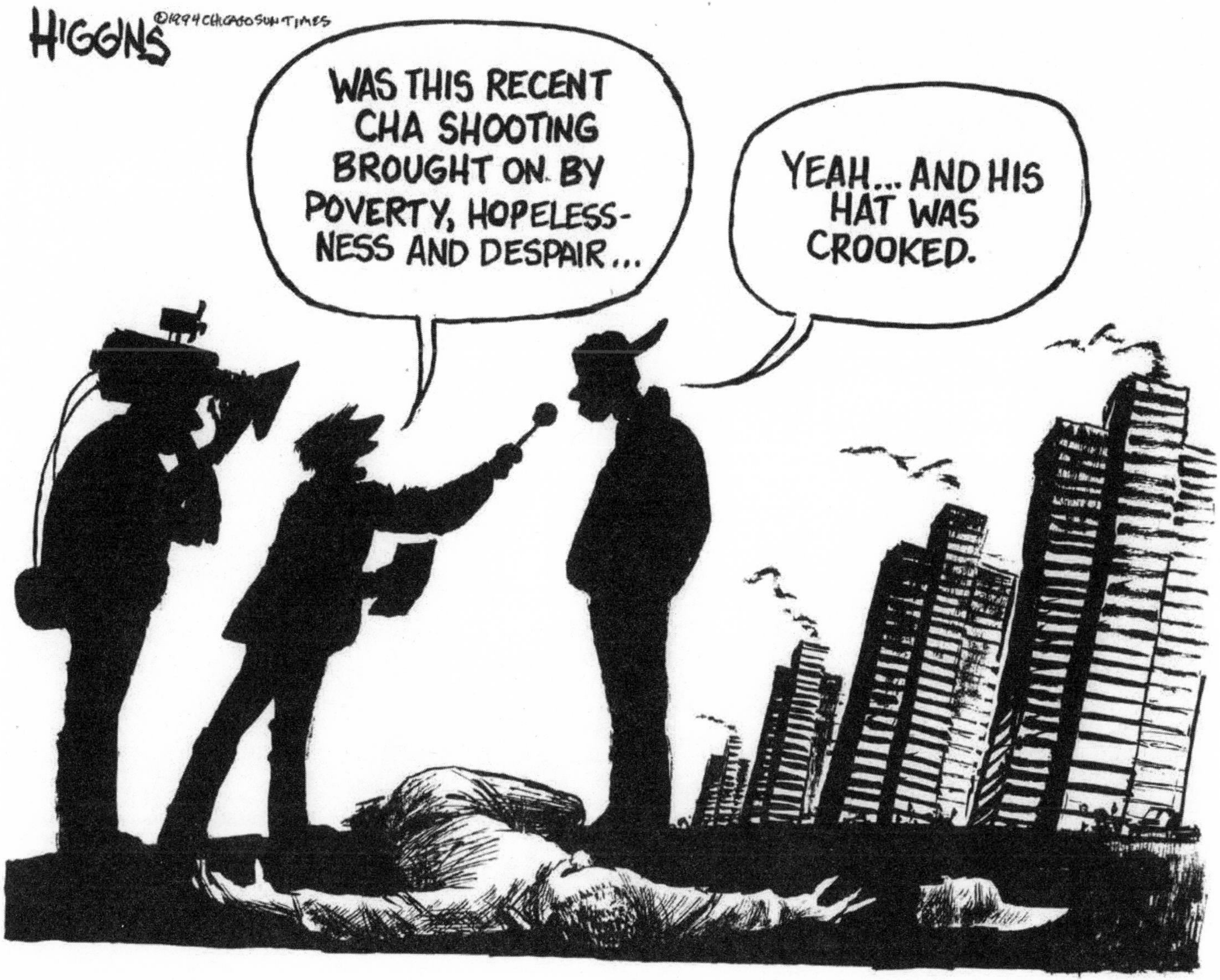
HIGGINS ©1994 CHICAGO SUN-TIMES
WAS THIS RECENT CHA SHOOTING BROUGHT ON BY POVERTY, HOPELESSNESS AND DESPAIR...
YEAH... AND HIS HAT WAS CROOKED.

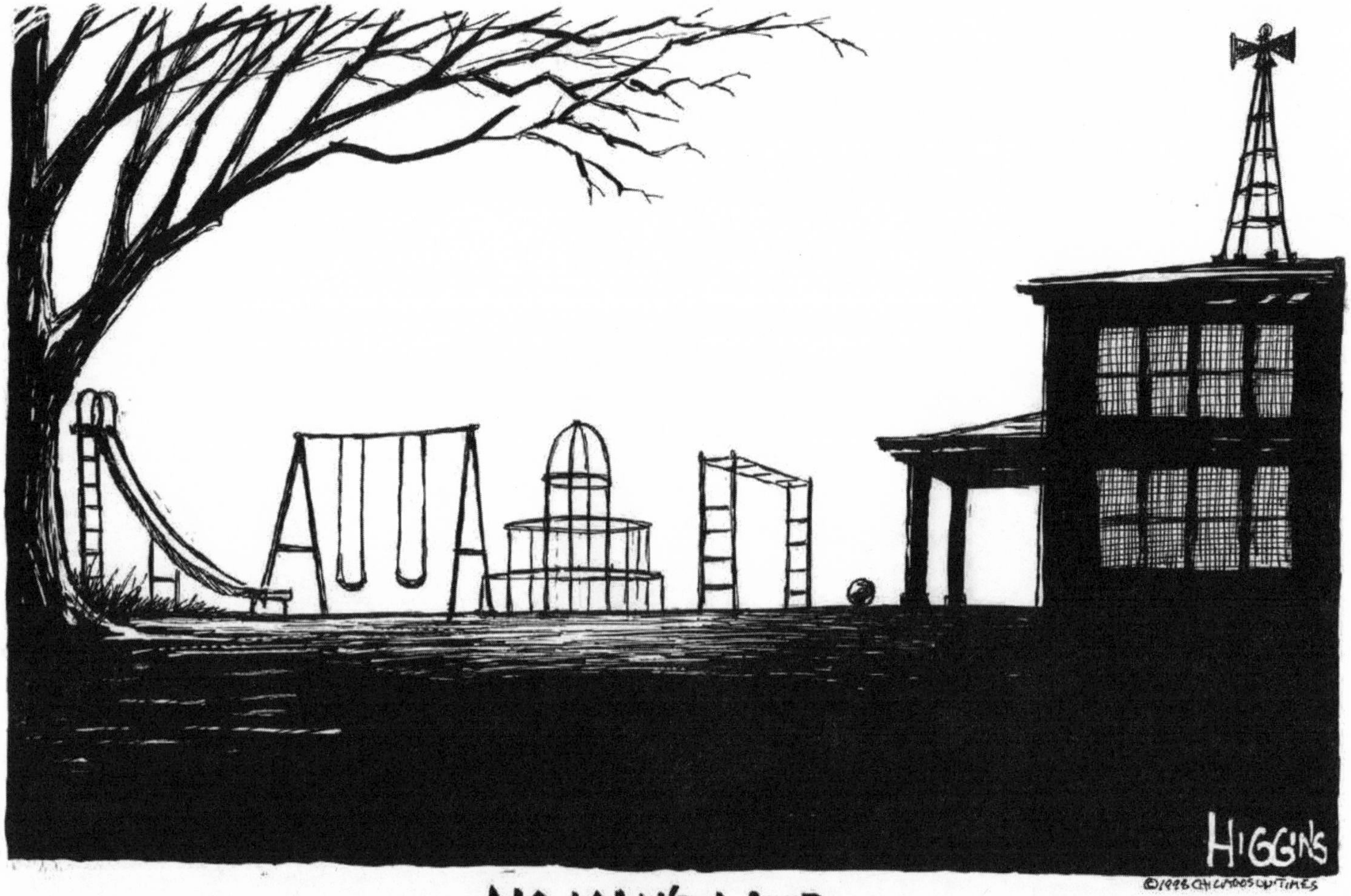
HIGGINS
©1998 CHICAGO SUN-TIMES

NO MAN'S LAND

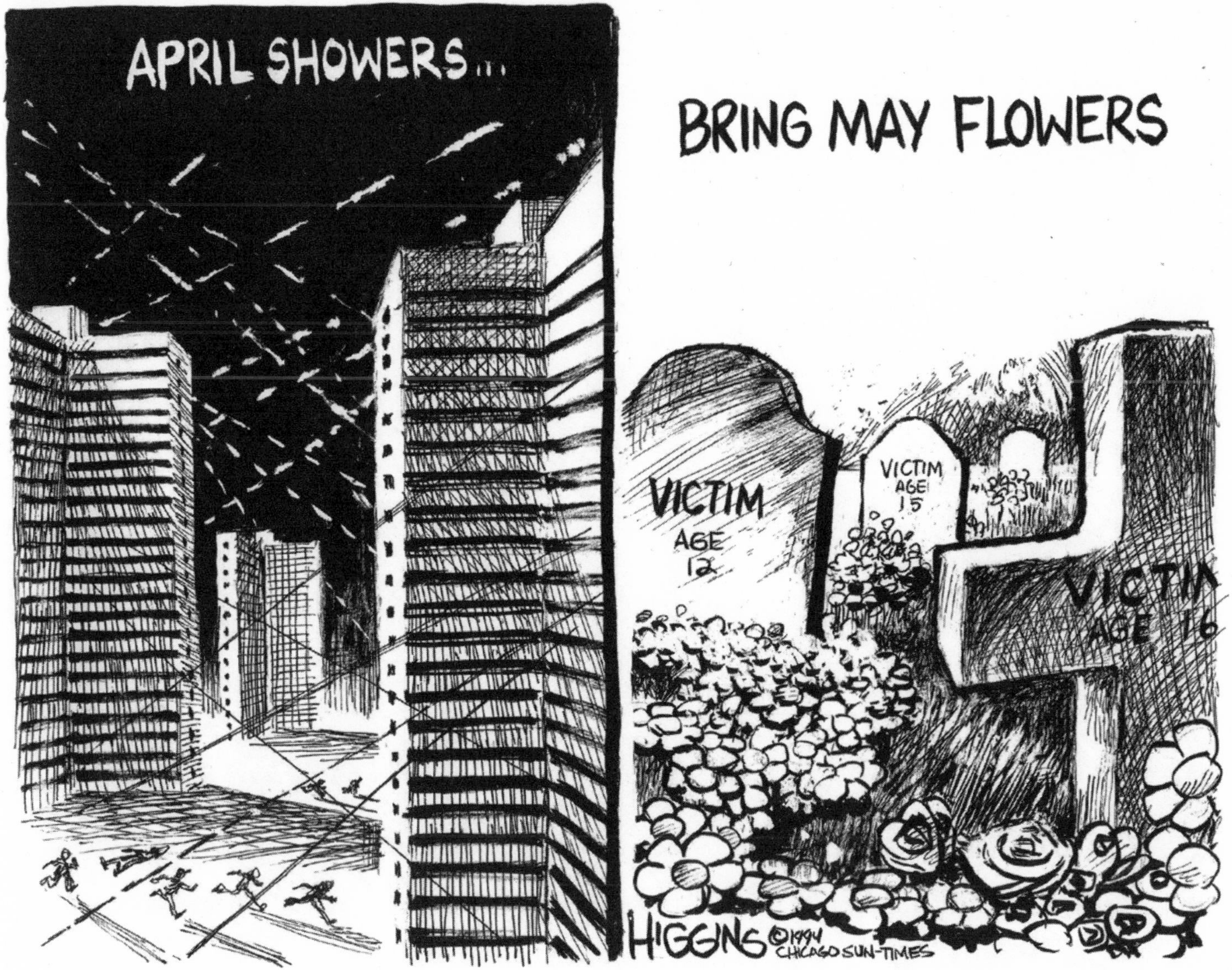
APRIL SHOWERS...
BRING MAY FLOWERS
VICTIM
AGE
12
VICTIM
AGE
15
VICTIM
AGE 16
HIGGINS ©1994
CHICAGO SUN-TIMES

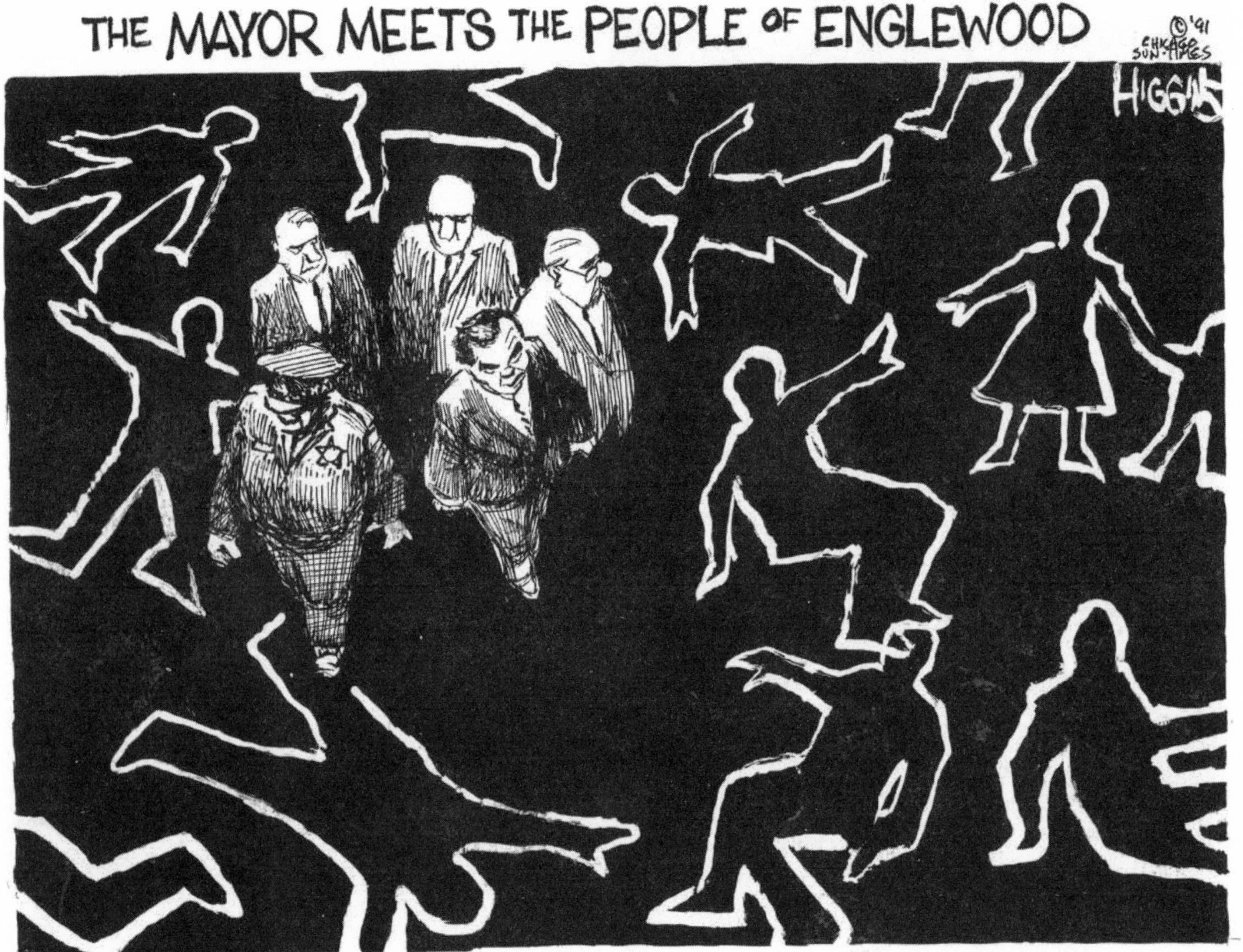
THE MAYOR MEETS THE PEOPLE OF ENGLEWOOD
© '91 CHICAGO SUN-TIMES
HIGGINS

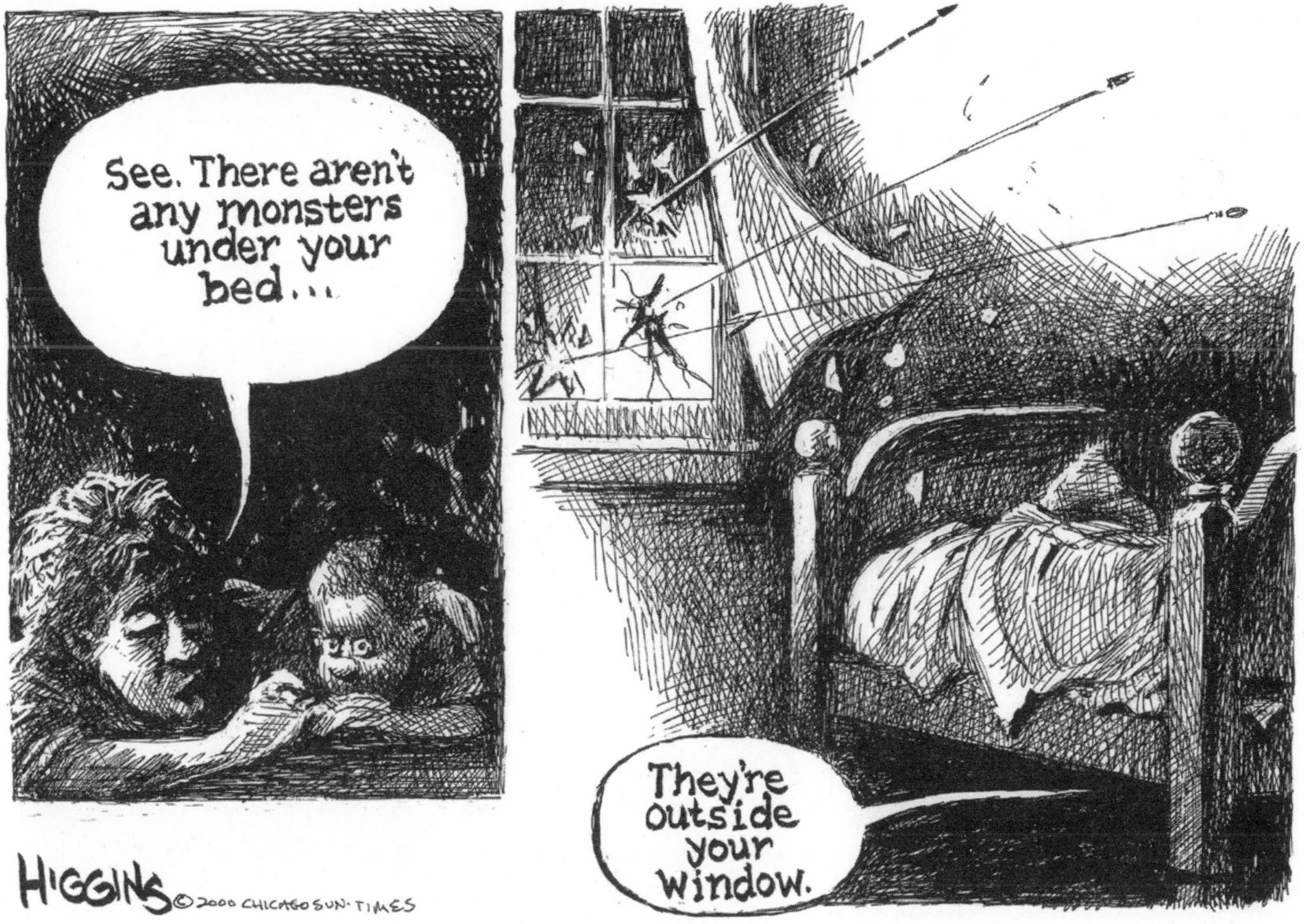
See. There aren't any monsters under your bed...
They're outside your window.
HIGGINS ©2000 CHICAGO SUN-TIMES

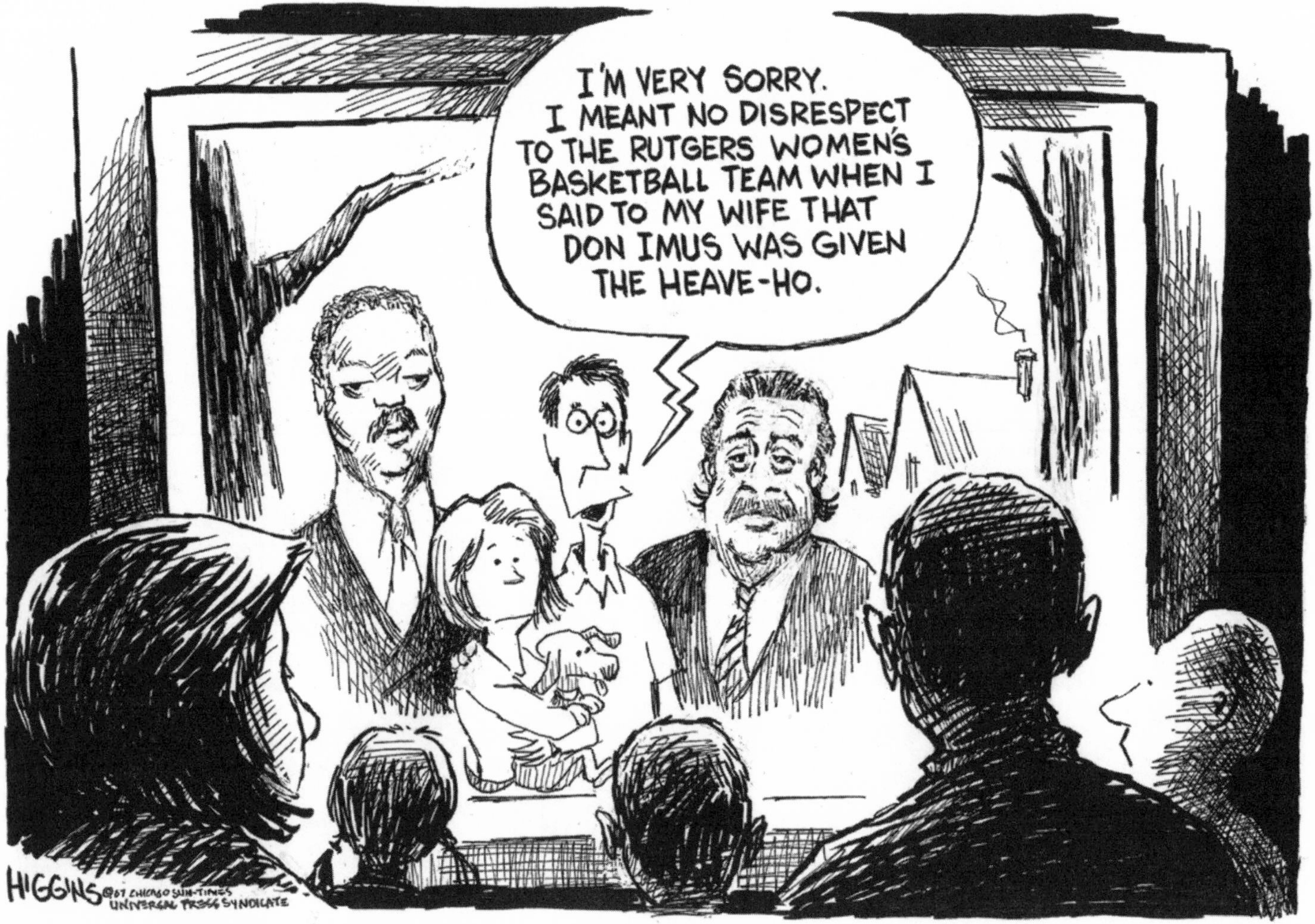
I'M VERY SORRY. I MEANT NO DISRESPECT TO THE RUTGERS WOMEN'S BASKETBALL TEAM WHEN I SAID TO MY WIFE THAT DON IMUS WAS GIVEN THE HEAVE-HO.
HIGGINS ©07 CHICAGO SUN-TIMES UNIVERSAL PRESS SYNDICATE

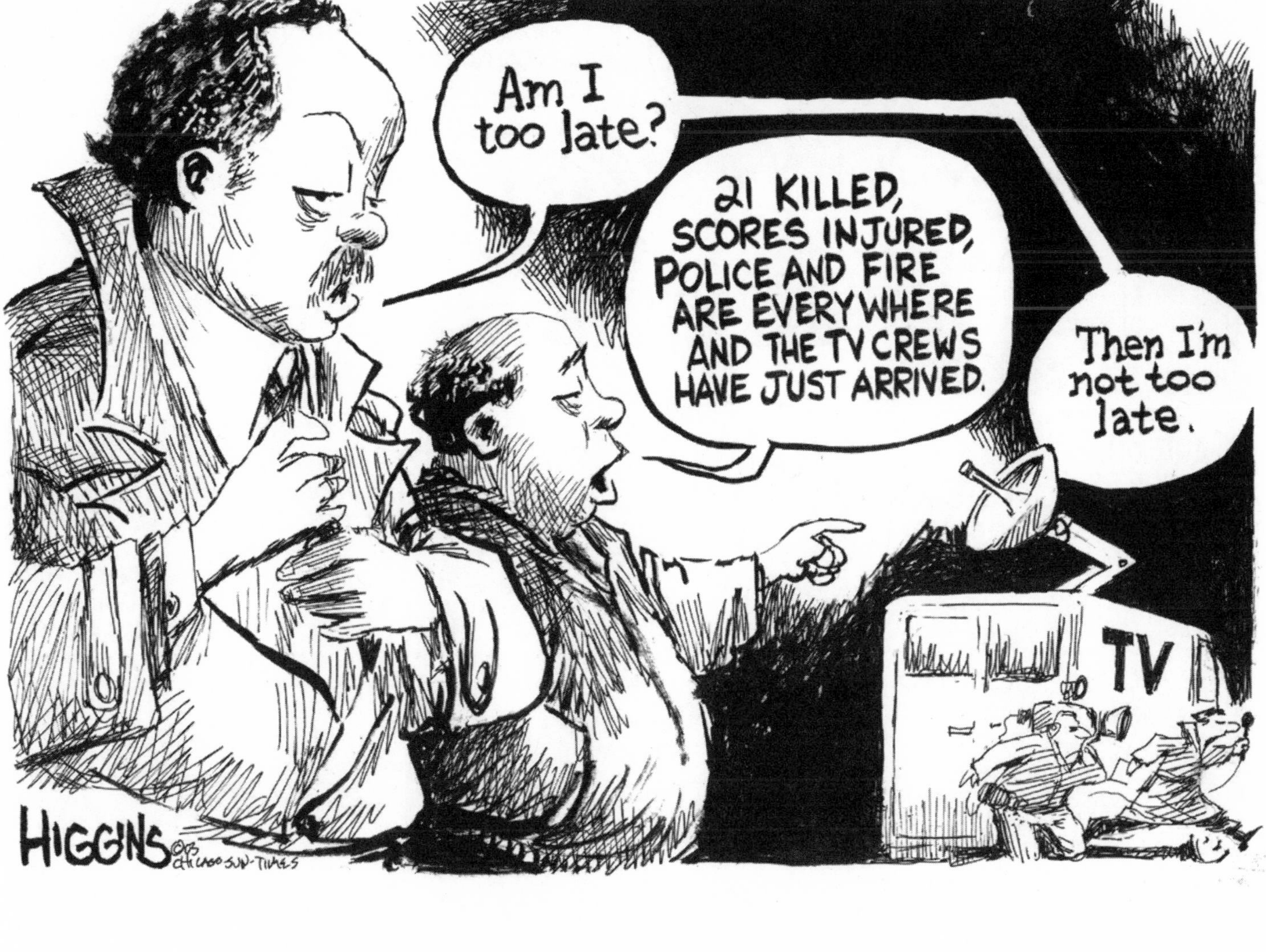
Am I too late?
21 KILLED, SCORES INJURED, POLICE AND FIRE ARE EVERYWHERE AND THE TV CREWS HAVE JUST ARRIVED.
Then I'm not too late.
TV
HIGGINS

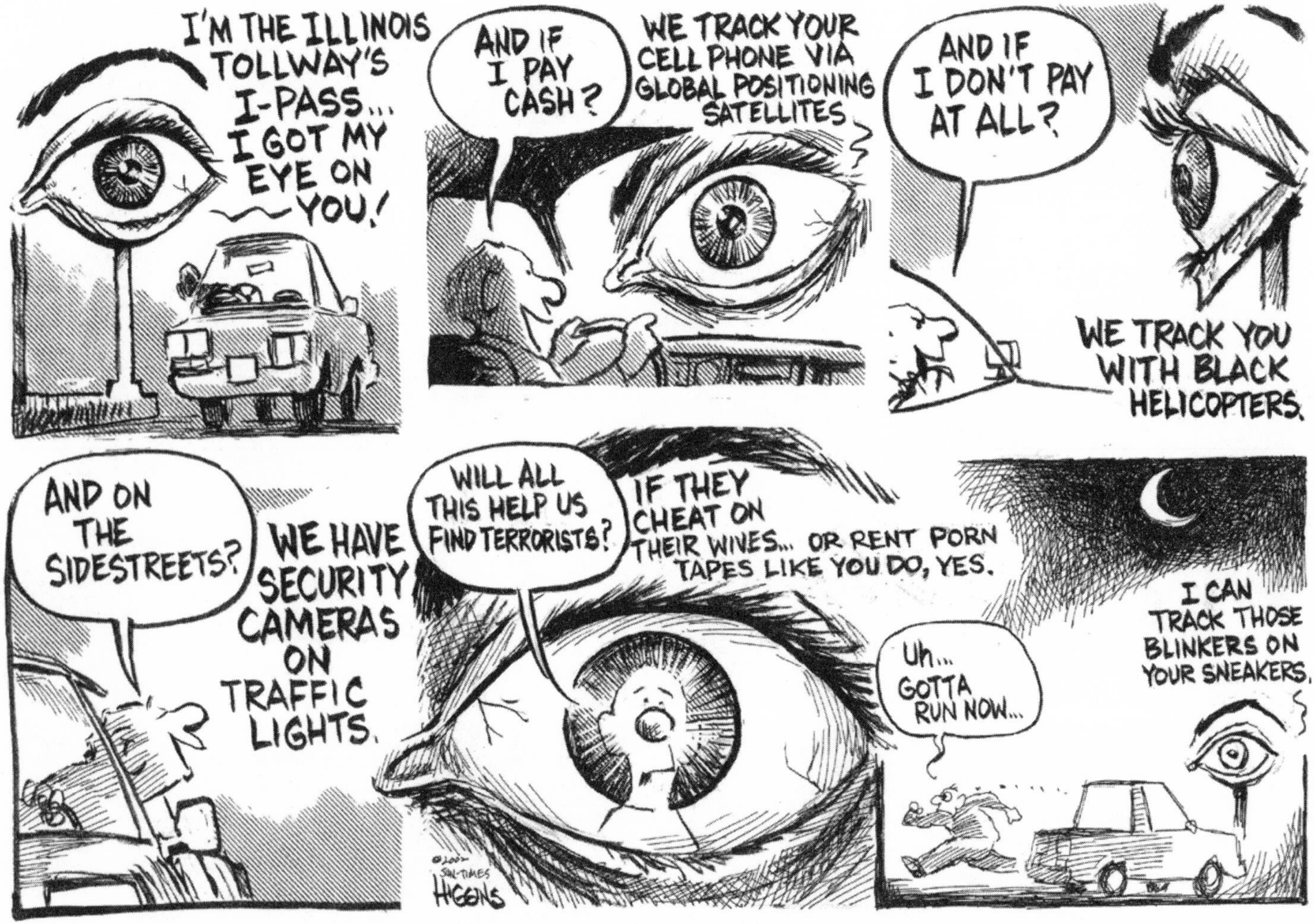
I'M THE ILLINOIS TOLLWAY'S I-PASS... I GOT MY EYE ON YOU!
AND IF I PAY CASH?
WE TRACK YOUR CELL PHONE VIA GLOBAL POSITIONING SATELLITES
AND IF I DON'T PAY AT ALL?
WE TRACK YOU WITH BLACK HELICOPTERS.
AND ON THE SIDESTREETS?
WE HAVE SECURITY CAMERAS ON TRAFFIC LIGHTS.
WILL ALL THIS HELP US FIND TERRORISTS?
IF THEY CHEAT ON THEIR WIVES... OR RENT PORN TAPES LIKE YOU DO, YES.
Uh... GOTTA RUN NOW...
I CAN TRACK THOSE BLINKERS ON YOUR SNEAKERS.
HIGGINS

PRETENDERS TO THE THRONE

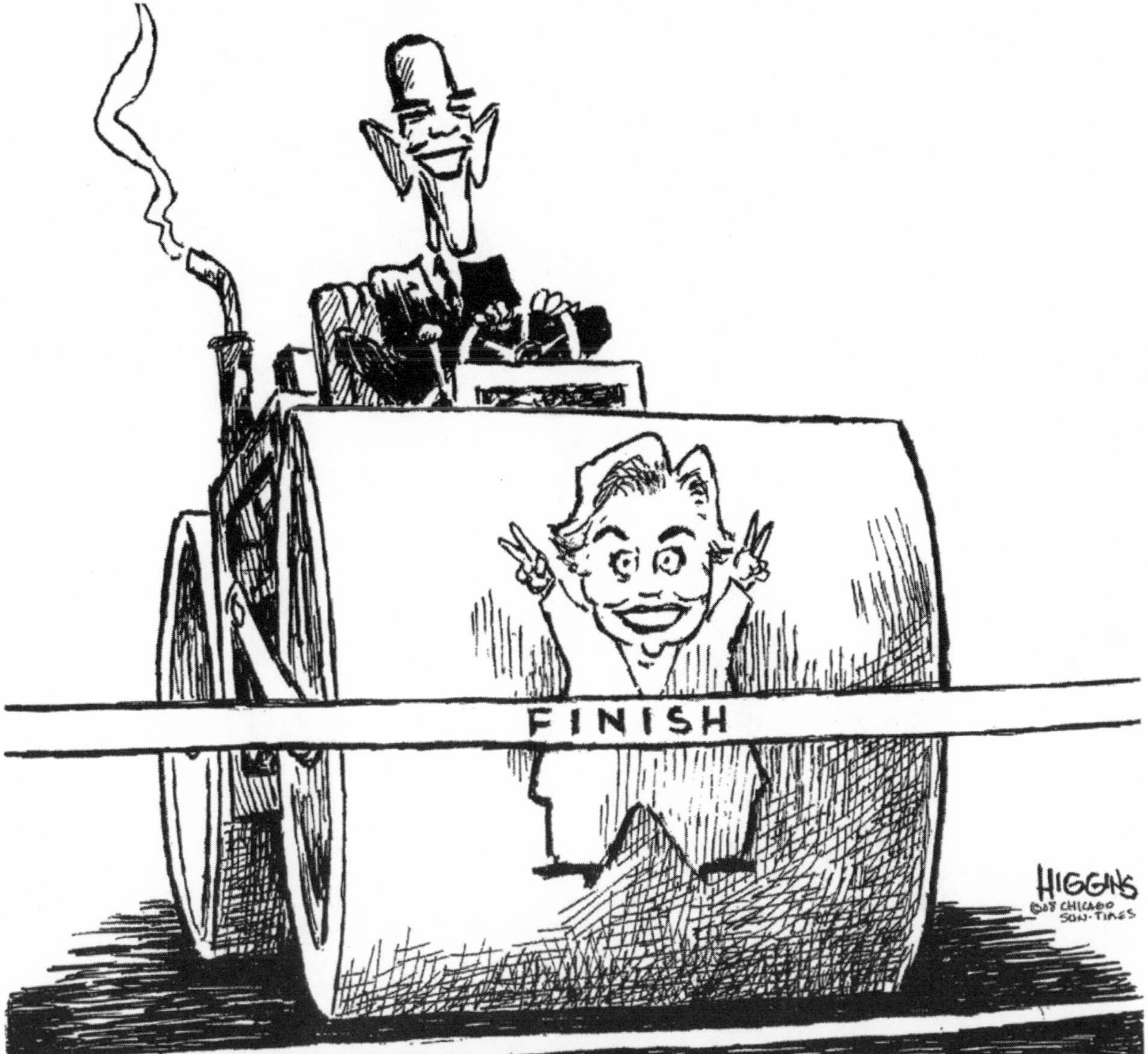
FINISH
HIGGINS
©08 CHICAGO SUN-TIMES

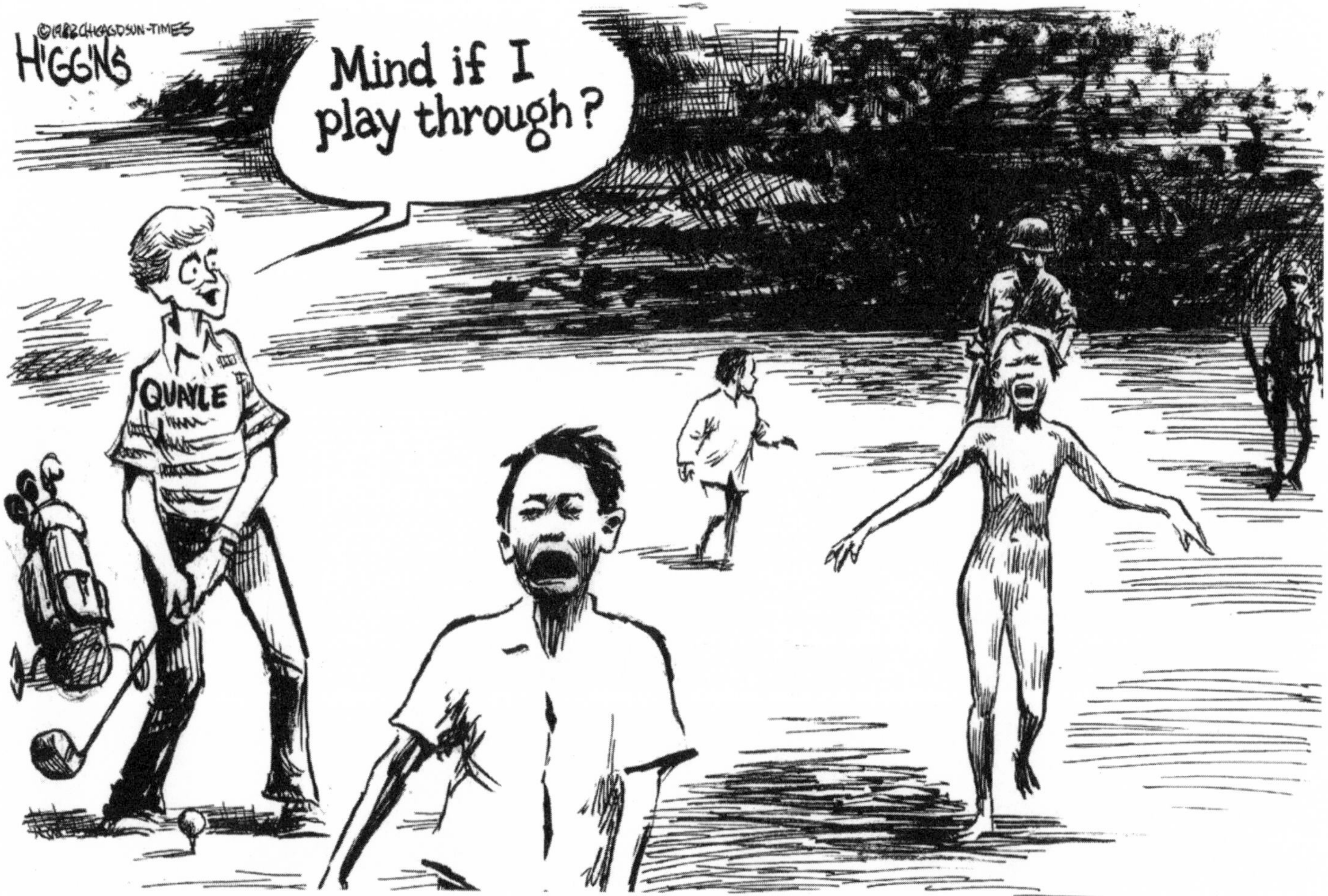
©1988 CHICAGO SUN-TIMES
HIGGINS
Mind if I play through?
QUAYLE

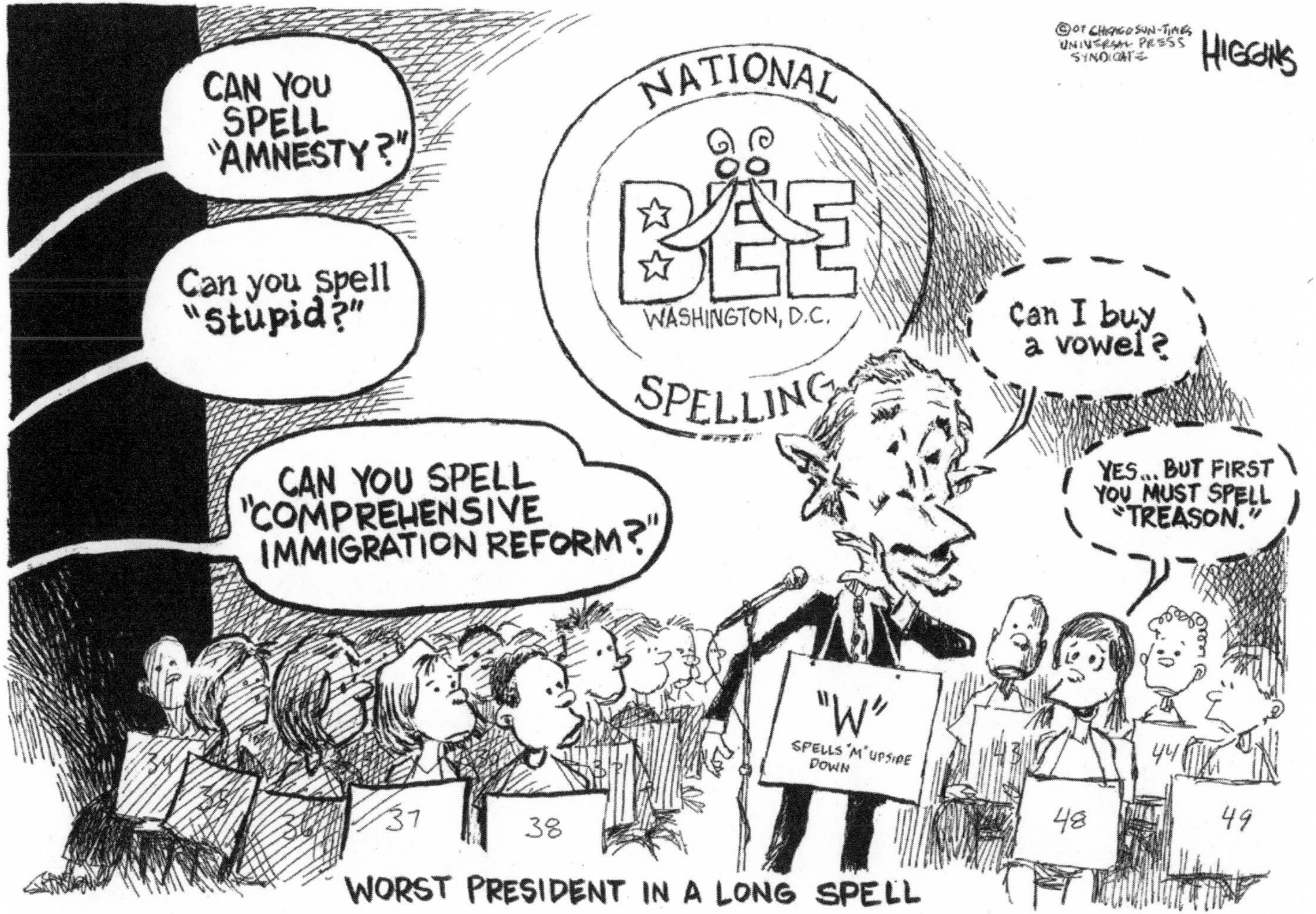
©07 CHICAGO SUN-TIMES UNIVERSAL PRESS SYNDICATE
HIGGINS
CAN YOU SPELL "AMNESTY?"
Can you spell "stupid?"
CAN YOU SPELL "COMPREHENSIVE IMMIGRATION REFORM?"
NATIONAL SPELLING BEE WASHINGTON, D.C.
Can I buy a vowel?
YES... BUT FIRST YOU MUST SPELL "TREASON."
"W" SPELLS "M" UPSIDE DOWN
34
35
36
37
38
43
44
48
49
WORST PRESIDENT IN A LONG SPELL

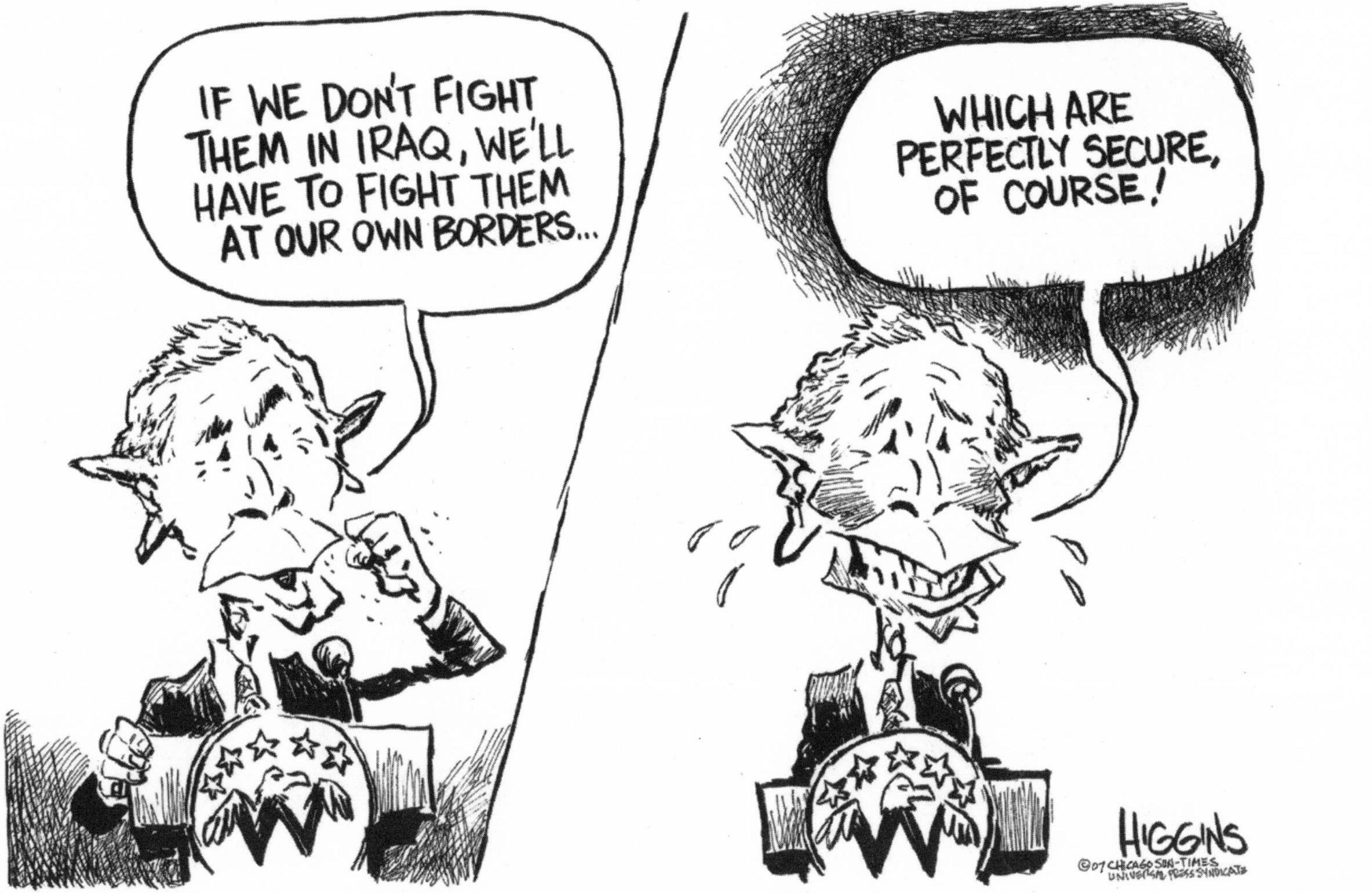
IF WE DON'T FIGHT THEM IN IRAQ, WE'LL HAVE TO FIGHT THEM AT OUR OWN BORDERS...
WHICH ARE PERFECTLY SECURE, OF COURSE!
HIGGINS
©07 CHICAGO SUN-TIMES UNIVERSAL PRESS SYNDICATE

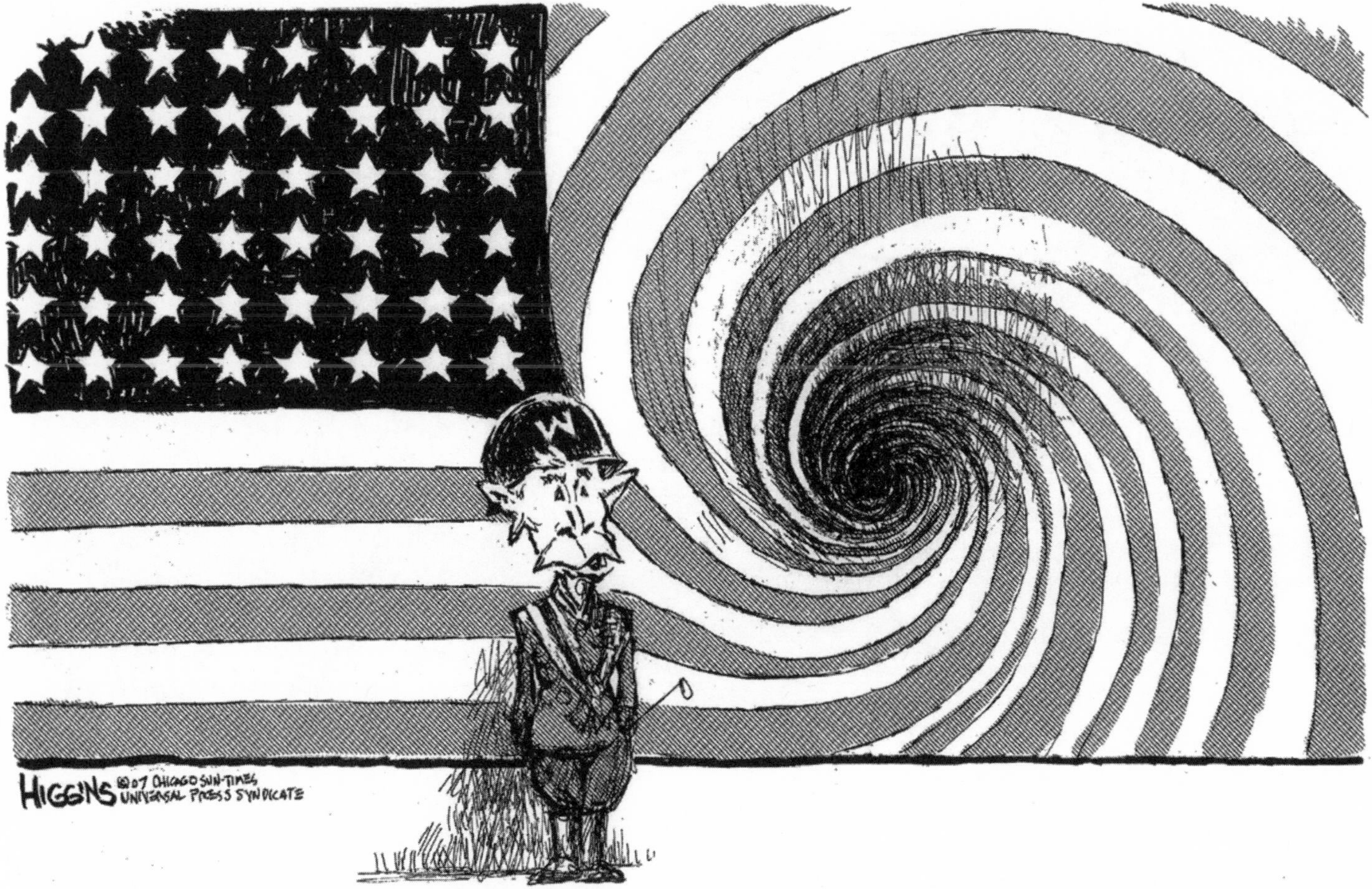
W
HIGGINS ©07 CHICAGO SUN-TIMES UNIVERSAL PRESS SYNDICATE

"Our surge in Iraq—The New Way Forward—is not open-ended..."

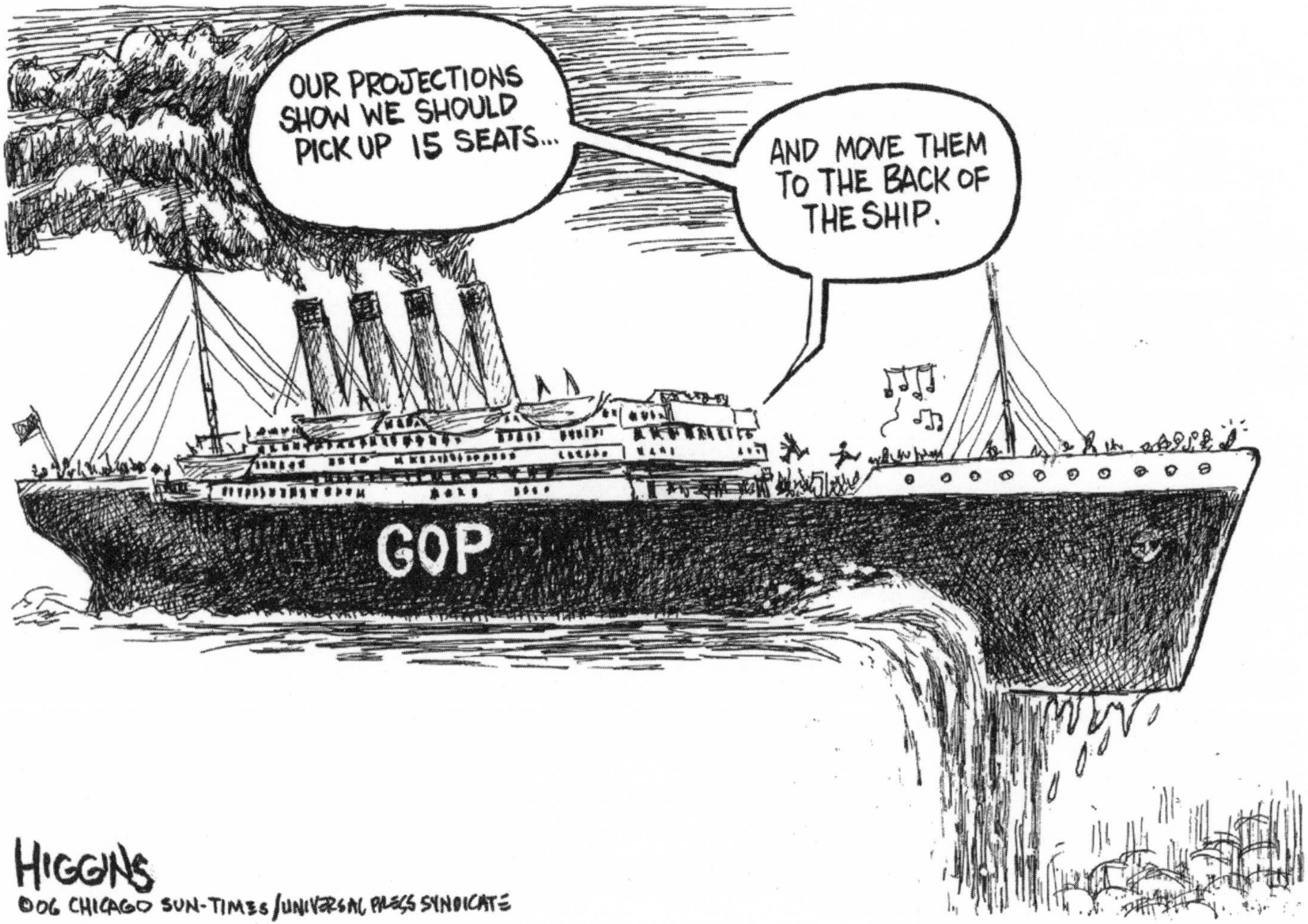
OUR PROJECTIONS SHOW WE SHOULD PICK UP 15 SEATS...
AND MOVE THEM TO THE BACK OF THE SHIP.
GOP
HIGGINS
©06 CHICAGO SUN-TIMES/UNIVERSAL PRESS SYNDICATE

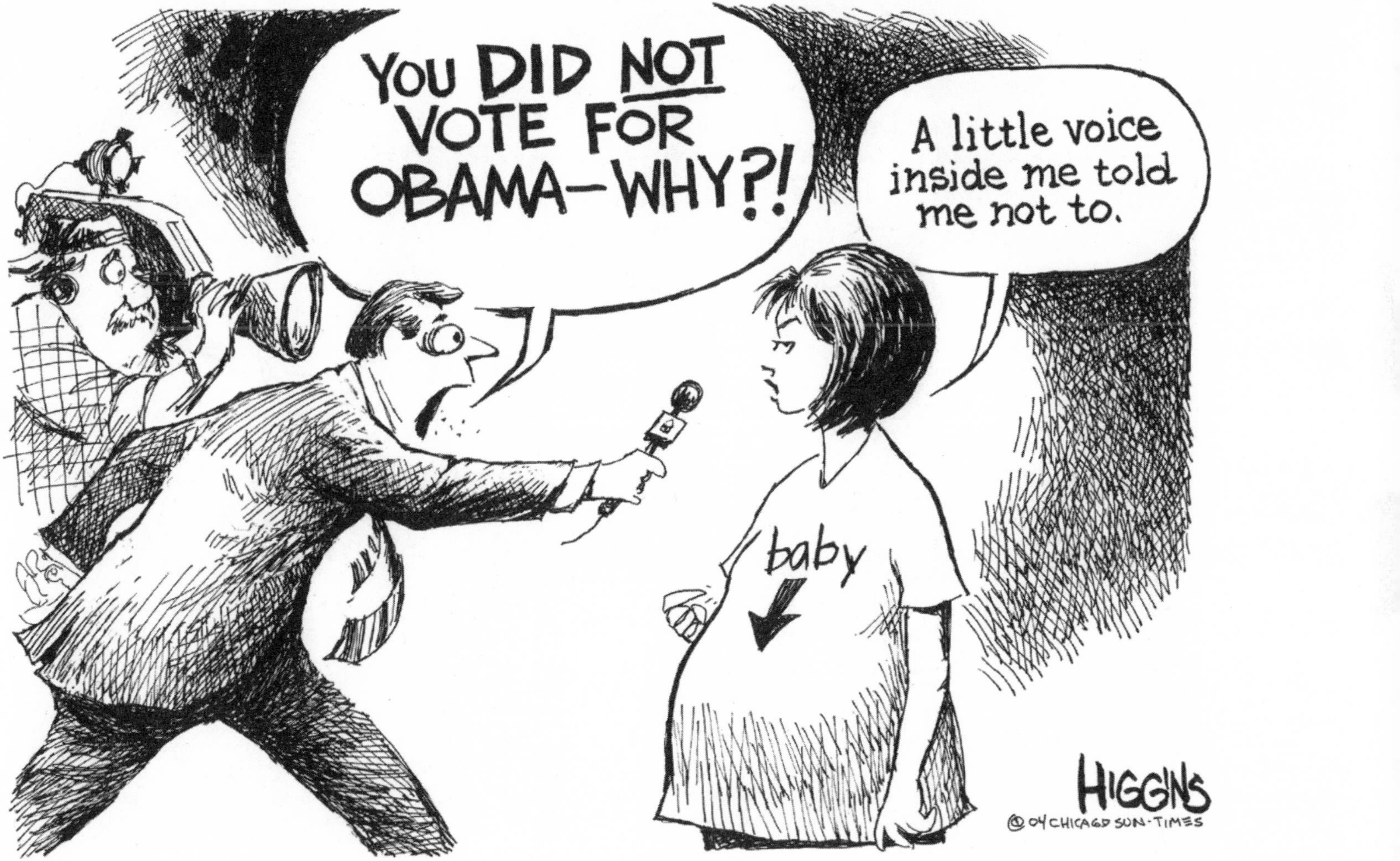
YOU DID NOT VOTE FOR OBAMA—WHY?!
A little voice inside me told me not to.
baby
HIGGINS
© 04 CHICAGO SUN-TIMES

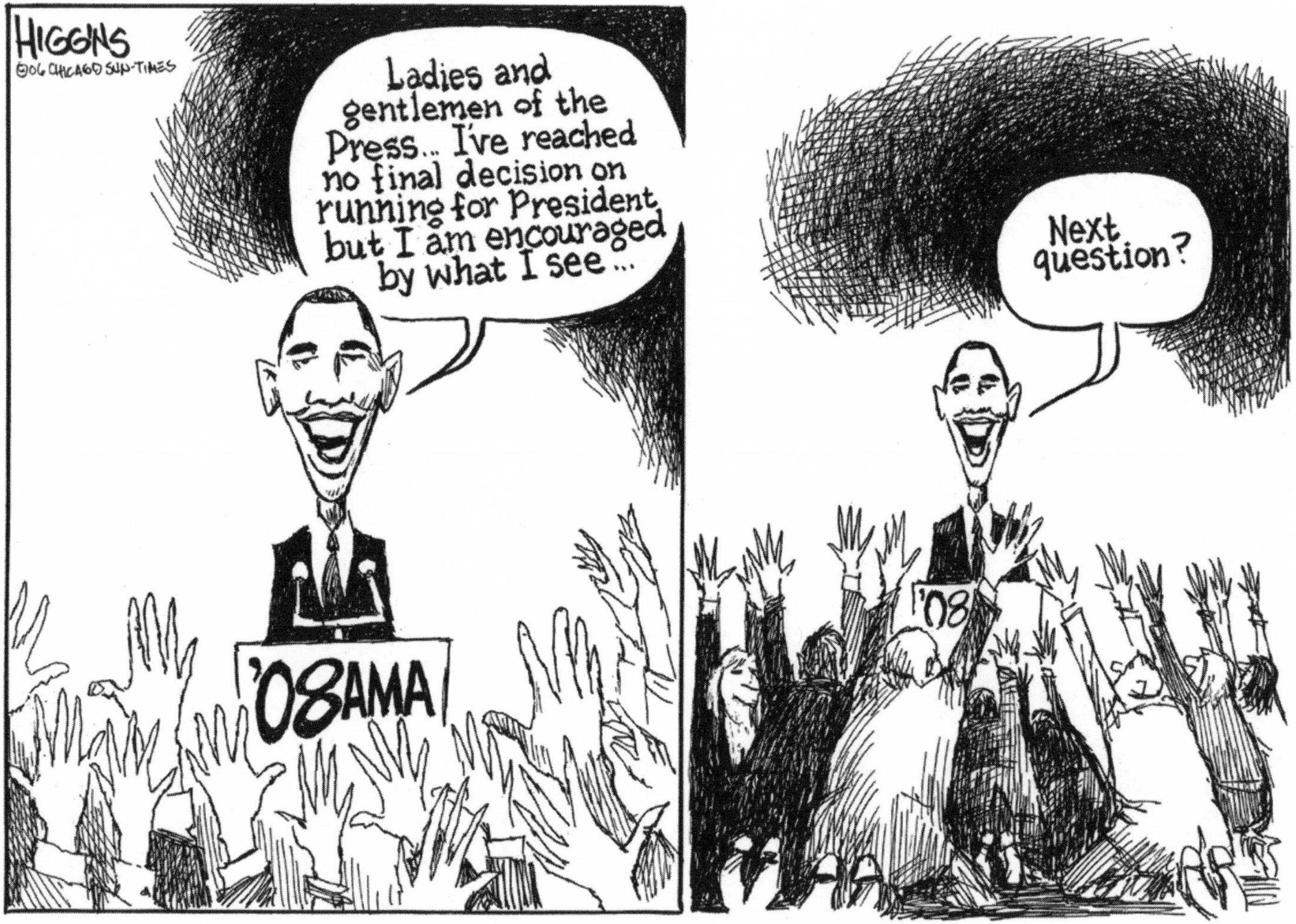
HIGGINS
©06 CHICAGO SUN-TIMES
Ladies and gentlemen of the Press... I've reached no final decision on running for President but I am encouraged by what I see...
'08AMA
Next question?
'08

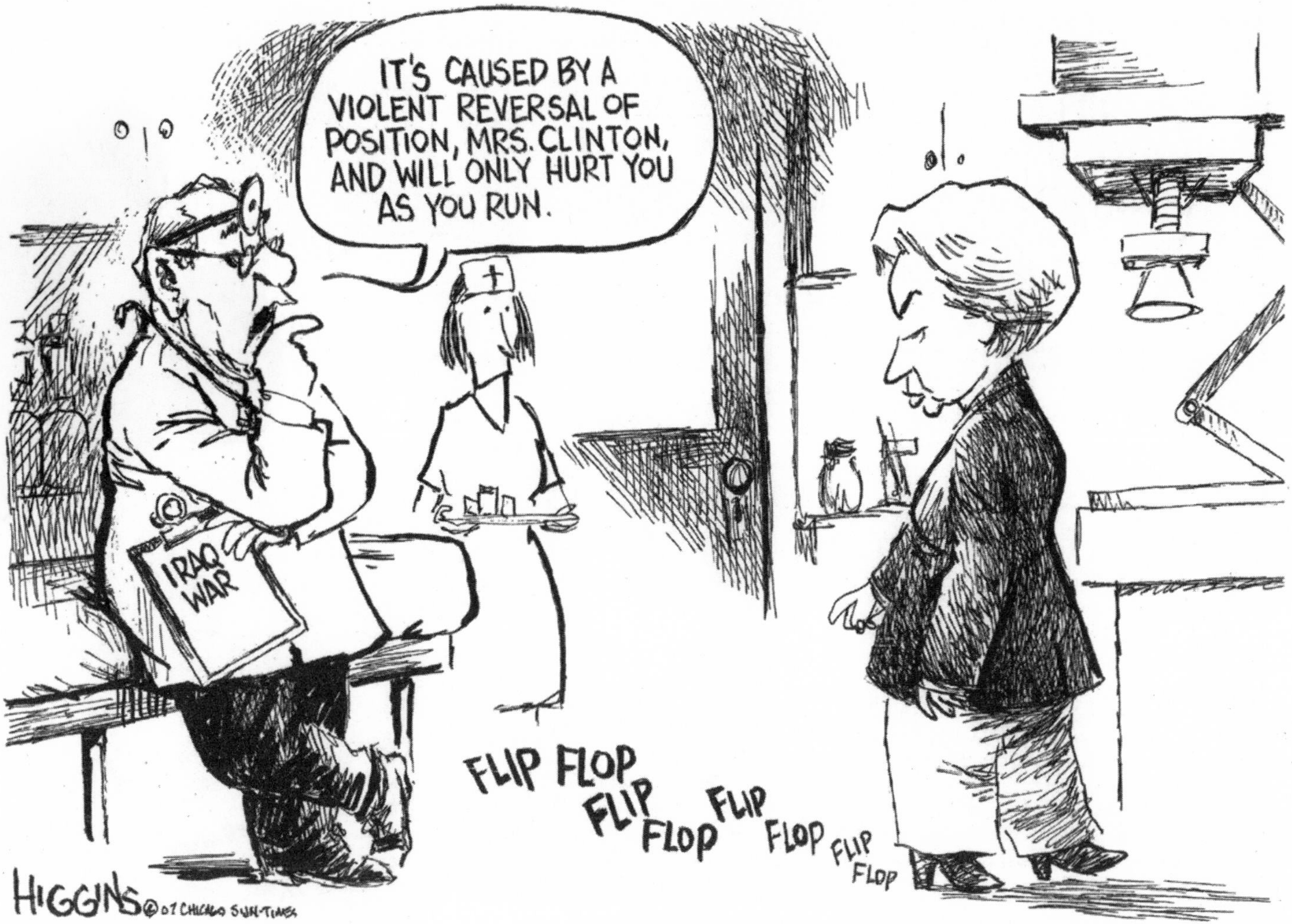
IT'S CAUSED BY A VIOLENT REVERSAL OF POSITION, MRS. CLINTON, AND WILL ONLY HURT YOU AS YOU RUN.
IRAQ WAR
FLIP FLOP FLIP FLOP FLIP FLOP FLIP FLOP
HIGGINS ©07 CHICAGO SUN-TIMES

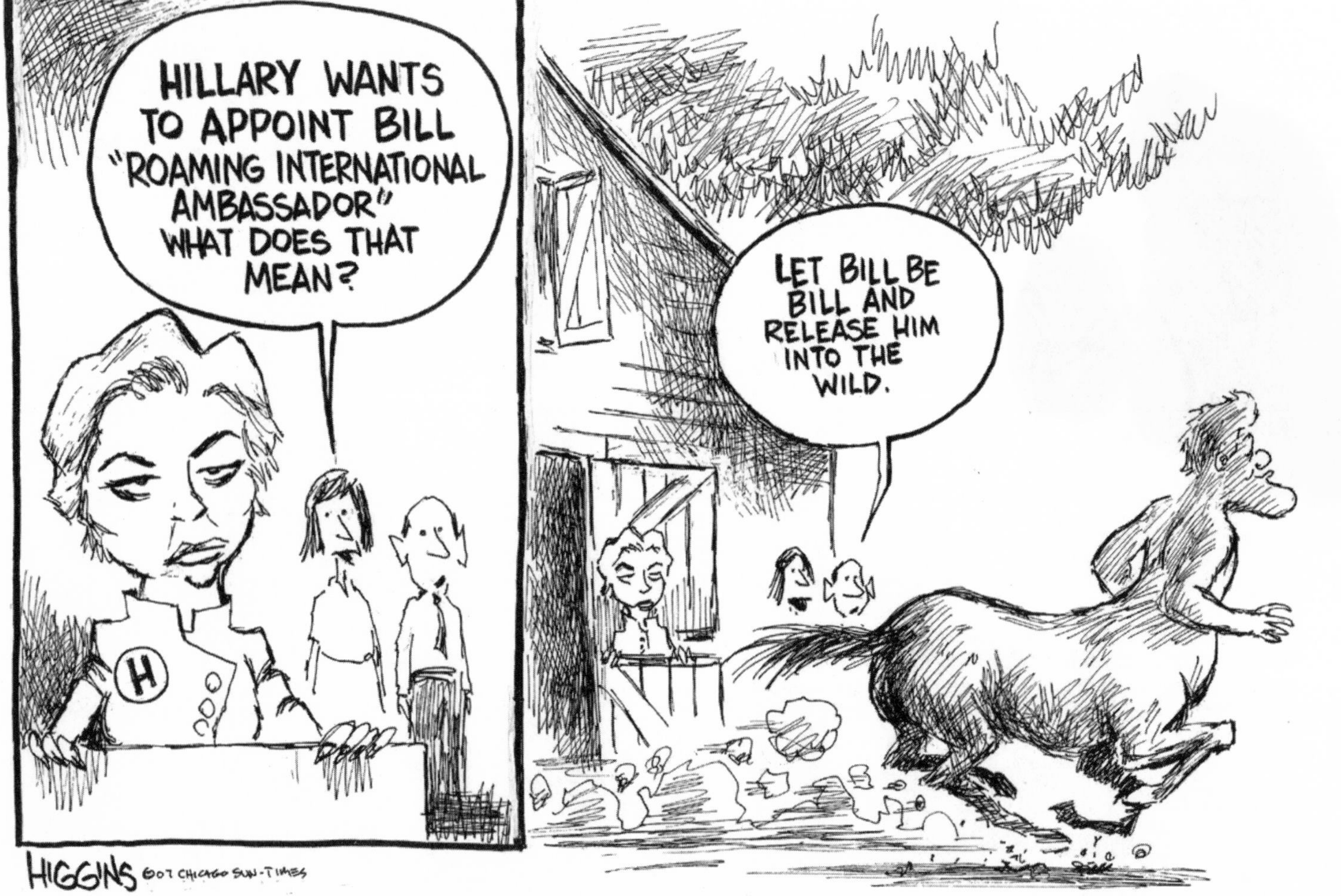
HILLARY WANTS TO APPOINT BILL "ROAMING INTERNATIONAL AMBASSADOR" WHAT DOES THAT MEAN?
LET BILL BE BILL AND RELEASE HIM INTO THE WILD.
H
HIGGINS ©07 CHICAGO SUN-TIMES

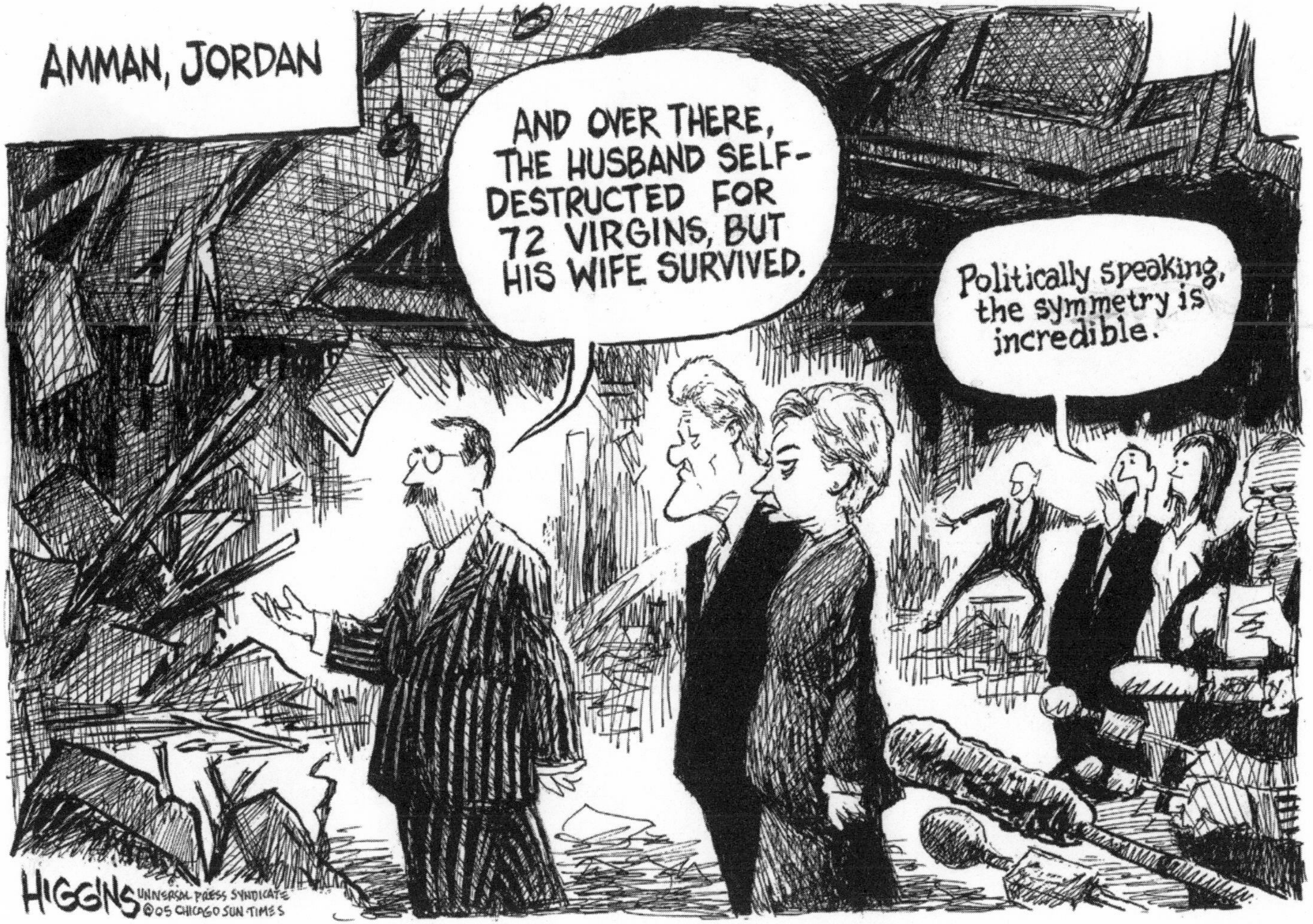
AMMAN, JORDAN
AND OVER THERE, THE HUSBAND SELF-DESTRUCTED FOR 72 VIRGINS, BUT HIS WIFE SURVIVED.
Politically speaking, the symmetry is incredible.
HIGGINS
UNIVERSAL PRESS SYNDICATE
©05 CHICAGO SUN-TIMES

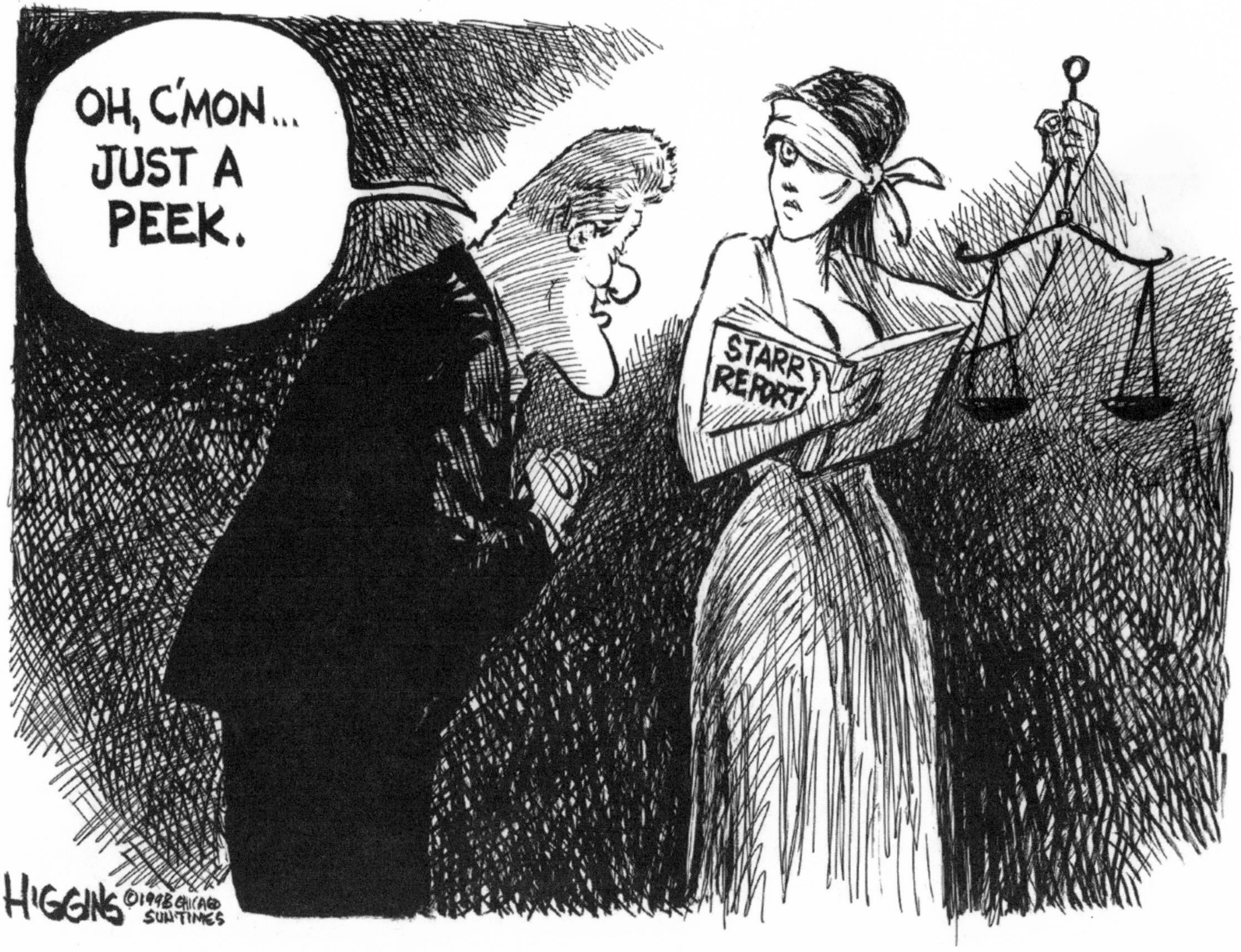
OH, C'MON... JUST A PEEK.
STARR REPORT
HIGGINS ©1998 CHICAGO SUN-TIMES

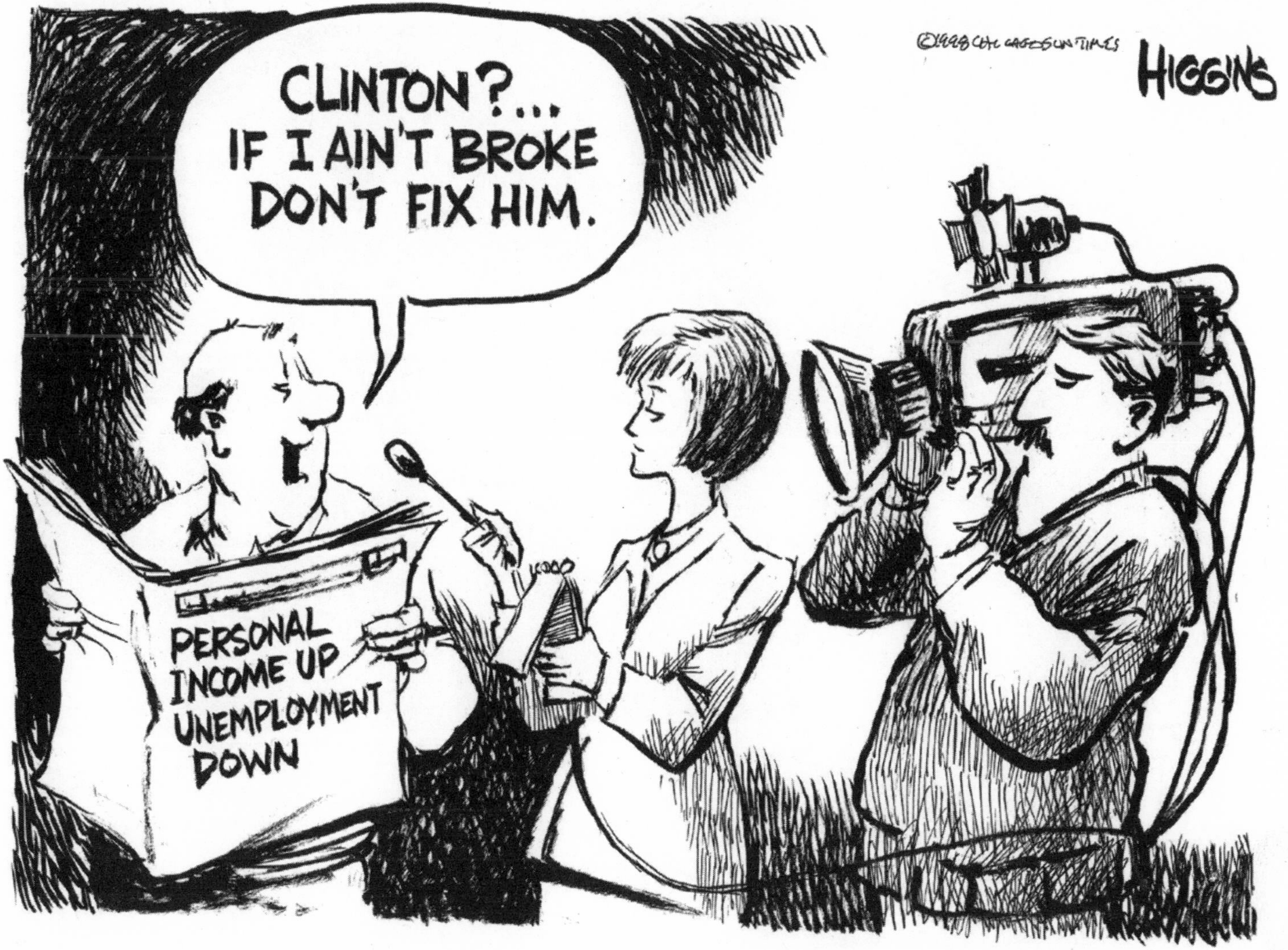
©1998 CHICAGO SUN TIMES
HIGGINS
CLINTON?... IF I AIN'T BROKE DON'T FIX HIM.
PERSONAL INCOME UP UNEMPLOYMENT DOWN

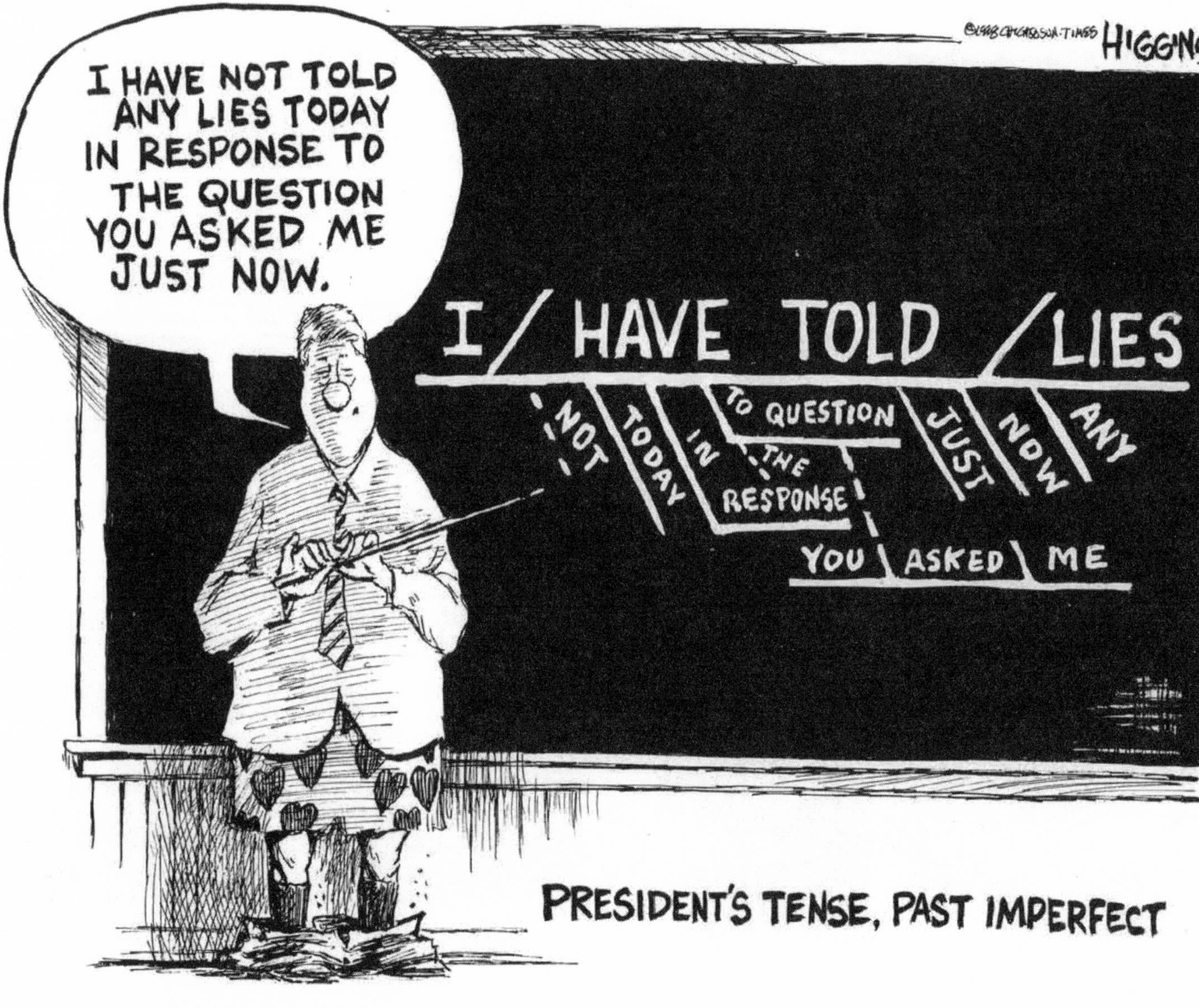
©1998 CHICAGO SUN-TIMES HIGGINS
I HAVE NOT TOLD ANY LIES TODAY IN RESPONSE TO THE QUESTION YOU ASKED ME JUST NOW.
I / HAVE TOLD / LIES
NOT
TODAY
IN
TO QUESTION
THE
RESPONSE
JUST
NOW
ANY
YOU \ ASKED \ ME

PRESIDENT'S TENSE, PAST IMPERFECT

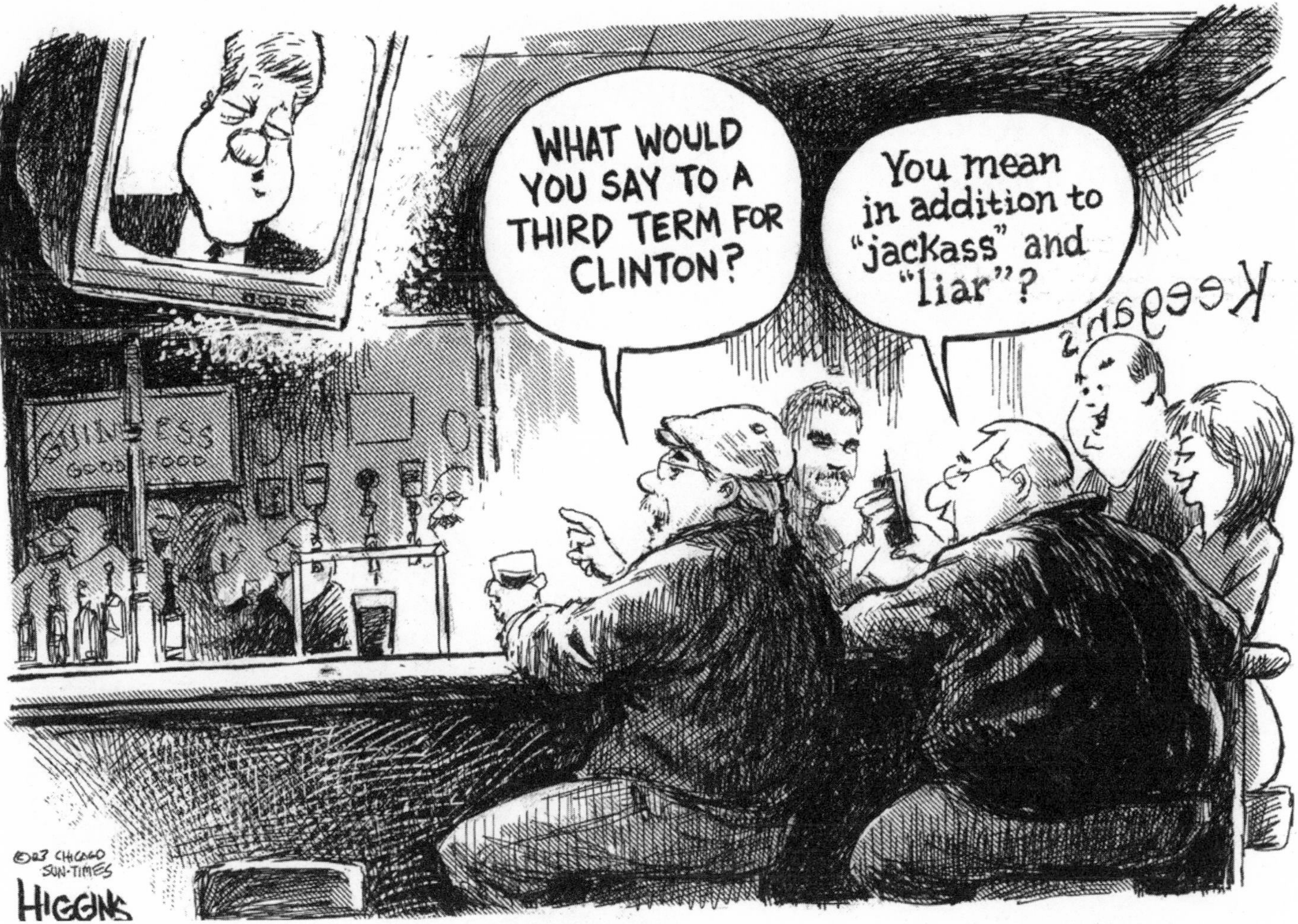
WHAT WOULD YOU SAY TO A THIRD TERM FOR CLINTON?
You mean in addition to "jackass" and "liar"?
Keegan's
GUINNESS GOOD FOOD
©03 CHICAGO SUN-TIMES
HIGGINS

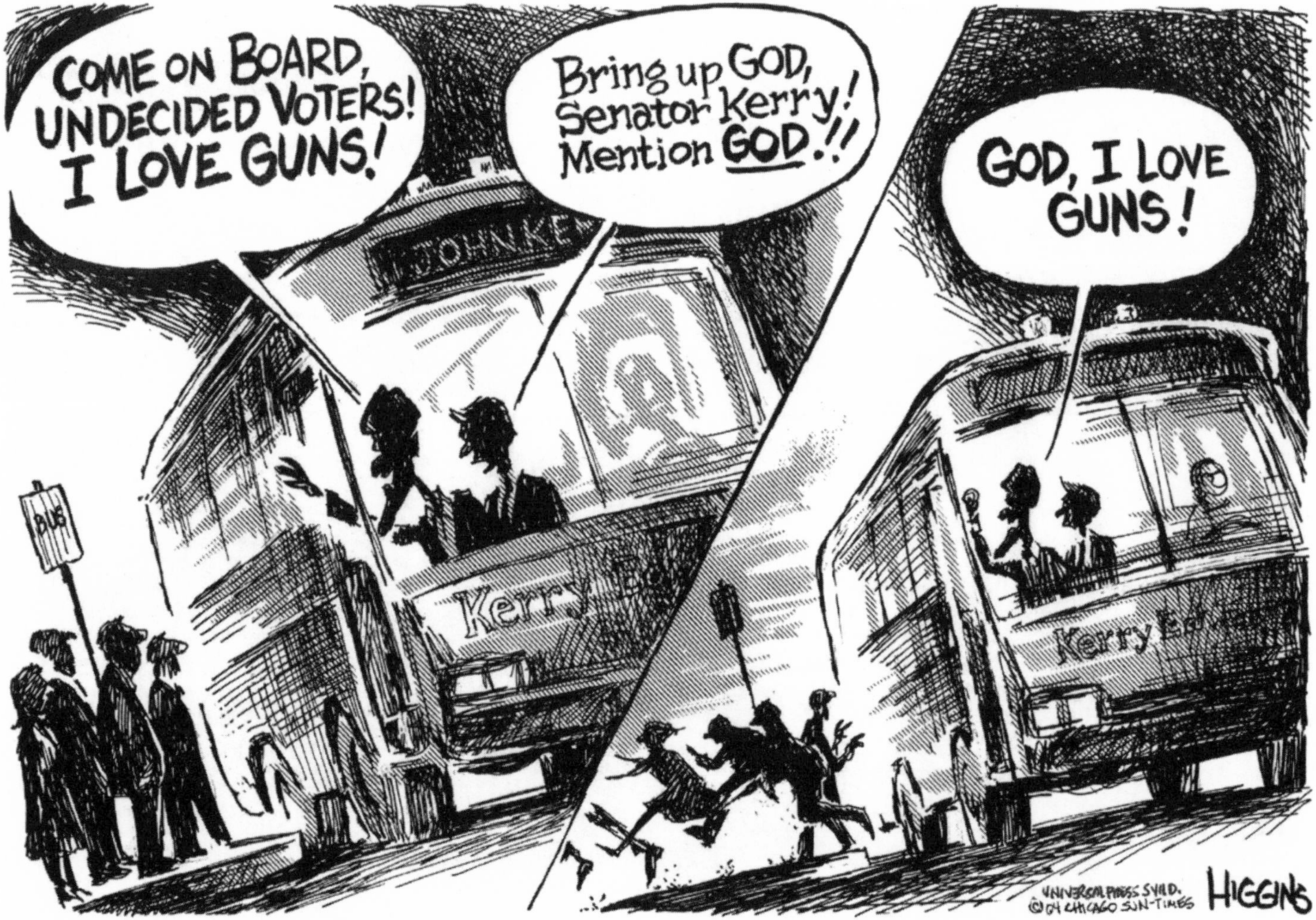
COME ON BOARD, UNDECIDED VOTERS! I LOVE GUNS!
Bring up GOD, Senator Kerry! Mention GOD!!!
BUS
Kerry
GOD, I LOVE GUNS!
UNIVERSAL PRESS SYND. ©04 CHICAGO SUN-TIMES
HIGGINS

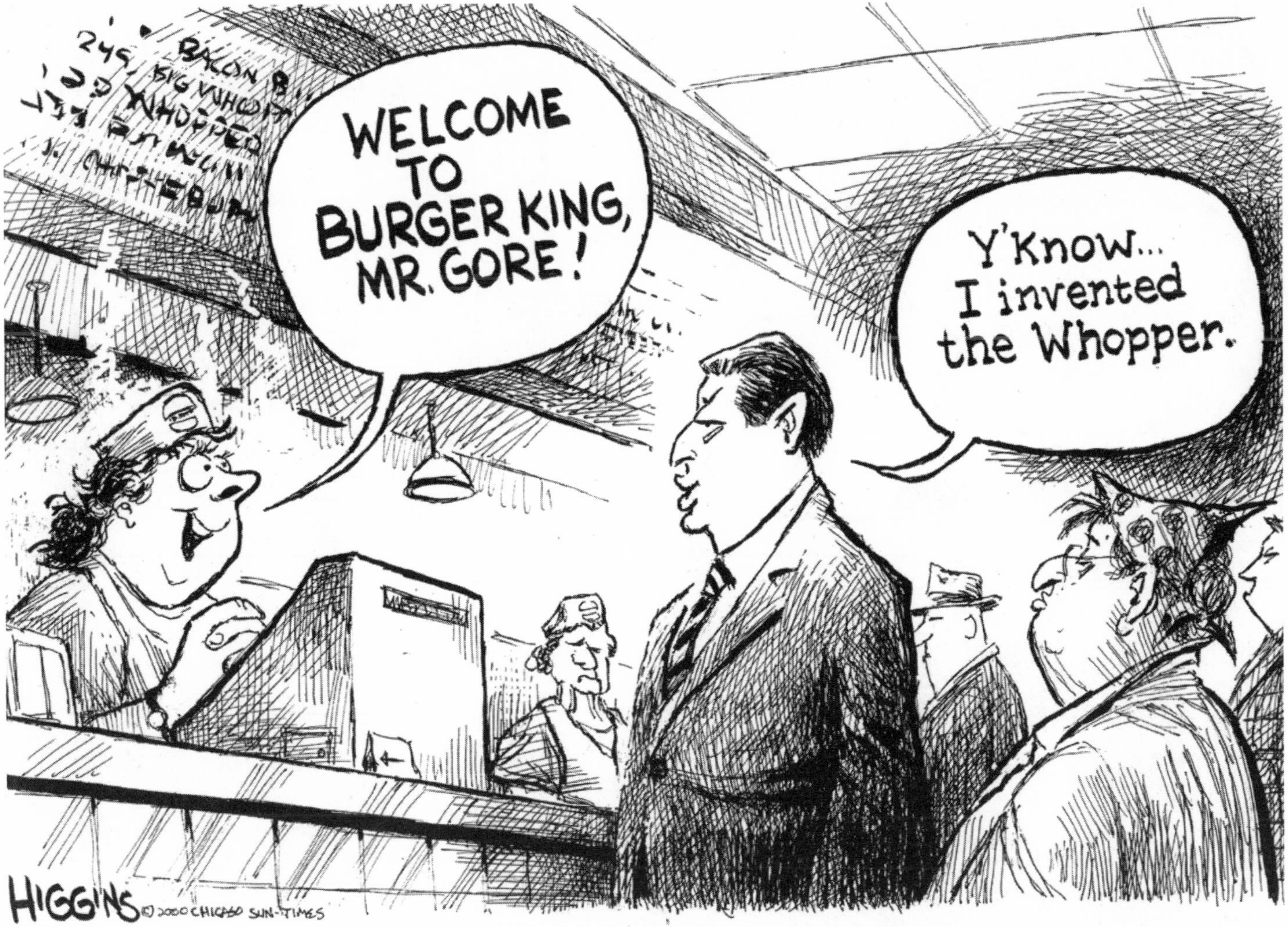
WELCOME TO BURGER KING, MR. GORE!
Y'Know... I invented the Whopper.
HIGGINS © 2000 CHICAGO SUN-TIMES

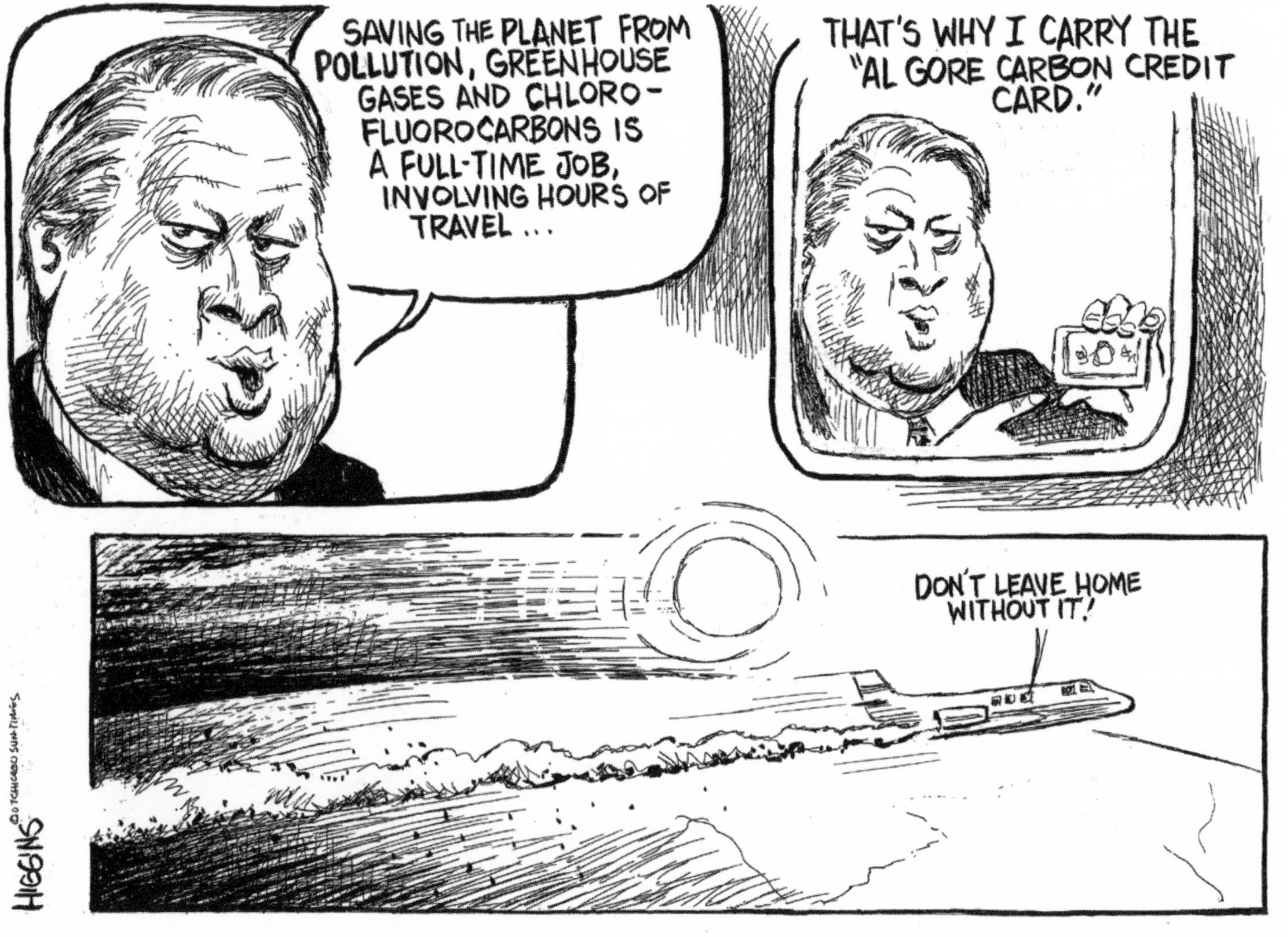
SAVING THE PLANET FROM POLLUTION, GREENHOUSE GASES AND CHLORO-FLUOROCARBONS IS A FULL-TIME JOB, INVOLVING HOURS OF TRAVEL ...
THAT'S WHY I CARRY THE "AL GORE CARBON CREDIT CARD."
DON'T LEAVE HOME WITHOUT IT!
HIGGINS

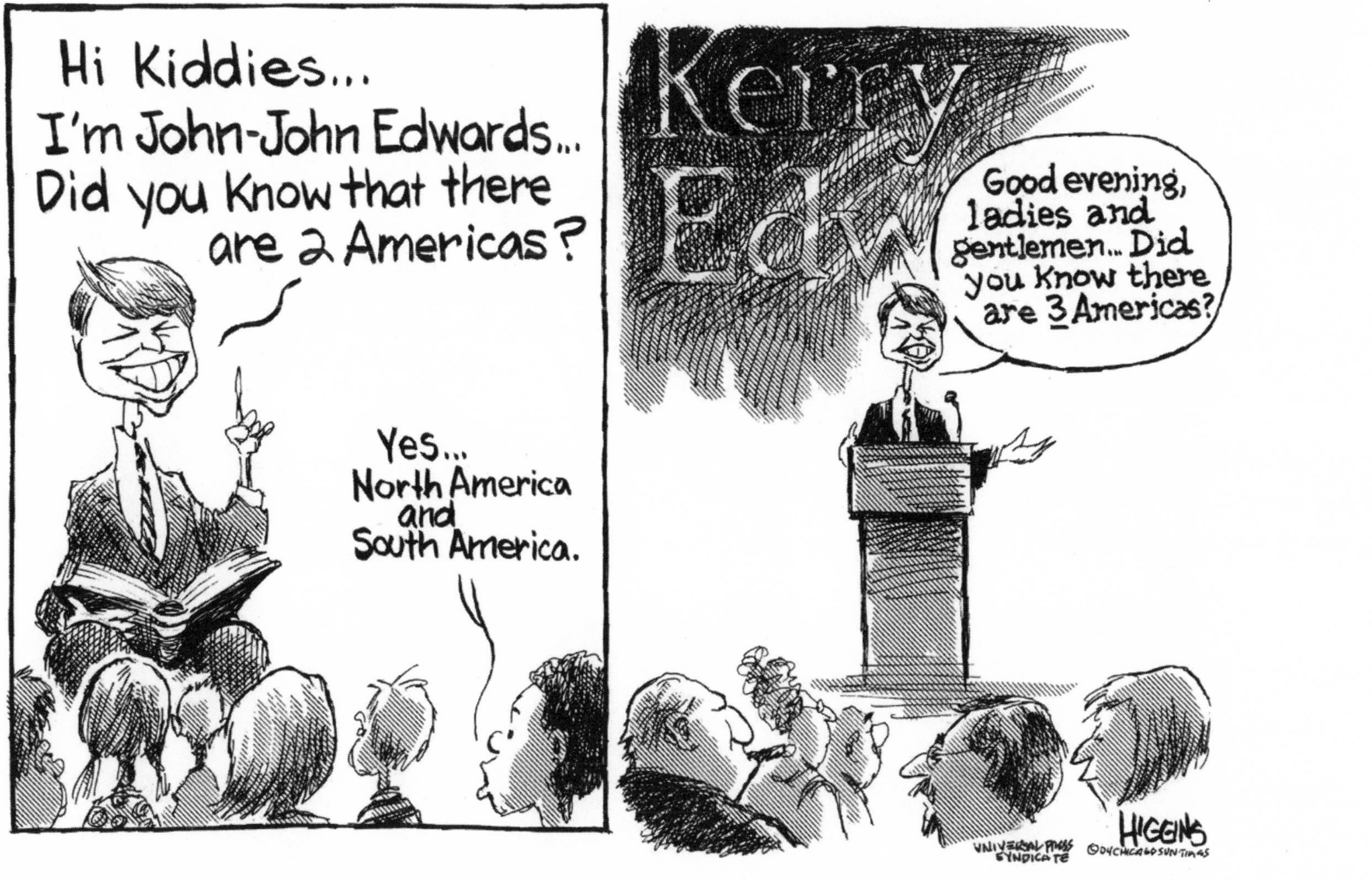

Hi Kiddies...
I'm John-John Edwards...
Did you Know that there are 2 Americas?
Yes...
North America and South America.
Kerry
Edw
Good evening, ladies and gentlemen... Did you Know there are 3 Americas?
HIGGINS
UNIVERSAL PRESS SYNDICATE
©04 CHICAGO SUN-TIMES

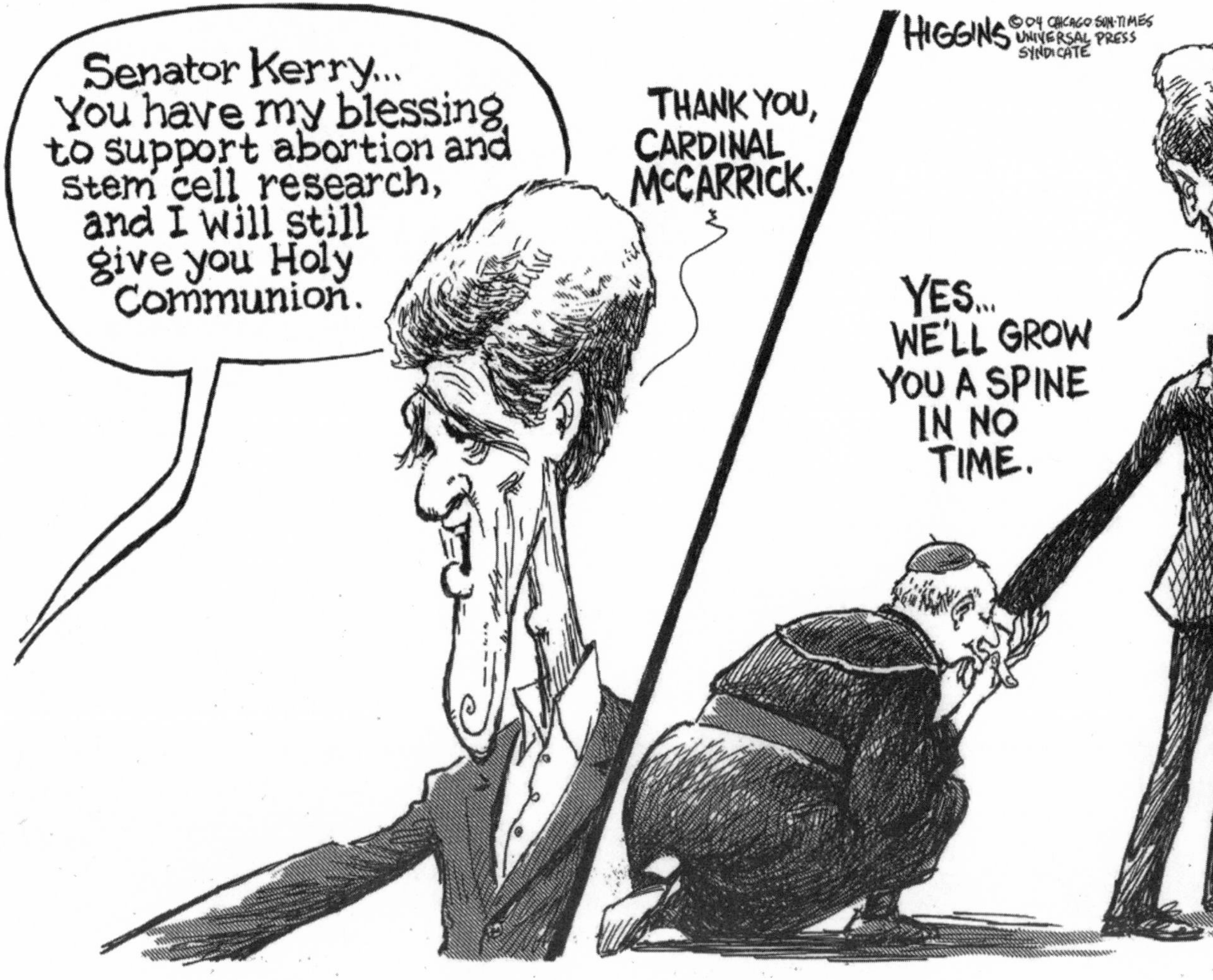
Senator Kerry... You have my blessing to support abortion and stem cell research, and I will still give you Holy Communion.
THANK YOU, CARDINAL McCARRICK.
HIGGINS © 04 CHICAGO SUN-TIMES UNIVERSAL PRESS SYNDICATE
YES... WE'LL GROW YOU A SPINE IN NO TIME.

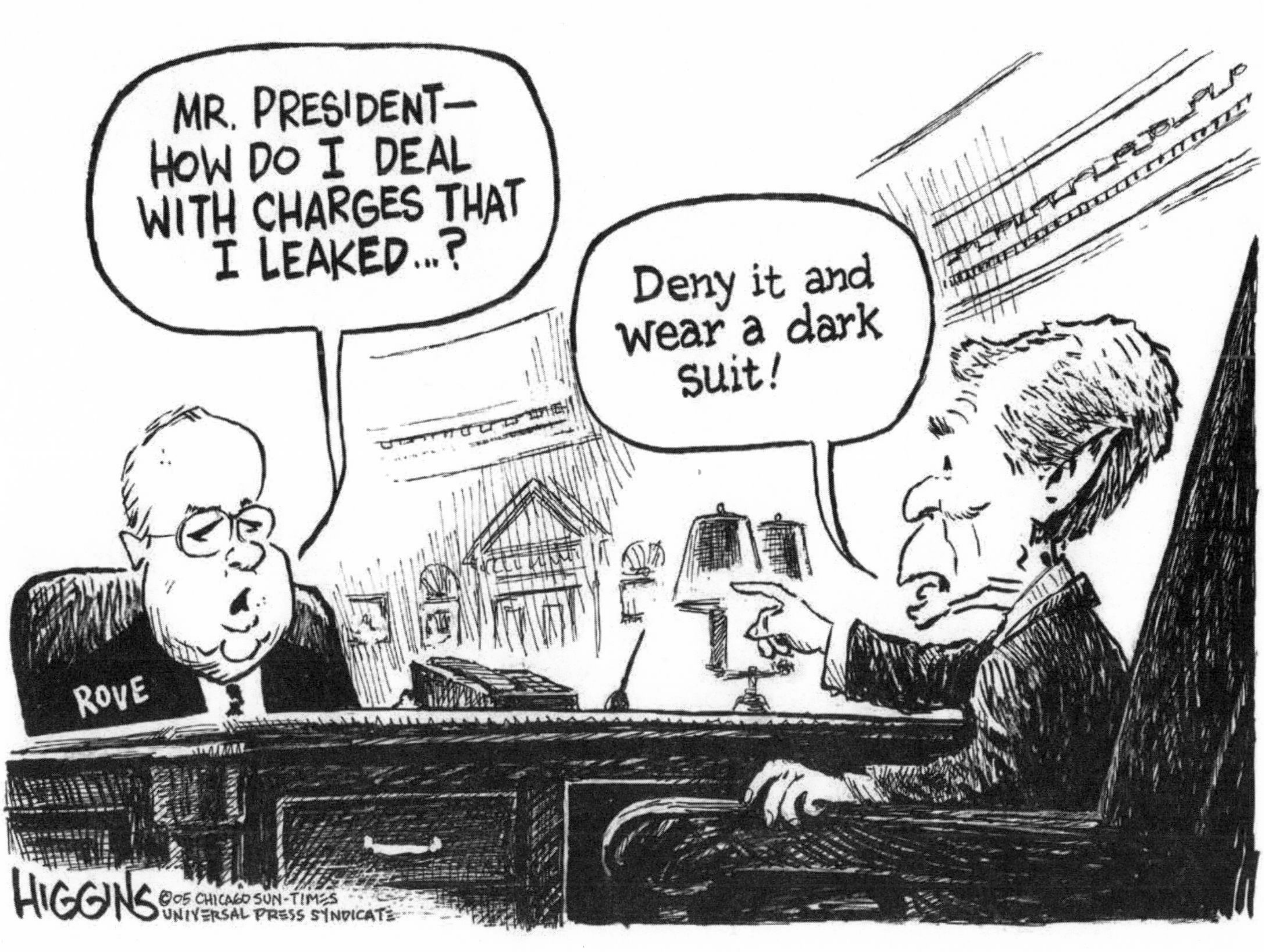
MR. PRESIDENT— HOW DO I DEAL WITH CHARGES THAT I LEAKED...?
Deny it and wear a dark suit!
ROVE
HIGGINS
©05 CHICAGO SUN-TIMES
UNIVERSAL PRESS SYNDICATE

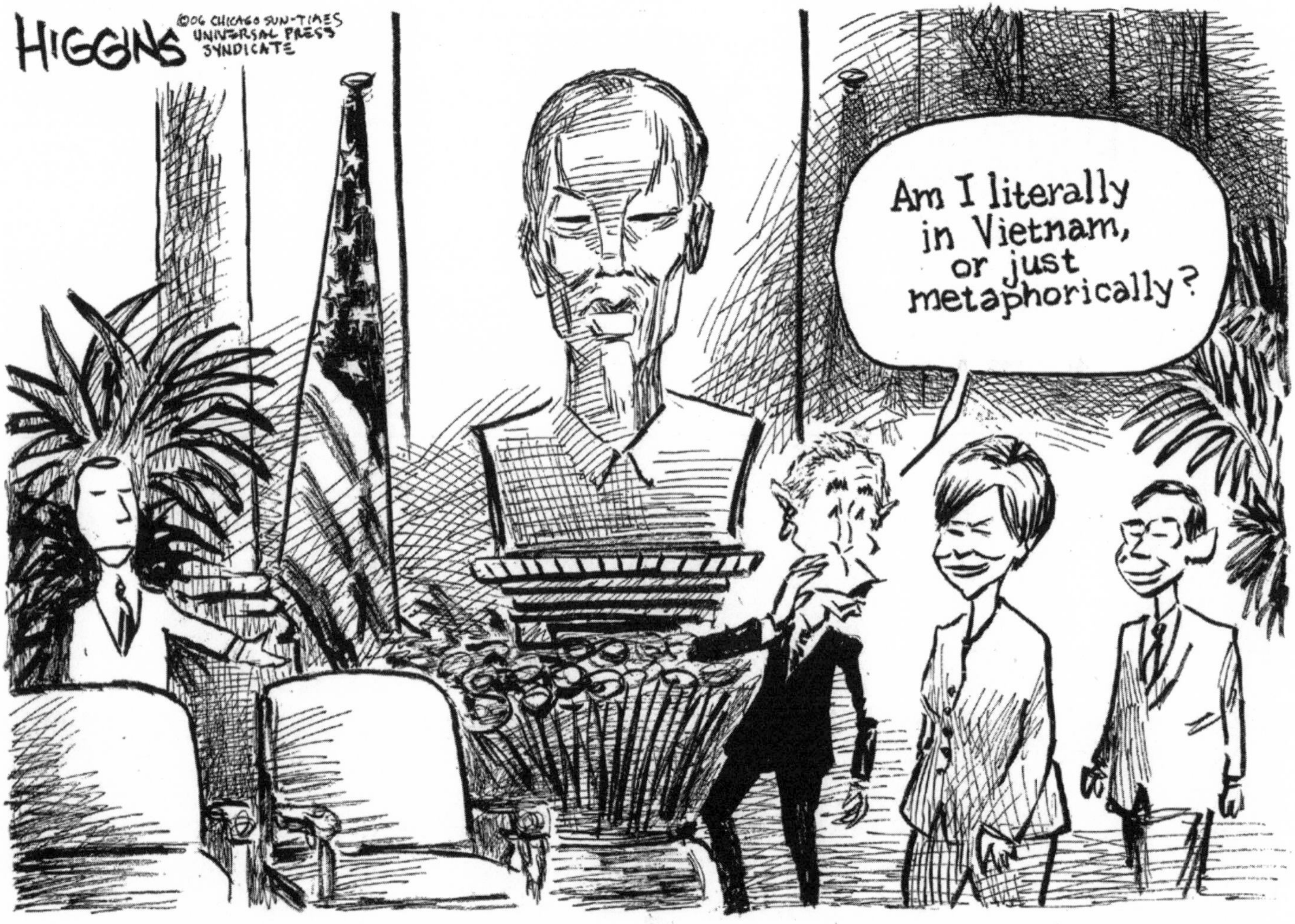
HIGGINS
©06 CHICAGO SUN-TIMES UNIVERSAL PRESS SYNDICATE
Am I literally in Vietnam, or just metaphorically?

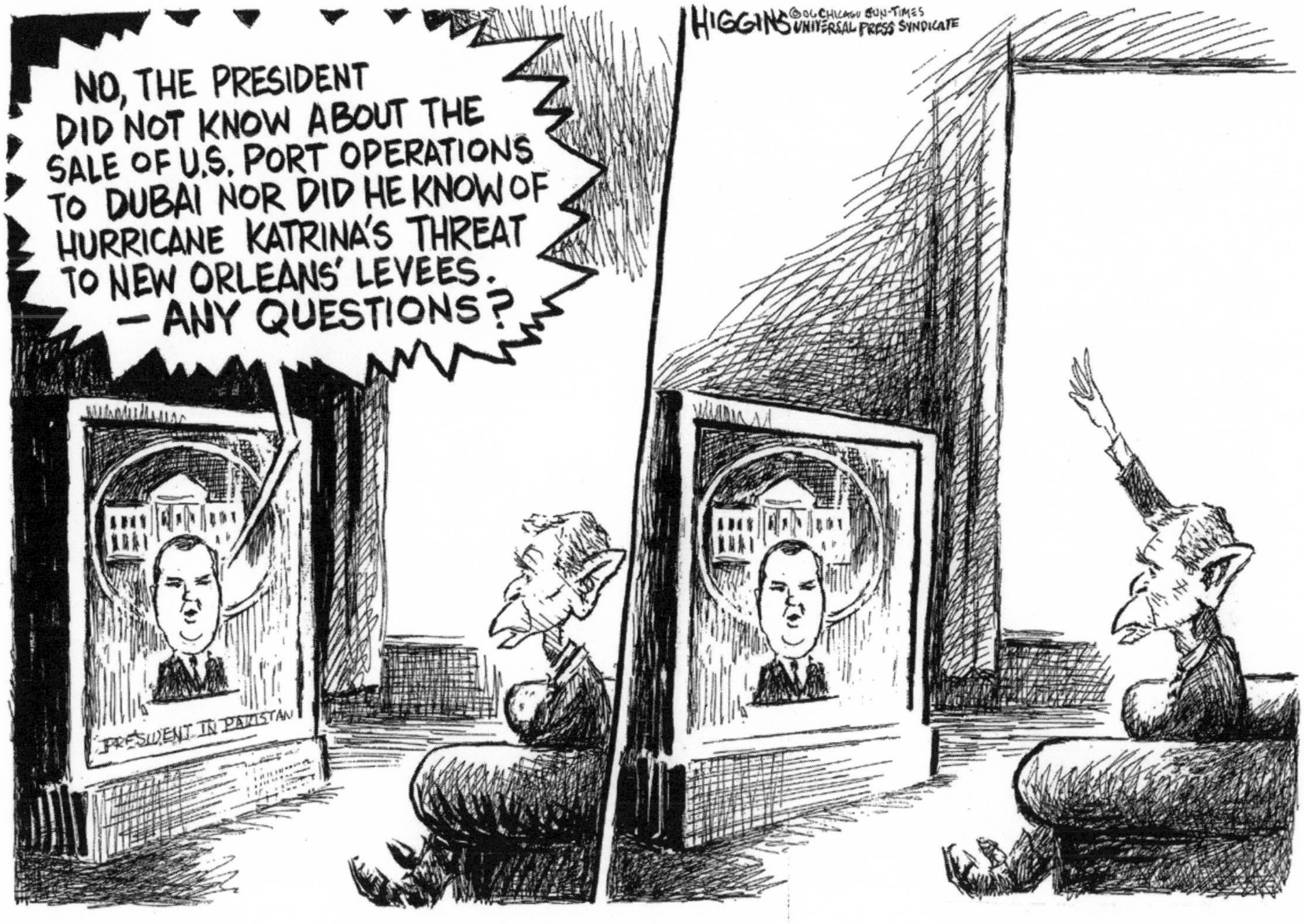
NO, THE PRESIDENT DID NOT KNOW ABOUT THE SALE OF U.S. PORT OPERATIONS TO DUBAI NOR DID HE KNOW OF HURRICANE KATRINA'S THREAT TO NEW ORLEANS' LEVEES. — ANY QUESTIONS?
PRESIDENT IN PAKISTAN
HIGGINS ©06 CHICAGO SUN-TIMES UNIVERSAL PRESS SYNDICATE

ECONOMY & CULTURE

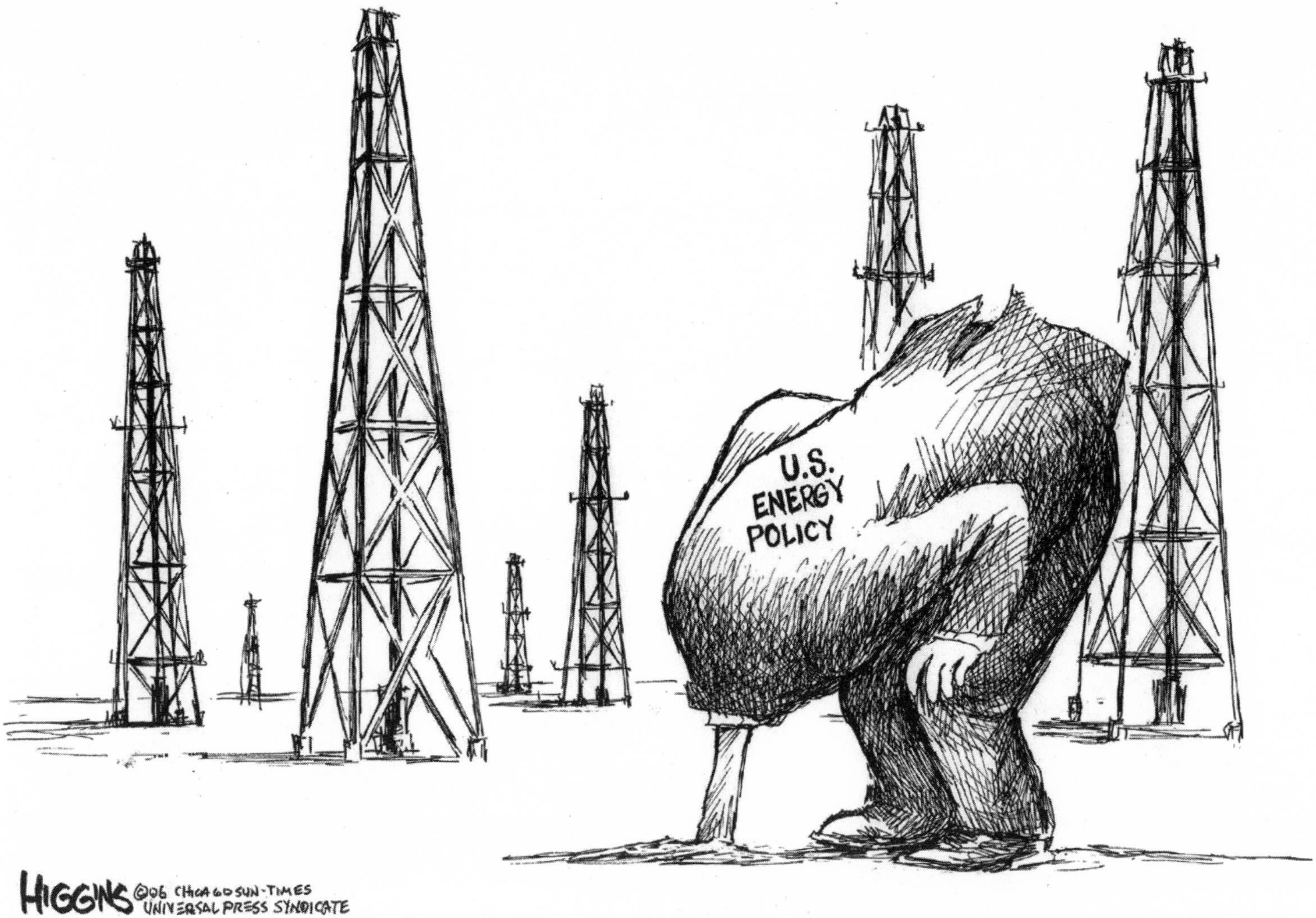
U.S.
ENERGY
POLICY
HIGGINS ©06 CHICAGO SUN-TIMES
UNIVERSAL PRESS SYNDICATE

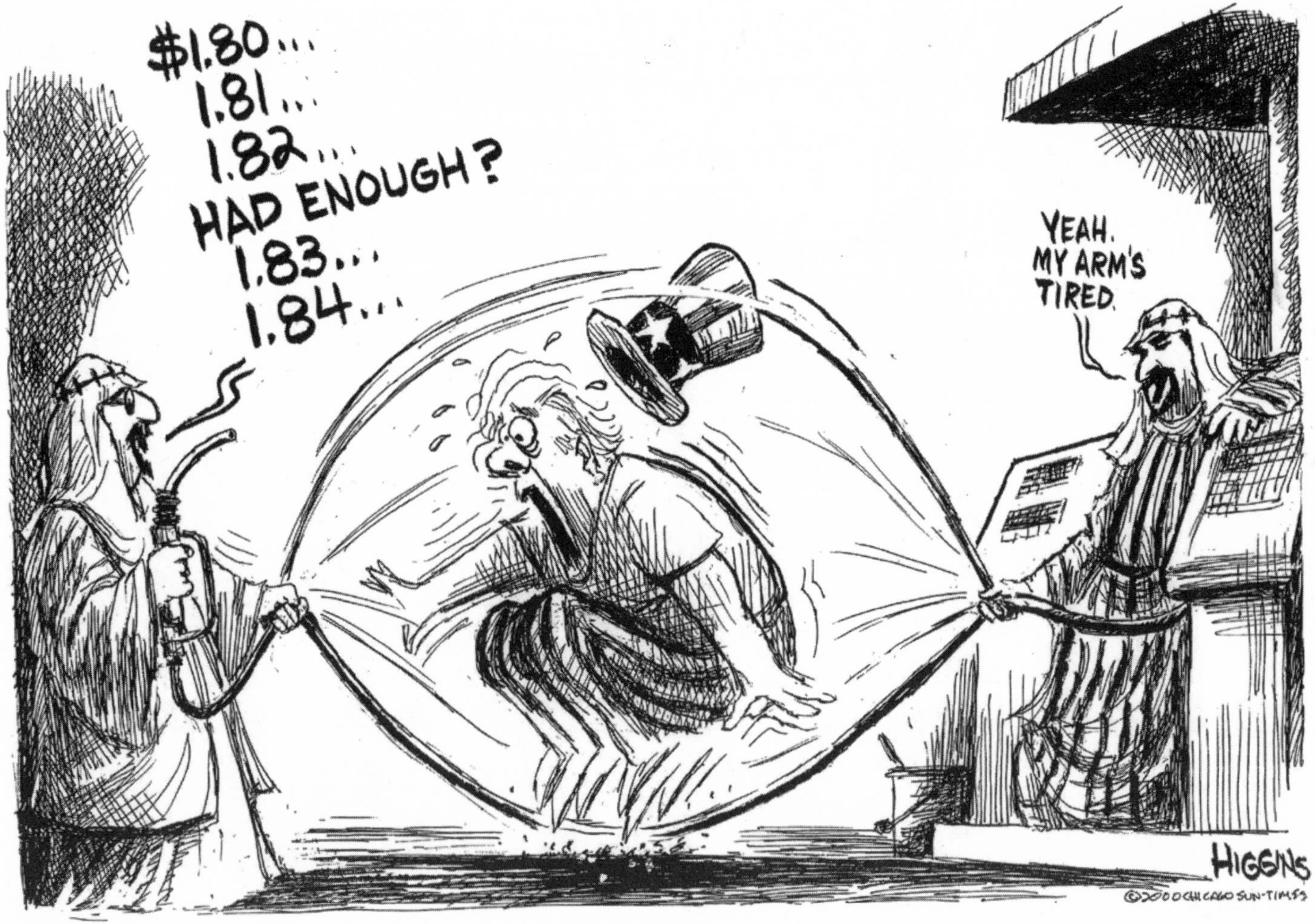
$1.80...
1.81...
1.82...
HAD ENOUGH?
1.83...
1.84...
YEAH. MY ARM'S TIRED.
HIGGINS
©2000 CHICAGO SUN-TIMES

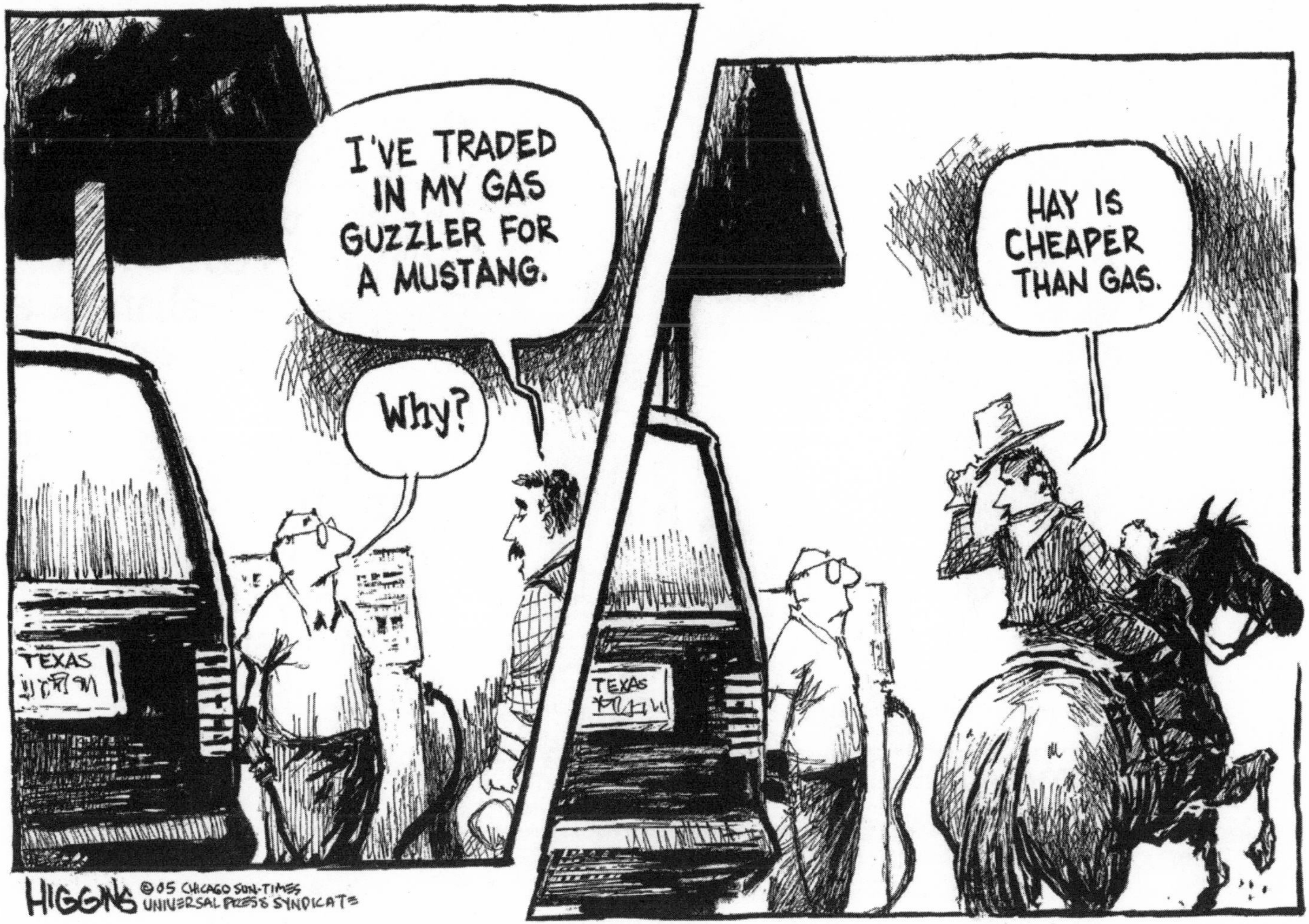
I'VE TRADED IN MY GAS GUZZLER FOR A MUSTANG.
Why?
TEXAS
HAY IS CHEAPER THAN GAS.
TEXAS
HIGGINS ©05 CHICAGO SUN-TIMES UNIVERSAL PRESS SYNDICATE

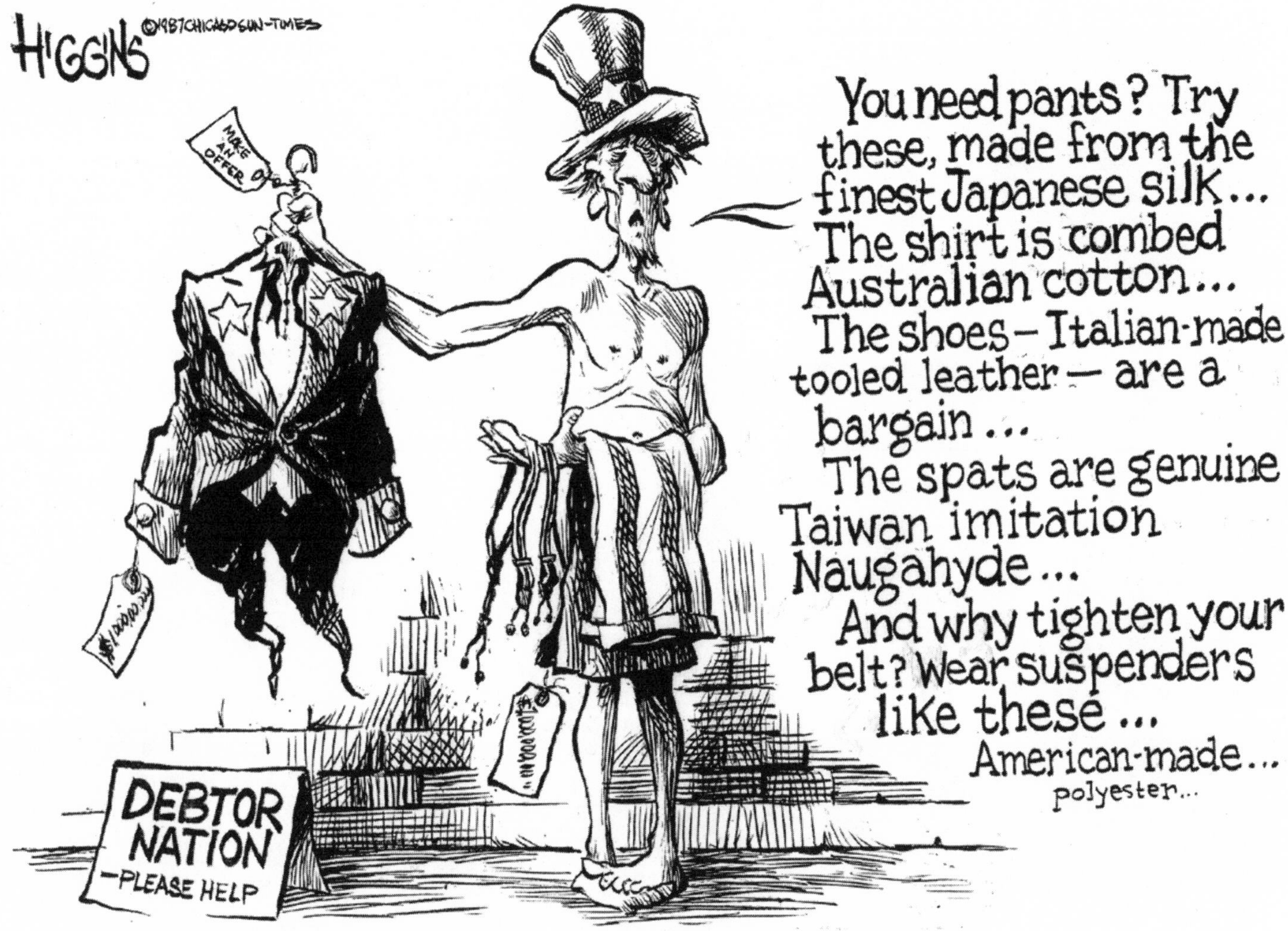
HIGGINS ©1987 CHICAGO SUN-TIMES
MAKE AN OFFER
You need pants? Try these, made from the finest Japanese silk...
The shirt is combed Australian cotton...
The shoes – Italian-made tooled leather – are a bargain...
The spats are genuine Taiwan imitation Naugahyde...
And why tighten your belt? Wear suspenders like these...
American-made...
polyester...
DEBTOR NATION
—PLEASE HELP

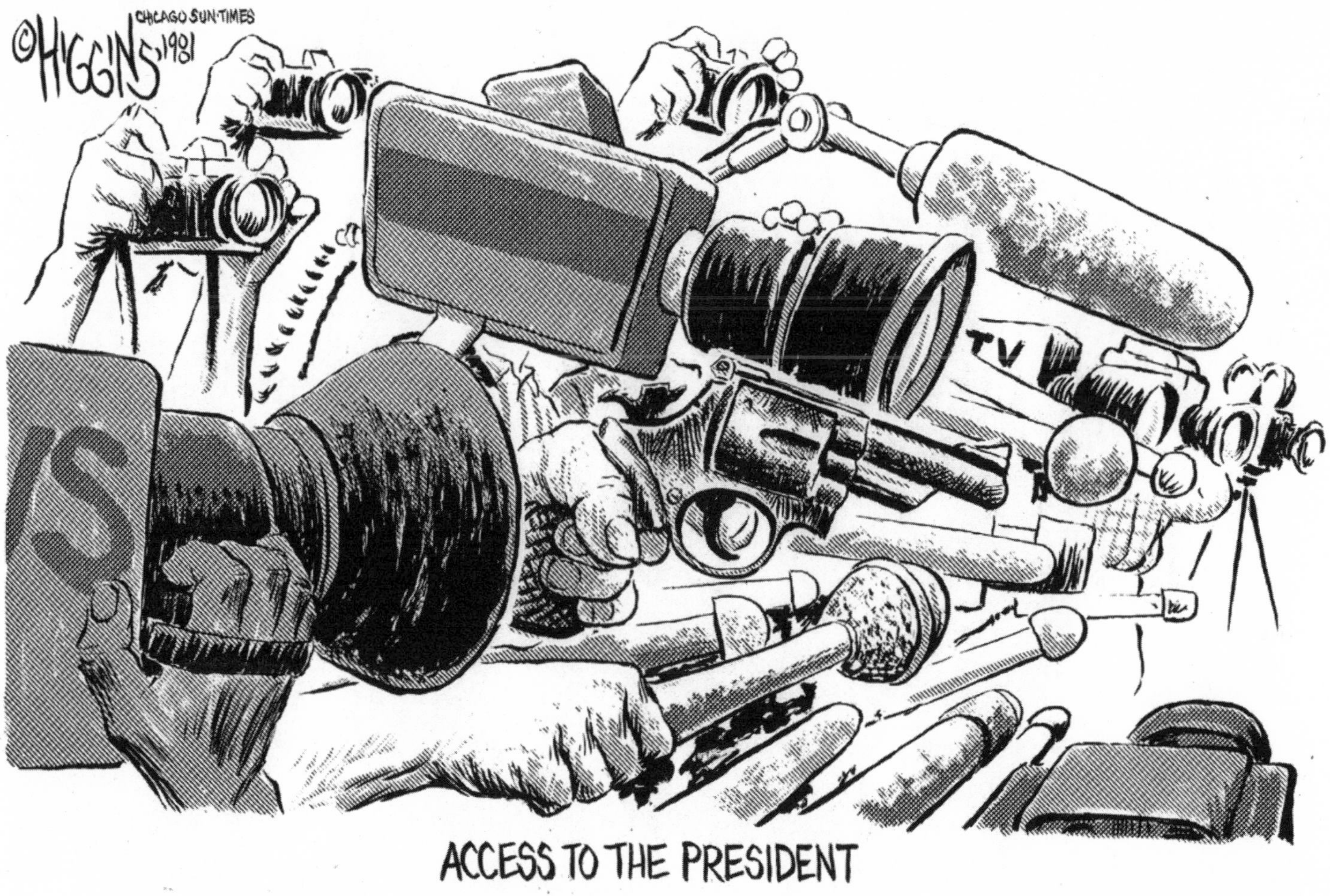
©HIGGINS 1981
CHICAGO SUN-TIMES
TV
ACCESS TO THE PRESIDENT

President Reagan is shot.

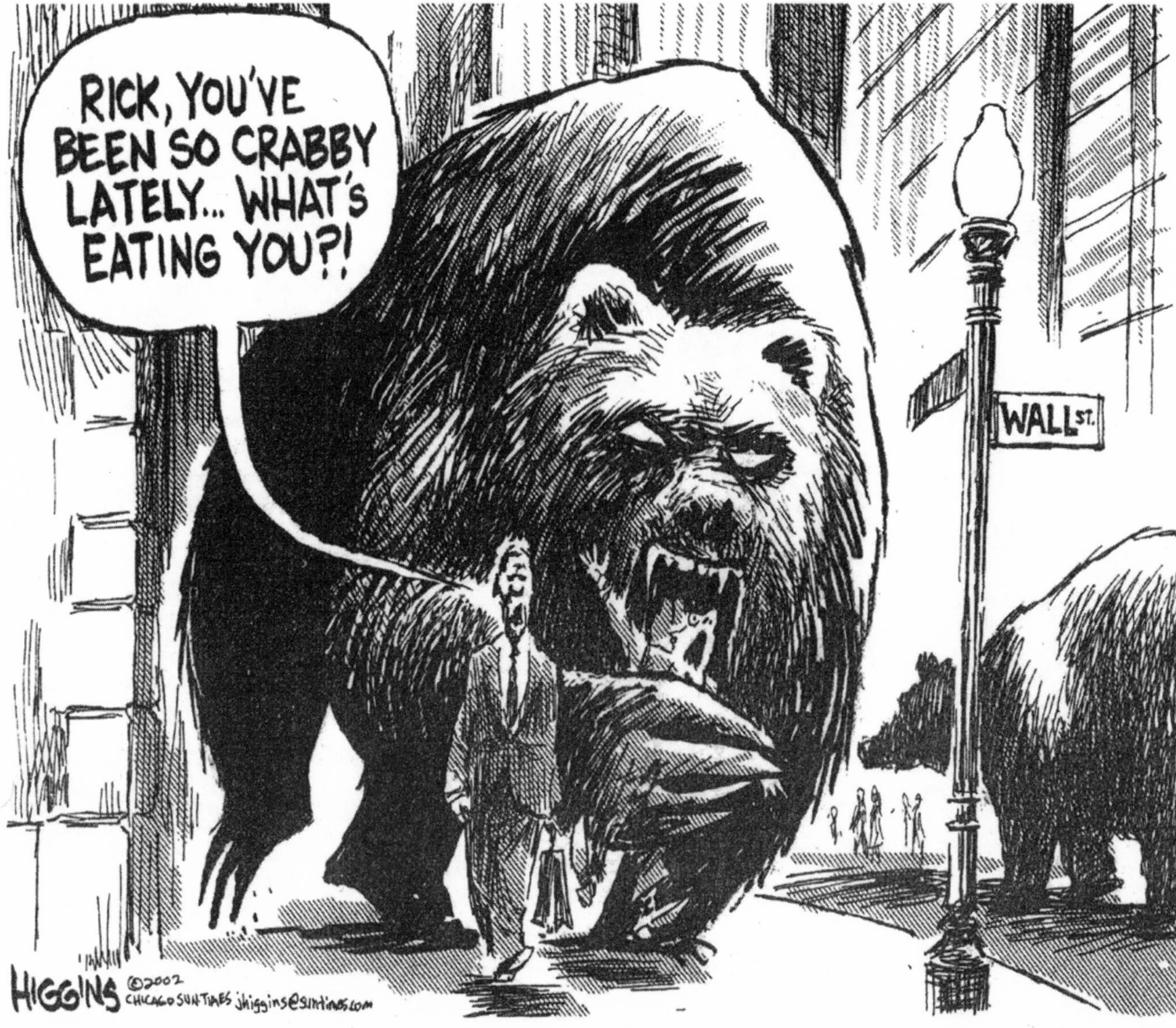
RICK, YOU'VE BEEN SO CRABBY LATELY... WHAT'S EATING YOU?!
WALL ST.
HIGGINS ©2002 CHICAGO SUN-TIMES jhiggins@suntimes.com

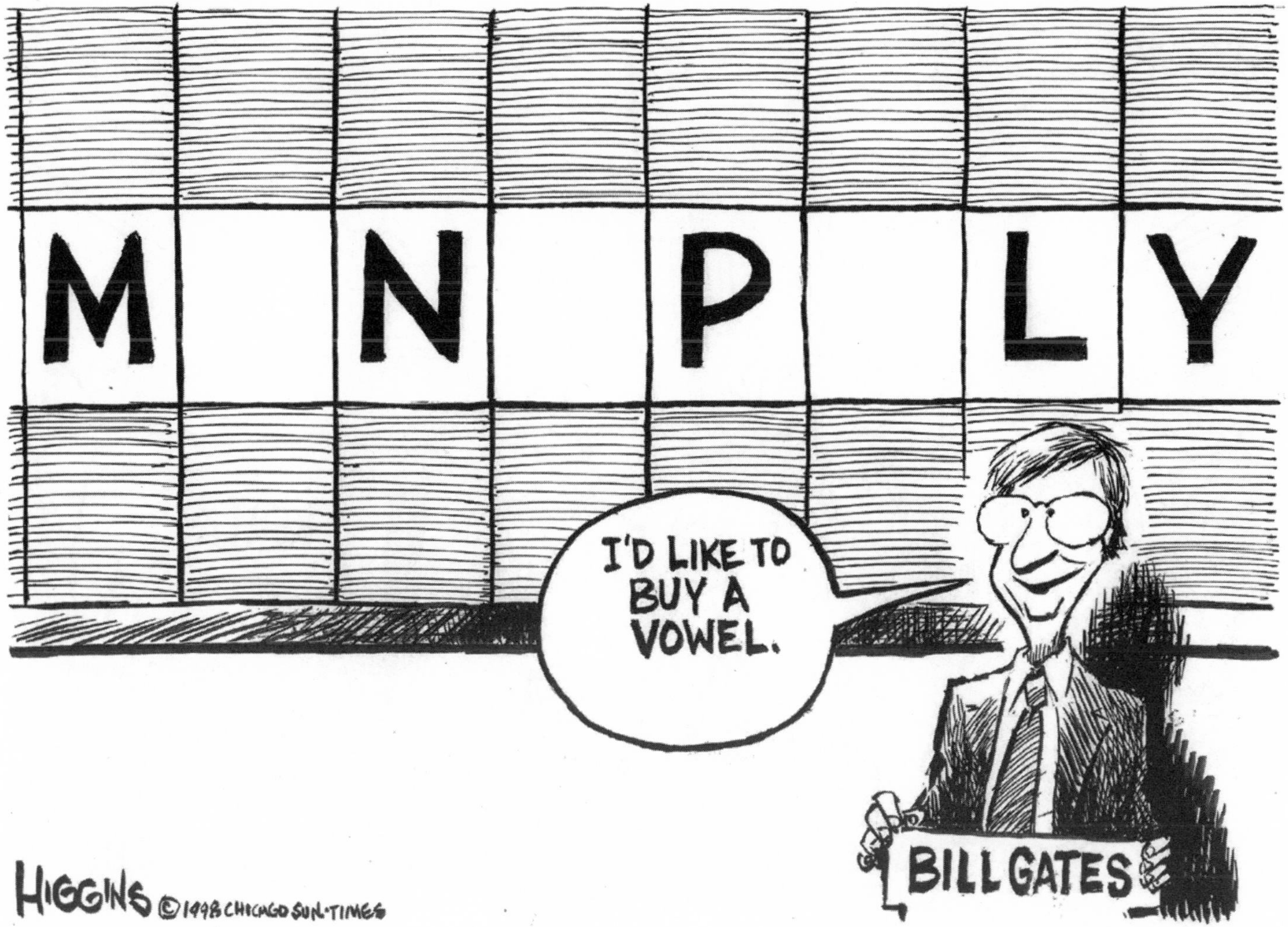
M N P L Y
I'D LIKE TO BUY A VOWEL.
BILL GATES
HIGGINS ©1998 CHICAGO SUN-TIMES

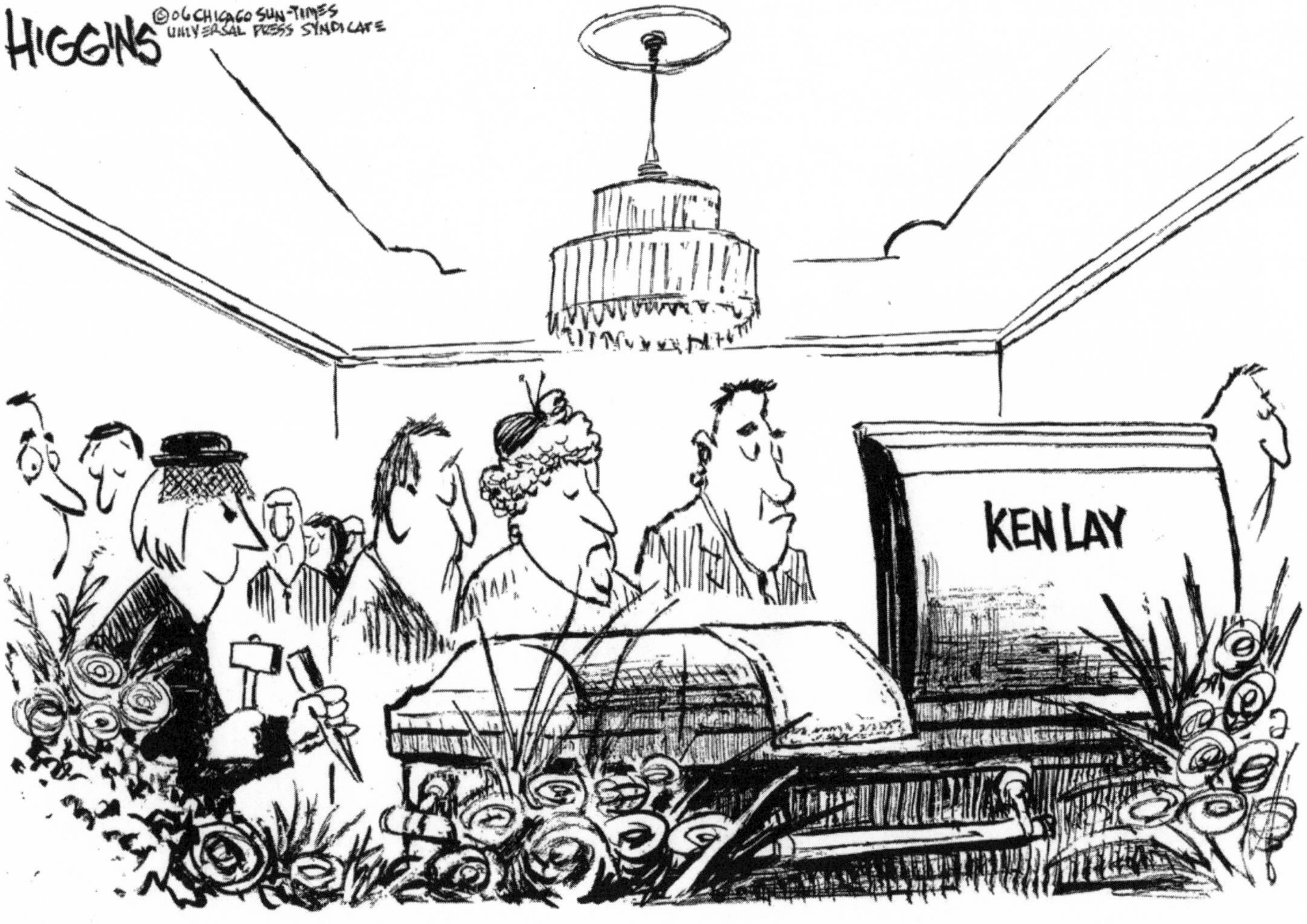
HIGGINS ©06 CHICAGO SUN-TIMES UNIVERSAL PRESS SYNDICATE
KEN LAY

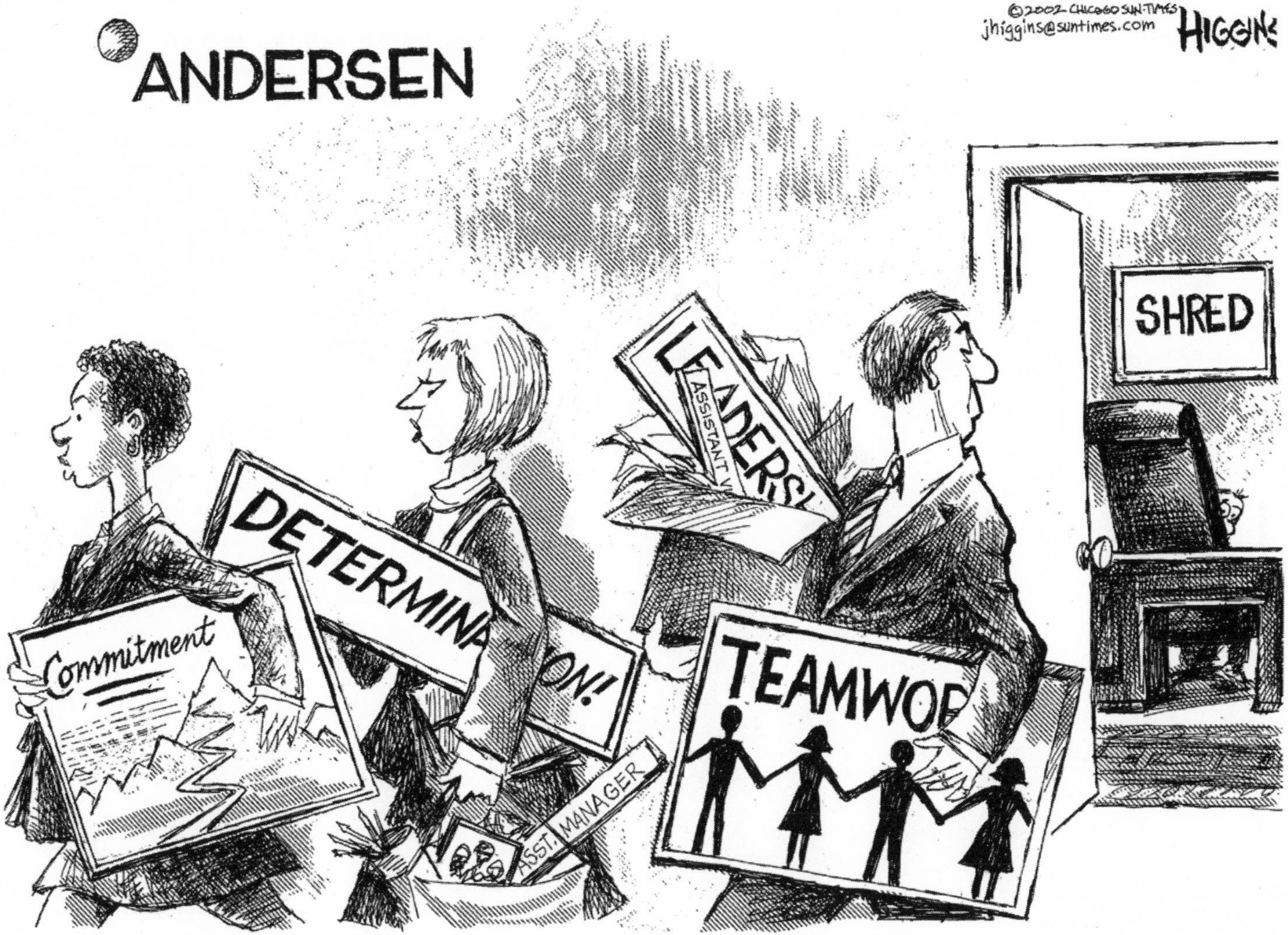
ANDERSEN
©2002 CHICAGO SUN-TIMES
jhiggins@suntimes.com
HIGGINS
SHRED
LEADERS
ASSISTANT V
DETERMINA
ON!
Commitment
TEAMWOR
ASST. MANAGER

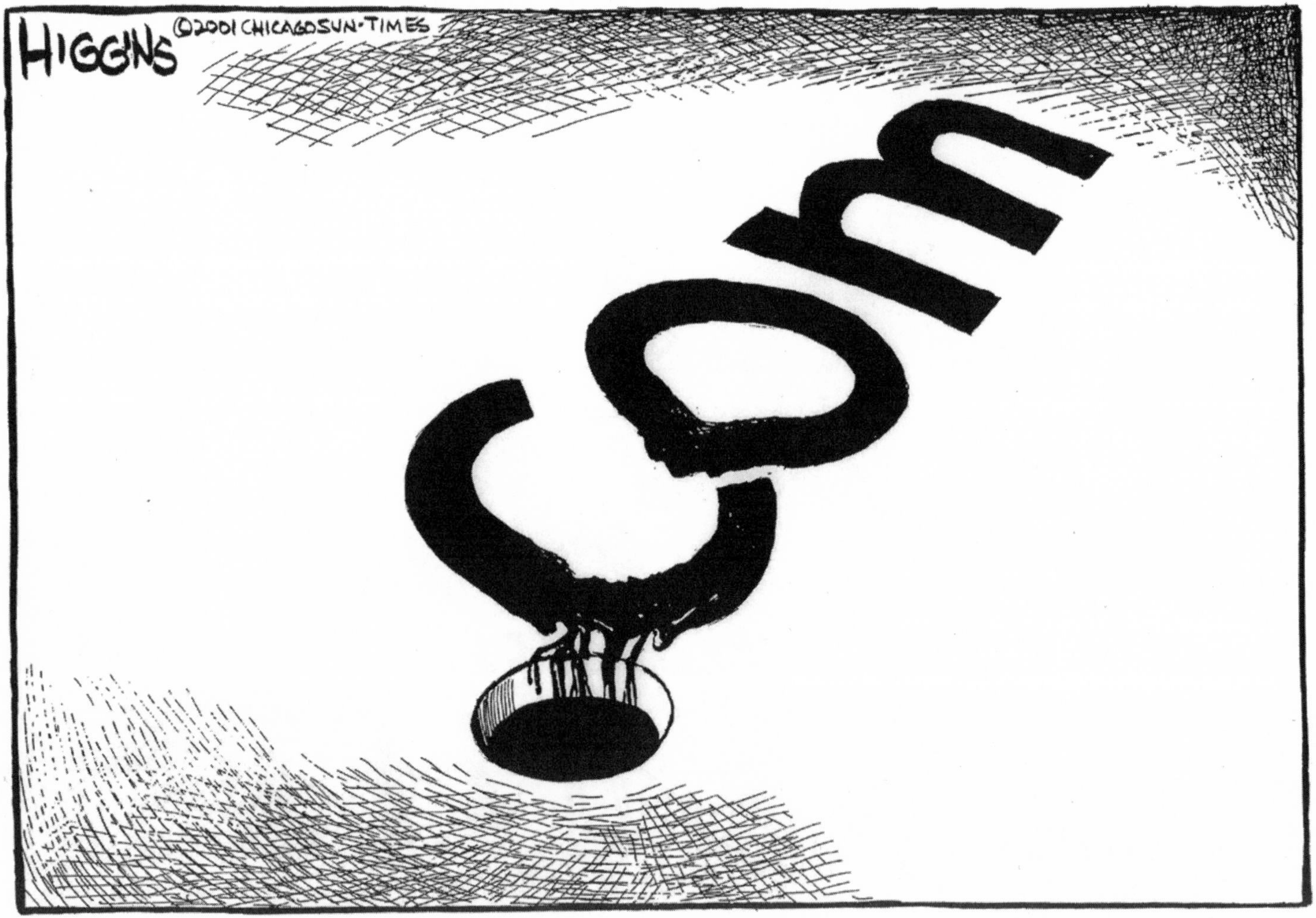
HIGGINS ©2001 CHICAGO SUN-TIMES
com

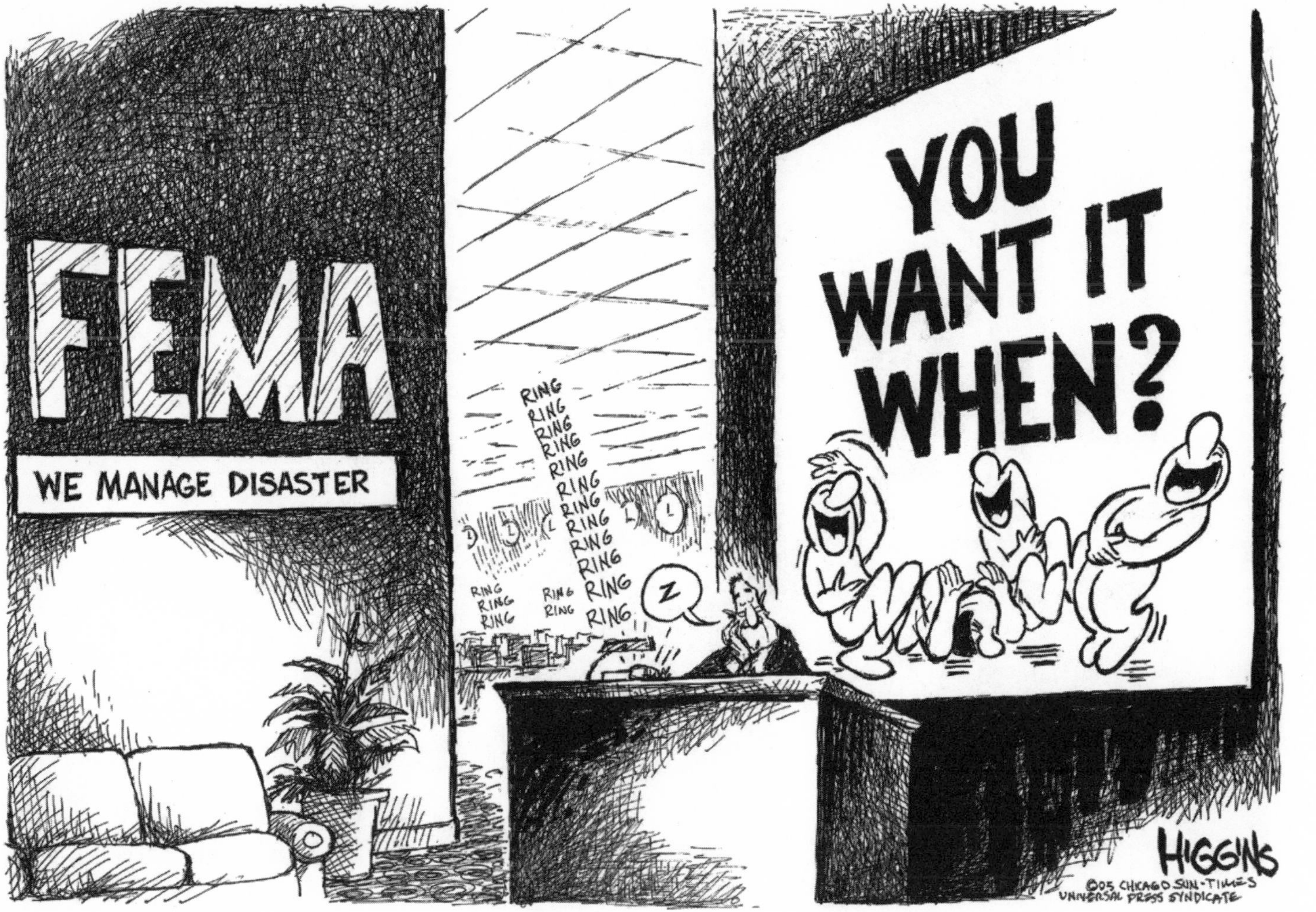
FEMA
WE MANAGE DISASTER
RING RING RING RING RING RING RING RING RING RING RING RING RING RING
RING RING RING
RING RING
Z
YOU WANT IT WHEN?
HIGGINS
©05 CHICAGO SUN-TIMES
UNIVERSAL PRESS SYNDICATE

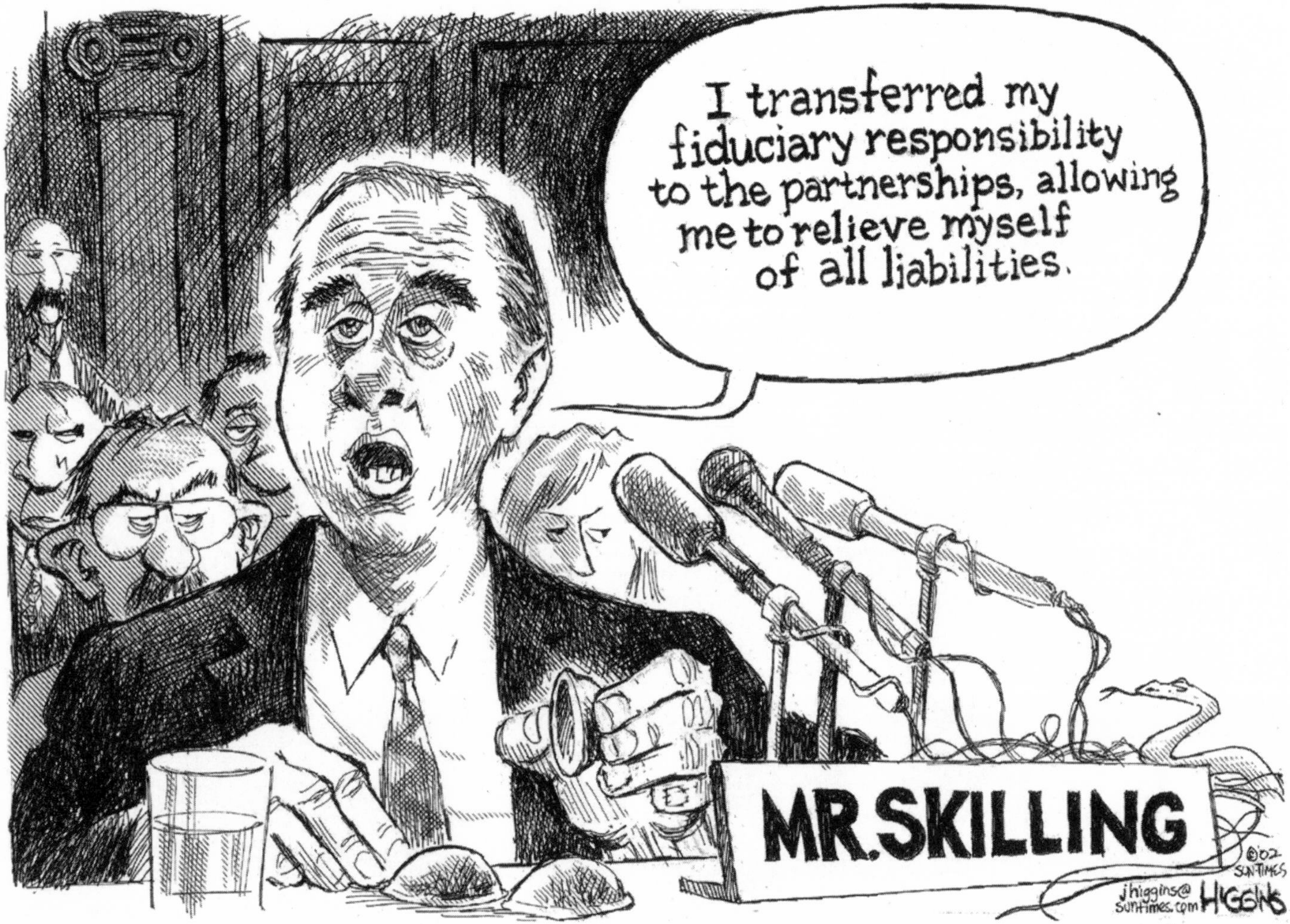
I transferred my fiduciary responsibility to the partnerships, allowing me to relieve myself of all liabilities.
MR. SKILLING
©'02 SUN-TIMES
jhiggins@suntimes.com
HIGGINS

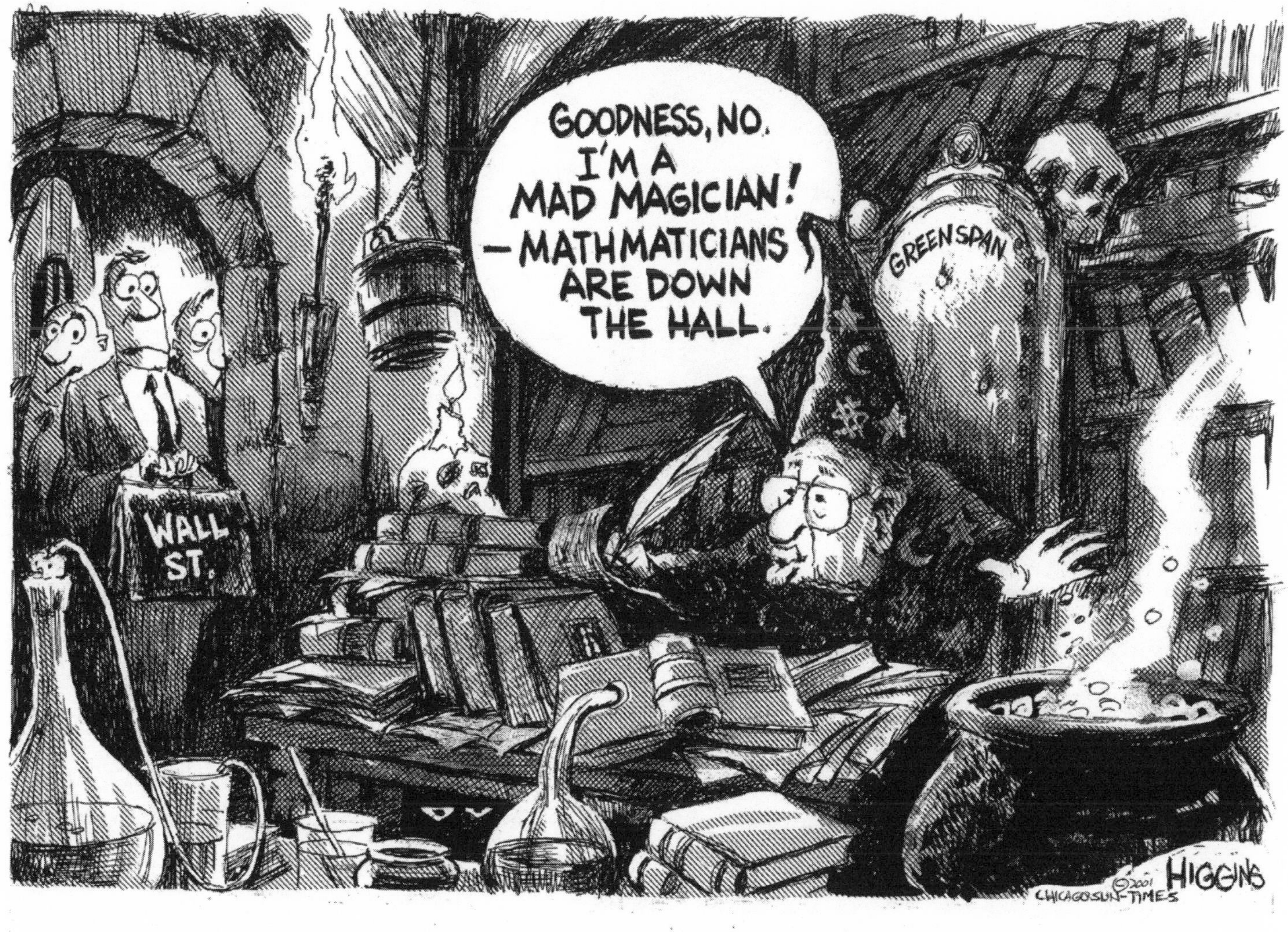

GOODNESS, NO. I'M A MAD MAGICIAN! —MATHMATICIANS ARE DOWN THE HALL.
GREENSPAN
WALL ST.
HIGGINS
©2001 CHICAGO SUN-TIMES

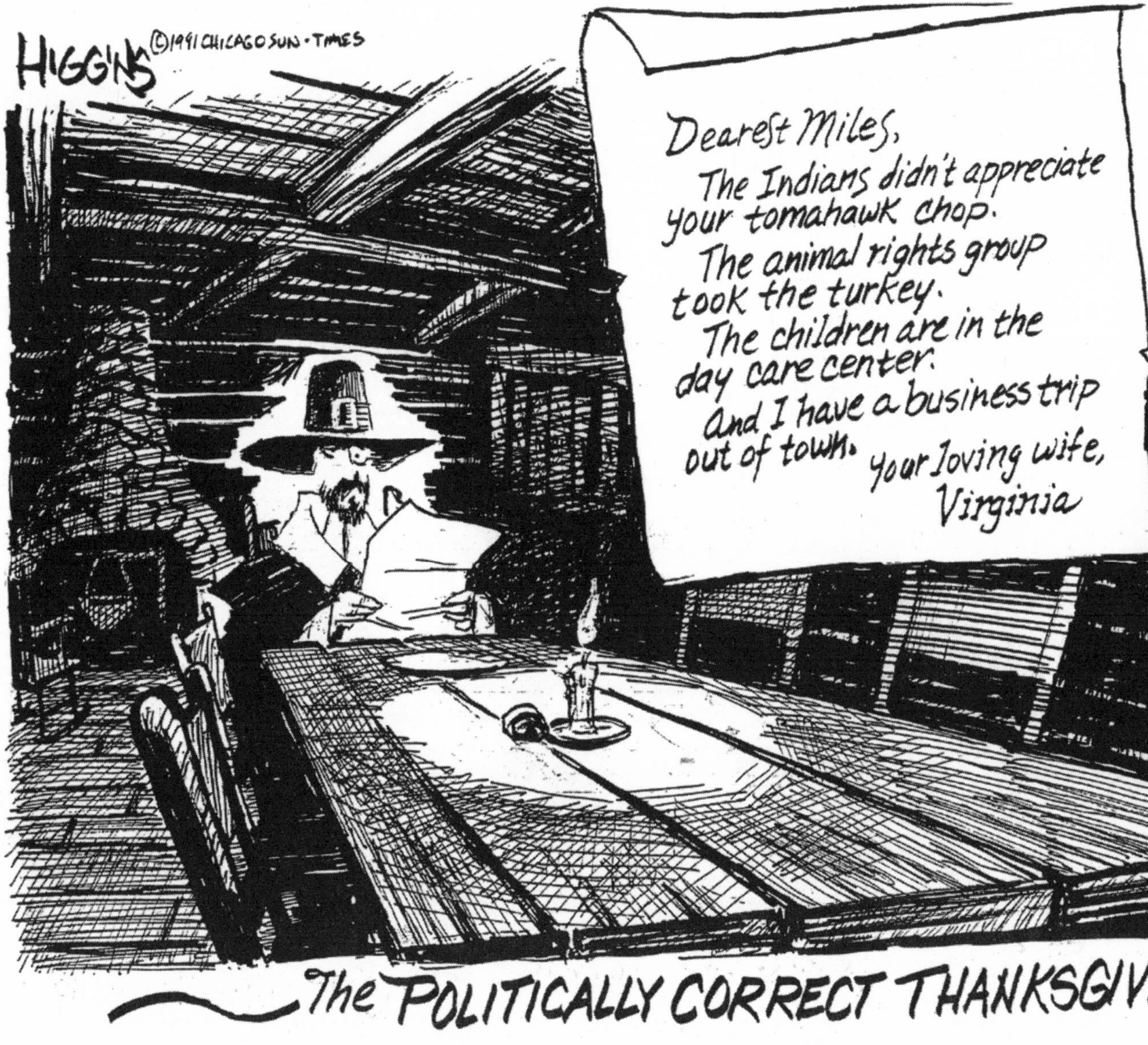
HIGGINS ©1991 CHICAGO SUN-TIMES
Dearest Miles,
The Indians didn't appreciate your tomahawk chop.
The animal rights group took the turkey.
The children are in the day care center.
And I have a business trip out of town.
Your loving wife,
Virginia
The POLITICALLY CORRECT THANKSGIVING

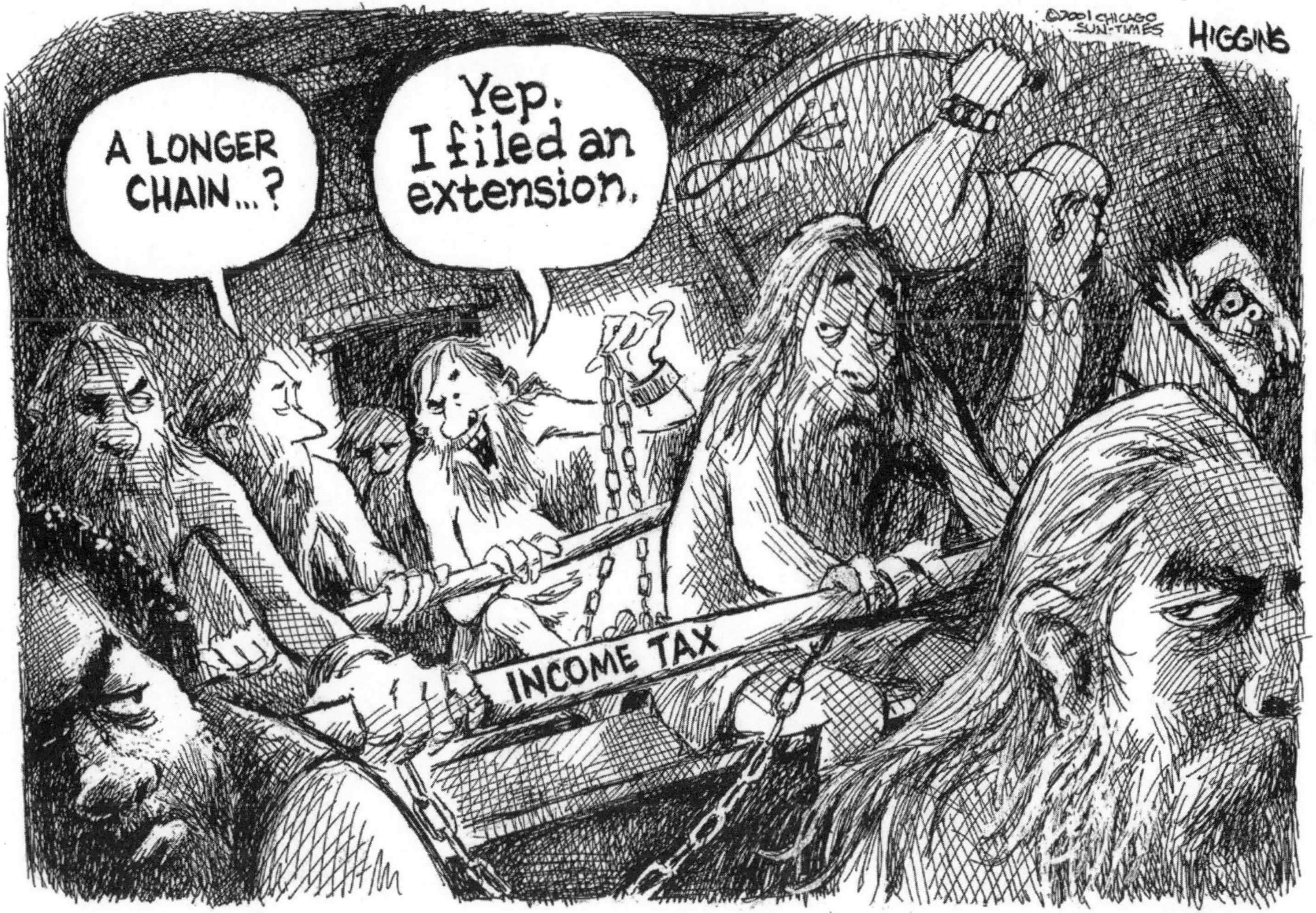

A LONGER CHAIN...?
Yep. I filed an extension.
INCOME TAX
©2001 CHICAGO SUN-TIMES
HIGGINS

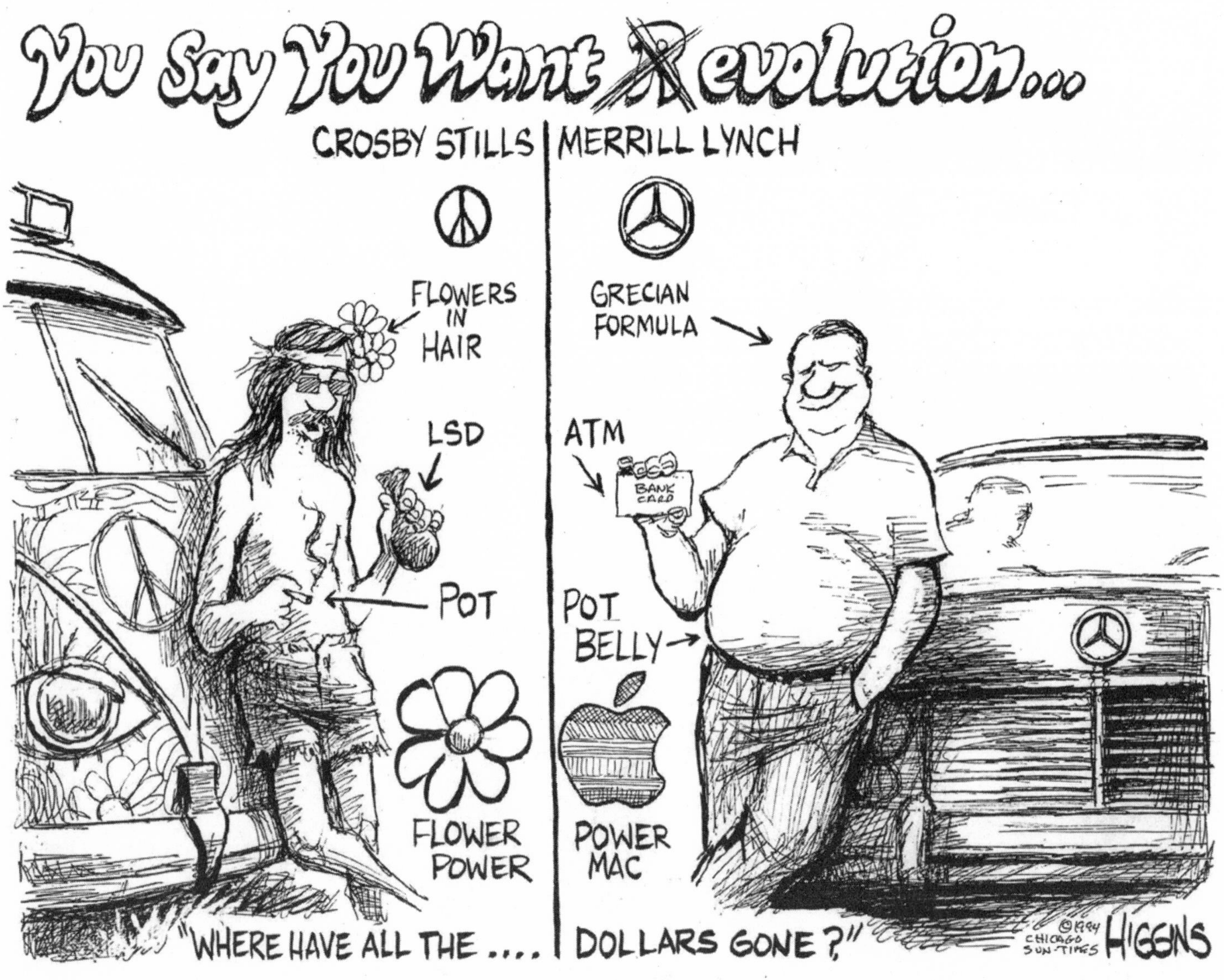

You Say You Want Revolution...
CROSBY STILLS
MERRILL LYNCH
FLOWERS IN HAIR
GRECIAN FORMULA
LSD
ATM
BANK CARD
POT
POT BELLY
FLOWER POWER
POWER MAC
"WHERE HAVE ALL THE ....
DOLLARS GONE?"
©1994 CHICAGO SUN-TIMES
HIGGINS

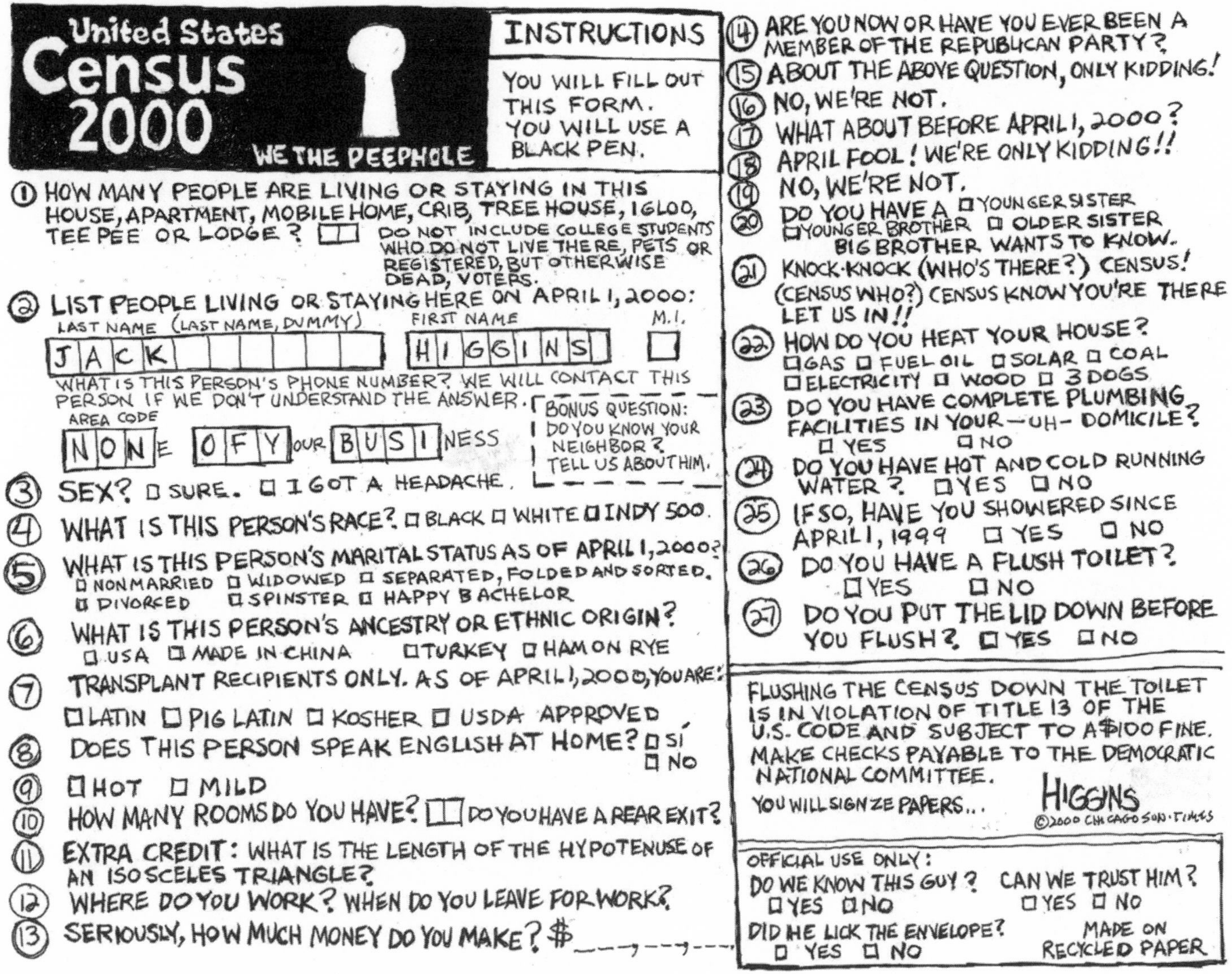

United States Census 2000
WE THE PEEPHOLE
INSTRUCTIONS
YOU WILL FILL OUT THIS FORM. YOU WILL USE A BLACK PEN.
① HOW MANY PEOPLE ARE LIVING OR STAYING IN THIS HOUSE, APARTMENT, MOBILE HOME, CRIB, TREE HOUSE, IGLOO, TEE PEE OR LODGE?
DO NOT INCLUDE COLLEGE STUDENTS WHO DO NOT LIVE THERE, PETS OR REGISTERED, BUT OTHERWISE DEAD, VOTERS.
② LIST PEOPLE LIVING OR STAYING HERE ON APRIL 1, 2000:
LAST NAME (LAST NAME, DUMMY) FIRST NAME M.I.
JACK HIGGINS
WHAT IS THIS PERSON'S PHONE NUMBER? WE WILL CONTACT THIS PERSON IF WE DON'T UNDERSTAND THE ANSWER.
AREA CODE
NONE OFYOUR BUSINESS
BONUS QUESTION: DO YOU KNOW YOUR NEIGHBOR? TELL US ABOUT HIM.
③ SEX? SURE. I GOT A HEADACHE.
④ WHAT IS THIS PERSON'S RACE? BLACK WHITE INDY 500.
⑤ WHAT IS THIS PERSON'S MARITAL STATUS AS OF APRIL 1, 2000?
NONMARRIED WIDOWED SEPARATED, FOLDED AND SORTED. DIVORCED SPINSTER HAPPY BACHELOR
⑥ WHAT IS THIS PERSON'S ANCESTRY OR ETHNIC ORIGIN?
USA MADE IN CHINA TURKEY HAM ON RYE
⑦ TRANSPLANT RECIPIENTS ONLY. AS OF APRIL 1, 2000, YOU ARE:
LATIN PIG LATIN KOSHER USDA APPROVED
⑧ DOES THIS PERSON SPEAK ENGLISH AT HOME? SÍ NO
⑨ HOT MILD
⑩ HOW MANY ROOMS DO YOU HAVE? DO YOU HAVE A REAR EXIT?
⑪ EXTRA CREDIT: WHAT IS THE LENGTH OF THE HYPOTENUSE OF AN ISOSCELES TRIANGLE?
⑫ WHERE DO YOU WORK? WHEN DO YOU LEAVE FOR WORK?
⑬ SERIOUSLY, HOW MUCH MONEY DO YOU MAKE? $___,___,___
⑭ ARE YOU NOW OR HAVE YOU EVER BEEN A MEMBER OF THE REPUBLICAN PARTY?
⑮ ABOUT THE ABOVE QUESTION, ONLY KIDDING!
⑯ NO, WE'RE NOT.
⑰ WHAT ABOUT BEFORE APRIL 1, 2000?
⑱ APRIL FOOL! WE'RE ONLY KIDDING!!
⑲ NO, WE'RE NOT.
⑳ DO YOU HAVE A YOUNGER SISTER YOUNGER BROTHER OLDER SISTER
BIG BROTHER WANTS TO KNOW.
㉑ KNOCK-KNOCK (WHO'S THERE?) CENSUS! (CENSUS WHO?) CENSUS KNOW YOU'RE THERE LET US IN!!
㉒ HOW DO YOU HEAT YOUR HOUSE? GAS FUEL OIL SOLAR COAL ELECTRICITY WOOD 3 DOGS
㉓ DO YOU HAVE COMPLETE PLUMBING FACILITIES IN YOUR—UH—DOMICILE? YES NO
㉔ DO YOU HAVE HOT AND COLD RUNNING WATER? YES NO
㉕ IF SO, HAVE YOU SHOWERED SINCE APRIL 1, 1999 YES NO
㉖ DO YOU HAVE A FLUSH TOILET? YES NO
㉗ DO YOU PUT THE LID DOWN BEFORE YOU FLUSH? YES NO
FLUSHING THE CENSUS DOWN THE TOILET IS IN VIOLATION OF TITLE 13 OF THE U.S. CODE AND SUBJECT TO A $100 FINE. MAKE CHECKS PAYABLE TO THE DEMOCRATIC NATIONAL COMMITTEE.
YOU WILL SIGN ZE PAPERS...
HIGGINS
©2000 CHICAGO SUN-TIMES
OFFICIAL USE ONLY:
DO WE KNOW THIS GUY? YES NO
CAN WE TRUST HIM? YES NO
DID HE LICK THE ENVELOPE? YES NO
MADE ON RECYCLED PAPER

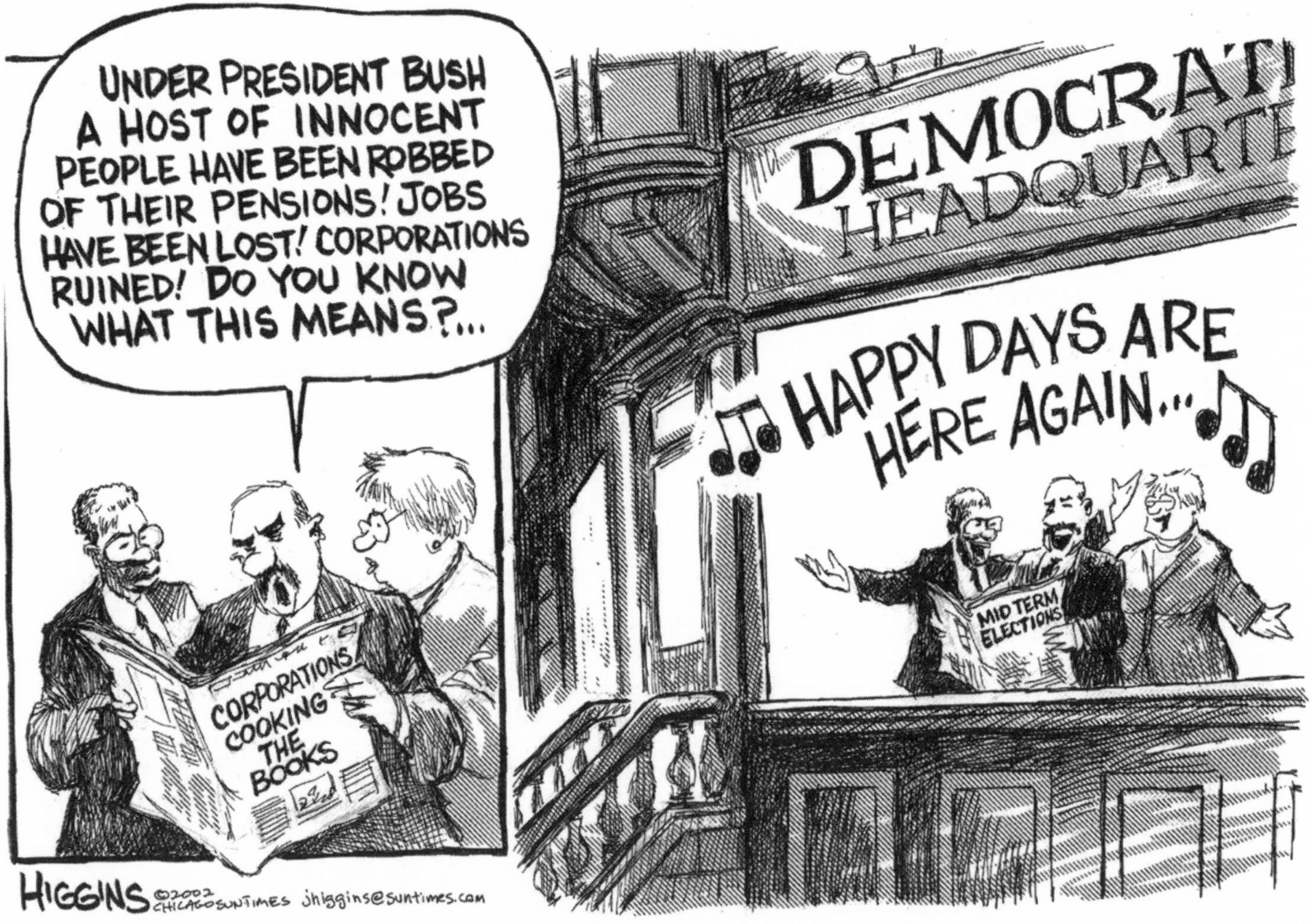

UNDER PRESIDENT BUSH A HOST OF INNOCENT PEOPLE HAVE BEEN ROBBED OF THEIR PENSIONS! JOBS HAVE BEEN LOST! CORPORATIONS RUINED! DO YOU KNOW WHAT THIS MEANS?...
CORPORATIONS COOKING THE BOOKS
DEMOCRAT
HEADQUARTE
HAPPY DAYS ARE HERE AGAIN...
MID TERM ELECTIONS
HIGGINS ©2002 CHICAGO SUNTIMES jhiggins@suntimes.com

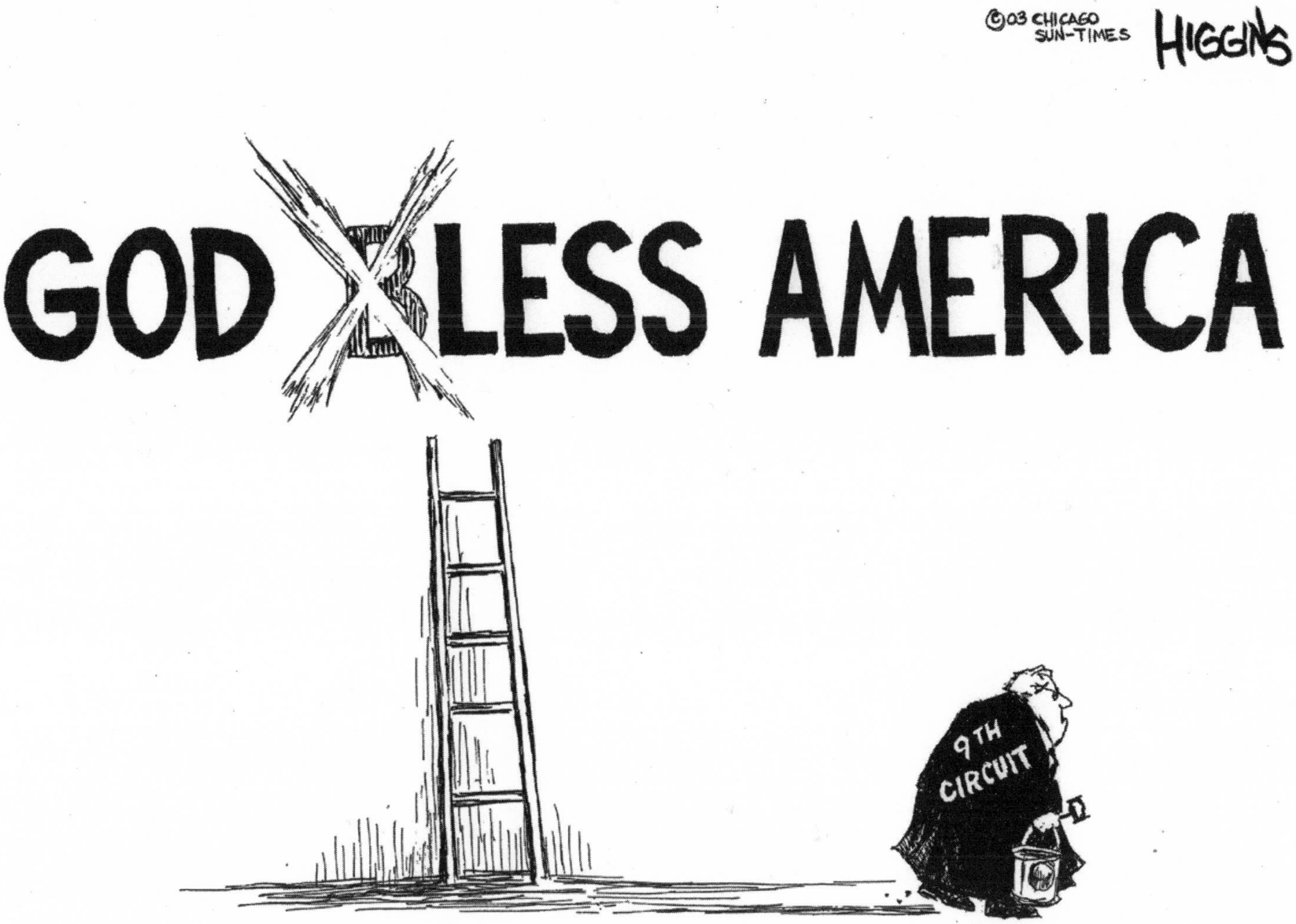
©03 CHICAGO SUN-TIMES
HIGGINS
GOD BLESS AMERICA
9TH CIRCUIT

ENVIRONMENT & HEALTH

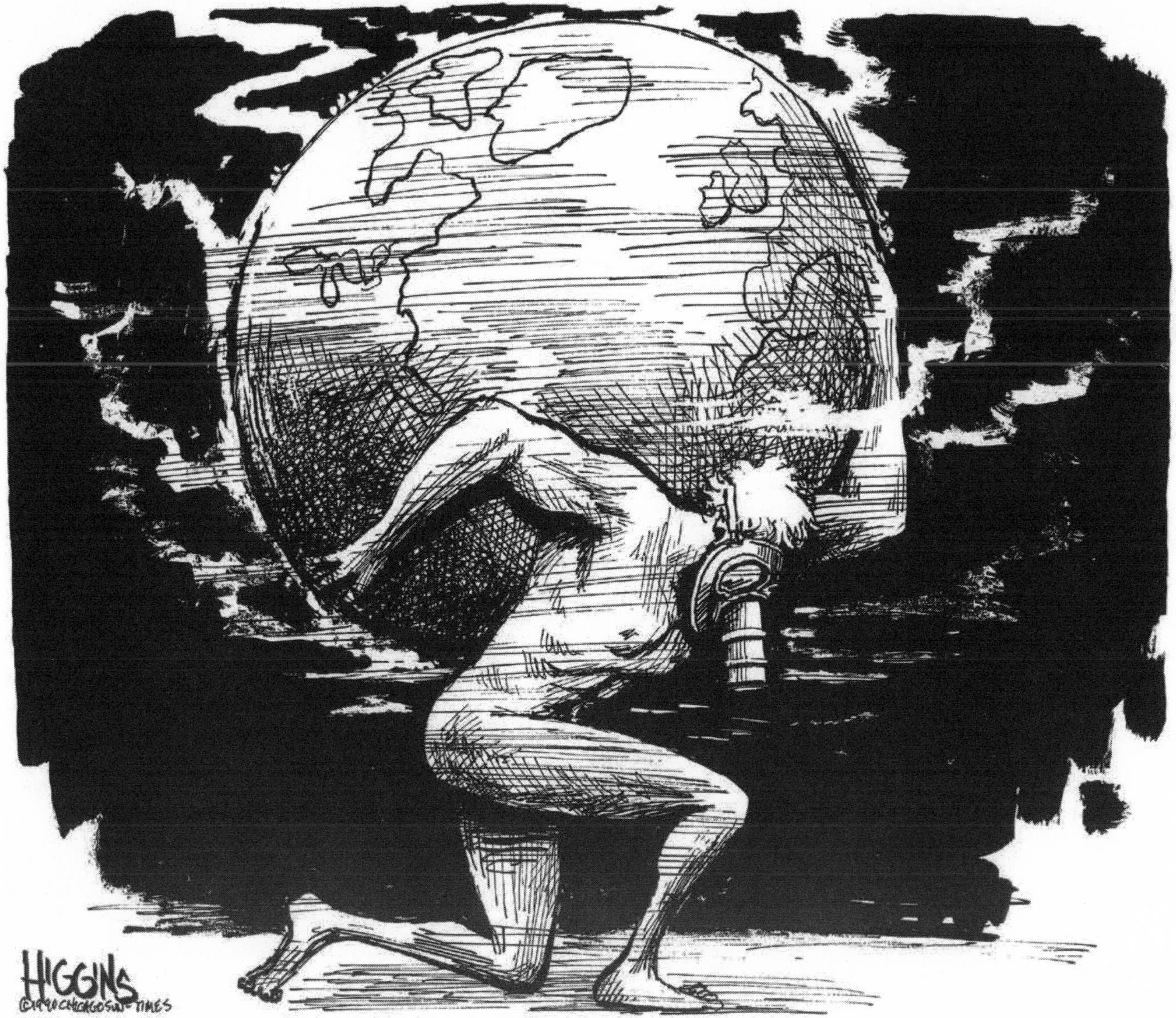
HIGGINS
©1990 CHICAGO SUN-TIMES

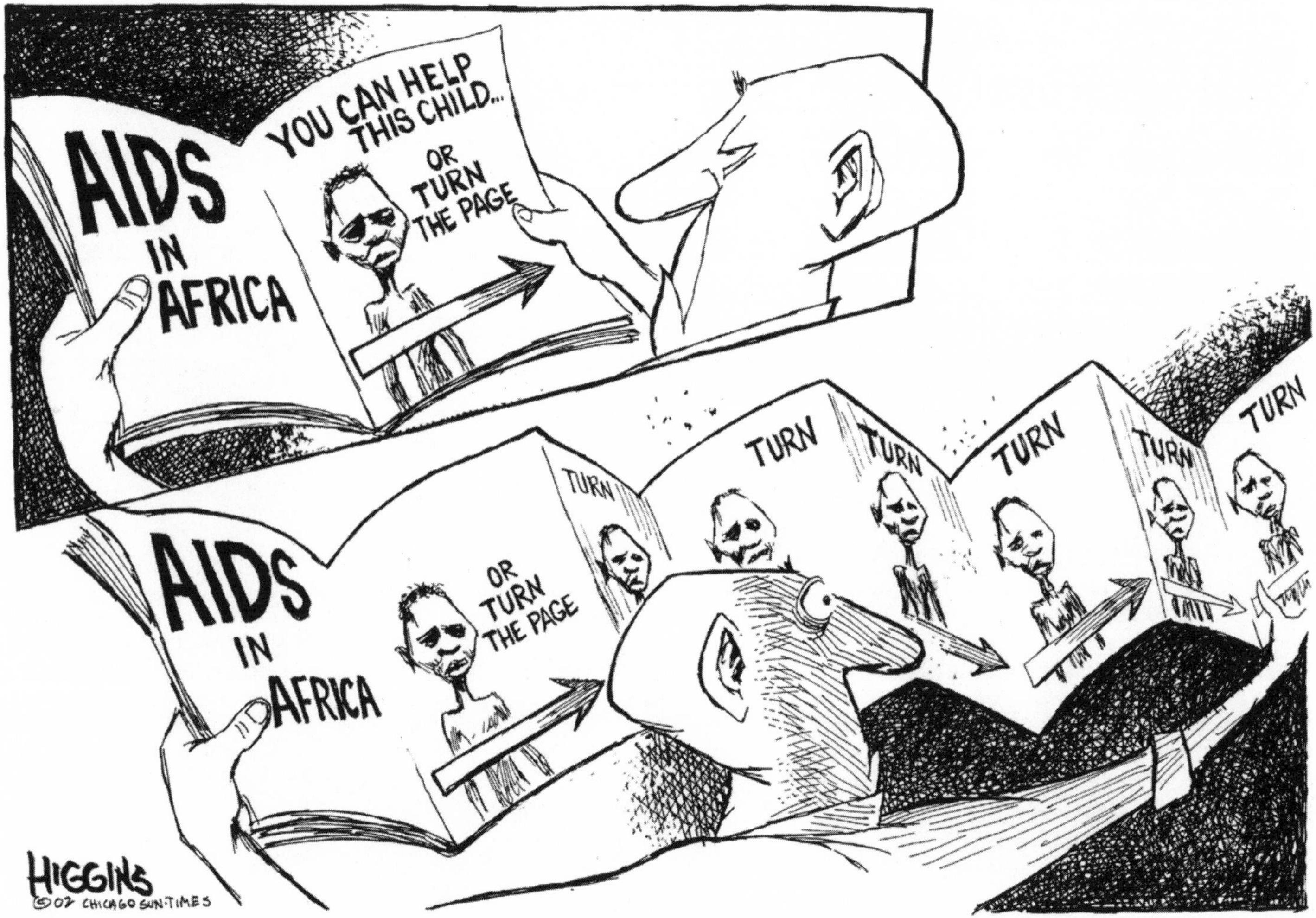
AIDS
IN
AFRICA
YOU CAN HELP
THIS CHILD...
OR
TURN
THE PAGE
AIDS
IN
AFRICA
OR
TURN
THE PAGE
TURN
TURN
TURN
TURN
TURN
TURN
HIGGINS
©07 CHICAGO SUN-TIMES

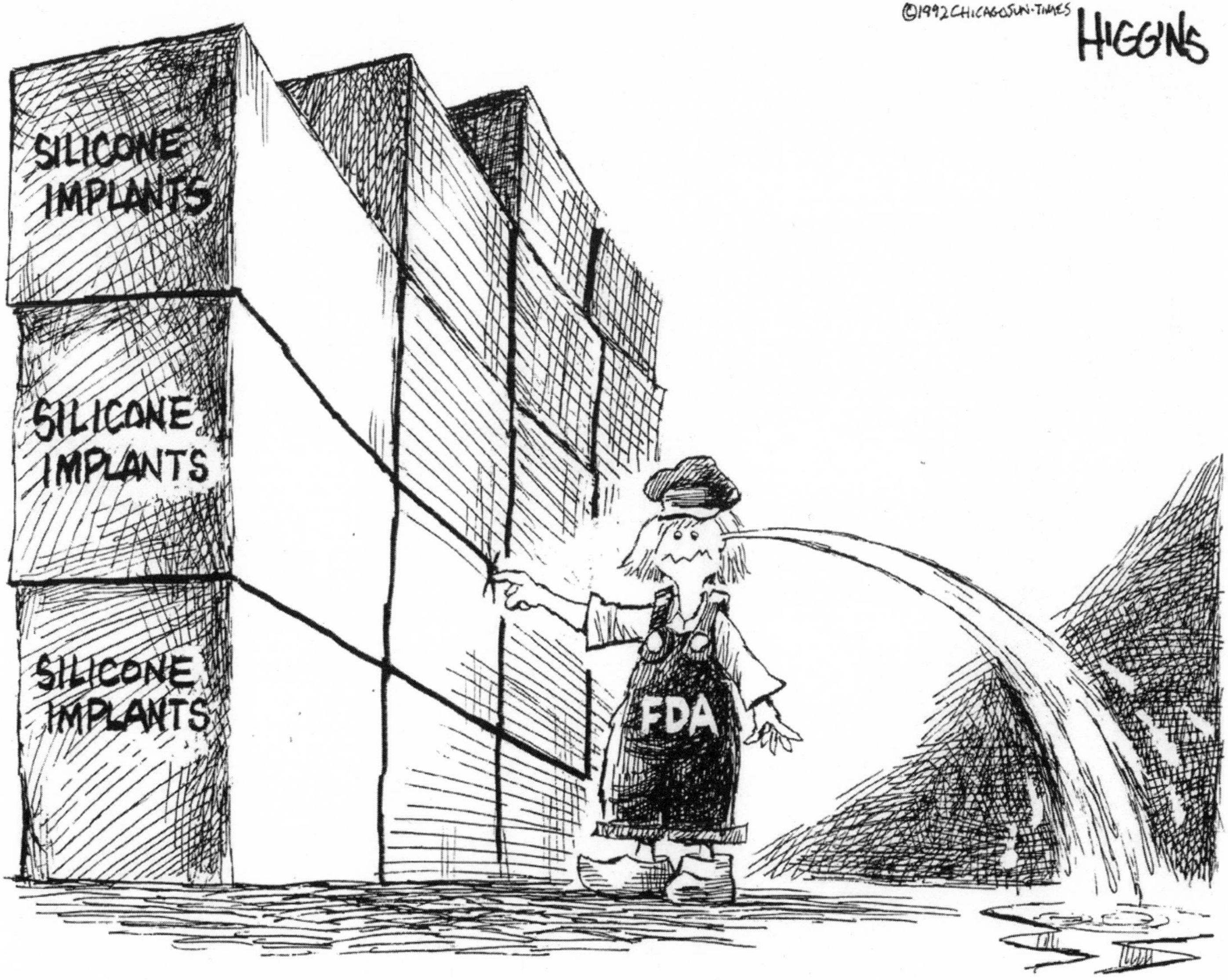
©1992 CHICAGO SUN-TIMES
HIGGINS
SILICONE IMPLANTS
SILICONE IMPLANTS
SILICONE IMPLANTS
FDA

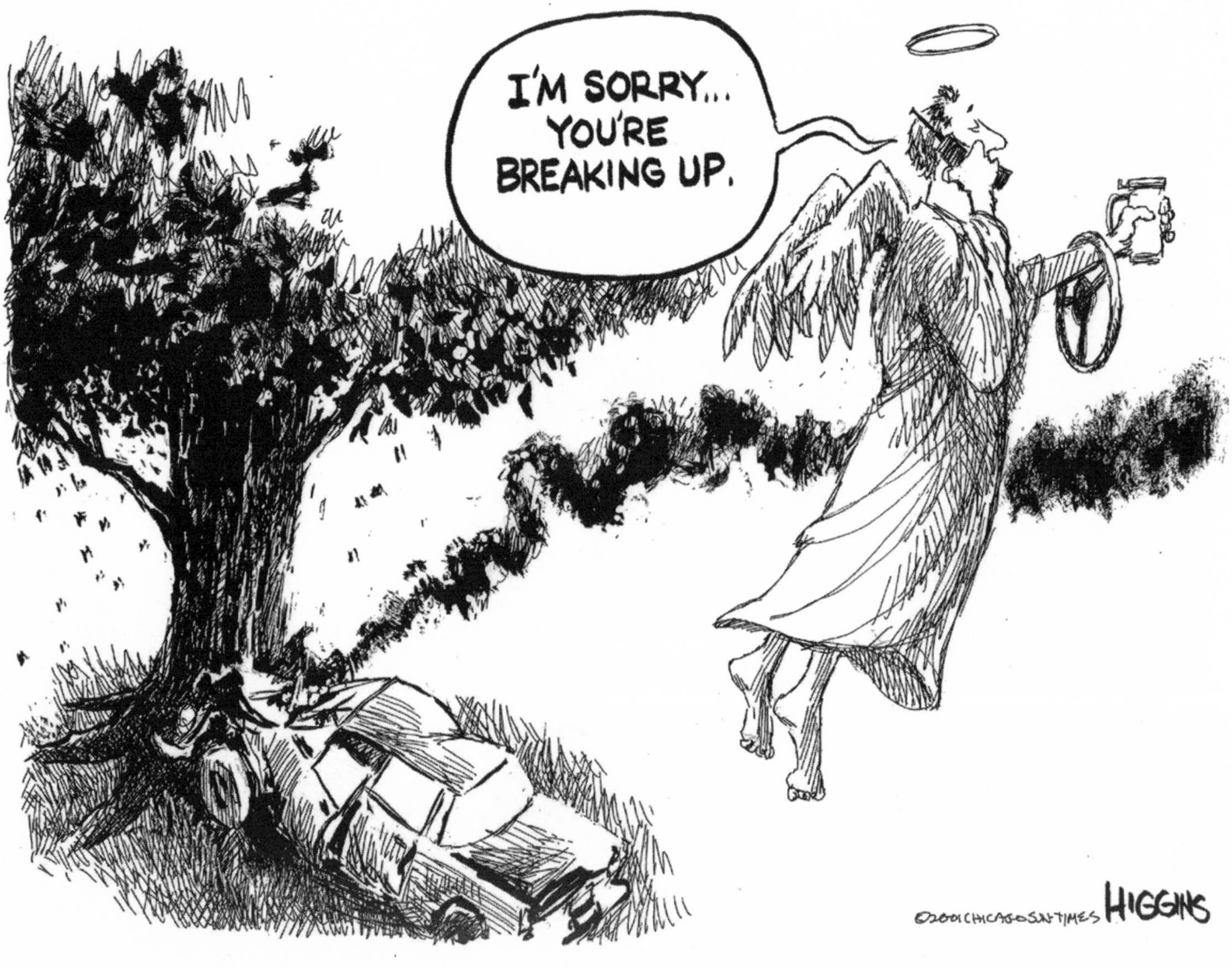
I'M SORRY...
YOU'RE
BREAKING UP.
©2001 CHICAGO SUN-TIMES HIGGINS

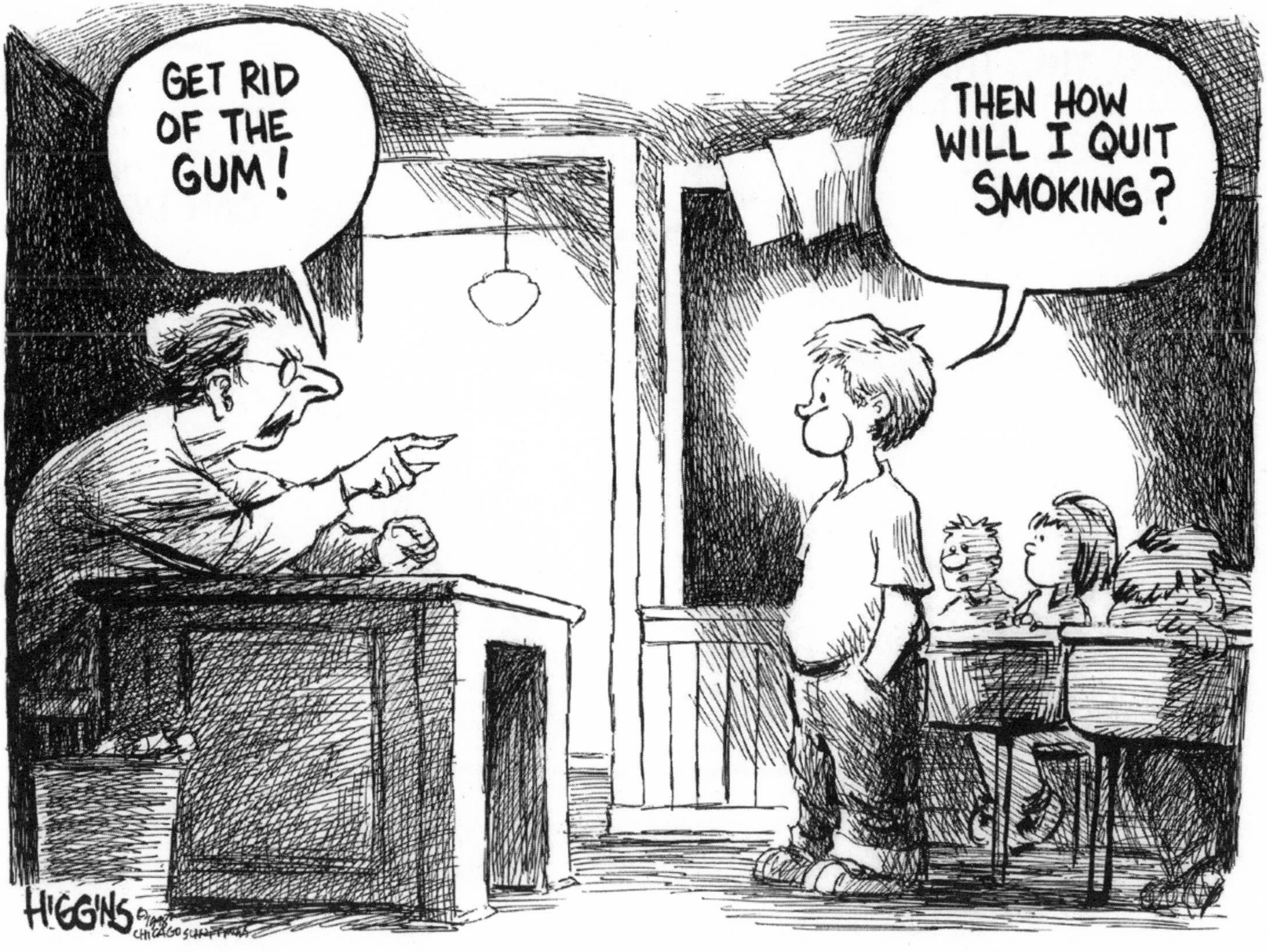
GET RID OF THE GUM!
THEN HOW WILL I QUIT SMOKING?
HIGGINS

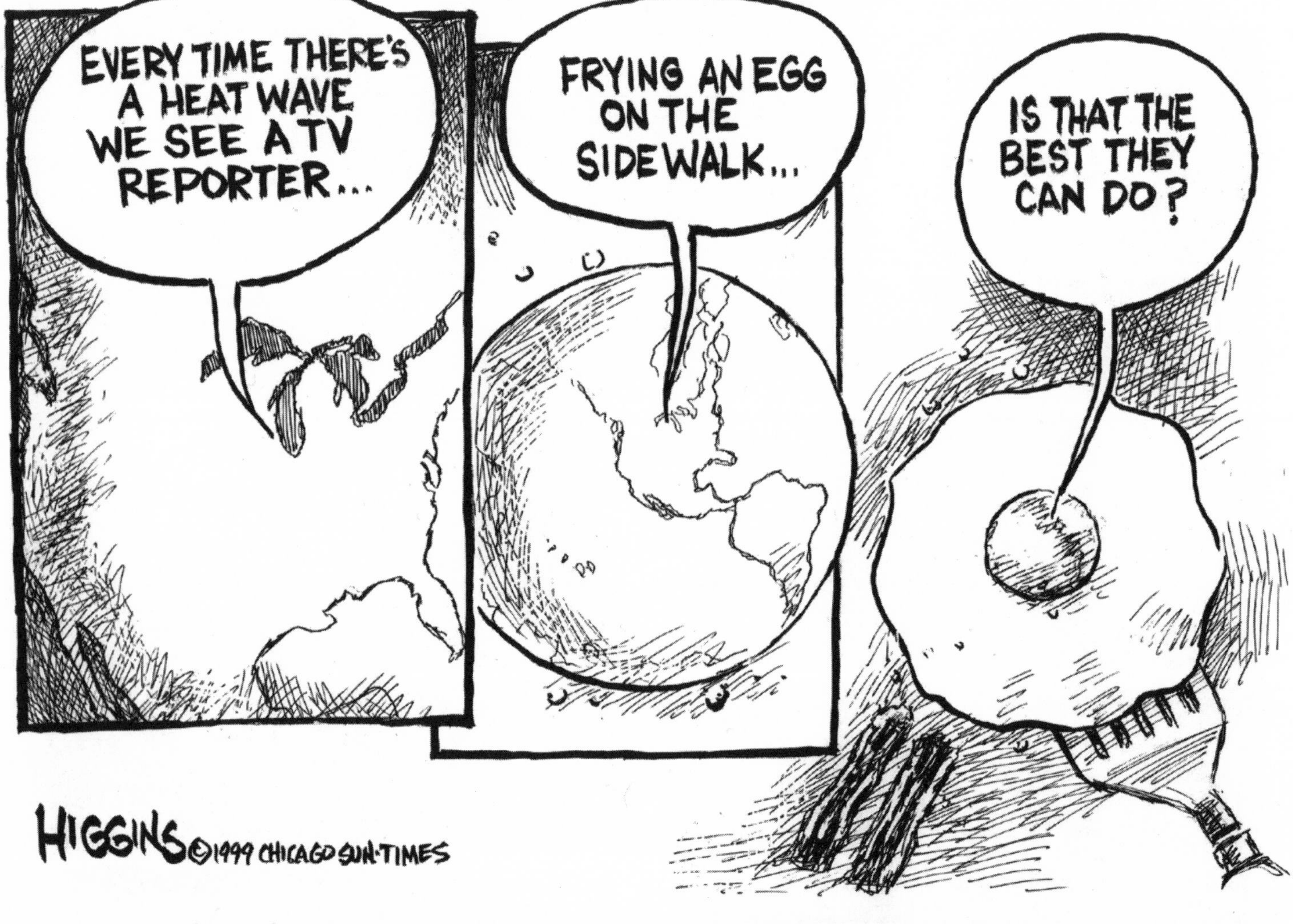
EVERY TIME THERE'S A HEAT WAVE WE SEE A TV REPORTER...
FRYING AN EGG ON THE SIDEWALK...
IS THAT THE BEST THEY CAN DO?
HIGGINS ©1999 CHICAGO SUN-TIMES

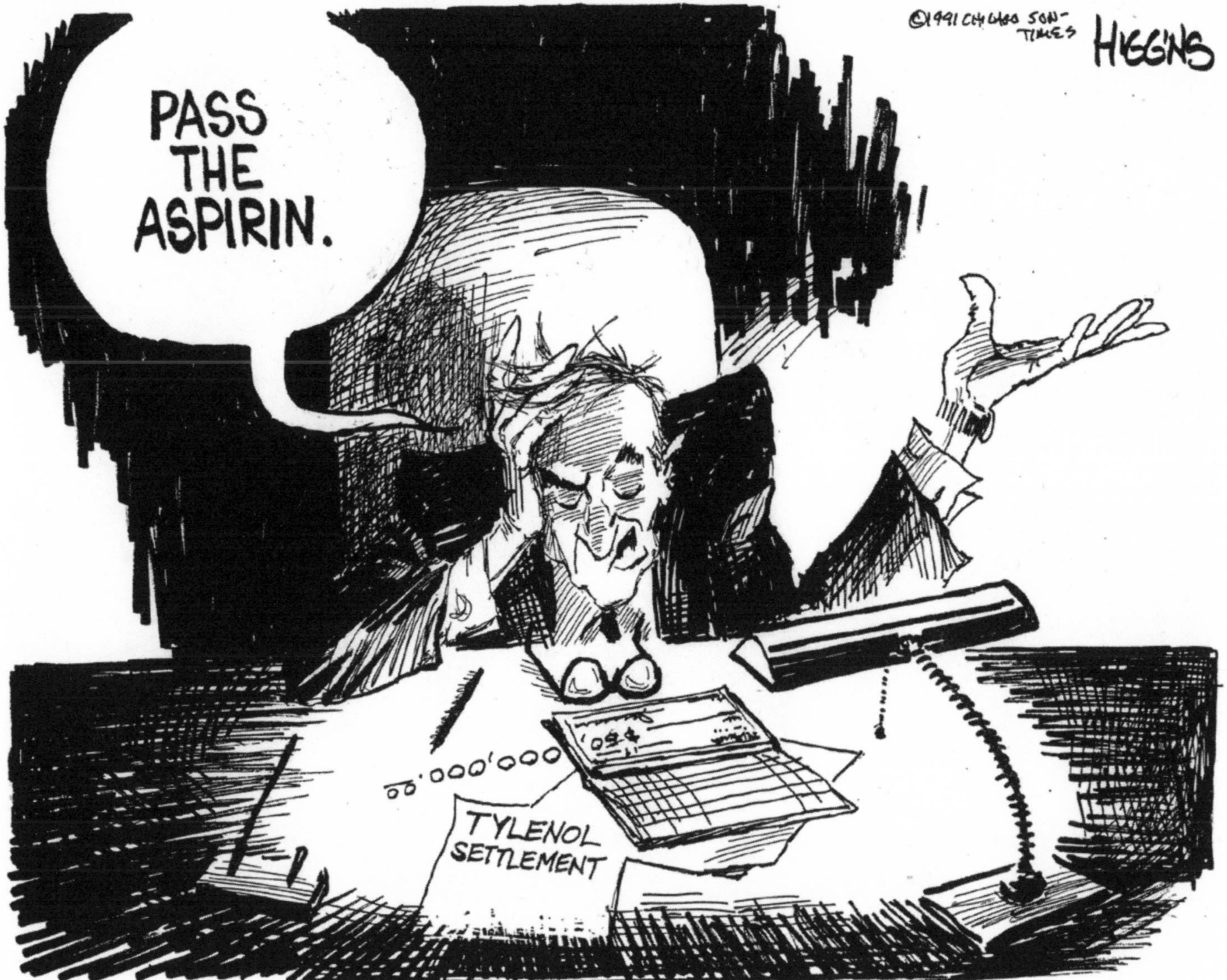

PASS THE ASPIRIN.
©1991 CHICAGO SUN-TIMES
HIGGINS
TYLENOL SETTLEMENT

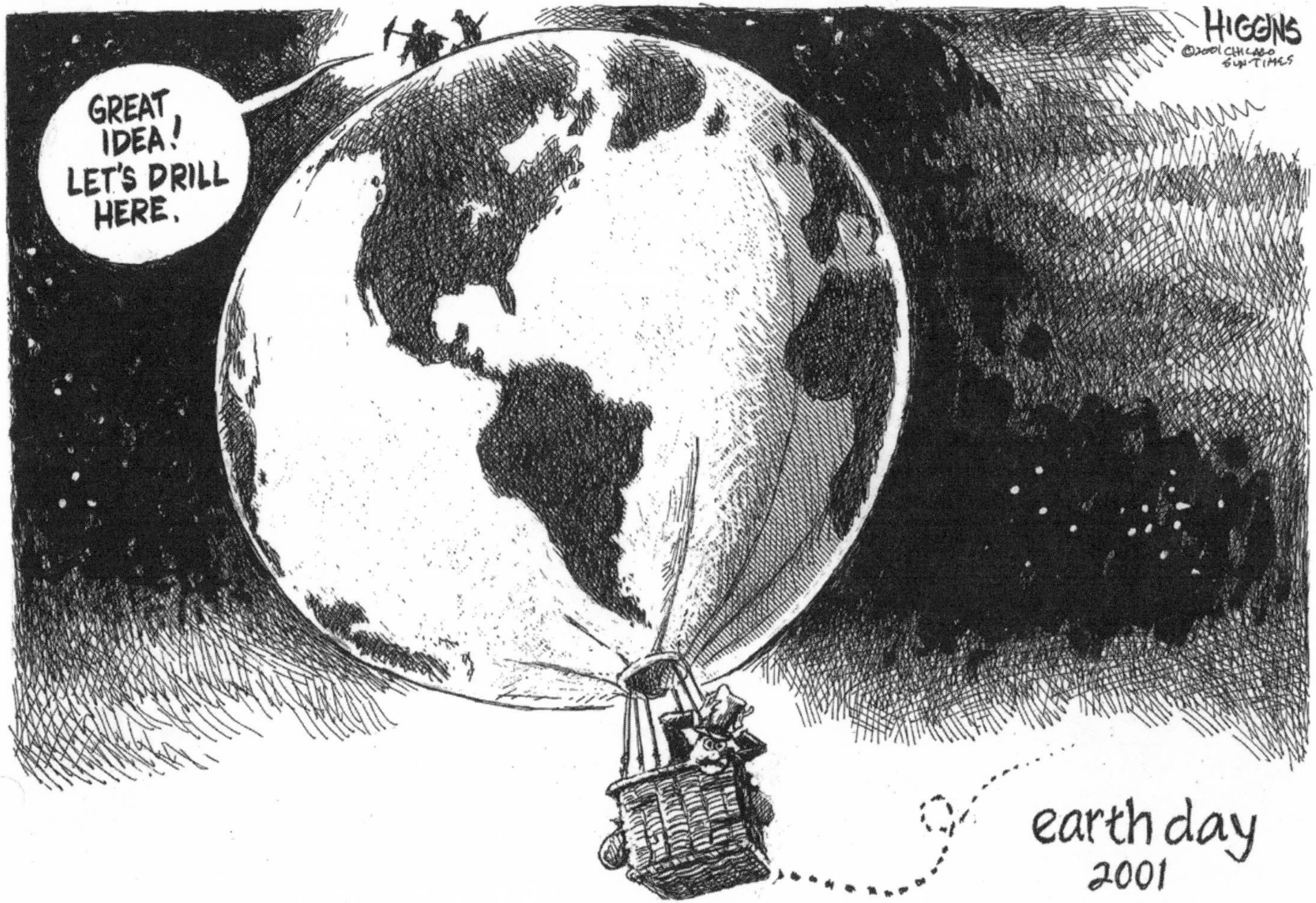
GREAT IDEA! LET'S DRILL HERE.
HIGGINS
©2001 CHICAGO SUN-TIMES
earth day
2001

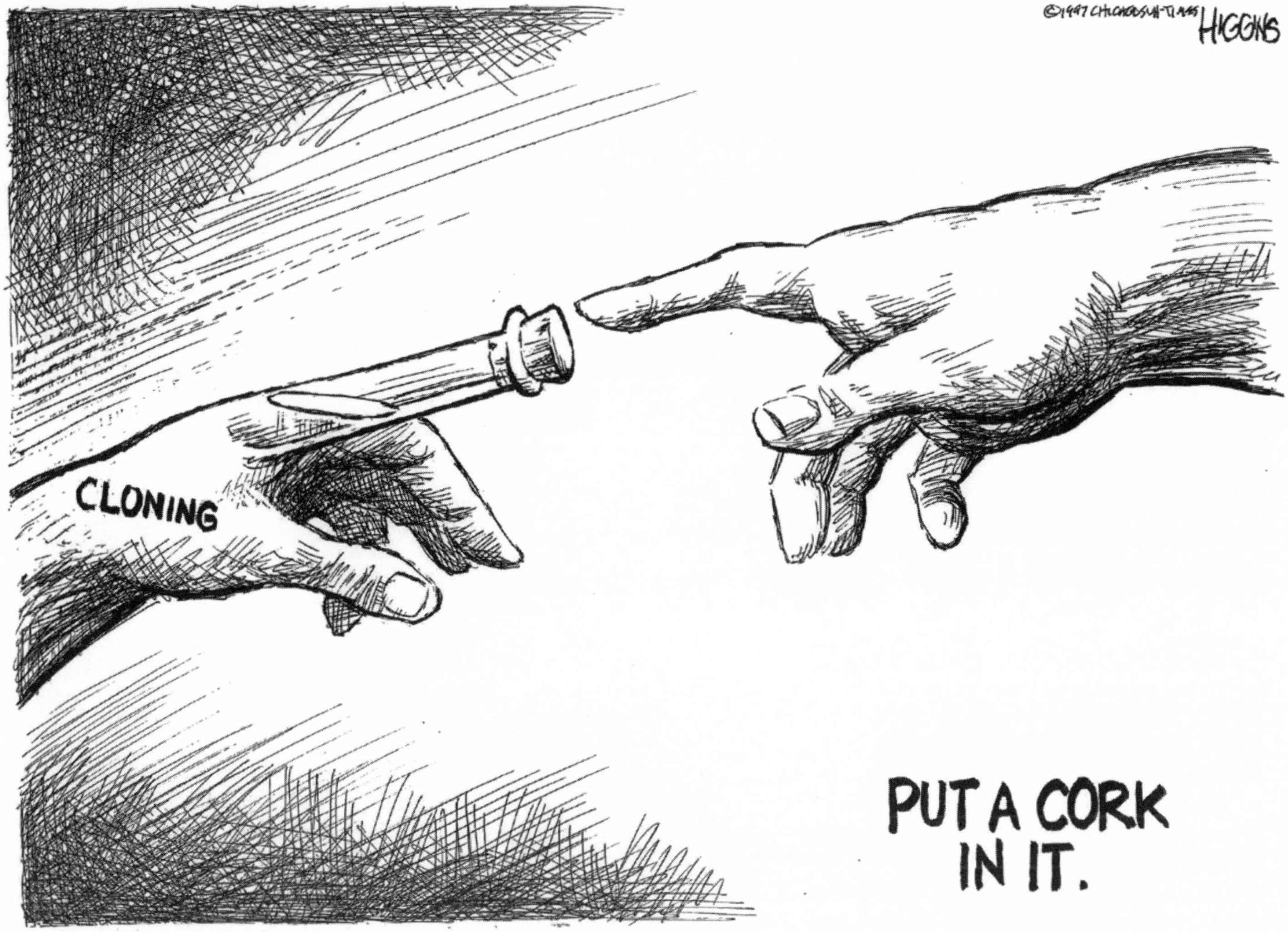
©1997 CHICAGO SUN-TIMES
HIGGINS
CLONING
PUT A CORK
IN IT.

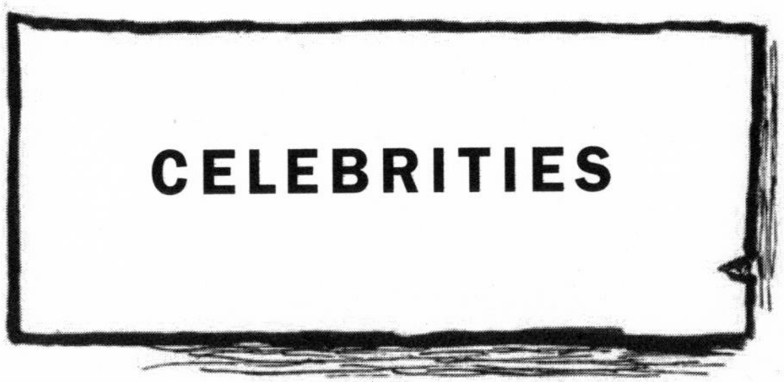

CELEBRITIES

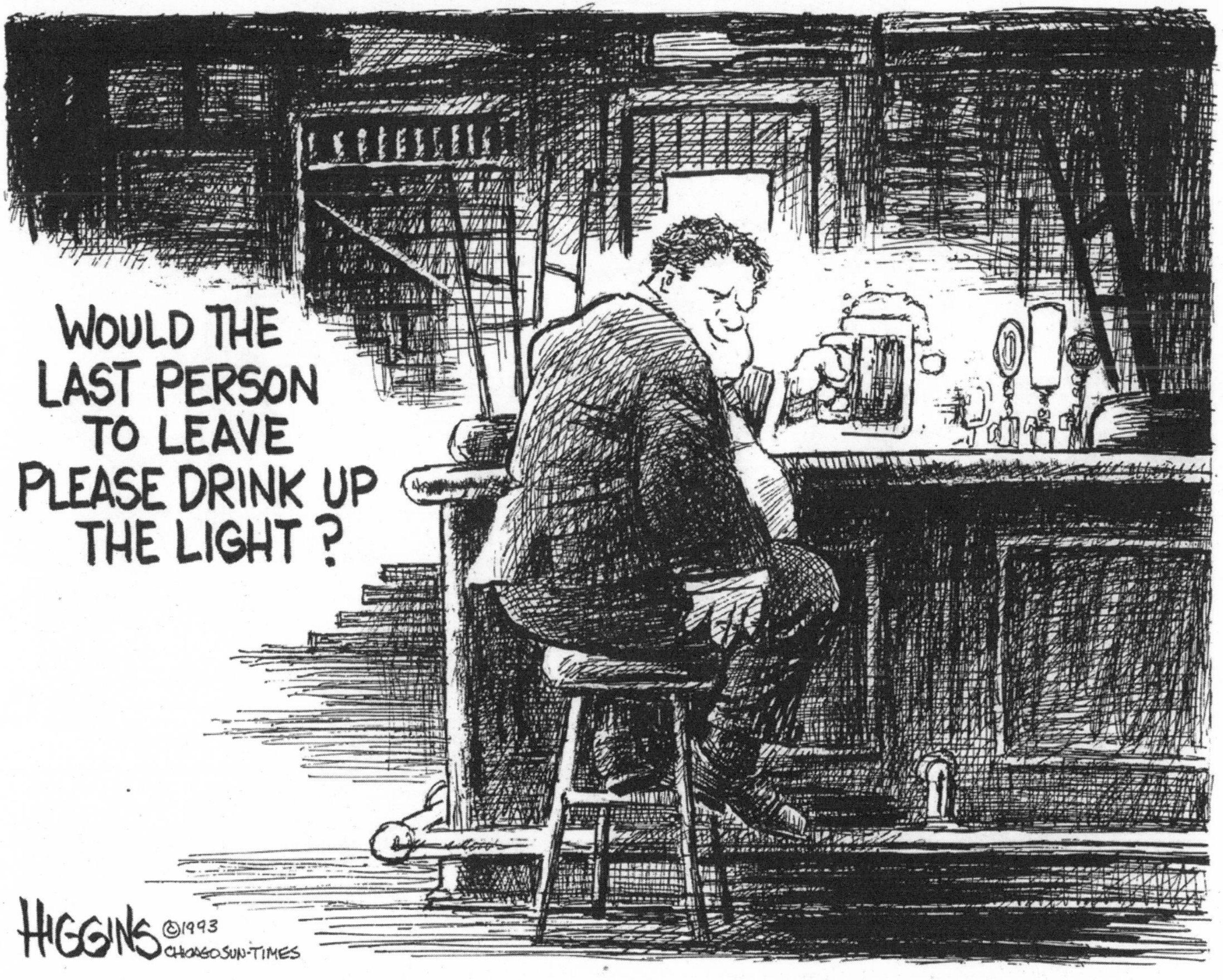
WOULD THE
LAST PERSON
TO LEAVE
PLEASE DRINK UP
THE LIGHT ?
HIGGINS ©1993
CHICAGO SUN-TIMES

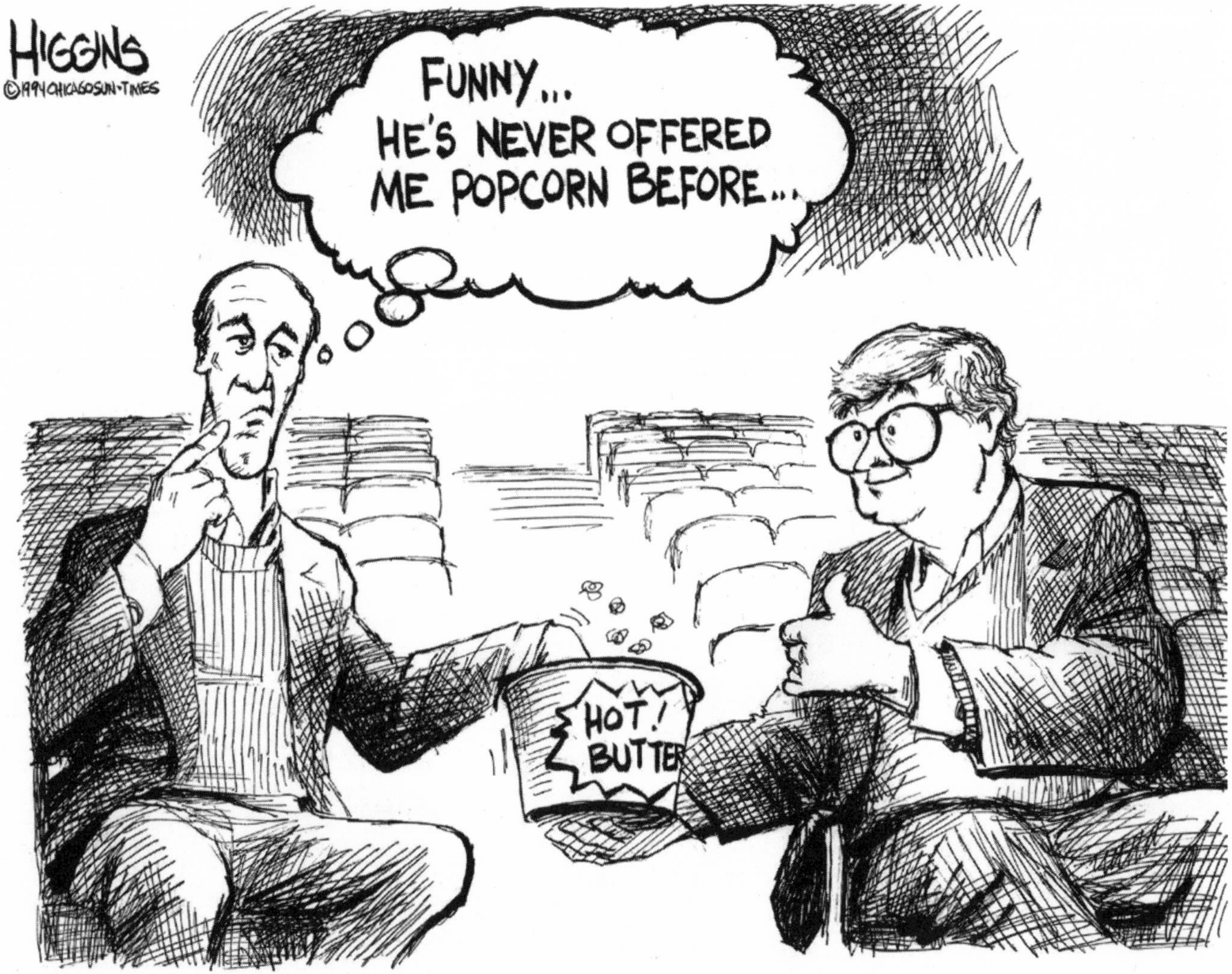
HIGGINS
©1994 CHICAGO SUN-TIMES
FUNNY... HE'S NEVER OFFERED ME POPCORN BEFORE...
HOT! BUTTER

Research in 1994 discovers that movie theater popcorn may be hazardous to your health.

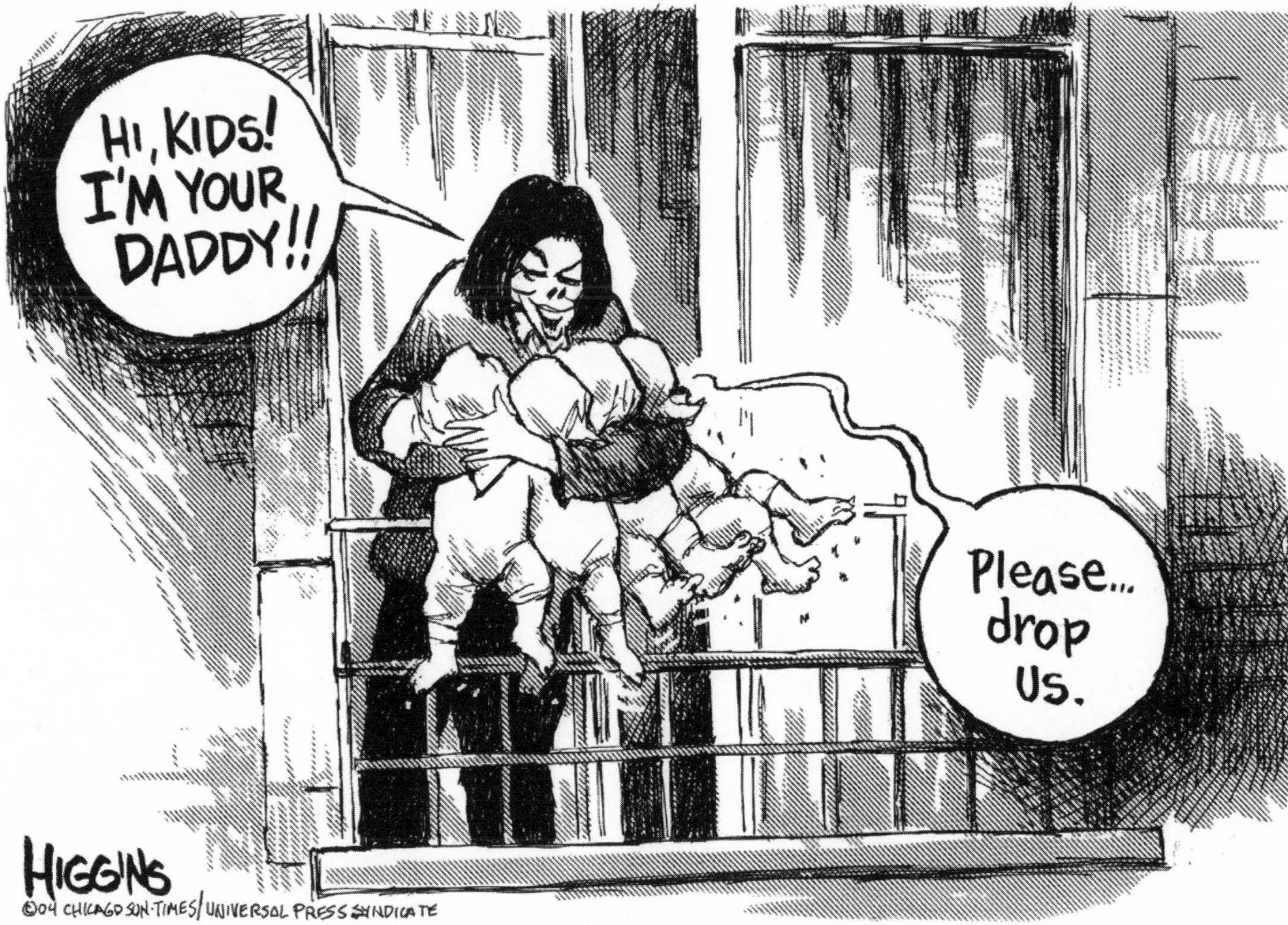
HI, KIDS! I'M YOUR DADDY!!
Please... drop us.
HIGGINS
©04 CHICAGO SUN-TIMES/UNIVERSAL PRESS SYNDICATE

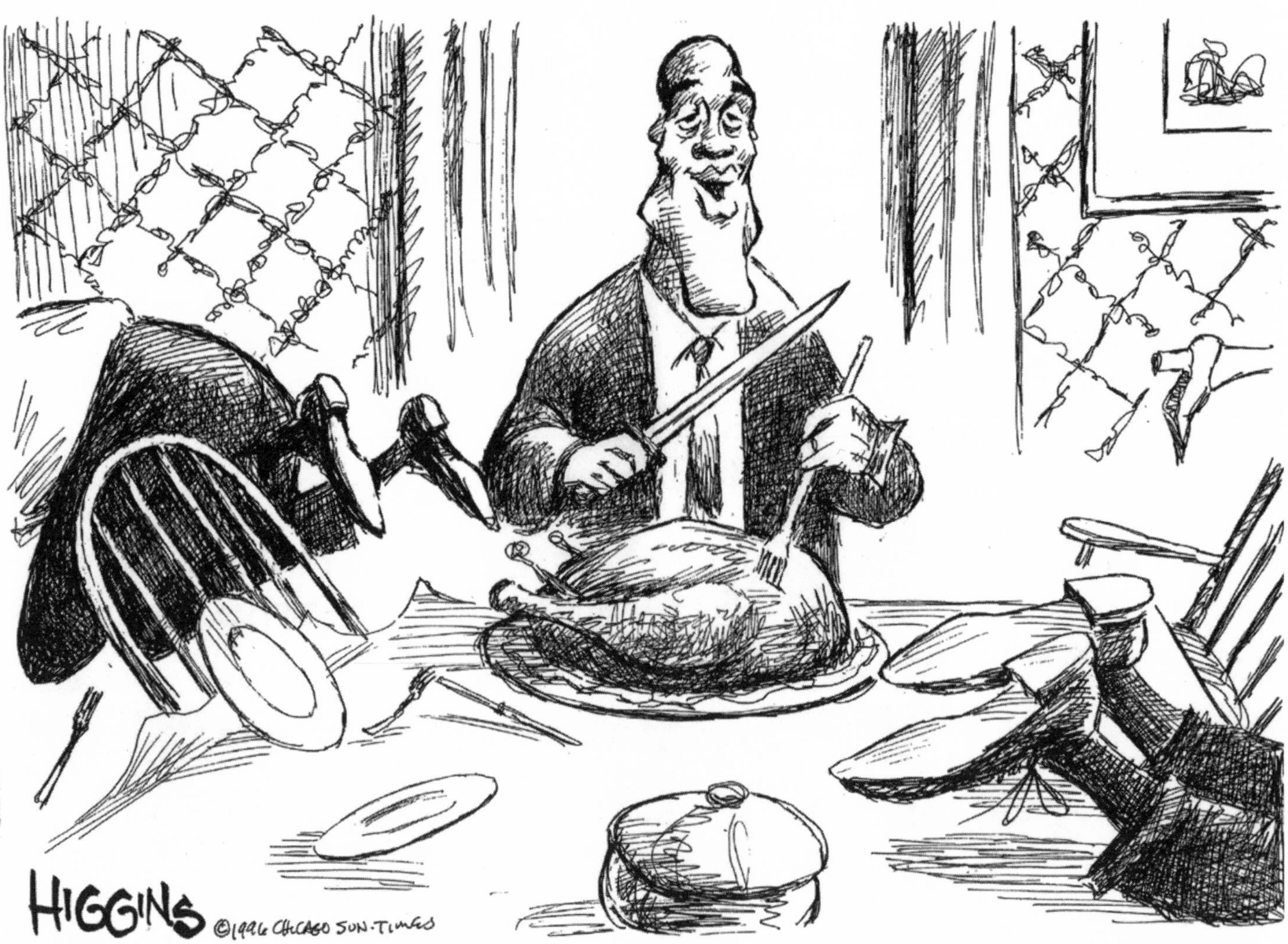
HIGGINS
©1996 CHICAGO SUN-TIMES

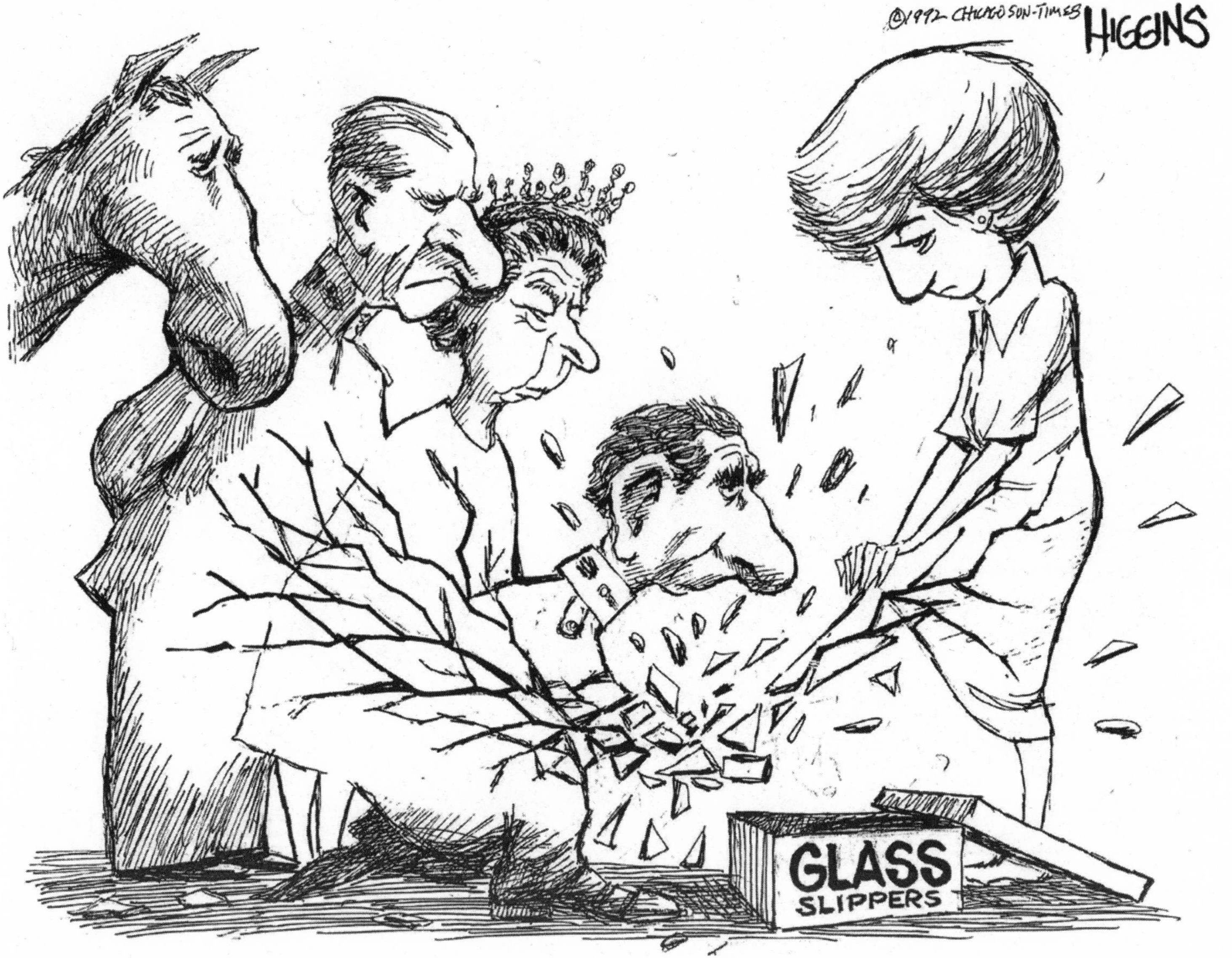
©1992 CHICAGO SUN-TIMES
HIGGINS
GLASS
SLIPPERS

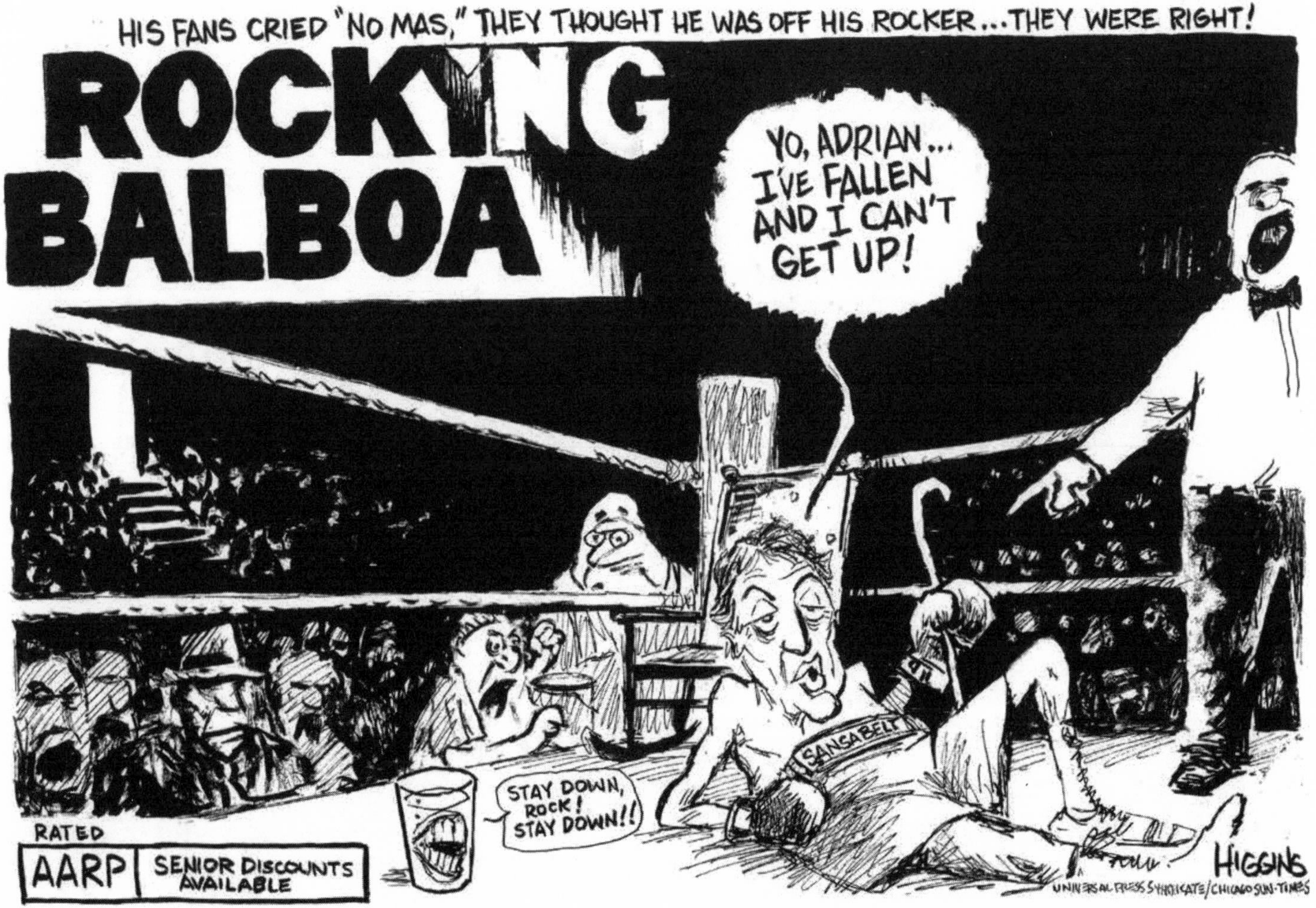
HIS FANS CRIED "NO MAS," THEY THOUGHT HE WAS OFF HIS ROCKER... THEY WERE RIGHT!
ROCKYNG BALBOA
YO, ADRIAN... I'VE FALLEN AND I CAN'T GET UP!
SANSABELT
STAY DOWN, ROCK! STAY DOWN!!
RATED
AARP
SENIOR DISCOUNTS AVAILABLE
HIGGINS
UNIVERSAL PRESS SYNDICATE/CHICAGO SUN-TIMES

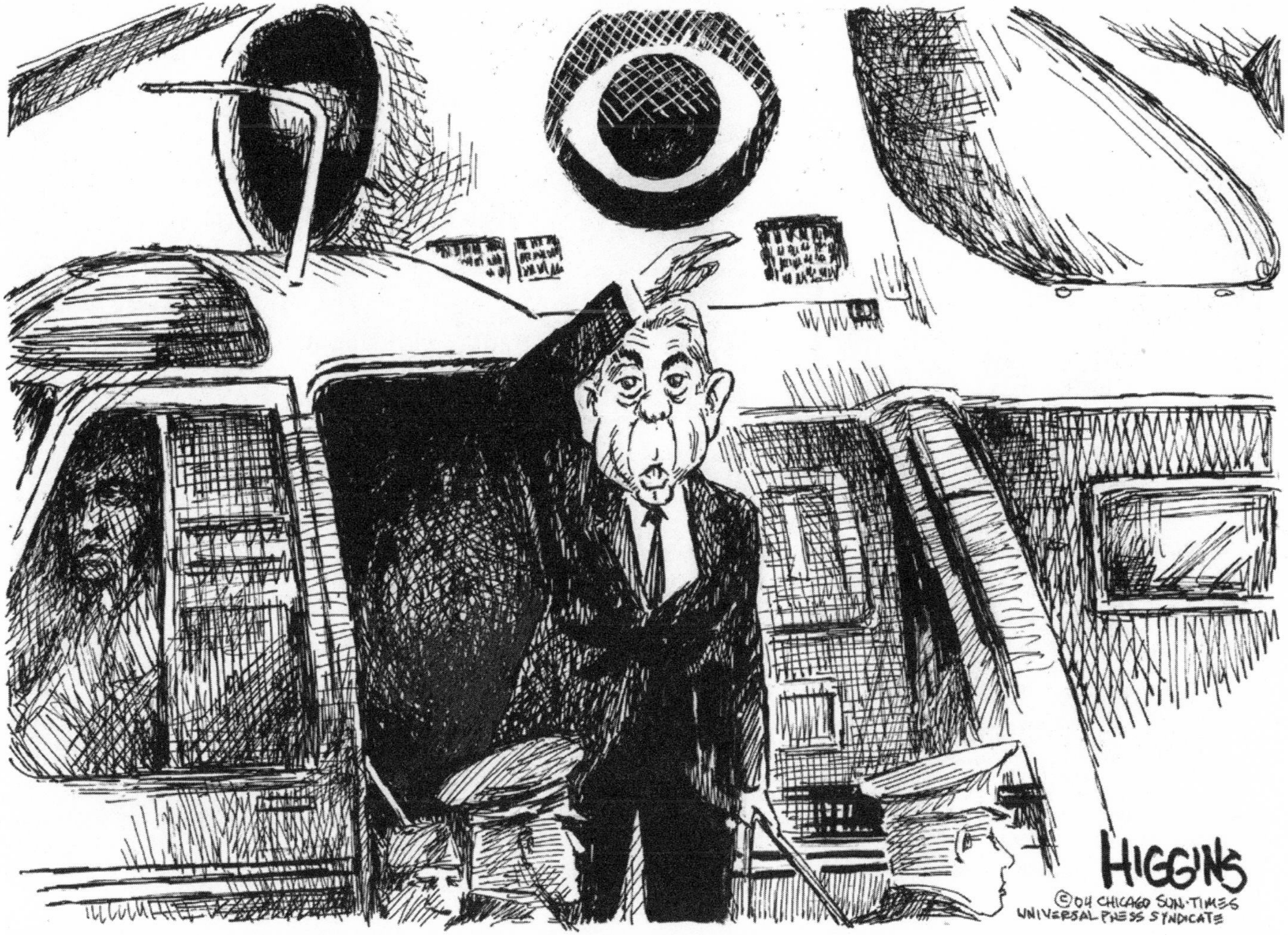
HIGGINS
©04 CHICAGO SUN-TIMES
UNIVERSAL PRESS SYNDICATE

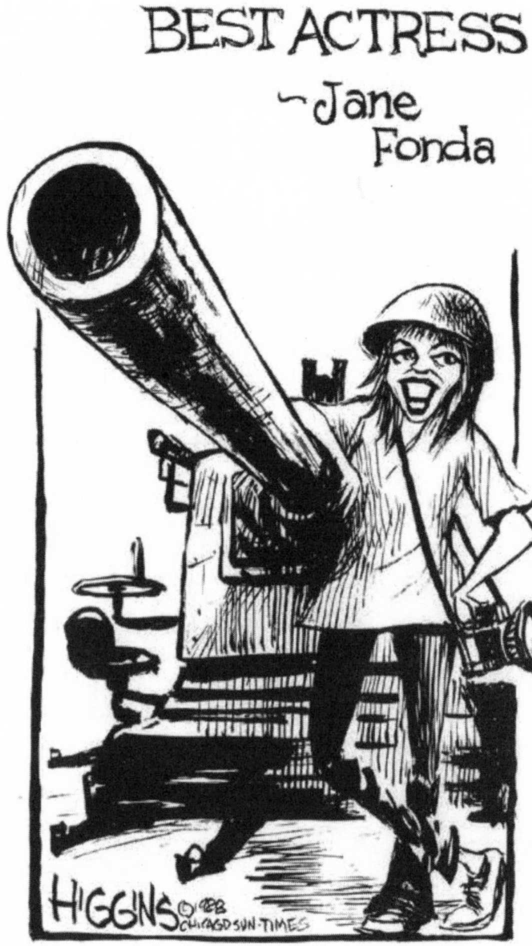
BEST ACTRESS
– Jane Fonda
HIGGINS ©1988 CHICAGO SUN-TIMES

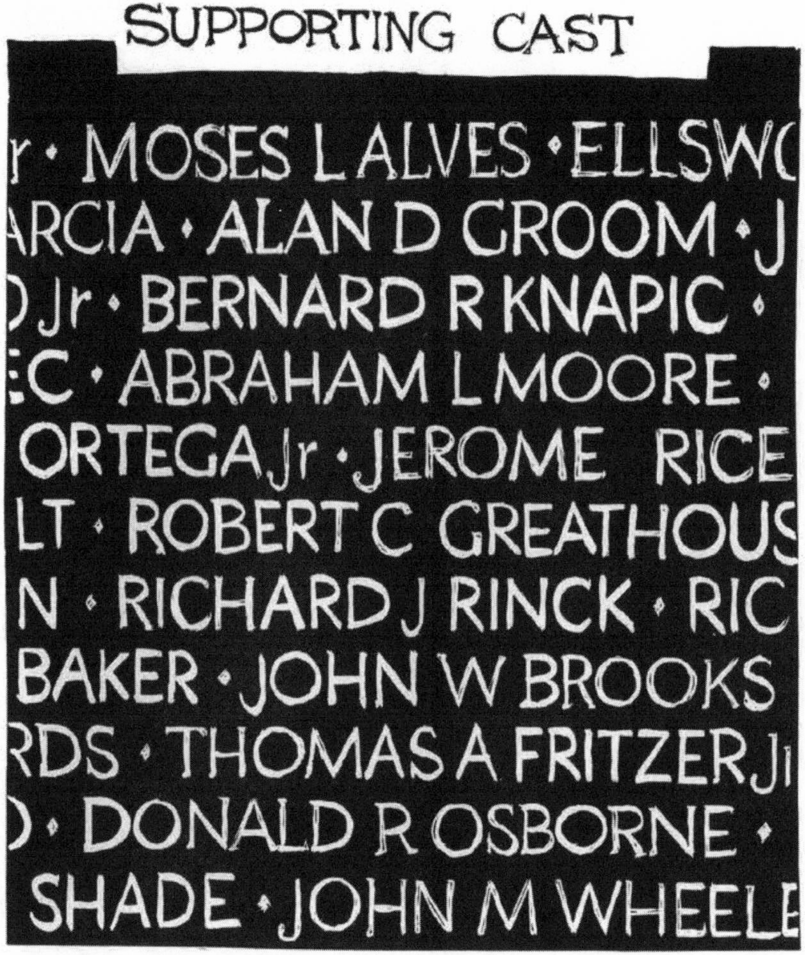
SUPPORTING CAST
r • MOSES L ALVES • ELLSW
ARCIA • ALAN D GROOM • J
D Jr • BERNARD R KNAPIC •
EC • ABRAHAM L MOORE •
ORTEGA Jr • JEROME RICE
LT • ROBERT C GREATHOUS
N • RICHARD J RINCK • RIC
BAKER • JOHN W BROOKS
RDS • THOMAS A FRITZER Jr
D • DONALD R OSBORNE •
SHADE • JOHN M WHEELE

FOREIGN
AFFAIRS

HAVE PEN, WILL TRAVEL

Over the years, I've been fortunate enough to take a break from a cartoonist's sedentary life and file cartoons from various ports of call, including Ireland, Cuba, Hungary, and the former Soviet Union.

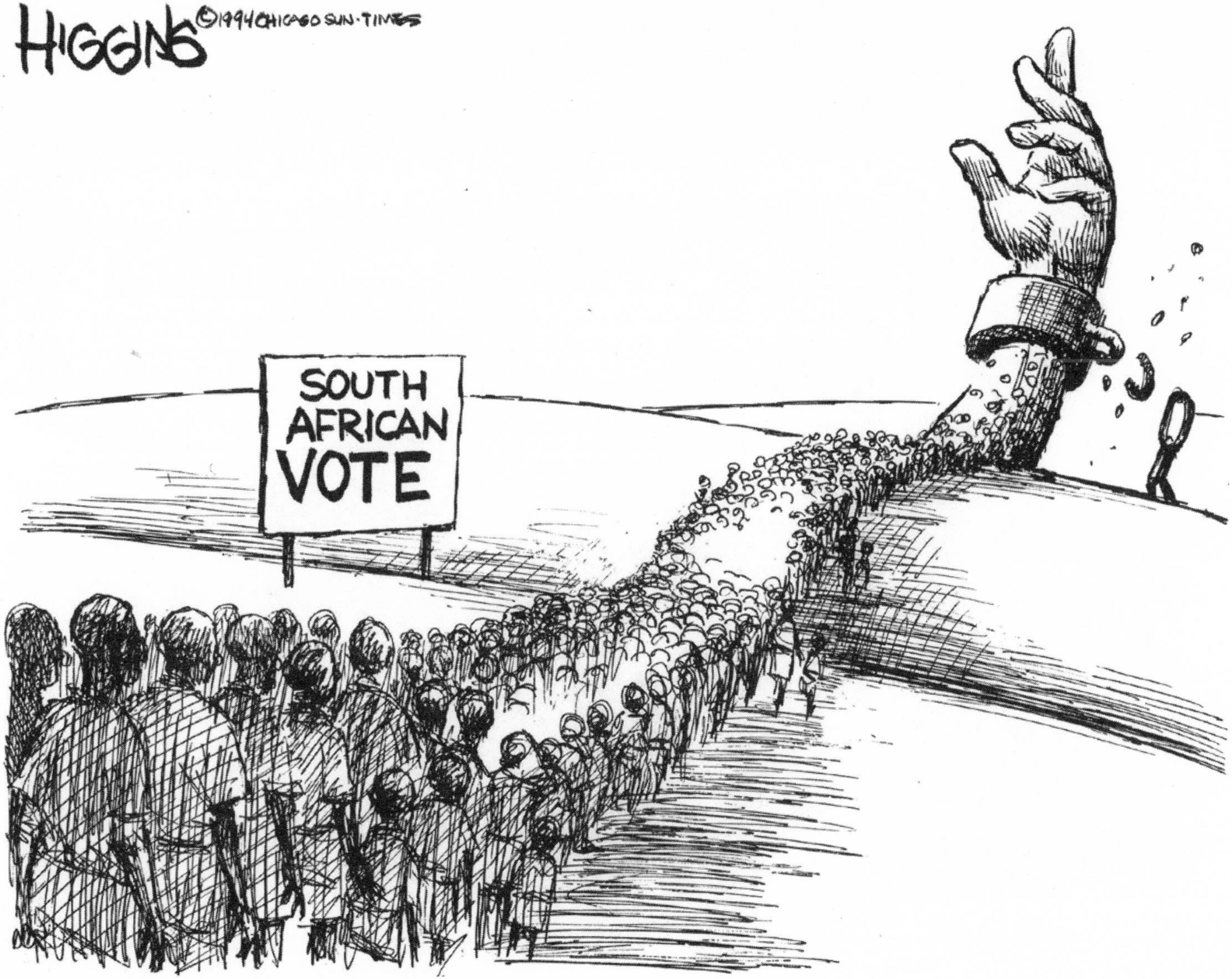
HIGGINS ©1994 CHICAGO SUN-TIMES
SOUTH AFRICAN VOTE

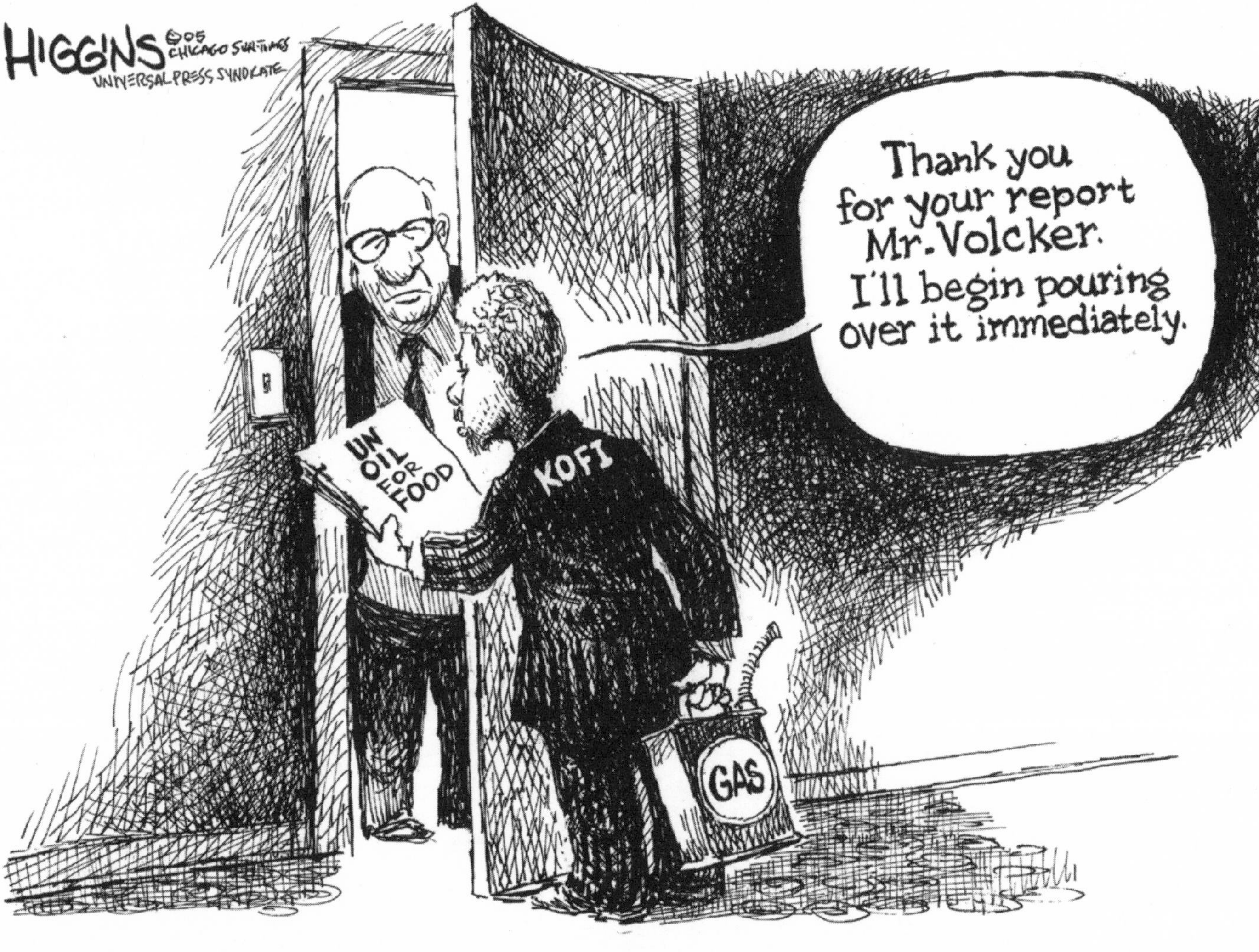
HIGGINS ©05 CHICAGO SUN-TIMES UNIVERSAL PRESS SYNDICATE
Thank you for your report Mr. Volcker. I'll begin pouring over it immediately.
UN OIL FOR FOOD
KOFI
GAS

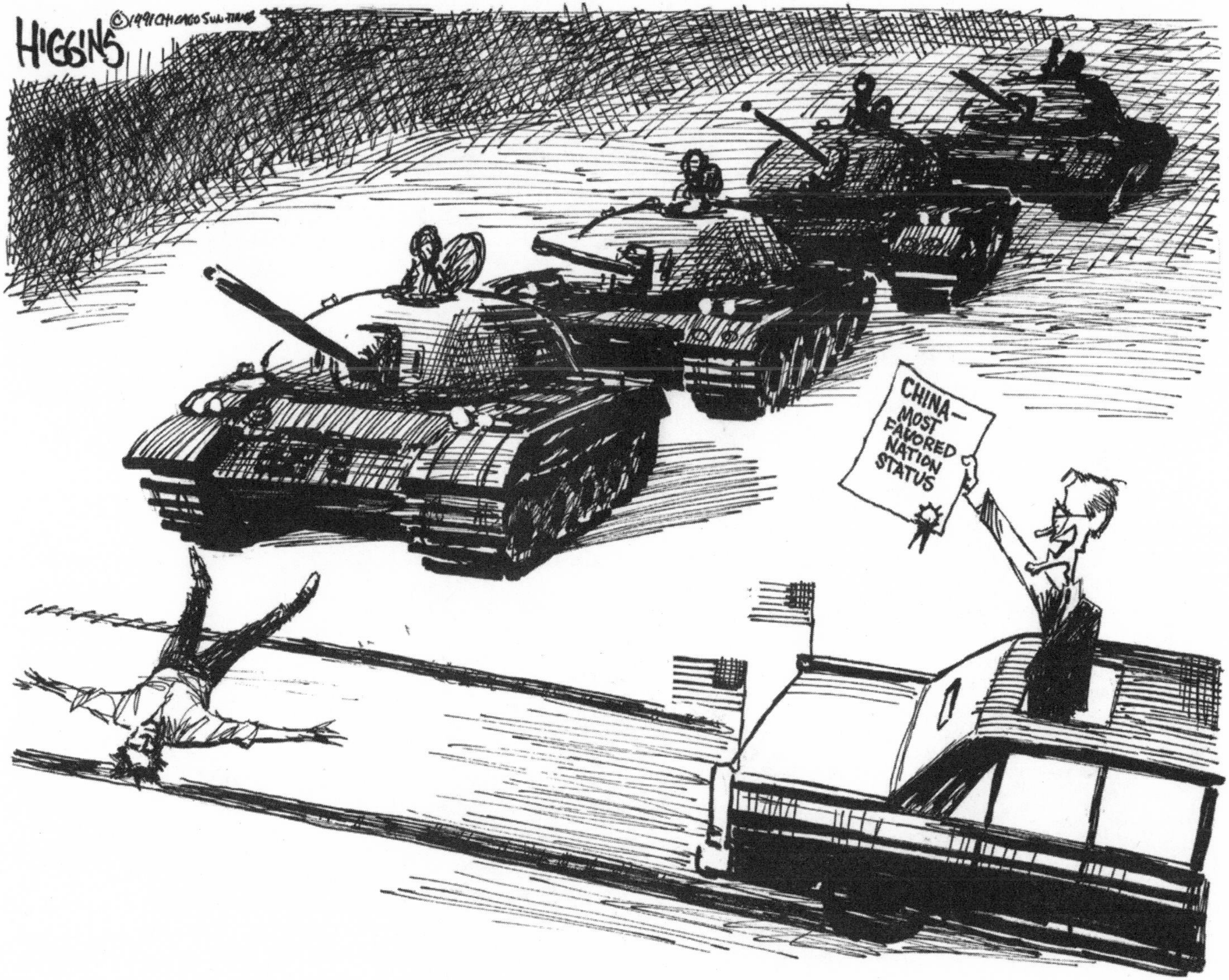
HIGGINS ©1991 CHICAGO SUN-TIMES
CHINA–
MOST
FAVORED
NATION
STATUS

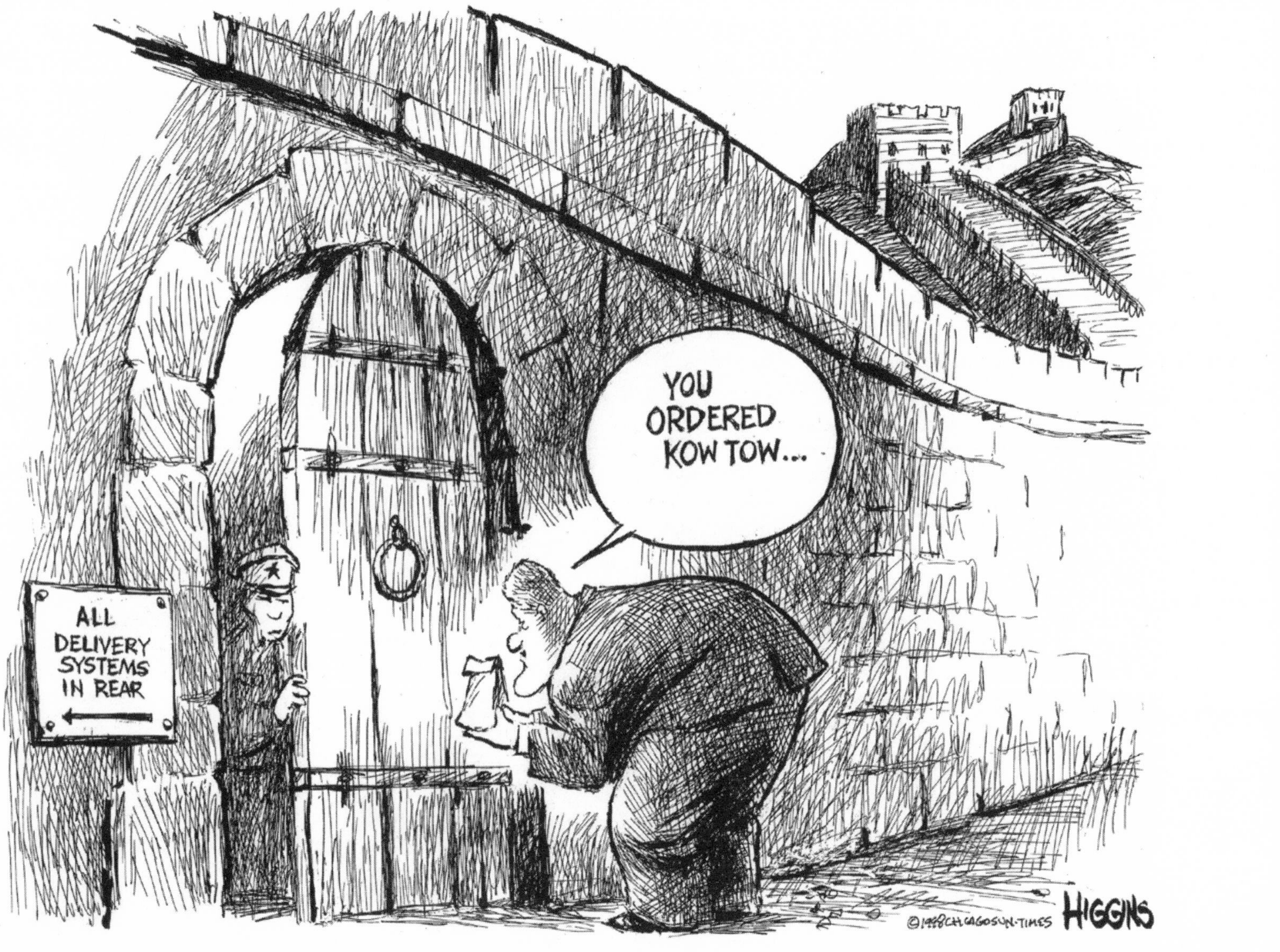
ALL
DELIVERY
SYSTEMS
IN REAR
YOU
ORDERED
KOW TOW...
©1998 CHICAGO SUN-TIMES
HIGGINS

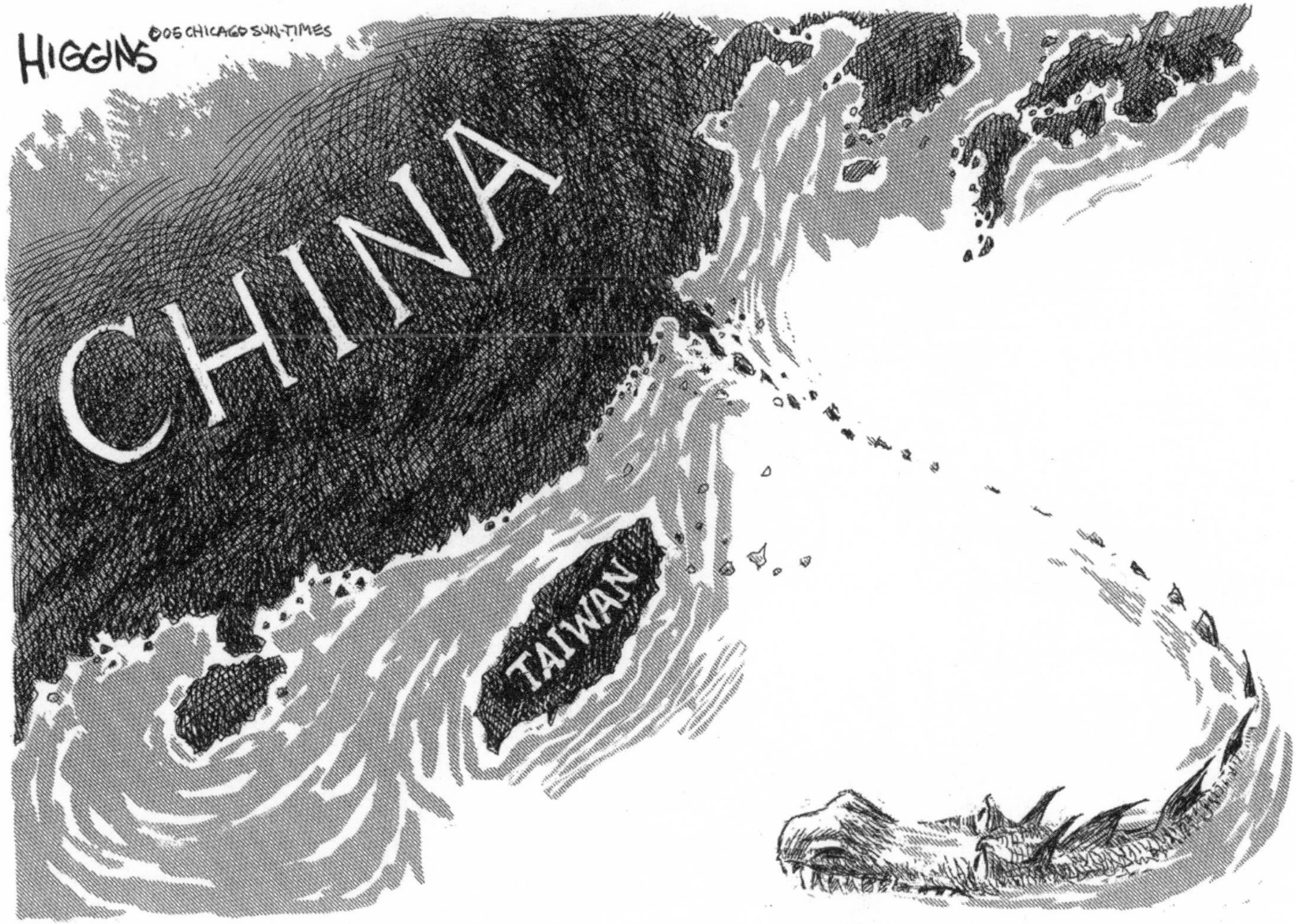

HIGGINS ©05 CHICAGO SUN-TIMES
CHINA
TAIWAN

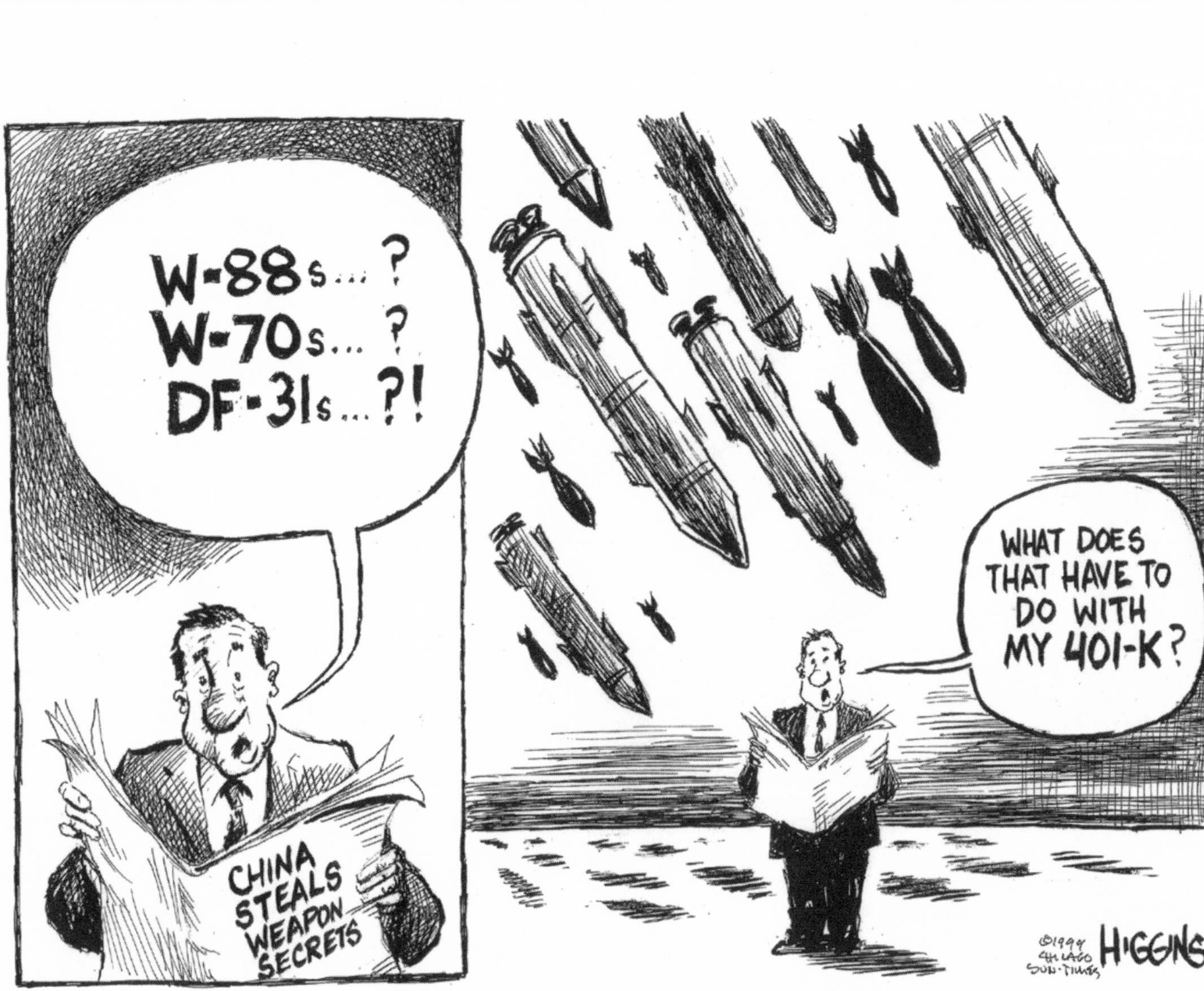
W-88s... ?
W-70s... ?
DF-31s...?!
CHINA STEALS WEAPON SECRETS
WHAT DOES THAT HAVE TO DO WITH MY 401-K?
©1999 CHICAGO SUN-TIMES
HIGGINS

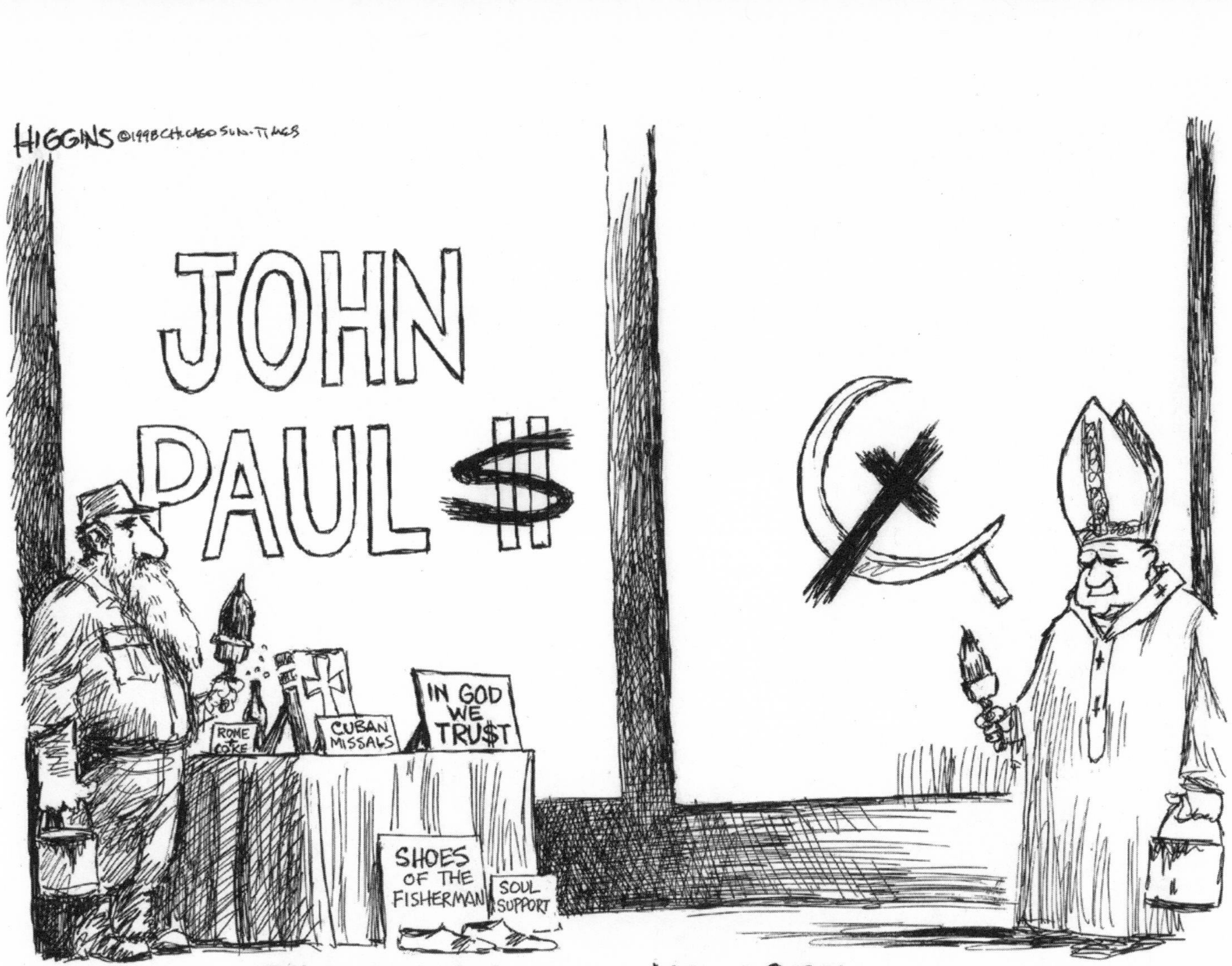
HIGGINS ©1998 CHICAGO SUN-TIMES
JOHN
PAUL II
$
ROME + COKE
CUBAN MISSALS
IN GOD WE TRU$T
SHOES OF THE FISHERMAN
SOUL SUPPORT

THE OLD MAN AND THE HOLY SEE

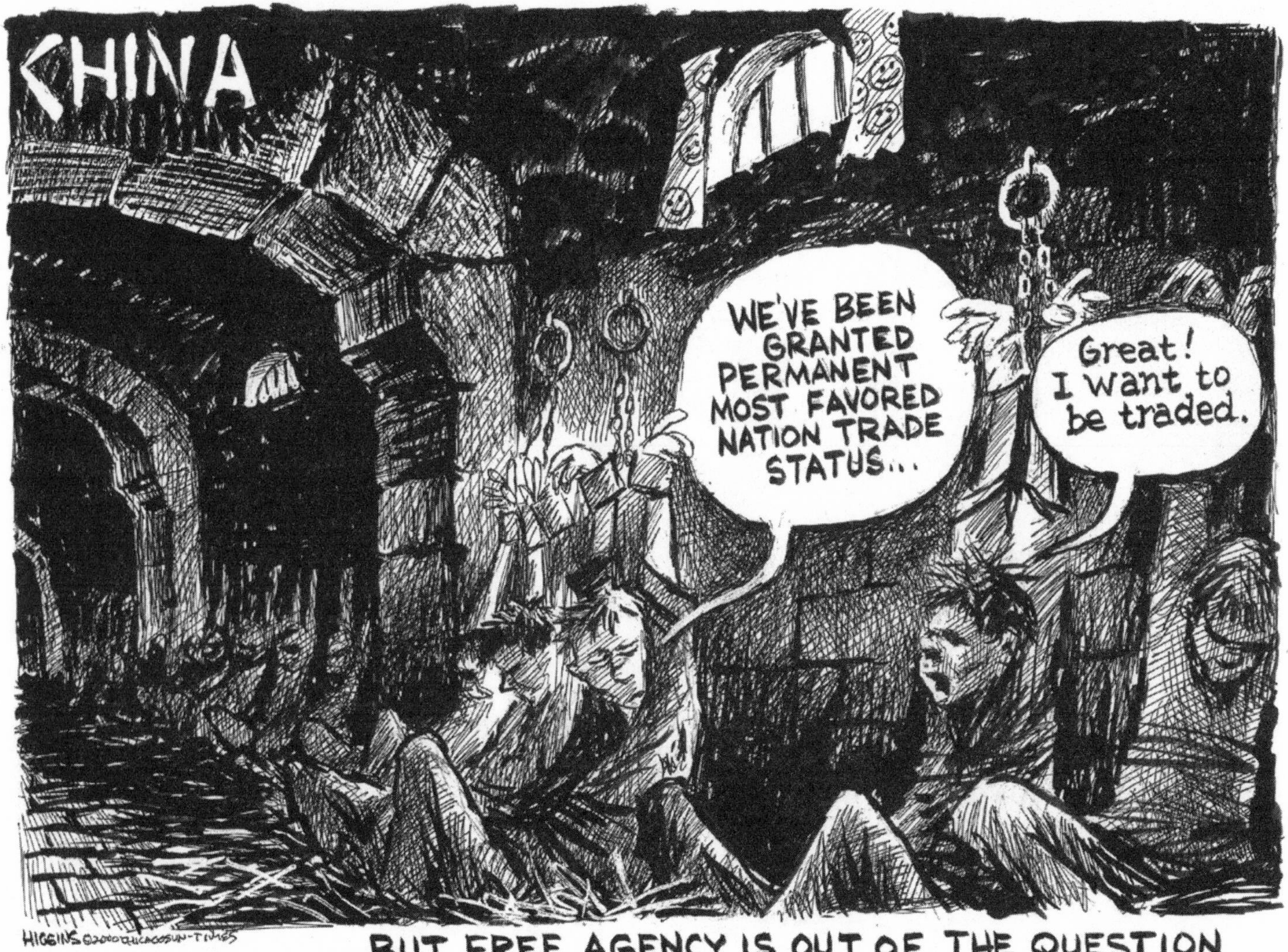
CHINA
WE'VE BEEN GRANTED PERMANENT MOST FAVORED NATION TRADE STATUS...
Great! I want to be traded.
HIGGINS ©2000 CHICAGO SUN-TIMES

... BUT FREE AGENCY IS OUT OF THE QUESTION

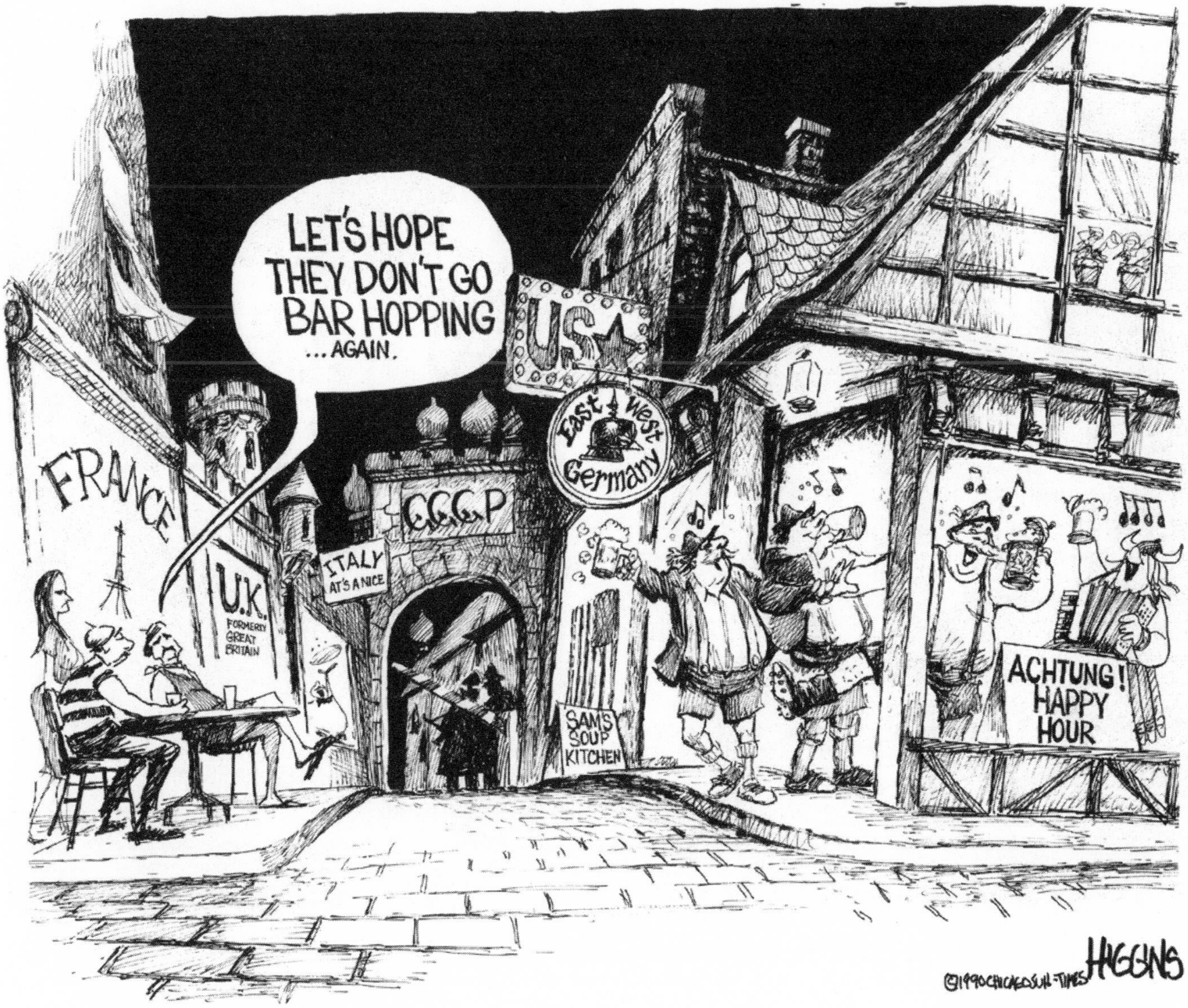
LET'S HOPE THEY DON'T GO BAR HOPPING ...AGAIN.
FRANCE
U.K. FORMERLY GREAT BRITAIN
ITALY AT'S A NICE
C.C.C.P
US
East West Germany
SAM'S SOUP KITCHEN
ACHTUNG! HAPPY HOUR
©1990 CHICAGO SUN-TIMES HIGGINS

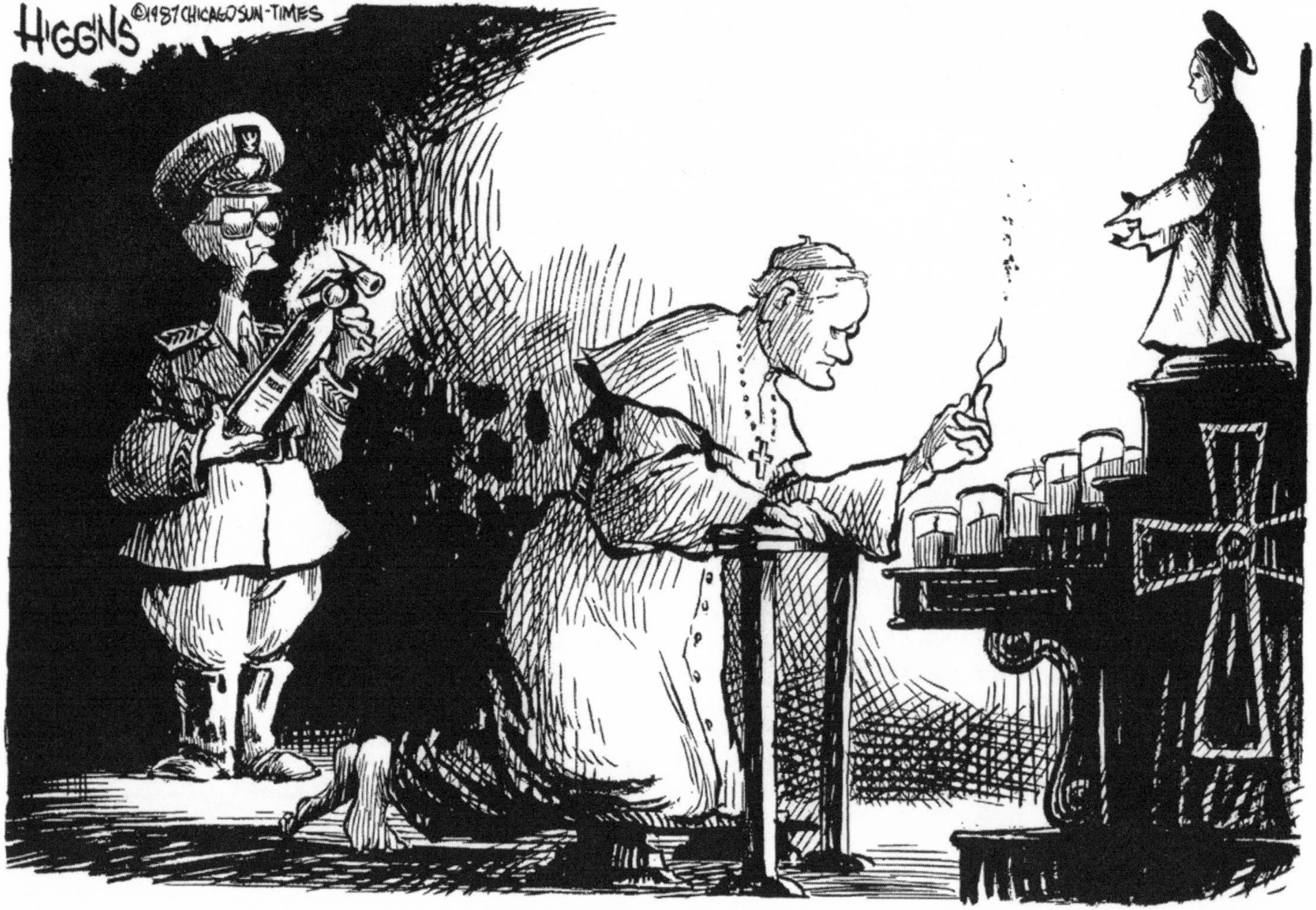
HIGGINS ©1987 CHICAGO SUN-TIMES

Picture the poorest pocket of a major U.S. city, plop Red Square in the middle. Add some beggars, public drunks, and enough pollution to choke Lenin's corpse and you have Moscow. I traveled to the Soviet Union in 1990 in the company of a group of editorial cartoonists.

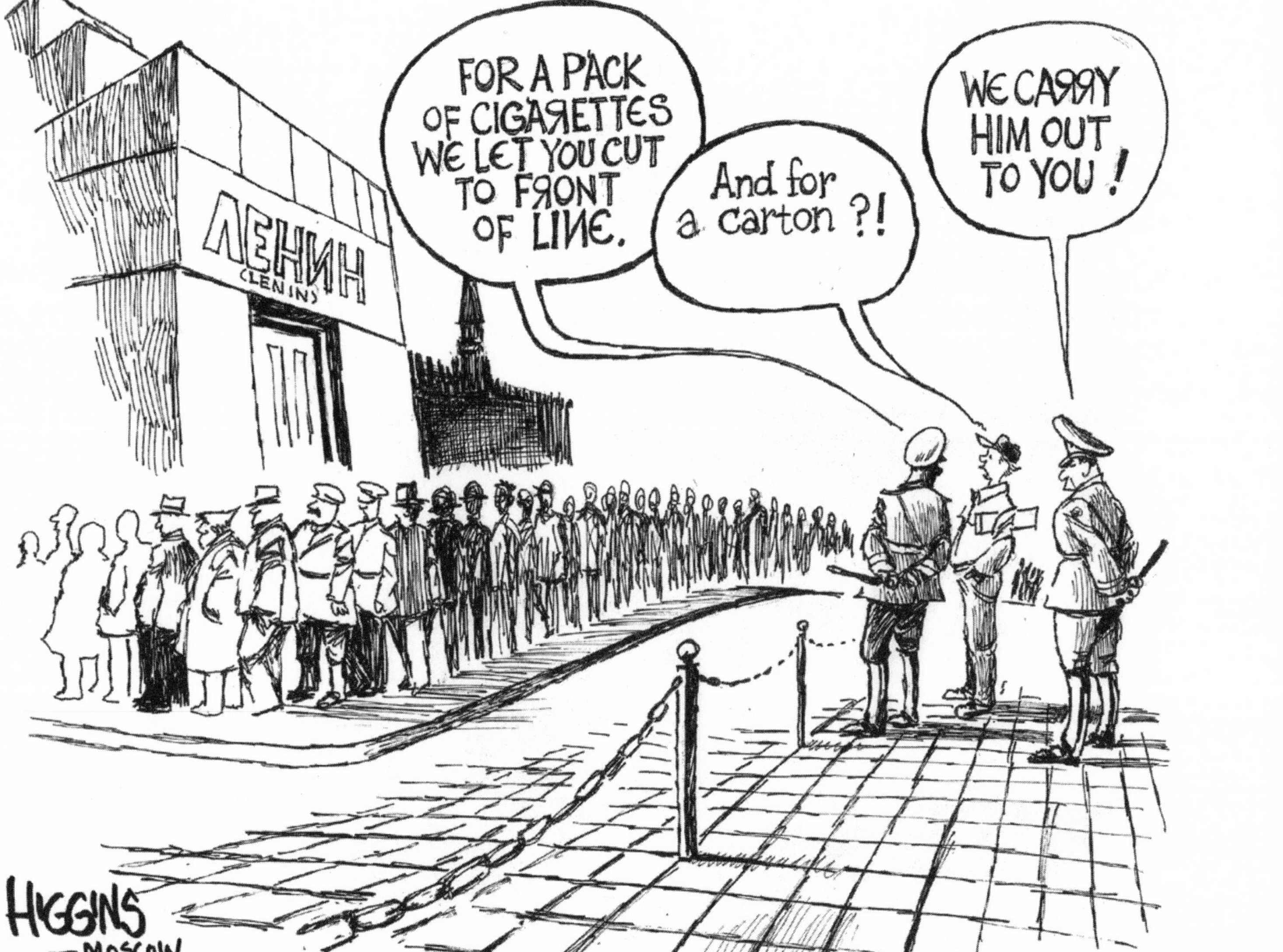
ЛЕНИН
(LENIN)
FOR A PACK OF CIGARETTES WE LET YOU CUT TO FRONT OF LINE.
And for a carton ?!
WE CARRY HIM OUT TO YOU !
HIGGINS —MOSCOW

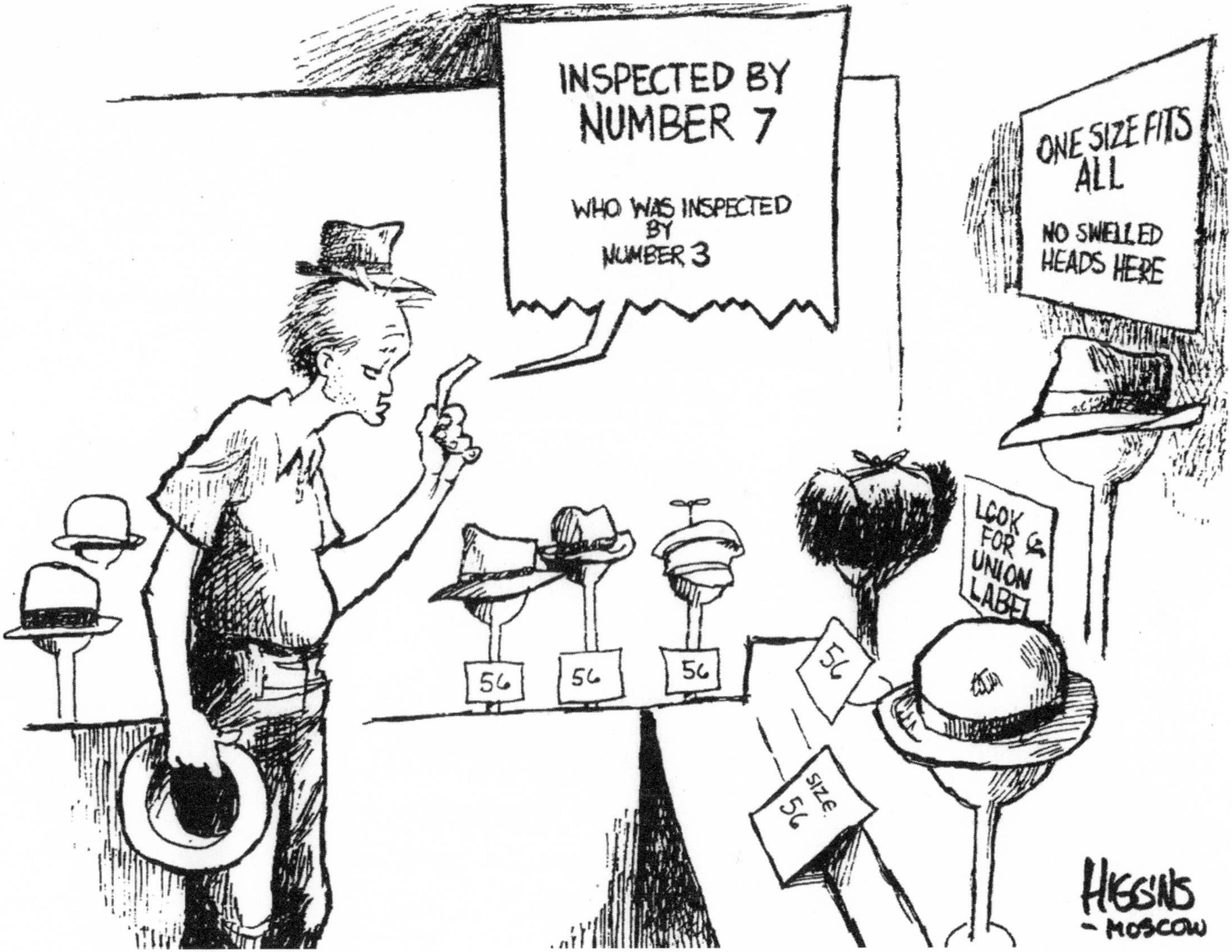
INSPECTED BY
NUMBER 7
WHO WAS INSPECTED
BY
NUMBER 3
ONE SIZE FITS
ALL
NO SWELLED
HEADS HERE
LOOK
FOR
UNION
LABEL
56
56
56
56
SIZE
56
HIGGINS
- MOSCOW

President Bill Clinton goes to Ireland to receive the Freedom of Limerick Award (insert your own dirty joke here). In one town square he visits, in County Kerry, there is a very prominent sign above a hair salon. It says "Monica's." Another example of "you can run, but you can't hide."

HIGGINS IN IRELAND

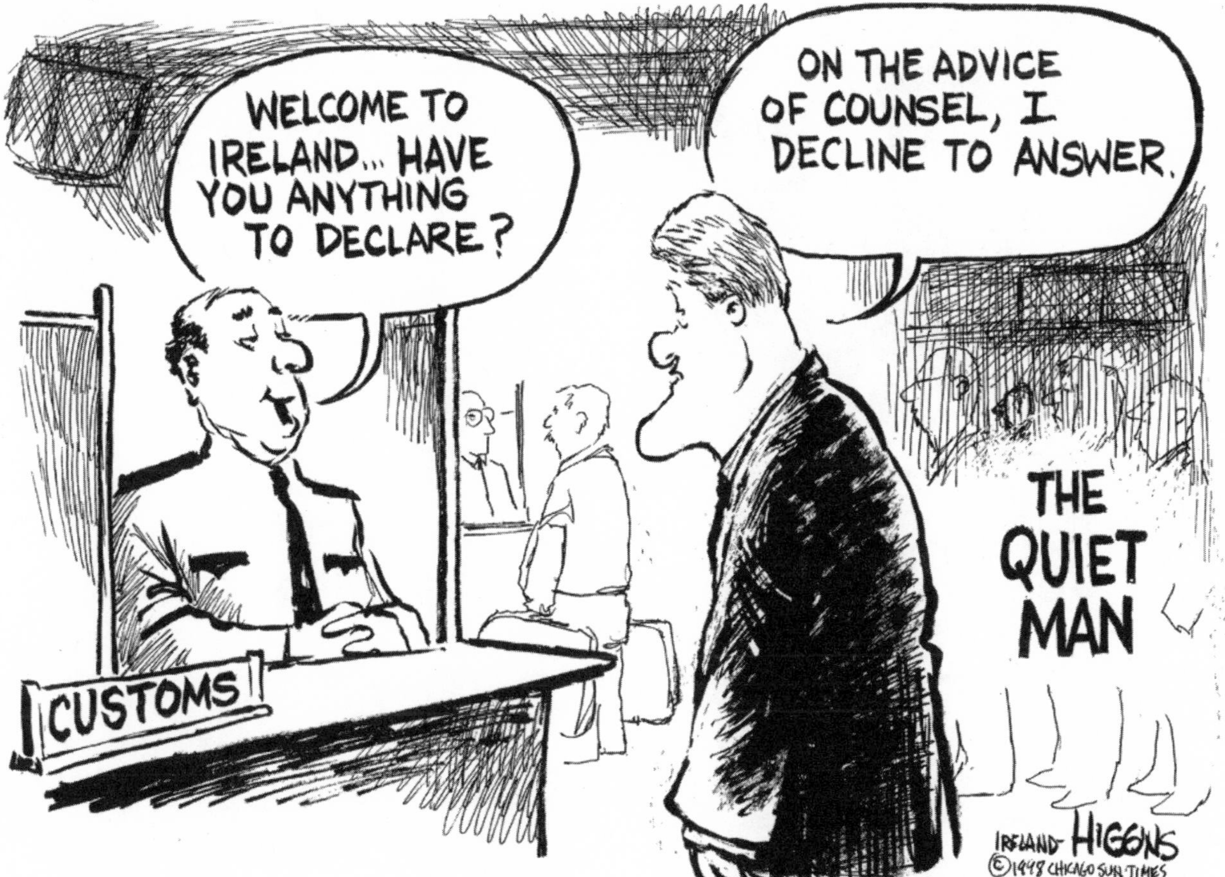
WELCOME TO IRELAND... HAVE YOU ANYTHING TO DECLARE?
ON THE ADVICE OF COUNSEL, I DECLINE TO ANSWER.
CUSTOMS
THE QUIET MAN
IRELAND HIGGINS
©1998 CHICAGO SUN-TIMES

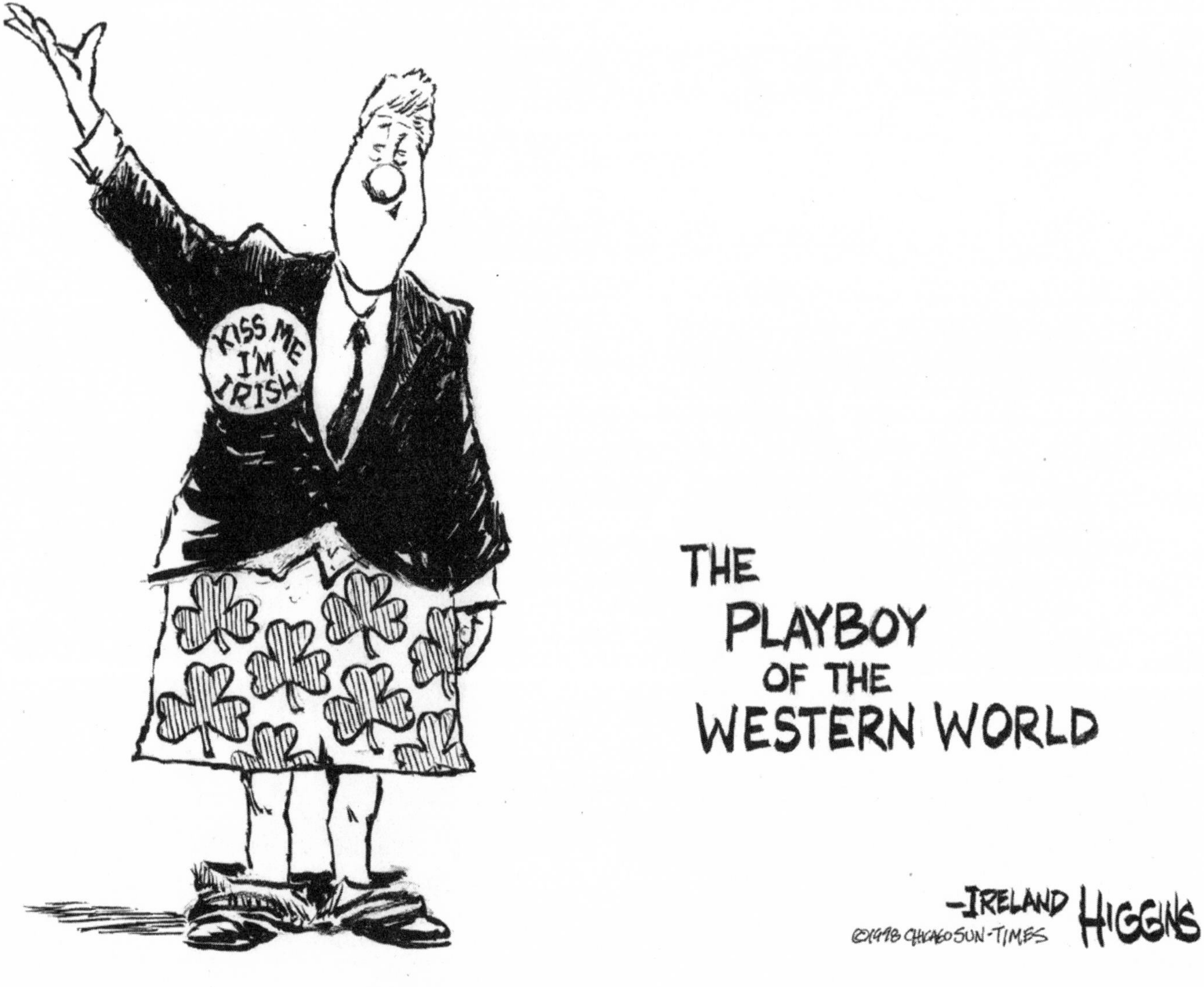
KISS ME I'M IRISH
THE PLAYBOY OF THE WESTERN WORLD
—IRELAND
©1998 CHICAGO SUN-TIMES
HIGGINS

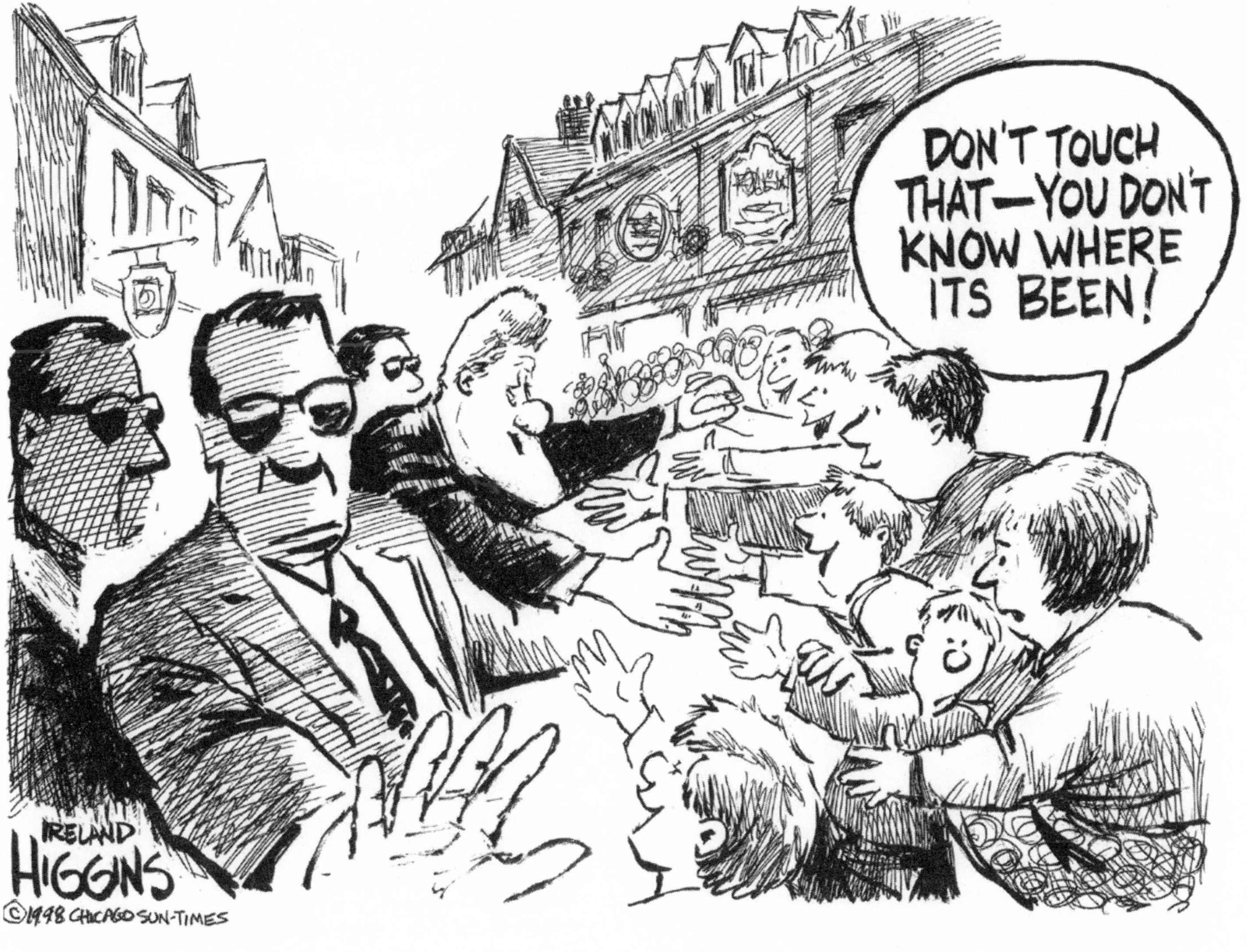
DON'T TOUCH THAT—YOU DON'T KNOW WHERE ITS BEEN!
IRELAND
HIGGINS
©1998 CHICAGO SUN-TIMES

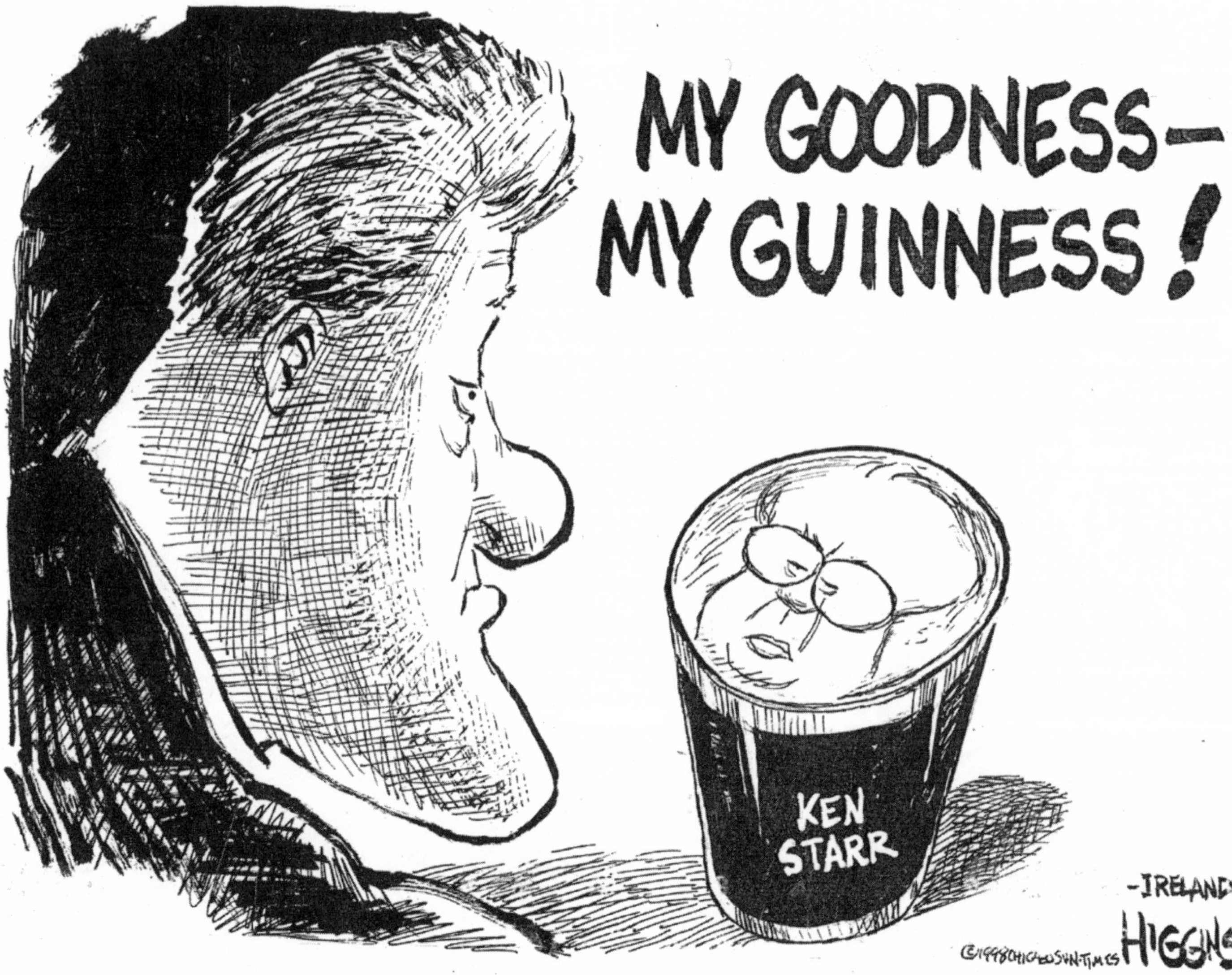
MY GOODNESS–
MY GUINNESS!
KEN
STARR
-IRELAND-
©1998 CHICAGO SUN-TIMES HIGGINS

In 1999, my wife and I accompanied a small group of political cartoonists to Cuba for a two-week tour of the island. During the trip, which was confined to an antiseptic environment in which only the party line was spoken, we made the most startling and intriguing discoveries about life in Havana.

Yet nothing we had seen previously compared with what we saw on our last day, when two young men took us on a four-hour "unofficial" trek through the city's Centro district. What we discovered were some of the saddest scenes of abject poverty you could imagine: buildings without roofs, doors, windows, or running water. In many cases, water buckets were hauled up by pulleys to the upper floors of dwellings. After forty years, the revolution was definitely showing its age. Our two teenage guides put themselves at risk by violating Cuba's "dangerousness" law, which prohibits their citizens from being too friendly with foreigners. At the end of our tour, they stopped at the edge of the neighborhood and told us we must go on without them because they were fearful of being seen talking with us outside of Centro. Here we saw some signs of capitalism on street corners as prostitutes plied their trade.

On another day, we took in a baseball game featuring a couple of the finest teams in captivity.

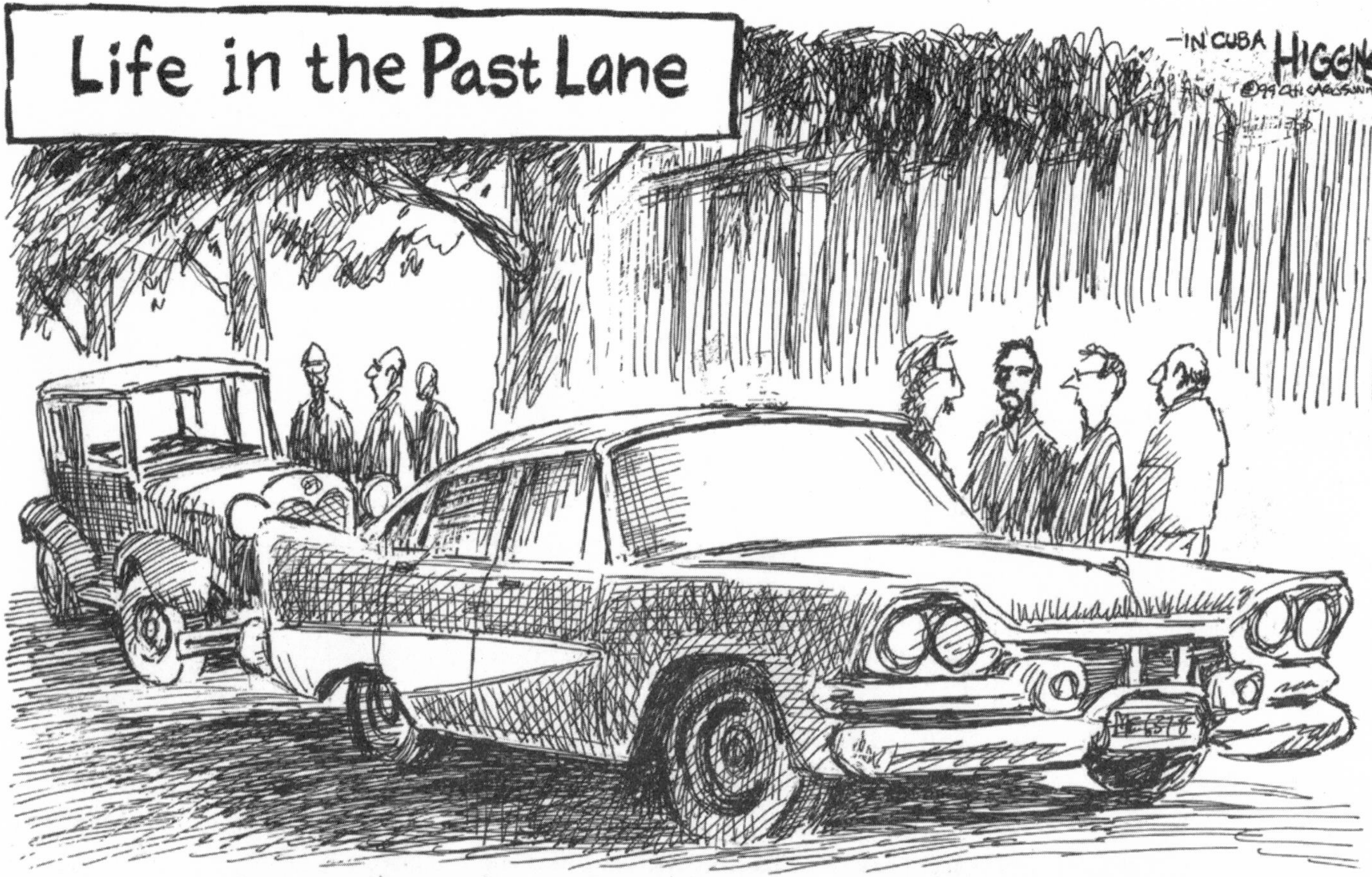
Life in the Past Lane
—IN CUBA
HIGGINS

Due to the embargo the streets of Havana hold a bumper crop of classic cars.

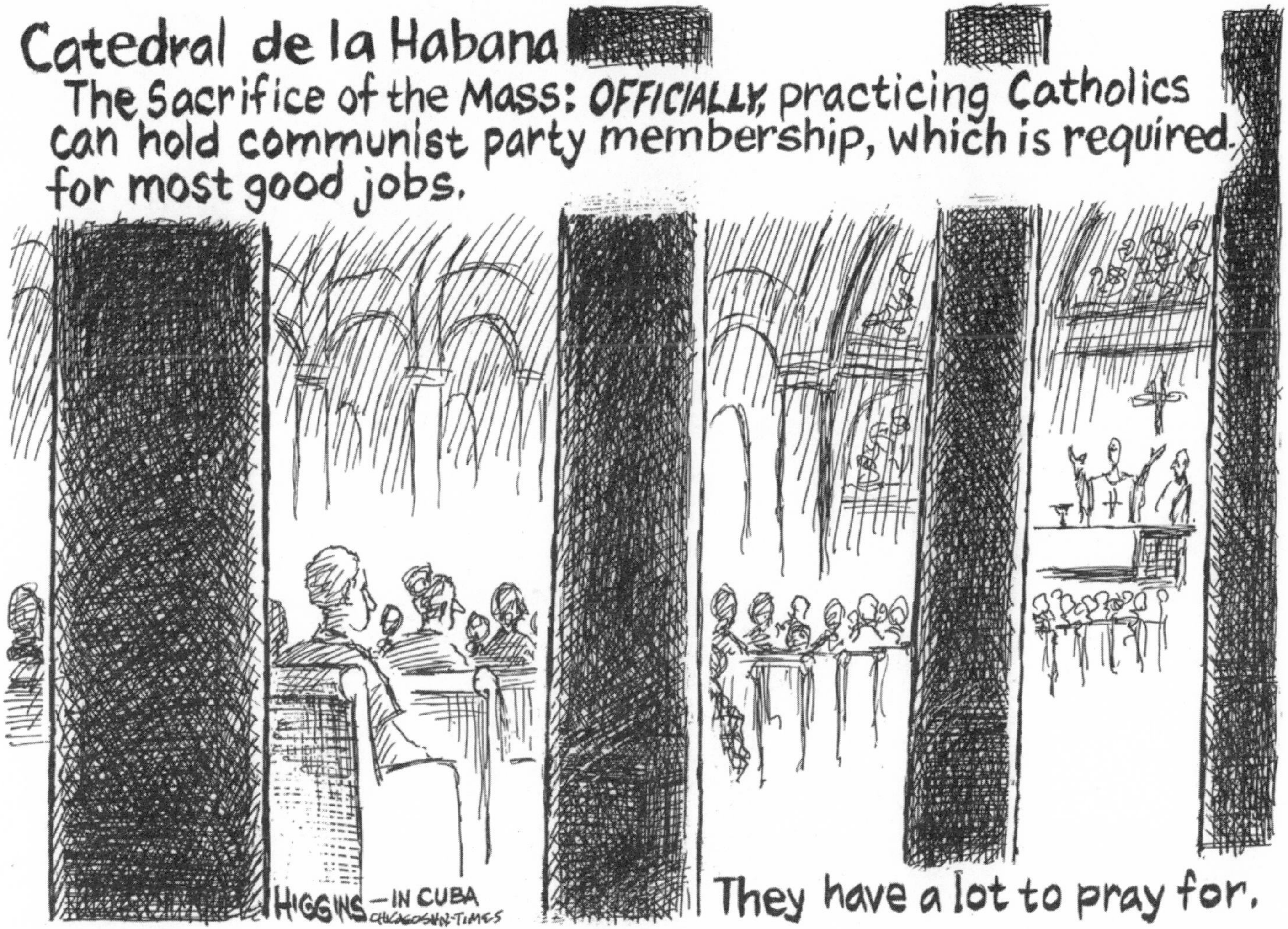
Catedral de la Habana
The Sacrifice of the Mass: OFFICIALLY, practicing Catholics can hold communist party membership, which is required for most good jobs.
HIGGINS—IN CUBA
CHICAGO SUN-TIMES
They have a lot to pray for.

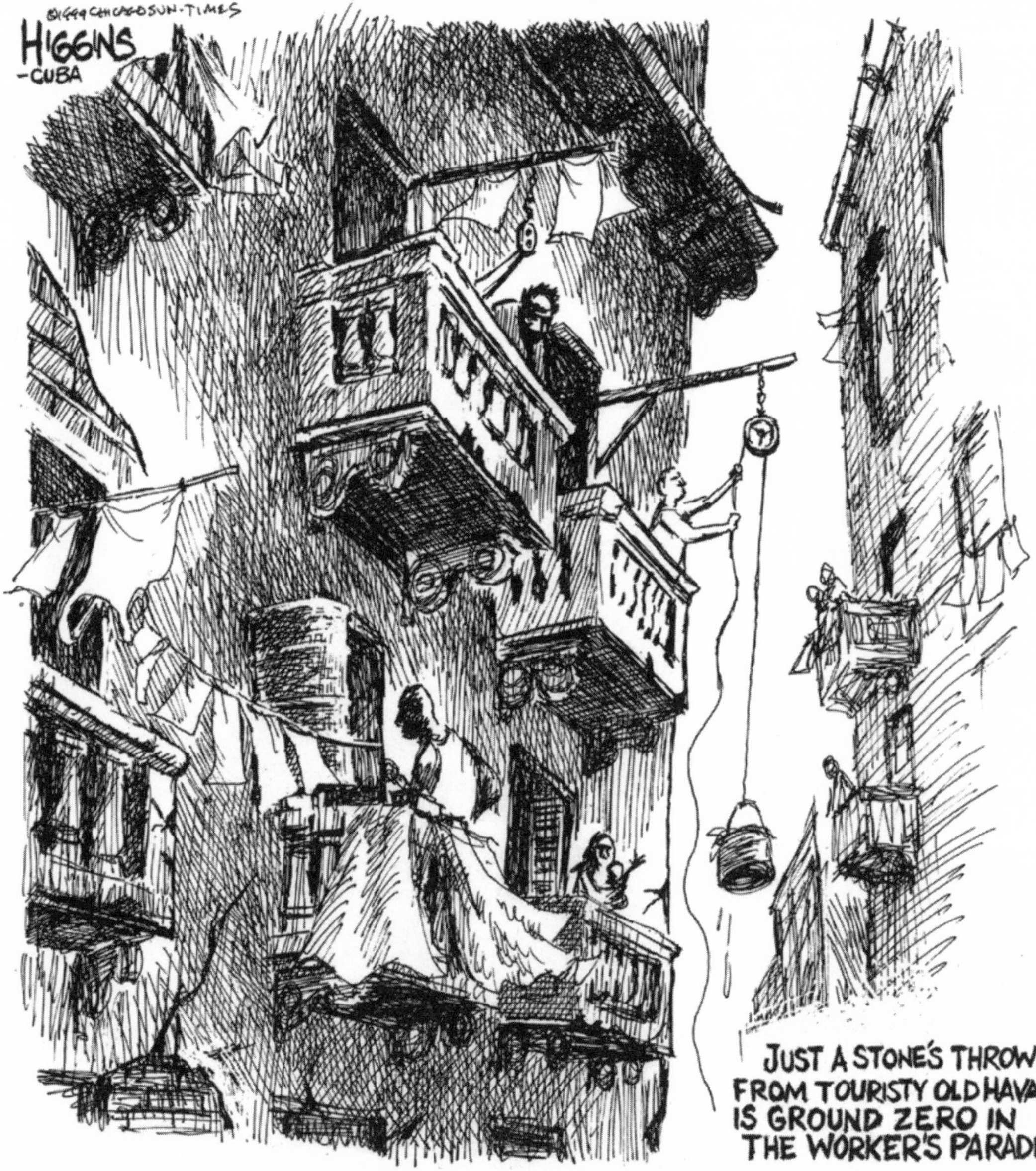
©1999 CHICAGO SUN-TIMES
HIGGINS
-CUBA
JUST A STONE'S THROW FROM TOURISTY OLD HAVANA IS GROUND ZERO IN THE WORKER'S PARADISE.

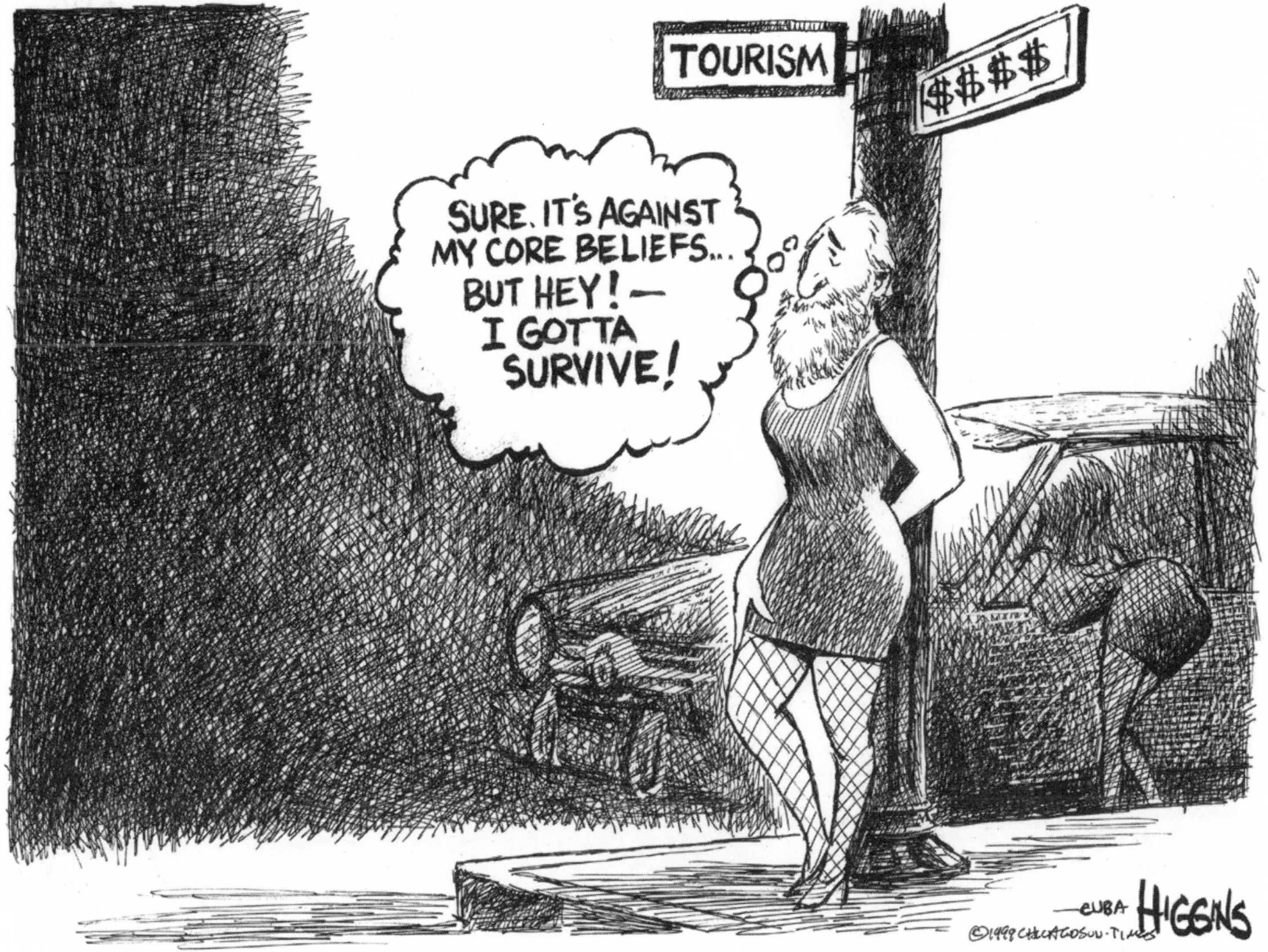
TOURISM
$$$$
SURE, IT'S AGAINST MY CORE BELIEFS... BUT HEY!— I GOTTA SURVIVE!
CUBA
HIGGINS

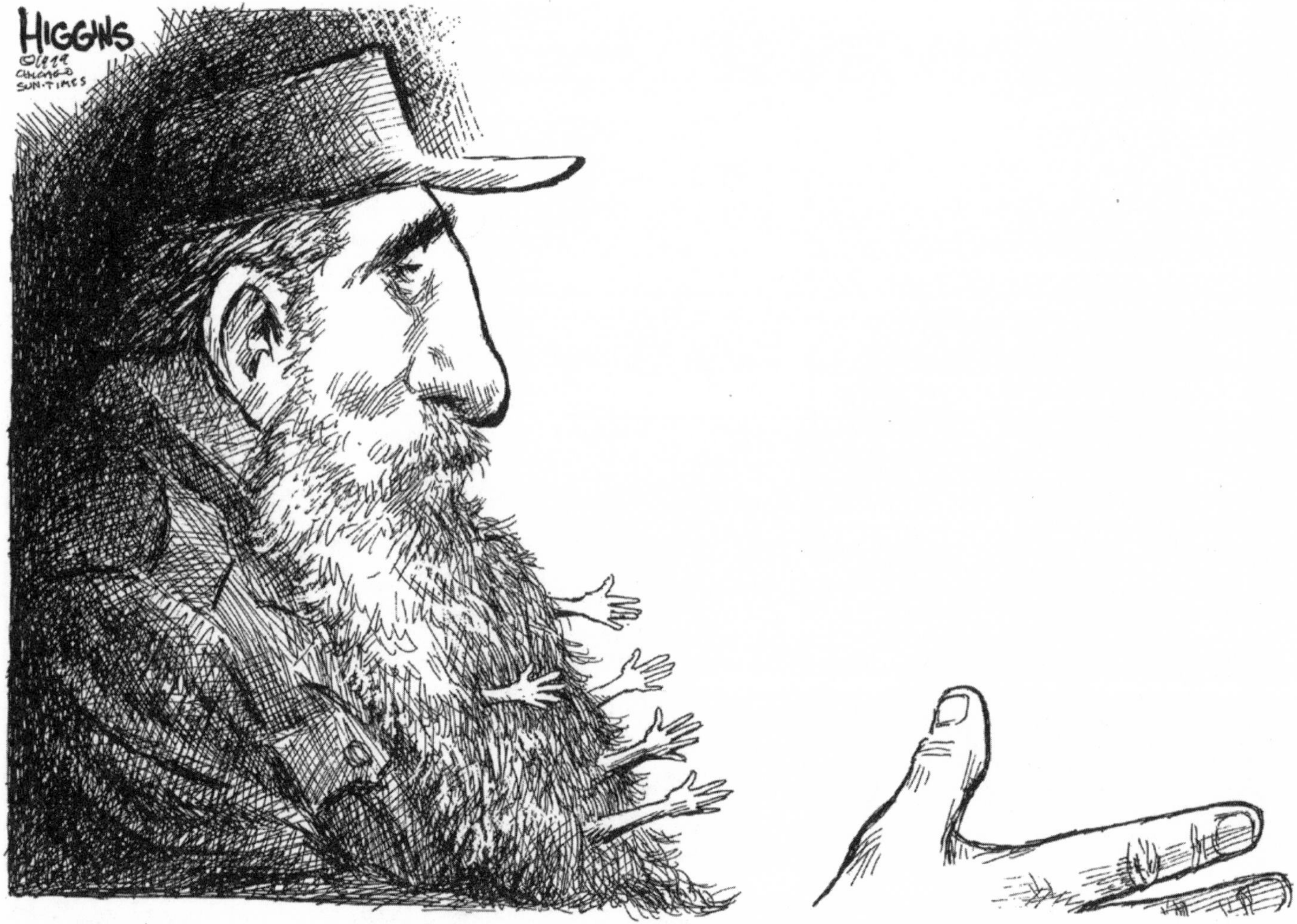
HIGGINS
CHICAGO
SUN-TIMES

Gramma

"WOULD YOUR GRANMA LIE TO YOU?"

HAVANA- SUNNY 85°
MIAMI- SNOW HIGH OF 32°

¡BUENOS DIAS!

HIGGINS
©CHICAGO SUN-TIMES/
UNIVERSAL PRESS
SYNDICATE

14 AUGUSTO 2006

¡CASTRO-SOCKO!

CAPTIVATING LEADER TAKES IT ON THE CHIN.

Abc dy QTRVXw. Abd but Aq mllnuxa
QUAK QUAK DUCKO OW POW BANG. THE SMall
YOUNG DOG. EVERY GOOD BOY DOES FINE

Hospitalized Cuban President Fidel Castro narrowly escaped death at his own hand Sunday, in Havana. Castro, seen here at his 80th birthday party, suddenly began punching himself as his bodyguard detail looked on in horror. With guns drawn, they debated for several minutes over how to disarm the assailant without injuring El Presidente.

"Fidel is not well," said one guard. "We did not want to see him harmed, yet at the same time we did not want to disrespect his wishes."

A solution arose when El Presidente's nurse, Juanita Anita Chavez Venezuela de la Revolucion, began slapping him, hoping to bring him to his senses.

Nurse de la Revolucion died of gunshot wounds Sunday in Havana. Services have been held.

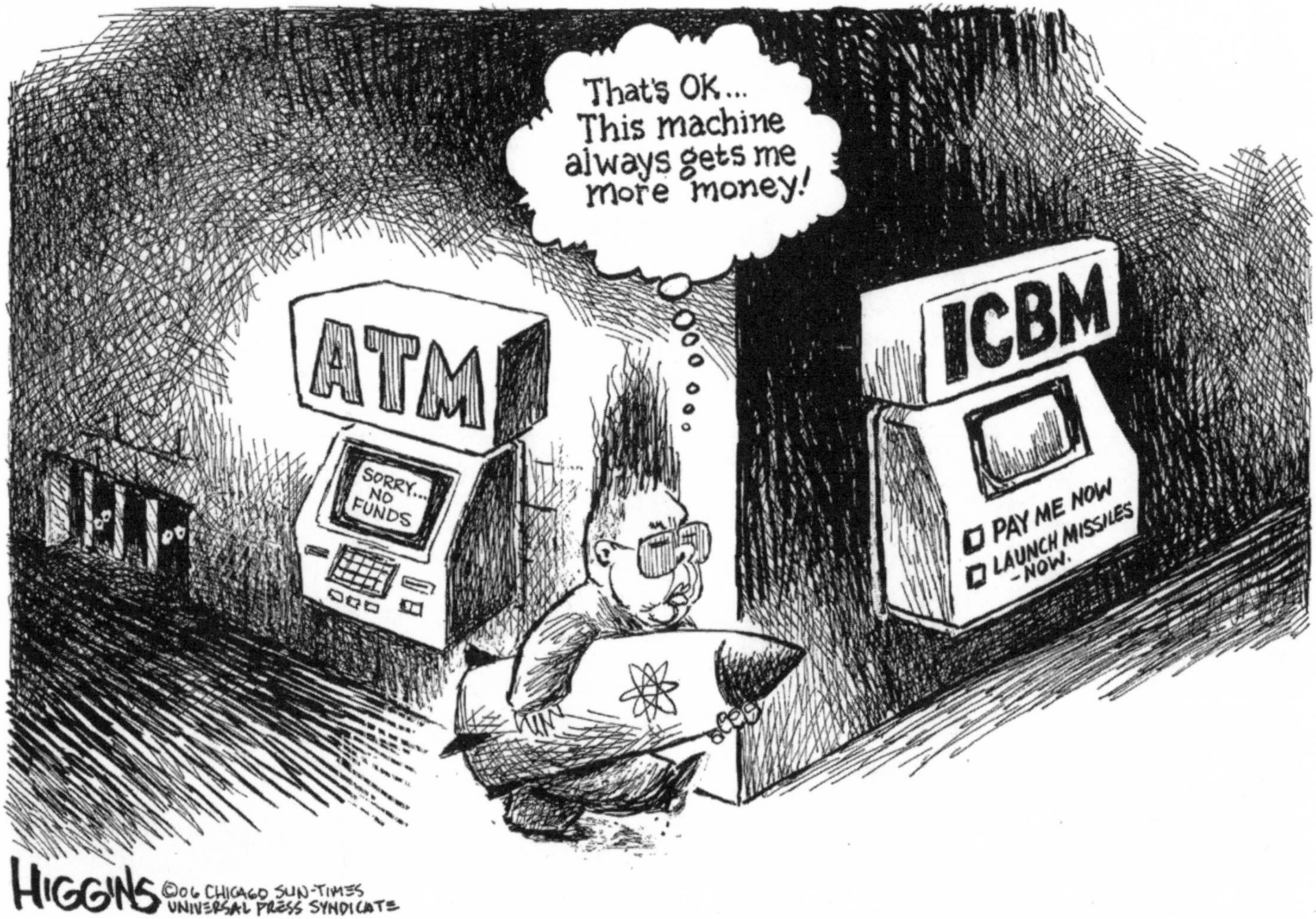
That's OK...
This machine
always gets me
more money!
ATM
SORRY...
NO
FUNDS
ICBM
PAY ME NOW
LAUNCH MISSILES
-NOW.
HIGGINS ©06 CHICAGO SUN-TIMES
UNIVERSAL PRESS SYNDICATE

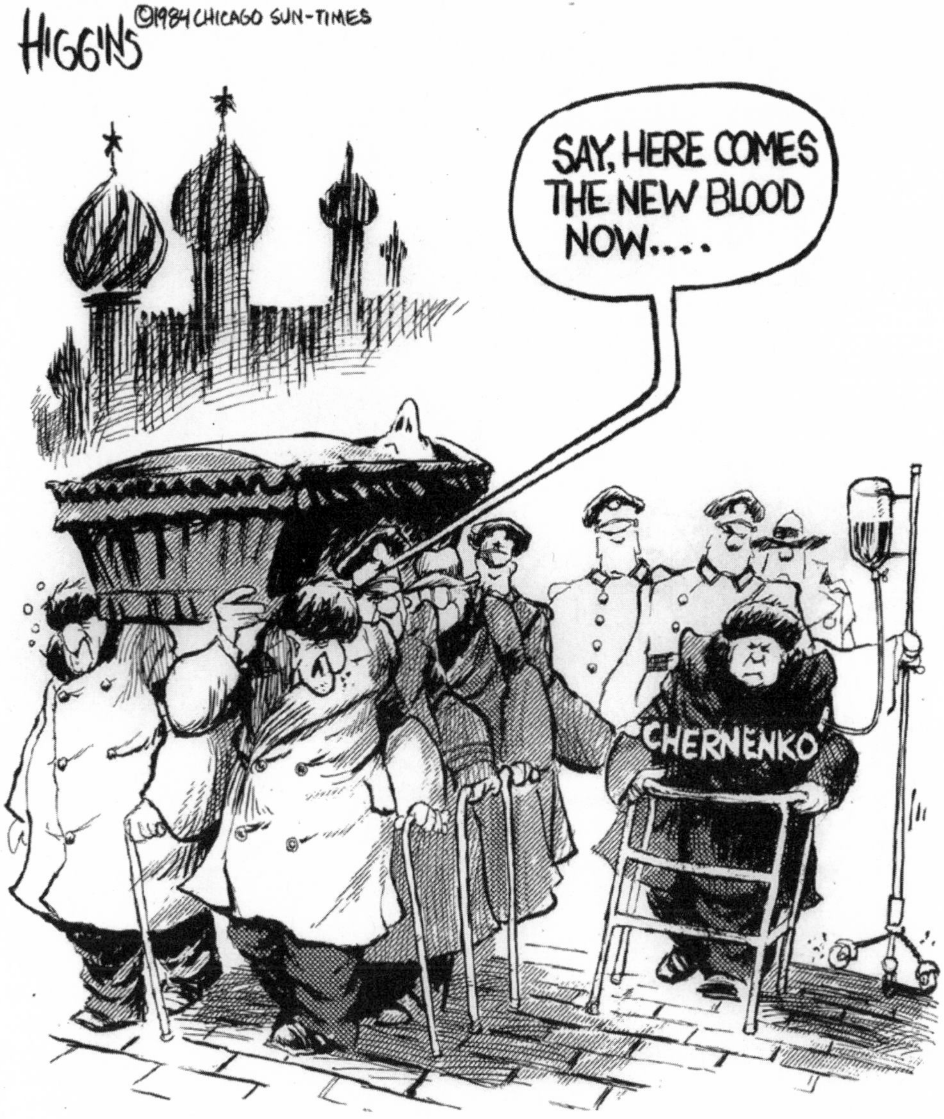
HIGGINS ©1984 CHICAGO SUN-TIMES
SAY, HERE COMES THE NEW BLOOD NOW....
CHERNENKO

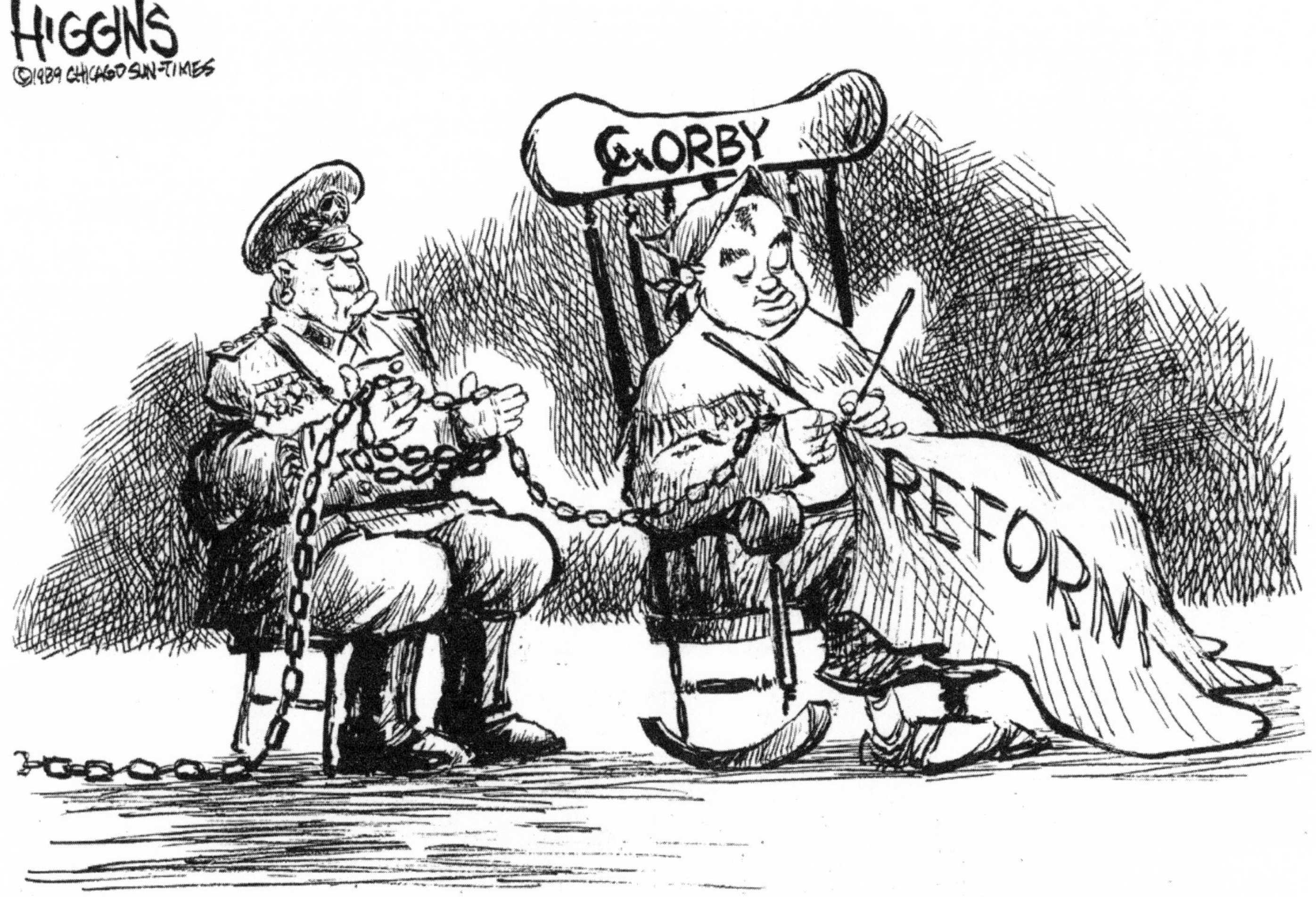
HIGGINS
©1989 CHICAGO SUN-TIMES
GORBY
REFORM

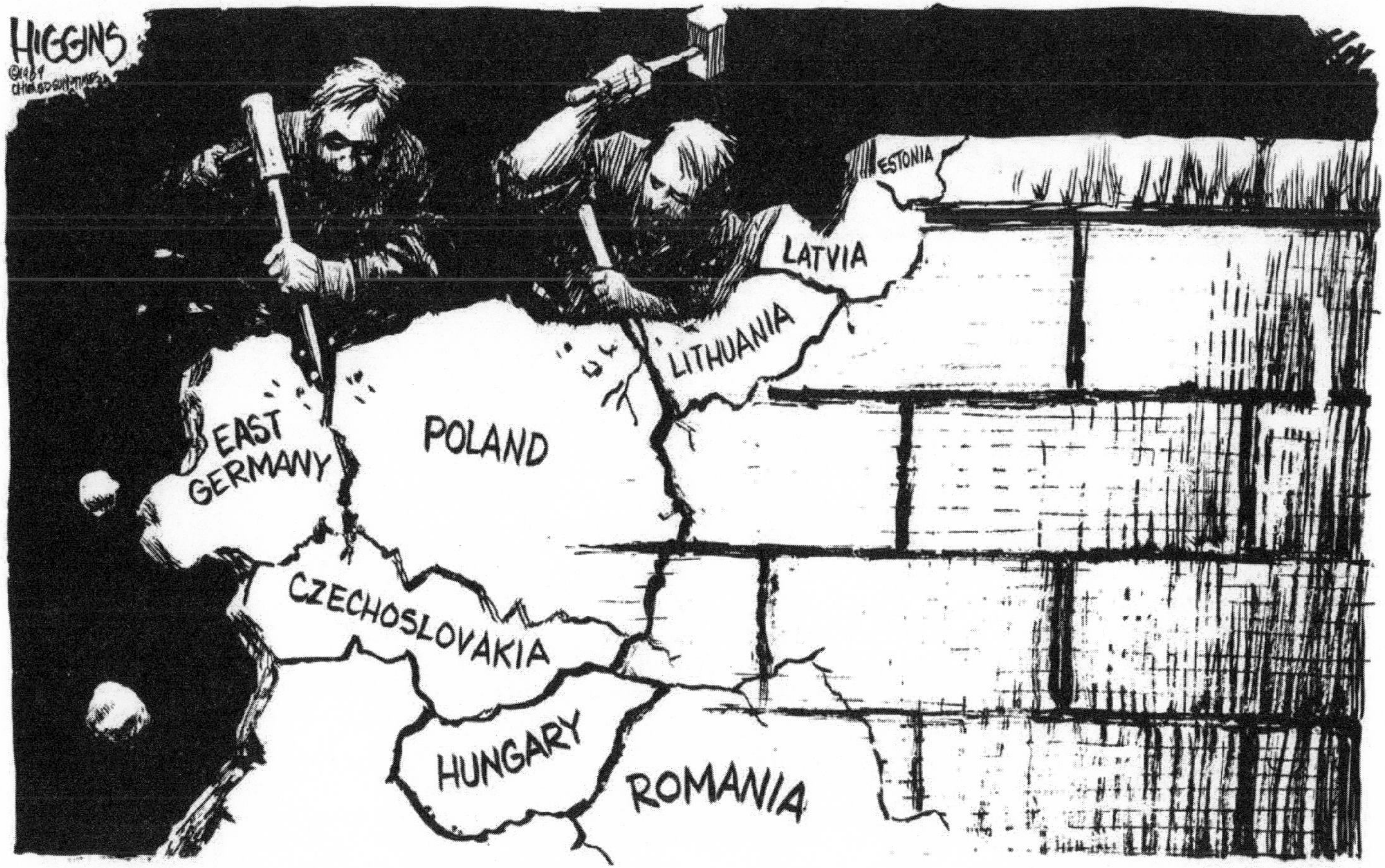
HIGGINS
©1989
CHICAGO SUN-TIMES
ESTONIA
LATVIA
LITHUANIA
EAST GERMANY
POLAND
CZECHOSLOVAKIA
HUNGARY
ROMANIA

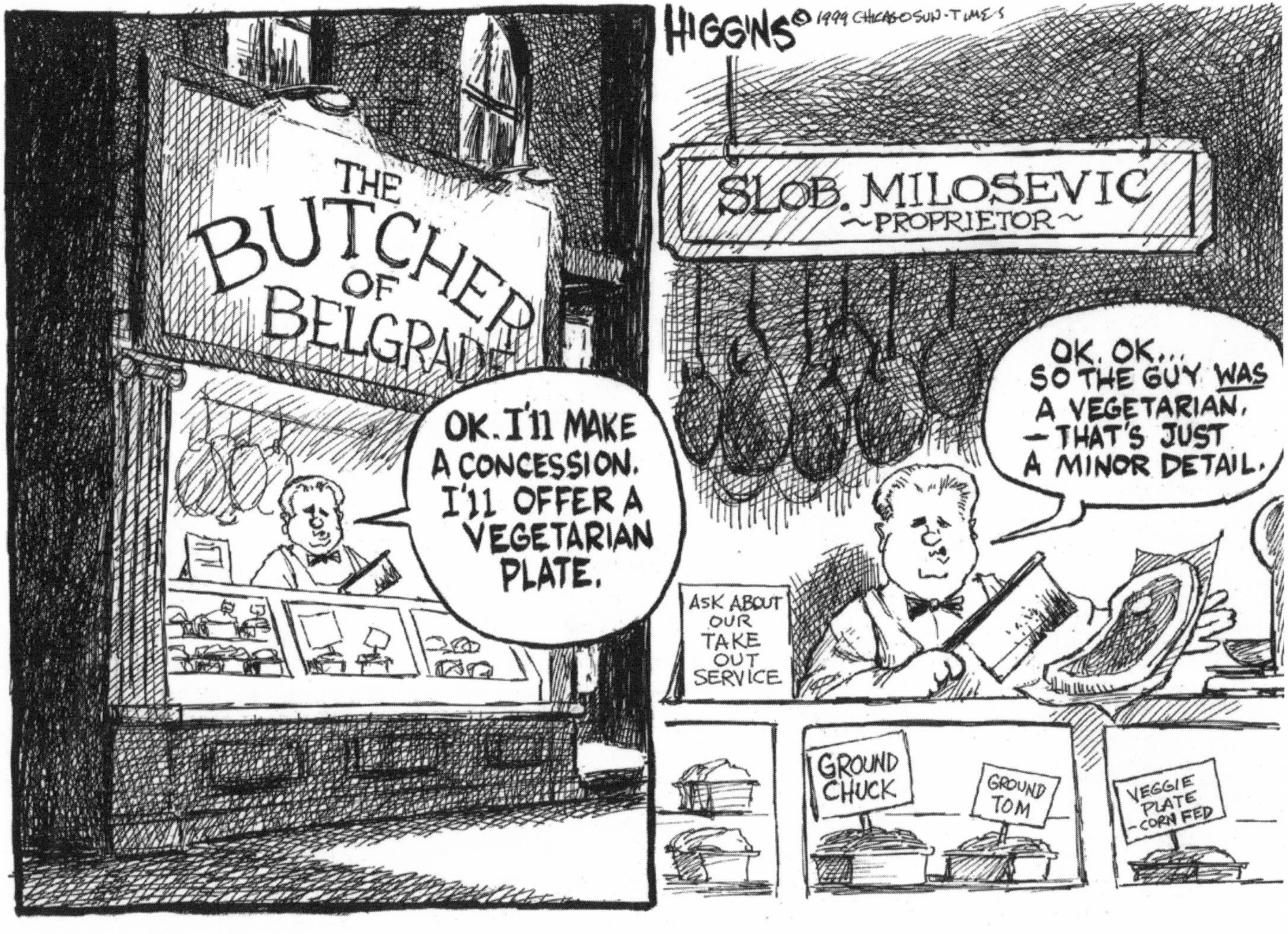
HIGGINS © 1999 CHICAGO SUN-TIMES
THE BUTCHER OF BELGRADE
OK. I'll MAKE A CONCESSION. I'll OFFER A VEGETARIAN PLATE.
SLOB. MILOSEVIC ~PROPRIETOR~
OK, OK... SO THE GUY WAS A VEGETARIAN. —THAT'S JUST A MINOR DETAIL.
ASK ABOUT OUR TAKE OUT SERVICE
GROUND CHUCK
GROUND TOM
VEGGIE PLATE —CORN FED

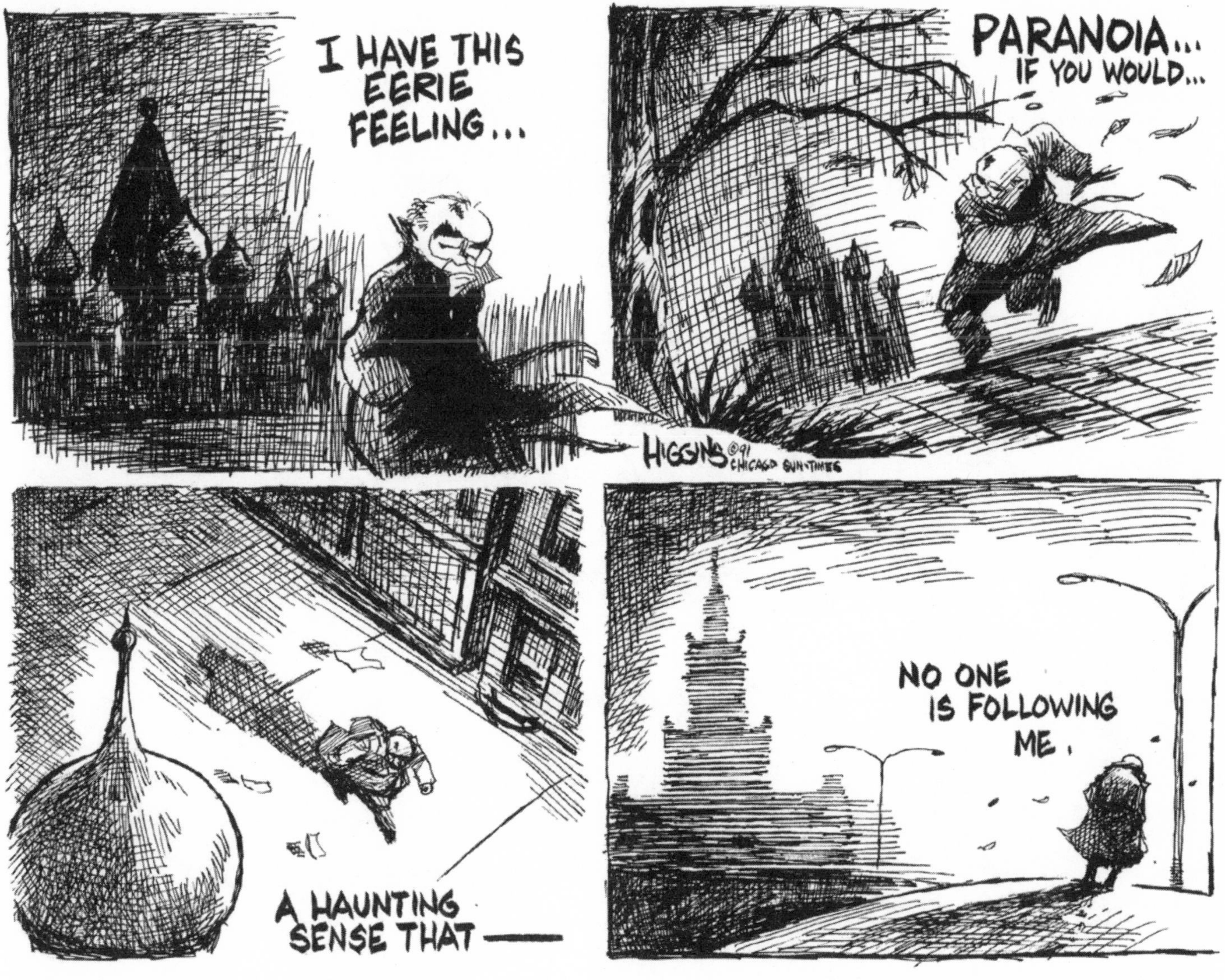
I HAVE THIS EERIE FEELING...
PARANOIA... IF YOU WOULD...
HIGGINS ©91 CHICAGO SUN-TIMES
A HAUNTING SENSE THAT —
NO ONE IS FOLLOWING ME.

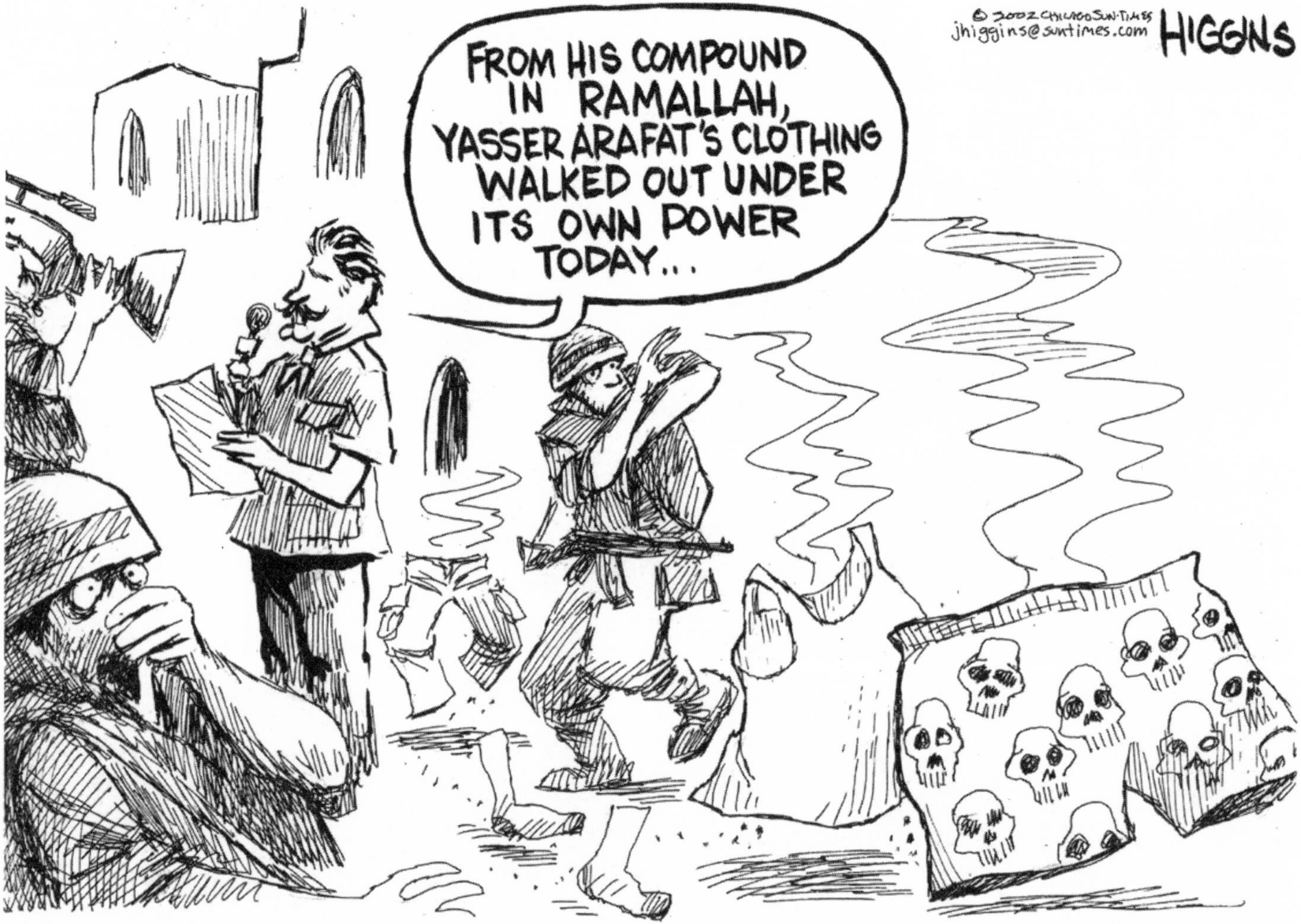
© 2002 CHICAGO SUN-TIMES
jhiggins@suntimes.com
HIGGINS
FROM HIS COMPOUND IN RAMALLAH, YASSER ARAFAT'S CLOTHING WALKED OUT UNDER ITS OWN POWER TODAY...

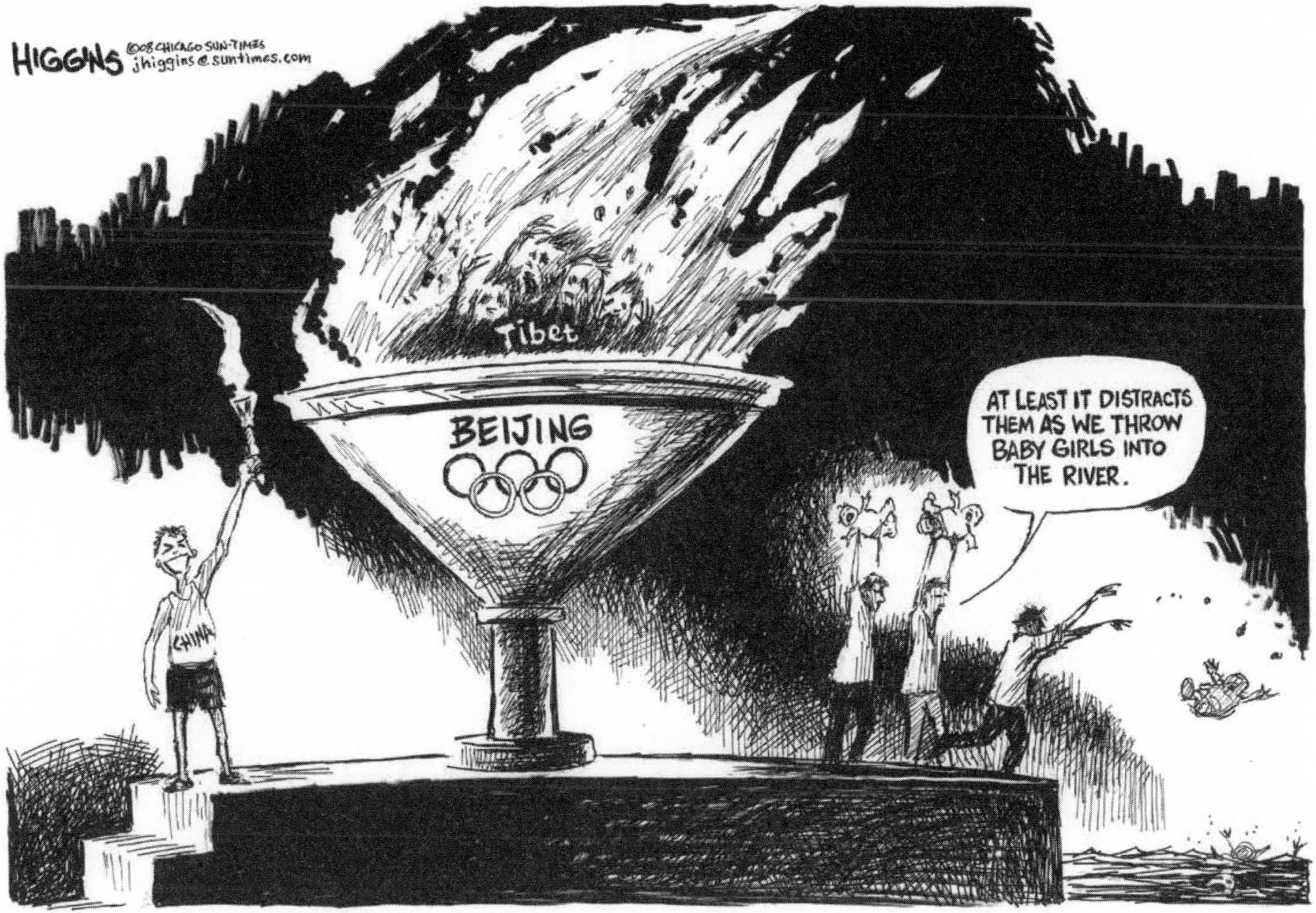
HIGGINS ©08 CHICAGO SUN-TIMES jhiggins@suntimes.com
Tibet
BEIJING
CHINA
AT LEAST IT DISTRACTS THEM AS WE THROW BABY GIRLS INTO THE RIVER.

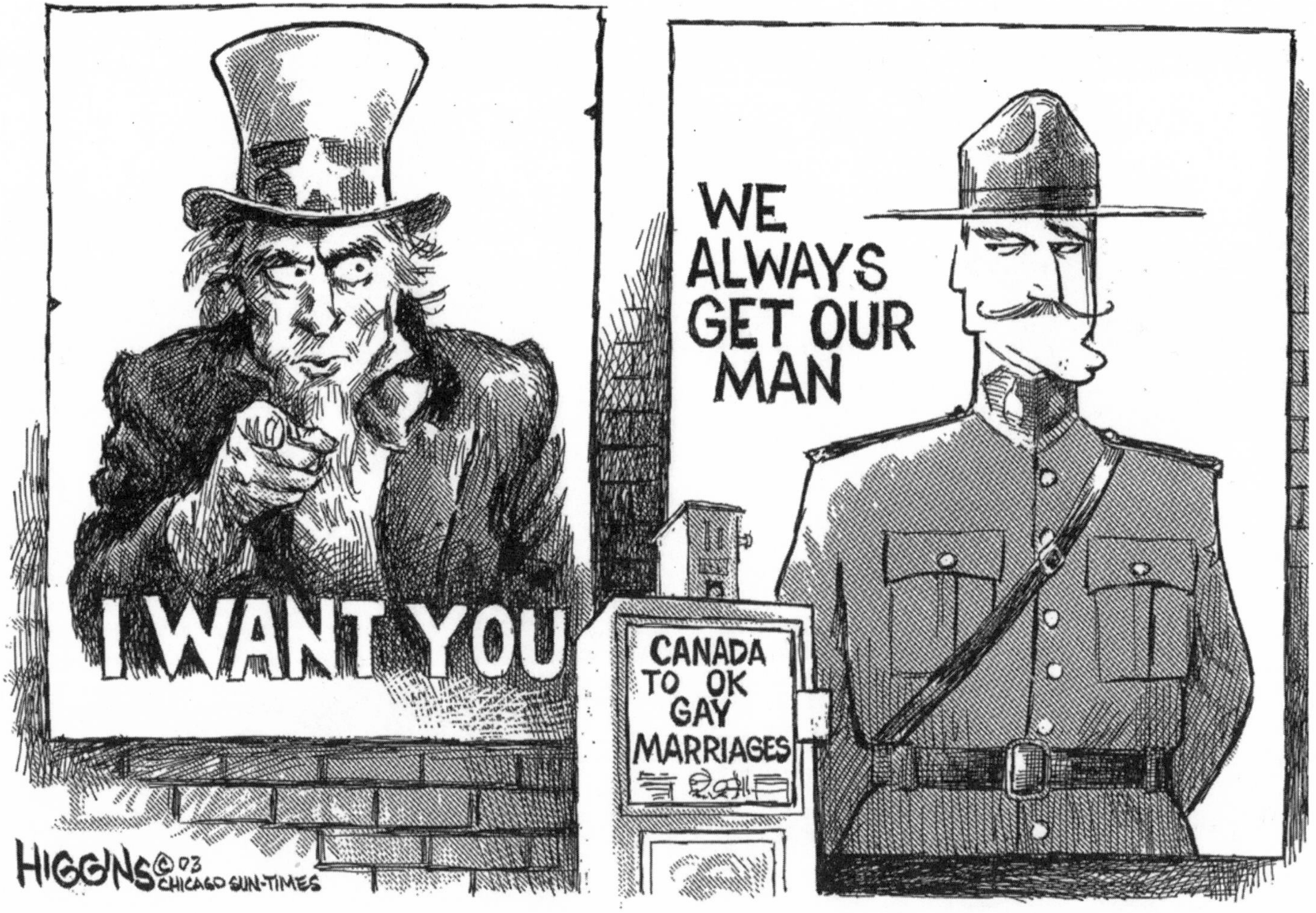
I WANT YOU
WE ALWAYS GET OUR MAN
CANADA TO OK GAY MARRIAGES
HIGGINS © 03 CHICAGO SUN-TIMES

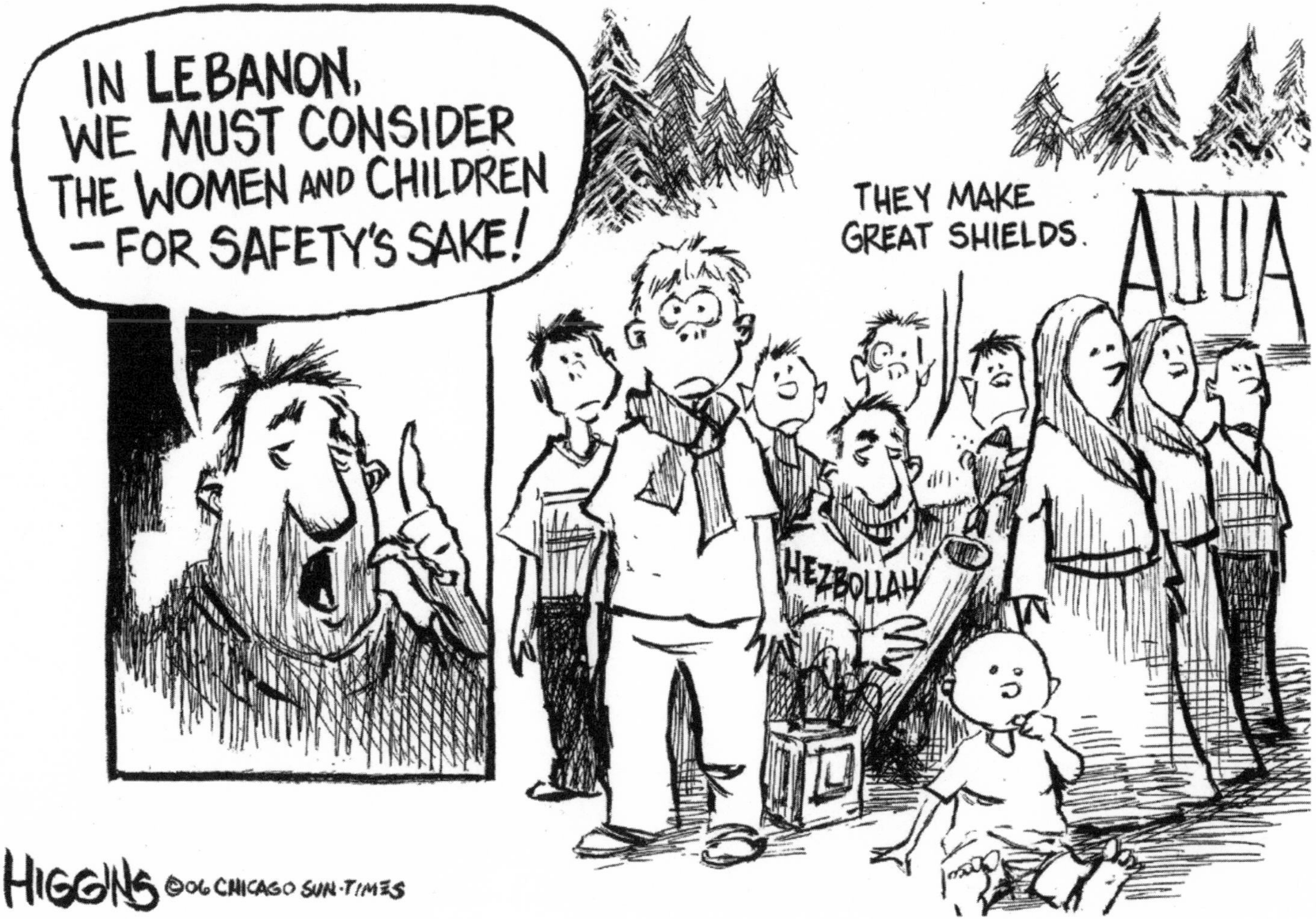

IN LEBANON, WE MUST CONSIDER THE WOMEN AND CHILDREN – FOR SAFETY'S SAKE!
THEY MAKE GREAT SHIELDS.
HEZBOLLAH
HIGGINS ©06 CHICAGO SUN-TIMES

9-11 & AFTER

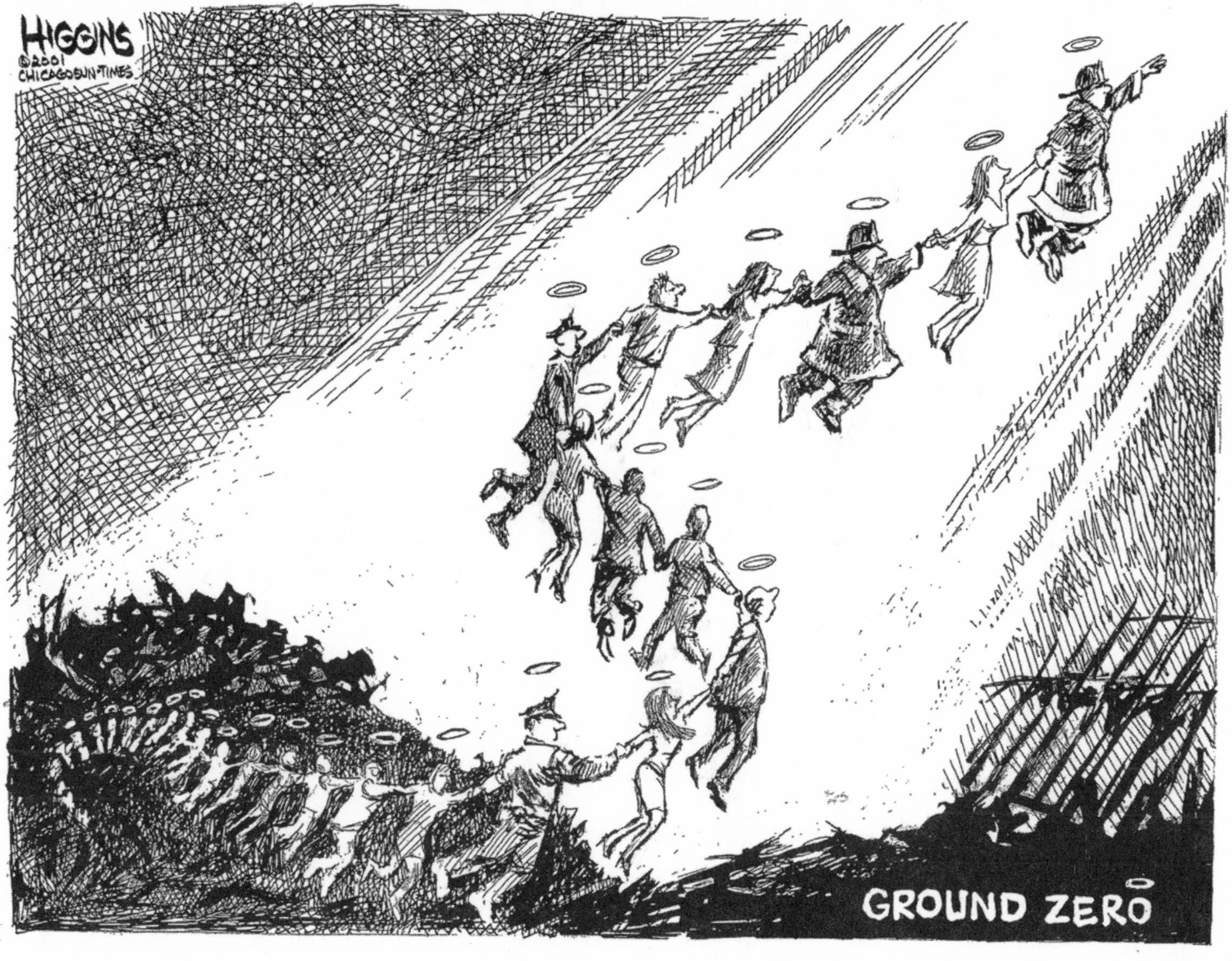
HIGGINS
©2001 CHICAGO SUN-TIMES
GROUND ZERO

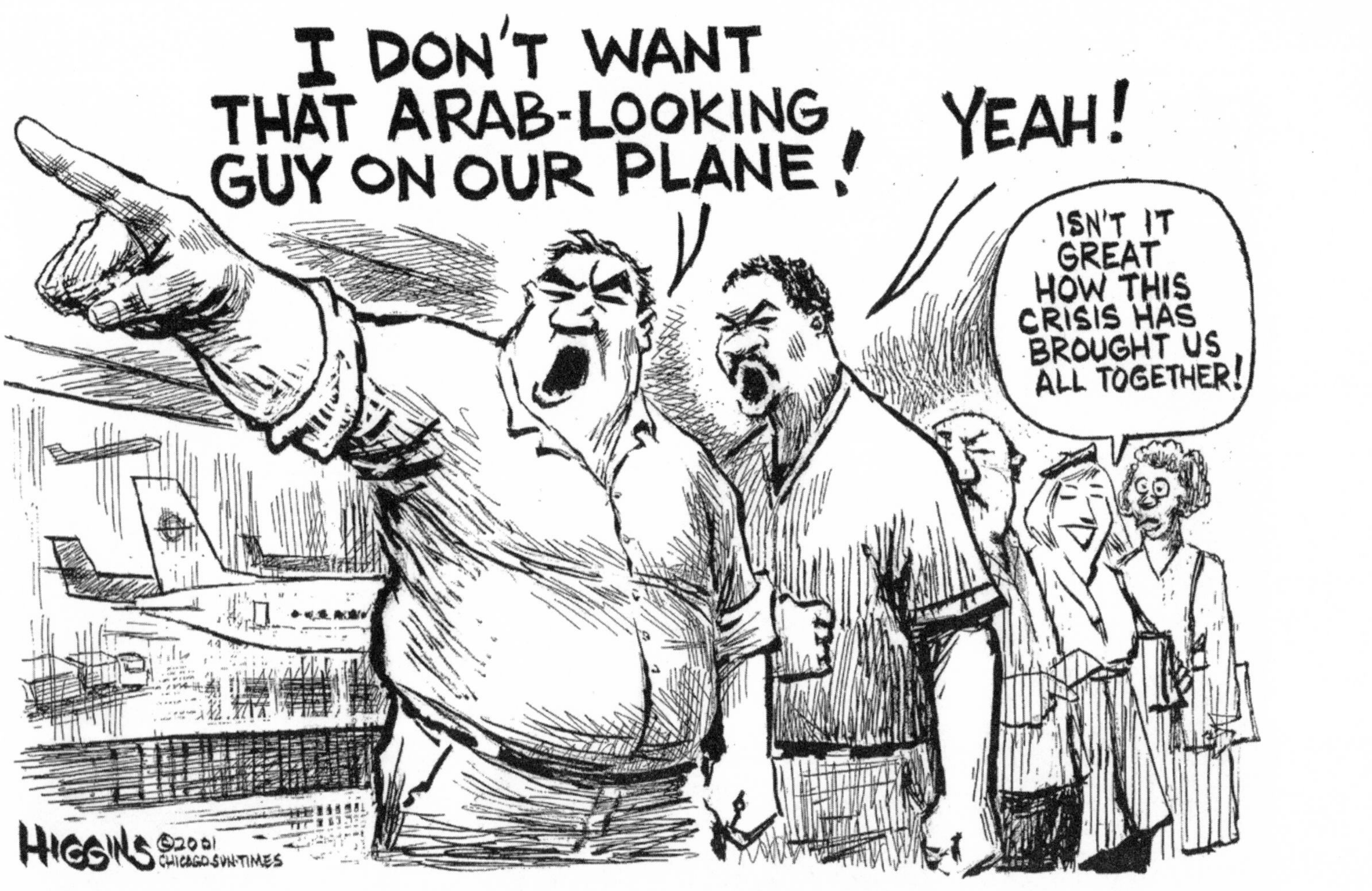
I DON'T WANT THAT ARAB-LOOKING GUY ON OUR PLANE!
YEAH!
ISN'T IT GREAT HOW THIS CRISIS HAS BROUGHT US ALL TOGETHER!
HIGGINS ©2001 CHICAGO SUN-TIMES

Blind fear, leading to anti-Arab sentiment, throws some Americans into a novel and perverse form of unity . . . . A Zogby poll shows blacks are equally likely as whites to racially profile when it comes to preflight screening.

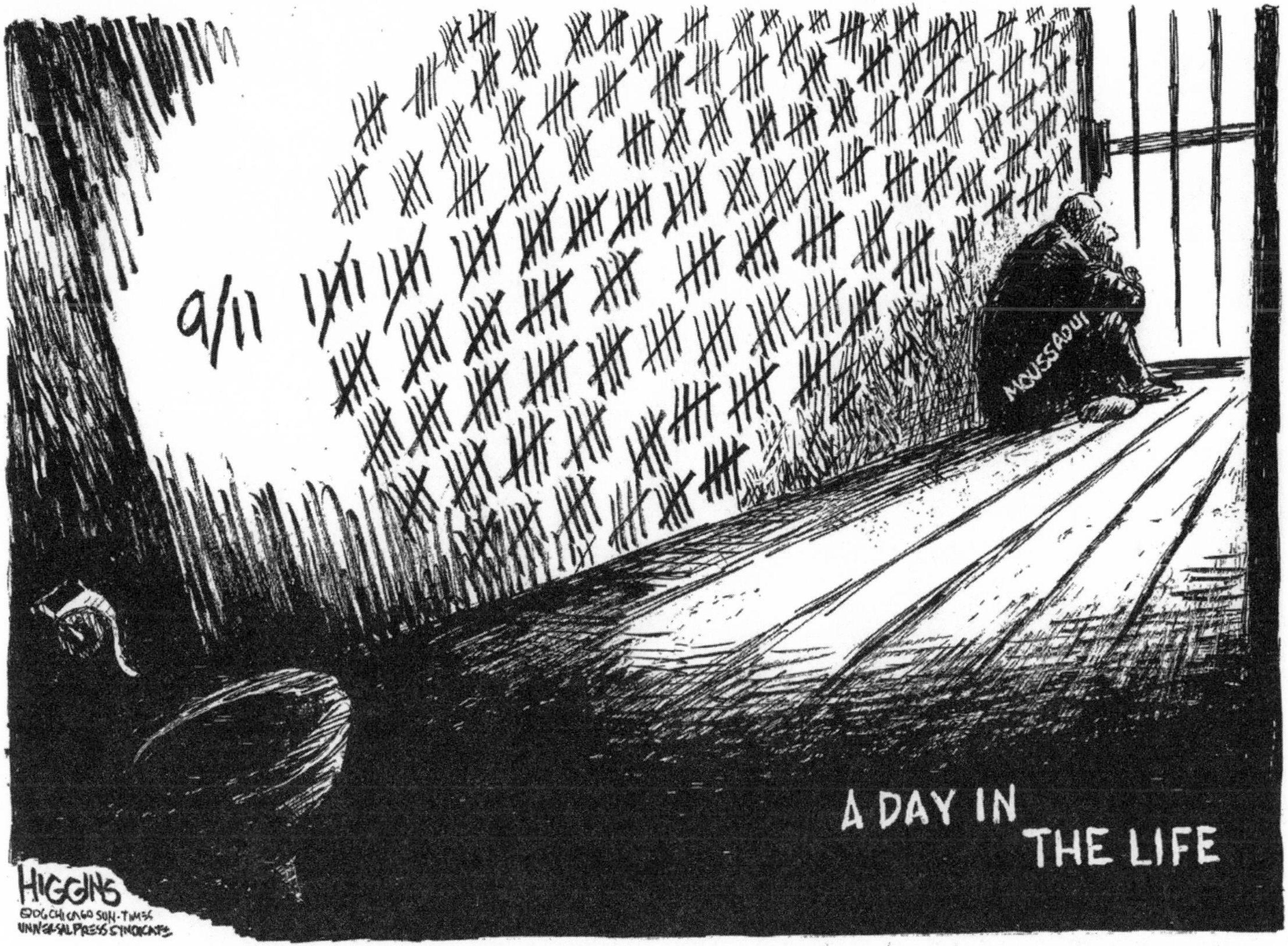

9/11
MOUSSAOUI
A DAY IN
THE LIFE
HIGGINS
©06 CHICAGO SUN-TIMES
UNIVERSAL PRESS SYNDICATE

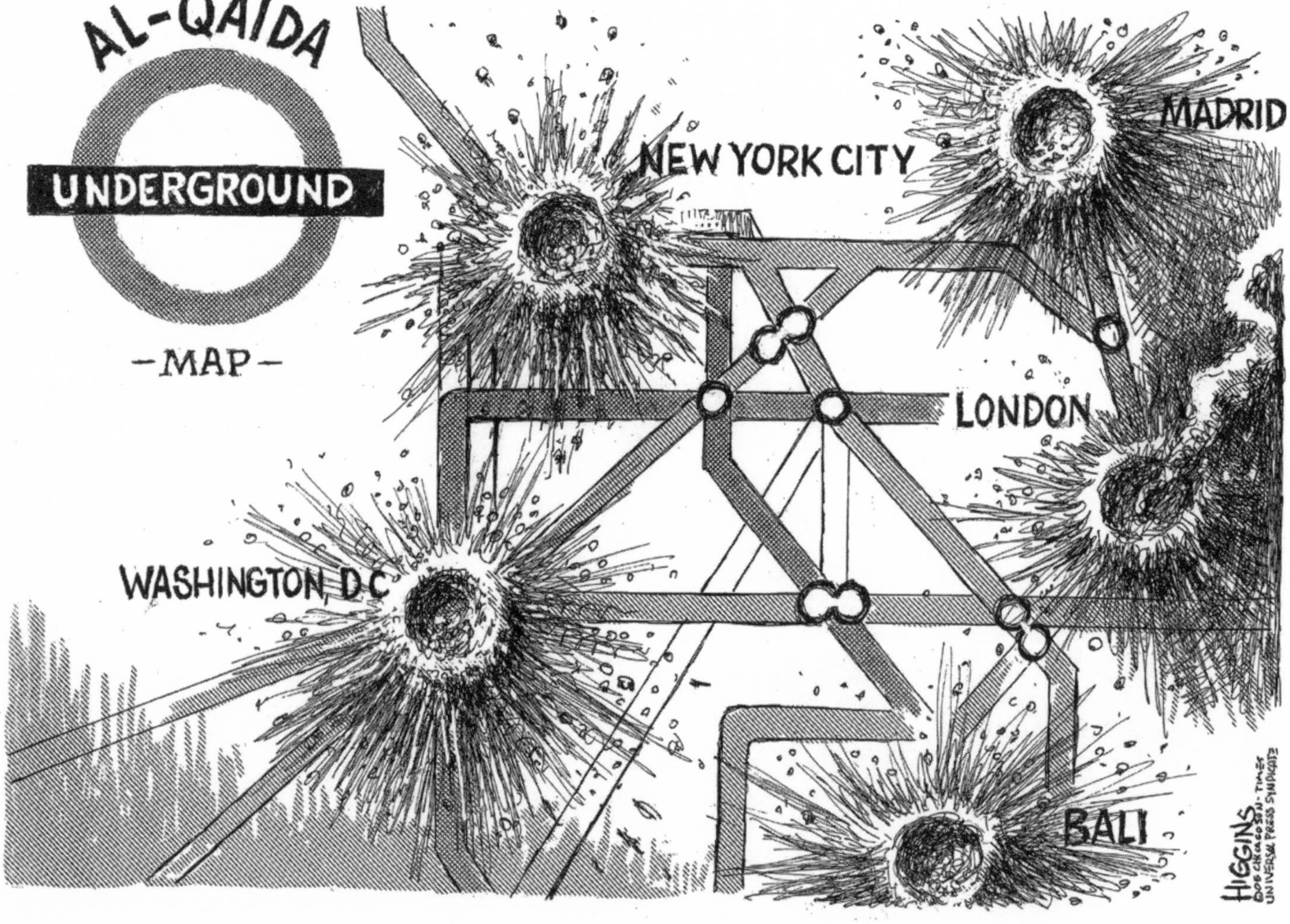

AL-QAIDA
UNDERGROUND
-MAP-
NEW YORK CITY
MADRID
LONDON
WASHINGTON, D.C
BALI
HIGGINS

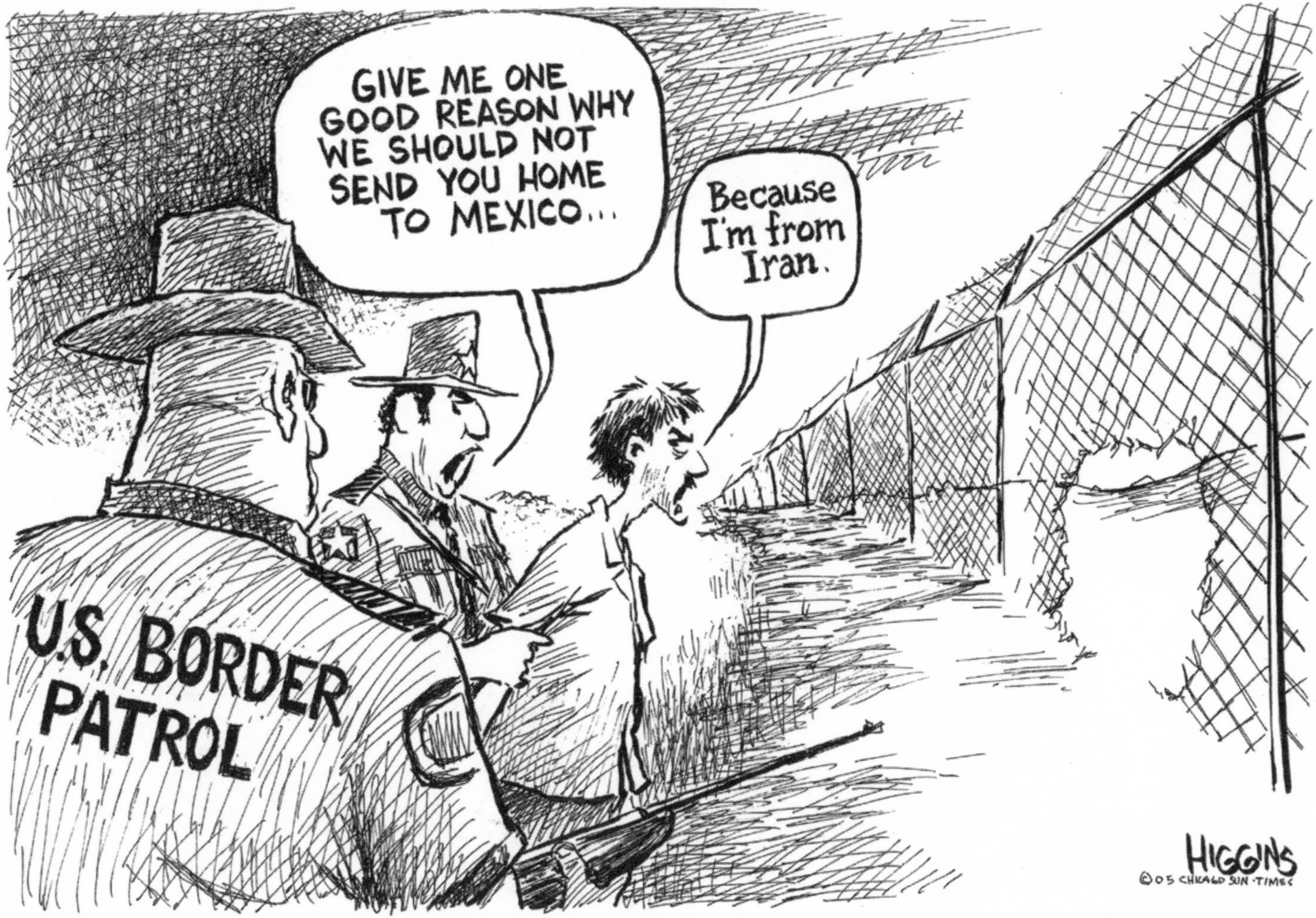
GIVE ME ONE GOOD REASON WHY WE SHOULD NOT SEND YOU HOME TO MEXICO...
Because I'm from Iran.
U.S. BORDER PATROL
HIGGINS
©05 CHICAGO SUN-TIMES

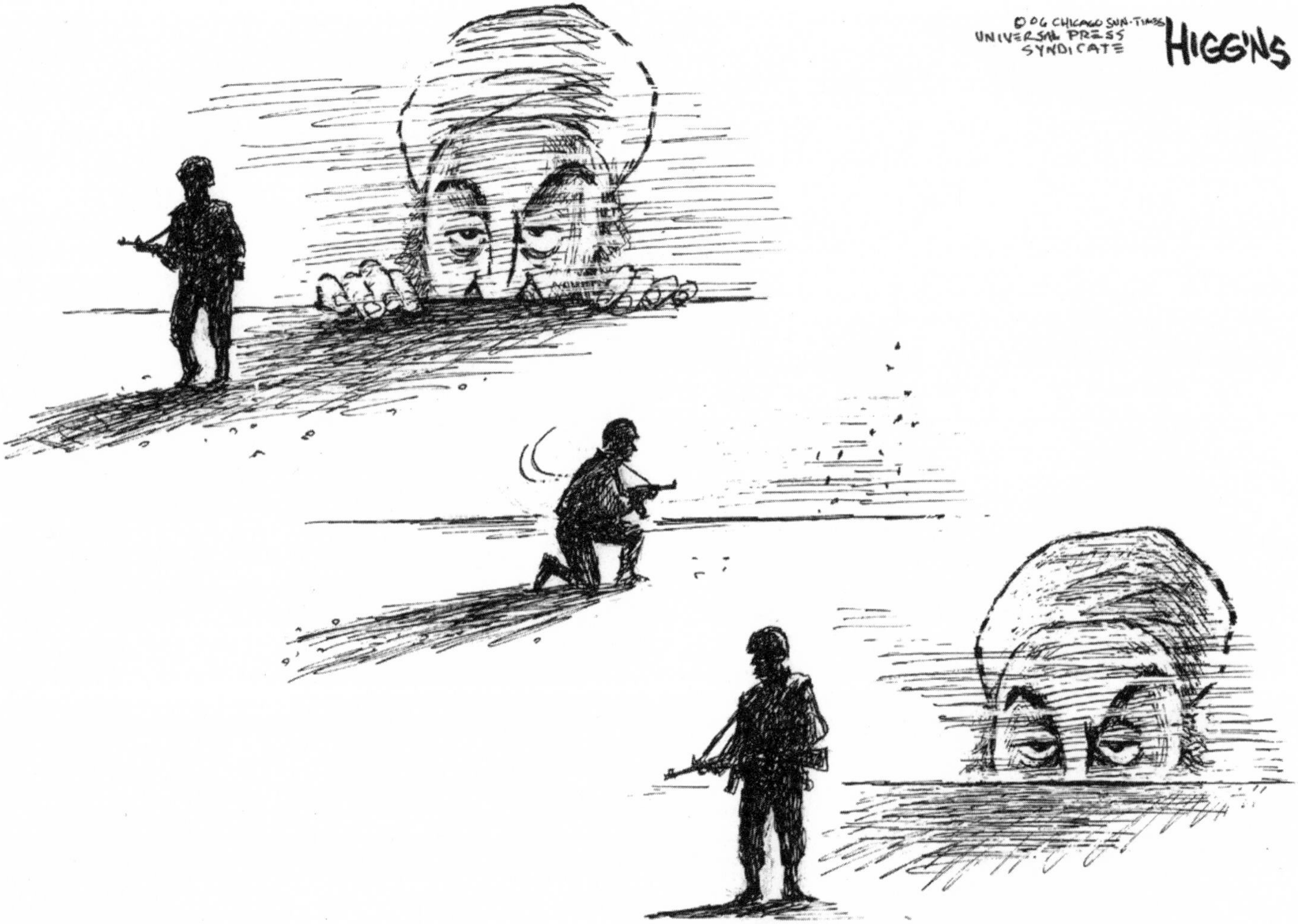
©06 CHICAGO SUN-TIMES
UNIVERSAL PRESS
SYNDICATE
HIGGINS

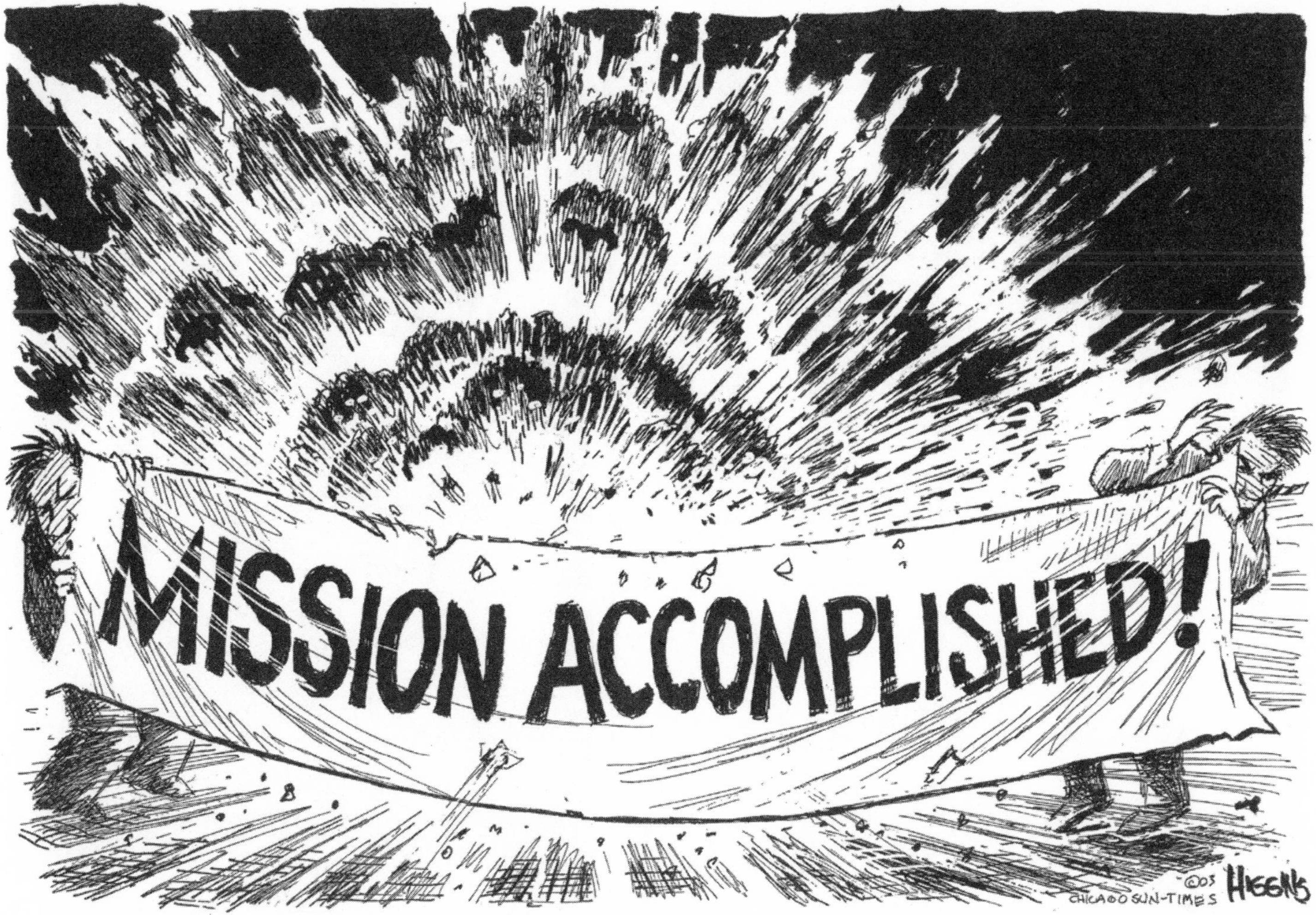
MISSION ACCOMPLISHED!
©03 CHICAGO SUN-TIMES
HIGGINS

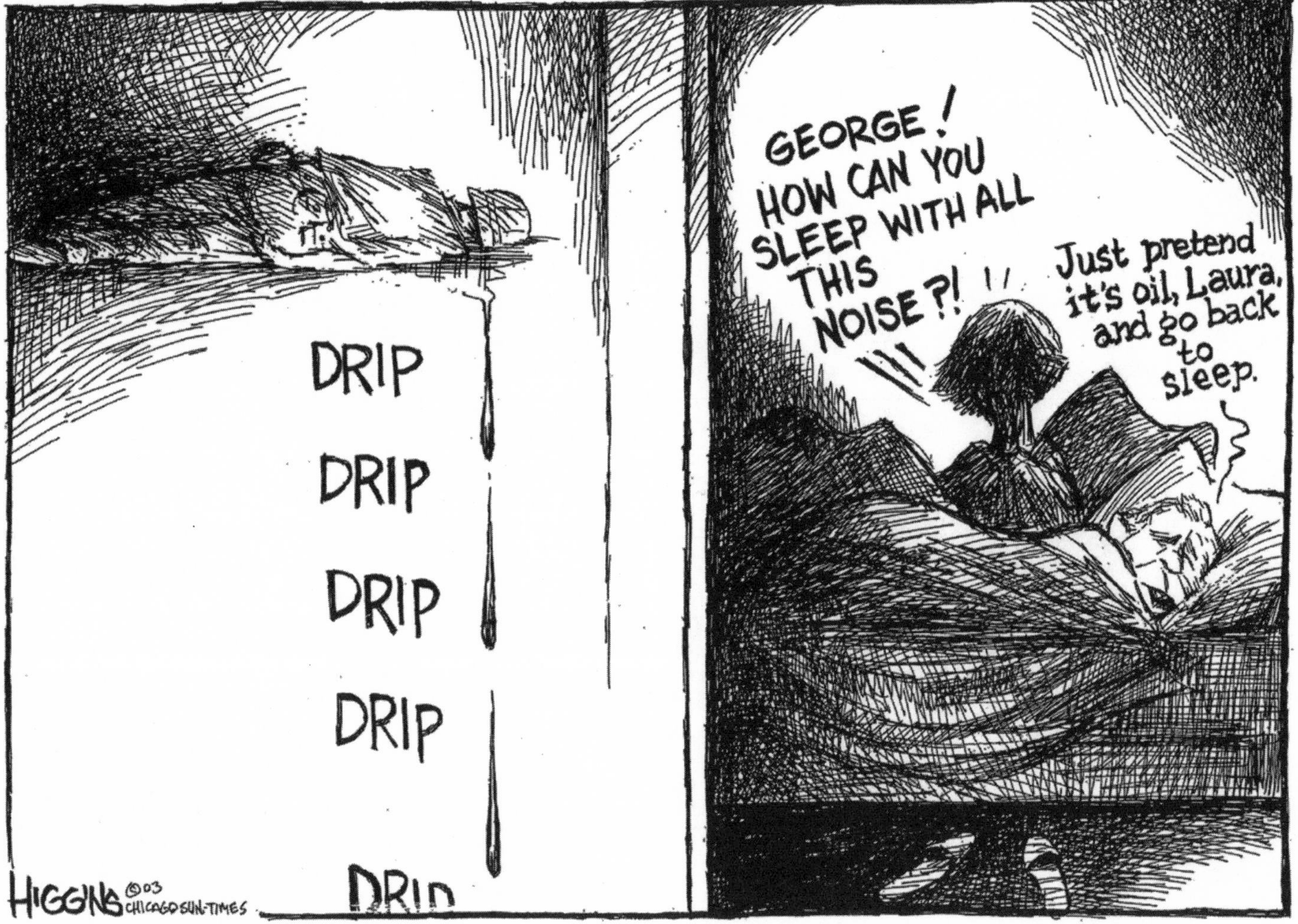
DRIP
DRIP
DRIP
DRIP
HIGGINS ©03 CHICAGO SUN-TIMES
GEORGE! HOW CAN YOU SLEEP WITH ALL THIS NOISE?!
Just pretend it's oil, Laura, and go back to sleep.

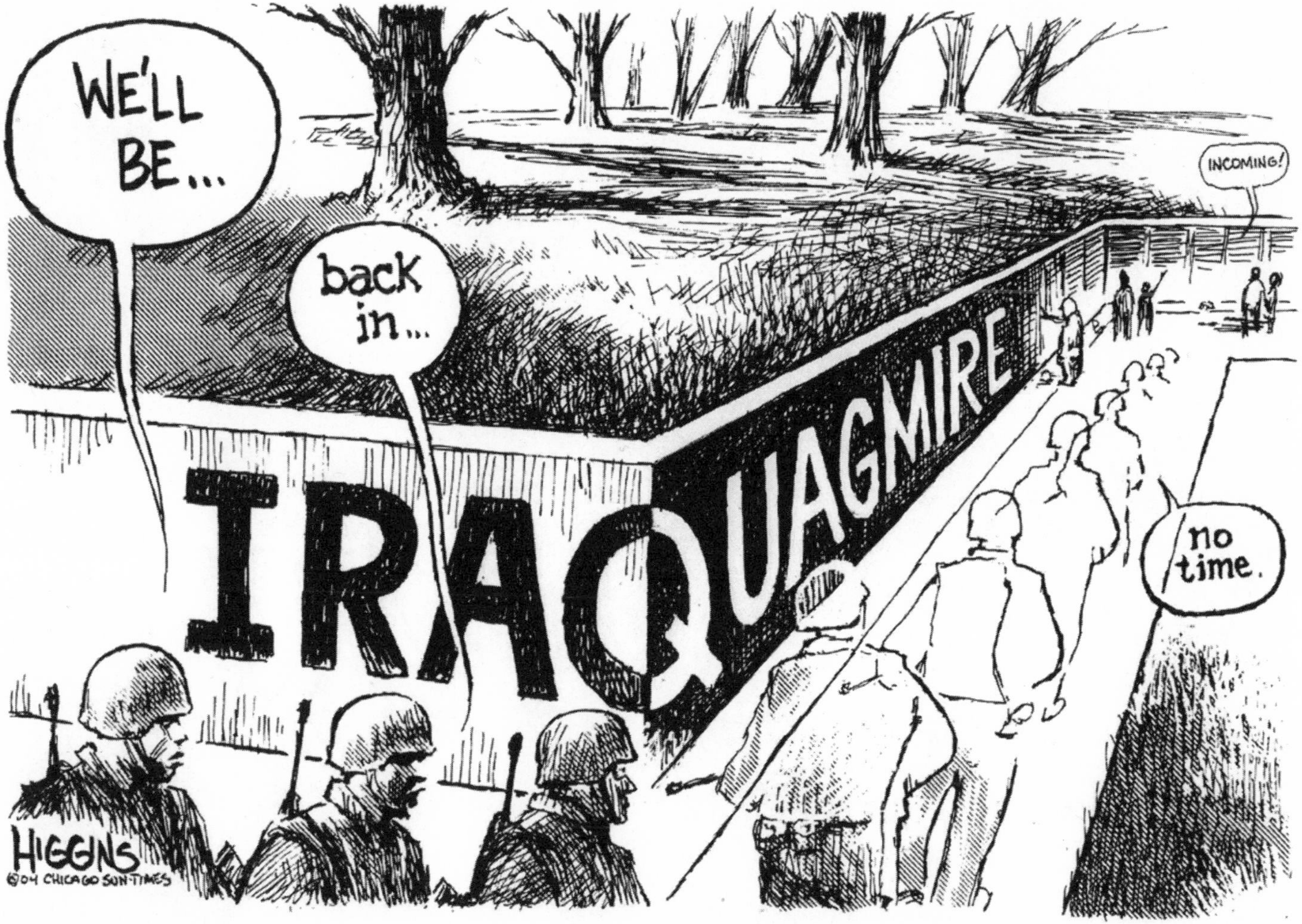
WE'LL BE...
back in...
IRAQUAGMIRE
no time.
INCOMING!
HIGGINS
©04 CHICAGO SUN-TIMES

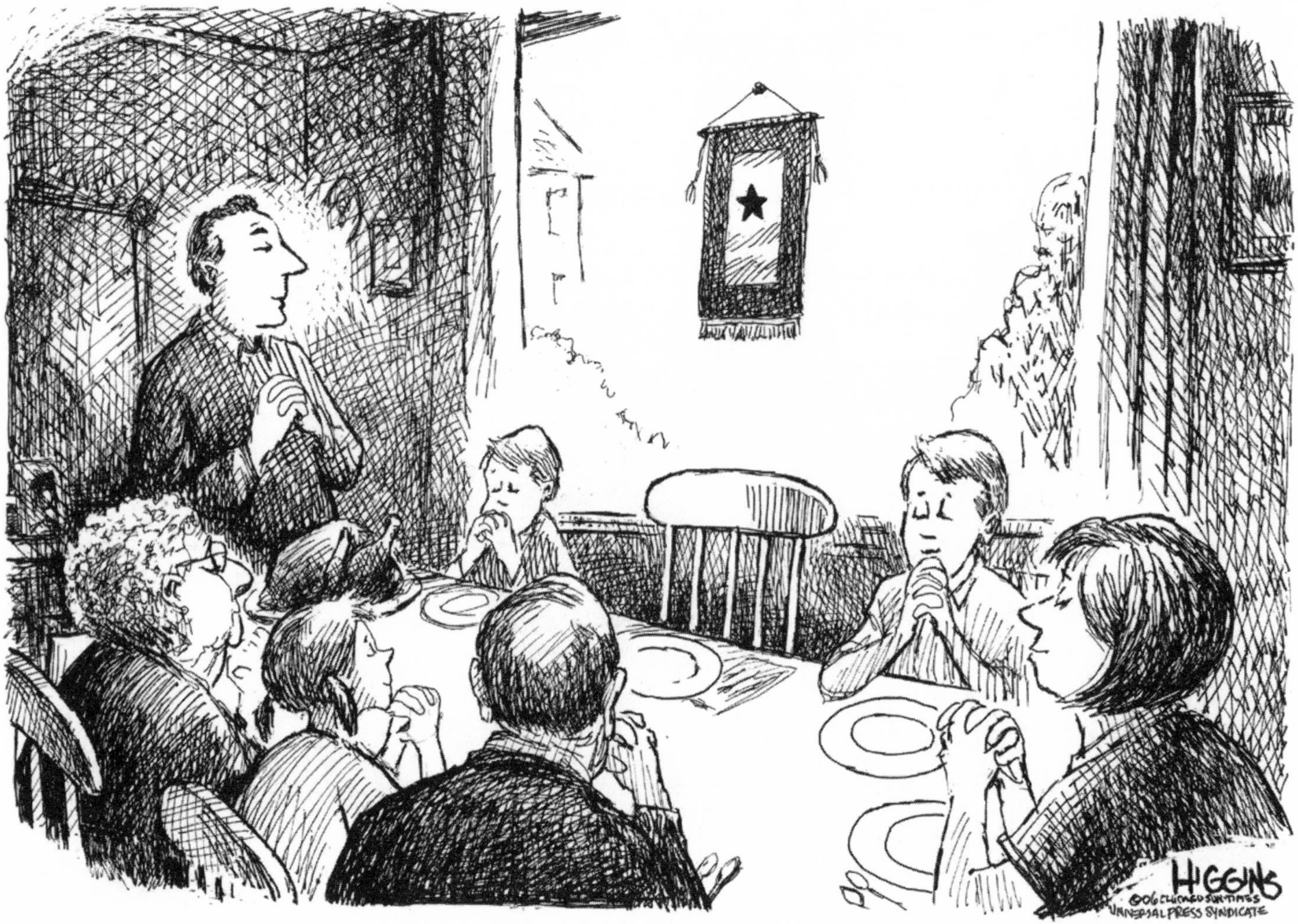
HIGGINS
©06 CHICAGO SUN-TIMES
UNIVERSAL PRESS SYNDICATE

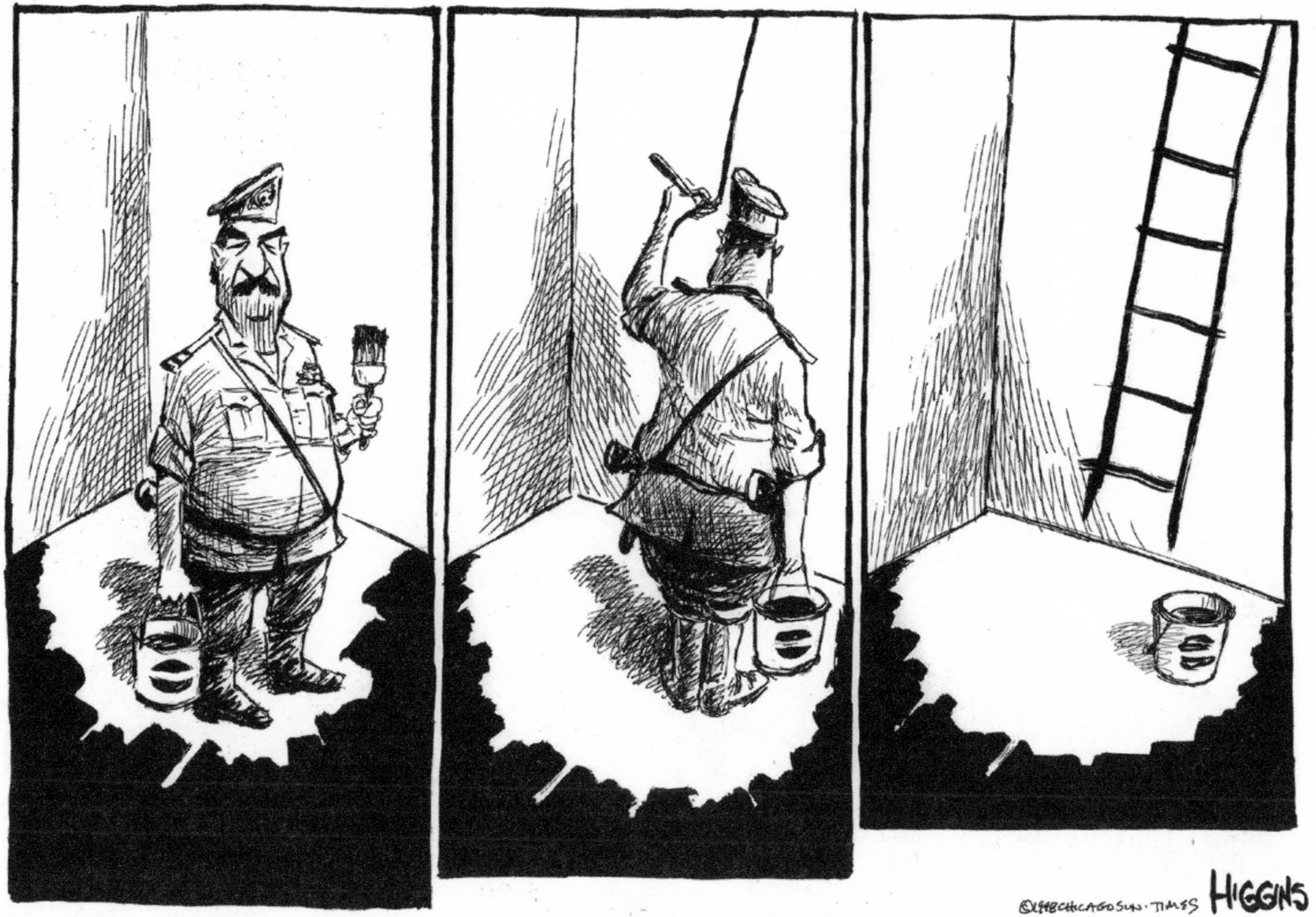
©1998 CHICAGO SUN-TIMES
HIGGINS

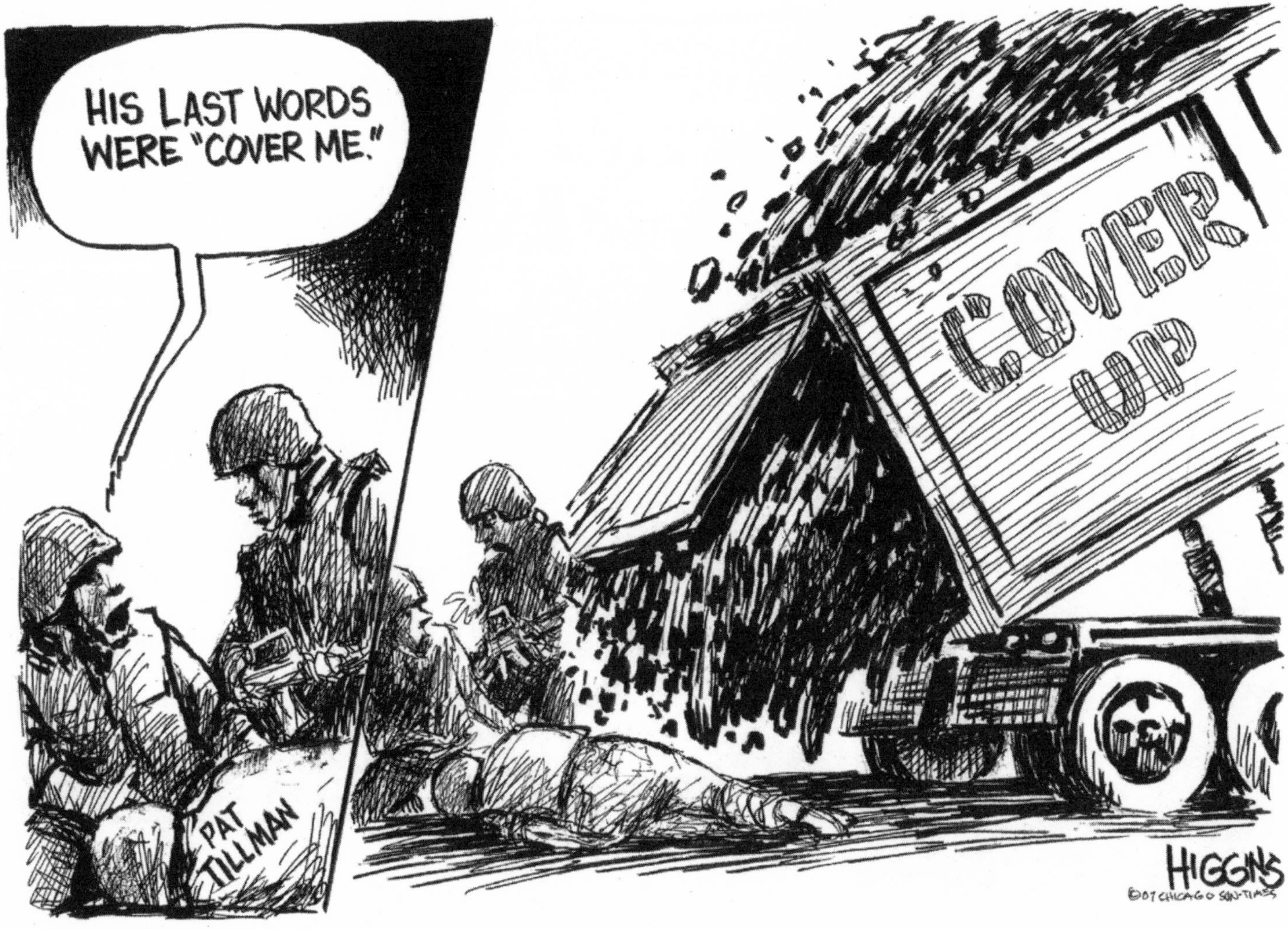
HIS LAST WORDS WERE "COVER ME."
PAT TILLMAN
COVER UP
HIGGINS
©07 CHICAGO SUN-TIMES

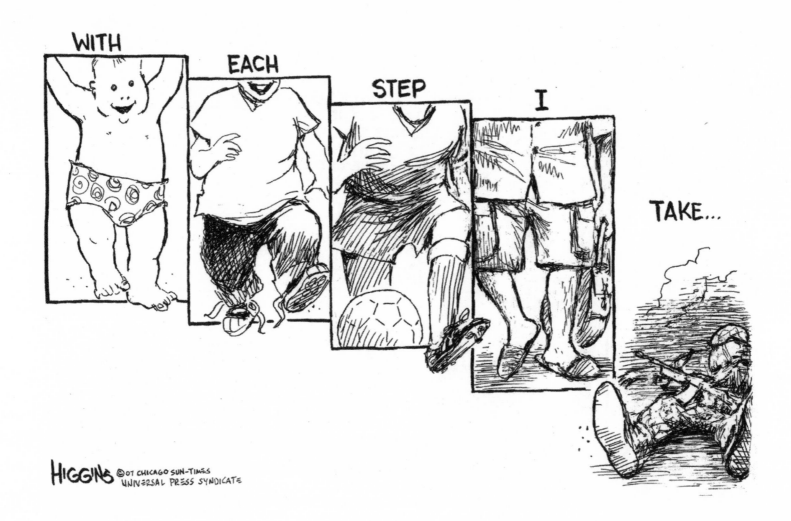

WITH

EACH

STEP

I

TAKE...

HIGGINS ©07 CHICAGO SUN-TIMES
UNIVERSAL PRESS SYNDICATE

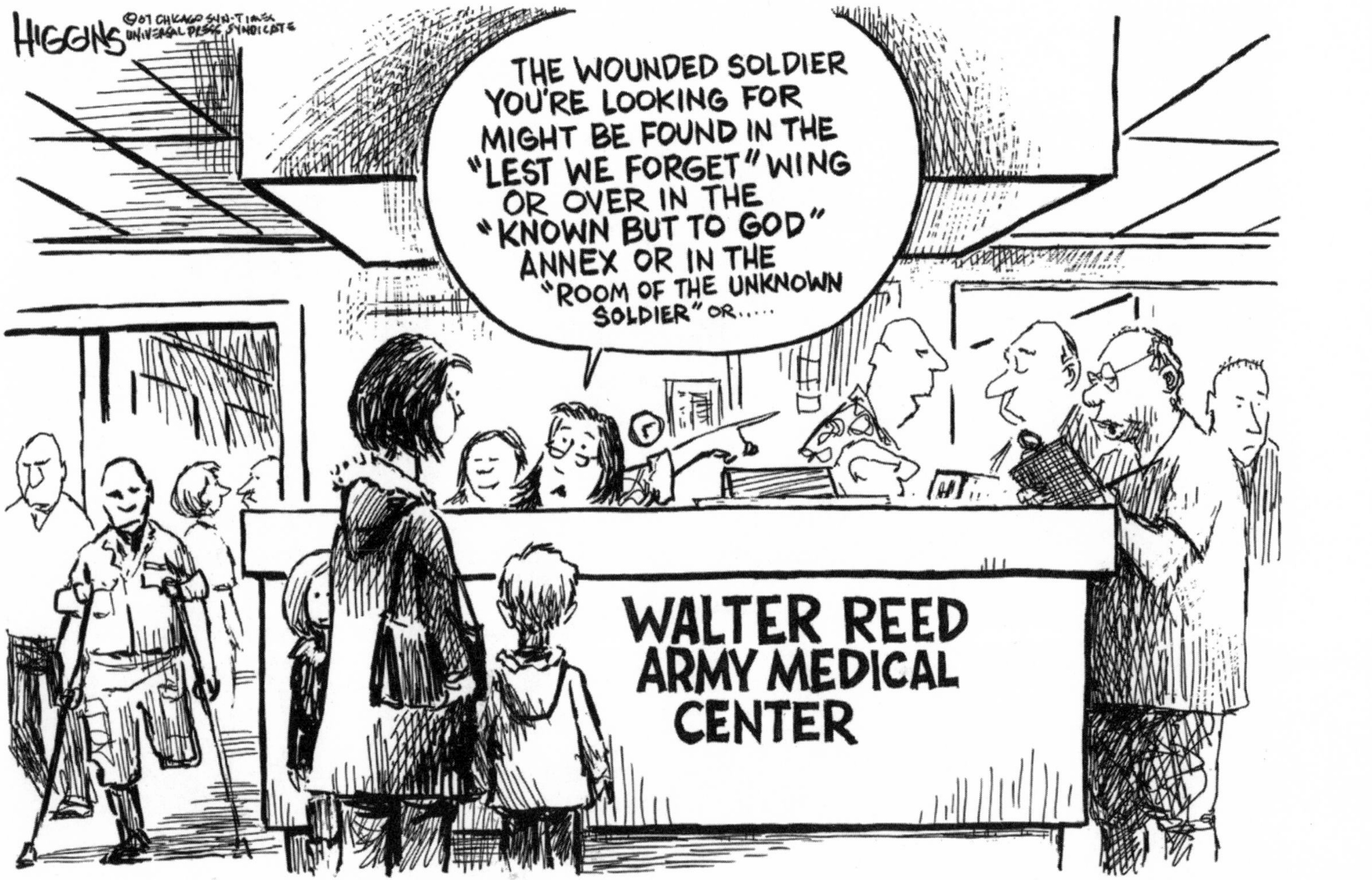
HIGGINS ©07 CHICAGO SUN-TIMES UNIVERSAL PRESS SYNDICATE
THE WOUNDED SOLDIER YOU'RE LOOKING FOR MIGHT BE FOUND IN THE "LEST WE FORGET" WING OR OVER IN THE "KNOWN BUT TO GOD" ANNEX OR IN THE "ROOM OF THE UNKNOWN SOLDIER" OR.....
WALTER REED ARMY MEDICAL CENTER

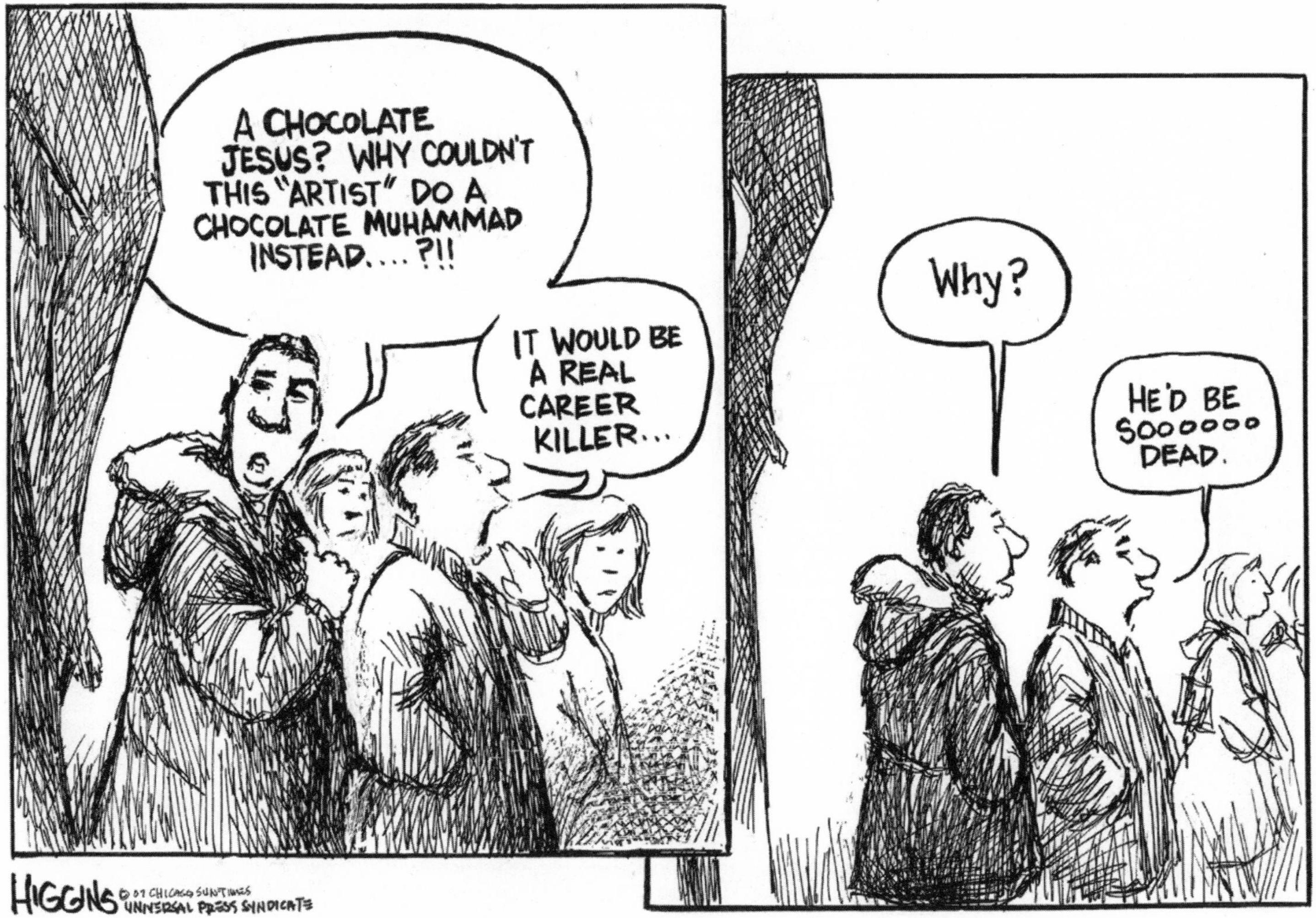
A CHOCOLATE JESUS? WHY COULDN'T THIS "ARTIST" DO A CHOCOLATE MUHAMMAD INSTEAD.... ?!!
IT WOULD BE A REAL CAREER KILLER...
Why?
HE'D BE SOOOOOO DEAD.
HIGGINS
© 07 CHICAGO SUN-TIMES UNIVERSAL PRESS SYNDICATE

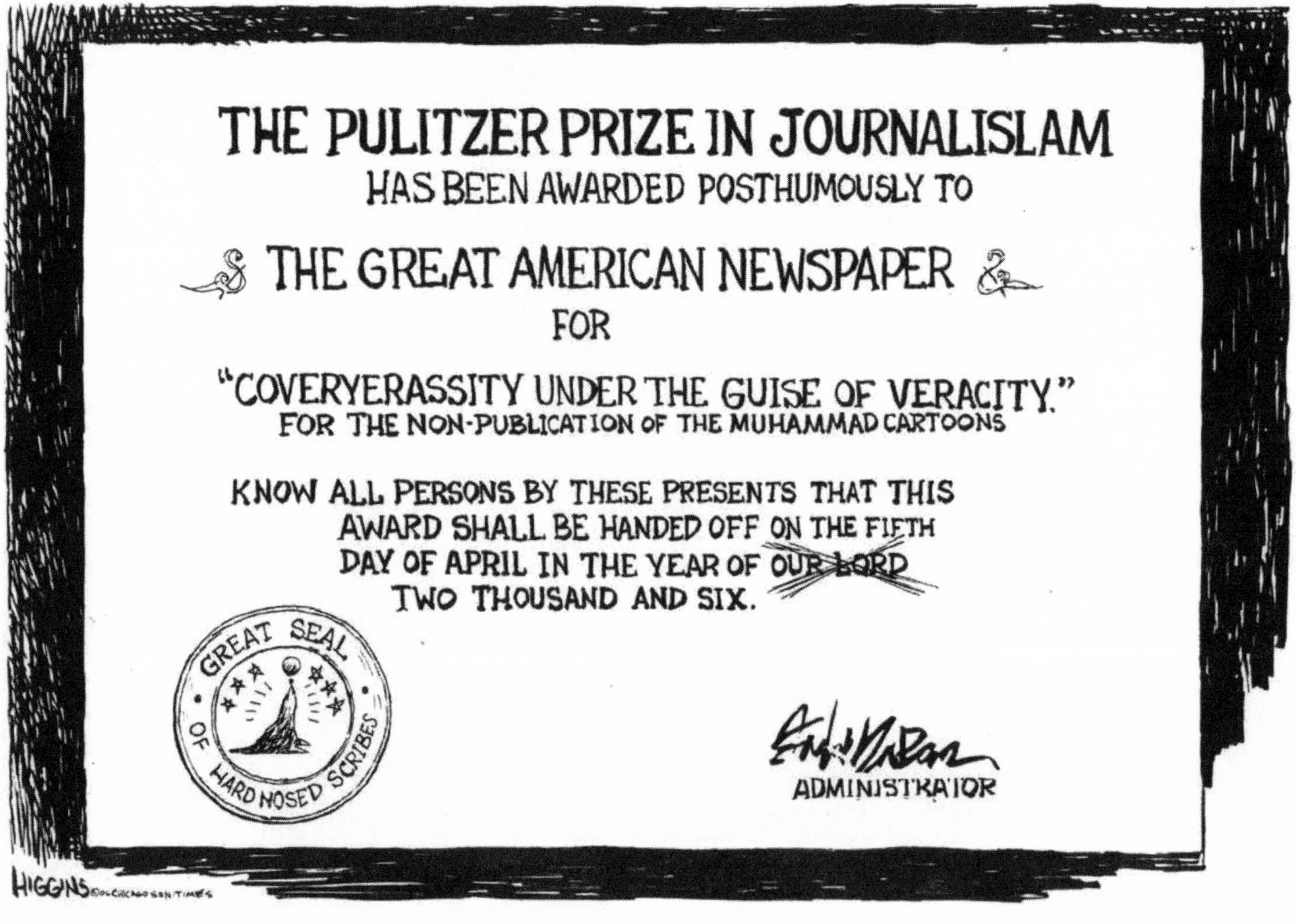
THE PULITZER PRIZE IN JOURNALISLAM
HAS BEEN AWARDED POSTHUMOUSLY TO
THE GREAT AMERICAN NEWSPAPER
FOR
"COVERYERASSITY UNDER THE GUISE OF VERACITY."
FOR THE NON-PUBLICATION OF THE MUHAMMAD CARTOONS
KNOW ALL PERSONS BY THESE PRESENTS THAT THIS AWARD SHALL BE HANDED OFF ON THE FIFTH DAY OF APRIL IN THE YEAR OF OUR LORD TWO THOUSAND AND SIX.
GREAT SEAL OF HARD NOSED SCRIBES
ADMINISTRATOR
HIGGINS

PORTRAITS
& PASSAGES

JACK HIGGINS

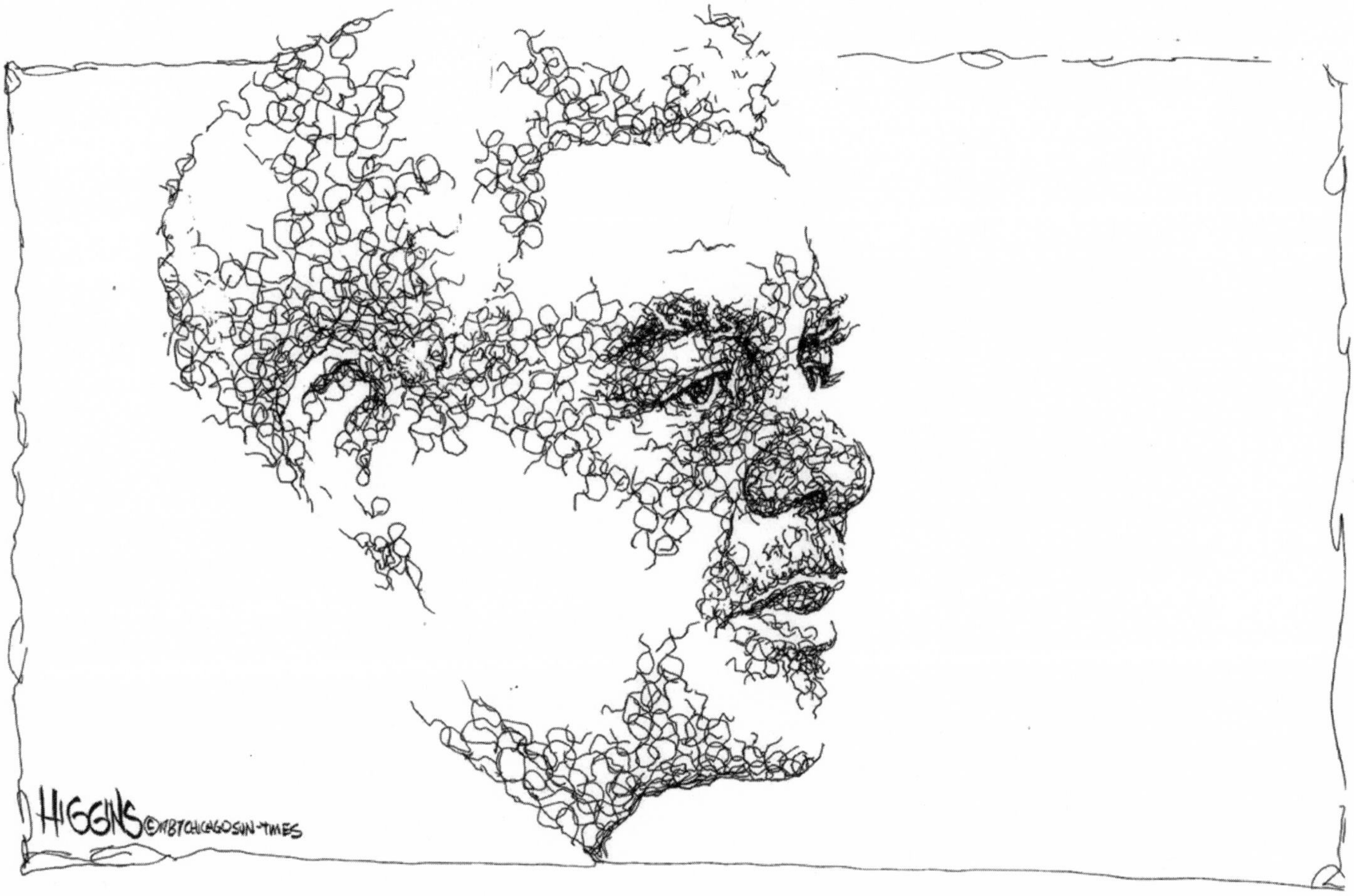
HIGGINS ©1987 CHICAGO SUN-TIMES

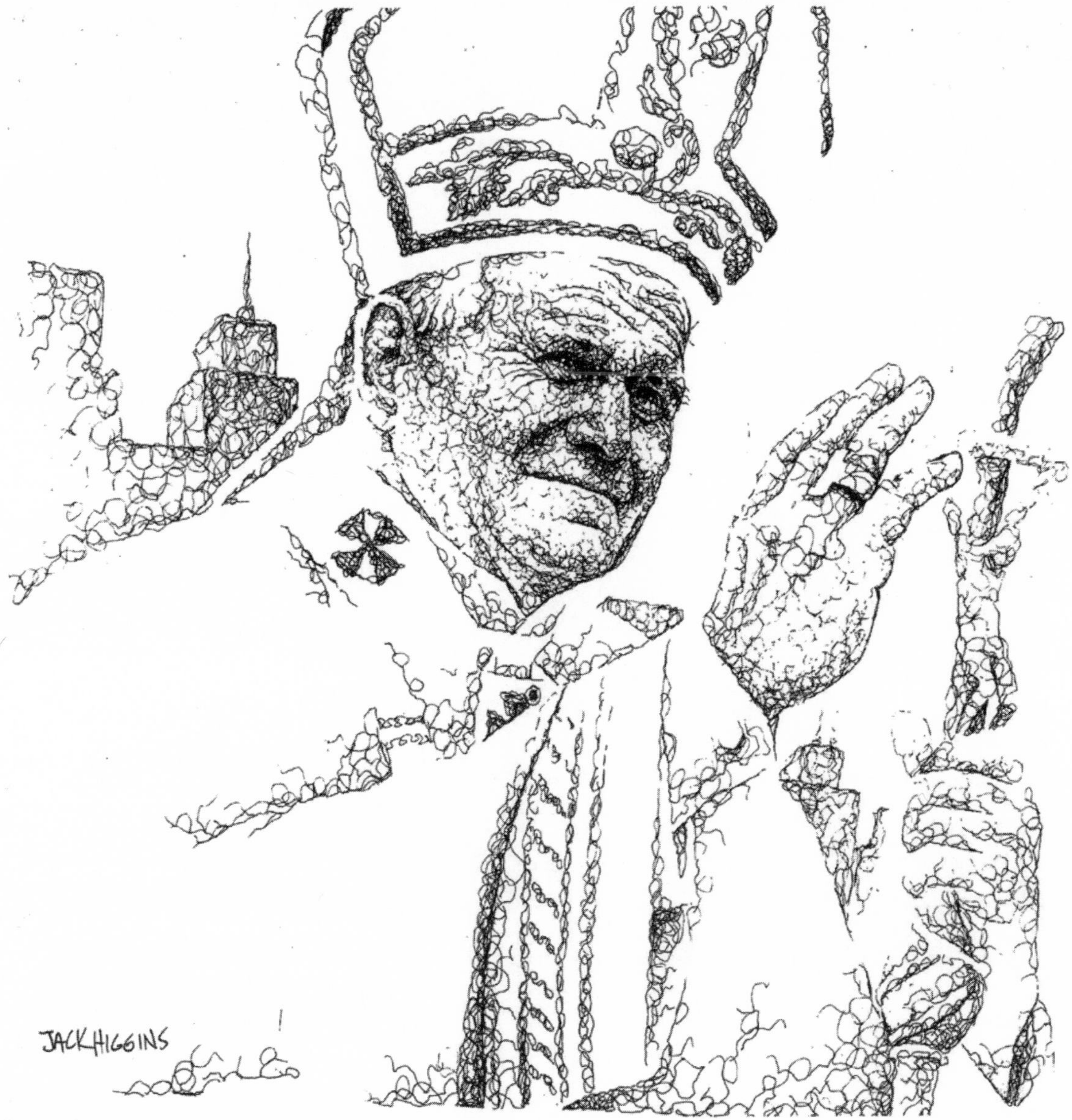
JACK HIGGINS

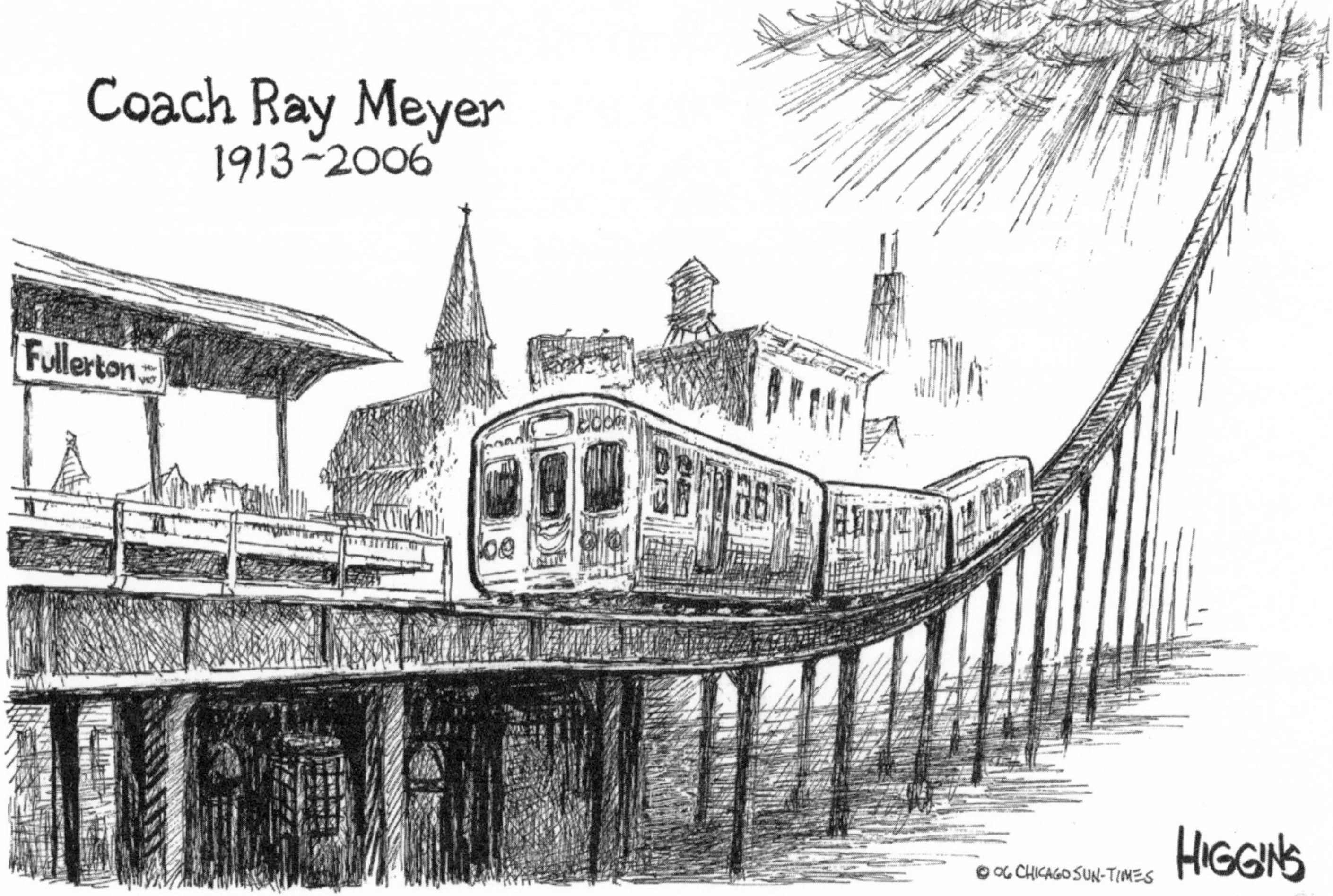
Coach Ray Meyer
1913–2006
Fullerton
© 06 CHICAGO SUN-TIMES
HIGGINS

THURSDAY, FEBRUARY 19, 1998 CHICAGO SUN-TIMES PAGE 112

Sports

HATS OFF TO HARRY:
Our writers recall their favorite memories of the Hall of Fame broadcaster. Pages 110-111.

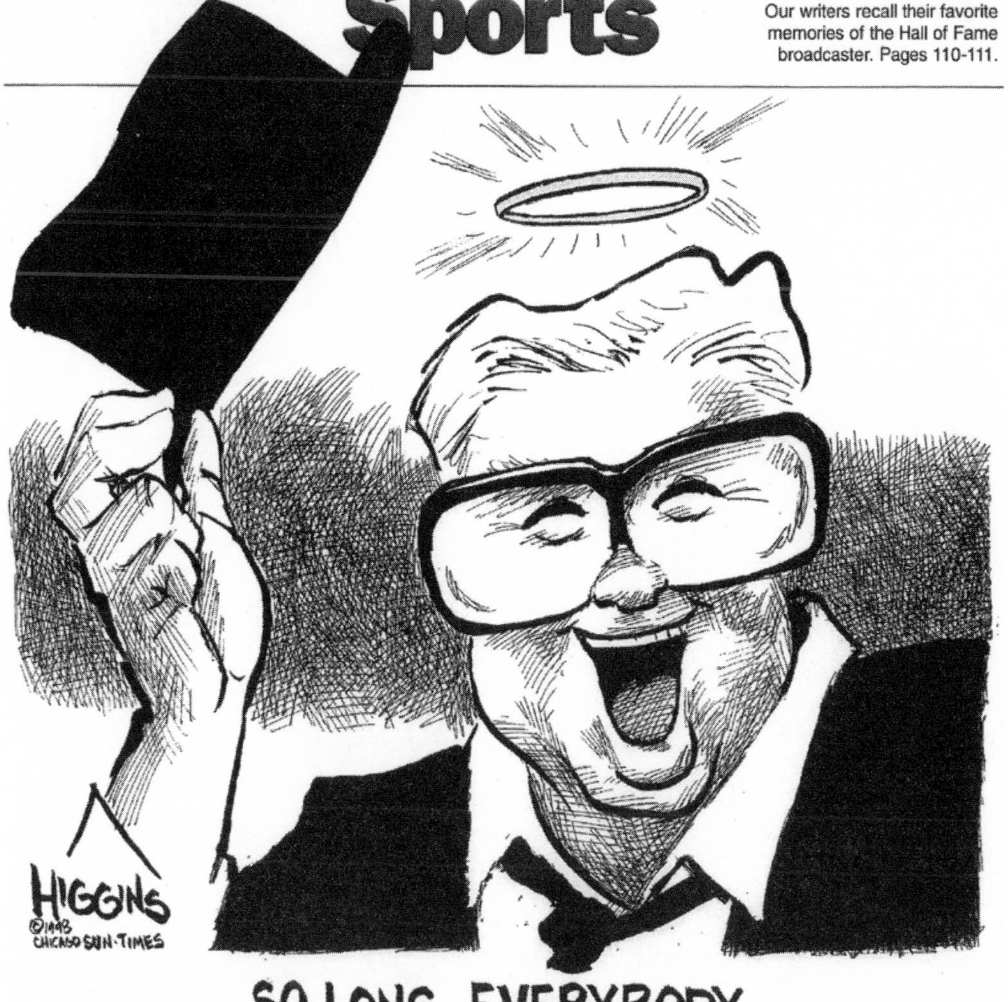
HIGGINS
©1998
CHICAGO SUN-TIMES

SO LONG, EVERYBODY

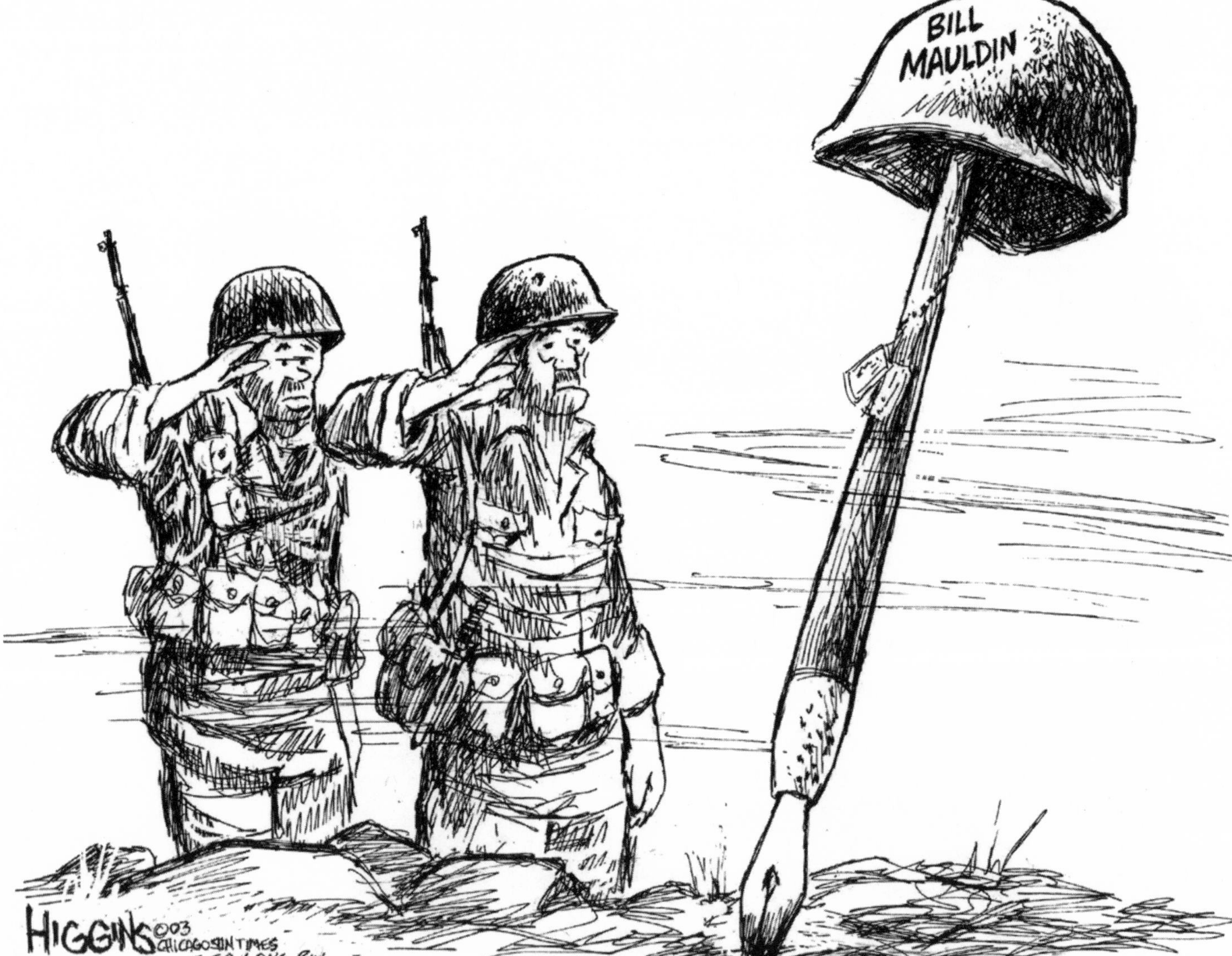
BILL
MAULDIN
HIGGINS ©03
CHICAGO SUN TIMES
SO LONG, BILL

A Seat in the
Upper Deck.

(as in Veeck.)

Higgins ©1986 CHICAGO SUN-TIMES

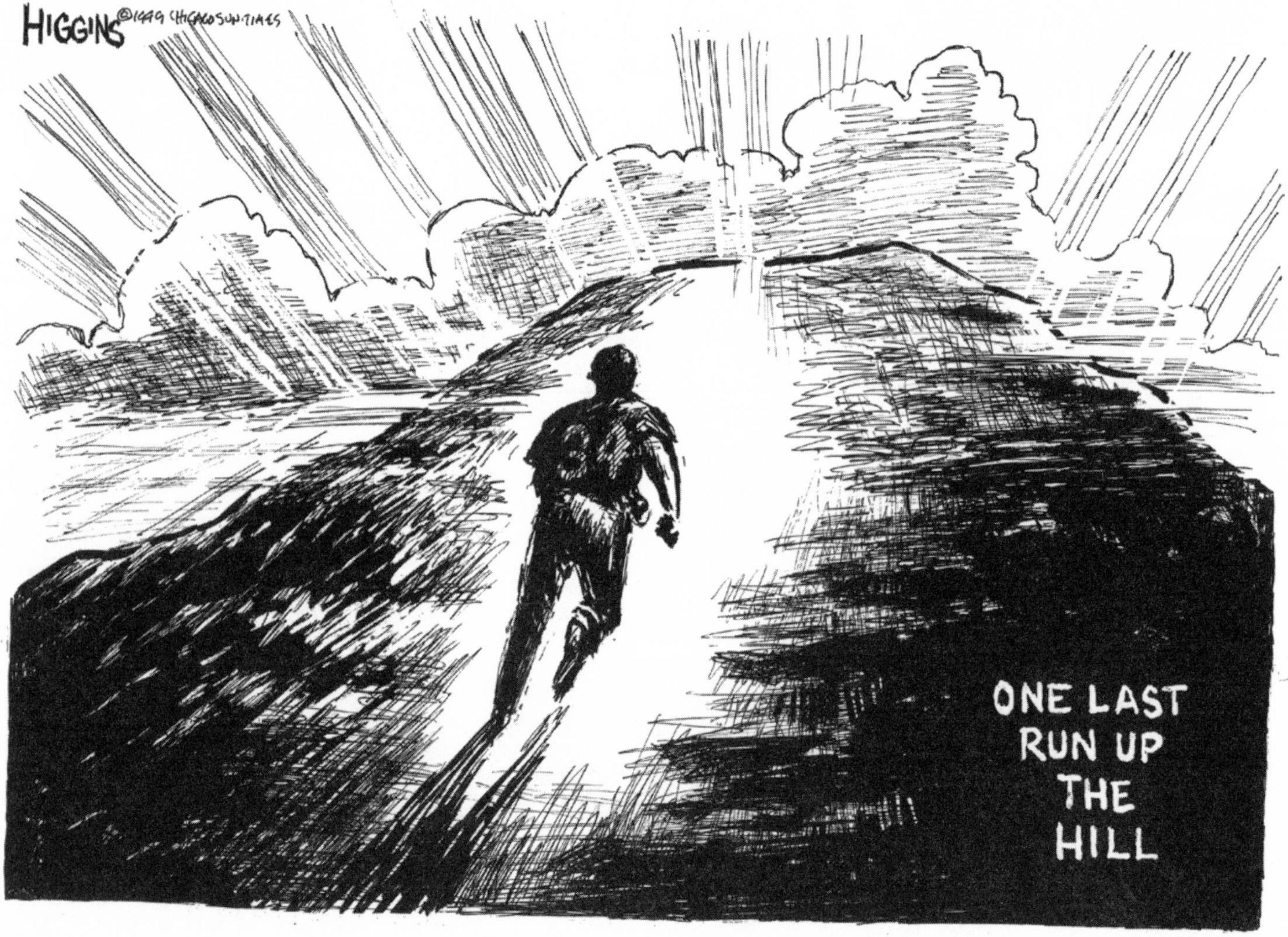
HIGGINS ©1999 CHICAGO SUN-TIMES
ONE LAST RUN UP THE HILL

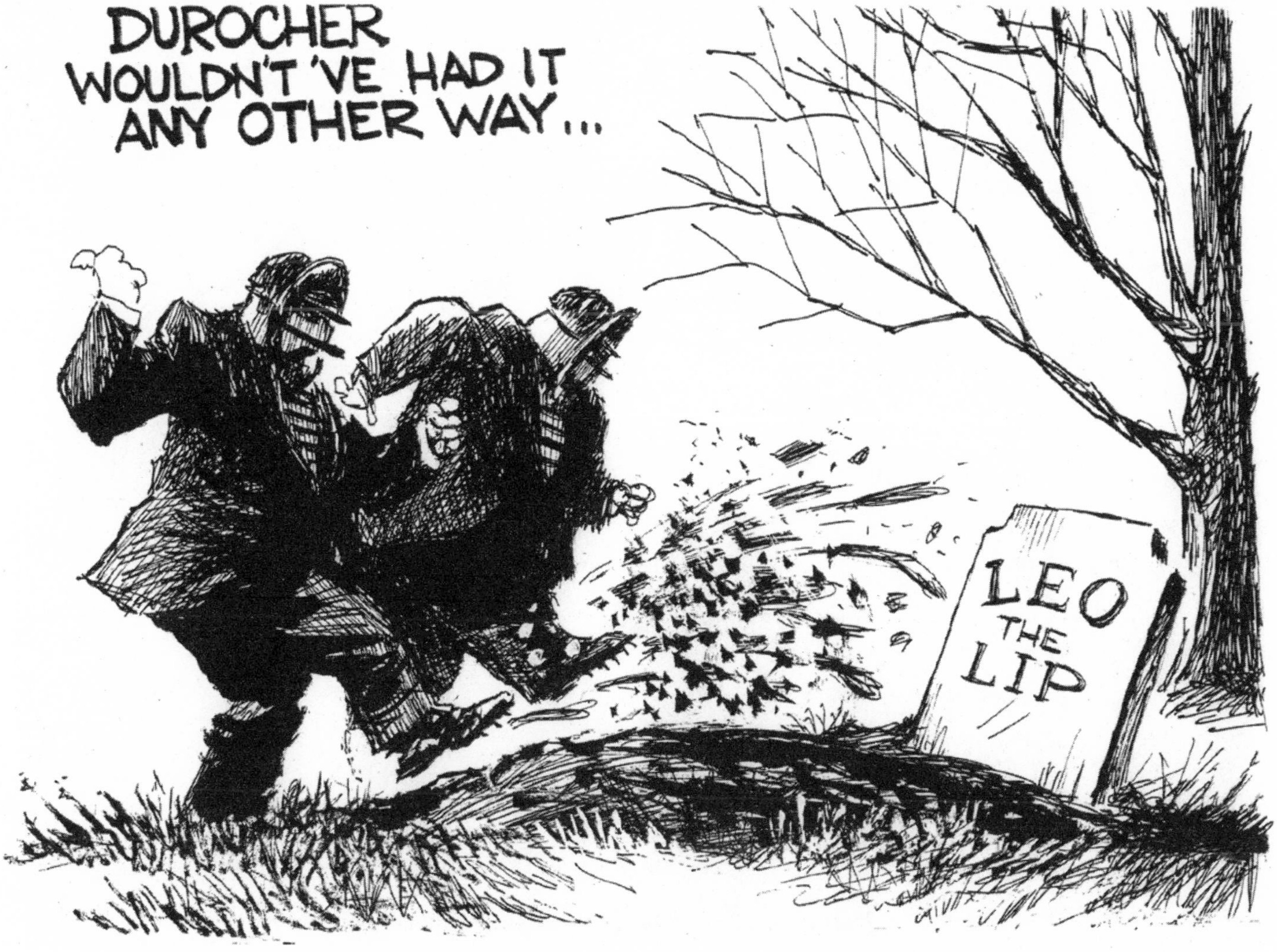
DUROCHER WOULDN'T 'VE HAD IT ANY OTHER WAY...
LEO THE LIP

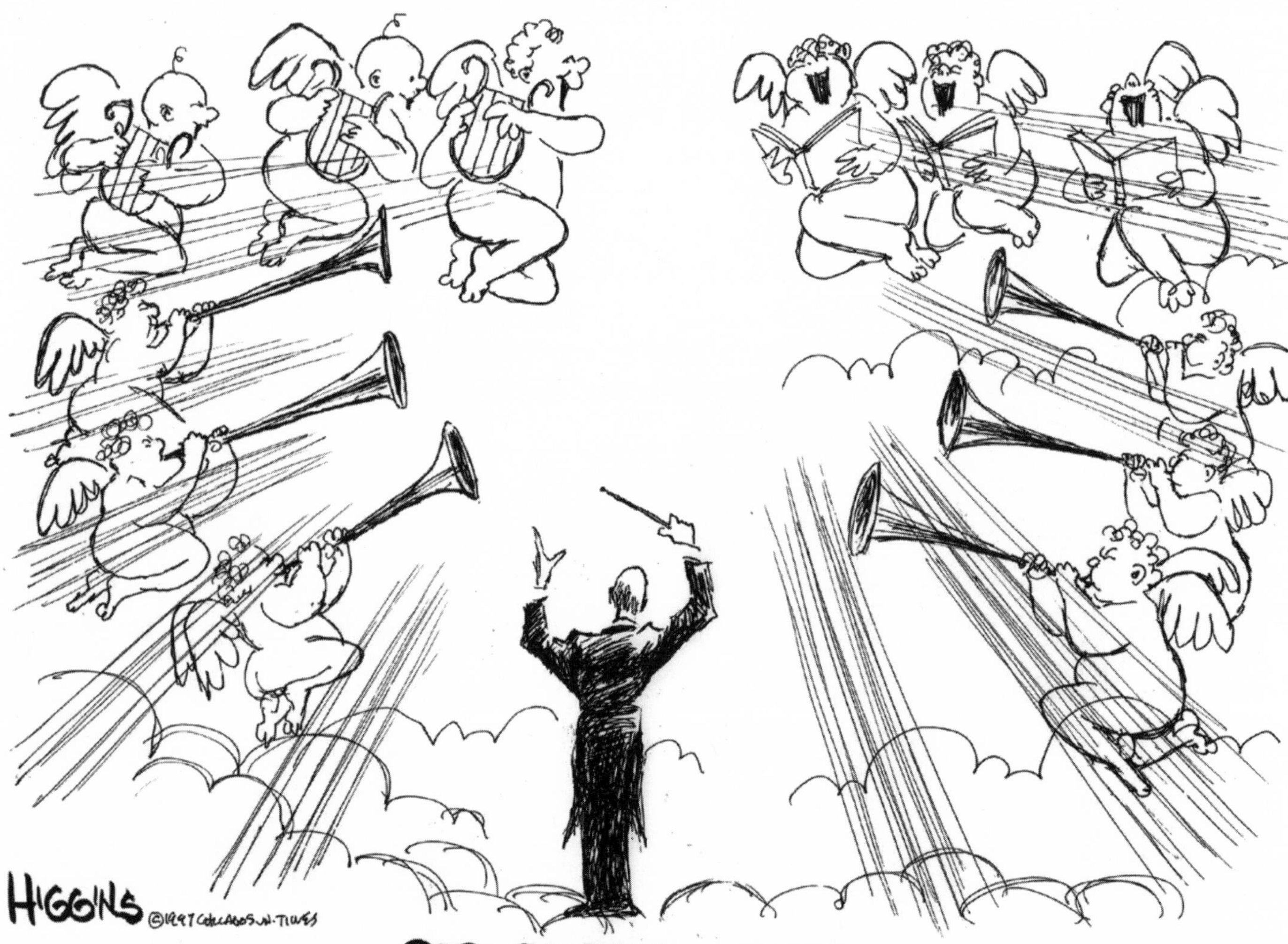
HIGGINS
©1997 CHICAGO SUN-TIMES

SIR GEORG SOLTI

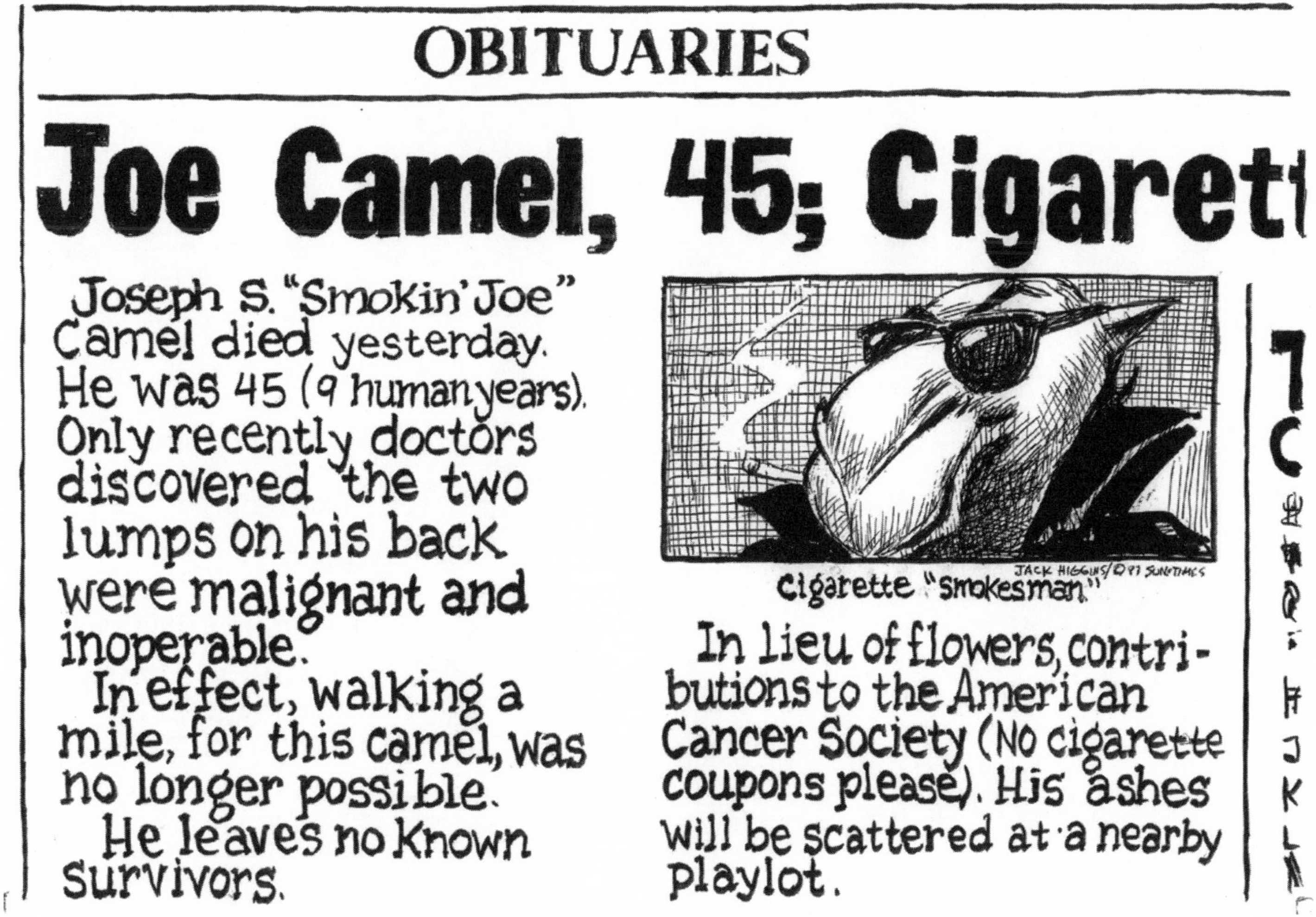
OBITUARIES
Joe Camel, 45; Cigarett
Joseph S. "Smokin' Joe" Camel died yesterday. He was 45 (9 human years). Only recently doctors discovered the two lumps on his back were malignant and inoperable.
In effect, walking a mile, for this camel, was no longer possible.
He leaves no known survivors.
Cigarette "smokesman."
In lieu of flowers, contributions to the American Cancer Society (No cigarette coupons please). His ashes will be scattered at a nearby playlot.

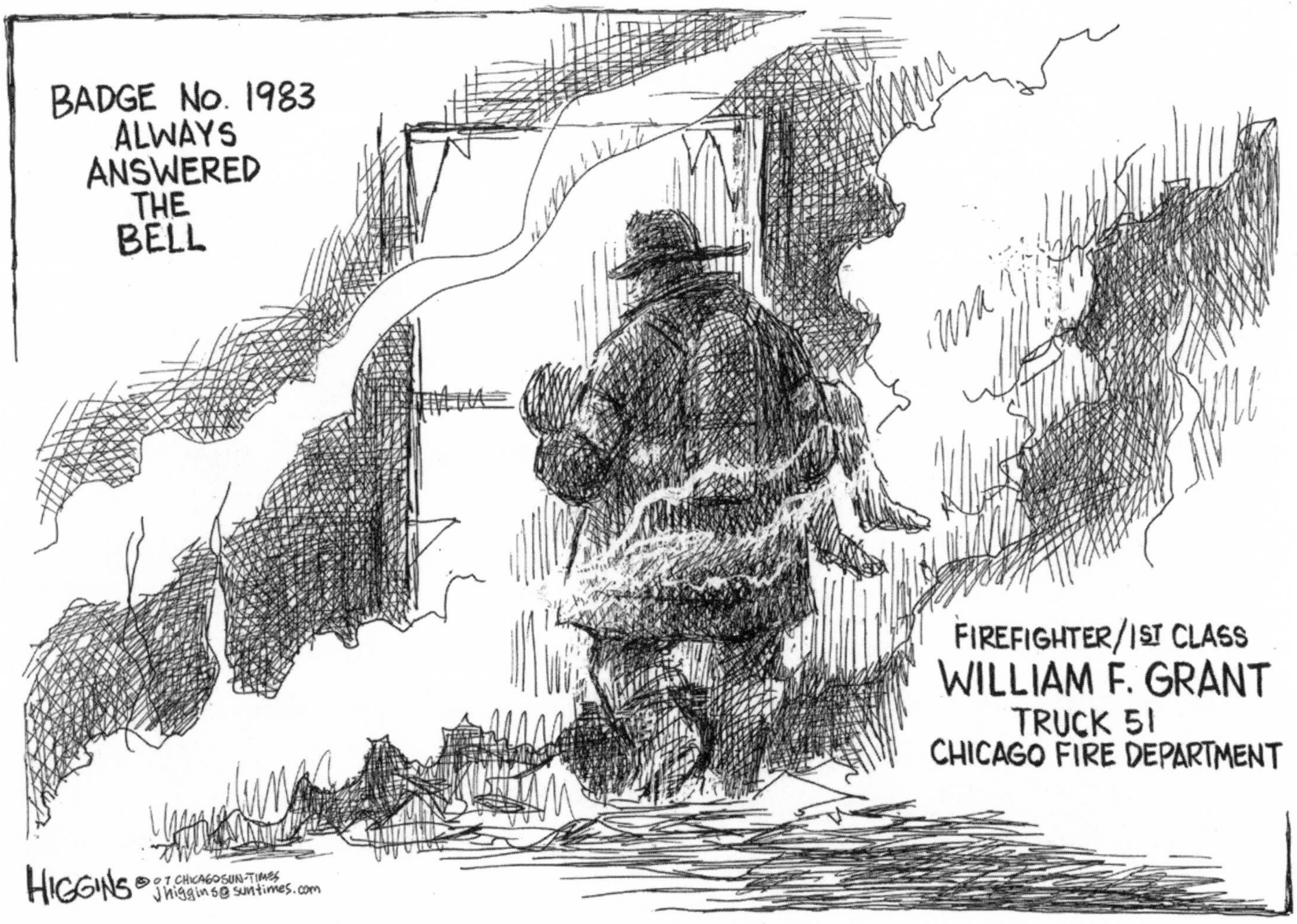
BADGE No. 1983 ALWAYS ANSWERED THE BELL
FIREFIGHTER/1ST CLASS
WILLIAM F. GRANT
TRUCK 51
CHICAGO FIRE DEPARTMENT
HIGGINS
© 07 CHICAGO SUN-TIMES
jhiggins@suntimes.com

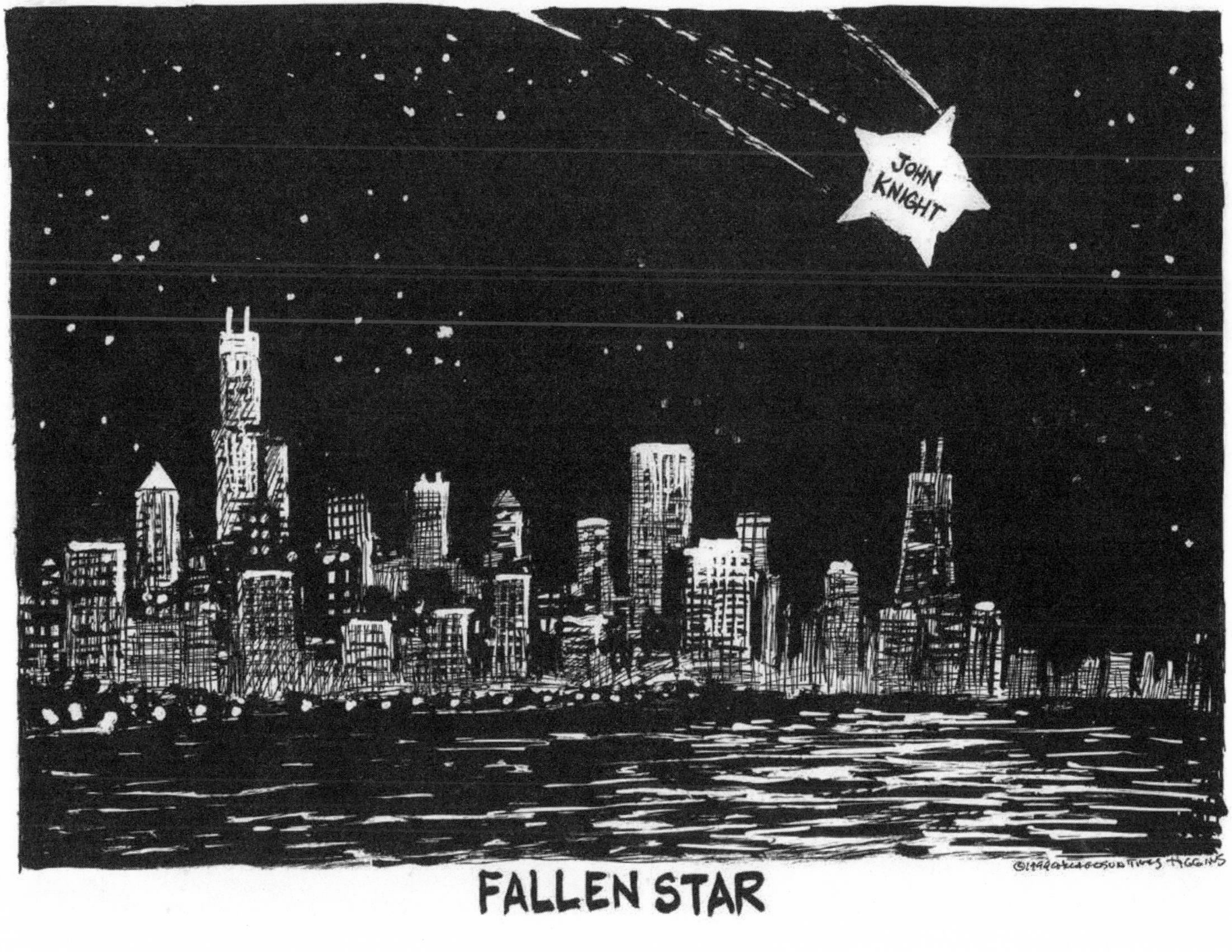
JOHN
KNIGHT

FALLEN STAR

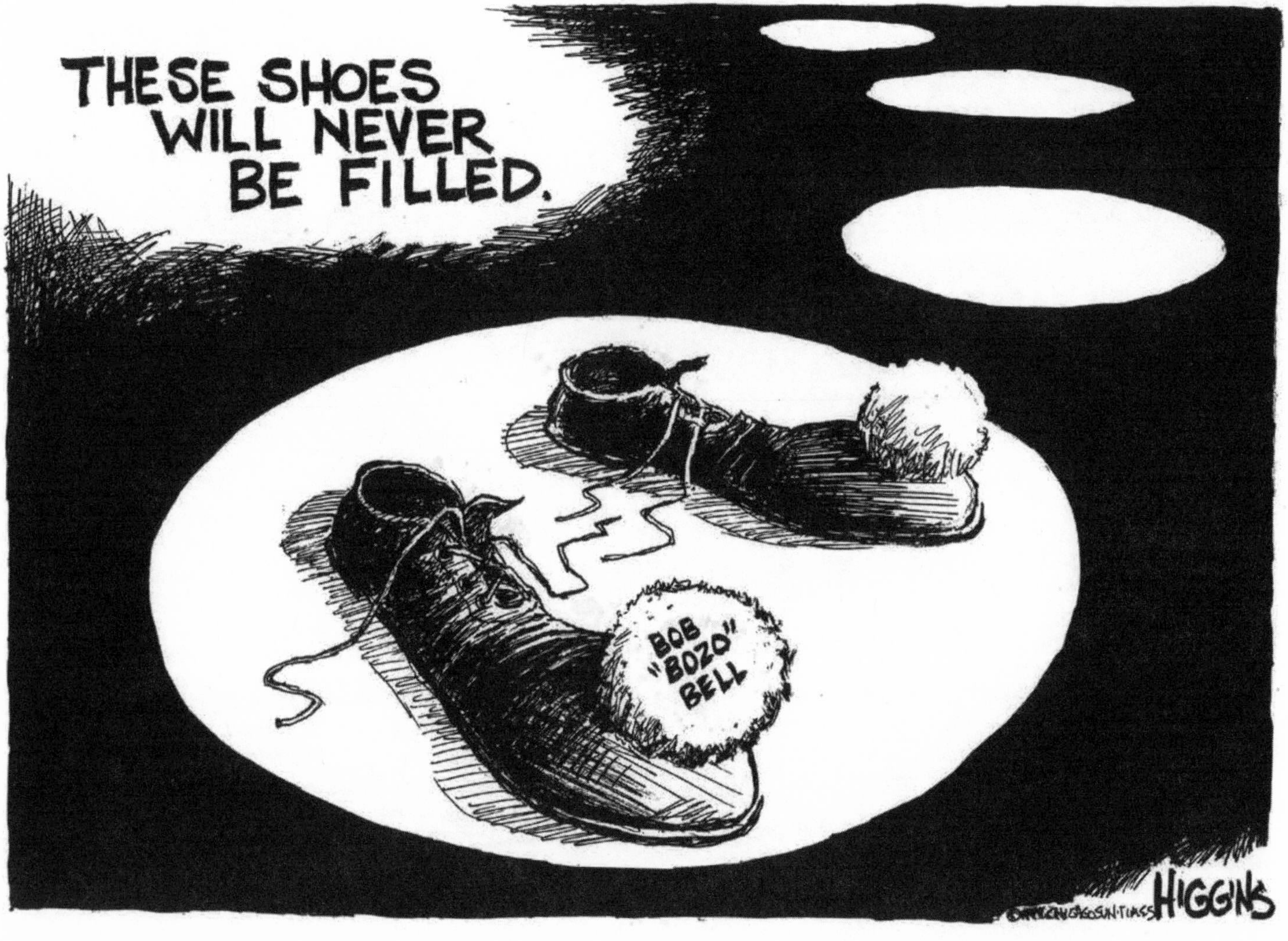
THESE SHOES WILL NEVER BE FILLED.
BOB "BOZO" BELL
HIGGINS

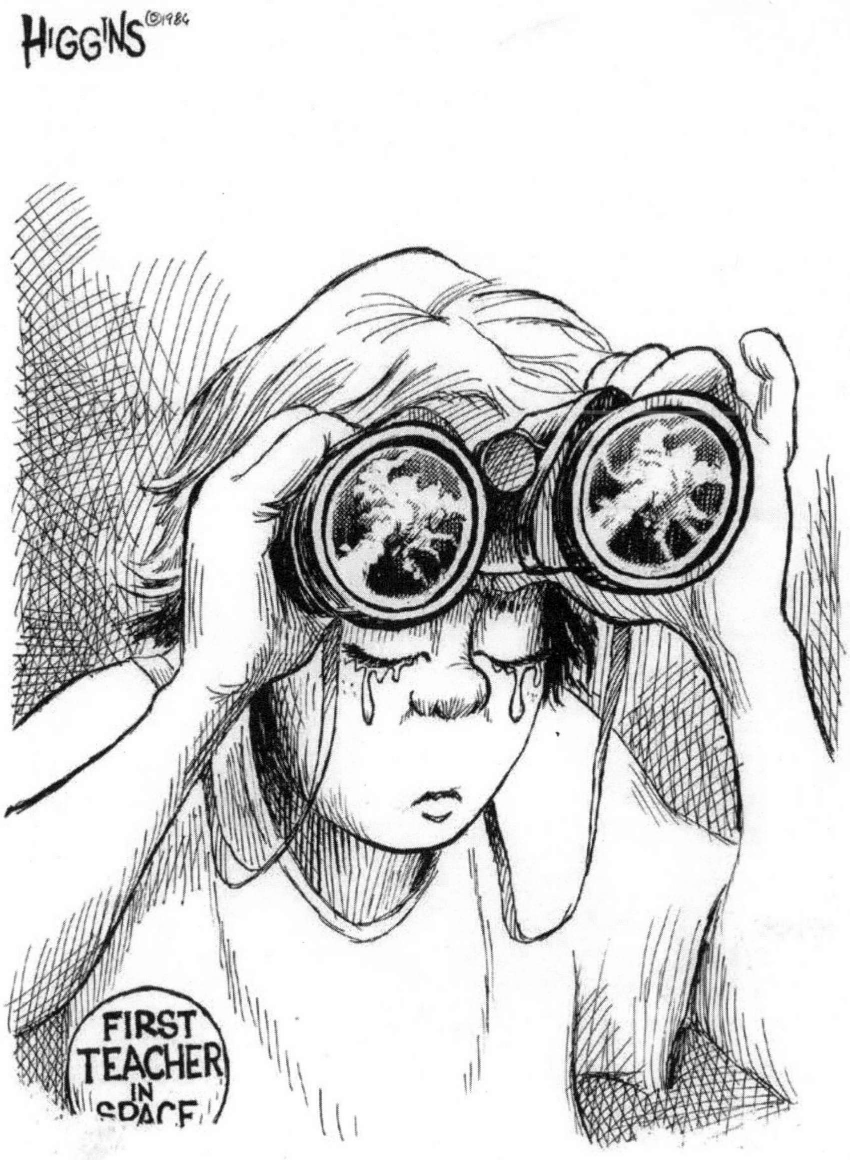
HIGGINS ©1984
FIRST
TEACHER
IN
SPACE

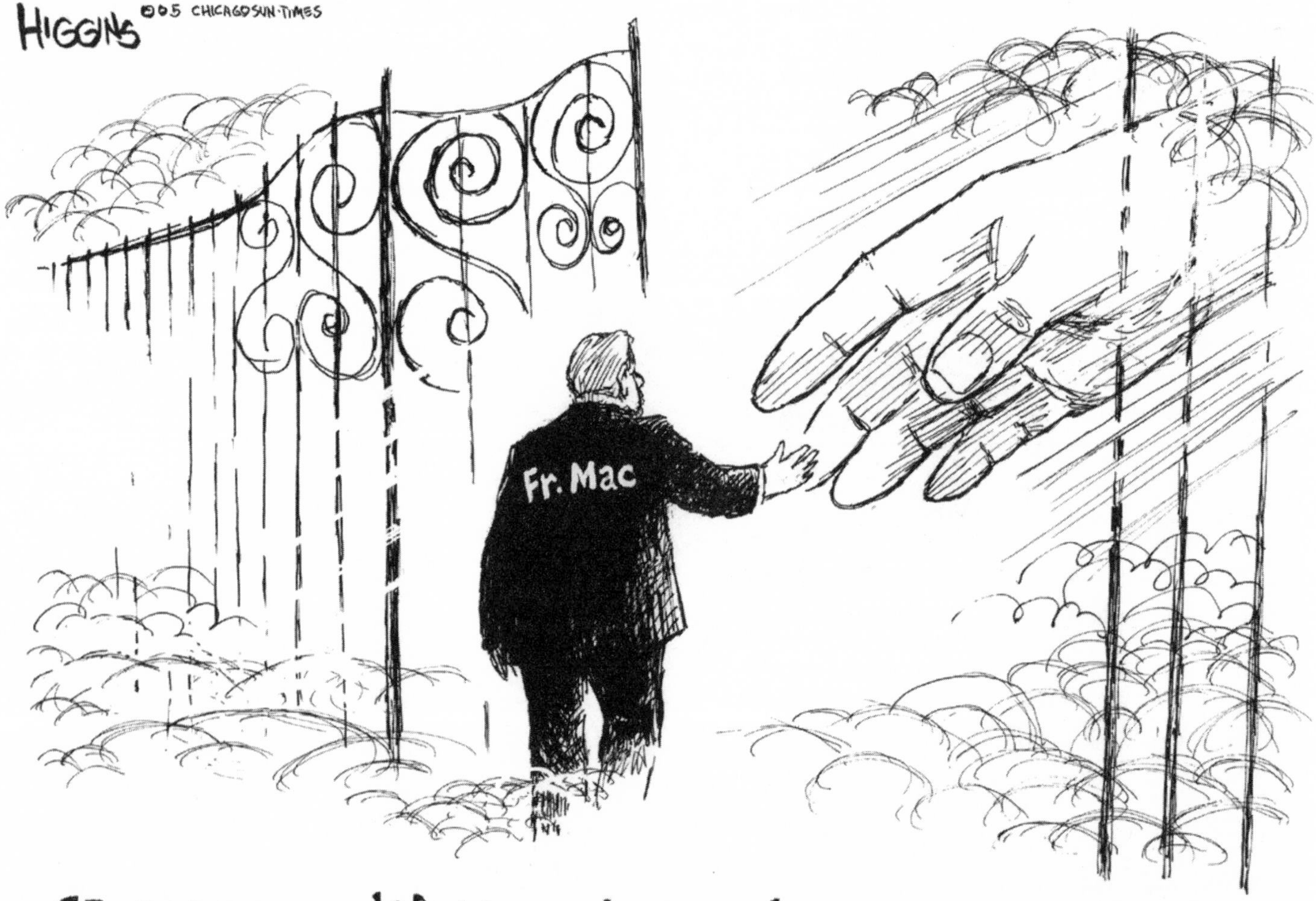
HIGGINS ©05 CHICAGO SUN-TIMES
Fr. Mac

95 seasons... lifetime clean-up hitter... safe at home.

Cyrus Freidheim Michael Cooke Tom + Debbie McNamee Don + Dawn Hayner Mary Mitchell
Linda + Steve Huntley Mabel +Dick Nardini Steve Warmbir Tom +Dodie Frisbie Jim Higgins
Joe O'Shaughnessy Michelle Stevens Eileen +George Peterson Leon + Carol Pitt Roy Moody
Nancy +Paul LoMaglio Rev. Michael Bowler Russ Andrew Allison Rosati John H. White Rose
Donna + Leo Murphy Donna Hyatt +Jim Parker Sue + John Alexander Paul Sullivan Brigid
Jerry Skizas Jeanne +Tim Rooney Bob Herguth Colette + Tom Durkin Bill 'Seb" Costin
Karen + Dennis McAuley Jenny Fleischman **Ray Coffey- RIP** Holly Coffey Carl Kipp
Dave Manthey MaryFran Dunne The Brothers McGovern John Ivers Lisa Jerstad Tommy
Jennifer Cacciatore Kathy + Jerry Schumacher Bob +Char Carley Nancy Casanova Brendan
Joe Kearns Tom Cronin

MERRY CHRISTMAS

Rev. Dudley Day
Carol + Pat Dwyer Rose Mary Barry PJ O'Dea
Jim Perner Judy + Tom Hynes Jim Wall Vicki Truax Harry Bendis St. Thomas More Parish
Lisa +Kevin Bahr Doreen +Dick Mitchell Barb +Dennis Byrne Keith Hale Dutchie Caray Jackie
Edie +Neil Steinberg Rich Harris +Ronna Feldman Ruth + David Nega Maggie + John Nocita
Lucy +Mark Wukas Dave McKinney Kevin Donlan Bill Zwecker Cliff Wirth Molly +Dave Kelly
Tommy Ward MaryPat McWalters Casey Ledowski Kerry +Willie Winters Candy +Ed Wooton
Anna Vasser Milt Rosenberg Pat + Jerry Hayes Sheila O'Grady + Dan Duffy Mike Sheahan
Phil Wright Brenda Warner Rotzoll Mark Suppelsa Trina Higgins Josie +Joe Guidice Missy
Howard Wolinsky Mark Brown Paige +Jim Wiser Patti +Terry Durkin Jim Wangler Jack Wright
Sandy Wojtynek Jim Hastings **Bunny Wronkiewicz-RIP** Carl Abbate Mary + Stuart Carlson
Rev. Tony Brankin Rob Chimberoff Katie +Barry Burdiak Sue +Chris Amafi Pete Belluomini
Laura +Bob Durkin Jim Conlon Kathy +Bill Figel Albert Dickens Kate Graham + Gordon Mayer
Mary +Peter Hayes Marilyn Geary Mary +Mike Houlihan Tapioca Sy Hickey Stella Foster
Andrew Herrmann Susie +Brian Lindell Dan McGrath Pat Sheahan Bill Strube Kate Grossman
Warner Saunders Kimbeth + Bernie Judge Colleen +Kevin Lamborn **Charlie Nicodemus-RIP**
Julie +Tim Kerrigan Rita +Tom Manion Dale McCullough Mary +Dick Locher Carol Marin
Nancy +Mark McDermott T. Brian Kelly Abdon Pallasch Joe Basile Joe Palm Sam Sianis
Nancy +Marty Manion Dirk Johnson Terry McEldowney Luke Fagan Pat Hickey Frank Golden
MaryAnn +Tim Monahan Chris +Mike Mulligan Barb +Bob Oster Joan Richardson Bob Mutter
Rev. Frank Phillips +the priests,brothers +parishioners of St. John Cantius Susan Randstrom
Nancy + Tom Figel Diane +Rich Egan Erin +Bill Durkin Rita + Harlan Draeger Ted Dixon
Suzanne + Dave Devane Alicia +Bill Derrah Kathleen +Nauge Daly Pat Summers Cronin
Lilly +Tom Roeser Ann +Thom Serafin **Hon. Edward Egan -RIP** Virginia + Peter Rooney
Marianne Murciano + Bob Sirott Terry Smirniotis Demetra Soter + Chris Doyle Ron Theel
Nancy Stuenkel Michael Thompson Susan +Ken Towers Marcy +Herman Vigerust Tom Spatz
John Vasilopoulos Pete Vernon Mike Flannery Celeste +Jim Durkin Dolores +Roger Flaherty
Richard Crowe- Boo! Tim Fitzgerald Tucker Sheahan Meg +John Rooney Ed + Dave Duffin
Bill Sianis Marge Fitch Karlene +Barry Cronin Tom Sullivan Richard Roeper Ernie Torres
Lina Curtin St. Ignatius College Prep. Jeanie Smyers Tony Dardano Patti Dudek
John Sheahan Lynn Sweet Michael Sneed Anne +Ed Burke Ray Long Bill Merchantz
Vicki +Larry Adams Bill Rosinski MaryAnn +Leo Burns Maureen Carroll Sue Neal
Mary Doherty +Bernard Callaghan Chaz +Roger Ebert Kitty + Jack Burns
Skip Carey **Bill Braden-RIP** Mike Miller Len Amari Marge + Bob Herguth
Mary Galligan +John Camper Herb Ballard Tim Novak Terri + Emmett Grady
Bob Foster John Holden Andy Shaw Diane + Dennis Gannon Elliott Harris
Pete Piotrowski Edward Gilbreth Nick Paloumpis Boz O'Brien Ken Paxson
Johanna +Jeff Borden Carol +Pete Petersen Anne +Larry Green Jim Ritter
Nona Novak Toby Roberts Bob Hilbert Sally +Joe Boniecki Ray Long
Carlos Hernandez Gomez Chester Polica Tuna Carey Nancy Batson Tommy
John Barron Ron Predovic Rosemary Higgins Bill Patterson
Earl Moses Dan Cahill Tim Carey Char +Zig Ulmanis Jack Lee
Betty + Todd Musburger Jim Barton Robin Robinson Brendan
Mike Brady Alice + Joe Sherman Ed Carroll Ralph Otwell
John "Big" Myers Char Searl Joe Waddell Pat Sheahan Jackie
Jim Casey Kathy +Pat Hayes Jim Frost Jack Conaty Bill Lee
Mike Gillis Lloyd Sachs Joe Power Marty Mullarkey Brigid

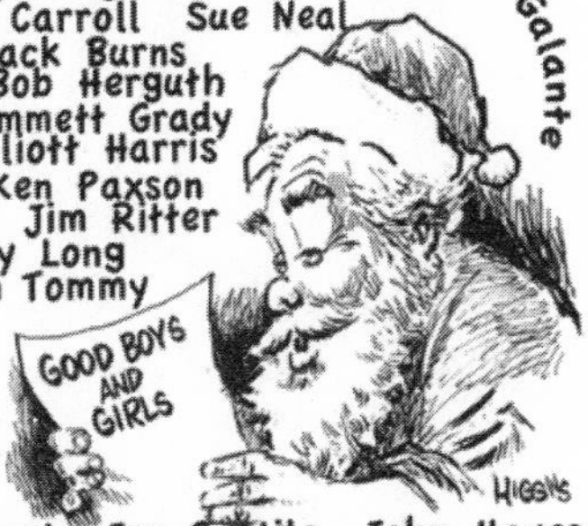
GOOD BOYS AND GIRLS
HIGGINS

Pat Byrnes Tom Gannon Mike Harvey Dom Najolia Scott Stewart Joe Gentile John Hayes
Johanna + Grant DePorter John Kadich John Kass Debbie O'Leary Nancy + Tom Manion
Darel Jevens Ron Magers Bob Kruse Bouch Kribech Dan Jedlicka Ernie Leggs Nick Manzie
10 Wools, 9 Potters, 8 Campillos, 7 Higgins, 5 Greers, 4 Helds, 3 Mordentes & a partridge in a pear tree!

Skinny Sheahan

Bill Galante

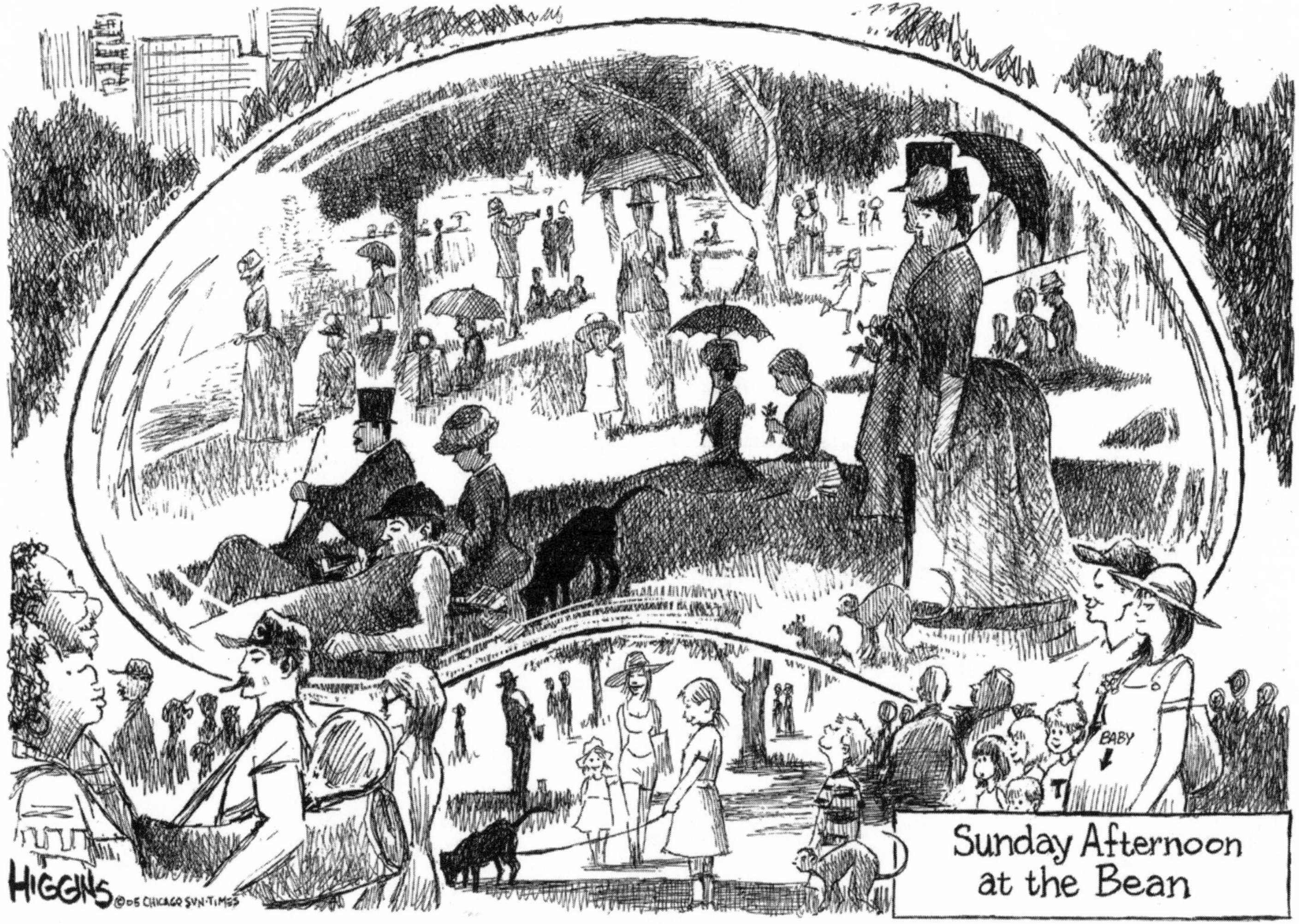
BABY
Sunday Afternoon at the Bean
HIGGINS ©05 CHICAGO SUN-TIMES

Portrait of the artist and his family.

About the Author

Jack Higgins is a political cartoonist based in Chicago whose work appears in publications worldwide. Among his many awards, he won a Pulitzer Prize in 1989, has twice won the Sigma Delta Chi, the Society of Professional Journalists Distinguished Service Award, and was named Illinois Journalist of the Year in 1996. He began his career drawing cartoons for the *Daily Northwestern*. He has been interviewed on the *Today* show, *NBC Nightly News with Tom Brokaw, Good Morning America,* and CNN. He has a bachelor's degree in economics from the College of the Holy Cross in Worcester, Massachusetts, and was recently honored with the school's Sanctae Crucis Award.